Lecture Notes in Computer Science 645

Edited by G. Goos and J. Hartmanis

Advisory Board: W. Brauer   D. Gries   J. Stoer

G. Pernul   A. M. Tjoa (eds.)

Entity-Relationship Approach – ER '92

11th International Conference
on the Entity-Relationship Approach
Karlsruhe, Germany, October 7–9, 1992
Proceedings

Springer-Verlag
Berlin Heidelberg New York
London Paris Tokyo
Hong Kong Barcelona
Budapest

G. Pernul   A M. Tjoa (Eds.)

Entity-Relationship Approach – ER '92

11th International Conference
on the Entity-Relationship Approach
Karlsruhe, Germany, October 7-9, 1992
Proceedings

Springer-Verlag

Berlin Heidelberg New York
London Paris Tokyo
Hong Kong Barcelona
Budapest

Series Editors

Gerhard Goos
Universität Karlsruhe
Postfach 69 80
Vincenz-Priessnitz-Straße 1
W-7500 Karlsruhe, FRG

Juris Hartmanis
Department of Computer Science
Cornell University
5149 Upson Hall
Ithaca, NY 14853, USA

Volume Editors

Günther Pernul
A Min Tjoa
University of Vienna, Institute for Statistics and Computer Science
Liebiggasse 4/3-4, A-1010 Vienna, Austria

CR Subject Classification (1991): H.2, H.1.0, H.3.3, H.4, H.5.2

ISBN 3-540-56023-8 Springer-Verlag Berlin Heidelberg New York
ISBN 0-387-56023-8 Springer-Verlag New York Berlin Heidelberg

Typesetting: Camera ready by author/editor
Printing and binding: Druckhaus Beltz, Hemsbach/Bergstr.
45/3140-543210 - Printed on acid-free paper

Foreword

Over the past fifteen years the Entity-Relationship Approach has evolved as an almost *de facto* standard for conceptual and logical design of databases and information systems. Continuing the tradition, the Eleventh International Conference on the Entity-Relationship Approach held in Karlsruhe, Germany, October 7-9, 1992, was organized to bring together researchers and practitioners to share ideas, encourage research and new developments, and raise issues related to the ER Approach.

The proceedings of the ER'92 conference contain the text of all the papers that were selected by the Program Committee and of the invited papers by leading experts in the field. To maintain the high technical quality of the conference all submitted papers went through an intensive review process. Out of the sixty-four submissions taken into consideration, twenty-two papers were selected for inclusion in the program. Technical quality, originality, significance, and clarity of presentation were the major criteria used in evaluating the papers.

The accepted papers describe original research in various areas related to the ER model and reflect the trend of recent years in extending the modeling power or in applying the model for the development of new applications. The papers address both theory and practice, and cover a wide range of database research activity including database design aspects, object-orientation, integrity constraints, query languages, knowledge-based techniques, and others.

This volume also includes the manuscripts of four invited speakers: Peter P. Chen shares his ideas on how to compare the constructs of the Entity-Relationship Approach with that of the Object-Oriented Approach to data modeling. Shamkant B. Navathe provides an analysis of the current state of the art in data modeling, methodologies, and database design tools and points out some directions in which he expects the entire field to move within the next ten years. August-Wilhelm Scheer develops a general architecture for integrated information systems and shows how data modeling fits into this architecture. Dennis Tsichritzis and his co-authors present some of their recent ideas and developments on the modeling of audio/video data which may signify a new challenge for the database community.

In addition to the presentation of the papers contained in the proceedings the conference hosted three tutorials: Ramez Elmasri addressed in his tutorial conceptual modeling of time, Shamkant B. Navathe and Sharma Chakravarthy discussed concepts and techniques inherent in heterogeneous databases, and Bernhard Thalheim presented the fundamentals of the Entity-Relationship model by taking a theoretical point of view.

Thanks are due to many people who contributed to the success of the conference. The invited speakers, the persons who contributed a tutorial, and all authors who have submitted papers for consideration should be given special credit. The members of the Program Committee and the external reviewers deserve a lot of thanks. Each submitted paper was reviewed three times, and to ensure a fair evaluation papers were reviewed a fourth time in cases the committee members did not agree. Special thanks are due to the Conference Chairman, Peter C. Lockemann, who did all the coordination and ground work. We gratefully acknowledge the conference organizers, especially Wolffried Stucky, the chairman of the Organization Committee. We would like to thank the involved secretariats in Karlsruhe and in Vienna, the chairpersons of the sessions and all other persons that have contributed to the conference. Finally, we thank all conference participants for the contribution to the field that their attendance represents.

Vienna, October 1992   G. Pernul, A M. Tjoa

Sponsorship

The conference is sponsored by

GI	Gesellschaft für Informatik
ERI	ER Institute

and in cooperation with

AICA	Associazione Italiana per l'Informatica ed il Calcolo Automatico
AFCET	Association Francaise pour la Cybernétique Economique et Technique
BCS	British Computer Society
OCG	Österreichische Computer Gesellschaft
SI	Schweizer Informatiker Gesellschaft

Industrial sponsorship

MPS Gabriel GmbH
Sun-Microsystems GmbH
Taylorix AG

Organization

Conference Chair:
P. Lockemann   (University of Karlsruhe, Germany)

Program Committee Chair:
A M. Tjoa   (University of Vienna and FAW Linz, Austria)

Organization Committee Chair:
W. Stucky   (University of Karlsruhe, Germany)

Organization Committee

W. Stucky (Germany, chairperson)	R. Richter (Germany)
K. Hogshead Davis (USA, US Co-chair)	P. Sander (Germany)
P. Jaeschke (Germany)	J. Wheeler (USA)
A. Oberweis (Germany)	

Program Committee

A M. Tjoa (Austria, chairperson)

C. Batini (Italy)
M. Bouzeghoub (France)
C. Breiteneder (Switzerland)
J. Bubenko (Sweden)
M. A. Casanova (Brazil)
S. Chakravarthy (USA)
V. De Antonellis (Italy)
K. R. Dittrich (Switzerland)
A. Dogac (Turkey)
J. Eder (Austria)
R. Elmasri (USA)
A. Furtado (Brazil)
M. Jarke (Germany)
H. Kangassalo (Finland)
G. Kappel (Austria)
T. W. Ling (Singapore)
V. M. Markowitz (USA)
R. Meersman (Netherlands)
S. B. Navathe (USA)
E. Neuhold (Germany)
P. A. Ng (USA)

A. Oberweis (Germany)
A. Olive (Spain)
C. Parent (France)
G. Pernul (Austria)
A. Pirotte (Belgium)
S. Ram (USA)
D. Reiner (USA)
C. Rolland (France)
G. Saake (Germany)
H. Sakai (Japan)
F. Saltor (Spain)
P. Sander (Germany)
G. Schlageter (Germany)
O. Sheng (USA)
S. Spaccapietra (Switzerland)
K. Tanaka (Japan)
B. Tauzovich (Canada)
B. Thalheim (Germany)
H. Thoma (Switzerland)
T. J. Teorey (USA)
Y. Wand (Canada)

Additional Referees

J. P. Alcàzar
A. Auddino
T. Berkel
J. Brunet
R. Busse
H. Dahlgren
O. De Troyer
G. Di Battista
G. Engels
P. Fankhauser
G. Fischer
S. Gatzia

C. - H. Goh
T. Hartmann
R. Herzig
P. Jaeschke
M. Jeusfeld
R. Jungclaus
M. Kaul
S. Kirn
J. Lee
S. P. Lee
P. Löhr-Richter
J. Ljungberg

M. Marmann
F. S. Mhknga
L. Mong-Li
T .C. Rakow
G. Santucci
M. Schrefl
W. Song
B. K. Tan Hee
Z. Tari
N. Vlachantonis
R. Wohed
Z. Zhu

Contents

Invited Papers (1)

Integrity

Database Design Aspects

Invited Paper (2)

Applications

Logical Aspects

Theoretical Aspects

Invited Paper (3)

User Interfaces and Query Languages

Object-Orientation

ER vs OO

Peter P. Chen

Address: Dept. of Computer Science, L.S.U., Baton Rouge, La 70803 U.S.A.

ER vs. OO

Peter P. Chen

Louisiana State University [*]
and
Massachusetts Institute of Technology

Extended Abstract

Is "OO" equal to "ER"? Is "OO" a subset of "ER"? Or, vice versa? These are the questions popped up in many people's minds these days. Both researchers and practitioners are looking for answers to these problems.

In this talk, we first review the basic concepts of the ER model and the OO paradigm. Then, we compare the constructs of the ER with that of the OO. In terms of the structural aspects, OO has fewer primitives than ER, and thus, can be considered as a subset of ER. Specifically, the OO utilizes primarily one type of relationship, which is a version of the "ISA" relationship in the ER. However, there are many more relationship types in the ER, which have not been addressed by the OO. We all know that the world is not made from type hierarchies only, and we need many different types of relationships to model the complex world.

In terms of dynamic aspects, ER can learn at least one thing from the OO. What ER can learn is the OO's *emphasis* on the dynamic behavior specification, and it is not crucial to learn the details of the OO specification schemes. Some people said, "ER is a subset of OO because OO includes the specification of the dynamics of entities." This statement is completely wrong. Actually, ER does have two parts, the "data (or structure)" part and the "process" part. However, in the past the "process" part was not emphasized since it was believed that if the data part is done right, the process part can be done easily. This is still true, but there is a need to specify the detailed steps on how to do process specifications once the data model has been done. So, the process part of the ER paradigm can be revitalized. Furthermore, in the ER world view, "data" and "processes" are in equal footing, while in the OO world view, "processes" are encapsulated with the data accessed. If we think deeply, the encapsulation of processes with data is a "packaging" issue and has nothing to do with the argument on whether OO has more dynamic behavior specifications than ER (or other paradigms). The OO's way of packaging processes

---

[*] Address: Dept. of Computer Science, L.S.U., Baton Rouge, LA 70803, U.S.A.

with data will work well in certain kinds of applications but not in other applications. Similarly, we can say the same thing about the conventional programming paradigm of packaging data with the same process. The ER's way of treating "processes" and "data" equally is a more balanced and more natural view and should be applicable to a wide spectrum of applications.

In conclusion, ER and OO can learn from each other. What needs to be done is to specify the details on how to make the ER model "active". An "active ER model" will emerge as the common model for both paradigms.

The Next Ten Years of Modeling, Methodologies, and Tools

Shamkant B. Navathe
College Of Computing
Georgia Institute Of Technology
Atlanta GA 30332-0280
e-mail: sham@cc.gatech.edu

EXTENDED ABSTRACT

1   Introduction

The field of data modeling and database schema design has been active for over twenty five years from the inception of commercial-scale data processing. As larger and larger databases came into existence, the need for having a comprehensive database design methodology became apparent. The management of the design problem called for tools to assist the designers. In this presentation, the author will trace the evolution of data models [1], and proceed to discuss the concomitant progression of methodologies and tools to aid the database designers and users. He will then propose an analysis of the current state of the art of modeling, methodologies, and tools and point out some directions in which he expects this entire field to move.

2   Data Modeling

Data modeling initially became established by providing a way for specifying the structures of data in actual database management systems. This led to the introduction of the network and the hierarchical models. Then the relational model was proposed as a mathematical basis for dealing with data, providing data independence and to supply a general framework to enable addressing the problems related to databases. They include modeling of constraints, security, distribution, redundancy as well as evaluating the goodness of designs of schemas in a formal way. Although recent DBMS implementations have adopted the relational model, a large amount of existing data (probably over 70% of it) is still in files or the hierarchical and network models. This has certain implications in terms of the need for data abstraction and reverse engineering tools.

Later, the focus has shifted to modeling data as seen by the application and the user. Basic data abstraction concepts of classification, generalization, aggregation, and identification were applied in different combinations and different degrees with a variety of representations (both diagrammatic and syntactic) to produce a plethora of "semantic" data models. The author traces this evolution of data models [1] with a particular mention of the entity-relationship approach and its extensions which are providing the basis for conceptual design in most commercial tools and methodologies today [2]. He then proceeds to discuss the recent developments affecting the commercial practice of data modeling: the binary modeling approach, the functional, and the object-oriented approaches. The author provides highlights of these approaches and analyzes the viability of the object-oriented approach to model the upcoming complex and challenging applications in scientific, geographical, biological, multi-media, engineering, and manufacturing applications. It is far from obvious that this approach will serve as a panacea for the emerging non-conventional applications.

A major current trend is to make databases more "active" which requires modeling the dynamics of the application environment together with its interaction with the database. Related areas include process and transaction modeling where a lot more remains to be done. The author will point out some research directions in modeling of meta-data and behavior, modeling of imprecise and ill structured information, the role of rules in active and deductive databases, and the process of "knowledge discovery" through conceptual clustering. Connections to information retrieval and knowledge representation areas will be brought out.

3 Methodologies

In spite of the volumes of research publications in the database area over the last two decades since the advent of the relational data model, database designers and practitioners have suffered badly from a lack of methodologies over the entire design spectrum. With the exception of a few projects such as DATAID in Italy [3,4], or the recent ESPIRIT projects including the one by Tsichritzis, Jarke, Vassiliou et al., that focussed on methodology and tools, little effort has been directed in this area. What exists out in the field today are cookbook approaches promoted by practitioners and vendors, many times with a very limited attention to some fundamental principles and basics for good database design. Some recent works, e.g., [5,6] by this author have started to put an emphasis on the methodological aspects of database design. In [2] we have already advocated that it is essential to merge application design, which is typically considered a part of software engineering, into the overall methodology for the design of databases. Methodologically, design of large application systems has received much more attention in the past leaving database design as a separate problem. We cannot afford to keep these two independent; and most organizations are trying to come to grips with this problem.

In the next decade, we need to see a major thrust to develop database design into a scientific discipline, rather than as an art. If we compare our accomplishments with other design disciplines, such as electrical circuit/chip design, design of machines and structures etc., we seem to be far behind, partly because the design problem we deal with is very poorly formed and has too many subjective human considerations. So we obviously cannot expect a universal design handbook for databases to emerge during the next few years. But it is this author's hope that with the advent of standards in data representation and transfer among systems, the common basic principles will still hold across systems and some stable methodologies will emerge. Research is needed on pragmatic metrics to guide database design. Future tools must span all phases of design including requirements analysis, conceptual design, logical and physical design , and also prototyping, testing, and benchmarking in an integrated fashion. With the trend toward active, deductive, heterogeneous databases, there is a further challenge on coming up with comprehensive design methodologies that will work for all types and sizes of databases and applications. In a recent research project, we have been developing methodologies for distributed database design [7].

4 Tools

All of the above discussion underscores a need for tools of a variety of types to make the life of users and designers easier while the complexity of the choices keeps going up. This complexity will rise because we will try to design applications against databases on different platforms using different models with different built-in interfaces. There is a need to have the tools communicate with a "common repository" of meta-data containing specification of requirements, design logs, design trade-offs, user profiles, rule bases, and a variety of additional information. The author will propose an architecture for supporting a suite of tools with a common data bus that draws meta information from the underlying information sources and assists the designer/user at various stages of design. These tools will have to support multiple models and languages, and possibly work with different methodologies and diagrammatic conventions.

The state of the art of tools that alleviate the above problems leaves a lot to be desired. Today, every vendor is promoting their own "workbench" of CASE tools specific to the design problem within their own DBMS with little regard to system independent conceptual design. There is a growing awareness among users of large databases that understanding the existing data and the applications that run against it is very important. This points to a need for better conceptual design and abstraction tools. Efforts like PDES (product data exchange using STEP) on an international level for a variety of product domains including electrical, mechanical products indicates the growing trend of other application areas benefitting from the concept of conceptual modeling.

We can expect future tools to address distribution, heterogeneity, active and deductive nature of databases in a variety of combinations. Reverse engineering/re-engineering of databases and applications will be a pressing need in years to come as the technology to access disparate systems with dissimilar models and representations becomes viable. So will be the tools for performing a joint data collection and analysis for database and application design. Graphics and better use of interfaces will positively influence the design of tools to come. The role of speech as a mode for input and/or output with these tools is questionable at best. The situation with natural language is not much different.

With the advent of the object based technology for databases, there is an imminent need to develop database design tools to work toward their design. The main difficulty lies in the absence of a common model, a lack of principles, and a sound theory of design in the object-oriented area. Some authors, particularly [8,9,10] have gained a fair amount of popularity and are likely to drive tool development efforts. One issue in favor of object-oriented database design is that it does not need separate models for conceptualization and implementation. The design in the chosen model is realized directly in the O-O DBMS.

Some tools have hitherto been totally ignored- e.g., tools to measure and deal with data quality and inconsistency problems. The multi-media movement will bring to the fore the need for designing additional tools such as authoring tools that can be used to define the navigation paths within multi-media information sources. Overall, a very large degree of innovative approaches are called for to develop tools that will embrace the emerging applications of tomorrow.

References

[1]   Navathe, S.B.,"Evolution of Data Modeling for Databases," Communications of the ACM, Vol. 35, No. 9, Sep. 1992.

[2]   Batini,C., Ceri, S. and Navathe, S.B., Conceptual Database Design : an Entity Relationship Approach, Benjamin Cummings, 1992.

[3]   Ceri, S. (Ed.), Methodology and Tools for Database Design, North Holland, 1983.

[4]   Albano,A., De Antonellis, Di Leva, A., (Eds .), Computer-aided Database Design: the DATAID project, North Holland, 1985.

[5]   Navathe, S.B., " Important Issues in Database Design Methodologies and Tools," in [4].

[6]   Navathe, S.B., and Pernul, G., "Conceptual and Logical Design of Relational Databases," in Advances in Computers, Vol. 35, (M.C. Yovits, Ed.), Academic Press, 1992.

[7]   Navathe, S. B., Ra, M., Varadarajan, R., Karlapalem, K., and Sreewastav, K., "A Mixed Partitioning Methodology for Distributed Database Design," UF-CIS Technical Report TR 90-17, University of Florida, 1990.

[8]   Booch, G., Object-oriented Design with Applications, Benjamin Cummings, 1991.

[9]   Coad, P., and Yourdon, E., Object-oriented Analysis, , Prentice Hall, 1990.

[10]   Rumbaugh, J., et al., Object-oriented Modeling and Design, , Prentice Hall, 1991.

Fundamentals of Cardinality Constraints

Bernhard Thalheim

Computer Science Dept., Rostock University, A.-Einstein-Str. 21, D-O-2500 Rostock

thalheim@informatik.uni-rostock.dbp.de

Abstract

The Entity-Relationship model is frequently used during conceptual database design phases. However, this model can be enriched and then used for the complete lifecycle of a database as an interface model. For this purpose, the concepts of the ER-model need to be theoretically well-founded. The aim of this paper is to show how the theoretical basis of one of the most important class of integrity constraints can be constructed and then used for the exploitation in practical database tasks. The concept of cardinality constraints is defined, generalized and used for the simplification of the design, for the improvement of maintenance programs and for the detection of problematic design decisions.

1 Introduction

Relationship types usually have certain restrictions that limit the possible combinations of entities participating in relationship instances. Cardinality or complexity constraints are the most commonly used class of constraints for binary relationship types. Cardinality constraints specify the number of relationships that an entity can participate in (maximal participation) and furthermore whether the existence of an entity depends on its being related to another entity via the relationship type (minimal participation). Often, there are considered only two values for the maximal participation: "one" and "many". For the minimal participation there are considered at least two values: "zero" or "one". Cardinality constraints can be considered as structural constraints since they limit the possible structure of the database. Sometimes the two participation constraints are independently considered. In [EN89], they are called cardinality ratio (maximal participation) and participation constraint (minimal participation). This separation is more intutive.

Cardinality constraints are already discussed over a longer period. But their properties are still not well understood in the case of n-ary relationship types. For this reason, we need a formal treatment of these. It does not mean that any database designer has to learn this abstract language and the abstract theory.

For database design it is only absolutely necessary to obtain the whole semantical information the desinger has. For this reason, building a design systems means also to integrate the theory into the tool. The practice shows that this integration is possible (see for instance [Tha92] or the overview on systems in [BCN92]).

Cardinality constraints are treated in different ways:

- The definitions of cardinality constraints are different. Either they are treating cardinality constraints from the entity visibility (how many entities can be seen via a relationship type from a certain entity) ["look accross"]) or they are treating cardinality constraints using the materialization of relationship types and the cardinality of these materialized sets under certain restrictions.

- The default assumptions in the case of a missing specification are different. In some cases, default assumptions are not allowed.

- There are different graphical representations for cardinality constraints of binary relationship types.

- There are different attempts for the generalization of the graphical representations for relationship types of higher arity [Fer91,NiH89,Teo89].

- The definition of the participation constraint (minimal participation) is either taken as a possible lower bound or as a strong condition.

- The meaning of cardinality constraints depends on the semantics, e.g. whether relationship types are based on a set interpretation or on a pointer interpretation.

These differences and the terminology differences (calling cardinality constraints, for instance, complexity, relative cardinality, connectivity, degree, uniqueness constraint or specifying the information on cardinality constraints by other constraints, e.g. key constraints) shows that there is a need in a unification of the definition and in a formal treatment. One effort for unification was made in [Fer91]. This paper aims to continue this attempt.

The paper is organized as follows. In the next part we give a formal definition of different kinds of cardinality constraints. Then we present some formal properties. In the last section, we show how these formal properties can and are to be used in database design.

2 Formal Definition of Cardinality Constraints

One formal ER-Model

Let us introduce the ER-model very briefly. For a more complete definition of our model we refer to [Tha89,Tha91',Tha92',Tha93].

An **entity type** E is a pair $(attr(E), id(E))$, where E is an entity set name, $attr(E)$ is a set of attributes and $id(E)$ is a non-empty generalized subset of $attr(E)$ called key or identifier.

Therefore concrete entities e of E can be now defined as tuples on $attr(E)$. A **data scheme** $DD = (U, \underline{D}, dom)$ is given by a finite set U of attributes, by a set $\underline{D} = D_1, D_2, ...$ of domains, and by an arity or domain function $dom : U \longrightarrow \underline{D}$ which associates with every attribute its domain. For a fixed moment of time t the present entity set E^t for the entity type E is a set E^t of tuples r on $attr(E)$ defined on DD such that
1. for any $A \in attr(E)$ and any $r \in E^t$: $r(A) \in dom(A)$ and
2. $id(E)$ is a key of E^t.

Given now entity types $E_1, ..., E_k$. A **relationship type** has the form $R = (ent(R), attr(R))$ where R is the name of the type, $ent(R)$ is a sequence of entity types, and of clusters of those and $attr(R)$ is a set of attributes from UN.

Given now a relationship type $R = (E_1, ..., E_n, \{B_1, ..., B_k\})$ and for a given moment t sets $E_1^t, ..., E_n^t$. A **relationship** r is then definable as an element of the Cartesian product $E_1^t \times ... \times E_n^t \times dom(B_1) \times ... \times dom(B_k)$. A relationship set R^t is then a set of relationships, i. e.
$$R^t \subseteq E_1^t \times ... \times E_n^t \times dom(B_1) \times ... \times dom(B_k) .$$

The relationship type is called relationship type of order 1. Analogously, relationship types of higher order [Tha89,Tha92'] can be defined hierarchically. Entity types could be therefore considered to be relationship types of order 0.

Cardinality Constraints

Let us define for $R = (R_1, ..., R_k, attr(R))$ where R_i is an entity or a relationship type and for each $i, 1 \le i \le k$, the **cardinality constraint**
$$comp(R, R_i) = (m, n)$$
specifies that in each database state an item e from R_i^t appears in R^t at least m and at most n times, e.g. $comp(R, R_i) = (m, n)$ iff for all t , all $e \in R_i^t$
$$m \le |\{r \in R^t | r(R_i) = e\}| \le n$$ where by $|M|$ is denoted the cardinality of M and by $r(R_i)$ is denoted the restriction of r to R_i.

Notice, that recursive components in relationship types are denoted by either their labels, e.g. in *Prerequisite* $= (Course, Course, \emptyset)$ as *Required:Course*, or by the component number, e.g. *(Course,1)*. This notation is used for the cardinality constraint too. For the simplification, we can use the number in the type sequence instead of the name. In this case we write $< 1, 3 >$ meaning the first and third type in the relationship type definition. If n is unbounded then it is denoted by $(m, .)$. The pairs (m, n) are partially ordered by the natural partial order $\le$.

This can be generalized to sequences of relationship types in $R = ((R_1, ..., R_k, attr(R))$. For each subsequence $R'_1...R'_m$, the generalized cardinality constraint $comp(R, R'_1...R'_m) = (l, p)$ specifies that in each database state the items from $R''^t_1, ..., R''^t_m$ appear in R^t at least l and at most p times, e.g. $comp(R, R'_1...R'_m) = (l, p)$ iff for all t , all $e_1 \in R''^t_1, ..., e_m \in R''^t_m$ $l \le |\{r \in R^t | r(R'_i) = e_i, 1 \le i \le m\}| \le p$.

If R_j is a cluster ($R_j = R_{j,1} + ... + R_{j,m}$ then the cardinality constraint notion can be generalized as follows for $R_{j,l}(1 \le l \le m)$:

$comp(R.R_{j,l}, R_i) = comp(R, R_{j,l}R_i)$.

In [ZNG90] an analogous cardinality constraint definition based on projections of relationship types is introduced (called flattened constraints and nested constraints). There it is claimed that using that using nested constraints always results in consistent specifications but flattening may lead to inconsistent specifications. However, there are nested specifications which are inconsistent (Fact 9).

For binary relationship types $R = (R_1, R_2, attr(R))$ between two entity or relationship types R_1, R_2, traditionally there are introduced special cardinality types: One-to-One, One-to-Many, Many-to-One and Many-to-Many. For instance, the many-to-one relationship type is characterized by

$comp(R, R_1) \le (1, 1)$ and $comp(R, R_2) \in \{(0, m), (1, m)\}$.

This notation can be extended also to arbitrary relationships. For a given relationship type $R = (E_1...E_k, attr(R))$ we can introduce similarly the notation of the $(n_1, m_1), (n_2, m_2), ..., (n_k, m_k)$ -relationship.

Obviously, these cardinality constraints are special functional dependencies. The semantics of functional dependencies and of cardinality constraints is different. Functional dependencies are two-tuple constraints. Cardinality constraints are restrictions.

For instance, for the relationship type
Lecture = (Professor, Course, Room, Semester { Time(Day,Hour)})
besides the trivial generalized cardinality constraints like

$(< 1 >, (1, .)), (< 2 >, (1, .)), (< 3 >, (1, .)), (< 4 >, (1, .)), (< 1, 3 >, (0, .)),$
$(< 1, 2, 3, 4 >, (0, 1)),$ and $(< 2, 3 >, (0, .)),$

we obtain nontrivial generalized cardinality constraints like

$(< 1, 2 >, (0, 3))$ - each professor can take a course only three times,
$(< 1, 4 >, (0, .))$ - there are professors which are absent for a term, and
$(< 2, 4 >, (1, 3))$ - each course is given in each term at least once but not
more than three times.

The last generalized cardinality constraint implies together with the last trivial generalized cardinality constraint the cardinality constraint $(< 2, 3, 4 >, (0, 3))$. The cardinality constraint $(< 1 >, (1, .))$ together with $(< 1, 4 >, (0, .))$ expresses the constraint that a new professor can not be absent for his/her first term.

Partial and Projected Cardinality Constraints

There can be used other notions for the cardinality constraint of the relationship type $R = (R_1, ..., R_k, attr(R))$ and the subsequence $R_1'...R_m'$ on R:

1. The $*$-cardinality constraint $comp^*(R, R_1'...R_m') = (l, p)$ specifies that in each database state the items from $R_1'^t \times ... \times R_m'^t \bigcap R^t |_{R_1',...,R_m'}$ appear in R^t at least l and at most p times, e.g. $comp(R, R_1'...R_m') = (l, p)$ iff for all t , all $r' \in R^t |_{R_1',...,R_m'}$ $l \leq |\{r \in R^t | r(R_1', ..., R_m') = r'\}| \leq p$.

2. The $+$-cardinality constraint $comp^+(R, R_1'...R_m') = (l, p)$ specifies that in each database state the items from $R^t |_{R_1'}, ..., R^t |_{R_m'}$ appear in R^t at least l and at most p times, e.g. $comp(R, R_1'...R_m') = (l, p)$ iff for all t , all $e_1 \in R^t |_{R_1'}, ..., e_m \in R^t |_{R_m'}$ $l \leq |\{r \in R^t | r(R_i') = e_i, 1 \leq i \leq m\}| \leq p$.

For each of these forms generalizations can be defined:

1. Instead of the interval $[l, p]$ of natural numbers a subset I of natural numbers could be used for the definition of Int-cardinality constraints. For instance, the Int-cardinality constraint $comp^*_{Int}(R, R_1'...R_m') = I$ specifies that in each database state the items from $R_1'^t \times ... \times R_m'^t \bigcap R^t |_{R_1',...,R_m'}$ appear in R^t i times for $i \in I$.

2. For each subsequence $R"_1...R"_n$ of the subsequence $R_1'...R_m'$, the projected cardinality constraint $comp(R[R_1'...R_m'], R"_1...R"_n) = (l, p)$ specifies that in each database state the items from $R"^t_1, ..., R"^t_n$ appear in $R^t |_{R_1',...,R_m'}$ at least l and at most p times, e.g. $comp(R[R_1'...R_m'], R"_1...R"_n) = (l, p)$ iff for all t , all $e_1 \in R"_1, ..., e_n \in R"_n$ $l \leq |\{r \in R^t |_{R_1',...,R_m'} |r(R"_i) = e_i, 1 \leq i \leq n\}| \leq p$.

Fact 1 *Given a relationship type* $R = (R_1, ..., R_k, \{A_1, ..., A_l\})$ *and a sequence seq on* R.
1. $comp^*(R, seq) \geq (1, 1)$ *,* $comp^+(R, R_i) \geq (1, 1)$ *.*
2. If $comp^*(R, seq) = (n_1, m_1)$, $comp^+(R, seq) = (n_2, m_2)$, *and* $comp(R, seq) = (n_3, m_3)$ *then* $m_1 = m_2 = m_3$ *and* $n_3 \leq n_2 \leq n_1$.

These results are valid also for projected cardinality constraints. The second fact can be generalized to Int-cardinality constraints according the minimal and maximal elements in I_i.

The cardinality constraint are generalized to carry more semantics. These generalization can be checked as easily as traditional cardinality constraints. For instance, if in the *Lecture* type a teacher can have either a sabbatical or he/she is teaching at least three but not more than five different courses then this can be expressed by the following two cardinality constraints:

$comp(Lecture, Professor\ Semester) = (0, 5)$
$comp^*(Lecture, Professor\ Semester) = (3, 5)$.

These constraints are equivalent to the constraint
$comp_{Int}(Lecture, Professor\ Semester) = \{0, 3, 4, 5\}$.

$comp(Lecture[Professor\ Course\ Semester], Course\ Semester) = (0,1)$ specifies that courses are given only by one professor in a term.
In the university example the cardinality constraint
$comp^+(Lecture, CourseSemester) = (0,3)$ expresses that each course is not given in each term and that courses are not given more than three times in a term whereas the cardinality constraint
$comp^+(Lecture, CourseSemester) = (1,3)$ expresses that each course is given in any term and there are not more than three parallel sessions.

In different books, the cardinality constraint is defined as a specific look-accross-constraint: For instance, for an n-ary relationship type $R = (E_1, ..., E_n, attr(R))$, $R.GLA_{max}(E_i, E_j)$ is the maximum number of entities of E_j^t that an entity from E_i^t can "see" when "it looks across" R at E_j^t , e.g.
$comp(R[E_i E_j], E_i) = (R.GLA_{min}(E_i, E_j), R.GLA_{max}(E_i, E_j))$.

Negated cardinality constraints can be defined using Int-cardinality constraints. It should be noticed that these notions can be also extended to projections in component types. However, the formal consideration of this most general cardinality constraint is out of the scope of this paper.

Representation in Diagrams

The diagrams can be also labeled by cardinality constraints. It should be noted that there is a little aggreement [BDK91] on what edge labels to use, and what they mean in ER-diagrams. The classical notation is the following for binary relationship types $R = (E_1, E_2, attr(R))$ (see for instance [EN89,Vos87]):
The edge $R \longrightarrow E_1$ is labeled
by $comp(R, E_2) = (n, m)$ or by 1 if $comp(R, E_2) \in \{(0,1), (1,1)\}$
or by n if $comp(R, E_2) \in \{(l, k | l \in \{0,1\}, l < k, k > 1\}$.
The edge $R \longrightarrow E_2$ is labeled
by $comp(R, E_1) = (n, m)$ or by 1 if $comp(R, E_1) \in \{(0,1), (1,1)\}$
or by n if $comp(R, E_1) \in \{(l, k | l \in \{0,1\}, l < k, k > 1\}$.

Since this notation can not be extended to ternary relationships in [Teo89] cardinality constraints for ternary relationships are marked by shaded areas in the relationship type triangle if the relationship type is "many". More concrete, for instance, the E_1-corner in the triangle which represents the relationship type $R = (E_1, E_2, E_3, attr(R))$ is <u>not</u> shaded if $comp(R, E_2 E_3) \leq (1,1)$. This notation is complicated and $comp(R, E_j)$-cardinality constraints are not represented. This proposal could be extended to quadrary relationship types but then we loose the information on the other cardinality constraints.
Other books avoid the question or present examples for binary relationship types. [TL82] states that "the semantics of ternary and higher-order relationship sets can become quite complex to comprehend". Another approach is pro-

posed in [Fer91][1] for ternary relationship types. For a given relationship type $R = (E_1, E_2, E_3, attr(R))$ and three different numbers i, j, k from $\{1, 2, 3\}$ the edge $R \longrightarrow E_i$ is labeled by $comp(R, E_i)$ and by $comp(R, E_j E_k)$. However this concept can not be generalized to quadrary types. It is repeating for $comp(R, E_j E_k)$ the labeling alike in Chen's original proposal for binary relationship types. There are also other labbeling proposals for other graph-oriented database models like the binary ER-model [Ris88,NiH89]. All these proposals do not show the whole picture. Our approach is general enough for the introduced types. A scheme should not show in general the whole semantic information in one shoot but software tools should allow browsing for picked objects [Tha92].

Given a relationship type $R = (R_1, ..., R_k, \{A_1, ..., A_l\})$. For $1 \leq j \leq k$, the edge $R \longrightarrow R_j$ can be labeled by $comp(R, R_j) = (n, m)$
  or by 1 if $comp(R, R_j) \in \{(0, 1), (1, 1)\}$
  or by n if $comp(R, R_j) \in \{(l, k | l \in \{0, 1\}, l < k, k > 1\}$.
For $1 \leq j \leq l$, the edge $R \longrightarrow A_j$ can be labeled by $dom(A_j)$.

A more complex labeling would be the following label for the diamonds: Given a relationship type $R = (R_1, ..., R_k, \{A_1, ..., A_l\})$. The diamond of the relationship type R is labeled by a subset of the set
$$\{(< i_1, i_2, ...i_j >, (n, m)) \mid 1 \leq j \leq k, 1 \leq i_1 < i_2 < ... < i_j \leq k,$$
$$comp(R, R_{i_1} R_{i_2} ... R_{i_j}) = (n, m)\} \ .$$

If edges are labelled then for n-ary relationship types each edge should be labeled with $3^{n-1} - 2^{n-1}$ generalized cardinality constraints and projected cardinality constraints or with $2^{n-1} - 1$ generalized cardinality constraints (e.g. for quadrary relationship types the edges should carry 19 resp. 7 pairs of cardinalities). It can be proven that there is a minimal set of cardinality constraints which would be sufficient for the representation of the cardinality constraints in the graph.

3 Properties of Cardinality Constraints

Monotonicity of Cardinality Constraints

For a given relationship type $R = (R_1, ..., R_k, \{A_1, ..., A_l\})$, sequences of components $seq = R'_1...R'_m$, $seq' = R''_1...R''_n$ the sequence seq' contains seq (denoted by $seq \sqsubseteq seq'$) if for each R'_i in seq there is an $R''_j = R'_i$ in seq. A function $f(R, seq)$ is monotone decreasing for containment of components on R if $f(R, seq) \geq f(R, seq')$ for $seq \sqsubseteq seq'$ and monotone decreasing for root expressions if $f(R[seq''], seq) \geq f(R[seq''], seq')$ for sequences $seq \sqsubseteq seq' \sqsubseteq seq''$ on R.

---

[1]He uses the visibility constraint. This constraint is introduced as a lookup cardinality constraint on the remaining entity types. Therefore it is equivalent to the proposed generalized cardinality constraint.

Obviously, if $seq \sqsubseteq seq'$ and $seq' \sqsubseteq seq$ then the cardinality constraints on the components seq and seq' are equal.

Using the definitions and properties we get directly the following Fact.

Fact 2 *The cardinality functions* $comp$, $comp^*$, $comp^+$ *are monotone decreasing for both component sequences and root expressions. The minimum and maximum of* I *in Int-cardinality constraints is monotone decreasing for both component sequences and root expressions.*

The lower bound 0 is inherited to all supersequences of component sequences. The lower bound 1 is inherited to all subsequences of components on R.

Directly, we get now that default assumptions can be based on monotonicity without restricting the schema.

Consequence 1 *If for* $R = (R_1, ..., R_k, attr(R))$ *the value of* $comp(R, R'_1...R'_m)$ *is unknown then this can be equivalently represented by the cardinality constraint* $comp(R, R'_1...R'_m) = (0, .)$.

These properties can be used also in design systems [Tha92] for the automatic detection of inconsistencies in the set of cardinality constraints. Let us discuss the use for an example proposed in [Fer91].

Salesmen (briefly S) work for a large manufactores of household items. They represent the *products* (P) in various *cities* (C). [Fer91] considers for the relationship type *Represents* $= (S, P, C, \emptyset)$ different conditions:

1. For any salesman and any city, there is only one product that the salesman can represent the product in that city.
2. For any salesman and any product, there is only one city that the salesman can represent the product in that city.
3. For any city and any product, there may be many salesmen representing the product in that city.
4. A salesman can partipate in *Represents* only once.
5. A salesman need not participate in the relationship.
6. Every product must have a salesman for every city which is representing the product in that city.[2]
7. Every city must participate in the relationship at least once.

These properties are to be represented by cardinality constraints:

$comp(Represents, C) = (1, ?)$	by 7.;	
$comp(Represents, S) = (0, 1)$	by 4. and 5.;	
$comp(Represents, P) = (?, ?)$;		
$comp(Represents, S\,P) = (?, 1)$	by 2.;	
$comp(Represents, C\,P) = (1, N)$	by 3. and 6.;	
$comp(Represents, S\,C) = (?, 1)$	by 1.	

Using Fact 2, we obtain the following system:

---

[2]The original formulation was the constraint "Every product must have a salesman representing it in every city." This constraint can not be represented by cardinality constraints.

$comp(Represents, C) = (1, N)$ by 7., 6. (derived) and 3. (derived);
$comp(Represents, S) = (0, 1)$ by 4. and 5.;
$comp(Represents, P) = (1, N)$ by 3. (derived) and 6. (derived);
$comp(Represents, S\,P) = (0, 1)$ by 2. and 5. (derived);
$comp(Represents, C\,P) = (1, N)$ by 3. and 6.;
$comp(Represents, S\,C) = (0, 1)$ by 1., 4. (derived) and 5. (derived).

If we change for instance the first restriction to " For any salesman and any city, there may be many products that the salesman can represent the product in that city." then this condition contradicts the fourth condition by Fact 2. We obtain furthermore that the first and the last condition can be omitted not changing the system.

Cardinality Constraints and Relational Constraints

Results from relational theory can be adapted to the entity-relationship model. Inclusion dependencies express partially cardinality constraints. Key dependencies [Tha91] can be expressed by cardinality constraints. Cardinality constraints can express domain dependencies [CoK83] or numerical dependencies [GrM85]. Therefore, the work on inclusion, domain and numerical dependencies [CFP84,CoK83,Mit83] can be used for cardinality constraints. Several results [Tha91] known on other types of constraints and known in the presence of incomplete information can be generalized to cardinality constraints.

Fact 3 (folklore) *Given the relationship type $R = (R_1, ..., R_k, attr(R))$.*
1. The cardinality constraint $comp(R, R'_1...R'_m) \leq (1, 1)$ is valid if and only if the functional dependency $R'_1...R'_m \longrightarrow R_1, ..., R_k$ is valid in R .
2. The constraint $comp(R, R') \geq (1, 1)$ is valid if and only if the inclusion dependency $R' \subseteq R[R']$ is valid in the scheme.
3. $comp^*(R, R'_1...R'_m) = (1, 1)$ if and only if $R'_1...R'_m \longrightarrow R_1, ..., R_k$ is valid in R.

In the second case, the cardinality constraint defines an into constraint [Kob85]. The cardinality constraint
$comp^*(Lecture, CourseSemesterProfessor) = (1, 1)$
expresses the validity of the functional dependency
$Lecture : \{Course, Semester, Professor\} \longrightarrow \{Room, Time(Day, Hour)\}$
in $Lecture^t$.

The property in Fact 2 seems to useful for the axiomatization of the set of generalized cardinality constraints. However the axiomatization problem is more complex for generalized cardinality constraints. It is easy to see that the set of generalized cardinality constraints is not k-ary axiomatizable [Tha91] by rules with k premises.

Fact 4 *The set of cardinality constraints is not axiomatizable.*

We show now that we need constraints which are more powerful than cardinality constraints if we use the model for complete database modeling and need generic operations. Generic operations are defined for relational algebras. After defining the structure in the relational model the operations *Insert*, *Delete* and *Update* are to be added to the data manipulation language if there exists a non-recursive definition. In schemata the definition of the generic functions depends from the definition of the types. If for instance, a type R is using the component type E then the *Insert* operation on R presumes the existence of corresponding elements in E. The *Delete* operation on E induces the application of this operation on type R too.

Fact 5 *The generic operations Insert, Delete and Update are well defined in entity-relationship schemes without additional integrity constraints. They are not defined in general for schemes with additional integrity constraints.*

The second part is based on the following counterexample adopted from [SST92]:
> *MarriedPerson* = (...)   ,
> *Marriage* = (*MarriedPerson*, *Spouse* : *MarriedPerson*, ...)   ,
> *comp*(*Marriage*, (*MarriedPerson*, 1)) = (1, 1) ,
> *comp*(*Marriage*, *Spouse*) = (1, 1) .

The *Insert* operation of a person requires the insertion of the corresponding spouse for which again the corresponding spouse should be inserted etc. However, the *Insert* operation is well defined if the following integrity constraint is valid: $\forall x, y\, (\, Marriage(x, y) \Rightarrow Marriage(y, x)\,)$.
In this case we can derive the correct *Insert* operation:
> *Insert_Couple_Into_Person(x,y)*   =
>   begin *Insert_Person(x)* ; *Insert_Person(y)* ;
>   *Insert_Marriage(x,y)* ; *Insert_Marriage(y,x)* end .

Satisfiability of Systems of Cardinality Constraints

Let us now consider the satisfiability of cardinality constraints. Generally, each ER scheme with a set of cardinality constraints is satisfiable by the empty database. However, if the set of cardinality constraints is not well-specified then the empty database may be the only finite instance of the scheme. Obviously, if the ER-scheme is using only cardinality constraints but not generalized cardinality constraints and is hierarchical then the scheme has also finite nonempty instances. The above discussed examples show already that hierarchical schemes with generalized cardinality constraints can be inconsistent.

A ER-scheme $\underline{S}$ with a set of cardinality constraints $\underline{C}$ is called consistent (strongly satisfiable) if there exists at least one database $DB = (r_1, ..., r_k)$ in $SAT(\underline{S}, \underline{C})$ in which all r_i are not empty.

This property is not trivial. If for instance
$comp(Prerequisite, Required : Course) = (1, 2)$ and

$comp(Prerequisite, Requires : Course) = (3,4)$

meaning that each course requires at least three and at most four prerequisites and each course is required from at least one and at most two courses then either $Course^t$ is empty or infinite. Suppose, $Course^t \neq \emptyset$. Then there exists at least one course c_1 which is required by at least three other courses. Let us assume that the requiring courses are c_1, c_2, c_3. Furthermore, c_2 is required by at least three others, e.g. c_1, c_2, c_3. The course c_3 is required by the at least three other courses. From the other side, the courses c_1, c_2, c_3 can require at most two other courses. Therefore, c_3 is required by three other courses, e.g. c_4, c_5, c_6 . We can repeat the same procedure for c_4, c_5. However, c_6 is to be required by at least three different courses, say c_7, c_8, c_9. Repeating this procedure we get an infinite set $Course^t$. The reason for this is the ratio in the recursion.

Let us consider first recursive relationship types. Given a relationship type $R = (R_1, ... R_n, attr(R))$ and the cardinality constraints $comp(R, R_i) = (x_i, y_i)$. Let us reorder the sequence of components in the relationship type according the components, i.e. $R = ((R_1, 1), ..., (R_1, q_1), ..., (R_k, 1), ...(R_k, q_k), attr(R))$ and $comp(R, (R_i, j)) = (x_{i,j}, y_{i,j})$, $1 \leq i \leq k, 1 \leq j \leq q_i$. Then for each database $(R_1^t, ..., R_k^t, R^t, ...)$ satisfying the cardinality constraints we obtain the condition $x_{i,j} \cdot | R_i^t | \leq | R^t | \leq y_{i,j} \cdot | R_k^t |$, $1 \leq i \leq k, 1 \leq j \leq q_i$.
Summarizing these conditions we derive the following statement.

Fact 6 *Given a relationship type*
$R = ((R_1, 1), ..., (R_1, q_1), ..., (R_k, 1), ...(R_k, q_k), attr(R))$ *with*
$comp(R, (R_i, j)) = (x_{i,j}, y_{i,j}), 1 \leq i \leq k, 1 \leq j \leq q_i$.
Then the ER scheme $\{R_1, ..., R_k, R\}$ with the cardinality constraints is consistent if and only if for all $i, 1 \leq i \leq k$ with $q_i > 1$ it is valid that
$max\{x_{i,j} \mid 1 \leq j \leq q_i\} \leq min\{y_{i,j} \mid 1 \leq j \leq q_i\}$.

Directly, we can conclude that for the above presented example the scheme with the cardinality constraints
$comp(Prerequis, Required : Course) = (1, 2)$ and
$comp(Prerequis, Requires : Course) = (a, 4)$
is inconsistent for $a \geq 3$ and consistent for $aleq2$. For recursive relationships, the relationship type and the cardinality constraints are consistent if and only if the intervals are overlapping.

Let us now generalize the approach of [LN90] where is proposed a nonconstructive solution. It can be shown generalizing the approach of [LN90] that there is a constructive criterion.
We introduce a labeled graph for ER-schemes $\underline{S} = \{E_1, ..., E_k, R_1, ..., R_m\}$ and a set of associated cardinality constraints $\underline{C}$: $G(\underline{S}, \underline{C}) = (V, E)$ where
$V = \{(E_1, 1), ..., (E_k, 1)\} \bigcup$
$\qquad \{(R_i, j) \mid 1 \leq i \leq m, R_i = (R_1', ..., R_n', attr(R_i), 1 \leq j \leq n\}$
$E = \{((R_j', 1), (R_i, j), y) \mid R_i = (R_1', ...R_n', attr(R_i)), comp(R_i, R_j') = (x, y)\} \bigcup$

$$\{((R_i, j), (R_i, 1), 1), ((R_i, 1), (R_i, j), 1) \mid R_i = (R'_1, ..., R'_n, attr(R_i)), 1 < j < n\}$$
$$\bigcup \{((R_i, j), (R'_j, 1), c^*(i, j)) \mid R_i = (R'_1, ...R'_n, attr(R_i))\} \bigcup$$
$$\{((R'_j, 1), (R_i, j), \infty) \mid R_i = (R'_1, ...R'_n, attr(R_i)), comp(R_i, R'_j) \text{ not defined }\} \bigcup$$
$$\{((R_i, j), (R'_j, 1), \infty) \mid R_i = (R'_1, ...R'_n, attr(R_i)), comp(R_i, R'_j) \text{ not defined }\}$$

where

$$c^*(i, j) == \begin{cases} \frac{1}{x} & \text{if } comp(R_i, R'_j) = (x, y) \geq (1, 1) \\ \infty & \text{otherwise} \end{cases}$$

For the above considered example we obtain the graph in Figure 1.

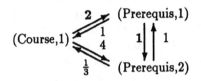

Figure 1: Graph for Prerequisites

Let $G = (V, E)$ where $V = \{v_i \mid 1 \leq i \leq n\}$ and $E = \{(v_i, v_j, c(i, j))\}$ a labeled graph. A sequence $p = v_1, ..., v_n$ of nodes from V with $(v_i, v_{i+1}, j) \in E$ for some j and all $i, 1 \leq i < n$ is called **path** and is called cycle if additionally $v_1 = v_n$.

The cycle is called simple if the elements in the sequence are pairwise different. For a sequence of nodes $p = v_1, ..., v_n$ of nodes from V with $(v_i, v_{i+1}, w_i) \in E$ the value $weight(p) = \prod_{i=1}^{n-1} w_i$ is called **weight** of p.

A critical cycle p is a simple cycle with a weight $weight(p)$ less than 1.

A critical cycle in Figure 1 is for instance the cycle *(Course,1), (Prerequis,1), (Prerequis,2), (Course,1)* . The weight of the cycle is $\frac{2}{3}$.

The following Fact shows that this condition is sufficient and necessary.

Fact 7 *Given a ER-scheme $\underline{S}$ and a set of associated cardinality constraints $\underline{C}$. $(\underline{S}, \underline{C})$ is inconsistent iff the graph $G(\underline{S}, \underline{C})$ contains a critical cycle.*

The computation whether the graph contains a critical cycle can be done by computing a special matrix product:
Let $G = (V, E)$ where $V = \{v_i \mid 1 \leq i \leq n\}$ and $E = \{(v_i, v_j, c(i, j))\}$ a labeled graph. Then we define an adjacency matrix $M_0(G)$ by

$$m_{i,j}^0(G) = \begin{cases} c(i, j) & \text{if } (v_i, v_j, c(i, j)) \in E \\ \infty & \text{otherwise} \end{cases}$$

Now we define inductively $M_{s+1}(G)$ as follows
$$m_{i,j}^{s+1}(G) = min\{m_{i,j}^s(G)\} \bigcup \{m_{i,k}^s(G) m_{k,j}^0(G) \mid 1 \leq k \leq n\} .$$
Now we can conclude the following fact.

Fact 8 *The graph $G(\underline{S}, \underline{C})$ contains a critical cycle iff there are s, i, j such that $m_{i,j}^{s+1}(G(\underline{S}, \underline{C})) < 1$.*

According to Fact 7 the implication problem of cardinality constraints differs for acyclic schemes and schemes containing a cycle. Using the equivalence to functional and inclusion dependencies and a result of [KCV83] we get that the implication problem of cardinality constraints for acyclic ER schemes is PSPACE-hard.

Let us now consider the question whether the properties of cardinality constraints are inherited by generalized cardinality constraints. Obviously, if there are given only generalized cardinality constraints then we can not derive conditions on cardinality constraints. But if there are given cardinality constraints and generalized cardinality constraints then we can derive inequalities using Fact 2. For instance, given the relationship type $R = (E_1, E_2, E_1)$ and the constraints $comp(R, (E_1, 1)) = (1, 2)$, $comp(R, (E_1, 2), E_2) = (3, 4)$ then we obtain using Fact 2 $comp(R, (E_1, 2)) \geq (3, 4)$ and by Fact 7 that $R^t = \emptyset$ for each t. Fact 6 can be generalized using the same proof.

Fact 9 *Given a relationship type*
$R = ((R_1, 1), ..., (R_1, q_1), ..., (R_k, 1), ...(R_k, q_k), attr(R))$ *with*
$comp(R, (R_i, j)) = (x_{i,j}, y_{i,j})$, $1 \leq i \leq k, 1 \leq j \leq q_i$, *and*
$comp(R, (R_i, j)(R_i, j')) = (x_{(i,j)(i,j')}, y_{(i,j)(i,j')})$, $1 \leq i \leq k, 1 \leq j < j' \leq q_i$.
Then the ER scheme $\{R_1, ..., R_k, R\}$ with the cardinality constraints is inconsistent if for some $i, 1 \leq i \leq k$ with $q_i > 1$ it is valid that

$$max\{\frac{x_{i,j}}{x_{(i,j)(i,j')}} \mid 1 \leq j < j' \leq q_i\} > min\{\frac{y_{i,j}}{y_{(i,j)(i,j')}} \mid 1 \leq j < j' \leq q_i\} .$$

4 Using Cardinality Constraints

Transformation of Schemes

Cardinality constraints can be used for the transformation of the schemes. Let us consider an abstract example and formulate the corresponding result.

Fact 10 *Given for the relationship type $R = (R_1, ..., R_k, attr(R))$ the cardinality constraint $comp(R, R'_1...R'_m) \leq (1, 1)$. The scheme obtained by replacing R by $R" = (R'_1, ..., R'_m, \emptyset)$ and $R^* = (R", R"_1, ..., R"_n, attr(R))$ and by replacing R by $R"$ in other relationship types where $\{R"_1, ..., R"_n\} \bigcup \{R'_1...R'_m\} = \{R_1, ..., R_k\}$ and $\{R"_1, ..., R"_n\} \bigcap \{R'_1...R'_m\} = \emptyset$ is equivalent to the given scheme. Furthermore, $comp(R^*, R") = (1, 1)$. In other integrity constraints R is to be replaced by $R"$.*

Fact 11 *If for the relationship types $R = (R_1, ..., R_k, attr(R))$, $R' = (R'_1, ..., R'_m, attr(R'))$ with $R = R'_j$ and $attr(R) \bigcap attr(R') = \emptyset$ the constraint $comp(R', R'_j) = (1, 1)$ is valid in R' then R and R' can be replaced by*

$R" = (R'_1, ..., R_{j-1}, R_1, ..., R_k, R_{j+1}, ..., R'_m, (attr(R') \bigcup attr(R)))$.
In integrity constraints R and R' are to be replaced by $R"$.

This can be used for simplifying or compactifying schemes. For instance, given
$R = (R_1, R_2, R_3, attr(R))$, $R_1 = (R_4, R_5, attr(R_1))$, $R_5 = (R_6, R_7, attr(R_5))$,
$comp(R, R_1 R_2) \leq (1,1)$, $comp(R_1, R_4) \leq (1,1)$, $comp(R_5, R_6) \leq (1,1)$.
Then an equivalent scheme is obtained replacing this subscheme in the scheme by
the following subscheme and replacing the corresponding cardinality constraints.
$R" = (R"_1, R_2, \emptyset)$, $R^* = (R", R_3, attr(R))$, , $R"_1 = (R_4, \emptyset)$,
$R_1^* = (R"_1, R"_5, attr(R_1))$, $R"_5 = (R_6, \emptyset)$, $R_5^* = (R"_5, R_7, attr(R_5))$.
This scheme is replacing the more complicated relationships types by three IsA-
relationships to the characterizing parts of the relationship types.
In the same sense, we can use (1,1)-cardinality constraints of relationship types
for compactification of schemes. Further, using this characterization (0,1)-cardi-
nality constraints can be omitted using an additional IsA type. This simplifies
the task of translation to network and relational schemes.
Given two relationship types $R_1 = (R_3, R_4, attr(R_1))$, $R_2 = (R_1, R_5, attr(R_2))$,
and the cardinality constraint $comp(R_2, R_1) = (1,1)$ and let $attr(R_1) \cap attr(R_2))$
$= \emptyset$. Then these two relationship types can be replaced by the equivalent relationship type $R_{12} = (R_3, R_4, R_5, attr(R_1) \bigcup attr(R_2))$.

Simplification of Schemes

We can use cardinality constraints also for the simplification of schemes. Nor-
mally, one-to-many relationship types are considered to be uncritical and for this
reason not revised. Let us consider the following example:
Person = ({ PName, ChildName } , { PName, ChildName }),
School = ({ SName, Address }, { SName }),
Connected = (Person, School, $\emptyset$) .
We get the following cardinality constraints:
$comp(Connected, Person) = (0,1)$, $comp(Connected, School) = (1,.)$.
However, it is valid also the cardinality constraint
$comp(Connected, Person[ChildName]) = (0,1)$.
Therefore, the concept *Person* is overloaded and should be simplified by the fol-
lowing scheme with the weak entity type *Child*.
Person' = ({ PName } , { PName }),
School = ({ SName, Address }, { SName }),
Connected' = (Child, School, $\emptyset$) ,
Child = ({ Childname }, { Childname, PersonsChild.Person' }),
PersonsChild = (Person, Child, $\emptyset$).
The last schema is extending the first but the key is to be reduced in the rela-
tionship *Connected'*.

Fact 12 *The following schemes are equivalent if the path constraint*
$R - S - T : A = B$ *and the cardinality constraints*
$comp(S, R) \geq (1,1)$, $comp(S, T) \geq (1,1)$ *are valid in the first schema:*

1. $R = (...A...)$, $S = (R, T, ...)$, $T = (...B...)$;
2. $S = (R', T', ..., A, ...)$ R', T' , where R' and T' are obtained from the types R, T after removal of A, B;
3. $S'' = (R, T', ...)$, R, T', where T' is obtained from T after removal of B.

For the proof of Fact 12 we use the set-theoretic interpretation.

Removal of Inconsistent Parts from Schemes

We can ask now whether it is possible to obtain from inconsistent schemes consistent subschemes.
Algorithm 1.
Given a ER-scheme $\underline{S} = E_1, ...E_n, R_1, ..., R_k$, a set of associated cardinality constraints $\underline{C}$, and a set $\underline{P} = \{p_i \mid 1 \le i \le m\}$ of critical cycles.
Step 1. Mark all entity and relationship types which are in a critical cycle of $\underline{P}$.
Step 2. Mark all relationship types which have components which are marked.
Step 3. Repeat step 2 until all possible relationship types are marked.
Step 4. Delete all marked entity and relationship types and associated cardinality constraints from the scheme.

Fact 13 *The scheme $(\underline{S}', \underline{C}')$ obtained from scheme $(\underline{S}, \underline{C})$ by algorithm 1 is consistent.*

Correction of Cardinality Constraints

We can exploit the weight function of paths also for **scheme corrections**. Let us consider paths p with $weight(p) = 1$.

Let us consider an abstract scheme: $R_2 = (R_1, R_3, \emptyset)$, $R_4 = (R_3, R_1, \emptyset)$, $comp(R_2, R_1) = comp(R_4, R_3) = (1, 1)$, $comp(R_2, R_3) = comp(R_4, R_1) = (0, 1)$. According to Fact 7 this scheme is consistent. Let us assume that one of the $(0, 1)$-cardinality constraints is proper in the database (R_1^t, R_2^t, R_3^t, R_4^t), for instance the first. Then there is an element c in R_3^t which is not related to an element in R_1^t by R_2^t. This element is related to one and only one element a in R_1^t by R_4^t. This element is related to another element c' of R_3^t by R_2^t. Via R_4^t we obtain another element a' in R_1^t. Now we get $(a', c'') \in R_1^t$. Further, $c'' \ne c$. Continuing this consideration we conclude that the database must be infinite in this case. If this scheme has a finite database then no such dangling c exists. Therefore we get $comp(R_2, R_1) = (1, 1)$, $comp(R_2, R_3) = (1, 1)$, $comp(R_4, R_3) = (1, 1)$, $comp(R_4, R_1) = (1, 1)$, .

Fact 14 *Given a ER-scheme $\underline{S}$ and a set of associated cardinality constraints $\underline{C}$ and a cycle p with $weight(p) = 1$. Then all cardinality constraints of the cycle are finite, i.e. for the graph $G(\underline{S}, \underline{C}) = (V, E)$ and the path $p = v_1, ..., v_n$ of nodes from V with $(v_i, v_{i+1}, j) \in E$ for some j the condition $j \ne \infty$ for all $i, 1 \le i < n$.*

The Fact can not be extended to paths with a weight higher than 1. In this case, dangling entities are possible. Using this Fact we can use now the following algorithm for correcting schemes.

Algorithm 2.

Given a ER-scheme $\underline{S} = E_1, ...E_n, R_1, ..., R_k$, a set of associated cardinality constraints $\underline{C}$, and a set $\underline{P} = \{p_i \mid 1 \leq i \leq m\}$ of cycles with weight 1.

Step. For each cycle and for the cardinality constraints $comp(R_i, R_j = (x, y)$ in the cycle: If $x = 0$ then correct x to 1.

Algorithm 2 and Fact 14 leads directly to the following Fact.

Consequence 2 *Given a ER-scheme $\underline{S}$ and a set of associated cardinality constraints $\underline{C}$. The scheme $(\underline{S}, \underline{C})$ is equivalent to the scheme $G(\underline{S}, \underline{C'})$ obtained by algorithm 2.*

5 Conclusion

We have developed a theory for cardinality constraints which could be used in database design for the solution of several problems. In the same manner, other constraints could be considered and theoretically based [Tha92',Tha93]. It is important that all these properties can be encorporated into design systems and then be used for the simplification of the design process.

References

[BCN92] C. Batini, S. Ceri, and S. Navathe, Conceptual database design, An entity-relationship approach. Benjamin Cummings, Redwood, 1992.

[BDK91] P. Buneman, S. Davidson, and A. Kosky, Theoretical aspects of schema merging. Proc. EDBT92, LNCS 580, 152-167.

[CFP84] M.A. Casanova, R. Fagin, and C.H. Papadimitiou, Inclusion dependencies and their interaction with functional dependencies. Journal of Computer and System Sciences, 28 1, 1984, 29–59.

[Che76] P. P. S. Chen. The Entity-Relationship Model: Toward a unified view of data. ACM TODS 1,1, 1976, 9–36.

[CoK83] S.S. Cosmodakis and P.C. Kanellakis, Functional and inclusion dependencies - A graph theoretic approach. Technical Report CS-83-21, Brown University, Dept. of Computer Science, 1983.

[EN89] R. Elmasri and S. H. Navathe, Fundamentals of database systems. Benjamin/Cummings Publ., Redwood City, 1989.

[Fer91] S. Ferg, Cardinality concepts in entity-relationship modeling. Proc. 10 ER-Conference (ed. T. Teorey), 1991, 1-30.

[GrM85] J. Grant and J. Minker, Inferences for numerical dependencies. Theoretical Computer Science 41, 1985, 271–287.

[KCV83] P.C. Kanellakis, S.S. Cosmodakis, and M.Y. Vardi, Unary inclusion dependencies have polynomial time inference problems. Technical report CS-83-09, Brown University, Dept. of Computer Science, 1983.

[Kob85] I. Kobayashi, An overview of database mangement technology. In Advances in Information System Science, ed. J.T. Tou, Vol. 9, Plenum Press, New York, 1985.

[LN90] M. Lenzerini and P. Nobili, On the satisfiability of dependency constraints in entity-relationship schemata. Information Systems, Vol. 15, 4, 1990, 453–461.

[Mit83] J.C. Mitchell, The implication problem for functional and inclusion dependencies. information and Control, 56, 3, 1983, 154–173.

[NiH89] G. M. Nijssen and T. A. Halpin. Conceptual schema and relational database design - a fact oriented approach. Prentice Hall, Sydney 1989.

[Ris88] N. Rishe. Database Design Fundamentals. Prentice-Hall, Englewood-Cliffs, 1988.

[SST92] K.-D. Schewe, J.W. Schmidt, B. Thalheim, and I. Wetzel, Integrity Enforcement in Object-Oriented Databases. Workshop Modelling Database Dynamics, Volkse 1992.

[Teo89] J.T. Teorey. Database Modeling and Design: The Entity-Relationship Approach. Morgan Kaufmann Publ. San Mateo, 1989.

[Tha89] B. Thalheim. The higher-order entity-relationship model and $(DB)^2$. LNCS 364, Springer 1989, 382–397.

[Tha91] B. Thalheim. Dependencies in Relational Databases. Leipzig, Teubner Verlag 1991.

[Tha91'] B. Thalheim, Concepts of database design. In: Trends in database management systems, (eds. G. Vossen, K.-U. Witt), Oldenbourg, München, 1–48 (in German).

[Tha92] B. Thalheim, The database design system (DB^2). Research and Practical issues in databases (eds. B. Srinivasan, J. Zeleznikow), Worlds Scientific, Singapore, 1992, 279-292.

[Tha92'] B. Thalheim, Foundations of entity-relationship modeling. Annals of Mathematics and Artificial Intelligence, 6, Nov. 1992.

[Tha93] B. Thalheim, Fundamentals of the entity-relationship model. Springer, Heidelberg, 1993.

[TL82] D. Tsichritzis and F. Lochovsky, Data Models. Prentice-Hall, 1982.

[Vos87] G. Vossen. Datenmodelle, Datenbanksprachen und Datenbank-Management-Systeme. Addison-Wesley, Bonn, 1987.

[ZNG90] J. Zhu, R. Nassif, P. Goyal, P. Drew and B. Askelid. Incorporating a model hierarchy into the ER paradigm. Proc. 9th ER Conference, ed. H. Kangassalo, 1990, 68–80.

Evaluation of Complex Cardinality Constraints

Jian Zhou and Peter Baumann

Fraunhofer–Institut für Graphische Datenverarbeitung (FhG–IGD)
Wilhelminenstr. 7, Darmstadt, Germany
email: {zhou, baumann}@igd.fhg.de

Abstract. In a previous paper, the *valence concept*, a general method to describe relationships, has been introduced along with a set-theoretic formal semantics. This approach is type-based, admits variants and detailed cardinality specifications, and can cope with incomplete intermediate states. Nevertheless, the resulting syntax is easy to understand.

In this paper, an implementation of the valence concept is outlined. Special emphasis has been placed on minimizing space and time overhead on instance level, but it turns out that data dictionary overhead also keeps within reasonable limits.

Please note that the valence concept is not a complete data model by itself, but a relationship model which can be embedded in a wide range of data models.

Key Words: Entity-Relationship model, Relationship semantics, Valence concept, April

1 Introduction

In the course of developing a data model for engineering design applications [1] based on the Entity-Relationship Model, current object and attribute modeling concepts proved to be developed enough for that purpose; support for specifying relationships in a general, flexible manner, however, turned out to be insufficient. The main critical points are

- cardinality specification over homogeneous and heterogeneous reference sets,
- variant relationships, and
- incremental construction of relationship instances.

The granularity of current cardinality specification capabilities is limited to compact intervals described by minimum and maximum bounds, e.g., *zero to five or four to infinity*. This is too coarse for many applications – think of a car which always has an even number of wheels, greater or equal to four. Besides, such constraints are restricted to homogeneous instance sets which span only one entity type; it is not possible to express conditions on heterogeneous entity sets (for example, a car must have twice as many wheels as axles). Although such cardinality constraints in principle could be monitored by a constraint manager (if available), it was felt that structure description should be as rich as possible to provide a high degree of model-inherent consistency.

Another issue is the need to model variants in the set of references comprising a relationship. Usual data abstractions, e.g., aggregates and sets, fail to express variants. In another approach, which has been adopted, e.g., by the expert system PLAKON [6], variant relationships are introduced by differentiating between **AND** branches for the usual *part_of* decomposition and **OR** branches representing choices among the items listed. However, such an approach allows only one kind of branching per nesting level, thus requiring auxiliary nodes for every variant. To the best of our knowledge, there is no model allowing to mix **AND** and **OR** branches.

Finally, incremental design should be supported in a way that incomplete intermediate states are allowed which means that references can be inserted into and removed from a relationship instance dynamically. Moreover, it should be possible to query the completeness status of a relationship instance at any time. Especially for design applications, such facilities seem indispensable.

The *valence concept* has been suggested in [2] to overcome these shortcomings. It allows to describe reference sets, so-called *valence bundles*, including detailed cardinality constraints and variants. Furthermore, it enables the database system to monitor design completeness, i.e., whether all specified references are present. Although based on a formal semantics, the resulting syntax is very suggestive and easy to understand. The valence concept does not require any special capability of the overall data model besides typing and object identity, hence it is neutral enough to be incorporated in virtually any ERM-based or object-oriented data model.

To prevent from misunderstanding, it should be noted that valences only deal with local properties of object graphs, i.e., the fan-out of a relationship graph node; global assertions like acyclicity in hierarchical relationships need further mechanisms. In this sense, it does not matter whether valences are used to describe complex objects or relationships.

Meanwhile , we have done two different implementations of the valence concept. In a first approach, valence definitions are mapped to finite automata whose task is to monitor admissibility and completeness of valence bundles. This version cannot cope with infinite upper bounds in cardinality ranges, and the exponential complexity of the construction algorithm makes is unacceptably slow. In a second approach, valence definitions are mapped to equation and unequation systems. This implementation covers all language constructs and, moreover, proved to be very efficient both in space and in time.

In this paper, the second implementation strategy shall be presented. To this end, the remainder of the paper is organized as follows. In the following section, a brief informal introduction to the valence concept is given. After a summary of the formal semantics in Section 3, a normal form is introduced in Section 4. These preparations are needed in Section 5, the central part of this paper, where the evaluation of valence definitions on type and instance level is explained. A brief look at space and time requirements is given in Section 6. Section 7 summarizes the plot.

2 Valences

In this section, an informal introduction to the valence concept is given, which, however, does not reveal the full expressiveness of the approach – please refer to the initial paper [2]. The running example used is drawn from garment industry, describing an ensemble of women's outer wear (see Figure 1 below).

Fig. 1: Complete instances of an *Ensemble*

Some terminology is required first. A *valence* is a binary, directed edge emanating from a relationship and directed towards another object (entity or relationship). A valence is called named, if a role is assigned to it. Valences are grouped according to the relationship instance they start from. The whole of valences belonging to a relationship instance forms its *valence bundle*. The description of valence bundles during type definition is done by means of the valence expression.

For the subsequent discussion, we focus on the description of an ensemble's parts on type level by specifying the valence bundle of the complex object type or relationship type *Ensemble* (for the purpose of this paper, the latter distinction does not make any difference).

First, assume the ensemble is made up from only one dress. The corresponding valence expression, then, is just as simple:

> *Dress*

This means that only one valence to an object of type *Dress* is allowed. Valences to objects of different types are described using the **and** operator. The expression

> *Dress* **and** *Jacket* **and** *Shoe*

allows for one valence to a *Dress*, a *Jacket*, and a *Shoe* object, resp. However, in real life one would like to wear two shoes; this can be overcome by specifying

> *Dress* **and** *Jacket* **and** *Shoe* **and** *Shoe*

or, abbreviated by a cardinality specification,

> *Dress* **and** *Jacket* **and** *2 Shoe*

An arbitrary number of references can be specified by employing the "*" – operator as an upper bound; for example,

> *0..1 Jacket* **and** *0..* Necklace*

means that an optional *Jacket* object and an arbitrary number *Necklace* objects may occur.

Whereas in summer stockings are not always necessary, one probably would like to wear warm stockings in winter, sometimes even more than only one pair. Hence, a subexpression is introduced allowing for an even, but otherwise arbitrary number of *Stocking* valences:

> *0..* (2 Stocking)*

Assume there is an alternative set of womens' outer wear consisting of a blouse and a skirt or trousers instead of a single dress. Such alternatives can be specified using the **xor** operator:

> *Dress* **xor** (*Blouse* **and** (*Skirt* **xor** *Trousers*))

It may be required to distinguish explicitly between a right and a left shoe. This is accomplished by roles; the expression

> *Shoe* **as** *Right* **and** *Shoe* **as** *Left*

associates the role names *Right* and *Left*, resp., with each valence to a *Shoe* object.

By combining all features introduced so far, a complete definition of an *En-*

semble's components can be given:

> (*Dress* xor (*Blouse* and (*Skirt* xor *Trousers*)))
> and *0..1 Jacket*
> and *0..* Necklace*
> and *0..* (2 Stocking)*
> and *Shoe* as *Right* and *Shoe* as *Left*

Fig. 2: the Complete definition of an *Ensemble*

In the classical ERM, a relationship may exist only if all references prescribed in the type definition are present. Contrary to this, the valence concept allows to establish a relationship piecemeal. This comes more close to the style of work in CAD, where usually partial results are brought in at different times. In order to determine whether a valence bundle contains all elements prescribed by the type definition, the status *design complete* is introduced. An object or a relationship is called *design complete* (or short: *complete*), if its valence bundle complies with one of the variants defined in the valence expression. If it complies only with a proper subset, the object's status is *incomplete*. Exceeding a cardinality constraint or inserting a valence to an object of a type not mentioned is forbidden.

In the next Section, we present a brief overview of the formal semantics.

3 Formal Semantics

Intuitively, a valence expression describes a set of alternative valence bundles, each of which in turn consists of a set of the referenced object identifiers. On type level, the object identifiers are replaced by type identifiers, hence the set becomes a multiset where multiple occurrences of the same type are tractable. The interpretation $I(V)$ of a valence expression V, therefore, is a set of multisets over type identifiers. We use $\sqcup$ and $\sqsubseteq$ to denote multiset union and containment, as opposed to the corresponding set operators $\cup$ and $\subseteq$.

We give a recursive definition of the interpretation function $I(V)$ of a valence expression V by providing five rules. The first rule starts the recursive definition by stating that a single type identifier represents one alternative consisting of exactly one valence of the mentioned type.

(1) Every type identifier

> T

is an expression. The interpretation is

> $I(T) = [\ T\ ]$

The following rule serves to connect expressions by **and**, **xor**, and **or**; further, parentheses are introduced.

(2) If A and B are expressions, then

> A and B
> A xor B
> A or B
> (A)

are also expressions. They are interpreted according to the following rules.

> $I(A$ and $B) = \{ M \mid M = M_A \sqcup M_B, M_A \in I(A), M_B \in I(B) \}$
> $I(A$ xor $B) = I(A) \cup I(B)$
> $I(A$ or $B) = I(A$ xor B xor $(A$ and $B))$
> $I((A)) = I(A)$

The following three rules describe cardinality constraints.

(3) Let A be a expression and m a natural number. Then,

> $m\ A$

is an expression. The interpretation is defined recursively as

> $I(0\ A) = [\ ]$
> $I(m\ A) = I(m'\ A$ and $A)$ with $m' = m - 1$ for $m > 0$

(4) Let m and n be natural numbers with $m < n$. Then,

> $m\ ..\ n\ A$

is an expression. It is to be interpreted as

> $I(m\ ..\ m\ A) = I(m\ A)$
> $I(m\ ..\ n\ A) = I(m\ ..\ n'\ A$ xor $n\ A)$ with $n' = n - 1$ for $m < n$.

(5) For $m \geq 0$,

> $m..\ *\ A$

is an expression. The interpretation is defined as

$$I(0..\ *\ A) = \{ M \mid M = \bigsqcup_{i=0}^{n} M_i, M_i \in I(A), n \in N_0 \}$$

> $I(m\ ..\ *\ A) = I(m\ A$ and $0\ ..\ *\ A)$ for $m > 0$.

A slight modification of the formalism allows to take into account role names. However, it is omitted here for reasons of simplicity as it does not affect the following discussion; the interested reader can refer to [2].

Based on this interpretation of a valence specification, admissibility and design completeness can be formalized. A valence bundle v is *design complete* wrt. a valence definition V iff its corresponding type multiset $t(v)$ corresponds with one of the alternatives in $I(V)$:

> $design\_complete(v, V) :\Longleftrightarrow t(v) \in I(V)$

For example, a valence bundle v_1 whose type multiset is
$t(v1) = [Dress, Stocking, Stocking, Shoe, Shoe]$ is design complete wrt. the *Ensemble* specification, whereas a valence bundle v_2 with
$t(v_2) = [Dress, Stocking]$ obviously is incomplete.

A valence bundle v is *admissible* wrt. a valence definition V iff its corresponding type multiset is a subset of one of the alternatives contained in $I(V)$:

> $admissible(v, V) :\Longleftrightarrow \exists v' \in I(V): t(v) \sqsubseteq t(v')$

The above example bundle v_2 is incomplete, yet admissible as an *Ensemble* valence bundle; an example for a non-admissible bundle would be *[Dress, Shoe,*

Shoe, Shoe, Cap], because (1) only two shoes are allowed and (2) a cap was not anticipated.

There is a number of algebraic laws obeyed by valence expressions and these can be used to transform valence expressions into equivalent forms. Here two valence expressions are considered equivalent if and only if their interpretations are the same. Table 1 shows some algebraic laws that hold for valence expressions *A*, *B* and *C* with integers *m* and *n*.

Some of the theorems are direct inferences of the formal definition given above,

Table 1. Algebraic properties of valence expressions

THEOREM	DESCRIPTION
A and *B* = *B* and *A*	and is commutative
A xor *B* = *B* xor *A*	xor is commutative
(*A* and *B*) and *C* = *A* and (*B* and *C*)	and is associative
(*A* xor *B*) xor *C* = *A* xor (*B* xor *C*)	xor is associative
A and (*B* xor *C*) = (*A* and *B*) xor (*A* and *C*)	and distributes over xor
A xor *A* = *A*	alternative is idempotent
m A and *n A* = (*m*+*n*) *A*	
0..* (*A* xor *B*) = 0..* *A* and 0..* *B*	relation between "0..*" and xor
0..* (*A* and 0..* *B*) = 0..* *A* and 0..* *B*	relation between "0..*" and and
0..* *A* and 0..* *A* = 0..* *A*	relation between "0..*" and and
0..* (0..* *A*) = 0..* *A*	"0..*" is idempotent

while others are not so evident. But usually, if we assume A and B to be type identifiers instead of arbitrary valence expressions, informal explanations for the verification of the theorems can be given. For example, let *S* and *T* be two type identifiers, we see that both valence expressions *0..* (S* xor *T)* and *0..* S* and *0..* T* specify nothing more than that the number of valence instance of type *S* and of type *T* are unlimited, hence

   0..* (S xor *T) = 0..* S* and *0..* T*

holds.

We can prove all of the theorems formally by demonstrating the equivalence of the two sets which comprise the interpretations of the two valence expressions in a valence expression respectively, but we have to omit the formal proofs here due to space limitation. The interested reader can refer to [7].

4 Normalization of the Valence Expression

The database management system monitors the cardinality constraints specified by valence expressions and performs queries to the completeness of relationship instances. Since the same cardinality constraints and completeness criteria may be expressed by very different forms of valence expressions, it is necessary to *normalize* a valence expression before it is evaluated by the database management system. Therefore, in this Section, we first design the normal form for valence expressions. Then, we propose an algorithm to normalize valence expressions.

4.1 The Normal Form of Valence Expressions

The *normal form* of valence expressions is designed in a way that the database management system can mechanically extract the cardinality constraints and completeness criteria from a normalized valence expression. It has the form of

$$T_1 \text{ xor } T_2 \text{ xor } \ldots \text{ xor } T_t \ . \tag{1}$$

Each $T_i(1 \leq i \leq t)$ is called *a term* and defined as

$$F_0 \text{ and } 0..* F_1 \text{ and } \ldots \text{ and } 0..* F_f \tag{2}$$

where $F_j(0 \leq j \leq f)$ is called *a factor* and has a form of

$$m_1 X_1 \text{ and } m_2 X_2 \text{ and } \ldots \text{ and } m_s X_s \ . \tag{3}$$

Here $m_k(1 \leq k \leq s)$ are nonnegative integers and $X_k(1 \leq k \leq s)$ are type identifiers. Each $m_k X_k$ is called an *atom factor*.

In the normal form above, each term represents a mutually exclusive variant of the valence bundles, thus the terms $T_i(1 \leq i \leq t)$ should be different from each other. Equivalent terms can be eliminated by Theorem $A \text{ xor } A = A$ in Table 1.

Within a term, F_0 comprises the mandatory component of the variant represented by a term, and the other factors, $F_j(1 \leq j \leq f)$, represent the optional components of the variant. Please notice that a term may have no optional components, that means F_0 itself is also a term, and that a term without the mandatory component is also permitted, which means the term itself is optional in the entire valence expression. Using Theorem $0..* A \text{ and } 0..* A = 0..* A$, the factors representing optional components, i.e. $F_j(1 \leq j \leq f)$, keep different.

The atom factors are basic elements of a normal form. Theorem $mA \text{ and } nA = (m+n)$ can be used to merge those atom factors having the same type identifier.

As an example, we now build up a normal form in a bottom-up way. Let's look at the valence expression describing the ensemble in Section 2. First we use atom factors to describe some basic components of an ensemble, such as

> *2 Shoe.*

Then, we define factors by connecting atom factors with ands to describe a group of components of an ensemble. For instance,

Jacket and *2 Shoe*

is a factor specifying two components of an ensemble. Furthermore, **ands** are used to connect factors to form a term, which describes a variant completely (note that a factor describes a variant partially). The term

Dress and *Jacket* and *0..* Necklace* and *2 Shoe*

describes a variant of an ensemble. Finally, all the variants of an ensemble are collected to a complete normal form by connecting the terms with with **xors**, yielding

(Dress and *2 Shoe* and *0..* Necklace* and *0..* (2 Stocking))*
xor *(Blouse* and *Skirt* and *2 Shoe* and *0..* Necklace* and *0..* (2 Stocking))*
xor *(Blouse* and *Trousers* and *2 Shoe* and *0..* Necklace* and *0..* (2 Stocking))*
xor *(Dress* and *Jacket* and *2 Shoe* and *0..* Necklace* and *0..* (2 Stocking))*
xor *(Blouse* and *Skirt* and *Jacket* and *2 Shoe* and *0..* Necklace*
      and *0..* (2 Stocking))*
xor *(Blouse* and *Trousers* and *Jacket* and *2 Shoe* and *0..* Necklace*
      and *0..* (2 Stocking))*

Fig. 3: The normal form describing an ensemble

The normal form above reveals that an ensemble has six variants, each of them consisting of several components. For instance, the variant described by the first term

(Dress and *2 Shoe* and *0..* Necklace* and *0..* (2 Stocking))*

specifies that one alternative of an ensemble can consist of a dress, a pair of shoes, several necklaces and several pairs of stockings. As we will see soon, a normal form can be manipulated more easily. In the second part of this Section, we propose the normalization algorithm.

4.2   The Normalization Algorithm

We now give an algorithm to normalize a valence expression. The algorithm is syntax-directed in that it uses the syntactic structure of the valence expression to guide the normalization process. The cases in the algorithm follow the cases in the definition of a valence expression. We first parse a valence expression into its constituent subexpressions. Note that the most basic subexpression, the atom factor, is already in its normal form. Then, guided by the syntactic structure of the valence expression, we combine these normalized subexpressions inductively using the rules below until we obtain the normal form for the entire expression.

1. For a type identifier T, its normal form is T.
2. Suppose A and B are two normalized subexpressions.
   (a) For the valence expression A and B, we normalize it using the distributivity of and over xor to "draw out" xor in each subexpression. Besides, we use other theorems in Table 1 to merge same terms, same factors, and atom factors having the same type identifiers.

(b) For the valence expression A **xor** B, we normalize it by **merging the same** terms in A and B.

(c) For the valence expression A **or** B, we normalize its equivalent form A **xor** B **xor** *(A and B))* using the rules 2(a) and 2(b).

(d) For the valence expression (A), its normal form is A.

3. Suppose A is a normalized subexpression and m and n are two natural numbers with $m \leq n$.

(a) For the valence expression m A, we first expand m A to a sequence of m occurrences of A connected by **and**. Then, we normalize it using the rule 2(a).

(b) For the valence expression $m..n$ A, we first break $m..n$ A down into alternatives whose cardinality specifiers run through all numbers between m and n. Then, we normalize the valence expression representing each alternative using the rule 3(a) and normalize the entire expression using the rule 2(b).

(c) For the valence expression m $..*$ A, which is equivalent to m A **and** $0..*$ A, we first normalize the subexpression $0..*$ A. Using Theorem

$$0..* (A \text{ xor } B) = 0..* A \text{ and } 0..* B,$$

we distribute "$0..*$" over **xor**. Using the theorems

$$0..* (0..* A) = 0..* A \qquad \text{and}$$
$$0..*(A \text{ and } 0..* B) = 0..* A \text{ and } 0..* B ,$$

we eliminate the nested "$0..*$". After merging the same terms, factors, and the atom factors having the same type identifiers, we obtain the normal form for $0..* A$. Then, using the rule 2(a) and 3(a), we normalize the entire expression.

Due to space limitation, we can only sketch the normalization algorithm and have to omit many details. To obtain a better understanding of the normalization process, the reader is encouraged to normalize the valence expression in Figure 2, using the algorithm sketched above; the result is given in Figure 3.

It can be proved that a normal form exists for every syntactically correct valence expression and is unique except for the commutativity and the associativity. In the next section, we show how to deduce cardinality constraints and completeness criteria from a normalized valence expression and how to evaluate them.

5 Evaluation Algorithms

In this Section, we propose our method to evaluate complex cardinality constraints on the base of a normal form. The evaluation includes two aspects. The first one is to check the admissibility of update operations, and second, the database management system keeps track of update operations so that it can tell the design completeness status of a relationship instance at any time. The two aspects of the evaluation are discussed in the two next subsections.

5.1 Cardinality Constraints

Cardinality constraints define an *upper bound* for each type in a valence expression. For example,

   Dress and *2 Shoe* and *0..* Necklace* and *0..* (2 Stocking)*

specifies that an alternative of an ensemble may have no more than one dress and two shoes, while the numbers of necklaces and stockings are unlimited. When a valence of a certain type is to be inserted, the database management system compares the number of the existing valences of this type with its upper bound and ensures that the upper bound will not be exceeded.

At type level, such cardinality constraints are described by an *upper bound array* which is subscripted by type identifiers. Each element of an upper bound array specifies the maximal admissible number of valences of a type. In the example above, the upper bound for *Dress*, *Shoe*, *Necklace* and *Stocking* valence is one, two, infinite, and infinite respectively, yielding the upper bound array

Dress	Shoe	Necklace	Stocking
1	2	∞	∞

At instance level, the database management system keeps track of insertions and deletions through maintaining a *counter array* in every relationship instance. Each element of a counter array records the current number of valences of a certain type. For example, an ensemble has a counter array of four counters C_{Dress}, C_{Shoe}, $C_{Necklace}$ and $C_{Stocking}$, which records the current numbers of the corresponding valences.

Before a valence of a certain type can be inserted, the appropriate counter in the relationship's counter array is increased by one. Then, the updated counter array is compared with a upper bound array element by element. If there is some counter in the updated counter array exceeds its upper bound, the insert operation will be rejected and the counter array restored.

The algorithm to calculate upper bounds is described in detail in [7]. Here we give the upper bound arrays for the entire normal form in Figure 3. Each of the upper bound array is subscripted by (*Dress, Blouse, Skirt, Jacket, Trousers, Shoe, Necklace, Stocking*).

Dress	Blouse	Skirt	Jacket	Trousers	Shoe	Necklace	Stocking
1	0	0	0	0	2	∞	∞
0	1	1	0	0	2	∞	∞
0	1	0	0	1	2	∞	∞
1	0	0	1	0	2	∞	∞
0	1	1	1	0	2	∞	∞
0	1	0	1	1	2	∞	∞

As demonstrated above, for each term in a normal form, an upper bound array will be produced. To decide the admissibility of an insert operation, a relationship's counter array will be compared with each term's upper bound array. An insertion is admissible if and only if it is admissible according to at least one term's upper bound array.

5.2 Completeness Criteria

In this Subsection, we describe how to express completeness criteria and how to evaluate completeness queries.

An Example. We first give an example to explain in detail what is completeness in the context of this paper. The normal form selected in the example is an abstract one so that each case of the query evaluation can be demonstrated concisely. Below is the normal form used in the example:

2 T and 3 S and 0..* (T and 2 U) and 0..* (3 V)

Three completeness criteria are specified by the normal form:

1. the number of the valences of type S must reach three;
2. the valences of type T is divided into two groups; the number of one group must be two and the number of another group must be a half of the number of valences of type U;
3. the number of valences of type V must be a multiple of the integer three.

Completeness criteria can be expressed by an equation system. The unknowns of the equation system represent the number of valences. In the equation systems, the unknowns are represented by the corresponding type identifiers. If a type identifier occurs more than one time, each occurrence has a corresponding unknown in the equation system and is represented by the type identifier subscripted by a small integer. In our example, we have unknowns S, U and V representing the number of valences of types S, U and V respectively; the valences of type T are divided into two groups and the number of each group is represented by two unknowns T_1 and T_2 respectively. From the three criteria listed above, we obtain four equations:

$$S = 3 \tag{4}$$
$$T_1 = 2 \tag{5}$$
$$2T_2 = U \tag{6}$$
$$V = 3X \tag{7}$$

A dummy unknown X is introduced which is restricted to nonnegative integers.

The four equations above reflect the constraints proposed by the data schema. On the other hand, the equation system must connect a relationship's current valence bundles with the data schema. For this purpose, four parameterized constants C_S, C_T, C_U and C_V are introduced, representing the current number of valences of type S, T, U and V respectively, and another four equations are added:

$$S = C_S \tag{8}$$
$$T_1 + T_2 = C_T \tag{9}$$
$$U = C_U \tag{10}$$
$$V = C_V \tag{11}$$

The two groups of equations above are merged into one equation system which is stored in the data dictionary. This equation system is called the *completeness equation system* of the valence expression.

When the completeness of a relationship is queried, the relationship's counter array replaces the four parameterized constants C_S, C_T, C_U and C_V in the completeness equation system. If the equation system has solutions in nonnegative integer domain, the second equation group is compatible with the first one. That means the number and type of the queried relationship's valences conform to the completeness criteria specified by the valence expression. The relationship is, therefore, complete. Since each unknown represents the number of valences, it is necessary for them to be nonnegative integers.

If a normalized valence expression consists of more than one term, each term has its own completeness equation system. When the completeness of a relationship is queried, the relationship's counter array replaces the parameterized constants in each completeness equation system and the solvability of each equation system is determined. The relationship is complete if and only if at least one completeness equation system is solvable in nonnegative integer domain. The rest of this Subsection will show how to put most effort into the construction of the data dictionary to decide the solvability efficiently.

Construct Completeness Equation System. We now introduce the algorithm which generates the completeness equation system from a normal form. To speed up the evaluation query, we diagonalize the completeness equation system before we save it in the data dictionary.

For each term of a normal form, the following algorithm constructs a completeness equation system for it. Let the term be of form

$$F_0 \text{ and } 0..*F_1 \text{ and } \ldots \text{and } 0..*F_f$$

where $F_i (0 \leq i \leq f)$ are factors which are represented as

$$F_i = m_{i,1} X_{i,1} \text{ and } m_{i,2} X_{i,2} \ldots \text{and } m_{i,s_i} X_{i,s_i} \ (0 \leq i \leq f)$$

where $s_i (0 \leq i \leq f)$ are the number of atom factors in factor F_i, $X_{i,j} (1 \leq j \leq s_i)$ are type identifiers and $m_{i,j} (1 \leq j \leq s_i)$ are integers. During constructing the equation system, the type identifiers are used to represent unknowns, and each occurrence of type identifiers corresponds to an unknown. Here is the algorithm:

```
1.   for each atom factor m_{0,j}X_{0,j} in F_0, 1 ≤ j ≤ s_0, do
2.        output equation     X_{0,j} = m_{0,j};
3.   for each factor F_i(1 ≤ i ≤ t) do
4.   begin
5.        if s_i > 1 then
6.            for j from 1 to s_i - 1 do
7.                output equation   m_{i,j+1}X_{i,j} = m_{i,j}X_{i,j+1};
8.        elseif s_i = 1 and m_{i,s_i} > 1 then
9.        begin
10.           let Dummy_i be a dummy unknown;
11.           output equation   X_{i,s_i} = m_{i,s_i}Dummy_i;
```

12.   **end**
13. **end**
14. **let** *setOfTypeIdentifier* **be the set**
      of all type identifiers of the term;
15. **for each** *typeId* **in** *setOfTypeIdentifier* **do**
16. **begin**
17.   **let** $X_{i_1,j_1}, X_{i_2,j_2}, \ldots, X_{i_u,j_u}$ **be** u **occurrences of** *type* **in the term;**
18.   **output equation** $\qquad X_{i_1,j_1} + X_{i_2,j_2} + \ldots + X_{i_u,j_u} = C_{type};$
      /* C_{typeId} **is parameterized counter recording**
      the number of valences of type *typeId* */
19. **end**

The loop from line 1 to 2 runs once for each type identifier in the first factor, the factor F_0, and produces the equations (4) and (5) in our example. The second loop, from line 3 to line 13, runs once for each factor constrained by an infinite cardinality, i.e. the factors $F_i (1 \leq i \leq f)$, and produces equations (6) and (7) in the example. The equations connecting the data schema with the current state of an relationship's valence bundles are produced by the third loop at lines 15-19. This loop runs on each type identifier once and produces equations (8) to (11).

The equation system constructed by the algorithm above can be written in matrix form as

$$A_{m \times n} X = b$$

where A is the coefficient matrix, X is the unknown vector and b is the constant vector. Below is the completeness equation system of our exemplary normal form introduced in Section 5.2.1.

$$A = \begin{bmatrix} 1 & 0 & 0 & 0 & 0 & 0 \\ 0 & 1 & 0 & 0 & 0 & 0 \\ 0 & 0 & 2 & -1 & 0 & 0 \\ 0 & 0 & 0 & 0 & 1 & -3 \\ 1 & 0 & 0 & 0 & 0 & 0 \\ 0 & 1 & 1 & 0 & 0 & 0 \\ 0 & 0 & 0 & 1 & 0 & 0 \\ 0 & 0 & 0 & 0 & 1 & 0 \end{bmatrix}, X = \begin{bmatrix} S \\ T_1 \\ T_2 \\ U \\ V \\ X \end{bmatrix}, b = \begin{bmatrix} 3 \\ 2 \\ 0 \\ 0 \\ C_S \\ C_T \\ C_U \\ C_V \end{bmatrix}$$

Note that the parameterized counters occur only in the constant vector b, so the coefficient matrix A can be fixed during the data schema definition. To minimize the overhead at instance level, we diagonalize the coefficient matrix A to a matric C of form

$$C = \begin{bmatrix} 1 & 0 & \cdot & 0 & c_{1,r+1} & \cdot & c_{1,n} \\ 0 & 1 & \cdot & 0 & c_{2,r+1} & \cdot & c_{2,n} \\ \cdot & \cdot & \cdot & \cdot & \cdot & & \cdot \\ 0 & 0 & \cdot & 1 & c_{r,r+1} & \cdot & c_{r,n} \\ 0 & 0 & \cdot & 0 & \cdot & & 0 \\ \cdot & \cdot & \cdot & \cdot & \cdot & & \cdot \\ 0 & 0 & \cdot & 0 & \cdot & & 0 \end{bmatrix}_{m \times n}$$

where r is the rank of $\mathbf{A}$ and m, n are the the dimensions of $\mathbf{A}$. The diagonalized matrix $\mathbf{C}$, the unknown vector $\mathbf{X}$ and the constant vector $\mathbf{b}$ together with the matrix transformations diagonalizing $\mathbf{A}$ are saved in the data dictionary.

Querying Completeness. Now we propose the algorithm to evaluate the query to the completeness, using the completeness criteria saved in the data dictionary.

When a relationship's completeness is queried, the parameterized counters in constant vector $\mathbf{b}$ are replaced by the relationship's counter array. Using the matrix transformations saved in the data dictionary, the constant vector $\mathbf{b}$ is transformed to d of form

$$
\mathbf{d} = \begin{bmatrix} d_1 \\ d_2 \\ \vdots \\ d_s \\ 0 \\ \vdots \\ 0 \end{bmatrix}_{m \times 1}
$$

where d_s is the last non-zero element in $\mathbf{d}$.

There are three cases concerning the solvability of the equation system:

1. if $s > r$, the equation system has no solution. Thus the relationship is not complete.
2. if $s \leq r$ and $r = n$, d is the unique solution of the equation system. Thus, the relationship is complete if and only if each $d_i (0 \leq i \leq s)$ is a nonnegative integer.
3. if $s \leq r$ and $r < n$, the equation system has multiple solutions. Since each unknown can be neither negative nor greater than the current number of the valences of the type which the unknown represents, the solution set must be finite. Thus, the relationship is complete if and only if at least one solution is in the nonnegative integer domain.

Continuing the example, we transform the coefficient matrix $\mathbf{A}$ and the constant vector $\mathbf{b}$ into $\mathbf{C}$ and $\mathbf{d}$, respectively:

$$
\mathbf{C} = \begin{bmatrix} 1&0&0&0&0&0 \\ 0&1&0&0&0&0 \\ 0&0&1&0&0&0 \\ 0&0&0&1&0&0 \\ 0&0&0&0&1&0 \\ 0&0&0&0&0&1 \\ 0&0&0&0&0&0 \\ 0&0&0&0&0&0 \end{bmatrix}, \mathbf{d} = \begin{bmatrix} 3 \\ 2 \\ C_U/2 \\ C_U \\ C_V \\ C_V/3 \\ C_S - 3 \\ 2(C_T - 2) - C_U \end{bmatrix}
$$

So we have $r = n = 5$. The value of s depends on the assignment of the relationship's counter array (C_U, C_V, C_S, C_T). Since $r = 5$, if the equation system is solvable,

$$C_S - 3 = 0 \text{ and } 2(C_T - 2) - C_U = 0$$

must hold. Furthermore,

$$C_V = 3X$$

must hold for a nonnegative integer X, i.e. C_V must be a multiple of three for the equation system to be solvable in integer domain. It is obvious that the conditions for completeness deduced here coincide with the three completeness criteria we listed in Section 5.2.1. The reader is encouraged to generate one or two completeness equation systems from the normal form of the ensemble example and to compare the completeness criteria deduced from the equation systems with intuitive expectations.

6 Performance Analysis

The amount of storage needed to evaluate the valence expression can be kept reasonably small. Let m be the number of terms and n be the number of different type identifiers. If we assume that the average occurrence times of each type identifiers is a small constant which can be omitted, at type level, the storage required for the upper bound arrays and the completeness equation systems can be expected in the average within $O(mn)$. At instance level, the extra storage needed for counter array is $O(n)$. In typical applications, both the amount of storage for the upper bound arrays and that for completeness equation systems can be kept within one kbyte. For instance, for the valence expression which we use to exemplify our evaluation method in Subsection 5.2, four integer counters are needed to record the current number of valences. In data dictionary, the storage for the upper bound arrays is 132 bytes and that for completeness criteria is 276 bytes. Therefore, the extra cost for an insertion is one read access to the data dictionary and one read/write access to the instance, which is usually required anyway. The cost for querying completeness is one read access to the data dictionary and one to the relationship instance.

7 Conclusion

The valence concept is a new refined relationship model for the family of ERMs. It is characterized by description of arbitrary cardinality constraints, definition of mutually excluding sets of references and specification of design-completeness. The purpose of this contribution is to develop an approach which can evaluate a valence expression efficiently. Comparing with the implementation in [2], the approach proposed here deals with the finite and infinite cardinalities uniformly. Because the main effort of the evaluation is put into the construction of the data dictionary, the necessary checks of type conformity cause little runtime overhead.

   The valences concept is integrated into the structurally object-oriented database system *APRIL* [1]. The query language of *APRIL* provides a built-in function *is_complete* ( ) to retrieve all relationship instances of a certain type which are in completeness states. Among the applications are VLSI design databases [4], a texture archive [5], and raster image databases [3]. Acceptance of the valence mechanism by database users is encouraging, both because of its ease of use and its quick response.

Acknowledgement

Thanks to Monique van Klev for preparing the fashion sketches.

References

1. P. Baumann, D. Köhler: *APRIL - Another PRODAT Implementation.* FhG Report Nr. FAGD-89i007, FhG-AGD Darmstadt 1989

2. P. Baumann: *Valence: A new Relationship Concept for the Entity-Relationship Model.* in: Lochovsky, F. (ed.): Entity-Relationship Approach to Database Design and Querying, Proc. of 8th Int. Conf., Toronto, 1989, North-Holland 1990, pp. 218 - 231

3. P. Baumann: *Language Support for Raster Image Manipulation in Databases.* Accepted for publication at: Workshop Graphics Modeling and Visualization in Science and Technology, April 1992, Darmstadt/Germany

4. P. Baumann, U. Jasnoch, D. Köhler, J. Zhou: *Communicating EDIF Objects: A Standard-Based Approach.* in: Ramnig, F.S.; Waxman, R. (eds.): Electronic Design Automation Frameworks, Charlotteville/USA, November 1990, North Holland 1991, pp. 229 - 238

5. P. Baumann, D. Köhler, G. Englert:*Das Texturarchiv als Beispiel für den Einsatz von nichtkonventionellen Datenbanktechniken* Proc. Workshop Intelligente integrierte Informationssysteme, Pila/Polen 24.-27.9.1990, pp. 156 - 175

6. B. Neumann, R. Cunis, A. Gnter I. Syska: *Wissensbasierte Planung und Konfiguration.* In: Brauer, W.; Wahlster, W. (eds.): Wissensbasierte Systeme, Informatik Fachberichte 155, Springer 1987, pp. 347

7. J. Zhou, P. Baumann: *Specification and Evaluation of Complex Cardinality Constrains.* FhG Report Nr. FIGD-92i008, FhG-IGD Darmstadt, May, 1992

Local referential integrity *

Gerti Kappel

Inst. für Statistik und Informatik

Universität Wien

Michael Schrefl

Inst. für Wirtschaftsinformatik

Universität Linz

Abstract

This paper introduces the concept of local referential integrity according to which an object may only reference objects belonging to the same composite object. For example, in production planning an employee of some department may only be scheduled to work on machines belonging to the same department. Usually, such a constraint must be stated explicitly by a predicate as "add on" to a database schema. Object-oriented data models have become popular for just the opposite. They represent implicitly integrity constraints which formerly had to be stated explicitly. Prominent examples, which so far have been studied independently, are referential integrity and composite objects. Local referential integrity combines both concepts by applying referential integrity within a composite object. We show that local referential integrity can be represented easily within an object-oriented database schema by using "local object classes" as domains of relationships. A local object class is a set of objects belonging exclusively to some composite object. Local referential integrity is maintained if any relationship from within a composite object to one of its local classes references a current member of that class.

Keywords: object-oriented database design, composite objects, referential integrity

1 Introduction

Object-oriented data models are influenced by two research directions, semantic data models and object-oriented programming languages. Models inspired by the former are termed "structurally object-oriented", those by the later "behaviorally object-oriented" [8]. Fully object-oriented data models cover both aspects, which are equally relevant in object-oriented design. We have addressed this topic in our previous research [12, 13] and have contributed to behavior modeling [27, 28] in particular. In this paper we continue our work by focusing on a specific aspect of structure modeling, local referential integrity.

Local referential integrity extends the well-known notion of referential integrity in the realm of composite objects. Referential integrity is satisfied if every object

---

*The research described in this paper is supported by FFF (Austrian Foundation for Research Applied to Industry) under grant No.2/279 and by SIEMENS Austria under grant GR 21/96106/5.

referenced exists [20, 21]. A composite object consists of several dependent component objects belonging exclusively to the composite object [14].[1] Local referential integrity means that in any object reference the referencing object and the referenced object belong to the same composite object. For example, consider a set of departments, each of them consisting of several employees and several machines. Furthermore, consider a relationship "works-on" relating an employee to a particular machine. Local referential integrity is satisfied if the machine referenced by an employee belongs to the same department as the employee.[2]

It is claimed that object-oriented data models provide for a natural representation of the real world and that they capture implicitly integrity constraints, which formerly had to be stated explicitly, e.g., in the relational model. The most prominent examples which support this claim are referential integrity and composite objects. The relational model requires to declare foreign key constraints in order to enforce referential integrity. A foreign key constraint expresses that the value of an attribute must be drawn from the set of primary key values of some relation. Object-oriented data models capture referential integrity implicitly in the declaration of directed relationships between object types. An instance of the source type of a relationship may only be related to some instance of the target type. Similarly, object-oriented data models support the semantics of composite objects. Whereas, for example, the deletion of composite objects in the object-oriented database ORION [16] implies the deletion of its component objects, the deletion of a tuple in the relational model requires explicit deletions of the tuples representing component objects, unless active database system concepts are used (see below).

Although object-oriented data models cover the semantics of referential integrity and composite objects, they fall short in supporting them in concert. As far as we know, none of the existing object-oriented database management system products and prototypes [4, 10] supports local referential integrity as a primary modeling concept. In case of lack of such support, several alternative solutions are possible.

1. Using predicates which define valid database extensions as "add-ons" to the database schema. Every local referential integrity constraint is specified by a separate and complex predicate. The predicates may be transformed into production rules which get executed whenever operations modifying an object reference occur [5, 11].

2. Using pre- and postconditions of type-specific operations. Every operation modifying an object reference checks in its pre- or post-condition whether the intended update is valid [18].

3. Using active database system concepts. Event-condition-action rules define how updates of object references are handled, if local referential integrity will be violated through the update [22].

---

[1]The notion has been extended to objects with exclusive independent component references, shared dependent component references, and shared independent component references[15]. Within this paper, however, we stick to the term's original semantics.

[2]In a draft version of the paper, we have used the term "intra-object referential integrity", which we abandoned in favor of "local referential integrity" due to helpful comments by H. Eder. Conversely, one of our referees suggested independently to use our original notion as the term "local" were semantically overloaded.

Each of these solutions requires to handle local referential integrity explicitly. This is opposite to the claim that object-oriented data models provide for a simple and natural representation of the real world.

This deficiency of object-oriented data models can be overcome by introducing a simple and intuitive representation of local referential integrity. We propose one in this paper. We suggest to use "local object classes" as domains of directed relationships. A local object class is a set of objects belonging exclusively to some composite object. Notice the following difference between the usual notion of "component object class" and our notion of "local object class". A component object class consists of all objects of a particular type which appear as components of *all* objects of some composite object class, whereas a local object class consists of all objects of a particular type which appear as components of a *single* object of some composite object class. Local referential integrity is maintained if any relationship from within a composite object to one of its local classes references a current member of that class.

Related approaches exist in the areas of semantic data modeling and of database programming languages. The semantic data model IFO [1] exhibits the concept of active domains, which are similar to local object classes. An active domain denotes the valid extension of some object type with respect to some object. There is no distinction between the intensional concept of a type and the extensional concept of a class, hence, active domains have to be computed every time some integrity constraint is checked. The object-oriented database programming language introduced in [2] distinguishes between types and classes. The class concept is used to specify extensional constraints, like inclusion constraints and referential integrity constraints. But, as the authors state, they do not support referential integrity within composite objects. To support referential integrity in the realm of composite objects is the major contribution of our paper.

The paper is organized as follows: In section 2, we give a sample problem statement. In section 3, we describe a simple object-oriented data model. We introduce the concept of "local object classes" and show how they can be used for representing local referential integrity constraints. In section 4, we extend our investigation to type and class hierarchies. We conclude with Section 5 by discussing current and future research topics.

2   A Sample Problem Statement

In this section, we give a simple problem statement which will be our running example throughout the paper. We omit any details which do not contribute to the essential points of this paper. Our sample problem statement covers selected parts of the conference organization problem posed by IFIP WG 8.1 [23].

An information system for organizing a set of conferences is to be designed. The system must keep track of the conferences organized and a set of persons involved or possibly interested in these conferences. In general, a conference is identified by an acronym and described by its full title. Every conference consists of a set of papers and a set of sessions. Each session has several slots, in which particular papers of the conference are presented. Notice the local referential integrity constraint that the slot and the paper presented in the slot must belong to the same conference.

Persons known by the conference organization system may participate in several conferences. As a participant of a particular conference, a person is described by a set of conference specific properties such as "has-paid" and "attends-conference-dinner". An author of a paper may be any person known by the conference organization system. But the chair of a session must be a person participating in the conference. Note the difference in the two local referential integrity constraints. The author of a paper must only be known by the conference organization database. But the chair and the session must belong to the same conference.

Working conferences are a special type of conference. Papers are distinguished into invited papers and submitted papers. They undergo a different reviewing process and are described by different properties, which are not relevant in our paper. Usually, a subset of all papers is accepted for presentation at the conference.

3 Object Types and Local Object Classes

In this section we define a simple object-oriented data model which supports local referential integrity, but does not consider type and class hierarchies. Type and class hierarchies will be discussed in the subsequent section.

We could extend any of several object-oriented data models [3, 7, 16] for our discussion. As no standard or commonly agreed to object-oriented data model exists [19] and as we do not expect all readers to be familiar with a particular model, we introduce a simple object-oriented data model. It contains essential features of object-oriented systems, but leaves out concepts and details not needed in this paper. Our purpose is not to introduce a new object-oriented data model, but to have a medium to convey our ideas.

The object-oriented data model exhibits three important features needed to handle local referential integrity in a natural way:

1. There is a clear distinction between *object types* and *object classes*. An object type defines the structure and the behavior of its potential instances. (Behavior is not discussed in this paper. The interested reader is referred to [13, 27]). An object class comprises a set of objects of a certain type.

2. Object classes are properties of objects. Such a property is called *local object class*, or shortly *local class*. The members of a local class are dependent on and belong exclusively to the object of which the object class is a property.[3] Thus, local object classes exhibit the semantics of composite object hierarchies.

3. The database is considered an object itself, the database object. Its local object classes correspond to the schema of a normal object-oriented database, and members of these local object classes correspond to independent objects stored in this database. Consequently, every object class is a local object class.

The idea of representing and enforcing local referential integrity is as follows: All objects in the database are organized in a locality hierarchy. At the type level, the

---

[3] "Local classes" differ from "cover aggregations" or "groupings" [24] in that their members are dependent on the object of which the object class is a property.

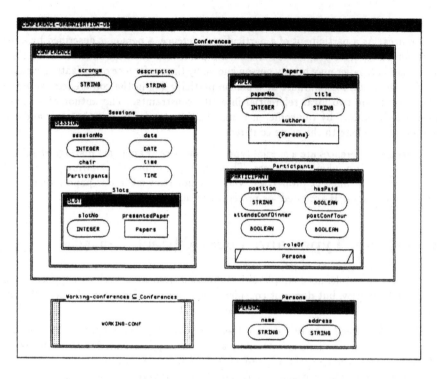

Figure 1: Object type CONFERENCE-ORGANISATION-DB

locality hierarchy is reflected by local classes. At the instance level, an object o is *local to* an object o', if o is a member of some local class of o'. An object o may reference another object o', if o' is local to some object o'' (i.e., is a member of some local class of o'') in the path from the referencing object o to the root of the locality hierarchy.

3.1 Object-Oriented Database Schema

We consider an *object-oriented database schema* to consist of a set of object types defining named properties which are distinguished into attributes, (directed) relationships, and local object classes.

As a notational convention, we write names of object types in uppercase letters. We start names of attributes and relationships by a lowercase letter, and names of local classes by an uppercase letter.

For a graphical representation of object types, we use an extended form of Object/Behavior Diagrams [13]. An object type is depicted by a box giving the name of the object type in a shaded bar at the top and showing its properties by nested ovals or rectangles, each giving the name and domain of the property. Attributes are shown by ovals, relationships by rectangles, and local classes by rectangles with double line borders depicting the domain of the local class. The domain of a local class may be given in a separate diagram to reduce representational complexity. In this case, the local class is depicted with shaded side bars giving the name of the domain but not its structure. Attributes and relationships may be declared multi-valued by enclosing the names of their domains in curly brackets.

Example: Figure 1 depicts part of the schema of an information system for organizing a set of conferences. The database is described by the object type CONFER-ENCE-ORGANISATION-DB with local object classes Conferences, Working-conferences, and Persons, which are used to keep track of a set of conferences, a set of working conferences in particular, and a set of persons being potential participants, sponsors or organizers. (The notation Working-conferences ⊆ Conferences defines Working-conferences to be a subclass of Conferences. For the moment ignore subclasses. They will be discussed later.)

The domain of an attribute is one of several predefined value types, such as INTEGER, STRING, and BOOLEAN. The domain of a local object class is an object type, referred to as its *member type*, and the domain of a relationship is a local object class, referred to as its *class domain*. The question which local object classes may serve as domain of a particular relationship is discussed below in subsection "Valid Database Schema".

Example: The local object class Conferences of CONFERENCE-ORGANISATION-DB has object type CONFERENCE as domain (cf. Figure 1). It defines the attributes acronym and description as well as the local classes Papers, Sessions, and Participants. Property Sessions has object type SESSION as domain, which in turn defines local class Slots with domain type SLOT defining the relationship presentedPaper with local class Papers as its domain. Local object class Working-conferences has object type WORKING-CONF as domain, which is depicted in a separate diagram (cf. Figure 3). Property Participants has object type PARTICIPANT as member type, which defines relationship roleOf with local class Persons as its domain. For the moment disregard this relationship, which will be discussed in detail further below.

3.2 Object-Oriented Database Extension

The extension of an object-oriented database consists of a set of objects. Each object is an instance of exactly one object type, is represented by a non-printable *object identifier*, and described by a value for each property defined at its type. For attributes, the value is a data value which is directly printable and stands for itself. For relationships, the value is the internal identifier of the object referenced. For local classes, the value is a set of object identifiers representing the current members of the class. Note: Local classes are considered properties of objects. If a local class *Class_name* is defined at an object type, *Class_name* does not refer to a unique class in the database. Rather, every instance of that object type has a local class identified by *Class_name*.

Example: Figure 2 depicts selected parts of a sample instance of object type CONFER-ENCE-ORGANISATION-DB. Internal object identifiers are represented by mnemonic names starting with the number symbol. Consider the members #DE92 and

#ER92 of class `Conferences`, which are instances of `CONFERENCE`. Both have a local class session with distinct members. (Only the extension for #ER92 is shown in Figure 2.)

The question which objects may be possibly referenced by a particular relationship of some object is discussed below in subsection "Valid Database Extension".

3.3 Valid Database Schema

In this subsection, we give rules for defining valid database schemas. We deliberately omit rules on naming. These are fairly straightforward and do not contribute to our discussion. For simplicity only, we assume names of object types and names of properties to be globally unique. Rather, we concentrate on the representation of local referential integrity at the type level.

As outlined above, local classes together with their member types reflect the locality hierarchy of objects at the type level. If type t has a local class c with member type t_c, every instance of t_c is *local to* some instance of t and we say t_c is a *local type of t*. In order that the position of an object type in the locality hierarchy of object types is unique, an object type may serve as member type of local classes of only one object type (*Single Locality Rule*) and an object type may not be transitively a local type of itself (*Acyclicity-Rule of Locality Hierarchy of Object Types*).

Example: Because object type `PERSON` is used as domain of local class `Persons` of object type `CONFERENCE-ORGANISATION-DB`, it may not be used as domain of local class `Participants` of object type `CONFERENCE`.

As the reader may notice, the single locality rule restricts the usage of object types to a narrow scope making it hard to represent situations in which entities of some type appear in different contexts. The concept of roles, introduced below, allows to model such a situation in a very intuitive, flexible and extendible way.

Local referential integrity is represented at the type level by using local classes as domains of relationships. To provide for a clear and simple organization of the database schema, we introduce a visibility rule for local classes similar to the scoping rules for nested procedure declarations in programming languages such as Pascal and Modula-2.

A local class c *is visible at* an object type t, if c is defined at t, or if there exists a type t' such that t is domain of some local class of t' and c is visible at t' (*Visibility Rule of Local Classes*). Note: Object type t' is unique because of the single locality rule of object types.

A class c may be used as domain of a relationship r defined at object type t, if class c is visible at t. (*Scoping Rule for Domains of Relationships*)

Example: Local class `Papers` of object type `CONFERENCE` is visible at object type `SLOT`, because `SLOT` is domain of local class `Slots` of object type `SESSION` which again is domain of local class `Sessions` of object type `CONFERENCE`. Therefore, local class `Papers` of object type `CONFERENCE` is visible at `SLOT` and can be used as domain of relationship `presentedPaper` of `SLOT`.

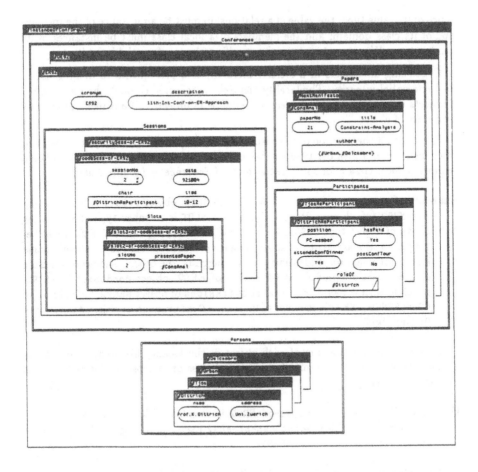

Figure 2: A sample instance of object type CONFERENCE-ORGANISATION-DB

A formal definition of a valid database schema, which also considers type and class hierarchies, is given in the appendix.

3.4 Valid Database Extension

In this subsection, we define the semantics of a valid database extension by giving rules on what constitutes a valid database extension.

Several rules are quite common and we will not discuss them in detail: Every object is direct instance of exactly one object type (*Unique Type Rule*). Every object possesses those properties defined at its type (*Property Induction Rule*). Every property possessed by an object is defined at its object type (*Type Consistency of Property Ownership*). The value of a property must be an instance of its domain (*Property Domain Satisfaction Rule*); i.e., the value of an attribute must be an instance of its value type; the value of a relationship must be an instance of the member type of its class domain; and the members of a local class must be instances of its member type. We concentrate on rules specific to local referential integrity.

Organizing all objects in a locality hierarchy is a prerequisite to making use of local referential integrity. The locality hierarchy is reflected through the membership of objects in local classes. An object o is *local to* an object o', if o is member of some local class of o'.

In order that the position of an object in the locality hierarchy of objects is defined, every instance of a member type t of a local class c of some object type t' must be a member of local class c for some instance of t' (*Existence of Locality Rule*).[4]

Example: Consider an instance of object type SLOT, object #slot2-of-oodbSess- -of-ER92 (cf. Figure 2). As object type SLOT is member type of local class Slots of object type SESSION, object #slot2-of-oodbSess-of-ER92 must belong to local class Slots of some instance of SESSION. As the mnemonic name for the internal object identifier already suggests, the object belongs to the slots of the object-oriented database session of ER92, object #oodbSess-of-ER92, which in turn is member of local class Sessions of object #ER92, an instance of CONFERENCE. #ER92 is member of local class Conferences of object #instance- OfConfOrgDB.

In order that the position of each object in the locality hierarchy of objects is unique, every object can be member of a local class of at most one object (*Unique Locality of Objects*).

Example: The object #oodbSess-of-ER92 is member of local class Sessions of object #ER92. Hence, #oodbSess-of-ER92 may not belong to the sessions of another conference, e.g, to #DE92.

Local Referential Integrity is satisfied, if an object references only objects that are local to some object in the path from the referencing object to the root of the locality hierarchy. More precisely, the value of a relationship r of object o with domain class c must be drawn from the extension of class c with respect to o. The extension of a local class c with respect to an object o is defined as follows: If c is a local class of o, the extension of c with respect to o is the set of members of c. If c is not a local class of o and if o is member of a local class c' of object o', the extension of c with respect to o is recursively defined as the extension of c with respect to o'. Note: Object o' is unique, because of the unique locality rule for objects.

Example: The extension of local class Papers with respect to object #slot2-of- -oodbSess-of-ER92 is the set of members of local class Papers of object #ER92. According to the local referential integrity rule, only these objects may be referenced by the relationship presentedPaper of object #slot2-of-oodbSess- -of-ER92. Thus, the local referential integrity rule ensures that only a paper submitted to ER92 - and not a paper submitted to some other conference - is presented in the object-oriented database session of ER92.

---

[4] As already outlined above, real world entities which can exist on their own ("independent entities") are modeled as members of local classes of the database object.

A formal definition of a valid database extension, which also considers type and class hierarchies, is given in the appendix.

3.5   Roles and Local Referential Integrity

Object-oriented systems represent real world entities as instances of the most specific object type in which they can be classified. This approach is appropriate only, if entities to be modeled can be partitioned into a set of disjoint object types and never change their type. Classification hierarchies of plants, animals, or technical parts are good examples.

Representing evolving objects using type hierarchies that require an object to be classified into a single most specific type is a tedious task. Entities need to be reclassified any time they evolve. E.g., if a person becomes a student a new student instance must be created, relevant information from the person instance must be copied to the student instance, all references to the person instance must be reset to the student instance, and finally, the obsolete person instance must be deleted.

Evolving objects can be handled most naturally by applying specialization at the object level rather than at the type level. A real world entity is represented by several objects, each representing it in a particular role. The objects of one entity are organized in a role hierarchy in which more special objects inherit property values and methods from more general ones. Object specialization has been proposed independently in [17, 29], and has been elaborated on more recently in [9, 25, 26].

Role hierarchies are specified at the schema level by role types. A role type defines the role-specific properties of objects in its role domain, which is a local object class. Any object in the role domain may acquire the role identified by the role type. In this case, a new instance of the role type is created and related by a *roleOf* relationship to the corresponding instance of the role domain. In object diagrams, the role domain of an object type is depicted by a special box labeled "roleOf".

For a valid database schema, the role domain of some type must be visible at that type, (*Scoping Rule for Role Domains*), and obviously, the role type hierarchy must be acyclic (*Acyclicity Rule of Role Type Hierarchy*).

Example: Figure 1 shows the role type PARTICIPANT with role domain Persons. The role-specific properties of a conference participant are his/her position, his/her payment status, and his/her attendance at the conference dinner and at the post conference tour.

Roles support representing and maintaining evolving objects in a very intuitive and flexible way: (1) Various roles of an entity share common structure and behavior. (2) Entities can acquire and abandon roles dynamically. (3) Roles can be acquired and abandoned independently of each other. (4) Entities can exhibit role-specific behavior. (5) Entities may occur multiple times in the same type of role. Several occurrences of the same entity in one type of role are distinguished by their different localities.

Example: Some person, e.g., Prof. Dittrich can participate in several conferences. In this case, Prof. Dittrich is represented by a person instance and by several participant instances, one for each conference participation. The person instance represents the common properties "name" and "address". Each participant instance represents Prof. Dittrich as participant of a particular conference giving the conference specific values of the attributes "position", "hasPaid", "attendsConfDinner", and "postConfTour".

For a database extension to be valid, every role instance must represent a role of some object in its role domain (*Local referential integrity of roleOf relationships*). If an entity occurs multiple times in the same type of role it must be local to different objects (*Role Qualification by Locality*). Finally, an object may not be local to and be role of the same object (*Proper Role Specialization*).

Example: Suppose object type `CONFERENCE-ORGANISATION-DB` has several databases as instances. Then, the local referential integrity of roleOf relationships requires that any person known by a particular database can become a participant of some conference in that very database, but not in a different one. In addition, the "role qualification by locality rule" ensures that a person is represented at most once as a participant of a given conference.

Using roles together with local referential integrity offers a major benefit in addition to those benefits of roles mentioned already above. The domain of a relationship specifies not only the type of object, but also the role and location in which a referenced object must appear. Thus, the semantics of relationships is defined more precise. Relationships carry a different semantics, if they refer to all entities of some type or only to those entities represented in a particular role and locality. The example below illustrates this.

Example: Consider relationship `chair` of object type `SESSION`. Its domain is the local class `Participants` of `CONFERENCE`. Hence, only somebody registered as participant of a conference can chair a session of that very conference. Had the domain of `chair` been defined to be `Persons` of `CONFERENCE-ORGANISATION-DB`, any person represented in a conference organization database could chair sessions of any conference represented in that database.

4 Subtypes and Subclasses

Specialization and inheritance are the most prominent features of object-oriented systems. Object types can be specialized into subtypes which inherit properties of their supertypes. Subtypes may introduce additional properties and may override properties inherited from the supertype.

We discuss the impact of type specialization on local referential integrity constraints in this section. In particular, we exhibit a set of rules for specializing object types such that local referential integrity constraints for instances of subtypes specialize, but do not arbitrarily override local referential integrity constraints for instances of supertypes. We restrict our discussion to single inheritance in this paper.

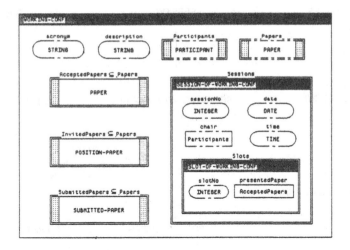

Figure 3: Object type WORKING-CONF

As types can be specialized into subtypes, classes can be specialized into subclasses. A subclass contains a subset of the members of its superclass.

Before discussing details, we give a small example. We use type and class hierarchy diagrams for depicting type and class hierarchies, and we use object diagrams for depicting the properties of an object type. Properties which are inherited but not overridden are depicted by dashed boxes.

Example: Figure 3 depicts object type WORKING-CONF which is a subtype of object type CONFERENCE (cf. the type hierarchy of Figure 4). The attributes acronym, and description, and the classes Participants and Papers are inherited from CONFERENCE unmodified. Local class Sessions is overridden. Its domain is specialized to object type SESSION-OF-WORKING-CONF, a subtype of SESSION. The local classes AcceptedPapers, SubmittedPapers, and InvitedPapers are introduced at object type WORKING-CONFERENCE as subclasses of Papers. Furthermore, the figure shows that object type SESSION-OF-WORKING-CONF specializes the domain of local class Slots to object type SLOT-OF-WORKING-CONF, which is a subtype of object type SLOT. SLOT-OF-WORKING-CONF specializes the domain of relationship presentedPaper to local class AcceptedPapers.

Figure 4 shows the type hierarchies with root types CONFERENCE, PAPER, SESSION, and SLOT.

Figure 5 shows the class hierarchy with root class Papers as seen at object type WORKING-CONF.

4.1   Additional Rules for a Valid Database Schema

In this subsection, we give rules for defining valid database schemas in the presence of type and class hierarchies. We concentrate on rules related to local referential integrity. An exhaustive list of rules is given in the Appendix.

53

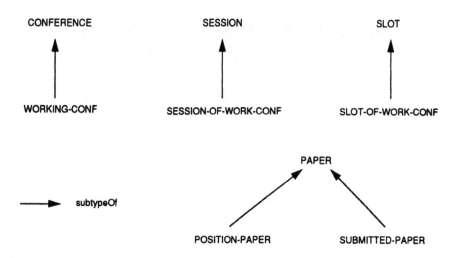

Figure 4: Type hierarchies with root types CONFERENCE, SESSION, SLOT and PAPER

A most desirable feature of a database is that every local referential integrity constraint is expressed entirely at the type level. For two instances o and o' of an object type, the path traversed to determine the extension of a local class c with respect to o should correspond at the type level to the path traversed to determine the extension of local class c with respect to o'. Both pathes should visit instances of the same object types. This *uniqueness property* provides for an efficient implementation of local referential integrity, as the path traversed for checking a local referential integrity constraint is known at the type level, and hence, for an instance of a given type, it is known already at compile time.

For a database schema without subtypes, the single locality rule for object types and the acyclicity rule for the locality hierarchy ensure this uniqueness property.

For a database schema with subtypes, the single locality rule for object types extends to the following *Coherent Usage Rule of Subtypes*: If object type t' is subtype of object type t which is local type of object type $\hat{t}$, then t' must be a local type of $\hat{t}$, or of a direct or indirect subtype of $\hat{t}$.

Example: Object type SUBMITTED-PAPER is subtype of object type PAPER. Object type PAPER is domain of local class Papers of CONFERENCE, and hence, a local type of CONFERENCE. Therefore, object type SUBMITTED-PAPER must be a local type of CONFERENCE or of a subtype of CONFERENCE. The latter is the case: SUBMITTED-PAPER is domain of local class SubmittedPapers of object type WORKING-CONF.

The acyclicity rule for the locality hierarchy is complemented by the *Orthogonality Rule for Locality and Subtype Hierarchies*. If an object type t is local or transitively local to an object type $\hat{t}$, then object types t and $\hat{t}$ belong to different type hierarchies, i.e., none is subtype of the other.

Example: Object type SUBMITTED-PAPER is a local type of WORKING-CONF. Therefore, both object types must belong to different type hierarchies, which is the

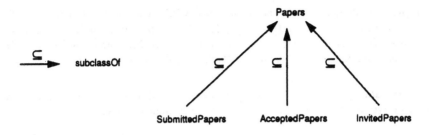

Figure 5: Class hierarchy with root class **Papers** as seen at object type **WORKING-CONF**

case. SUBMITTED–PAPER belongs to the type hierarchy with root PAPER, and
WORKING-CONF belongs to the type hierarchy with root CONFERENCE (cf. Figure 4).

The orthogonality rule for locality and subtype hierarchies and the coherent usage
rule of subtypes lead to stratified layers of object types. Object types in the $(i+1)$-st
layer are local types of object types in the i-th layer. Every subtree of a type hierarchy
rooted at an object type that is a local type of some other object type includes only
object types of the same layer. Notice that the concept of roles, as introduced above,
can be employed to model situations in which entities of some object type appear in
several layers of the locality hierarchy. For space limitations, we can not elaborate
further on this subject here.

As already indicated above, local referential integrity constraints should only be
specialized, and not overridden arbitrarily at subtypes. This is ensured by the remaining rules. The first three of them concern the target of local referential integrity
constraints, local classes. The last one states how relationships may be redefined at
subtypes.

Introduction Rule for Subclasses: A subclass may only be introduced at the same
type, or at a direct or indirect subtype of the object type introducing the superclass.

Example: Object type WORKING-CONF introduces local class AcceptedPapers as a
subclass of Papers. The introduction rule for subclasses is satisfied, because
Papers is introduced by object type CONFERENCE of which WORKING-CONF is a
subtype.

Specialization Rule for Member Types of Subclasses: The member type of a subclass must be identical to, or a direct or indirect subtype of the member type of its
superclass.

Example: Local class AcceptedPapers of WORKING-CONF is defined to be a subclass
of Papers. The member types of both classes are the same. Therefore, the
specialization rule for member types of subclasses is satisfied.

Specialization Rule for Member Types of Classes: If a local class is inherited from
a supertype, the member type may only be overridden to a subtype.

Example: The domain of local class `Sessions` of `CONFERENCE` is object type `SESSION`. As `WORKING-CONF` is a subtype of `CONFERENCE`, the specialization rule for member types of classes requires that the domain of local class `Sessions` of `WORKING-CONF`, object type `SESSION-OF-WORKING-CONF`, is a subtype of `SESSION`.

Specialization Rule for Domains of Relationships: If a relationship is inherited from a supertype, its domain class may only be overridden to a subclass.

Example: The domain of relationship `presentedPaper` of `SLOT` is local class `Papers`. As `SLOT-OF-WORKING-CONF` is a subtype of `SLOT`, the specialization rule for domains of relationships requires that the domain of relationship `presentedPaper` of `SLOT-OF-WORKING-CONF`, local class `AcceptedPapers`, is a subclass of `Papers`.

4.2 Additional Rules for a Valid Database Extension

The rules for a valid extension of a database schema with subtypes and subclasses are rather straightforward. We will not discuss them in detail. The interested reader is referred to the Appendix. We only remark that the rules for a valid schema have been defined in a way such that the definition of local referential integrity given above for a database extension of a schema without subtypes is still valid.

5 Conclusion

We have introduced an important concept for constraint modeling in object-oriented database design, local referential integrity. Local referential integrity extends the well-known notion of referential integrity to the realm of composite objects. It is satisfied if in any object reference the referencing object and the referenced object belong to the same composite object.

We have shown how local referential integrity can be supported in an object-oriented data model by using "local object classes" as domains of relationships. Whereas previous approaches require to treat local referential integrity explicitly by "add ons" to the database schema - such as predicates, pre- and postconditions of operations, or event-condition-action rules - our approach captures referential integrity implicitly by the database schema. This is in line with the common claim of object-oriented systems to provide for a natural and simple representation of the real world.

We have considered only single inheritance in this paper. An extension to multiple inheritance is necessary as certain situations can not be modeled by single inheritance. For example, multiple inheritance is needed if in a subtype t' of t the member types t_c of a class T_d and t_d of a subclass d of c are specialized to t_c' and t_d', respectively. Then according to the specialization rule for member types of classes, t_d' must be a subtype of t_d, and according to the specialization rule for member types of subclasses, t_d' must also be a subtype of t_c'. Thus, the member type of the superclass can not be specialized using single inheritance. (But the member types of the subclasses may be specialized. Therefore both rules are needed for the single inheritance case.)

Local referential integrity can be included as a primary concept for data modeling in any object-oriented design technique. If the implementation model does not support local classes, local classes must be mapped into set-valued properties and local referential integrity enforced explicitly by one of the traditional approaches outlined in the introduction.

References

[1] S. Abiteboul and R. Hull, "IFO: A formal semantic database model," in *ACM Transactions on Database Systems* , vol. 12 , no. 4, pp. 525-565, Dec. 1987.

[2] A. Albano, G. Ghelli and R. Orsini, "A Relationship Mechanism for a Strongly-Typed Object-Oriented Database Programming Language," in *Proceedings of the 17th VLDB Conference*, pp. 165-175, Barcelona, 1991.

[3] P. Butterworth, A. Otis and J. Stein, "The GemStone Object Database Management System," in *Communications of the ACM*, vol. 34, no. 10, pp. 64-77, October 1991.

[4] *Communications of the ACM, Special Issue on Next-Generation Database Systems*, vol. 34, no. 10, October 1991.

[5] S. Ceri and J. Widom, "Deriving Production Rules for Constraint Maintenance," in *Proceedings of the 16th VLDB Conference*, pp. 566-577, Brisbane, 1990.

[6] P.P. Chen, "The Entity-Relationship Model - Toward a unified view of data," in *ACM Transcations on Database Systems*, vol. 1, no. 1, pp. 9-36, 1976.

[7] O. Deux, "The O2 System," in *Communications of the ACM*, vol. 34, no. 10, pp. 34-48, October 1991.

[8] K. Dittrich, "Object-Oriented Database Systems: The Next Miles of the Marathon," in *Information Systems*, vol. 15, no. 1, pp. 161-167, 1990.

[9] G. Gottlob, G. Kappel and M. Schrefl, "Semantics of Object-Oriented Data Models - The Evolving Algebra Approach," in *Next Generation Information System Technology, Proceedings of the First International East/West Database Workshop*, ed. J.W. Schmidt and A.A. Stogny, pp. 144-160, Springer LNCS 504, 1991.

[10] *IEEE Transactions on Knowledge and Data Engineering, Special Issue on Database Prototype Systems*, vol. 2, no. 1, March 1990.

[11] M. Jeusfeld and M. Jarke, "From Relational to Object-Oriented Integrity Simplification," in *Proc. of 2nd Int.Conf on Deductive and Object-Oriented Databases*, ed. Delobel, Kifer, and Masunaga, pp. 460-477, Springer LNCS 566, 1991.

[12] G. Kappel and M. Schrefl, "A Behaviour Integrated Entity Relationship Approach for the Design of Object-Oriented Databases," in *A Bridge to the User, Proceedings of the 7th Int. Conf. on ER Approach*, ed. C. Batini, pp. 311-328, North-Holland, 1989.

[13] G. Kappel and M. Schrefl, "Object/Behavior Diagrams," in *Proceedings of the 7th International Conference on Data Engineering*, pp. 530-539, IEEE Computer Society Press, Kobe, Japan, April 1991.

[14] W. Kim et al, "Composite Object Support in an Object-Oriented Database System," in *Object-Oriented Programming Systems Languages and Applications (OOPSLA), Special Issue of SIGPLAN Notices*, ed. N. Meyrowitz , vol. 22, no. 12, Dec. 1987.

[15] W. Kim, E. Bertino and J.F. Garza, "Composite Objects Revisited," in *Proceedings of the ACM-SIGMOD Conf. on Management of Data, SIGMOD Record*, vol. 18, no. 2, pp. 337-347, Portland, June 1989.

[16] W. Kim, J.F. Garza, N. Ballou and D. Woelk, "Architecture of the ORION Next-Generation Database System," in *IEEE Transactions on Knowledge and Data Engineering*, vol. 2, no. 1, pp. 109-124, March 1990.

[17] W. Klas, E.J. Neuhold and M. Schrefl, "On an object-oriented datamodel for a knowledge base," in *Research into Networks and Distriubted Application - EUTECO*, ed. R. Speth, North-Holland, 1988.

[18] C. Lecluse and P. Richard, "Database Schemas and Type Systems for DBPL," Technical Report Altair 55-90, August 1990.

[19] D. Maier, "Why isn't there an object-oriented data model?," in *Information Processing 89 - IFIP World Computer Congress*, ed. G.X. Ritter, pp. 793-798, North-Holland, 1989.

[20] V.M. Markowitz, "Referential Integrity Revisited: An Object-Oriented Perspective," in *Proceedings of the 16th VLDB Conference*, pp. 578-589, Brisbane, 1990.

[21] V.M. Markowitz, "Safe Referential Integrity Structures in Relational Databases," in *Proceedings of the 17th VLDB Conference*, pp. 123-132, Barcelona, 1991.

[22] C.B. Medeiros and P. Pfeffer, "Object Integrity Using Rules," in *ECOOP'91*, ed. P. America, pp. 219-230, Springer LNCS 512, July 1991.

[23] T.W. Olle, "System Design Specifications for a Conference Organization System," in *Computerized Assistance During the Information System's Life Cycle*, ed. T.W. Olle, A.A. Verrijn-Stuart and L. Bhabuta, pp. 497-539, North-Holland, 1988.

[24] J. Peckham and F. Maryanski, "Semantic Data Models," in *ACM Computing Surveys*, vol. 20, no. 3, pp. 153-189, Sept. 1988.

[25] B. Pernici, "Objects with Roles," in *Proceedings of the ACM/IEEE Conf. of Office Information Systems*, pp. 205-215, Cambridge, MA, April 1990.

[26] J. Richardson and P. Schwarz, "Aspects: Extending Objects to Support Multiple, Independent Roles," in *Proceedings of the ACM-SIGMOD Conf. on Management of Data, SIGMOD Record*, ed. J. Clifford and R. King, vol. 20, no. 2, pp. 298-307, Denver, June 1991.

[27] M. Schrefl, "Behavior Modeling by Stepwise Refining Behavior Diagrams," in *Proceedings of the 9th Int. Conf. on Entity Relationship Approach*, pp. 113-128, Lausanne, October 1990.

[28] M. Schrefl and G. Kappel, "Cooperation Contracts," in *Proceedings of the 10th Int. Conf. on ER Approach*, pp. 285-307, Oct. 1991.

[29] E. Sciore, "Object Specialization," in *ACM Transactions on Information Systems*, vol. 7, no. 2, pp. 103-122, April 1989.

Appendix

Definition 1: An object-oriented database schema is a tuple $ODB_{Schema} = (T, V, A, R, C, introducedAt, hasMemberType, attrDom, relDom, multiplicity, roleDom, subtypeOf, subclassOf)$, where T, V, A, R, and C are finite sets, representing object types, predefined value types, attributes, relationships, and local classes, respectively, and where the remaining elements are the following functions.

1. The total function $introducedAt : C \cup R \rightarrow T$ maps a relationship or local class to the most general object type in the type hierarchy at which the relationship or local class is defined.

2. The partial function $hasMemberType : C \times T \rightarrow T$ maps a local class c and an object type t to an object type t' that serves as member type of local class c for all instances of t. The function is undefined if c does not belong to t, or if the inherited domain of c is not overridden at t.

3. The total function $attrDom : A \rightarrow V$ maps each attribute a to a predefined value type v. The domain of an attribute may not be overridden at subtypes, which is guaranteed by the specification of $attrDom$.

4. The partial function $relDom : R \times T \rightarrow C$ maps a relationship r and an object type t to a local class c that serves as class domain of r for all instances of t. The function is undefined if r does not belong to t, or if the inherited domain of r is not overridden at t.

5. The total function $multiplicity : A \cup R \rightarrow \{`sv', `mv'\}$ states for each attribute and relationship whether it is single-valued or multi-valued.

6. The partial function $roleDom : T \rightarrow C$ maps a role type t to its role domain c.

7. The partial function $subtypeOf : T \rightarrow T$ maps a subtype to its supertype.

8. The partial function $subclassOf : C \rightarrow C$ maps a subclass to its superclass.

For simplicity we define the predicates $isSubtypeOf(t, t')$ and $isSubclassOf(c, c')$. The predicate $isSubtypeOf(t, t')$ is true iff $subtypeOf(t) = t'$, and the predicate $isSubclassOf(c, c')$ is true iff $subclassOf(c) = c'$. If $p(x, x')$ is a predicate, we denote the transitive closure of $p(x, x')$ by $p^+(x, x')$, and the transitive and reflexive closure by $p^*(x, x')$.

Definition 2: *Auxiliary predicates and functions*

1. For $x \in C \cup R, t \in T$, the boolean predicate $belongsTo(x, t)$ is true, if x is defined at or inherited by t:
$$belongsTo(x, t) := \exists t' \in T : introducedAt(x) = t' \wedge isSubtypeOf^*(t, t')$$

2. For $c \in C, t \in T$, the function $hasMemberType_i : C \times T \rightarrow T$ extends the partial function $hasMemberType : C \times T \rightarrow T$ to all pairs $(c, t) \in C \times T$ for which $belongsTo(c, t)$ holds:
$hasMemberType_i(c, t) :=$

$$\begin{cases} hasMemberType(c, t) & \text{if } hasMemberType(c, t) \text{ is defined} \\ hasMemberType_i(c, t') & \text{if } hasMemberType(c, t) \text{ is not defined and} \\ & \exists t' \in T : subtypeOf(t) = t' \\ \text{is not defined} & \text{otherwise} \end{cases}$$

3. The function $relDom_i : R \times T \rightarrow T$ extends the partial function $relDom : R \times T \rightarrow T$ to all pairs $(r, t) \in R \times T$ for which $belongsTo(r, t)$ holds:
$relDom_i(r, t) :=$

$$\begin{cases} relDom(r, t) & \text{if } relDom(r, t) \text{ is defined} \\ relDom_i(r, t') & \text{if } relDom(r, t) \text{ is not defined and} \\ & \exists t' \in T : subtypeOf(t) = t' \\ \text{is not defined} & \text{otherwise} \end{cases}$$

4. The function $roleDom_i : T \rightarrow C$ extends the partial function $roleDom : T \rightarrow C$ to subtypes of T: $roleDom_i(t) :=$

$$\begin{cases} roleDom(t) & \text{if } roleDom(t) \text{ is defined} \\ roleDom_i(t') & \text{if } roleDom(t) \text{ is not defined and} \\ & \exists t' \in T : subtypeOf(t) = t' \\ \text{is not defined} & \text{otherwise} \end{cases}$$

5. For $t, \hat{t} \in T$, the boolean predicate $isLocalTypeOf(t, \hat{t})$ is true, if t is used as member type of some local class of $\hat{t}$, or, if t is not used as member type of any object class and there exists a supertype t' of t such that t' is a local type of $\hat{t}$:
$isLocalTypeOf(t, \hat{t}) :=$

$$\begin{cases} true & \exists c \in C : belongsTo(c, \hat{t}) \wedge hasMemberType(c, \hat{t}) = t \text{ holds} \\ true & \not\exists c \in C : belongsTo(c, \hat{t}) \wedge hasMemberType(c, \hat{t}) = t \text{ and} \\ & \exists t' \in T : subtypeOf(t) = t' \wedge isLocalTypeOf(t', \hat{t}) \text{ holds} \\ false & \text{otherwise} \end{cases}$$

6. For $t, \hat{t} \in T : islocalTypeOf_i(t, \hat{t}) :=$

$$\begin{cases} true & \text{if } isLocalTypeOf(t, \hat{t}) \text{ holds} \\ true & \text{if } isLocalTypeOf(t, \hat{t}) \text{ does not hold and} \\ & \exists \hat{t}' \in T : subtypeOf(\hat{t}) = \hat{t}' \wedge isLocalTypeOf_i(t, \hat{t}') \text{ holds} \\ false & \text{otherwise} \end{cases}$$

7. For $c \in C$ and $t \in T$ the boolean predicate $visibleAt(c, t)$ states whether local class c is visible at object type t:
$visibleAt(c, t) :=$
$belongsTo(c, t) \vee \exists \hat{t} \in T : isLocalTypeOf(t, \hat{t}) \wedge visibleAt(c, \hat{t})$

8. For $t, \bar{t} \in T$: the boolean predicate $isRoleTypeOf(t, \bar{t})$ is true, if instances of t represent instances of $\bar{t}$ in a particular role:
$isRoleTypeOf(t, \bar{t}) := roleDom_i(t)$ is defined $\wedge$
$\exists \hat{t}, \exists \bar{t}' : isSubtypeOf^*(\bar{t}, \bar{t}') \wedge hasMemberType(roleDom_i(t), \hat{t}) = \bar{t}'$

Definition 3: *Valid Database Schema*

1. Scoping rules
   (a) $\forall r \in R, t \in T : relDom(r, t)$ is defined $\Rightarrow visibleAt(relDom(r, t), t)$
   (b) $\forall t \in T : roleDom(t)$ is defined $\Rightarrow visibleAt(roleDom(t), t)$

2. Single locality of object types
   $\forall t, t', t'' \in T : isLocalTypeOf(t, t') \wedge isLocalTypeOf(t, t'') \Rightarrow t'' = t'$

3. Existence of domains of relationships
   $\forall r \in R : introducedAt(r) = t \Rightarrow \exists c \in C : relDom(r, t) = c$

4. Existence of member types of classes
   $\forall c \in C : introducedAt(c) = t \Rightarrow \exists t' \in T : hasMemberType(c, t) = t'$

5. Acyclicity of subtype hierarchy
   $\forall t \in T : \neg isSubtypeOf^+(t, t)$

6. Acyclicity of locality hierarchy
   $\forall t \in T : \neg isLocalTypeOf_i^+(t, t)$

7. Acyclicity of role type hierarchy
   $\forall t \in T : \neg isRoleTypeOf^+(t, t)$

8. Acyclicity of subclass hierarchy
   $\forall o \in O : \neg isSubclassOf^+(o, o)$

9. Orthogonality of subtype and locality hierarchies
$\forall t, t' \in T : isLocalTypeOf_i^+(t, t') \Rightarrow \neg(isSubtypeOf^*(t, t') \vee isSubtypeOf^*(t', t))$

10. Orthogonality of subtype and role hierarchies
$\forall t, t' \in T : isRoleTypeOf^+(t, t') \Rightarrow \neg(isSubtypeOf^*(t, t') \vee isSubtypeOf^*(t', t))$

11. Specialization rule for domains of relationships
$\forall t, t' \in T, \forall r \in R : isSubtypeOf(t, t') \wedge belongsTo(r, t') \Rightarrow$
$isSubclassOf^*(relDom_i(r, t), relDom_i(r, t'))$

12. Specialization rule for member types of classes
$\forall t, t' \in T, \forall c \in C : isSubtypeOf(t, t') \wedge belongsTo(c, t') \Rightarrow$
$isSubtypeOf^*(hasMemberType_i(c, t), hasMemberType_i(c, t'))$

13. Specialization rule for role domains
$\forall t, t' \in T: roleDom(t)$ is defined: $isSubtypeOf(t, t') \Rightarrow$
$\exists c' \in C : roleDom_i(t') = c' \wedge isSubclassOf^*(roleDom(t), roleDom_i(t))$

14. Introduction rule for subclasses
$\forall c, c' \in C : isSubclassOf(c, c') \Rightarrow$
$isSubtypeOf^*(introducedAt(c), introducedAt(c'))$

15. Specialization rule for member types of subclasses
$\forall t \in T, \forall c, c' \in C : isSubclassOf(c, c') \wedge belongsTo(c, t) \wedge belongsTo(c', t) \Rightarrow$

$isSubtypeOf^*(hasMemberType_i(c, t), hasMemberType_i(c', t))$

16. Coherent usage of subtypes
$\forall t, t', \hat{t} : isSubtypeOf(t', t) \wedge isLocalTypeOf(t, \hat{t}) \Rightarrow$
$\exists \hat{t}' : isSubtypeOf^*(\hat{t}', \hat{t}) \wedge isLocalTypeOf(t', \hat{t}')$

Definition 4: An object-oriented *database extension* is a tuple $ODB_{ext} = (O, D, instOf, roleOf, E, Rval, Aval)$ where O and D are finite sets representing all objects and all data values in the database. The remaining elements are the following functions and relations.

1. The total function $instOf : O \to T$ maps each object in the database to the object type which it is an instance of.

2. The partial function $roleOf : O \to O$ maps an object o to another object o' of which it is a role; o and o' model the same real world object in different contexts.

3. For $o, o' \in O$ with $o \neq o', c \in C : (o', c, o) \in E$ with $E \subset O \times C \times O$ if the object o is member of the local class c of the object o'.

4. For $o, o' \in O$ with $o \neq o', r \in R : (o', r, o) \in Rval$ with $Rval \subset O \times R \times O$ if o' references o through r.

5. For $o \in O, d \in D, a \in A : (o, a, d) \in Aval$ with $Aval \subset O \times A \times D$ if d is value of attribute a of object o.

Definition 5: Auxiliary predicates and functions

1. For $o, o' \in O$ the boolean predicate $isLocalTo(o, o')$ is true, if o is member of some local class c of o':
$isLocalTo(o, o') := \exists c \in C : (o', c, o) \in E$

2. For $o \in O$ and $t, t' \in T$ the boolean predicate $kindOf(o, t)$ is true, if o is an instance of t, or an instance of some direct or indirect subtype t' of t:
$$kindOf(o, t) := \exists t' \in T : instOf(o, t') \wedge isSubtypeOf^*(t', t)$$

3. The function $ext : C \times O \rightarrow 2^O$ maps a class c and an object o to the extension of c with respect to o:
$ext(c, o) :=$

$$\begin{cases} \{o' \in O \mid (o, c, o') \in E\} & \text{if } belongsTo(c, instOf(o)) \\ ext(c, o') & \text{if } \neg belongsTo(c, instOf(o)) \wedge \exists o' : isLocalTo(o, o') \\ \emptyset & \text{otherwise} \end{cases}$$

Definition 6: *Valid Database Extension*

1. Unique locality of objects
$$\forall o, o', o'' \in O : isLocalTo(o, o') \wedge isLocalTo(o, o'') \Rightarrow o' = o''$$

2. Existence of locality
$$\forall o \in O, t \in T : instOf(o) = t \wedge \exists t' \in T : isLocalTypeOf(t, t') \Rightarrow \exists o' \in O : isLocalTo(o, o')$$

3. Proper role specialization
$$\forall o, o', o'' \in O : isLocalTo^*(o, o') \wedge roleOf(o) = o'' \Rightarrow o' \neq o''$$

4. Role qualification by Locality
$$\forall o, o', \hat{o} \in O : roleOf(o) = roleOf(o') \wedge isLocalTo(o, \hat{o}) \wedge isLocalTo(o', \hat{o}) \wedge$$
$$(kindOf(o, instOf(o')) \vee kindOf(o', instOf(o))) \Rightarrow o = o'$$

5. Proper multiplicity of attributes
$$\forall x \in A, \forall y', y' \in D : multiplicity(x) = \text{`sv'} \wedge$$
$$((o, x, y') \in Aval \wedge (o, x, y'') \in Aval)) \Rightarrow y' = y''$$

6. Proper multiplicity of relationships
$$\forall x \in R, \forall y, y' \in O : multiplicity(x) = \text{`sv'} \wedge$$
$$((o, x, y') \in Rval \wedge (o, x, y'') \in Rval)$$
$$\Rightarrow y' = y''$$

7. Type consistency of class ownership
$$(o, c, o') \in E \Rightarrow belongsTo(c, instOf(o))$$

8. Type consistency of class membership
$$(o, c, o') \in E \Rightarrow kindOf(o', hasMemberType_i(c, instOf(o)))$$

9. Subclass-superclass membership
$$(o, c, o') \in E \wedge isSubclassOf(c, c') \Rightarrow (o, c', o') \in E$$

10. Type consistency of relationship ownership
$$(o, r, v) \in Rval \Rightarrow belongsTo(r, instOf(o))$$
$$roleOf(o) \text{ is defined} \Rightarrow roleDom(instOf(o)) \text{ is defined}$$

11. Local referential integrity

    (a) $(o, r, o') \in Rval \Rightarrow o' \in ext(relDom_i(r, instOf(o)), o)$

    (b) $\forall o \in O : instOf(o) = t \wedge roleDom(t) \text{ is defined} \Rightarrow \exists o' \in O : roleOf(o) = o' \wedge o' \in ext(roleDom(t), o)$

Entity Tree Clustering -
A Method for Simplifying ER Designs

Otto Rauh[a] and Eberhard Stickel[b],

a Berufsakademie Mosbach, Arnold-Janssen-Str. 9-13, W-6950 Mosbach
b Berufsakademie Stuttgart, Rotebühlplatz 41, W-7000 Stuttgart 1

Abstract. Entity Tree Clustering (ETC) is a method for clustering entity sets in large ER designs in order to improve the clarity of these designs. The procedure is stepwise so that clustered designs on different levels are achieved. Parenthood connections are used to build increasingly complex entity sets out of primitive ones. No semantical extensions of the original ER model are necessary because these connections are identified by their cardinalities alone.

1 Introduction

1.1 Motivation

Detailed ER designs of whole firms or even parts of them are very complex and therefore difficult to understand. Small parts of the whole design, which would be easy to read, cannot give the overall understanding of the system. Clustering designs is a possibility to present a complex system in an understandable way.

1.2 What we expect from a clustering method

There are four points we want to emphasize:

- Clustering should be done step by step. Thus the users of the designs can move between the different levels as they like.
- Only understandable terms should be used on any level. We might have to use abstractions in order to simplify a design but we should never leave the common terminology of the discipline.
- We should be able to automate the procedure without having to input additional data besides those incorporated in the basic design. Otherwise it would be too expensive to hold the clustered design up to date.
- The method should be applicable to 'normal' ER designs. In particular, no semantic extensions to the model should be necessary.

1.3 Contributions to the clustering problem

Preliminary work stems from two directions:

- papers on the data abstraction techniques classification, generalization, aggregation, and association (see Smith [1977], Codd [1979], and Hammer [1981]),
- numerous articles on complex objects and part-of hierarchies (see e.g. Lorie [1983] and Katz [1985], who were among the first).

There are some special contributions to the clustering problem too, see for example Vermeir [1983], Feldman [1986], Teory [1989], Wiborny [1991], and Mistelbauer [1991]. Among them Teory offers the greatest variety of clustering mechanisms. Besides Chen's distinction between strong and weak entities (Chen [1976]) he uses data abstractions and constraints between relationship sets as a basis for clustering operations. Because there are conflicts between these operations, he prescribes a sequence that should be observed. Thus there is a rudimentary algorithm. Unfortunately we need a semantically enhanced ER model as a basis for it, including all kinds of data abstractions and constraints between relationship sets.

Mistelbauer's contribution is a pragmatic one. He begins with ER designs with hierarchically ordered entity sets according to their cardinalities. This is a common feature of Mistelbauer's approach and ours. But there are major differences too. Though in Mistelbauer's solution the clustering operations depend on this hierarchical ordering, they are not done automatically. All the grouping decisions have to be put in additionally. The complex entity sets that are created this way have to be disjunctive, which is a radical constraint.

2 Characteristics of Entity Tree Clustering

Now we want to introduce Entity Tree Clustering (ETC), a clustering method with the following characteristics:

- it is based on an algorithm which can be implemented (and in fact has been implemented).
- it can be applied to designs that are expressed in a relatively sparse ER model. Compared with the original model we only need a more detailed declaration of the cardinalities.
- the complex entity sets that are the result of the clustering process may have common parts.

The basic principle of our algorithm is as follows: The primitive entity sets of the basic design are gradually merged so that they become more and more complex. Merging means that certain entity sets are absorbed by others, becoming entity set-valued attributes of these other entity sets. The absorptions are done on the basis of "parenthood connections" between the entity sets which we do not have to declare explicitly. If we choose the Bachman version of the ER model, all these connections can be identified by the cardinalities alone.

3 The role of cardinalities

Only those entity sets can be merged that are connected via relationship sets. Which of the two entity sets participating in a relationship set is absorbed by the other depends on a special form of parenthood between them. Parenthood itself is dependent on cardinalities.

To express cardinalities we use the well-known (min:max)-notation. Let *cardinality* = {(0:1), (1:1), (0:n), (1:n)}. Then we can put together a transitive relation *Par* ⊆ *cardinality* × *cardinality* that tells us which of two connected entity sets is a parent of the other one:

$$\{((1:1), (0:1)),$$
$$((0:1), (0:n)),$$
$$((0:1), (1:n)),$$
$$((1:1), (0:n)),$$
$$((1:1), (1:n))\}.$$

Suppose there is a relationship set *A-B* between entity sets A and B and the cardinalities are c_a and c_b respectively. If $(c_a, c_b) \in Par$ we call A a parent of B and, in the clustering process, B is absorbed by A.

To make sure that all relationship sets in an ER schema to be clustered are parenthoods we have two things to do before clustering begins:

1. We convert the ER schema into its Bachman form. That means we eliminate all complex relationship sets by adding associative entity sets. We use the term complex relationship set to denote all relationship sets of degree higher than two and all binary relationship sets with cardinalities m-to-n. Let us look at Fig. 1 for two examples. Originally, there was a complex relationship set *Pro-Room* with cardinalities ((0:n),(0:n)) between *Project* and *Room* which has been decomposed by an associative entity set with the same name. Now both *Room* and *Project* are parents of *Pro-Room* according to relation *Par*. In the same way the complex relationship set between *Room* and *Department* was decomposed by adding the associative entity set *Dep-Room*.

2. Every pair of entity sets connected by a relationship set with cardinalities ((0:1), (0:1)) or ((1:1), (1:1)) is immediately transformed into a single entity set.

Why do we use parenthoods as a basis for clustering? Let us look at them more closely in order to find out which sorts of relationship sets result in a parenthood. Roughly speaking, there are three sorts of them:

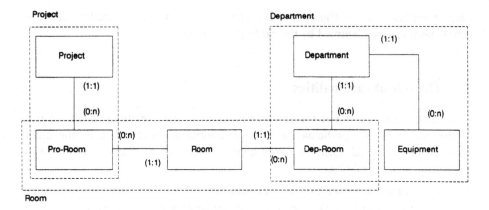

Fig. 1: Bachman form of ER schema

- relationship sets between associative entity sets and their components as described above,
- relationship sets between weak entity sets (Chen [1976]) and their strong counterparts,
- relationship sets that coincide with certain types of data abstraction, namely generalization, aggregation, and classification.

Weak entity sets

The cardinality on the side of the strong entity set is always (1:1), because a weak entity set is by definition existentially dependent on its strong counterpart. On the side of the weak entity set the cardinality is less determined; it can take the values (1:n), (0:n) or, more seldom, (0:1). Every weak entity set can be absorbed by the strong one it belongs to. The broken line in Fig. 2 indicates that both *Degree* and *Résumé* are absorbed by *Employee*, yielding a complex entity set *Employee*.

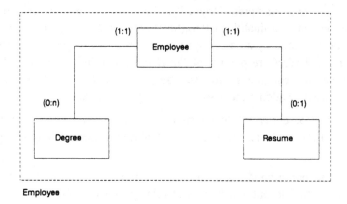

Fig. 2: Strong and weak entity sets

Generalization (Kind-of connections)

The cardinality on the side of the more general entity set is always (1:1), the one on the other side is (0:1) (cf. Fig. 3). We can use this sort of connections for clustering as follows: if two entity sets are connected this way the more special one is absorbed by the more general.

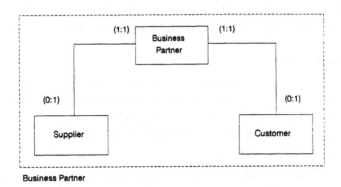

Fig. 3: Generalization

Classification and aggregation

When we classify, we seek to group things that have a common structure or exhibit a common behavior (Booch [1991], p. 133). Classification may be used in ER modeling in two ways. Firstly, every entity set is derived from classifying the entities it contains. Secondly, and this is the relevant form of classification in this context, entities of type A may be grouped into entities of type B which are classes of the entities of A (cf. Fig. 4, left side). A slightly different form of grouping is aggregation. Aggregation is based on part-of relationships whereas classification is based on instance-of relationships. Fig. 4, right side, contains an example for aggregation.

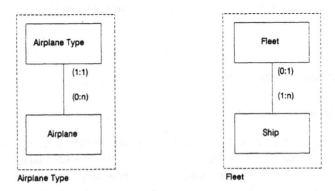

Fig. 4: Classification and aggregation

In a narrow version of grouping every group member can only participate in at most one group entity (Fig. 4). Thus the cardinality on the side of the group entity set is (0:1), or (1:1) if there is an existential dependency, whereas we have (0:n) or (1:n) on the side of the member entity sets. This narrow version does not cover all situations that may occur in reality. In the case of aggregation an entity may participate in more than one group entity of the same type, which would imply a complex relationship set between group and member entity set. Thus not any part-of relationship can be directly represented by a parenthood.

Associative entity sets

Every associative entity is existentially dependent on each of its component entities and is connected to exactly one entity of each component type. Therefore the cardinalities on the sides of the component entity sets are all (1:1) (cf. Fig. 1). Thus an associative entity set has all its components as parents and, in the clustering process, is absorbed by each of them.

Parenthoods of this kind may be seen as an alternative, though not a complete subsitute, for part-of relationships in the wider sense mentioned above. Let us look at Fig. 1 again. Before decomposition *Room* was connected with *Project* and *Department* by two complex relationship sets. Both of them can be interpreted as part-of relationships. Because of the parenthoods resulting from decomposition, *Pro-Room* is absorbed by *Project*, standing there for the rooms, and *Dep-Room* is absorbed by *Department*, again representing the rooms.

In summary, we can say that for every absorption in the clustering process the absorbing entity set has at least one of the following two characteristics:
- it is on a higher level of abstraction than the absorbed one,
- the absorbed entity set is existentially dependent on it.

When clustering is done completely, the resulting entity sets are on the highest possible level of abstraction (according to the basic schema) and they are not existentially dependent on any other entity set, which means that they are kernel entity sets.

4 The clustering process

4.1 Complex object structures

The relation *Par* may be used to derive the structures of the complex objects which are to be built during the clustering process. Fig. 5 shows the ER diagram which will serve us as the basic design. Every complex object type may be represented as a tree whose nodes are entity sets and whose edges are relationship sets. The roots of these trees are entity sets that have no parents. Beginning with a root we find the

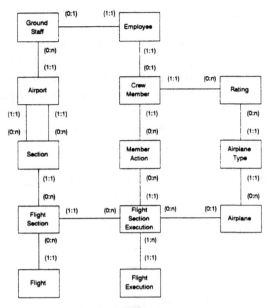

Fig. 5: Basic schema

other nodes by looking for its children, then looking for the children of these children, and so on. When we come upon an entity set that has no child we have reached a leaf of the object tree. Fig. 6 shows the complex objects contained in our basic design. Instead of the cardinalities we use arrows to indicate which of two connected nodes is the parent and which is the child. If the arrow has a continuous line the child is existentially dependent on its parent, otherwise it is not. We call the node at the starting point of a continuous arrow an existential parent.

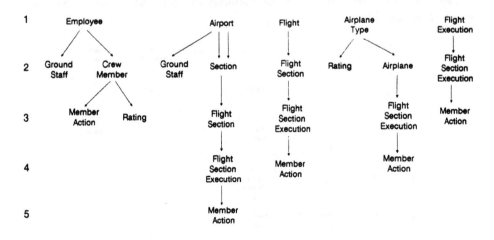

Fig. 6: Complex objects contained in the basic schema

4.2 Clustering strategies

Fig. 7 shows our basic design once again including the additional information about the hierarchical structures of the complex objects. We may follow these structures during the clustering process. Beginning with the maximum level (level 5 in our example) the entity sets on this level are absorbed by their parents, becoming entity-valued attributes. We may then proceed to level 4 and absorb all entity sets located on this level. The clustering process ends when all entity sets on level 2 are absorbed by their parents which are all root entity sets.

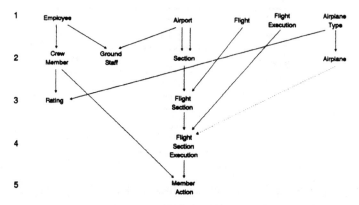

Fig. 7: LAP strategy

An alternative clustering strategy is represented by Fig. 8. If we follow Fig. 7 the children are absorbed as late as possible. We call this method, which results in a relatively slow clustering process, LAP-strategy (as Late As Possible). In contrast, the strategy represented by Fig. 8 is fast, although the overall number of rounds remains the same. We call this the EAP-strategy (as Early As Possible) and shall use it in our algorithm.

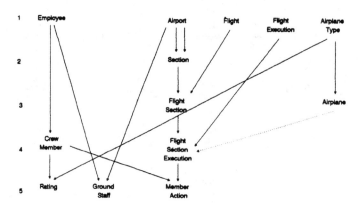

Fig. 8: EAP strategy

4.3   Absorption rules

When an entity set is absorbed by a parent it becomes an entity-valued attribute of this parent. Entity sets having more than one parent are absorbed by each of them. If a child is only connected with one other entity set (which is a parent, of course), this relationship set disappears when the child is absorbed. If a child is connected with more than one other entity set (which might be parents and non-parents) we have to create new relationship sets between these entity sets when the child is absorbed. Suppose, E is an entity set that is to be absorbed. The new relationship sets are built according to the following rules:

1.   If E has more than one existential parent, we build a chain of binary relationship sets between these parents.

2.   Every entity set that is connected with E but is not an existential parent of E is to be connected with an existential parent of E through a binary relationship set, if E has an existential parent at all.

3.   If E is connected with more than one entity set but has no existential parents, each of these entity sets is connected with each other via a binary relationship set.

4.   If E is engaged in a recursive relationship set, recursive relationship sets for each of E's parents are created.

The cardinalities of the newly created relationship sets are not taken into consideration in this version of the algorithm. Parenthoods alone are not sufficient to determine cardinalities, we would also need the cardinalities of the basic schema (see section 6). Fig. 9 contains some examples. The undirected connections represent relationship sets which were created previously in the clustering process. Fig. 9a shows the absorption of an entity set D that is connected with three existential parents. According to rule 1 a chain of binary relationship sets is built

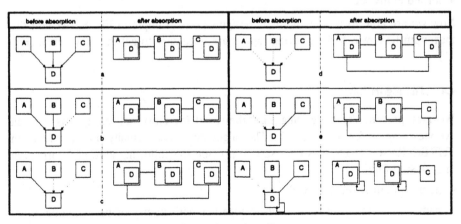

Fig. 9: Absorption rules

between A, B, and C. Please note that these relationship sets are sufficient to assign exactly the same C-entities to an A-entity that could be assigned via D in the basic design. Because A, B and C now contain D, relationships can be recorded on the level of the absorbed D-entities (Fig. 10). It doesn't matter how the entity sets in the chain are ordered, because any existential parent can serve as a link.

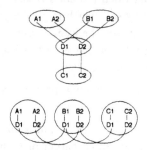

Fig. 10: Relationships between complex objects

In the examples shown in Figs. 9b and 9c rule 2 is applied additionally. Non-existential parents like C in Fig. 9b do not contain a C-entity for each D-entity. Therefore it might be impossible to get from an A-entity to its corresponding B-entities via C. C cannot serve as a link when we assign A-entities to B-entities or vice versa.

The application of rule 3 is shown in Figs. 9d and 9e. In both cases there are no existential parents at all which could serve as links. This is why A, B and C have to be connected in pairs. The only difference between 9d and 9e is that C is not parent of D in 9e. The relationship set between C and D was created during one of the preceding clustering rounds.

Fig. 9f shows how a recursive relationship set is passed on to the parents of the absorbed entity set.

Now we are able to cluster the basic design of our example in Fig. 8. Because the maximum level was 5, 4 clustering rounds are necessary to get the final result (Fig. 11).

4.4 The algorithm

We now present the underlying algorithm used for clustering entity sets. For an overview we refer to Fig. 12. The algorithm was actually implemented in TURBO-PASCAL 5.5. It is necessary to provide the following kind of information in an ASCII file:

- names of entity sets involved;
- names of relationship sets involved together with names of participating entity sets as well as their cardinalities in (min:max)-notation.

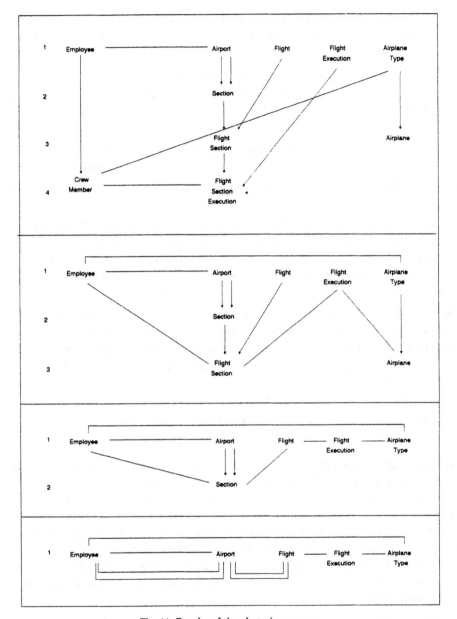

Fig. 11: Results of the clustering process

Before presenting the actual algorithm we once more explicitly state the necessary prerequisites for its application:

1. No relationship sets of order greater than two do exist. Any such relationship sets should be resolved by introducing associative entity sets with corresponding binary relationship sets.

2. No m-to-n relationship sets do exist in the data model that is supposed to be clustered. If there are any such relationship sets they should be resolved into two 1-n-relationship sets by introducing an associative entity set.

3. No 1-1-relationship sets with cardinalities (1:1) and (1:1) on both sides do exist. Any such relationships imply an invertible one-to-one relationship between the participating entity sets. In this case the entity sets may be considered identical and they are clustered immediately.

4. No 1-1-relationships with cardinalities (0:1) and (0:1) on both sides do exist. Any such relationships imply possible one-to-one relationships between the participating entity sets. In this case the entity sets are also clustered immediately.

In the first step of the algorithm root entity sets are determined. If E denotes a given entity set then it is simply checked whether in all relationship sets in which E participates E is the parent. If no root entity set can be found the algorithm terminates. In this case no clustering is performed. Note, however, that in all practical applications considered so far this never did happen.

In the second step a hierarchy of entity sets is built. Note that in general we get a special kind of graph structure which for simplicity will be called a **quasi-tree structure**. Since an entity set may occur as a child in more than one relationship set we do not in general get a tree structure. However it is possible to recursively define hierarchic levels of an entity set as follows:

a root entity set E has level $l(E): = 1$;

for an entity set E that is not a root its level l is defined by:

$$l(E) := 1 + \max \{l(E') \mid E \text{ is a child of } E'\}.$$

The algorithm terminates if the level of an entity set exceeds the number of entity sets in our basic design. In this case we have a sequence $E_1,...,E_k$, $E_{k+1}=E_1$ of entity sets where E_i is parent of E_{i+1} for $i=1,..,k$. This is called a direct ($k=2$) or indirect ($k>2$) cycle. In this case we would not get a quasi-tree structure as required above. Therefore the algorithm terminates. Clearly we only have edges between nodes on different hierarchic levels since m-n-relationships have been resolved and no cycles exist. Thus it is possible to parse our quasi-tree in postorder. Different branches of the quasi-tree are traversed more than once but the parsing algorithm finally terminates.

In the third step the quasi-tree structure is examined once more. The strategy of our algorithm is to cluster entity sets as early as possible (EAP). Suppose now that the maximum level of an entity set in our quasi-tree is m. If E is an entity set with level l having no children then the level of this entity set is 'pulled down' to m. In general we examine all children of a given entity set E. If E is not a leaf we compute

$$l' := \min \{l(E') \mid E' \text{ is a child of } E\}.$$

We then set

$$l(E) := l' - 1.$$

However, this procedure is not applied to root entity sets. A root entity set always has level $l = 1$. To compute l' we once more traverse the quasi-tree structure in postorder.

Now we are able to start the clustering process on the highest level. This is the fourth step of the algorithm. All entity sets on level m are clustered in this step. To be explicit all entity sets on level $l = m$ are added to their parent entity sets as entity-valued attributes.

It is necessary to adjust relationship sets the clustered entity set was involved in. Let E be a clustered entity set. If E is engaged in a recursive relationship set, this relationship set is passed on to each of E's parents. This is simply done by placing a marker.

We then check whether an existential parent E' does exist. If this is the case we may proceed as follows:

All nonrecursive relationship sets where the entity set E was involved are transformed into relationship sets where E' takes over the part of E.

If there is more than just one existential parent we may as well build a linked list of existential parents. In this case relationship sets between E and an existential parent P are successively modelled as relationship sets between P and the last existential parent found. For every non existential parent of E a relationship set between this entity set and an existential parent is created.

Note that the newly created relationship sets typically are m-n-relationship sets which we denote as complex relationship sets. In our actual program we used different data types to model relationship sets of our quasi-tree (edges) and newly created complex relationship sets.

Suppose now that no existential parent of the entity set E does exist. We then proceed as follows:

For each nonrecursive relationship set where the entity set E is involved and every parent entity set of E a complex relationship where the parent entity set takes over the part of E is created.

The fourth step of the algorithm may be repeated, if so desired, until the clustering level reaches $l = 1$.

Note that it is possible to extract the required information about entity sets and corresponding relationship sets from a commercial CASE tool (e.g. IEW of Knowledgeware). After running the algorithm the output, namely the resulting clustered entity sets with the existing relationship sets, may be fed back into this tool. This way it is possible to automate the visualization process.

```
┌─ *ER-CLUSTERING-PROCESS
└─ Algorithm
┌─ For Each relationship set do
│  ┌─ If relationship set is of order greater two
│  │    resolve by introducing asociative relationship set
│  └
│
│  ┌─ If m-n-relationship
│  │    resolve by introducing associative relationship set
│  └
│
│  ┌─ If 1-1 relationship sets of type ((1:1) and (1:1)) or ((0:1) and (0:1)) exist
│  │    perform clustering immediately
│  └
└

┌─ If no root entity set exists
│    exit program - clustering is performed
└─ Else
     build hierarchy of entity sets
   ┌─ If cycle is detected
   │    exit - direct or indirect cycle
   └

     tree-order:=order of tree built
     pull-down-levels
     level:=tree-order
   ┌─ While level>=2 do
   │    find all clustering candidates on level
   │  ┌─ For Each clustering candidate do
   │  │    found-existential-parent:=false
   │  │  ┌─ For Each parent entity-set do
   │  │  │    add clustering candidate to parent entity set
   │  │  │  ┌─ If clustering-candidate participates in recursive relationship set
   │  │  │  │    establish recursive relationship set involving parent entity set
   │  │  │  └
   │  │  │
   │  │  │  ┌─ If found-existential-parent=false
   │  │  │  │    check for existential parent
   │  │  │  │  ┌─ If existential parent
   │  │  │  │  │    found-existential-parent:=true
   │  │  │  │  │    fix existential parent
   │  │  │  │  └
   │  │  │  └
   │  │  └
   │  │
   │  │  ┌─ If found-existential-parent
   │  │  │  ┌─ For Each parent entity set of clustering candidate do
   │  │  │  │    create/update complex relationship between parent entity set and an existential parent
   │  │  │  │  ┌─ For Each complex relationship where clustering candidate is involved do
   │  │  │  │  │    substitute an existential parent for clustering candidate
   │  │  │  │  └
   │  │  │  └
   │  │  └─ Else
   │  │     ┌─ For Each parent entity set of clustering candidate do
   │  │     │
   │  │     │  ┌─ For Each parent entity set of clustering candidate do
   │  │     │  │    create/update relationship between parent entity sets
   │  │     │  └
   │  │     │
   │  │     │  ┌─ For Each complex relationship where clustering candidate is involved do
   │  │     │  │    substitute parent entity set for clustering candidate
   │  │     │  └
   │  │     └
   │  └
   │    level:=level-1
   └
```

Fig. 12: The clustering algorithm

Root Entity Sets Discovered:
        Employee
        Airport
        Flight
        Flight Execution
        Airplane Type
        Total Number: 5

Tree Structures:
sysroot level 0
    Employee level 1
        Crew Member level 2
            Member Action level 3
            Rating level 3
        Ground Staff level 2
    Airport level 1
        Ground Staff level 2
        Section level 2
            Flight Section level 3
                Flight Section Execution level 4
                Member Action level 5
    Flight level 1
        Flight Section level 2
            Flight Section Execution level 3
                Member Action level 4
    Flight Execution level 1
        Flight Section Execution level 2
        Member Action level 3
    Airplane Type level 1
        Rating level 2
        Airplane level 2
            Flight Section Execution level 3
            Member Action level 4

Clustering Process on Level 5
Entity Set Ground Staff added to
    Entity Set Airport
    Entity Set Employee
Existential Parent of entity set Ground Staff exists: Airport
Detected relationship between Ground Staff and Employee
 created/updated relationship between Airport and Employee
Entity Set Rating added to
    Entity Set Airplane Type
    Entity Set Crew Member
Existential Parent of entity set Rating exists: Airplane Type
Detected relationship between Rating and Crew Member
 created/updated relationship between Airplane Type and Crew Member
Entity Set Member Action added to
    Entity Set Flight Section Execution
    Entity Set Crew Member
Existential Parent of entity set Member Action exists: Flight Section Execution
Detected relationship between Member Action and Crew Member
 created/updated relationship between Flight Section Execution and Crew Member

Fig. 13: Extract of clustering documentation

5 Conclusion

A method for clustering ER schemas has been presented in this paper. The basic idea is to use parenthoods as given in the relation *Par* and to absorb the children into their parent entity sets. Relationship sets involving absorbed entity sets have to be rebuilt on a higher level of abstraction. The algorithm was implemented in Turbo-Pascal and a sample documentation is included in the paper.

In its present form ETC shows neither the contents nor the cardinalities of the newly created relationship sets. The algorithm could be extended to determine these useful additional informations. Fig. 14 shows a cardinality function $z = f(x,y)$ in tabular form (cf. [Rauh 1992] and [Rauh 1992a]). Suppose B has to be absorbed by both A und C. Then a new relationship set A-C between A and C replaces A-B and B-C . We can use the table on the right to determine the cardinality z out of cardinalities x and y. Fig. 15 shows how the function is applied to a part of our basic schema. According to our rules entity set *Ground staff* has to be absorbed by *Employee* and *Airport* as well. In order to determine the cardinality on the right we set $x := (0{:}1)$ and $y := (1{:}1)$. The table in Fig. 14 tells us that $z = (0{:}1)$. The cardinality on the left is determined in the same way.

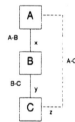

x \ y	0:1	1:1	0:m	1:m
0:1	0:1	0:1	0:m	0:m
1:1	0:1	1:1	0:m	1:m
0:m	0:m	0:m	0:m	0:m
1:m	0:m	1:m	0:m	1:m

Fig. 14: Cardinality function

There seem to be possibilities to show the contents of the new relationship too. We might simply give it the name of the absorbed entity set (Fig. 15). There are situations where we need additional information about the contents of the relationship sets in the basic schema, e.g. when multiple connections between entity sets exist. But this is a subject for further work.

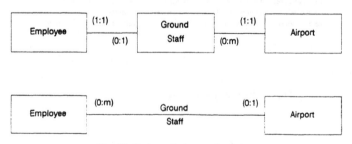

Fig. 15: Basic and clustered schema

References

Booch, G. [1991]. *Object oriented design with applications*, Redwood City, California: Benjamin/Cummings

Chen, P.P. [1976]. "The Entity-Relationship Model: Toward a Unified View of Data", *ACM Trans. on Database Systems*, March 1976

Codd, E.F. [1979]. "Extending the database relational model to capture more meaning", *ACM Trans. on Database Systems*, Dec. 1979

Feldman, P., Miller, D. [1986]. "Entity Model Clustering: A Data Model By Abstraction", *Computer Journal 29/4*, 1986

Hammer, M. and McLead, D. [1981]. "Database description with SDM: a semantic database model", *ACM Trans. on Database Systems*, Sept. 1981

Katz, R.H. [1985]. *Information Management for Engineering Design*, Springer-Verlag

Lorie, R., and Plouffe, W. [1983]. "Complex Objects and Their Use in Design Transactions", *Proc. ACM International Conference on Management of Data, Database Week*, San Jose, Calif., May 1983

Mistelbauer, H. [1991]. "Datenmodellverdichtung: Vom Projektdatenmodell zur Unternehmens-Datenarchitektur", *Wirtschaftsinformatik 4/91*

Rauh, O. [1992]. "Die Unterscheidung von originären und ableitbaren Daten im Entity-Relationship-Modell". In Rau, K.-H. and Stickel, E. (eds), *Daten- und Funktionsmodellierung*, Wiesbaden: Gabler, 1992

Rauh, O. [1992a]. "Some Rules for Handling Derivable Data in Conceptual Data Modeling". *Proc. International Conference on Database and Expert Systems Applications (DEXA 92)*, to appear Sept. 1992

Smith, J., and Smith, D. [1977]. "Database Abstractions: Aggregation and Generalization", *ACM Trans. on Database Systems*, July 1977

Teory, T.J., Wei, G., Bolton, D.L., Koenig, J.A. [1989]. "ER Model Clustering as an Aid for User Communication and Documentation in Database Design", *Communications of The ACM*, 32/8, 1989

Vermeir, D. [1983]. "Semantic hierarchies and abstractions in conceptual schemata", *Inform. Systems 8/2*, 1983

Wiborny, W. [1991]. *Datenmodellierung - CASE - Datenmanagement*, Bonn u.a.: Addison-Wesley

A Temporal Statistical Model
for Entity-Relationship Schemas

J-L Hainaut

Institut d'Informatique - University of Namur
rue Grandgagnage, 21 - B-5000 Namur (Belgium)
jlh@info.fundp.ac.be

Abstract. This paper is about the statistical description of the contents of an existing or future database. This information, very often neglected in database design methods, is essential for database optimisation and physical tuning for instance. The paper defines an extension of the E-R model to specify the size of the populations of entity types, relationship types, domains, attributes, and of their interconnections. It proposes a minimum set of statistics together with the relations that organise them. It analyses the problem of computing these statistics by using the relations as derivation rules. Data statistics are then considered as time-dependent quantities. Finally, the paper proposes translation rules that allows the preservation of the statistics when their supporting schema is restructured. This statistical model has been implemented in a commercial CASE tool.

Keywords : data statistics, physical design, simulation, optimisation, database modeling, database design, schema transformation.

1. INTRODUCTION

During database design [2, 3], producing an efficient schema is an important activity which is often neglected or at least underestimated. There are several causes for this situation. The major one is certainly that logical and physical database optimisation is a difficult problem. In particular, it has triggered very few researches that could lead to practical results usable by database professionals. Advices from the *Administrator Guides* of commercial DBMS are often below the minimum level of decency and very few CASE tools offer any help in this realm. The second reason is that optimisation needs precise input data on population statistics and usage statistics of the (future) data. This statistical information is difficult to collect and to interprete, and even more difficult to maintain during the design activities. Availability of precise and coherent statistical information on the data is also the main requirement for related activities such as simulation and query processing.

This paper is about the statistical description of the data, be they existing or in project. It is about its structure, its consistency, its computability, its temporal behaviour and its transformation.

It is organised as follows. Section 2 presents the concepts of a generic E-R model that is to support all the phases of database design, including conceptual, logical and physical design activities. Section 3 proposes an extension of this model to describe main statistical aspects of data. Section 4 analyses the problem of measuring basic statistics *vs* computing derived statistics. Section 5 extends the concepts of section 3 to the evolution of these statistics over time. Section 6 is dedicated to schema transformation with special consideration to statistics translation.

2. A GENERAL-PURPOSE ENTITY-RELATIONSHIP MODEL

Designing a database is generally decomposed into several processes, starting from, say, requirements collection, and ending with DDL schema generation and tuning. These processes define a set of standard products, such as the validated conceptual schema or the executable DDL schema. This set of products can also be perceived as a set of states of the database schema. According to this view, a large part of database design consists in applying design processes to a source schema (generally a conceptual schema) in order to *transform* it into an executable database schema that satisfies a given set of design criteria such as semantic correctness, readableness, efficiency and executability. Such a *transformational view* of database design has been described in [11]. It is based on two basic principles, namely a **common data model** for all the design processes and a **transformation toolset** for schema restructuring.

Transforming a conceptual schema down to executable specifications in a DBMS DDL is based on a *unique generic model* to express database structures in any of their possible states. This unique model allows a neutral definition of the design processes, as well as a high flexibility in the design strategies used by the designers. For instance, a conceptual transformation can be used on a physical schema as well. The generic model is an extension of the E-R model that can express both conceptual and technical structures. It has been described in [11] and its formalization can be found in [8]. Since we shall mainly concentrate on the statistical aspects of the model, we shall give only a short, informal, introduction to its main components.

The *generic specification model* is made up of six generic objects classified into high-level objects that define macrostructures (schema, entity type, relationship type and space) and low-level objects that define microstructures (attribute and group). Some objects (relationship type and group) can be given additional characteristics specifically aimed at describing technical or physical structures.

Entity type : represents any information unit that can be perceived or manipulated as a whole, at any level of the design process. According to the abstraction level in a given design method, it can be used to model either conceptual entities or logical or technical objects (such as record types, tables, segment types, etc). *Is-a* relations define specialisation hierarchies. We shall call *population* of an entity type the set of all the entities of that type at an instant of reference.

Relationship type : represents any significant aggregate of at least two (not necessarily distinct) entity types. Each position in the aggregate is called a *role*[1] that is played by an entity types. The number of roles is called the *degree* of the relationship type. The *cardinality properties* of a role are a couple of integers specifying in how many (min-max) relationships an entity must and can appear in that role (N stands for ∞). We shall call *population* of a relationship type the set of all the relationship of that type at an instant of reference.

Besides the graphical representation suggested in figure 1, we shall make use of a more concise notation as follows [8] :

```
MOVE(FROM[0-N]:WAREHOUSE,TO[0-N]:WAREHOUSE,[0-N]:PRODUCT,DATE:..,QTY:..)
```

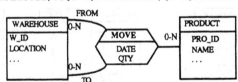

Fig. 1. Example of a relationship type of degree 3 with attributes

It can be used to model both conceptual relationships and technical constructs. At a technical or programming level, a relationship can be perceived not only as a conceptual association between entities, but also as an access mechanism to navigate through (technical) entities; therefore, a binary relationship type can support zero[2], one or two *access paths*, each defined from the *origin* role toward the *target* role (Figure 2). This concept can be seen as an abstraction of CODASYL set types, IMS parent/child relationship, TOTAL paths, ADABAS file coupling, relational tuple linkage, etc.

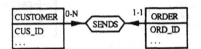

Fig. 2. A relationship type supporting two access paths

Space : is a collection of entities, possibly of different types. At the technical level, a space can model objects such as files, dbspaces, tablespaces, areas and datasets. When needed, a space can be represented graphically by a grey ellipsis surrounding its entity types (Figure 7).

---

[1] The roles of a relationship type have distinct names. When there is no ambiguity, a role has the same name as its entity type. In that case it does not appear in the schema, nor in the concise notation.

[2] For instance a conceptual E-R schema has no access paths.

Attribute : is associated with a parent object, i.e. an entity type, a relationship type or a compound attribute. An attribute can be atomic or compound. It is qualified by cardinality properties expressed as a couple of integers stating how many (min-max) values can and must be associated with the parent object (the default values are 1-1 and will be ignored in graphical representations). Any number of attributes (including zero) can be associated with an entity type or a relationship type. An attribute is defined on a *domain*, which is a reference value set.

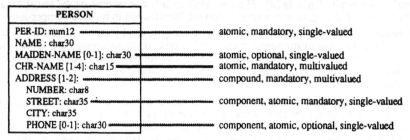

Fig. 3. Various types of attributes

Group : the group is a simple and powerful construct with which one can model entity and relationship identifiers, referential integrity, intra- and inter-entity attribute redundancy, logical access, statistical support, etc. A group is a collection of attributes and/or roles and is associated with an entity type or a relationship type. A group can have some specific functions regarding its parent entity or relationship type. It can be for instance :

• an **identifier**[3] (in figure 4, an EMPLOYEE is identified by its EMP-ID and its origin SUBSIDIARY, a MOVE relationship is identified by its date and its source and destination WAREHOUSES, a SCHEDULE is identified by TEACHER + TIME values and by TIME + PLACE values)...

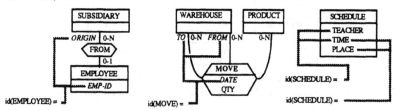

Fig. 4. Representation of identifiers as groups of attributes/roles

• a **reference** (inclusion, equality, copy) to other attributes (in the example below, SUBS-ID + EMPL-ID is a *foreign key* that references to EMPLOYEE)...

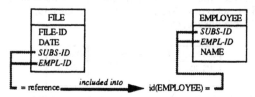

Fig. 5. Representation of an inclusion constraint (here a referential constraint or foreign key) as the inclusion of a group into another one.

• or, at the technical level, an access mechanism called **access key** (abstraction of indices, calc keys, hash organization, etc). In figure 6, FILE-ID is both an identifier and an access

---

[3] When possible, the components of the identifier will be underlined in the graphical representation. Otherwise, we shall use the explicit notation : id(E):component1,component2, ..

key to FILE; DATE and the EMPLOYEE entity it is coming FROM constitute an access key to FILE (i.e. given an EMPLOYEE entity and a DATE value, one can gain a quick and selective access to the concerned FILE entities).

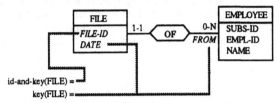

Fig. 6. Representation of an access key as a group of attributes/roles. This example is typical of CODASYL (indexed set types) and IMS structures.

We shall call *value of a group* a list of elements obtained by replacing each component of a group by one of its instances, namely a domain value for an attribute and an entity for a role.

Besides its intrinsic properties, an object can be characterized according to other facets : naming, statistical and informal specification (e.g. narrative semantics, technical notes, design justification). See [11] for details. The following section will develop the statistical facet.

This generic model can be specialized into dedicated models such as normalized E-R, binary E-R, Merise, IEW, Bachman's DSD, CODASYL, relational, IMS, COBOL file structures, etc. This specialization is done by a set of constraint rules that states the conditions a schema must satisfy in order to be declared *model-compliant*.

3. TIME-INDEPENDENT STATISTICAL MODEL OF DATA

The statistical model allows the specification of statistics on future or existing data, structured according to the E-R model. It describes the size of entity, relationship, attribute and domain populations and of their relations. As such it is an extension of the E-R model .
Though the statistics that will be proposed are often strongly related, we shall present them classified according to the main data object type they describe.

In many cases, the statistics are not constants, but are rather time-dependent quantities. In this section, we shall consider statistical descriptions related to a reference time point, i.e. description of a snapshot of the future or existing data at a given time. Time-dependent evolution of these descriptions will be discussed in section 5.

3.1 Statistical description of entity types

The most obvious statistics are N_E the average size of the population of entity type E.
Example : $N_{PRODUCT} = 6,000$

The statistical relations between entity type A and any subset of m direct subtypes $B_1, B_2, \ldots, B_m$ of A must satisfy the following rules :

$N_{Bi} \leq N_A$ for any i in [1-m]   rel.1

$N_A \geq \Sigma_i N_{Bi}$ for i in [1-m]   if the B_i's form a disjonction   rel.2

$N_A \leq \Sigma_i N_{Bi}$ for i in [1-m]   if the B_i's form a covering   rel.3

As a consequence, we have also :

$N_A = \Sigma_i N_{Bi}$ for i in [1-m]   if the B_i's form a partition   rel.4

3.2 Statistical description of relationship types

Let $R(r_1[m_{r1}-M_{r1}]:E_1, r_2[m_{r2}-M_{r2}]:E_2, \ldots, r_n[m_{rn}-M_{rn}]:E_n)$ be the structure of relationship type R with degree n. The role r_i is taken by entity type E_i and its cardinality properties are $m_{ri}-M_{ri}$.

Let N_R be the average number of instances of R. We can define for each role a *participation* probability function Π_r defined as follows :

$\Pi_{ri}(k)$ gives the probability that an E_i entity participates in exactly k instances of R as r_i. k must satisfy the condition $m_{ri} \leq k \leq M_{ri}$

Building Π_{ri} for each role of each relationship type in a schema is unrealistic in most situations. Therefore, a simpler version will be proposed, in which we keep only two participation statistics, namely $\Pi0_{ri}$, the probability that an entity participates in no R instances[4] and μ_{ri}, the average number of instances in which entities participate. They are defined as follows :

$$\Pi0_{ri} = \Pi_{ri}(0) \qquad\qquad\qquad \text{rel.5}$$
$$\mu_{ri} = \Sigma_k\,\Pi_{ri}(k) \times k, \text{ for k in } [m_{ri},M_{ri}] \qquad\qquad \text{rel.6}$$

The first statistics N_R derives from the others through the important relation :

$$N_{Ei} \times \mu_{ri} = N_R \text{ for i in } [1-n] \qquad\qquad\qquad \text{rel.7}$$

In addition we have the obvious properties :

$$m_{ri} \leq \mu_{ri} \leq M_{ri} \qquad\qquad\qquad\qquad \text{rel.8}$$
$$m_{ri} > 0 \quad \Rightarrow \quad \Pi0_{ri} = 0 \qquad\qquad\qquad \text{rel.9}$$

We can immediately derive another statistics, the average number of instances in which *participating* entities participate (i.e. excluding those which don't participate in any instance) :

$$\mu'_{ri} = \mu_{ri} / (1-\Pi0_{ri}) \qquad\qquad\qquad\qquad \text{rel.10}$$

Example :   let R be buys ([0-N] :CUSTOMER, [0-N] :PRODUCT)
$$\mu_{PRODUCT} = 60$$
$$\Pi0_{PRODUCT} = 0,4$$
$$\mu'_{PRODUCT} = 60/(1-0,4) = 100$$

There is an average of 60 customers per product; 40% of products are not bought; for products that are actually bought, there is an average of 100 customers.

These relations imply some consequences that are important for checking the consistency of statistics, and to ease their definition.

1. Statistics μ_{ri} of role r_i of R can be inferred from statistics μ_{rj} of any other role r_j of R. Indeed, we have :

$$\mu_{ri} = N_{Ej} \times \mu_{rj} / N_{Ei} \qquad\qquad\qquad\qquad \text{rel.11}$$

This property states that statistics μ_r needs to be measured for one role of R only.

    Example :   let R be LINE ([1-N] :ORDER, [0-N] :PRODUCT, [0-N] :SUPPLIER)

$N_{ORDER} = 8,000$ $\mu_{PRODUCT} = 8,000\times3/6,000 = 4$

$N_{PRODUCT} = 6,000$ $\Rightarrow$ $\mu_{SUPPLIER} = 8,000\times3/200 = 120$

$N_{SUPPLIER} = 200$

$\mu_{ORDER} = 3$

2. Statistics N_E of entity type E can be inferred from statistics μ_r of any relationship type R in which it appears in role r :

$$N_E = N_R / \mu_r \qquad\qquad\qquad\qquad\qquad \text{rel.12}$$

    Example : let R be SUPPLIES ([0-N] :COMPANY, [0-N] :PRODUCT)

$N_{COMPANY} = 600$

$\mu_{COMPANY} = 40$ $\Rightarrow$ $N_{PRODUCT} = 600\times40/12 = 2,000$

$\mu_{PRODUCT} = 12$

3. According to rel.8, we have :

$$m_{ri} = M_{ri} \Rightarrow \mu_{ri} = m_{ri} \qquad\qquad\qquad\qquad \text{rel.13}$$

Consequently, if $m_{ri} = M_{ri} = 1$, we have also for any role r_j of R :

$$\mu_{rj} = N_{Ei} / N_{Ej} \qquad\qquad\qquad\qquad\qquad \text{rel.14}$$

---

4 Note that the statistics $\Pi0_{ri}$ is as precise as function Π_{ri} when $M_{ri} = 1$. Indeed, $\Pi_{ri}(1) = 1-\Pi0_{ri}$.

Example : let R be SENDS([0-N]:CUSTOMER,[1-1]:ORDER)

$N_{CUSTOMER} = 600$

$N_{ORDER} = 1,800$ $\Rightarrow$ $\mu_{CUSTOMER} = 1,800 / 600 = 3$

4. In any (recursive) relationship types, all the roles taken by the same entity type have the same μ_r statistics.
Indeed,

$$N_E \times \mu_{ri} = N_E \times \mu_{rj} \qquad\qquad \text{rel.15}$$

implies,

$$\mu_{ri} = \mu_{rj} \qquad\qquad \text{rel.16}$$

Example : let R be MOVE(from[0-N]:STOCK,to[0-N]:STOCK,[0-N]:PRODUCT)

$N_{STOCK} = 80$ $\mu_{from} = 2,000\times40/80 = 1,000$

$N_{PRODUCT} = 2,000$ $\Rightarrow$ $\mu_{to} = 2,000\times40/80 = 1,000$

$\mu_{PRODUCT} = 40$

In particular, the statistics of any role of a relationship type having a *one* role[5] (for instance a binary *one-to-many* relationship type) cannot be greater than 1.

Example : let R be is-son-of(son[0-1]:PERSON,father[0-N]:PERSON)
the statistics of both roles cannot exceed 1. In other words, the fact that a person cannot have more than one father implies that persons cannot have more than one son in the average. For instance,

$\mu_{son} = 0,3$ $\Rightarrow$ $\mu_{father} = 0,3$

Though it is quite correct, this result is far from intuitive at first glance[6].

5. For any role with cardinality properties 0-1, we have,

$$\Pi0_{ri} = 1 - \mu_{ri} \qquad\qquad \text{rel.17}$$

3.3 Statistical description of attributes

Let us consider attribute A of parent object E with cardinality properties [m_A-M_A] and domain D.

There are two statistics concerning domain D :

N_D the number of values in D[7].

λ_D the average length of the values in D, in any convenient unit.

The first statistics of attribute A are,

N_A the number of distinct domain values that appear in A[8].

λ_A the average length of the values of A[9].

The other statistics describe and quantify the connection[10] between A values and instances of E,

---

5 I.e. a role r such that $M_r = 1$

6 Of course, the μ' statistics would have been more intuitive. If we suppose that $\Pi0_{father} = 0.85$, then $\mu'_{son}=1$ and $\mu'_{father}=2$. Note that in any case, $\Pi0_{son}\leq\Pi0_{father}$. Why ?

7 Often, this number is rather large, and can be considered as practically infinite. Such is the case with machine domains such as long character strings, long integers, floating-point numbers, etc. In these cases, statistics N_D is of no value. There exist situations in which the notion is useful, such as those using geographic names, department names, etc.

8 I.e. the values that are actually attached to a parent object instance.

9 I.e. that actually appear in A. This statistics measures individual values, and not lists of values.

10 This notion of connection suggests a strong similarity with relationship types, as it is common in binary models. This suggests too a similar treatment of the statistical description, based for instance on probability functions such as $\Pi_{A/E}(k)$ indicating the probability that an E instance has k values of A and $\Pi_{E/A}(k)$ indicating the probability that an A value is shared by k instances of E. For the same reason as for relationship types, these functions will prove too complex to build in many cases, and have been replaced by a simpler model.

$\mu_{A/E}$,   that specifies the average number of A values corresponding to an instance of E.

$\mu_{E/A}$,   that specifies the average number of E instances corresponding to a value of A.

$\Pi 0_{A/E}$,   that specifies the probability that an E instance has no A values.

Some immediate properties :

$$N_A \leq N_D \qquad \text{rel.18}$$
$$m_A \leq \mu_{A/E} \leq M_A \qquad \text{rel.19}$$
$$m_A > 0 \quad \Rightarrow \quad \Pi 0_{A/E} = 0 \qquad \text{rel.20}$$
$$N_E \times \mu_{A/E} = N_A \times \mu_{E/A} \qquad \text{rel.21}$$
$$\text{if A values have fixed-length 1, } \lambda_A = \lambda_D = 1 \qquad \text{rel.22}$$

We can derive two secondary statistics,

- the average number of A values for E instances that actually have A values (i.e. excluding those which don't have A values) :

$$\mu'_{A/E} = \mu_{A/E} / (1 - \Pi 0_{A/E}) \qquad \text{rel.23}$$

- the average length of A values for E instances that actually have A values :

$$\lambda'_A = \lambda_A / (1 - \Pi 0_{A/E}) \qquad \text{rel.24}$$

Example :   let E be entity type EMPLOYEE with attribute PHONE[0-5]; let's use abbreviation E for EMPLOYEE and P for PHONE;

```
N_E = 1,200
N_P = 900
μ_P/E = 1.5
μ_E/P = 2
Π0_P/E = 0,2
μ'_P/E = 1.5/(1-0,2) = 1.875
```

There is an average of 1.5 telephones per employee and 2 employees per telephone; 20% of the employees have no telephone; employees who do have telephones have an average of 1.875 telephones.

By similarity with the statistical description of relationship types, the following relations can be derived immediately from the definitions given above.

1. Inference of statistics $\mu_{A/E}$ or $\mu_{A/E}$:

$$\mu_{A/E} = \mu_{E/A} \times N_A / N_E \qquad \text{rel.25}$$
$$\mu_{E/A} = \mu_{A/E} \times N_E / N_A \qquad \text{rel.26}$$

2. Inference of statistics N_A :

$$N_A = \mu_{A/E} \times N_E / \mu_{E/A} \qquad \text{rel.27}$$

3. Inference from rel.19 :

$$m_A = M_A \quad \Rightarrow \quad \mu_{A/E} = m_A \qquad \text{rel.28}$$

Consequently, if $m_A = M_A = 1$, we have also :

$$\mu_{E/A} = N_E / N_A \qquad \text{rel.29}$$

Remarks.

1. It can be noted that the description of attributes seems asymmetrical when compared with that of (binary) relationship types. Indeed, there is no such statistics as $\Pi 0_{E/A}$, stating the probability that an A value corresponds to no E entities. Should it exist, it would be 0 in any case. On the contrary, this notion is pertinent for domain values, since they are not mandatorily appearing as A value. However, it has not be included in the model. If needed, it can be computed as $1 - N_A/N_D$.

2. Another basic statistical function can be though of as lacking in the model, namely the distribution function according to the actual values of attribute A (or more generally domain

D of A). It would give the probability that an E entity has a given value v as attribute A. It could be defined as,

$$\Pi V_A(v), \text{ for } v \in D$$

This function has been discarded to keep the model simple. However, this has been used in specific problems such as query optimization in some commercial SQL DBMS.

3.4 Statistical description of groups

The statistical description of a group is important for access keys, for instance, but the following principles are valid for any group, whatever its function[11]. A goup G is attached to a parent object E, which is an entity type or a relationship type.

The proposed statistics are :

N_G, the average number of distinct values of G that appear in the database,

μ_G, the average number of E instances corresponding to a value of G[12].

Let's first consider a group G made of *more than one component*[13]. We have the property :

$$0 \leq N_G \leq N_E \qquad \text{rel.30}$$

if group G is an identifier, we have :

$$N_G = N_E \qquad \text{rel.31}$$
$$\mu_G = 1 \qquad \text{rel.32}$$

If G *includes one component only* (which is necessarily an attribute A), we have :

$$N_G = N_A \qquad \text{rel.33}$$
$$\mu_G = \mu_{E/A} \qquad \text{rel.34}$$

Since relation rel.21 of statistical descriptions of attributes is still valid :

$$N_E \times \mu_{A/E} = N_G \times \mu_G \qquad \text{rel.35}$$

if $m_A = M_A = 1$, we have also :

$$\mu_G = N_E / N_G \qquad \text{rel.36}$$

if G is an identifier, $\mu_G = 1$, so that, $\qquad$ rel.37

$$N_G = \mu_{A/E} \times N_E \qquad \text{rel.38}$$

3.5 Statistical description of spaces

A space S is described by,

$\mu_{E/S}$, that specifies the average number of E entities that are contained in space S,

In a consistent (e.g. finished) logical schema, the population of each entity type is completely assigned to at least one space. Therefore, considering that E has been associated with spaces $S_1, S_2, ..., S_p$, we have,

$$N_E = \Sigma_i \mu_{E/Si} \qquad \text{for i in } [1-p] \qquad \text{rel.39}$$

however, in an inconsistent schema, we have,

$$N_E \geq \Sigma_i \mu_{E/Si} \qquad \text{for i in } [1-p] \qquad \text{rel.40}$$

---

11 This function can be simply to support the statistics.

12 In fact, at a certain level of abstraction, the relationship between a group and its parent object can be perceived as somewhat similar to a relationship type between two entity types. Therefore, we could have proposed a more precise description based on a probability function $\Pi_G(k)$ indicating the probability that a group value is associated with k instances of the home object. For the same reason as for relationship type and attributes, a simpler model based on μ_G only has been adopted. Note that $\Pi_G(0) = 0$ since group values not related to a home object instance are discarded from the model. Therefore, there is no such concept as $\Pi 0_G$.

13 For technical reasons that are beyond the scope of this paper, the components of G are constrained to be single-valued

3.6 Summary

The basic statistics that make up the proposed model are illustrated in figure 7.

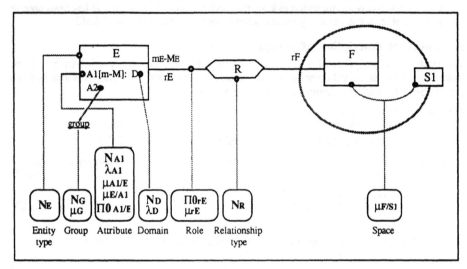

Fig. 7. The components of the statistical model

4. COMPUTABLE STATISTICAL SPECIFICATIONS

Until now the statistical specifications of a schema appear as a set of statistics, a set of inter-statistics relations and a set of constants assigned to the statistics. From an algebraic point of view, the specifications appear as a system of variables (the statistics) and equations (inter-statistics relations) together with one solution (statistics values).

Practically speaking, things appear differently. Since some variables can be derived from the others, the problem is to distinguish the *independent* or **basic variables,** to which we must assign values, from the *dependent* or **derived** variables, the values of which will be computed.

For instance, $N_R = N_{Ei} \times \mu_{ri}$ suggests to calculate N_R from the N_{Ei} and μ_{ri} of an arbitrary role, and therefore to consider N_{Ei} and μ_{ri} as basic variables and N_R as a derived variables. Unfortunately, an inter-statistics relation is basically *undirected*, i.e. it can be used to define any of its variables as a function of the other ones. For instance, the expression above can be seen also as a way to calculate the μ_{ri} from N_{Ei} and N_R or even to calculate all the μ_{ri} of R from one of them.

Deciding what are the basic statistics and what are the derived ones results in a system of *computable specifications*[14]. A given set of undirected specifications can generate a fairly large set of computable systems [5]. Finding them, and more specifically choosing one of them is not a straighforward task. The problem is twofold :

how to determine basic and derived statistics of a given schema and

how to determine the order in which the derived statistics must be computed

We propose a procedure to find computable specifications. It is described in appendix.

---

[14] To make the problem more pragmatic, let's say that computable specifications can be easily implemented into a primitive spreadsheet processor that allows forward computing only, or into a purely sequential program in any 3rd generation language.

5. EVOLUTION OF STATISTICS

In all generality, we cannot consider that E-R statistics are constant over time. Some entity populations will grow while others will remain constant or even shrink. When estimating the volume and the performances of a database for instance, it is important to get an evolving picture of these figures during a given period. The model presented in section 3 allows the description of a given state of data, but it is unable to describe its evolution except as a mere sequence of independent states. In fact we would like to include in the model concepts and laws that describe the temporal behaviour of the statistics. With such extensions, we will be able to study the future evolution of the data from the statistical point of view.

An important by-product of the classification procedure proposed in appendix is to determine the statistics for which a temporal analysis has to be carried out. Indeed, only the basic statistics must be associated with a temporal description.

In general, statistics S classified as basic is defined by a function f_S that can be of one of the following forms :
   - constant (i.e. S is time-independent)
   - temporal function $f_S(t)$;
   - function of other statistics;

Let's examine shortly each of them.

Constants

Some statistics may time-independent, and therefore constant, e.g. $N_{COUNTRY} = 185$

Temporal functions

Here are some examples of analytic or semi-analytic functions : proportional, linear, quadratic, exponential, periodic, segmented, etc, in t.

Many phenomena can be described as evolving *linearly*. Their statistics, say S, are said linear over time, i.e. that they can be expressed as,

$$S(t) = S_0 + \delta_S \times t$$

where $S(t)$ is the value of S at time t

            S_0 is the value of the S at the starting time

            δ_S is the absolute variation of S per unit of time

For instance, a current customer population of 20,000 with a yearly growth of 10% w.r.t. the current value can described as follows :

$$N_C = 20,000 + 2,000 \times t$$

Besides this simple case, logarithmic and exponential behaviours are also frequent, exhibiting saturation or explosive evolutions. They can be modeled through *logarithmic or exponential functions*. Going back to the customer example, if the 10% growth is defined w.r.t. the population of the previous year, the expression will be the following (t is in years) :

$$N_C = 20,000 \times (1 + 0,1)^t$$

Periodic functions can be used to describe statistics behaviours presenting a regular and repeating pattern. Such will be the case in hospital, where the demand for specific services depends on the period of the year, of the month or of the week, and in industries related to seasonal activities or products.

A *segmented function* is made up of a sequence of contiguous time segments, each of them being of a simple analytical form. A periodic function can be segmented as well. In this case, the period is both segmented and repeating.

Other functions

Statistics can be declared as being an explicit function of other statistics, independently of (but consistently with) the derivation rules, or being an explicit function of the previous state(s). For instance, the N_E statistics of SECRETARY can be declared as being half that of

ENGINEER. Such functions make the classification procedure more complex since additional dependencies and derivation rules must be taken into account. Moreover, some specifications may prove *uncomputable*, that is, they cannot be transformed (easily) into a computable system, due to cyclic dependency relations. Such a problem is beyond the scope of this paper and we shall ignore this possibility (see [5]).

6. SCHEMA TRANSFORMATION

6.1 Introduction

A (schema) transformation is most generally considered as an operator by which a data structure S1 is replaced by another structure S2 which has some sort of equivalence with S1. Schema transformation is a ubiquitous concept in the database realm. This concept is particularly attractive in database modeling and design, and has been proposed as basic design tools by several authors. Proving the equivalence of schemas [12], refining a conceptual schema [4], integrating two partial schemas [1, 11], producing a DBMS-compliant schema from a conceptual schema [3, 5, 12], restructuring a physical schema [2], DB reverse engineering [9], are basic design activities that can be carried out by carefully chosen schema transformations.

Though developing this concept and its formalization is beyond the scope of this paper (see [10] for a more formal treatment), we shall sketch the main definitions and properties that will be important for statistics processing and propagation.

A **transformation T** is an operator that replaces a source construct C in schema S by another construct C'; C' is the target of C through T, and is noted   C' = T(C)
A transformation T is defined by, (1) a minimal precondition P that any construct C must satisfy in order to be transformed by T, (2) a maximal postcondition Q that T(C) satisfies. T can therefore be written T = <P,Q> as well. P and Q are pattern-matching predicates that identify the components and the properties of C and T(C), and more specifically : the components of C that are preserved in T(C), the components of C that are discarded from T(C), the components of T(C) that didn't exist in C.
A transformation T1 = <P,Q> is *reversible*[15], or *semantics-preserving*, *iff* there exists a transformation T2 such that, for any construct C, P(C) ⇒ T2(T1(C)) = S. T2 is the reverse of T1, and conversely. We have the following property : T2 = <Q,P>

In some cases, it is possible to give a more readable representation of a transformation by expressing C and T(C) graphically, assuming that the graphical language is powerful enough.

Due to the limited scope of the paper as far as this topic is concerned, we shall limit the development as follows :
- we shall specify transformations through graphical expressions,
- we shall consider semantics-preserving transformations only,
- among the large number of possible transformations, we shall choose three of them that cover the most important needs when producing relational and CODASYL-like schemas.
The reader will find in [10] and [11] more in-depth studies of the problem.

In the context of comprehensive database design methods and tools, transforming conceptual structures is essential but not sufficient. The other aspects of the specifications must be adapted as well, in order to preserve the design characteristics and decisions. In particular, access structures, names, statistics, informal descriptions, etc, must all be translated into equivalent specifications in the transformed schema. We shall concentrate on the statistics-preservation properties of the transformations and ignore the other aspects in the following.

---

[15] In fact, the issue is a bit more complex, since a transformation must be defined not only by a mapping T between schemas but also by a mapping t between data populations (instances) of the schemas. Two kind of semantics preservation can be defined, namely *reversibility* and *symmetrical reversibility* [8]. T1 is reversible iff, *for any instance s of schema S such that P(S)*, s = t2(t1(s)); T1 is symmetrically reversible iff both T1 and T2 are reversible, i.e., in addition to the property mentioned above, *for any instance s' of S' such that Q(S'), s' = t1(t2(s'))*. For simplicity, we shall ignore this distinction in this paper.

The point is of particular importance since gathering and validating the statistics of a future or existing database is a complex and costly task. It is essential that the statistical specifications in a schema be preserved when this schema is transformed.

The idea of transforming statistics on a conceptual schema into statistics on a logical or physical schema can be questioned. Indeed, statistics are mainly useful for performance evaluation, query optimisation or simulation, i.e. for problems related with logical and physical structures. Therefore, it would have been more realistic to collect these statistics for the final, physical schema, and therefore to ignore the problem of transforming statistics.

The answer is rather straighforward :
- collecting statistics at the conceptual level is much easier and more natural since they describe conceptual objects. Therefore, users can be involved in this process;
- the conceptual schema is more stable than physical schemas, which may evolve according to changes in the performance requirements and in the state of the technology;
- conceptual schemas, as well as physical schemas, may be transformed for other reasons than pure top-down implementation; view derivation and integration are only two examples.

This section describes three major schema transformations together with their statistics translation rules. These rules are also reversible, so that the transformations can be used both ways. It should be noted that the proposed rules are independent of the nature of the statistics, be they constants or temporal functions.

6.2 *Relationship type* ⇔ *entity type* **transformation**

This transformation is aimed at replacing complex relationship types R of degree n (e.g. that are *many-to-many* or recursive, or with a degree greater than 2, or with attributes) by an equivalent entity type R, *plus* binary *one-to-many* relationship types r1, r2, .., rn. It can be used during the conceptual analysis phase, as well as in the implementation phases, when such a simplification of the schema narrows the structural gap between the conceptual model and the DBMS model. Note that due to the reversibility of the operation, it can be used to transform an entity type into a relationship type as well, a useful operator in database reverse engineering [9]. This transformation derives from the generic transformation proposed in [10].

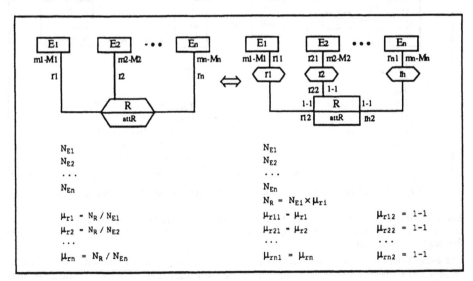

Fig. 8. Transformation of a relationship type into an entity type, and conversely.

Figure 9 illustrates the transformation with a practical example. In statistics names, some naming conventions have been adopted to unambiguously designate roles : for instance, SL.LINE designates role LINE in relationship type SL.

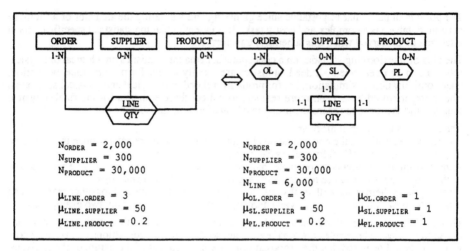

Fig. 9. Example of the transformation of a relationship type into an entity type, and conversely

6.3 *Relationship type* ⇔ *attribute* transformation

Through this transformation, a binary, one-to-many relationship type R is replaced by reference attributes refA (i.e. a foreign key) *plus* a referential constraint. Together with the previous transformation, they constitute the basic operators that allows the translation of arbitrary relationship types into relational structures. Being reversible, it can be used to transform reference attributes into a relationship type (in database reverse engineering for instance).

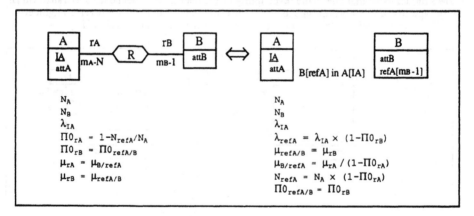

Fig. 10. Transformation of a relationship type into reference attributes, and conversely.

This transformation is fully reversible if the cardinality properties of rA are 0-N or 1-N (or 0-1 or 1-1 of course). Other cases need additional integrity constraints that would make the development more complex without any profit.

The complexity of the definitions of λ_{refA}, $\mu_{B/refA}$ and N_{refA} is due to the fact that there can be less refA distinct values in B than there are IA values in A. Figure 11 illustrates the transformation with a practical example. In statistics names, abbreviations have been used to shorten expressions : E stands for EMPLOYEE and D for DEPART.

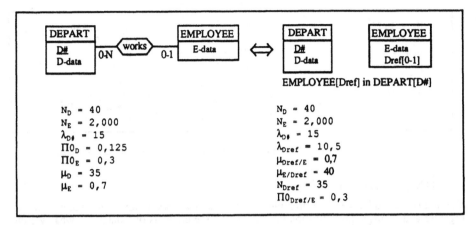

Fig. 11. Example of the transformation of a relationship type into an attribute, and conversely

6.4 *Attribute ⇔ Entity type* transformation

This transformation is mainly intended to extract a multivalued attribute B and to replace it by an entity type EB *plus* a one-to-many relationship type R[16]. Together with the previous transformation, they constitute the basic operators to translate multivalued attributes into relational structures. It derives from the generic transformation proposed in [10].

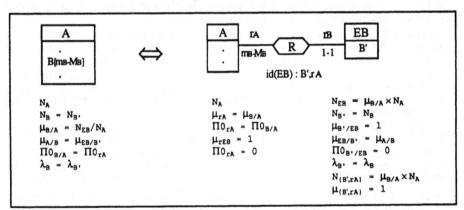

Fig. 12. Transformation of an attribute into an entity type, and conversely.

Figure 13 gives a practical example. In statistics names, abbreviations have been used to shorten expressions : E stands for EMPLOYEE, P for PHONE, EP for E-EMP and P' for PHONE'.

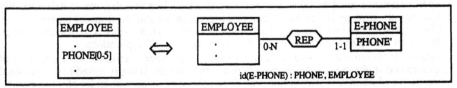

---

[16] There exists another general transformation that can extract any attribute, whatever its cardinality properties. It would have produced a many-to-many relationship type in this case, an undesired complex structure that would have needed further transformations for, say, producing a relational schema. More on this in [8].

$$N_E = 1,200 \qquad\qquad N_E = \qquad\qquad\qquad N_{EP} = 1,800$$
$$N_P = 900 \qquad\qquad \mu_E = 1.5 \qquad\qquad N_{P'} = 900$$
$$\mu_{P/E} = 1.5 \qquad\qquad \Pi 0_E = 0.2 \qquad\qquad \mu_{P'/EP} = 1$$
$$\mu_{E/P} = 2 \qquad\qquad \mu_{EP} = 1 \qquad\qquad \mu_{EP/P'} = 2$$
$$\Pi 0_{P/E} = 0.2 \qquad\qquad \Pi 0_{EP} = 0 \qquad\qquad \Pi 0_{P'/EP} = 0$$
$$\lambda_P = 12 \qquad\qquad\qquad\qquad\qquad\qquad \lambda_{P'} = 12$$
$$N_{\{P',E\}} = 1,800$$
$$\mu_{\{P',E\}} = 1$$

Fig. 13. Example of the transformation of an attribute into an entity type, and conversely.

7. CONCLUSIONS

The statistical model we have presented in this paper allows a simple and natural way to organise and manage quantification information on the contents of a database, whatever the level of abstraction at which this database is described.

It is clear that collecting statistics before the database is implemented is both difficult and tedious. The goal of this paper is to formalise these statistics and their management in order to determine the minimal set of useful quantities to collect, and to propose techniques to maintain them without any loss during all the activities of database design. In particular, this maintenance (translation through schema transformation) garantees that the statistics can be collected at the most natural level, i.e. on the conceptual schema, and will propagate down to the physical schema without designer interaction.

Due to its limited scope, the paper has not discussed possible usage of this statistical description. Let's mention some of the most obvious applications :
- computing the volume of a future database, and its evolution; this application requires some additional information on the physical length of attribute values, on the representation of null values, on physical data storage and on the physical organisation of indices for instance.
- estimating the cost of critical queries and applications; knowing the access strategies of the applications, it is fairly easy to compute the number of logical accesses (number of entities processed); these results can be converted into physical accesses if physical storage parameters are known.
- query optimisation; finding optimal access strategies cannot be based on the knowledge of the logical schema only; knowledge on statistics on the data is also essential.
- logical/physical design. Choosing the optimal data structures w.r.t. the performance of a set of critical applications needs two analytical tools : generating equivalent schemas [7] [10], and evaluating the cost of the applications [6]. The best schema minimizes the total cost [6].

Though its merits, the model proposed in this paper is far from comprehensive. Let us mention some problems still to be discussed and some natural extensions.
- correlations between statistics cannot be described; besides the analytical relations between statistics presented in section 3, it is impossible to declare real world relationships between statistics. For instance, unmarried persons have not the same statistics about their children than married ones.
- update statistics must be taken into account as well. In particular, create/delete/modify statistics are strongly linked to the temporal aspects of the statistical model presented here. These statistics can be either specified explicitly, or they can be inferred from knowledge on the access strategies and frequencies of the update queries and applications.
- data usage statistics must also be taken into account in order to estimate the access time of queries and application. Update and data usage statistics are strongly linked to the statistical model. In addition, this information provides a precise decision support for physical design.
- the model presented is based on the idea that all the objects of a schema are described by all the statistics of their type. For instance, all attributes are supposed to be associated with the five statistics evoked in figure 7. This is not realistic. The user (i.e. the designer) must be allowed to decide what are the quantities (s)he needs. The concept of consistent and computable system of statistics must be revised accordingly.

Many of the statistical extensions of the E-R model presented in this paper have been incorporated in TRAMIS, an commercial CASE tools dedicated to database design support, from conceptual analysis to optimised DDL generation [11]. This tool allows the specification of static statistics (described in this paper), as well as of dynamic (update and data usage) statistics. The specifications are checked when they are recorded in the repository, and propagation according to the derivation rules is carried out automatically. Statistical specifications are maintained through schema transformation (TRAMIS offers a toolset of about 20 transformations). TRAMIS generates detailed and summary reports on static and dynamic statistics. These reports are used by the designer to decide the optimal logical and physical structures to implement. In addition, the DDL generator makes use[17] of the statistics to generate optimized DBMS schema. Temporal aspects of statistics are still to be implemented.

8. ACKNOWLEDGEMENT

Thanks to M. Cadelli, B. Decuyper, O. Marchand, of the TRAMIS team for their contribution to TRAMIS. Thanks also to CONCIS, the company with the help of which TRAMIS has been specified, developed and which distributed the first version. Finally, thanks to all the members of the DB Laboratory of EPFL, Lausanne, who welcomed me so kindly and so competently during my sabbatical leave. Particular thanks to Stefano who gave me meaningful remarks and advices on this paper.

9. REFERENCES

[1] Batini, C., Lenzerini, M., Moscarini, M., *View integration, in Methodology and tools for data base design*, Ceri, S., (Ed.) North-Holland, 1983

[2] Batini, C., Ceri, S., Navathe, S., B., *Conceptual Database Design*, Benjamin/ Cummings, 1992

[3], Bert, M., N., and al., *The logical design in the DATAID Project : the EASYMAP system*, in *Computer-Aided Database Design : the DATAID Project*, Albano and al. (Ed.), North-Holland, 1985

[4] Giraudin, J-P., Delobel, C., Dardailler, P., *Eléments de construction d'un système expert pour la modélisation progressive d'une base de données*, in Actes Journées Bases de Données Avancées, Mars,1985

[5] Geoffrion, A., M., *An Introduction to Structured Modeling*, Management Sciences, Vol. 33, No. 5, 1987

[6] Hainaut, J-L., *Some Tools for Data Independence in Multilevel Data Base Systems*, in Proc of the IFIP TC2/WC on Modelling in Data Base Management Systems, Nice, North-Holland, 1977

[7] Hainaut, J-L., *Theoretical and practical tools for database design*, in Proc. 6th Inter. Conf. on Very Large Data Bases, 1981

[8] Hainaut, J.-L., *A Generic Entity-Relationship Model*, in Proc. of the IFIP WG 8.1 Conf. on *Information System Concepts: an in-depth analysis*, North-Holland, 1989.

[9] Hainaut, J-L., *Database Reverse Engineering, Models, Techniques and Strategies*, in PreProc. of the 10th Conf. on Entity-Relationship Approach, San Mateo, 1991

[10] Hainaut, J-L., *Entity-generating Schema Transformation for Entity-Relationship Models*, in Proc. of the 10th Conf. on Entity-Relationship Approach, San Mateo, North-Holland, 1991

[11] Hainaut, J-L., *Database CASE Tool Architecture : Principles for Flexible Design Strategies*, In Proc. of CAiSE-92 Conference, Manchester, LNCS Springer-Verlag, 1992

[12] Kobayashi, I., *Losslessness and Semantic Correctness of Database Schema Transformation : another look of Schema Equivalence*, in Information Systems, Vol. 11, No 1, pp. 41-59, January, 1986

[13] Spaccapietra, S., Parent, C., *View Integration : A Step Forward in Solving Structural Conflicts*, Res. Report , EPFL, Lausanne (CH), August 1990. To appear in IEEE Trans. on Knowledge and Data Engineering, October, 1992

[14] Reiner, D., Brown, G., Friedell, M., Lehman, J., McKee, R., Rheingans, P., Rosenthal, A., *A Database Designer's Worbench*, in Proc. of Entity-Relationship Approach, 1986

Appendix - Deriving computable statistical specifications

Let us propose some preliminary considerations.

1. The problem can be stratified according to two levels. The first level consists in classifying statistics N_E, N_R and μ_r related to entity types, relationship types and roles into basic and

---

[17] A limited usage until now. Incorporating optimisation heuristics for schema restructuration and generation is planned for the next version.

derived. Indeed, these statistics are strongly related and appear as more fundamental than the others. In the second level, we will classify all the other statistics.

2. The statistics of some E-R constructs depend fully on conceptual properties. This is the case of roles such that $m_r = M_r$ (e.g. the most common case $1-1$). Let us call *a locking role* such a role. Indeed, it offers no freedom to determine its participation statistics.

Let us call *defined*, statistics that have already been classified and *undefined*, statistics that still have to be classified. The problem is solved when all the statistics are defined.

The procedure is described through a structured collection of *rule sets* together with a *strategy* (meta-rules) indicating how to apply the rules.

First step : classification of N_E, N_R and μ_r

Classification rule

Rule 0 : A statistics is either defined or undefined. A statistics is defined *iff* it is either basic or derived.

E&R rules[18]

Rule 1 : The N_E statistics of entity types E participating in no locking roles are classified as basic.

Rule 2 : The statistics μ_r of locking roles r are derived [rel.13]

Rule 3 : When entity type E appears in role r of relationship type R, if N_E and μ_r are defined and N_R is undefined, then N_R can be classified as derived [rel.7]

Rule 4 : When entity type E appears in role r of relationship type R, if N_R and μ_r are defined and N_E is undefined, then N_E can be classified as derived [rel.12]

Rule 5 : When entity type E appears in role r of relationship type R, if N_R and N_E are defined and μ_r is undefined, then μ_r can be classified as derived [rel.11]

Strategy for classifying statistics N_E, N_R and μ_r

1. apply the **classification** and **E&R** rules until no further N_E, N_R or μ_r statistics can be defined,
2. while undefined N_E, N_R or μ_r statistics still exist, do
   2.1 choose one undefined N_E, N_R or μ_r statistics and classify it as basic
   2.2 apply the **classification** and **E&R** rules until no further N_E, N_R or μ_r statistics can be defined,

The choice of the undefined statistics in step 2.1 leads to several substrategies. One can think of a hierarchy according to which we choose undefined statistics of entity types first. We think that it is better to be guided by the *naturalness* of the chosen statistics, i.e. by the ease of finding its value (and function) in the real world. This choice depends on conceptual and practical consideration and cannot be fully automated. It involves human interaction.

Examples : let's consider the relationship type HAS([1-N]:ORDER, [1-1]:LINE) with the following final statistical specifications (let's ignore μ_{LINE}) : $N_{ORDER} = 20,000$, $N_{LINE} = 60,000$, $\mu_{ORDER} = 3$, $N_{HAS} = 60,000$. Stating that *there is an average of 3 lines per order* is more natural that stating that *there are 60,000 lines of order*. Therefore, we shall declare $\{N_{ORDER}, \mu_{ORDER}\}$ as basic and $\{N_{LINE}, N_{HAS}\}$ as derived.

The situation is different for the similar relationship type SENDS([0-N]:CUSTOMER, [1-1]:ORDER) with the following final statistical specifications(let's ignore μ_{ORDER}) : $N_{CUSTOMER} = 4,000$, $N_{ORDER} = 20,000$, $\mu_{CUSTOMER} = 5$, $N_{SENDS} = 20,000$. Now, stating that *there are 20,000 orders* is more natural that stating the average number of orders per customer. Therefore, $\{N_{CUSTOMER}, N_{ORDER}\}$ are basic and $\{\mu_{CUSTOMER}, N_{SENDS}\}$ are derived.

Second step : classification of the other statistics

Role rules (complement)

Rule 6 : For role r_E, if $m_r > 0$ or $M_r = 1$ then $\Pi 0_{rE}$ is derived else it is basic [rel.9] [rel.17]

Domain rules

Rule 7 : For domain D, N_D is basic.

Rule 8 : For domain D, if its format is fixed-length, then λ_D is derived else it is basic [rel.22]

---

[18] To keep things (rather) simple, we have not included the rules related to *is-a* relations.

Attribute rules
Rule 9 : For attribute A of E, if $m_A = M_A$ then $\mu_{A/E}$ is derived else it is basic [rel.27]
Rule 10 : For attribute A of E, if $\mu_{A/E}$ and N_A are defined and $\mu_{E/A}$ is undefined, then $\mu_{E/A}$ is derived [rel.26]
Rule 11 : For attribute A of E, if $\mu_{E/A}$ and $\mu_{A/E}$ are defined and N_A is undefined, then N_A is derived [rel.27]
Rule 12 : For attribute A of E, if N_A and $\mu_{E/A}$ are defined and $\mu_{A/E}$ is undefined, then $\mu_{A/E}$ is derived [rel.25]
Rule 13 : For attribute A of E, if $m_A > 0$ then $\Pi 0_{A/E}$ is derived else it is basic [rel.20]
Rule 14 : For attribute A of E, if λ_D is derived then λ_A is derived else it is basic [rel.22]

Group rules - set 1
Rule 15 : For mono-component group G (with component A), if N_A is defined and N_G is undefined, then N_G is derived [rel.33]
Rule 16 : For mono-component group G (with component A), if $\mu_{E/A}$ is defined and μ_G is undefined, then μ_G is derived [rel.34]
Rule 17 : For mono-component group G (with component A), if $\mu_{A/E}$ and N_G are defined and μ_G is undefined, then μ_G is derived [rel.35]   :
Rule 18 : For mono-component group G (with component A), if $\mu_{A/E}$ and μ_G are defined and N_G is undefined, then N_G is derived [rel.35]
Rule 19 : For multi-component group G, if G is an identifier, then N_G is derived [rel.31]
Rule 20 : For group G, if G is an identifier, then μ_G is derived [rel.32] [rel.37]

Group rules - set 2
Rule 21 : For mono-component group G (with component A), if N_G is defined and N_A is undefined, then N_A is derived [rel.33]
Rule 22 : For mono-component group G (with component A), if μ_G is defined and $\mu_{E/A}$ is undefined, then $\mu_{E/A}$ is derived [rel.34]
Rule 23 : For mono-component group G (with component A), if N_G and μ_G are defined and $\mu_{A/E}$ is undefined, then $\mu_{A/E}$ is derived [rel.35]

Space rules
Rule 24 : For space S and entity type E, $\mu_{E/S}$ is basic.

Strategy for classifying the other statistics

3. apply **Role rules** until no further $\Pi 0_{rE}$ statistics can be defined,
4. apply **Domain rules** until no further N_D or λ_D statistics can be defined,
5. apply **Attribute rules** until no further $\mu_{A/E}$ or $\mu_{E/A}$ or N_A or $\Pi 0_{A/E}$ or λ_A statistics can be defined,
6. apply **Group rules - set 1** until no further N_G or μ_G statistics can be defined,
7. while undefined N_G or μ_G statistics still exist, do
   7.1 choose one undefined N_G or μ_G statistics, and classify it as basic,
   7.2 apply **Group rules - set 1** until no further N_G or μ_G statistics can be defined,
8. apply **Group rules - set 2**
9. apply **Attribute rules**
10. if needed, apply **Space rules**

Final step : computing ordering

When all the statistics are defined, they can be considered as computable. Indeed, knowing the value (or the temporal function) of each basic statistics, all the derived statistics can be evaluated through the derivation rules (rel.1 to rel.40) that are mentioned in each inference rule that classify a derived statistics. In addition, the order in which the derived statistics have been classified defines a *preorder relation* on them. Through topological sorting, this preorder gives also a correct sequence of computations that can be followed either to compute the derived statistics, or to write a sequential computing program[19]. Indeed, the expression of a derived statistics makes use of statistics that are either basic, or already evaluated.

---

[19] This can be demonstrated easily.

Semantic Similarity Relations
in Schema Integration

William W. Song, Paul Johannesson, Janis A. Bubenko Jr.

SYSLAB, Department of Computer and Systems Sciences
Royal Inst. of Technology and Stockholm University
ELECTRUM 230, S-16440, Kista, Sweden
and
Swedish Institute of Systems Development (SISU)
Box 1250, S-16428, Kista, Sweden

Abstract. To find similarities between objects of different schemata at the semantic level is a crucial problem in schema integration. To identify such similarities it is necessary to form a set of semantic characteristics the objects may have. In this paper, we present a set of such characteristics and a set of semantic similarity relations. The relations are classified into four groups, weak semantic relation, compatible semantic relation, equivalence semantic relation, and mergeable semantic relation. We also propose a schema integration tool, which makes use of the semantic relations to integrate objects of different schemata.

Keywords. view integration, schema integration, semantic similarity, entity-relationship model, conceptual schema design

1. Introduction and assumptions

View integration is an important concept in database design, information system design, and knowledge base system design. With the number of databases and conceptual schemata steadily growing, the need to re-use existing resources is accentuated. The task to integrate data from different systems is critical and hard. Semantic conflicts which arise in systems evolution and integration must be solved with specific methods, which are not considered in ordinary information system and database design methodologies. Semantic conflicts arise due to different user and designer perceptions of the universe of discourse. To some extent, view integration includes both schema integration and database integration [2]. *Schema integration* produces a global conceptual schema of a set of proposed database schemata through resolving the conflicts among different users' views. *Database integration* produces a virtual view of a collection of databases. In this paper we address the problems of schema integration.

The goal of schema integration is either 1) to create a global schema, which takes in all possible user's views and makes these views consistent by solving the conflicts among the component schemata; or 2) to provide a common access or interface to local (or component) schemata in which the user's diverse requests (or views) are represented. We assume, in agreement with [2, 11, 13], that the schema integration process consists of five iterating steps: canonization (pre-integration), comparison, conciliation, merging (integration), and restructuring. 1) In the canonizing step the intra-schema conflicts and inconsistencies are detected against some predefined criteria or requirements, such as "an entity type is not allowed to connect to an attribute by a relationship". 2) The comparison step performs a pairwise comparison of objects of the schemata to be integrated and finds possible object pairs which may be semantically similar. The object pair set so generated is called the semantic similarity relation with respect to some properties, such as synonym, equal key attributes and equal context. 3) In the conciliation step, a variety of user assisted techniques are used to resolve conflicts and mismatched objects. 4) The merging step generates an integrated schema from two component schemata. In 5), the last step, restructuring, the objective is to check the consistency of the integrated schema and build correspondences between the component schemata and the integrated schema. The main problems of schema integration are summarised in the following section.

1.1 Problems of schema integration

The major problems lie in understanding of the *intended meaning* of objects in different schemata, such as attributes, relationships, and entities as well as the semantic associations between them. The difficulties of acquiring semantics are manifold and reflect difficulties in the acquisition and representation of people's perceptions of the reality, in achieving correct reflections of schemata to these perceptions, and in the stipulation of the meaning of schema objects. We prefer the point of view that a good schema integrator is so built that it can collect as much information as possible from the component schemata for semantic comparison and then offer suggestions to the user, who then makes the final decisions in schema integration.

Key problems of schema integration, addressed in this paper are how to identify semantic similarity between objects from different schemata based on certain criteria (the *semantic similarity relation* means that two objects may be related through their features, such as their names, their key attributes or their contexts). We make use of names of objects, and contexts of object to form such criteria. The semantic similarity between objects is built on the basis of these criteria. Most of the criteria are provided in the knowledge bases.

1.2 Basic assumptions

In the following we make a list of assumptions which concern different aspects of schema integration. These aspects include those of the principle of concepts, semantic relations, and the use of a semantic dictionary and a taxonomy structure. In addition, we assume that a time dimension is applied to the integration of schema and their objects.

1) The concept principle
We assume that a concept, represented by an entity type, a relationship type, or an attribute in a schema, can be uniquely determined by a set P of properties. We also assume a *key* property set K, a subset of P. K can uniquely determine P. To which semantic relation an object (or concept) pair belongs depends on the closeness (or the number of shared properties) of their property sets. We do not care about which are the elements in the property set. As an illustration, we suggest some properties of the concept 'car'. For example, assume that 'car' is an entity type. Its attributes can be its

properties, such as 'registration number', 'manufacturer', and 'color'. Its contexts can be its properties, such as 'has engine', 'is owned by people'. The words underlined could be relationship types in a schema. Its properties can also be obtained from other concepts. Suppose that we have known O1 already (which has been, for example, defined in the knowledge bases), and O2 is synonymous to O1. Then O2 can have all the properties of O1.

2) Semantic similarity relations

A semantic similarity relation (in the sequel we will often use 'semantic relation' for short) is considered to be defined on the set of concepts S . We propose four types of semantic relations between a pair of objects, all based on the comparison of concept properties. They are:

(1) *weak semantic relation*: - an object pair belongs to this relation if the property sets of the two objects are overlapping;

(2) *compatible semantic relation* - an object pair belongs to this relation if the key property sets of the two objects are overlapping;

(3) *equivalent semantic relation*: - an object pair belongs to this relation if the key property sets of the two objects are identical; and

(4) *mergeable semantic relation*: - an object pair belongs to this relation if the property sets of the two objects are identical.

3) The semantic dictionary and the taxonomy structure

In addition to the use of an integration rule base, which were used in most methodologies for schema or view integration since the mid eighties, we presume the use of a semantic dictionary and a taxonomy structure. The semantic dictionary is similar to a synonym dictionary. We apply here a two grade synonym scale to concept pairs, namely, strong-synonym and weak-synonym, and use the terms 'synonym' and 'similar' for them (we might have used a spectrum of similarities, with 'synonym' and 'not similar' as extremes; this is a future research topic).

The taxonomy structure includes two hierarchical structures, a **subset** relationship and a **coverage** relationship. The subset relationship has the conventional meaning. A set of object classes {E1, E2, ..., En} covers an object class E if{E1, E2, ..., En} is a partition of E. The taxonomy is further described in section 4.1.

4) The assumption of the time dimension

The time dimension is introduced to the integration approach for two reasons. The first reason is to provide the integration *process* with a possibility for back-tracking and decision tracing. We assume that every schema carries a time reference, indicating when the schema was created. For the same reason, all objects of a schema carry a time reference as well. Obviously, the schema creation time should be earlier than or equal to the creation time of its objects. The second reason is that the time dimension and decision recording provides us a possibility to check the schemata for different 'well-formedness' criteria, such as the completeness and minimization of an integrated schema [2].

1.3 Related research

A comprehensive survey of the view integration research area can be found in [2]. Most of the works in this area address the methods of view integration [1, 3, 6, 9, 12,

15, 17, 19], while the other works focus on the structural components of schemata [4, 10, 11, 13, 16, 20, 21]. Since the mid eighties, most of the view integration research has been based on the entity relationship model or some extension to it. It is interesting that more and more research works seem to concentrate on some specific aspects of the view integration problem. These works include qualitative analysis of attributes [11, 21], schema structures [20] and mapping constraints [10], and quantitative analysis of object similarity and resemblance [3, 8, 14, 16, 17].

An original integration method, based on the principle of unification of structures and similar to logical unification in Prolog, is described in [3]. View integration is viewed as 'an incremental design process which starts with a rough sketch of a conceptual schema which is enriched by successive integration of different views'. 'The integration of a given view is seen as a unification process of two data structures'. The authors base the structural unification on three notions: equivalence, similarity and dissimilarity. A *similarity vector* is introduced to quantitatively describe the interpretation of the different components varying from equivalence to dissimilarity.

In [12], view integration is considered as the activity of designing a global structure (integrated schema) starting from individual component structures (views). The authors focus on the domain knowledge of objects in component schemata. The precise relationships between the domains of pairs of classes from different views are specified as one of the following possibilities: 1) identical domains; 2) contained domains; 3) overlapping domains; and 4) disjoint domains.

In [8], the authors introduce the view integration tool (MUVIS) which applies an expert system to help integrate views. The integration methodology follows [12] with an improvement, where the object equivalence is determined by comparing the aspects of each object domain and computing a *weighted probability of similarity*. In addition, a transformation from the extended entity relationship model (EERM) to the semantic data model (SDM) is described in order to reduce the complexity of the integration.

An interactive tool is introduced in [14] to assist database designers and administrators (DDA) in integrating schemata. It collects the information required for integration from a DDA, performs essential bookkeeping, and integrates schemata according to the semantics provided. The equivalence class specification is based on the equivalence of attributes. Two attributes are determined to be equivalent based on several characteristics, including uniqueness, cardinality, domain, etc. A further detail discussion on the characteristics of attribute can be found in [11].

The schema integration process is investigated in the context of a logic based modeling language in [9]. The author presents two basic forms for integration assertions: object equality assertions and extension relationship assertions to represent the equivalent constructs of conceptual schemata. The schema integration process is performed based on the assertions thus obtained.

An expert system to help users to integrate databases at the conceptual level is described in [17]. The objectives of the schema integration system are to help the user in finding the overlap, determining whether conflicts exist, modifying the schemata and defining mappings between the constructs of the two schemata. One of the most interesting aspects is that the author introduces a *resemblance function* to quantify the similarity between a pair of constructs in such a way that an integrator is presented with lists of pairs of constructs or group of constructs, ordered by this measure of similarity, which can be used to assert equivalences, introduce modifications or generate mappings.

Consequently, it is obvious that object similarity plays an important role in the schema comparison step. Even more important is to base such similarity on semantic associations between objects. Current researches are restricted to the informal description and application of such similarity. In this paper, we attempt to formally define such similarity and thus collect more related information to assist the user's assertions with the aids of the knowledge bases.

1.4 Overview of this paper

The paper deals with two problems. The first is to abstract and define semantic similarity relations, their members being pairs of possibly similar or equivalent objects. The second is to devise a semantic dictionary and a taxonomy structure in order to provide support for the building and classification of the semantic similarity relations. In the next chapter, the model, ER+, an extension of the ER model [5] is introduced. ER+ contains richer semantic features than the original ER model, such as generalization, and coverage. Then the *schema structure*, used in this paper, is described. It consists of two kinds of information of objects. One is the basic information of objects, which includes so called *internal information* of objects, such as their name, creation-time, definition, etc. The other, called *external information* of objects, represents associations between objects. Semantic similarity relations, introduced in section 1.2, are defined and described in chapter 3, which play an important role in our integration tool. In Chapter 4 we describe the integration tool. We focus here on two components: the *integration knowledge bases* and the *integration processor*. The integration knowledge bases contain knowledge components such as synonym and subset relationships. The integration processor carries out tasks such as collection of semantic associations, consistency checking, etc. The last chapter concludes the paper and suggests future research.

2. The ER+ model and the schema structure

2.1 The ER+ model

The model ER+ proposed here is an extension of the basic ER model [5]. The basic ER model contains a set of entity types and a set of relationships which associate two entity types. An entity type has one or more attributes. A formal definition of the basic ER model can be found in [5, 7]. In addition to the components of the basic ER model, the ER+ model possesses richer semantic features. These are:

(1)   A relationship type, expressed by an arrow, connects an entity type, the domain of the relationship, with one or more entity types, the ranges of the relationship. Each relationship type has a *mapping constraint*, described by the predicate

rel_map(Rel_id, [(M1:N1), (M2:N2)]),

where Rel_id is a global identifier of this relationship type, (M1:N1) represents that the domain entity must participate in at least M1 and at most N1 instances of the relationship type Rel_id, and (M2:N2) indicates that the range entity must participate in at least M2 and at most N2 instances of the relationship.

For example, the mapping constraint of the relationship type 'owns' in the schema

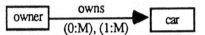

indicates that an owner may have zero up to many cars and a car must be owned by at least one owner.

(2)   An entity type must have at least one attribute. The entity type is called the domain of its attributes. Each attribute has a *cardinality* denoted by a predicate as

attr_card(Attr_id, [(M:N)]),

where Attr_id is the global identifier of the attribute, and the cardinality (M:N) indicates that the domain entity participates in this attribute at least M and at most N times.

(3)   Each entity type, relationship type or attribute has a time dimension included in their basic information, indicating when the object was created or modified. The reason to apply the time dimension is to keep the component schemata unchanged during the integration process. The predicate expression for the time dimension is

creation_time(Object_id, Time),

where Object_id is the global identifier of a schema, or a schema object (an entity type, a relationship type, or an attribute).

(4)   Two kinds of generalization relationships, the *is_subset_of* relationship and the *is_covered_by* relationship, are used in the ER+. As follows, we define the two relationships. Let A and B be two object classes.

Definition 2.1 A *is_subset_of* B means that if x is a member of A then x must be a member of B.

Definition 2.2 A *is_covered_by* B, where B is a set of entity classes, B1, B2, ..., Bn, means that $A = B1 \cup B2 \cup ... \cup Bn$, where Bi « Bj = Ø, i≠j.

We use the following predicates to denote these two relationships

is_subset_of(Sup_entity, Sub_entity),

and

is_covered_by(Sup_entity, [Sub_entity_list]).

Here, the first predicate indicates that Sub_entity is a subset of Sup_entity and the second one indicates Sup_entity is covered by its subset list [Sub_entity].

2.2 Schema structure

We present here the definitions of all object types used in the schema integration process. They are: schema, entity type, relationship type, and attribute. An object type carries two kinds of information, *basic information* and *extended information*, which are defined below.

Definition 2.3 The *basic information* of an object type is defined as a quintuple:

object_type(Identifier, Name, Definition, Time, Original),

where
a) Identifier is a globally unique 'internal name' of this object maintained during the whole integration process. It is invisible to the user,
b) Name is the 'external name' given by the user when the object type is created or modified during the schema integration process,
c) Definition is a text by which a user can further define and describe the object type, such as its narrative definition, purpose, usage, etc.
d) Time indicates the time when the object type is created, and
e) Original is a set whose elements are the identifiers of object types in 'preceding' schemata from which the current object type is generated.

For example, when merging objects A of schema X and B of schema Y we obtain a new object C in the integrated schema Z, we say the original of C is a set {A, B}. The purpose of maintaining the object original is to make tracing and back-tracking possible.

The extended information of object types is different depending on the types.

Definition 2.4 The *extended information* of a *schema* is defined as a triple:
schema_ex_info(Identifier, Entity_type_list, Rel_type_list),

where
a) Identifier is a globally unique internal name of the schema (invisible to the user),
b) Entity_type_list is a set whose elements are the identifiers of all entity types of this schema, and
c) Rel_type_list is a set whose elements are the identifiers of all relationship types of this schema.

Definition 2.5 The *extended information* of an *entity type* is defined as a quadruple:

entity_ex_info(Identifier, Schema_id, Attr_list, Rel_type_list),

where
a) Identifier is a globally unique internal name of the entity type (invisible to the user),
b) Schema_id is the identifier of the schema to which the entity type belongs,
c) Attr_list is a set whose elements are the identifiers of all attributes of the entity type, and
d) Rel_type_list is a set whose elements are the identifiers of all relationship types which are connected to the entity type.

Definition 2.6 The *extended information* of a *relationship type* is defined as a quadruple:

  relationship_ex_info(Identifier, Domain, Range, Map),

where
a) Identifier is the globally unique internal name of the relationship type (invisible to the user),
b) Schema_id is the identifier of the schema to which the relationship type belongs,
c) Domain is the identifier of the entity type which is the domain of the relationship, and
d) Range is the identifier of the entity type which is the range of the relationship,
e) Map, the mapping constraint, has been defined in Section 2.1.

Definition 2.7 The *extended information* of an *attribute type* is defined as a triple:

  attribute_ex_info(Identifier, Domain, Card),

where
a) Identifier is a globally unique internal name of the attribute (invisible to the user),
b) Domain is the identifier of the entity type which has this attribute, and
c) Card, the cardinality, as defined in Section 2.1.

These definitions are graphically illustrated by the following meta-schema (self-explanatory):

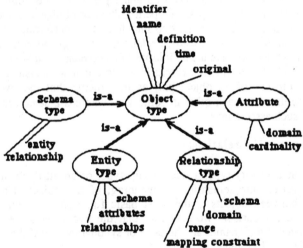

3. Semantic similarity relations

Objects of the component schemata may be related in a variety of ways. Possibly the names of the objects are the same, or the key attributes indicate that one domain is contained in another, or their contexts support a subset relation between two objects. Our tool for schema integration is built on the basis of such semantic similarity relationships, which may exist between objects or object sets in the component schemata. As discussed before, an object may represent an entity type, a relationship type, or an attribute. In general, two objects are considered to be related if, for example, 1) they have same the name or synonymous names (for entity types, relationship types and attributes), 2) at least one corresponding pair of their relationship types are related (only for entity types), or 3) their contexts are related (this holds for entity types and relationship types as well). The context of an entity type includes all relationship types which are connected to the entity type, and all the entity types on the range side of the relationship types. The key issue here is to analyze the possible semantic relations which may be relevant in an integration process.

The following assumptions form the basis which supports us to construct the semantic relations. They include three cases: 1) Two objects with the same name indicate that they may refer to the same object in reality. Finding two objects with the same name is intuitive and can be done directly by examining the object names in a schema. 2) Two objects with synonymous names indicate that they might refer to the same object in reality. In this case we presume a semantic dictionary, which keeps track of all the synonymous words in our universe of discourse. The details of the semantic dictionary will be discussed later. 3) Two objects with one of their names being the short form of the other (For example, AI stands for Artificial Intelligence) suggest that they refer to the same object in reality. All the short forms together with their normal forms are also kept in the semantic dictionary.

By investigating these properties, we find that a pair of objects could be related in different ways in terms of how many properties this pair of objects shares. Therefore, the semantic relations can be classified into four different groups, namely, *weak relation*, *compatible relation*, *equivalent relation*, and *mergeable relation*. Before we define these relations, we give the definitions of *basic name equivalence*, *weak name equivalence* and *object-related associations*. Note that we consider the *semantic similarity relation* of an object pair as to indicate that the two objects are semantically related to each other in some way whereas a *semantic relation* is a collection of such associations.

3.1 Basic semantic relations

The name[1] of an entity type, a relationship type, or an attribute in a schema is assumed to reflect the semantic, the meaning, of the object. Therefore name comparison between objects is the most basic function in schema integration. Through name comparison, we may find that the two objects are equivalent or somehow related if their names are the same or synonymous, or if they possess some other relationships, like generalization.

> **Definition 3.1** *Basic name equivalence* - Let Obj1 and Obj2 be two entity types, relationship types or attributes. Obj1 is basic name equivalence to Obj2 if
> 1) one object name is the same as the other, or

---

[1]In this context we use the terms 'name' and 'word' alternatively.

2) one object name is synonymous to the other, or
3) one object name is the short form of the other.

The situation that one object name is synonymous to the other is provided by a semantic dictionary. We assume that the two objects involved in this association have exactly the same meaning which forms the basis of equivalence of the semantic relations discussed later. Furthermore, since it is often difficult to judge whether two words have exactly the same meaning, we introduce another association called *weak name equivalence*. This association means that the names of two objects are not synonymous, i.e., they do not share exactly the same 'meaning'. But, their meanings are quite close (or near), for instance the concept, 'people' and 'masses'[2]. This association is defined as

> **Definition 3.2** *Weak name equivalence* - Two objects are considered as *weakly name equivalent* if their names have closely related meanings.

In the semantic dictionary, this association is stored as weak_synonym(Name1, Name2). The aim to have this association is to leave the user with more freedom to judge what the exact semantic associations between two objects are.

> **Definition 3.3** *Object-related association* - Two objects are *object-related* if they have one of the following semantic associations or relationships:
> 1) the basic name equivalence,
> 2) the weak name equivalence,
> 3) one of the objects is the subset of the other,
> 4) two objects have a coverage association.

The last two items only apply to entity types. The use of the object-related association is to provide the basis for the later definitions of the weak relations.

3.2 Mapping constraints and cardinalities

The associations between objects are not only stipulated by their conceptual features, such as attributes, contexts, etc, but also constrained by their quantities, which have been described as cardinalities for attributes and mapping constraints for relationship types. In this section, we elaborate the discussion of such quantitative constraints.

Consider an association between an entity, say, Student, and one of its attributes, say, Name, (i.e. domain(Name, Student)). Each student has at least one name. The cardinality of Name to Student can be written in predicate as attribute_cardinality(Name_id, [(1:M)]). The Name_id indicates the global identifier of the attribute Name. We compare two cardinalities of two different attributes and conclude the mapping relations between them. The possible situations of cardinalities are *equal* and *compatible* .

---

[2]See BigThesaurus (a computerized dictionary, THEBIG THESAURUS™, 1986-88 Deneba Systems, Inc) under the entry people.

Definition 3.4 *Cardinality equal* - Let Attr1 and Attr2 be two attributes, and their cardinalities (M1:N1) and (M2:N2). The cardinalities of Attr1 and Attr2 are equal if
1) Attr1 and Attr2 possess basic name equivalence or weak name equivalence,
2) M1 = M2, N1 = N2.

Definition 3.5 *Cardinality compatible* - The cardinalities of Attr1 and Attr2 are compatible if one of the following cases holds:

case 1 dAttr1 $\subseteq$ dAttr2 and M1 $\geq$ M2 and N1 $\leq$ N2;

case 2 dAttr1 $\cap$ dAttr2 $\neq \emptyset$ and the [M1:N1] and [M2:N2] are intersected;

case 3 dAttr1 $\cap$ dAttr2 $= \emptyset$ and no limitation to the cardinalities.

Here, dAttr1 is the set of all the instances (or the extension) of the attribute Attr1, and so is dAttr2. For instance, suppose that 'color' is an attribute. The extension of 'color' could be a set of 'red', 'yellow', etc.

Now we define possible situations of mapping constraints of relationship types. Suppose that Rel1 and Rel2 are two relationship types and their mapping constraints are Map1 = [(M1:N1), (P1:Q1)] and Map2 = [(M2:N2), (P2:Q2)]. The possible cases for the relation between Map1 and Map2 are *mapping equal* and *compatible* .

Definition 3.6 *Mapping equal* - Let Rel1 and Rel2 be two relationship types, and their mapping constraints [(M1:N1), (P1:Q1)] and [(M2:N2), (P2:Q2)]. Their domains are denoted as DOM1 and DOM2 and their ranges RNG1 and RNG2. Rel1 and Rel2 are mapping equal if
1) Rel1 and Rel2 are of basic name equivalence,
2) dDOM1 = dDOM2,
3) dRNG1 = dRNG2, and
4) all the corresponding items of their mapping constraints are equal.

Here, dDOM1 is the set of all the instances (or the extension) of the domain DOM1, so are DOM2, RNG1, and RNG2. This explanation is also used for the following definition.

Definition 3.7 *Mapping compatible* - Let Rel1 and Rel2 be two relationship types, and their mapping constraints [(M1:N1), (P1:Q1)] and [(M2:N2), (P2:Q2)]. For simplicity, we use notations $\Rightarrow$ Rel1 and $\Leftarrow$ Rel1 to represent the intervals (M1:N1) and (P1:Q1), a subset of the natural number set. A similar notation is used for the intervals (M2:N2) and (P2:Q2). Their domains are denoted DOM1 and DOM2; their ranges RNG1 and RNG2. Rel1 and Rel2 are mapping compatible if
1) Rel1 and Rel2 are of basic name equivalence or weak name equivalence,
2) one of the following cases holds:

    case 1:   if

        dDOM1 $\cap$ dDOM2 $\neq \emptyset$ and dRNG1 $\cap$ dRNG2 $\neq \emptyset$,
           then

        $\Rightarrow$ Rel1 $\cap$ $\Leftarrow$ Rel1 $\neq \emptyset$ and $\Rightarrow$ Rel2 $\cap$ $\Leftarrow$ Rel2 $\neq \emptyset$;
    case 2: otherwise, no limitation.

An detailed discussion about mapping constraints and view integration can be found in [10].

3.3 Attribute semantic relations

It is quite common and essential to compare and contrast objects by their attributes [11], since a combination of attributes (in particular, key attributes) of a certain entity type may uniquely determine the entity type. For example, assume that we have two entity types 'Non-registered Student' and 'Registered Student'. The attribute 'registration number' of the entity type 'Registered Student' may distinguish the former entity type from the latter.

The semantic relations between attributes of two objects may help the user to judge whether the two object types are semantically related to each other. In particular, the semantic relations between two key attributes will play an important role in the determination of the semantic relations between their domains. Here follows the definition of a key attribute.

> **Definition 3.8** *Key attributes* - Let Ent be any entity type defined in ER+. The attribute set of Ent is
> $A = \{A1, A2, ..., An\}$.
> The key attribute set is denoted as
> K, where K ® A,
> and K can uniquely determine the entity type Ent and its attribute set A as well.

Informally we can say that two entity types are *mergeable* if their key attribute sets are equal because the key attributes determine their domain entity type. In terms of the extended information of the attributes, the semantic relations between two attributes are dependent on three factors: their names, their domain entity types and their cardinalities.

> **Definition 3.9** *Weak attribute relation* - Two attributes are *weakly related* if they are object-related.

> **Definition 3.10** *Attribute compatible relation* - Let Attr1 and Attr2 be two attributes. The attributes Attr1 and Attr2 are *compatibly related* if
> 1) they satisfy the basic name equivalence or the weak name equivalence,
> 2) their cardinalities are compatible.

> **Definition 3.11** *Attribute equivalent relation* - Let Attr1 and Attr2 be two attributes. The attributes Attr1 and Attr2 are *equivalently related* if
> 1) they are of basic name equivalence,
> 2) their cardinalities are mapping equal.

> **Definition 3.12** *Attribute mergeable relation* - Two attributes are considered as *mergeably related* if
> 1) they are of attribute equivalent relation, and
> 2) their domain entities can be merged.

The reasons to define the semantic relations between attributes are 1) to support the definitions of the semantic similarity relations between entity types, 2) to help the user to make assertions about merging the attributes.

3.4 Relationship semantic relations

Relationship comparison in schema integration plays an important role, since a relationship not only associates two entities but also dominates them. In other words, a relationship needs a subject which carries out the action represented by the relationship and an object which accepts the action. Therefore the relationship, or the action, demands that its subject should possess some particular features which stipulate a semantic category (the category here means a set, each of whose elements can be a subject of this relationship) of which the subject is an element. Similarly, the object is also an element of a semantic category. The semantic category is intensionally a set of features, and extensionally, a group of things which possess these features. For instance, the relationship type 'attends' in the statements 'author attends a conference' and 'submitter attends a conference' imply that 'author' and 'submitter' as subjects should belong to the same semantic category, which has the feature 'can attend', on one hand. On the other hand, 'attends' stipulates that 'conference' should be an element of the semantic category having the feature 'can be attended'. Inversely, relationships are of course affected by their subjects and objects. In our ER+ model, subjects and objects are called domains and ranges respectively.

Furthermore, relationship types are also constrained by the number of the domains and ranges participating in the relationship types, which have been discussed in section 3.2. Based on this, we give the following definitions of relationship equivalence.

> **Definition 3.13** Inverse relationship - Suppose that Rel is a relationship defined as a relation[3]:
>
> Rel (Ent1, Ent2),
>
> where Ent1 and Ent2 are the domain entity type and range entity type of Rel respectively. The inverse relationship type of Rel, denoted as Rel^{-1}, is defined as a relation
>
> Rel^{-1}(Ent2, Ent1) = Rel (Ent1, Ent2),
>
> where Ent2 and Ent1 are the domain and range entity types of Rel^{-1}.
> The mapping constraint of Rel^{-1} is [(M2:N2), (M1:N1)] if the mapping constraint of Rel is [(M1:N1), (M2:N2)].

Now we proceed to define equivalence relations between relationship types.

> **Definition 3.14** *Weak relationship relation* - Two relationship types are considered to be *weakly related* if the two relationship types are object-related or one relationship type is the inverse of the other.

---

[3]This relation is different from the semantic relation we apply in the paper. Its definition is referred to the book, *Elements of the Theory of Computation*, by H. Lewis and C. Papadimitriou, p.9. The same to the next.

Definition 3.15 *Relationship compatible relation* - Two relationship types are considered to be *compatibly related* if
1) the two relationship types are basic name equivalence or weak name equivalence or one relationship type is the inverse of the other, and
2) their mapping constraints are mapping compatible.

Definition 3.16 *Relationship equivalent relation* - Two relationship types are considered to be *equivalently related* if
1) the two relationship types are basic name equivalence or one relationship type is the inverse of the other, and
2) their mapping constraints are of mapping equal.

Definition 3.17 *Relationship mergeable relation* - Two relationship types are considered to be *mergeably related* if
1) the two relationship types are equivalently related, and
2) their domains are mergeably related, and
3) their ranges are mergeably related.

The aims to define the semantic similarity relations between relationships are 1) to help defining the semantic relations between entity contexts and 2) to support the user's assertions for merging relationships.

3.5 Context semantic relations

An entity type of a schema may be connected to several other entity types of that schema by relationship types. Here the relationship types are considered binary[4]. As can be seen, an entity type can be characterized by its *context* just as it can be characterized by its key attributes. Moreover, to compare the contexts of two entity types can often help in the better perception of slight difference between the two entity types. Taking as an example these two statements 'The student will get Ph.D next month' and 'The student will get BSc. next month'. 'Student' in the former statement implies a postgraduate whereas 'student' in the latter is an undergraduate student.

Before defining the *context equivalence* relations, we illustrate this concept through an example. In the following figure, we have two schemata (a) and (b).

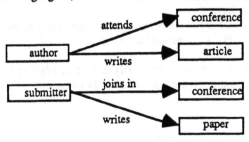

---

[4]In this paper, we also use multi-tuple relationships, for example *is_covered_by*.

By the contexts 'attends conference' and 'joins in conference' of the entity types 'author' and 'submitter', people hardly have problem in recognizing that these two entity types have a close meaning by their semantic knowledge of the meaning of these words. That is, the participating entity types could have same meaning or they share partially the same meaning. In other words, they possess at least one same feature, 'can be a member of a conference'. The entity types 'author' and 'submitter' having this feature together with the relationship type 'writes' form the contexts of 'article' and 'paper' so that the latter two entity types, 'article' and 'paper', are related to each other. Before defining the semantic relations between contexts, we first define the concept of an <u>entity context</u>.

Definition 3.18 *Entity context* - Let Ent be an entity type. The set of relationship types associated to Ent are $[Rel_1, Rel_2, ..., Rel_n]$, and all the entity types being the ranges of the relationship types $[Rel_1, Rel_2, ..., Rel_n]$ are denoted $[Ent_1, Ent_2, ..., Ent_n]$. Then <u>the context of the entity type</u> Ent is the set context(Ent) = $\{(Rel_i, Ent_i) \mid 1 \le i \le n\}$.

Definition 3.19 *Weak context relation* - Let Ent1 and Ent2 be two entity types, Cntx1 = (Rel1, Ent1') $\in$ *context(Ent1)* and Cntx2 = (Rel2, Ent2') $\in$ *context(Ent2)*. Ent1' and Ent2' are two entity types which are connected to the entity types Ent1 and Ent2, respectively, by the relationship types Rel1 and Rel2. *context(Ent1)* and *context(Ent2)* are *weakly related* if Rel1 and Rel2 are weakly related.

Definition 3.20 *Context compatible relation* - Let Ent1 and Ent2 be two entity types, Cntx1 = (Rel1, Ent1') $\in$ *context(Ent1)* and Cntx2 = (Rel2, Ent2') $\in$ *context(Ent2)*. *context(Ent1)* and *context(Ent2)* are considered to be *compatibly related* if
1) Rel1 and Rel2 are of relationship compatible relation, and
2) Ent1' and Ent2' are compatibly related.

Definition 3.21 *Context equivalent relation* - Let Ent1 and Ent2 be two entity types, Cntx1 = (Rel1, Ent1') $\in$ *context(Ent1)* and Cntx2 = (Rel2, Ent2') $\in$ *context(Ent1)*. *context(Ent1)* and *context(Ent2)* are considered to be *equivalently related* if
1) Rel1 and Rel2 are of relationship equivalent relation, and
2) Ent1' and Ent2' are equivalently related.

The role[5] the context semantic similarity relations play is to assist the user's judgement of the semantic relations between entity types.

---

[5]We plan in our future work to add degree to the context. For example, Cntx1 and Cntx2 are two elements of *context(Ent1)* and Cntx3 and Cntx4 are two elements of *context(Ent2)*. Ent1 and Ent2 are two entity types. Suppose that Cntx1 is compatible to Cntx3, Cntx2 compatible to Cntx4. Then we say that, *context(Ent1)* is compatibly related to *context(Ent2)* with a degree, Deg = 2.

3.6 Entity semantic relations

The semantic relations defined above are mainly used for the definitions of the semantic similarity relations between entity types. In this integration tool, the first and major objective is to find out all the possible semantic similarity relations between entity types. It might be noticed that the entity semantic relations were used somewhere in the definitions above. As a matter of fact, these definitions are recursive. For instance, to merge two key attributes is dependent on the semantic relation between their domain entity types, whereas, inversely, their domains may be dominated by these key attributes. In addition, entity types also give the quantitative constraints to the relationship types and the attributes the entity types participate in, i.e. mapping constraints and cardinalities.

> **Definition 3.22** *Weak entity relation* - Two entity types are *weakly related* if at least one of the following conditions holds:
> 1) they are object-related,
> 2) their key attributes are weakly related,
> 3) their contexts are weakly related.

> **Definition 3.23** *Entity compatible relation* - Two entity types are *compatibly related* if at least one of the following conditions holds:
> 1) they are of basic name equivalence or weak name equivalence,
> 2) their key attributes are compatibly related,
> 3) their contexts are compatibly related.

> **Definition 3.24** *Entity equivalent relation* - Two entity types are *equivalently related* if
> 1) they are of basic name equivalence, or
> 2) all their key attributes are equivalently related, or
> 3) their contexts are equivalently related.

> **Definition 3.25** *Entity mergeable relation* - Two entity types are *mergeably related* if they have been confirmed by the user and/or they are equivalently related.

3.7 A summary of the semantic relations

We have presented three semantic similarity relation groups respectively for the representation of similarities between attributes, between relationship types, and between entity types, and a supporting semantic relation group for the representation of associations between entity contexts. Each group contains three to four kinds of semantic relations, i.e., weak, compatible, equivalence, and mergeable semantic similarity relations.

Among these object pairs, we focus on the associations between entity types, since our schema integration objective first of all is to integrate the entity types, when they share same properties, with the aid of similarity relations between other object pairs. We also focus on the equivalence relation, since the object pairs in this relation will directly help the user to integrate the object pairs.

4. The integrator architecture

Conventional schema integrators lack, in general, 1) a deeper analysis of the semantic similarity relations, 2) consistency checking of schemata and evolution of the integrator's knowledge bases, and 3) recording and maintenance of the integration process decisions. In our integrator, we maintain three integration knowledge bases which provide the facts and rules, such as semantic similarity relations, hierarchical relations and deductive rules. Based on these knowledge bases, the integrator can build up a group of corresponding objects which are related in names, attributes, or contexts, check the consistencies, and make assertions for object integration. The architecture of the integrator is shown in the figure below. A brief description of the architecture is presented after illustrating the similarity concepts by an example.

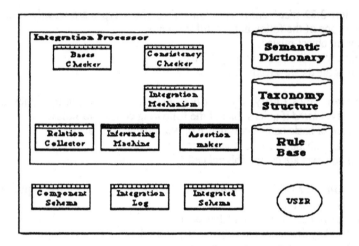

4.1 An example

The following two schemata describe information about conference management. We illustrate two points in this example. One is how to make use of integration knowledge bases to form the semantic similarity relations. The other is to depict the association collection step. The part content of the knowledge bases is illustrated below.

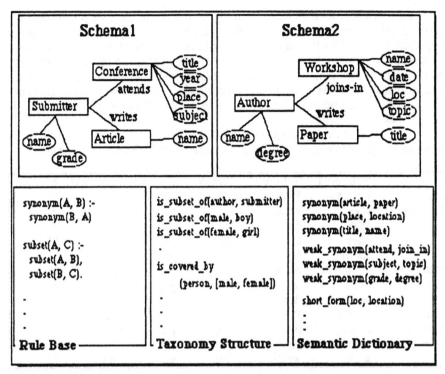

For the sake of simplicity, we take only entity types into account. The entity types *Article* and *Paper* are obviously weakly, compatibly, and equivalently related because they are synonymous (by looking up the semantic dictionary and following the definitions 3.22, 3.23, and 3.24 in section 3.6). The entity types *Submitter* and *Author* are weakly related because of the subset relationship (by looking up the taxonomy structure and following the definitions 3.22 in section 3.6). Context(*Conference*) and context(*Workshop*) are compatibly related through checking definition 3.20, since the relationship types *attends* and *joins-in* are compatibly related.

Similar situations can be found for relationship types and attributes. Consider the attribute *place* and the attribute *loc*. By looking up the semantic dictionary, we know that *loc* is the short form of *location* and *location* is synonymous to *place*. So by applying the rule:

> synonym(A, B) :-
>> synonym(A, C),
>> short_form(B, C).

we have *loc* synonymous to *place*. Furthermore, according to definition 3.11, we acquire that *loc* is equivalently related to *place*.

All possible semantic similarity relations are listed in the following table. The question mark ? means that the user's decisions and assertions are required. Note that the dash mark - indicates that no such relations can be deduced from the knowledge bases according to the definitions hereinbefore.

When the user's decisions are required during the integration step, we present him all possible information to assist in making assertions. Suppose that the user's judgement is needed for the similarity association of the entity types *Conference* and *Workshop*. A **dialogue box** will be displayed with all attribute pairs together with their similarity relations (e.g., equivalent(*place, loc*)) and all the contexts (e.g., compatible(*attends, joins-in*) and compatible(*Submitter, Author*)). In the dialogue box, a possible suggestion is also given, say, equivalent(*Conference, Workshop*). If the user makes the decision

equivalent(Conference, Workshop)

then a new suggestion may be triggered, say, mergeable(*Conference, Workshop*).

	Schema1	Schema2	Weak	Compat.	Equival.	Merg.
Entity:	Conference	Workshop	yes	yes	?	?
Attribute:	title	name	yes	yes	?	?
	year	date	-	-	-	-
	place	loc	yes	yes	yes	?[6]
	subject	topic	yes	yes	?	?
Entity:	Submitter	Author	yes	yes	no	no
Attribute:	name	name	yes	yes	yes	no[7]
	grade	degree	yes	yes	?	no
Entity:	Article	Paper	yes	yes	yes	yes
Attribute:	name	title	yes	yes	?	?
Relationship:	attends	joins-in	yes	yes	?	no
	writes	writes	yes	yes	yes	?

4.2 Integration knowledge bases

The integration knowledge bases are the most important components in the integrator since all the possible relations between objects from the component schemata are found in terms of the facts in these bases. Also the assertions made on the similarity relations, discussed above, are based on the knowledge in these knowledge bases. The knowledge bases include a semantic dictionary (SD), a taxonomy structure (TS), and a rule base (RB).

(1) Semantic Dictionary
In the semantic dictionary, words are stored in pairs. Each pair of the words indicate that the words have the same meaning or a close meaning. The format of a fact in the semantic dictionary is:

Relation_name(Word1, Word2).

---

[6]Whether the object pair 'place' and 'loc' belongs to the attribute mergeable relation also depends on the association of their domains 'Conference' and 'Workshop'. For example, if the user asserts that 'Conference' and 'Workshop' are mergeable, then 'place' and 'loc' are also mergeable. If 'Conference' and 'Workshop' are not mergeable then neither are 'place' and 'loc'.

[7]In this case that 'Submitter' is a subset of 'Author', if the attributes of 'Submitter' are equivalent to those of 'Submitter', the former attributes are considered to be inherited from the latter attributes. Due to the limitation of space, we do not discuss this case further.

The Relation_name indicates that Word1 and Word2 have a peculiar semantic relationship, like synonym. In our current semantic dictionary, we adopt only three semantic relations for the Relation_name: synonym, short_form_of, and weak_synonym. The facts in the SD can be obtained from dictionaries like a synonym dictionary, or an abbreviation dictionary. The second way to expand the SD is that, following the user's assertions, related word pairs have the same semantic relations as synonym, etc. Then these words pairs are added to the SD in a process where the user's advice is emphasised.

(2) Taxonomy Structure
The taxonomy structure contains many sub-structures. Each sub-structure is a tree. The child nodes inherit all the characteristics from their parent nodes and possess their own characteristics different from those of their parent as well. In other words, the parent node is the genus and the child node is the species. The root is the top genus and the leaves are the finest species (see figure below).

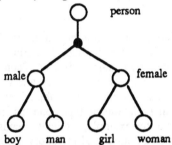

Male is a subset of person. The set male inherits all the features of person. Note here we use a black dot to represent the 'is_covered_by' relationship between person and male, female. The format of the hierarchy relation in the TS is

Relation_name(Node1, Node2).

The Relation_name indicates the hierarchy relationships between Node1 and Node2. These relationships could be 'is_subset_of' or 'is_covered_by', which have been defined in Section 2.1. The expansion of the TS depends on the assertions deduced from the object relations or assertions made by the user.

(3) The rule base
Two groups of rules are stored in the rule base. The first group contains rules which deal with generally used inferencing operations in schema integration. These operations are used to derive relations between objects. For example, if A is synonymous to B, then B is also synonymous to A. Another example is that if A is subset of B and B is subset of C, then A is subset of C. The second group provides the rules which directly serve for the integration cases, such as dropping redundant objects, creating new objects, and so on. For example, if two entity types can be merged, their attributes, if equivalently related, should be merged too.

4.3 The integrator

The integration tool has an integration processor which provides capability to check the consistency of the component schemata as well as of the integrated schema after integration, to collect all possible semantic relations between entity types, relationship types, and attributes, to let the user make assertions based on the semantic similarity relations collected, and to check the knowledge bases whether they need modified. These capabilities are carried out by the function blocks Consistency Checker, Integration Mechanism, Relation Collector, and Base Checker. The functionality of these blocks is discussed in this section.

(1) Relation Collector

The task of this block is to make use of the semantic relations defined in chapter 3, to take in and compare all the objects in the component schemata, and to find out all the possible relations between the objects which are somehow semantically related to each other. The results the relation collector obtains are stored in the Integration Log and will be provided to the function block Assertion Maker. The format of the results is

Relation_name(Object1, Object2, Type),

which means that Object1 and Object2 have the semantic relation Relation_name of one of the semantic similarity types *attribute, relationship, context*, or *entity*.

(2) Consistency Checker.

This function block carries out a number of tasks. First, when the component schemata are input, it checks name conflicts. According to the SD, it will first search for synonymous and homonym names, if any. Then it will present these name conflicts to the user since the integrator is not allowed to modify the component schemata. Second, it checks any incorrectly objectified relationships. Inappropriate objectification means that a relationship type connects an entity type with an attribute of some other entity type, for example, 'Student attends course-number'. Instead, it should be 'Student attends a course' and the entity 'Course' has an attribute 'course-number' [4]. If the checker detects any inappropriate objectifications, it presents them to user. Third, it checks the consistencies among cardinalities and mapping constraints during the collecting of semantic relations. Fourth, the consistency checker will examine the integrated schema and see whether there are any name conflicts, mapping inconsistencies and redundancies. If there are any, it will present them to user and make an attempt to restructure the schema.

(3) Integration Mechanism

The main task of the function block Integration Mechanism is to merge the objects in the component schemata and produce the integrated schema. It has two sub-blocks: Assertion Maker and Inferencing Machine. As an interface to the user, the assertion maker takes in the semantic relations in the integration log and presents to the user these relations which should be confirmed, for example, those object pairs which are equivalently related but not mergeably related. When an object pair is presented to the user for confirmation, all the information related to this confirmation is given to user and possible conclusions are also suggested by the function sub-block. The possible suggestions are that the object pair is *mergeable, containing, overlapping*, or *disjoint but mergeable*.

The inferencing machine is an interface to the knowledge bases. Each time this sub-block is triggered, it uses the facts and rules in the knowledge bases to re-build the semantic relations in the integration log. The two sub-blocks are triggered alternatively. For instance, at the beginning, all the object pairs stored in the log are of object related relations. Then the inferencing machine works. Some relations become compatible relations and equivalent relations. The equivalent relations will be sent to user by Assertion Maker. When this process finishes, the integration mechanism begins to produce the integrated schema.

(4) Base Checker
One of the functions of Base Checker block is to gradually modify the semantic dictionary and the taxonomy structure. This modification is based on the intermediate results stored in the integration log and can be carried out under the control of the person who has the authority to control it. For example, when a new pair of synonymous words are found, the Base Checker will, after an authorized user's confirmation, look into the SD and check whether the word pair already exists in the SD. If not, it will be added to the SD. If the pair exists, the checker will see whether they are consistent, and so forth. The same gradual evolution holds for the TS. The second function is to check whether the knowledge bases are consistent and non-redundant. For example, an inconsistency holds if

$$synonym(a, b)$$

in the SD and

$$is\_subset\_of(a, b)$$

in the TS. The Base Checker will inform user with this inconsistency and ask for user's decision.

5. Conclusion and future work

To find out all the possible semantic associations between schema objects, to establish semantic similarity relations and hence to provide as much information as possible for assertion making, is a time consuming task in schema integration. To build and apply domain knowledge bases also plays an important role in schema integration. We have proposed an integration tool which uses a semantic dictionary and a taxonomy structure to build up semantic similarity relations from the pairwise comparison between objects in the component schemata. The user's assertions of the objects are based on these semantic relations. The tool also tries to offer possible suggestions when user's decisions are required. In addition, the tool provides consistency checking both for the component schemata and the integrated schema as well. Our main contributions concern the following issues.

1) The generation of the semantic relations
The semantic relations found between objects are crucial to the assertion making no matter how the assertion making is fulfilled by the integrator or the user. We select a set of properties for the collection of these semantic associations. These properties are obtained from the knowledge bases, the object names, and the contexts of entity types. We propose four different semantic relations, weak relation, compatible relation, equivalent relation, and mergeable relation, which the objects from the component schemata may match to. The introduction of these four relations helps us in finding object pairs; each pair is related in some way according to the property set and hence supports our assertion making and integration task. Still, more properties like these are expected to improve this performance.

2) The use of integration knowledge bases
The formation and use of semantic knowledge is essential in conceptual schema modeling as well as in the integration of schemata. What we have done is initial

work. Only a few types of semantic relations are used in our semantic dictionary and taxonomy structure. Our future work will extend the scope of the dictionary.

3) The evolution of integration knowledge bases

A very rich semantic is contained in the objects of conceptual schema. In other words, when a schema is designed, the designer is always trying to use the objects in the schema to express richer and more correct semantic so that the reality of interest could be well reflected. Therefore, to obtain semantic meanings of new words directly from the component schemata together with the existing word semantic meanings should be a main path to enrich the knowledge bases and make them evolve.

More research is needed in the area of semantic similarity relations. One problem in the exploration of semantic in schemata is the possibility of reuse of knowledge of the schemata history. Real schemata are semantically rich. In particular, the collocation of relationships (usually verbs) with entities (usually nouns) ([18], p.408) gives rise of a rigid restriction to the association among relationships and entities. This restriction mainly depends on the semantic of such collocation of words. In other words, the objects in schemata interact and constrain one another. We should make use of the schemata processed before as knowledge or information resources for our current schema integration. We call it the 'reusability of knowledge of schemata'.

References

1.   Batini, C. and M. Lenzerini. *A Methodology for Data Schema Integration in the Entity Relationship model.* **IEEE TOSE. SE-10**(6): 650-664, 1984.

2.   Batini, C., M. Lenzerini and S. B. Navathe. *A Comparative Analysis of Methodologies for Database Schema Integration.* **ACM Computing Surveys.** 18(4): 323-364, 1986.

3.   Bouzeghoub, M. and I. Comyn-Wattiau. *View Integration by Semantic Unification and Transformation of Data Structures.* **the 9th Int'l Conf. on Entity-Relationship Approach.** Lausanne, Switzerland. 1990

4.   Bubenko, J. j. *Knowledge for Schema Restructuring and Integration Tools.* **SYSLAB, DSV. SYSLAB IWN No. 1.** 1985.

5.   Chen, P. P. *The Entity-Relationship Model - Toward a Unified View of Data.* **ACM TODS.** 1(1): 9-36, 1976.

6.   Dayal, U. and H.-Y. Hwang. *View Definition and Generalization for Database Integration in a Multidatabase System.* **IEEE TOSE. SE-10**(6): 628-644, 1984.

7.   Gogolla, M. and U. Hohenstein. *Towards a Semantic View of an Extended Entity-Relationship Model.* **ACM TODS.** 16(3): 369-416, 1991.

8.   Hayne, S. and S. Ram. *Multi-user View Integration System (MUVIS): An Expert System for View Integration.* **IEEE 6th Int'l Conf. on Data Engineering.** Los Angeles. 1990

9.   Johannesson, P. *A Logic Based Approach to Schema Integration*. **10th International Conference on Entity-Relationship Approach**. San Fransisco. 1991

10.   Johansson, B.-M. and C. Sundblad. *View Integration: A Knowledge Problem*. Department of Computer and Systems Sciences, University of Stockholm. **SYSLAB WP No. 115**. 1987.

11.   Larson, J., S. Navathe and R. Elmasri. *A Theory of Attribute Equivalence in Database with Application to Schema Integration*. **IEEE TOSE. SE-15**(4): 1989.

12.   Navathe, S., R. Elmasri and J. Larson. *Integrating User Views in Database Design*. **IEEE Computer. 19**(1): p. 50-62, 1986.

13.   Navathe, S. B., T. Sashidhar and R. Elmasri. *Relationship Mergeing in Schema Integration*. **10th Int'l Conf. on Very Large Data Base**. Singapore. 1984

14.   Sheth, A. P., J. A. Larson, A. Cornelio and S. B. Navathe. *A Tool for Integrating Conceptual Schemas and User Views*. **IEEE 4th Int'l Conf. on Data Engineering**. Los Angeles. 1988

15.   Song, W. *View Integration: A Case Learning*. DSV, SU/KTH, Sweden. **SYSLAB WP No. 185**. 1990.

16.   Song, W. W. *An Approach to Conflict Detection and Assertion Making in Schema Integration*. Department of Computer and System Sciences. **SYSLAB IWN No. 47**. 1991.

17.   Souza, J. M. d. *SIS - A Schema Integration System*. **the 5th British National Conference on Databases (BNCODS)**. 1986

18.   Sowa, J. F. "Conceptual Structures: Information Processing in Mind and Machine." 1984 Addison-Wesley Publishing Company.

19.   Spaccapietra, S. *View Integration with the ERC Approach*. University of Bourgogne-IUT, France. **Research Report No. 8802**. 1988.

20.   Spaccapietra, S. and C. Parent. *View Integration: a step forward in solving structural conflicts*. Laboratoire de Bases de Donnees, Dept. d'informatique, Ecole Polutechnique Federale de Lausanne. **Research Report**. 1990.

21.   Wangler, B. *On the Use of Abstractions in Database Modeling: Propagation of Mapping Constraints under Attribute Abstraction*. Department of Computer and systems Sciences, University of Stockholm. **SYSLAB Report No. 61**. 1988.

Classifying and Reusing Conceptual Schemas

S. Castano V. De Antonellis

Dipartimento di Elettronica e Informazione - Politecnico di Milano
Piazza Leonardo da Vinci 32 - 20133 Milano
Email: {deantone,castano}@ipmel2.elet.polimi.it

B. Zonta

Dipartimento di Scienze dell'Informazione - Università di Milano
via Comelico 39/41 - 20135 Milano

Abstract. The paper presents a methodological approach to guide the application engineer to construct a Library of Entity-Relationship schemas, classified by means of indexing criteria and clustering techniques, and to extract reusable components from the existing selected schemas. Reusable components are defined as generic entities with associated meta-entities providing guidelines for reuse in a given application. Generic entities are derived from the analysis of the entities belonging to similar schemas within clusters of the Library. A set of reuse guidelines in form of meta-entities are given, suggesting how generic entities can be modified and tailored according to the needs of the application to be developed.

1 Introduction

The ever growing complexity of software applications, and the need to develop information systems that can be readily adapted to changes in user requirements, has led to an increasing demand for methods and tools for reusing knowledge, processes and results of previously developed applications in order to improve productivity and quality of the development and maintenance process [1, 4, 15]. In both the frameworks of software engineering and information systems development, the traditional approaches based on the *design by transformation* paradigm, according to refinement and/or abstraction strategies, are being extended to adopt, in an integrated way, the *design by reuse* paradigm. According to this paradigm, applications are developed not from scratch, but tailoring and personalizing reusable components [5, 21]. The possibility of reusing components at any development level (requirements, design, code) is strongly dependent on their capacity to behave as generic solvers of problems existing in a wide range of specific situations. Genericity is an essential property to support the reuse of components as pointed out in [21], and allows the definition of a minimal set of reusable components to represent the significant problems of the application domain under consideration [16, 18, 21]. The extraction of reusable components relies on the availability of a Library containing selected pre-existing conceptual schemas which can be readily accessed and analysed according to similarity criteria [12, 17]. Several approaches to reusability are being proposed and experimented in the object-oriented area [14, 25, 13, 22, 4, 9]. An approach to define reusable components following the F-ORM object-oriented approach [7, 8], is presented in [5].

In this paper we consider reusability of Entity-Relationship schemas [3]. The problem is properly set since E-R schemas are widely and intensively produced in most organizations and their reuse can significantly improve design productivity. Precisely, we present a methodological approach for building a Library of Entity-Relationship schemas, classified by means of indexing criteria and clustering techniques, and for extracting reusable components from the existing selected schemas. Reusable components are defined as generic entities with associated meta-entities providing guidelines for reuse in a given application. Generic entities are derived from the analysis of the entities belonging to similar schemas within clusters of the Library. Guidelines associated to a reusable component provide a set of design suggestions about ways to incorporate that component in an application by means of possible adaptations and transformations. Responsible for the definition and maintenance of the Library and of the reusable components is the *application engineer* who is concerned with the following activities:

- organization of existing selected schemas in the Library according to a classification model, to support their search and retrieval by the application developer [11, 18, 20, 10];

- definition of the reusable components, extracting generic entities from schemas in the Library and defining corresponding meta-entities for their reuse [19, 25].

The proposed approach guides application engineers in both the activities. The paper is organized in the following way. Sect. 2 illustrates the model for the construction of the Library of E-R conceptual schemas. Sect. 3 focuses on the extraction of generic entities. In Sect.4, methods to define reusable components are discussed. In Sect.5, concluding remarks are given.

2   Construction of a Library of Conceptual Schemas

The analysis of about a hundred E-R schemas led us to conclude that an E-R schema is a kind of document suitable for automatic indexing. In fact, a schema appears to be a document, structured at both syntactic and semantic levels, ever belonging to a well identifiable (sub)domain. The structure of an E-R schema is constituted by interrelated elements labeled with meaningful names. These interrelated elements form a significant unit which, in turn, can be given a name, that is, the title of the schema. The linguistic labels of the schema elements, constitute, at least in principle, relevant terms for the description of the schema subject and are, therefore, good candidates for becoming descriptors of that schema. In practice, however, often the interpretation of a label cannot be immediate, because of the frequency of abbreviations, jargon, foreign words, or general terms which could be applied to any field and be specified only by their context (see, for instance, the schema in 2.1, where a credit dossier is called simply "dossier"). To overcome this obstacle, it is convenient, not to say necessary, to introduce normalizing interventions at the very moment of the label coinage [6]. Possible normalizations require to: eliminate articles, unnecessary prepositions, and the like; choose, among possible synonyms, those which are more pregnant in meaning (not "dossier" but "credit" or "credit dossier"); avoid, when possible, foreign words, acronyms and abbreviations.

In this section we present a methodological approach to the construction of a Library of conceptual schemas. The schemas descriptors, SDs, are extracted and used to compute the similarity coefficients of the schemas belonging to the same application, in order to arrange them into cluster hierarchies, which facilitate their retrieval also through browsing operations (Sect.2.1 and Sect.2.2). According to the proposed approach, a prototypal tool, CLAU (CLassificazione AUtomatica), has been developed to interactively support the application developer in building a Library of schemas. Specifically, whenever a new application arrives at the Library, CLAU extracts from its schemas the relevant terms for the arrangement of the schemas within the application and the classification of the application within the Library. CLAU is implemented in QUINTUS PROLOG in the programming environment UNIX SUN.

2.1 Extraction of Schema Descriptors

We have decided to candidate only the labels of the entities to become schema descriptors. In fact, we have found that the labels of relationships and attributes are usually not very expressive, in that the former are mostly made up by composing the names of the two related entities (e.g., "guarantee-guarantor") or by quite generic words (e.g., "concerns"), and the latter are often shared by a number of different entities (e.g., "code", "date"). For the sake of brevity, leaving out "labels of", we will from now on speak simply of "entities".

Given a schema S, the procedure for the extraction of schema descriptors (SDs) from its entities (Es) consists in two basic steps:
- to assign to each E of S a weight W;
- to establish a threshold for the choice of the SDs from the weighted Es.

Since for the entities of the same schema there is the assumption of a unique name, the weight evaluation of an entity cannot be based on a quantitative criterion, such as its frequency, but on a combination of evaluation criteria taking into account structural properties of the schema.
For each E, we consider:
- number of adjacent Es, that is, entities which are in direct relationship with E;
- number of proper attributes of E.

In addition, for each E taking part in an is-a hierarchy we consider:
- level number of E in the hierarchy: 1 for the root, from 2 on for the descendants;
- number of Es which are direct descendants of E;
- number of Es which are direct collaterals of E.

The weight W of each entity E is computed as the sum of the single values. For instance, in the conceptual schema "Credit Dossier" (from [2]) in Fig.1, for each entity, the single values and their global weights are shown in Table 1.

Entity		HL	DC	DD	AD	PA	W
1.	*provisional dossier*	1	--	1	3	3	8
2.	*requested dossier*	2	--	1	--	4	7
3.	*proposed dossier*	3	--	1	2	3	9
4.	*submitted dossier for resolution*	4	--	2	--	2	8
5.	*accepted dossier*	5	1	1	--	3	10
6.	*refused dossier*	5	1	--	--	1	7
7.	*activated dossier*	6	--	--	--	1	7
8.	*client*	1	--	4	--	4	9
9.	*credited client*	2	3	--	1	3	9
10.	*natural person*	2	3	--	--	1	6
11.	*company*	2	3	--	--	1	6
12.	*guarantor*	2	3	--	1	--	6
13.	branch	--	--	--	2	1	3
14.	issuing bureau	--	--	--	2	1	3
15.	*guarantee*	--	--	--	3	3	6
16.	credit mode	--	--	--	3	2	5
17.	utilization	--	--	--	3	1	4
18.	technical form	--	--	--	1	2	3
19.	contract	--	--	--	1	2	3

(HL=hierarchical level; DC=direct collateral; DD=direct descentant;
AD=adjacent; PA=proper attribute; W=weight)

Tab.1 Weights for the "Credit Dossier" schema

The threshold weight is computed as the sum of the Ws of the entities divided by the their number, i.e., as the average weight. In our example: 119/19=6. Only the entities with a weight equal to or greater than the threshold become SDs. In the Table 1 the SDs are in italic.

We have observed that the criteria by which weights are assigned to hierarchical entities may lead to exclude from the SDs some entities which have a few or null adjacent entities and proper attributes, but are, nevertheless, quite relevant for the classification of the schema in the Library and the consequent retrieval. On the other hand, considering also the possible inherited attributes and relationships in the weight computation would have led the lowest hierarchical levels to values which would be too high for the threshold computation, often such to exclude from the SDs every entity which did not belong to that hierarchy. The hierarchical structure, moreover, does not provide *per se* any indication on the relevance of its components: sometimes the greatest information pregnancy is found at the low levels while the high ones have rather a structural function; other times, the low levels represent details not very significant in the general schema context.

The previous considerations have led us to the conclusion that no kind of computation could guarantee a correct admission-exclusion of hierarchical entities from the SDs. As a consequence, a compromise has been adopted: all the hierarchical entities of a schema are raised to the rank of SDs, though their weights are under the threshold.

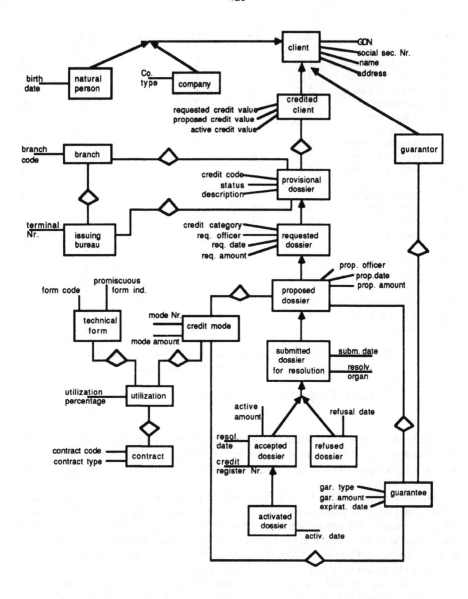

Fig.1 The conceptual schema "Credit Dossier"

It can also happen, as we have seen, that some of the most significant terms for the characterization of the schema are absent, or only partially specified, among the SDs. It is convenient, therefore, to invite the designer to point out the relevant terms in the name or title of the schema. These terms too will become SDs, receiving in any case the highest relevance values. In our example it will be "credit dossier" to join the SDs with the top weight 10.

Schema-card. When the schemas of an application are released to the Library, a Schema-card is associated to each schema. Beside the name of the schema and the reference to the application, a Schema-card contains the list of the SDs together with their weight, the total number of terms, and possibly other information. In Fig.2 the card of the schema presented in Fig.1, belonging to the application 111, is shown.

Starting from information on SDs contained in the Schema-cards referring to the same application, schemas are submitted to pairwise comparisons and classified hierarchically according to cluster generation procedures of an agglomerative, or bottom up, type.

> *Schema name:* Credit dossier
> *Version:* final
> *Designer:* X.Y.
> *Weighted SDs:* credit dossier, accepted dossier (10);
>   proposed dossier, client, credited client (9);
>   provisional dossier, submitted dossier for resolution (8);
>   requested dossier, refused dossier, activated dossier (7);
>   natural person, company, guarantor, guarantee(6)
> *Total Nr. of terms:* 19
> *Model:* E-R
> *Schema code:* 111.1
> *References:* None

Fig.2 Schema-card for the "Credit Dossier" schema

2.2 Schema Similarity and Classification

The SDs of each schema of the same application are considered as a cluster [24] and are matched with the SDs of all the other schemas in the application, giving rise, for N schemas, to N(N-1)/2 pairwise comparisons and as many similarity coefficients. Such coefficients are computed by means of the function [23]:

$$\frac{2 \text{ (Nr. of SDs shared by schemas S1 and S2)}}{\text{Nr. of SDs in S1 + Nr. of SDs in S2}}$$

For each pair of schemas, there are three possible cases:

1)   The schemas do not share any SD:
   - numerator is 0,
   - quotient is 0,
   - similarity coefficient is 0.

From a hierarchical point of view, no common ancestor exists for them beside the root of the cluster tree representing the whole application.

2)   The schemas share at least one SD and has at least a different one:
   - numerator is an even number smaller than denominator,
   - quotient is a decimal number smaller than 1,
   - similarity coefficient is a decimal number fixed between two thresholds, for instance, between 0.01 and 0.99.

From a hierarchical point of view two subcases can be distinguished:

a) both schemas have at least one different SD. As a potential common ancestor, they have a schema which contains only the shared SDs and which is, therefore, their cluster centroid.

b) all the SDs of one schema are contained in the other (when one of the addends at the denominator is the half of the numerator). The contained schema can be considered an ancestor of its container and so a cluster centroid for both.

3) The two schemas have no SDs other than the common ones:
   • numerator and denominator are equal,
   • quotient is 1,
   • similarity coefficient is 1.

They are to be considered identical, at least in this context. Only by examining the SD weights and possibly the non-SD terms, can we evaluate the actual identity.

In our example, we have considered 28 schemas. The number of pairwise comparisons has been 378, resulting in as many similarity coefficients. Here we show, for brevity, the application of the adopted similarity formula only to the comparison between the Schema-card presented in Fig.2 (code 111.1) and the Schema-card presented in Fig.4, extracted from the schema shown in Fig.3 (code 222.1).

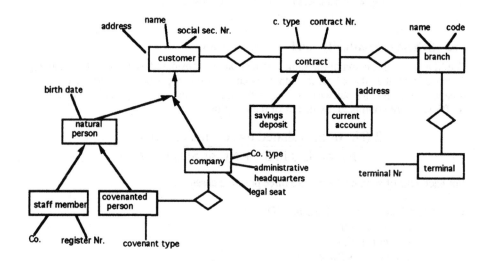

Fig.3 The conceptual schema "Customer Register"

The common SDs are 3: natural person, company, contract. The similarity coefficient, therefore, is:

$$\frac{2*3}{14+8} = 0.3$$

As evident, in the similarity computation the different weights assigned to the same descriptors in the various schemas have not been taken into account, because that would have lowered the similarity coefficients too much.

> *Schema name:* Customer register
> *Version:* final
> *Designer:* W.Z.
> *Weighted SDs:*   customer, company(7); contract ,natural
>   person, staff member, covenanted person(6);
>   savings deposit, current account (4).
> *Total Nr. of terms:* 10
> *Model:* E-R
> *Schema code:* 222.1
> *References:* None

Fig.4 Schema-card for the "Customer Register" schema

The similarity pairs of items so obtained are then listed in a decreasing order together with their similarity coefficients. Suppose that the order of the compared pairs for the schemas A, B, C, D, E, be:

DE	1.00
AB	0.70
AD	0.65
AE	0.60
CD	0.55
CE	0.50
AC	0.40
BD	0.30
BE	0.28
BC	0.22

with the corresponding similarity matrix:

	A	B	C	D	E
A	·	0.70	0.40	0.65	0.60
B	0.70	·	0.22	0.30	0.28
C	0.40	0.22	·	0.55	0.50
D	0.65	0.30	0.55	·	1.00
E	0.60	0.28	0.50	1.00	·

Since DE is the pair with the higher similarity coefficient, the cluster DE is constructed.

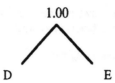

1.00

D   E

In the tree representation, the two schemas correspond to the leaves, while the node, marked by the similarity coefficient, represents their virtual centroid, that is a schema which would contain only the SDs common to both schemas, in our case all.

As for the next steps, two clustering strategies have been experimented and compared, precisely those known in literature as single link and complete link. In brief, in order to include a new item in a cluster, the single link clustering takes into account only the coefficient of the new item with the last clustered ones; while the complete link clustering requires knowing the coefficients of the new item with all the others of the list. With the first strategy, which obviously involves less computation, a small number of large clusters is obtained: it is, therefore, expedient when the items in question belong to the same or close domain. On the contrary, the second strategy produces a larger number of smaller clusters, pointing out more precisely equalities and differences between items which belong to various domains. Because of the supposed homogeneous nature of the schemas of the same application, the single link technique has been chosen in order to privilege retrieval recall rather than precision.

The matrix, therefore, is updated by picking up, as a new similarity coefficient between (DE), on the one part, and A,B,C, on the other, the highest values of D and E, when considered separately. For instance: AD=0.65 and AE=0.60, then A(DE)=0.65.

	A	B	C	DE
A	.	0.70	0.40	0.65
B	0.70	.	0.22	0.30
C	0.40	0.22	.	0.55
DE	0.65	0.30	0.55	.

The remaining pairs are processed in the following order:
AB=0.70; (AB)(DE)=0.65; ((AB)(DE)) C = 0.55, giving rise to the final tree:

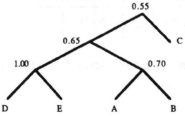

0.55

0.65   C

1.00   0.70

D   E   A   B

3 Definition of Reusable Components

The Library of schemas constitutes the starting point for defining reusable components. In fact, the application engineer has to extract generic entities from the existing classified schemas and then provide guidelines for their reuse. A *generic entity* is defined as an entity with a set of attributes which is "minimal" for the entities belonging to the similar schemas grouped in a given cluster of the Library. The application engineer compares the similar schemas belonging to a given cluster and by means of the "generalization abstraction" [3] mechanism defines a generic entity starting from the set of specific entities existing in the cluster schemas. Since a generic entity defines the minimal set of attributes required for characterizing a certain class of objects, different specializations of the generic entity are possible, according to the specific applications to be designed. In this way, reusable entities can be differently integrated in more than one application, possibly enriching them with attributes and relationships typical of the application to be modeled.

In this section, we describe a methodological approach for the definition of generic entities starting from entities belonging to schemas of the same cluster. Selected a cluster in the Library of schemas, possibly according to a predefined similarity threshold, schema-cards of the cluster schemas are compared with the purpose of selecting the entities having some level of "semantic affinity" between them. *Semantic affinity* exists between entities in different schemas if they describe distinct classes of objects having several common properties in the schemas. In the following, we describe the comparison process in the case of two entities E_1, E_2, belonging to different schemas. It can be easily extended to the case of n>2 entities. Two entities E_1 and E_2 are selected according to a predefined level of semantic affinity, and the application engineer evaluates the opportunity of defining a corresponding generic entity.

The following situations can occur:

• *E_1, E_2 have the same name in both schemas*
• *E_1, E_2 have different names in the schemas*

If E_1 and E_2 have the same name in the two schemas, they are automatically selected, as they belong to similar schemas, and, consequently, there exists an high probability of semantic affinity between them. Moreover, it is high probable that E_1 and E_2 describe the same class of objects in the two schemas (object identity), i.e., they are equally defined in the two schemas.

If E_1 and E_2 have different names in the two schemas, the procedure followed is based on the analysis and evaluation of the neighbor properties of each E_i, that is:
- attributes;
- generalization and specialization entities,
- entities participating in adjacent relationships with E_i.

The idea is that neighbor properties give information about the semantics of an entity, and consequently are useful for establishing the level of semantic affinity between E_1 and E_2 in the two schemas. The following "affinity coefficients" are used to compute the level of semantic affinity of E_1 and E_2:

- *Attribute Affinity*

  The attributes of E_1, E_2 are examined, to find out those equal in both the entities. The attribute affinity of E_1 and E_2, $AA_{(E_1,E_2)}$, is computed using the following function:

$$AA_{(E_1, E_2)} = \frac{2 \text{ (attributes common to } E_1 \text{ and } E_2)}{\sum_{i=1}^{2} \text{ attributes of } E_i}$$

- *Hierarchy Affinity*

  If E_1 and E_2 belong to generalization hierarchies, ascendant and descendant entities of E_1 and E_2 are examined, to find out those common to both the hierarchies. The hierarchy affinity of E_1 and E_2, $HA_{(E_1,E_2)}$, is computed using the following function:

$$HA_{(E_1, E_2)} = \frac{2 \text{ (ascendants and descendants common to } E_1 \text{ and } E_2)}{\sum_{i=1}^{2} \text{ ascendants and descendants of } E_i}$$

  If generalization hierarchies are not defined for both E1 and E2, then this coefficient is "not applicable". If a generalization hierarchy exists for only E_1 (E_2), $HA_{(E_1,E_2)}$ returns a value different from zero only if E_2 (E_1) belongs to the hierarchy of E_1 (E_2).

- *Adjacency Affinity*

  Adjacent entities of E1 and E2 are examined, to find out those common to both E_1 and E_2, i.e., the adjacent entities having the same name in both the schemas of E_1, E_2. The adjacency affinity of E_1 and E_2, $ADA_{(E_1,E_2)}$, is computed using the following function:

$$ADA_{(E_1, E_2)} = \frac{2 \text{ (adjacent entities common to } E_1 \text{ and } E_2)}{\sum_{i=1}^{2} \text{ adjacent entities of } E_i}$$

Each coefficient can assume values between 0 and 1. The value 0 represents a situation of absence of affinity (no commonalities exist between E_1 and E_2 for that coefficient), while the value 1 represents a situation of identity (E_1 and E_2 are equally defined in both schemas, with respect to the coefficient). Intermediate values describe situations of more or less affinity, corresponding to more or less commonalities (i.e., equal neighbor properties) between E_1 and E_2 in both schemas.

For E_1 and E_2 the affinity coefficients are computed and all the computed values are summarized to determine the Global Affinity, $GA_{(E_1,E_2)}$, of E_1, E_2, that is,

$$GA_{(E_1,E_2)} = AA_{(E_1,E_2)} + HA_{(E_1,E_2)} + ADA_{(E_1,E_2)}$$

Three cases can be considered:

- $GA_{(E_1,E_2)} = 0$

  All the affinity coefficients are equal to zero. In this case, we can speak of "no semantic affinity", meaning that E_1 and E_2 describe classes of objects with different properties in the two schemas. E_1 and E_2 are not selected for defining the corresponding generic entity.

- $GA_{(E_1,E_2)} = 3$

  All the affinity coefficients are equal to one. In this case, we can speak of "identity", meaning that E_1 and E_2 describe the same class of objects with equal properties in the two schemas. The corresponding generic entity is defined in the same way as E_1 (E_2), choosing one of the two names, or a third different name.

- $0 < GA_{(E_1,E_2)} < 3$

  Affinity coefficients have a value between zero and one. In this case, we can speak of "semantic affinity", meaning that E_1 and E_2 describe classes of objects with more or less common properties in the two schemas. In this case a threshold value of acceptance of 0.3 is established. Entities exceeding such a threshold are selected and the corresponding generic entity is defined for them.

For example, given the "client" and "customer" entities of the "Credit Dossier" and "Customer Register" schemas presented in Fig.1 and Fig.3 respectively, we obtain the attribute affinity $AA_{(client,customer)} = 0.86$, the hierarchy affinity $HA_{(client,customer)} = 0.66$, and the adjacency affinity equal to zero. Then, the global affinity is $GA_{(client,customer)} = 1.52$ and the two entities are selected for the generic entity extraction.

The selected pair $<E_i, E_j>$ (entities having the same name in the two schemas, or entities having different names exceeding the established threshold value of 0.3) is proposed to the application engineer who evaluates whether a generic entity can be effectively defined for the proposed pair. The application engineer examines entities names and neighbor properties from a semantic point of view, that is, he/she analyzes the meaning and the role of each E_i in both schemas. Depending on the semantics of E_1 and E_2, the following cases can be recognized:

- *Identity*

  E_1 and E_2 have the same name and the application engineer establishes that they indicate the same class of objects, by means of the semantic analysis. In this case, the generic entity E is defined with the same name and properties of the two entities;

- *Semantic affinity*

  E_1 and E_2 have same or different names and they describe classes of objects having several common properties. By a semantic analysis of the names and of the neighbor properties of E_1 and E_2, the application engineer can recognize one of the following cases:

  i)   synonyms: the two names indicate the same class of objects. In this case, the application engineer can select one of the two names, or a third name for the corresponding generic entity. An example of synonyms are the "customer" and "client" entities in the "Credit Dossier" and "Customer Register" schemas presented in Fig.1 and Fig. 3, respectively;

ii) iperonym: one of the two entities is an iperonym of the other (e.g., E_1 is an iperonym of E_2), meaning that the name of E_1 indicates a class of objects which is a generalization of that described by E_2. The generic entity E is defined with the same name of the iperonym, e.g., E_1 (as this name already indicates a generalization entity). Let us consider the "Customer Register" schema in Fig.3. The entity "contract" is an example of iperonym entity for the "savings deposit" entity in the same schema; E_1 and E_2 are restructured and the common attributes of E_1 and E_2 are defined for E;

iii) collaterals: E_1 and E_2 are at the same level of genericity with respect to the class of objects identified by their names and their neighbor properties. The application engineer selects a name that generalizes the names of E_1 and E_2, and defines the generic entity E with that name. An example of collaterals are the "savings deposit" and the "current account" of the "Customer Register" in Fig.3.

For the pair $<E_1, E_2>$ selected by semantic analysis, the corresponding generic entity E is defined factoring out the attributes common to both the entities. For example, the "client" and "customer" entities of the "Credit Dossier" and "Customer Register" schemas, presented in Fig.1 and Fig.3 respectively, can be selected and the generic entity named "Customer" is defined for them. For the "Customer" entity the attributes "address", "name", and "social sec.nr." are defined, since they are common to both the considered entities in the two schemas.

4   Representing Reuse Guidelines as Meta-Entities

Reusable components are described as generic entities and associated meta-entities, defined according to the template shown in Fig.6. A meta-entity is defined to describe how a generic entity E can be reused and tailored to be exploited in different views of one or more applications. In a meta-entity the "dependencies" and "guidelines for reuse" composite attributes are defined, describing, respectively, the types of dependencies characterizing the generic entity E and the suggestions for reusing E to construct different views. A "meta-of" one-to-one relationship is also defined between the meta-entity and the corresponding entity E which the meta-entity refers to (see Fig.7).

Use of the E-R model in the definition of both the generic entities and the corresponding meta-entities, and of the application conceptual schemas allows a homogeneous approach in the development process.

For an entity E, attributes of the corresponding meta-entity specify information concerning:

Entity dependencies. An entity usually has some form of dependency with other entities in a schema [3]. The main types of dependencies among entities in an E-R schema derive from both relationships and generalization hierarchies.

Types of dependencies defined for a generic entity E in the corresponding meta-entity M can be classified as follows:

• *Adjacent entities.* They are the entities that could participate in an adjacent relationship with E. The list of adjacent entities gives suggestions about the possible ways of defining relationships involving E. Several adjacent entities can be specified, corresponding to different ways of aggregating E.

Meta-entity Template
meta-entity: <meta-entity name >
composite attributes:
>   *dependencies*
>>   *adjacent entities,*   < list of entities/relationships>
>>   *specialization entities,*   < list of entities >
>   *guidelines for reuse*
>>   *guidelines*   < textual description >
>>   *suggested types of reuse,* < list of views names >
>>   *suggested actions,*   < list of rules >

Fig. 6 Meta-entity template

Relationship: Meta-of
connected entities: (1,1) < entity name >
                                     (1,1) < meta-entity name >

Fig. 7 Meta-of relationship

- *Specialization entities.* They are the entities which can be specialization of E. For each entity in the list, the set of additional attributes characterizing the entity in reference to E are given. The list of specialization entities guides designers in defining specialization hierarchies for E, enriching and detailing E for describing more specific classes of objects.

Guidelines for reuse. A list of suggested types of reuse is given, specifying what are the possible views that can be modeled reusing E. Depending on the selected view, rules for constructing the schema involving E for that view/application are specified. Such rules describe actions for incrementally defining the context of E, that is the adjacent relationships for E and, possibly, a specialization hierarchy for E. Moreover, rules indicating how to refine E by adding more specific attributes, i.e., typical of the view under consideration, are given.

In the following, we describe how the application engineer defines a meta-entity M for the generic entity E extracted from the selected pair $<E_1, E_2>$ of entities.

- For E, the adjacent entities e_i and the connecting relationships r_i are listed in the attribute "adjacent entities", with the following format:

$$(r_i, e_i)$$

An example of adjacent entities for the "Customer" generic entity is ("holds", "contract"), expressing the relationship existing between the entities "customer" and "contract" in the "Customer Register" schema in Fig.3. Adjacent entities give information on possible ways of aggregating E with other entities, enabling designers studying possible contexts characterizing E. More accurated suggestions on how to realize complete contexts for E, with several relationships and possibly generalization hierarchies, are given in form of rules in the "suggested actions" attribute of M.

- For E, possible specialization entities d_i are listed in the "specialization entities" attribute, with the following format:

$$(d_i , \{(\text{attribute, domain})\})$$

where d_i indicates the name of the specialization entity, followed by the set of pairs (attribute, domain), specifying the attributes (and corresponding domains) to be added to E to obtain the specialization entity d_i. E_1, E_2 are also listed as specializations of E. Examples of specialization entities for the "Customer" generic entity are: "natural person, (birth-date, date)", "company, {(Co. type, integer), (administrative headquarters, text(50)), (legal seat, text(20))}", "credit client, {(requested credit value, integer), (proposed credit value, integer), (active credit value, integer)}", expressing some of the possible specializations in the "Credit Dossier" and "Customer Register" schemas. In general, specialization entities can be useful for designers to study how E can be specialized and enriched with new attributes, i.e., for defining more detailed classes of objects. More accurated suggestions for defining specialization hierarchies for E are given in form of rules, as they depend on the specific view considered in reusing E.

- For E, the possible views in which E can be used for modeling applications are defined. In particular, are listed the views where E_1 and E_2 are used. For example, the views in which "Customer" can be reused are "credit" and "register". For each selected view, the rules for incrementally constructing the view starting from E are defined in the "suggested actions" attribute of the "guidelines for reuse" composite attribute of M. Such rules have the form:

IF (view name) THEN <actions>

where:

- view name: indicates one of the possible views in which E can be reused;
- actions: indicate the sequence of operations needed for tailoring and modifying E. In particular, according to the chosen view, actions can be specified for: adding new attributes to E in order to increase its level of detail; aggregating E with adjacent entities; defining specializations hierarchies for E. Example of rules for reusing the "Customer" generic entity for modeling the "register" and "credit" views are defined as follows:

IF (register) THEN
 define a relationship between "Customer" and "contract" using the tuple:
   ("holds", "contract");
 define the specialization entity "natural person" for "Customer" using the tuple:
   ("natural person", (birth date, date)); ....
IF (credit) THEN
 add to "Customer" the (General Direction Number, integer) attribute;
 define the specialization entity "credit client" for "Customer", using the tuple:
 ("credit client", {(requested credit value, integer), (proposed credit value, integer), (active credit value, integer)} .....

5 Concluding Remarks

A methodological approach for the classification of Entity-Relationship conceptual schemas into a Library and for their reuse has been discussed in this paper. Two main phases have been defined:

i) *Classification of Entity-Relationship schemas in a Library.* Input of the phase are conceptual schemas of existing applications. Output of the phase are the schemas grouped in clusters according to similarity criteria. Methods for automatic indexing of E-R schemas and for their clustering have been presented.

ii) *Definition of reusable components in terms of generic entities and meta-entities.* Input of the phase are the schemas grouped by similarity in the Library. Output of the phase is a set of generic entities and corresponding meta-entities. Each generic entity factors out the commonalities of all the entities in the grouped schemas. Suggestions about ways of aggregating and specializing generic entities are given in the corresponding meta-entities, in form of rules guiding the definition of several views for the considered generic entity.

The proposed approach is being experimented in the framework of the Italian National Research Council Project "Sistemi Informatici e Calcolo Parallelo", INFOKIT. The major contribution of the approach consists in the definition of a set of techniques and criteria which are the basis not only for the automatic indexing of schemas and their clustering according to similarity levels, but also for the extraction and definition of reusable components. Further research work is needed to complete the approach for the aspects related to the analysis of dynamic properties of entities (i.e., their behavior in the processes in which are involved) and to provide automatic support in classifying generic entities and meta-entities in the Library. Tools for the automatic derivation of reusable entities from the analysis of existing components are also being investigated within the INFOKIT and ITHACA-Esprit N.2705 projects.

Acknowledgements. This work has been supported by by the Italian National Research Council Project "Sistemi Informatici e Calcolo Parallelo", L.R.C. INFOKIT, by the ITHACA Esprit Project N.2705, and by MURST 40%.

References

1. ACM Issue on Object-Oriented Design, September 1990

2. C. Batini, G. De Petra, M. Lenzerini, G. Santucci: La progettazione concettuale dei dati, Franco Angeli Editore, 1986

3. C. Batini, S. Ceri, S. Navathe: Conceptual Database Design, Addison Wesley, 1991

4. T.J. Biggerstaff, A.J. Perlins (eds.): Software Reusability- Concepts and Models, vol.I, ACM Press, Addison-Wesley, 1990

5. S.Castano, V. DeAntonellis, B. Pernici: Requirements reuse. ITHACA Report, ITHACA.POLIMI-UDUNIV, 1992

6. V. De Antonellis, B. Zonta: A disciplined Approach to Office Analysis. IEEE TSE, Vol. 16, No. 8, pp. 822-828, 1990

7. V. DeAntonellis, B. Pernici, P. Samarati: F-ORM: Functionality in Object with Roles Model. In: 2nd Int. Conf. on Dynamic Aspects on Information Systems, Washington, DC, July 1991

8. V. DeAntonellis, B. Pernici, P. Samarati: F-ORM METHOD: A F-ORM Methodology for Reusing Specifications. In: IFIP WG 8.4 Working Conf. on Object Oriented Aspects in Information Systems, Quebec, October 1991

9. V. DeAntonellis, B. Pernici: The ITHACA Object Oriented Methodology: Application Developer Manual", ITHACA Report, ITHACA.POLIMI-UDUNIV.E.8.1, October 1991

10. P. Devanbu, R.J. Brachman, P.G. Selfridge, B.W. Ballard: LaSSIE: A Knowledge-Based Software Information System. Communications of the ACM, Vol.34 N.5, May 1991

11. G. Di Battista, H. Kangassalo, R. Tamassia: Definition Libraries for Conceptual Modelling. In: Proc. VII International Conference on Entity-Relationship Approach, pp. 245-260, North Holland

12. W.B. Frakes, B.A. Nejmeh: Software reuse through information retrieval. In: Proc. 20th Ann. HICSS (Kona,HI), January 1987

13. M.G. Fugini, O. Nierstrasz, B. Pernici: Application Development through Reuse: the Ithaca Tools Environment. ACM SIGOIS Bulletin, August 1992

14. B. Henderson, J.M. Edwards: The Object-Oriented System life-cycle. Comm. of the ACM, September 1990

15. W. Tracz (ed.): Software Reuse: Emerging Technology. Computer Society Press, Washington D.C., 1988

16. M.F. Kilian: A Note on Type Composition and Reusability. OOPS Messenger, 1991

17. Y.S. Maarek, D.B. Berry, G.E. Kaiser: An Information Retrieval Approach for Automatically Constructing Software Libraries. IEEE TSE, Vol.17, N.8, August 1991

18. R. Prieto-Diaz: Domain Analysis for Reusability. In: Proc. of COMPSAC '87, 1987, pp.23-29

19. R. Prieto-Diaz, P. Freeman: Classifying Software for Reusability. IEEE Software, Vol.4., N.1, January 1987

20. R. Prieto-Diaz: Implementing Faceted Classification for Software Reuse. Communications of the ACM, Vol.34 N.5, May 1991

21. Proceedings of REBOOT Workshop on Reuse, Esprit Project 5327, Grenoble, September 1991

22. H.B. Reubenstein, R.C. Waters: The Requirements Apprentice: Automated Assistance for Requirements Acquisition. IEEE TSE, Vol.17, N.3, March 1991

23. G. Salton, Ch. Buckley: Term Weighting Approaches in Automatic Text Retrieval. Information Processing and Management, 24, 5, pp.513-523, 1989

24. P. Willet: Recent Trends in Hierarchic Document Clustering: A Critical Review. Information Processing and Management, 24, Nr. 5, pp. 577-97, 1988

25. R. Wirfs-Brock, R.E. Johnson: Surveying Current Research in Object-Oriented Design. Communications of the ACM, Vol.33, N.9, September 1990

Embedding Data Modelling in a General Architecture for Integrated Information Systems

A.-W. Scheer

IWi, Institut für Wirtschaftsinformatik

Im Stadtwald, Geb. 14.1

D - 6600 Saarbrücken

1. Information Systems Design Methods

The application of data modelling has long evolved beyond mere database development. In object-oriented analysis data modelling concepts are used to define the relationships between object classes [17,21]. Several approaches have been developed to integrate heterogeneous systems via the data models associated with them [5,7]. In many information systems design methods (ISDM) data modelling has become a key activity to capture the "static" requirements of an information system [9,12,25]. These methods aim to remove software development from the sphere of handicrafted one-off production to the organizational form of industrial production, the form then being referred to as the software factory [1, p.2].

The multiplicity of methods available can be distinguished according to whereabouts in the software development process their support is focussed, and according to their chosen perspective on the problem (e.g. data-, event-, or function-driven). An impression of the number of available methods can be obtained from standard texts on software engineering e.g. Balzert[1], Sommerville[23] or from the conference reports of the Working Group 8.1 published by IFIP [13].

The multiplicity of methods, which are often only marginally distinguishable from each other, has led to considerable difficulties in surveying the methods and has impeded the development of computerized tools based on these methods. As a result attempts are being made to create a methodology (theory of methods) for the development methods.

Typical questions which the framework provided by such a methodology should help to answer are [22,14, p.2]:

1. Are there really so many fundamentally different ways of designing a computerized information system ?
2. If not, how similar are these ways, and if so, why are the ways so different ?
3. Is there an optimal way to develop an information system ?
4. Where does the development process begin and end ?
5. What does the end product of the design process look like?
6. How many levels are needed to achieve a development result?
7. Should only one methodology be employed for a specific type of information system or are several methods required for different systems? If so, which criteria should be used to determine the method to be used?

In addition to answering these questions, with the aim of categorising and evaluating the methods, there is another set of reasons in considering ISDM (Information System Design Methods). These reasons result from the fact that in general complex development projects involve several partners who may implement diverse development methods and whose working results overlap. In this situation, only a conceptual framework which allows the categorisation of the various methods, and consequently their conformities and discrepancies, can generate mutual understanding. The fact that such a conceptual framework can also lead to uniformity in the use of methods is, of course, also relevant.

Computerized information systems for business economics are particularly characterised by an increasingly high degree of complexity. Integrated data processing, which supports the common use of data by diverse applications, and the implementation of comprehensive EDP oriented global enterprise models (CIM in industrial firms, computerized retail information and control systems in trading firms, electronic banking in banking firms) mean that many internal and external partners are involved in the development of an information system. A conceptual framework, or architecture, is required to allow the coordinated division of labour in the implementation of such projects.

Architecture is generally understood as the art of construction. Applying this concept to information systems implies that the individual building blocks which constitute the information system need to be described in terms of their:

- type,
- functional properties,

- interactions.

Application of the term architecture to information processing concepts is commonplace. Attempts to justify the application of architectural concepts to information systems in etymological terms are made by Krcmar[10] and Strunz.[24] However, the author believes that the application of the concept should be regarded as the result of a colloquial understanding rather than in terms of an etymological explanation. Associated with the term architecture are concepts such as planning, the following of rules, the structuring or coordination of several partners, which correspond to problems within information systems. Furthermore, the term has largely been adopted from the American literature, and is also applied to the description of hardware and database systems.[11]

In addition to that part of the architecture which defines the components and their interaction - the "what" that is established in the description of an information system - the "how" must also established, that is, the procedural method for creating an information system.

An information system architecture facilitates the use of tools for automating the development process. It is common knowledge that the development of large software systems is associated with considerable costs and risks. Consequently, efforts are being made to automate software production by developing a comprehensive set of tools.[15,8,2,16]

Many of the methods that are commonly used at present for developing information systems are the result of empirical findings rather than theoretical models. Some of the approaches to developing a methodology also attempt to integrate the existing methods into a conceptual framework, rather than deriving the methodology theoretically.

For this reason the following treatment derives the architecture of integrated business information systems from a general business economics process chain model. The emphasis on the business economics applications background does not represent a significant restriction. Rather, it emphasizes the considerable significance of the integration principle of information systems, which is typical of business economics applications, refers to the area from which the vast majority of application examples in this book are taken, and indicates that special applications systems (e.g. process automation) will receive less attention. The architecture of Integrated information systems (ARIS) which is developed should therefore be regarded as a generally applicable proposal.

The ARIS architecture constitutes a framework in which integrated applications systems can be developed, optimized and converted into EDP-technical implementations. At the same time it demonstrates how business economics can examine and analyse information systems in order to translate their contents into EDP-suitable form.

Process chains are an important support for business information systems.[20] Examples of process chains are the entire order handling process from order acceptance through material management, production to dispatch, or the development of a product from the initial idea through to the release of the fully tested product for production. The elements of a process chain are the individual processes. A process is an occurrence of some duration which is started by an event and completed by an event. Start and result events thus define the beginning and end of the process (see figure 1).

The object of the processing can be the transformation of materials used into products (materials produced). In terms of Gutenberg's theory of production,[4] further factors of production - the use of human labour and equipment in the form of production machines or information technology devices - are needed to achieve this transformation. The rules for combining the basic factors are specified as processing rules for describing the process.

Parallel to the process of material transformation, and closely linked with it, is the process of information transformation. The event as an occurrence at a specific timepoint (e.g. in the form of a production order) initiates the process of production. In contrast to a process, an event requires neither time nor resources. The result is then the completion of the order as result event and the part S5. A result event can also be a change in status of an already familiar object. The order completion report is therefore the change in status of the production order. It is quite possible that several events in conjunction initiate a process, or that several events are the result of a process.

To control the process, conditions in the task environment need to be included, to provide parameters for the processing rules, for example. In the case of production these might be descriptions of the product to be created or the components needed (inventories). During processing these data can be altered, for example, inventories reduced by assigning components to the customer order.

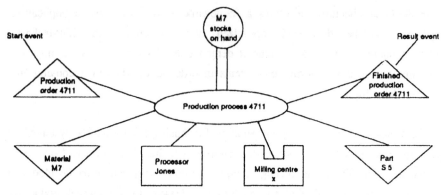

Fig. 1: Elements of a process chain

Alterations to the conditions in an environment resulting from the processing function are always the consequence of the events generated by the execution of the process. Examples might be the establishment of a new entity (customer, article, etc.) or alterations to an attribute value. This state of affairs characterizes the conventional definition of a process as the transformation of input data into output data. The individual events and the alterations which are based on them only become visible when the processes are described in detail. The alteration represented in figure 1 by counter-arrows is thus a rough representation of the transformation process. Only two specific events are highlighted, which represent the start and the result of a process.

Depending on the kind of process the transformation of either material or information can be predominant. In considering production processes, such as are analysed in the context of business economics production theory, the material transformation is dominant. In contrast, for more strongly administrative processes, such as order processing, bookkeeping, planning and design, the information transformation process is dominant. It must be emphasized, however, that the two processes are intertwined, that is, material transformation also involves information transformation and alterations to information can also give rise to material alterations. These interdependences are made particularly obvious by the use of modern technical production processes in which machines are controlled by control programs (NC programs) and feedback concerning the execution of the process is automatically recorded by the information system. For this reason production-oriented and information-oriented equipment are regarded as of equal significance.

Information systems are used to support specific applications. These can be viewed at various levels of abstraction. At the lowest level of abstraction shown in figure 1 the individual instances of the "order handling" process chain are represented. The event "receipt of production order 4711" initiates the processing function "production process 4711" for order 4711. A specific employee, Mr. Jones, is responsible for this. Details of the stock levels for the article and materials referred to in the order are required for production.

Abstracting from the individual properties of particular production processes generates the standard process of production shown at abstraction level 2 in figure 2. Here the description of the individual process "production" defines the general rules for the transformation of material and information, which are controlled by the specific status of the stock level data in the way in which they are used. The combination of similar objects into a single concept type is referred to as classification. Similarity between elements arises when elements of the same class can be described by the same characteristics.

The specific individual production orders are thus amalgamated into the class PRODUCTION ORDER, the individual production processes to the class PRODUCTION PROCESS, etc.

Business economic information systems are generally described at this second level. Consequently they relate to specific application areas and constitute a general processing framework for individual processes.

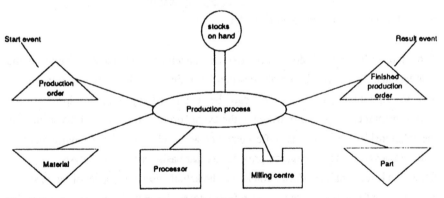

Fig. 2: Production process: abstraction level 2

Further abstraction from the application, i.e. from whether a production process, an order processing or a bookkeeping process is being described, generates the general process chain model of level 3 shown in figure 3. Reference to the application is thereby abandoned and a level reached at which the fundamental structure of the processing of a process chain is described.

The temporally-specific factors, such as order placement or order confirmation are amalgamated into the class EVENTS, all time-taking occurrences are amalgamated into the class PROCESS, all environmental descriptions to the class ENVIRONMENTAL CONDITIONS, all materials (auxiliary materials, equipment and other materials) to the class MATERIALS, etc.

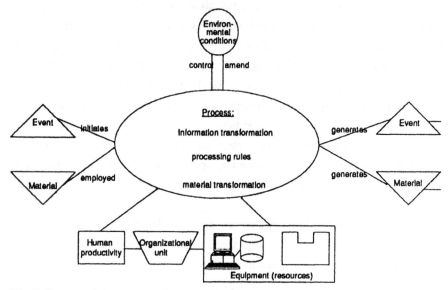

Fig. 3: Process chains: abstraction level 3

The graphic for level 3 does not show all conceivable relationships between the components. Thus, specific employees can be assigned both to organizational units and to equipment, or an event can be explained by relationships between environmental conditions. For example the event "order placement" can be defined as the relationship between a specific customer as an element of the environment or time. However, the representation provides a clear basis for further analysis.

Since this level contains information about the actual descriptive level of the business economics information system, it is referred to as the meta-level. At this level the approaches, procedures and concepts to be used to describe the underlying real levels are established. At level 2 diverse description procedures can be applied. At level 3, however, the elements to be described by this procedure are fixed.

This abstraction is also a classification, since once again similar objects are amalgamated into conceptual types. The level 2 objects are thereby elements (instances) of the level 3 classes.

The amalgamation into classes is an intellectual procedure and as such is not free from subjective elements. For example, intermediate classes could have been formed, in that first the classes "rush orders" and "normal orders" be established for specific customer orders which would then be amalgamated as the class "orders". This implies that, particularly at level 2, several class hierarchies are possible.

The class structure at level 3 is also not the only possible one. However, it does contain the essential concepts for describing the business economic and informational facts, and thereby constitutes a suitable starting point for further analysis.

In the following, this initial model will be used to derive an architecture within which information systems can be described, and which can be used to provide support for process chains.

Once the ARIS architecture has been established, the individual components can be considered in more detail, leading to a more detailed description of level 2, including the descriptive processes commonly used. These then can be analysed and the general elements including their relationships to level 3 can be established.[18] The ARIS architecture provides the framework for this analysis, and must therefore be constructed in such a way as to allow these detailed considerations.

To this end the starting model will be further structured, in order to simplify the descriptive subject matter. Thereafter a descriptive language will be established for describing at level 3 all the objects used at level 2. This also allows all the various software design methods used at level 2, and the constructs that they employ, to be represented in a uniform language.

The architecture provides the framework for storing models of level 2. These are then filed in a meta-database, or a repository.

Level 3 therefore consists of:

-    the general procedural method for deriving the architecture,
-    the descriptive building blocks and components (architecture),
-    the descriptive language for a detailed description of the building blocks and components for classifying the conceptual world of level 2,
-    models for representing the elements of a descriptive approach (meta-models),

- a database for storing the level 2 models described in accordance with the architecture (repository).

2. Derivation of the ARIS Architecture by Structuring the Process Chain Model

The components of an information system to be described from the business economics standpoint, including their relationships to each other, are therefore conditions, events, and processes; the factors of production materials, human labour (employees), and equipment (differentiated between production equipment and information technology equipment); and organizational units which provide their structure. Since each element can be related to every other element this generates a complex structure. Multiple relationships can also arise. For example, the relationship between the process and human labour also depends on the equipment provided in support of the execution of the process. Furthermore relationships can also arise within relationships, indicating how conditions depend on each other, or how events can be linked together, for example.

In order to reduce the complexity, therefore, three steps are undertaken:

1. the abstraction from factors that are irrelevant to information processing,
2. the amalgamation of elements into more general descriptive views.
3. the reduction of relationships using a phased, or procedural, model.

2.1 Concentration on the Transformation of Information

In order to reduce the number of components to be analysed and to ensure simplicity, the physical material transformation process is no longer treated as an independent descriptive component of the architecture. Instead it is considered as part of the environment of the process chain, which is described by conditions. The same applies to the production equipment used in the transformation of material. This also enters the informational representation via the concept of the environmental condition. As a result of the close links between the real and the information transformation, however, information about the material transformation process continues to be reflected in the description of the environment conditions. For example, in a PPC system a process chain model for material transformation is represented by the bills of materials and work schedules. Here, the operations to be carried out (e.g. sawing, drilling, milling), the equipment to be used and the materials needed are described. However, these are recorded by a PPC system as environmental descriptions (in the database). The operations in this information transformation process in which these data are used as environmental conditions, are process planning, work scheduling, production control and operational data collection, for example.

The broad concept "environmental condition" is therefore used to absorb all those components of an information system which are not to be handled from their own descriptive viewpoint.

Human productive capacity - employees - are divided into those involved in the production process, who are also regarded as part of the environment, and those users who are directly involved with the information system. Fig. 4 indicates this altered approach by circling the elements involved. This approach signifies that, from the information processing viewpoint, the production process is not viewed from the physical standpoint of the use of materials, human labour and equipment, but merely in terms of the data alterations resulting from the physical production process. Thus, only the data-related representation is considered.

The information technology equipment, however, continues to be relevant as the foundation for the information system. The same applies to that human productivity which is directly linked with the information system via the user. The aggregation of employees or equipment into organizational units also continues to be a relevant component.

2.2 Creating Views

The process chain model resulting from the concentration on informationally relevant factors is still complex. Consequently, individual descriptive elements are further aggregated.

The process-specific view also gives rise to considerable redundancy. The same environmental conditions, events, users, etc., can be responsible for several processes. In order to avoid this redundancy the process chain model is broken down into individual views, which are then described independently, and thus with less redundancy (see figure 5).

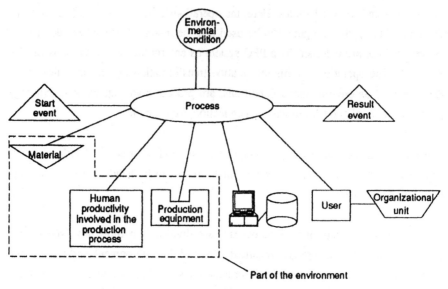

Fig. 4: Elements of the "environmental conditions" component

First, events and environmental conditions are represented by data. They are represented as information objects using a uniform data view. The recording of events as part of a data view is common to many software development methods.[14, S.43]

The description of process rules and the process structure provides the process or function view. The term "function" is therefore often used interchangeably with the terms "process" or "process chain", because it is often used in the literature in association with functionally-oriented system design.

Because of their close connections, components user and organizational unit are aggregated into a single element. Users are assigned to organizational units and these are constructed on the basis of criteria such as "same function" or "same work object". This view is referred to as the organizational view.

Information technology equipment constitutes the fourth descriptive area, the resource view. This reduces the six descriptive elements to four, whereby further simplification is achieved by the concentration of the terms equipment and user on the relationship with information transformation. In creating these views, however, the links between the views are lost. For this reason an additional view, referred to as "control", will be introduced later to record the relationships between the viewpoints.

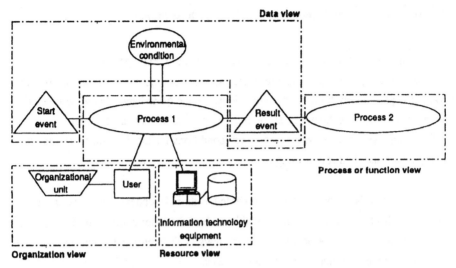

Fig. 5: Process chain model views

In addition to reducing complexity and redundancy within the descriptive subject matter, the formation of views also has the advantage that one component (that is, one view) can already be developed without the other views being available. This means, for example, that later the data model for a system can be created without the functions being comprehensively defined. Insofar as details from one view are absolutely essential for the description of another view these can be established in general form by this view and then further specified by the view responsible.

The division between views cannot always be absolutely strictly maintained, as a result of the relationships existing between them. For example, the description of processes within the function view might also usefully specify events which initiate or result from processes, although these are partially recorded in the data model. The strict requirements of the definition of information objects do not then need to be maintained.

The boundaries between the meta-levels and the description of an application are not always clear. For example, the organizational viewpoint is on the one hand described as part of the ARIS architecture in the meta-information model, on the other hand "organization" is a business application which can be represented in an application-specific "organization" data model.[19]

2.3 Breakdown of the Resource View Using a Phase Model

Given the multiplicity of components, such as CPU, peripherals, networks, programming systems or database systems, the resource view of an information system is particularly broad and multifarious. On the other hand, this view is only of importance from the business economics viewpoint in that, as foundation for the information system, it provides framework conditions for the description of the other components and their relationships.

For this reason the resources are not regarded as an independent descriptive area, but rather, the resource view is handled within each of the other component descriptions. Furthermore the description of the other views is differentiated according to their proximity to the information technical resources.

This process of transforming the business economics factors into the EDP-technical implementation is often described by differentiated phase models.[14, p.37] The following treatment adopts a five stage layering approach to implementing and running a business economics application model.

In the first step an EDP-oriented semantic starting position is created. This is the result of an actual analysis of the process chains with planned concepts built upon it. This process chain analysis should make the fundamental benefits of the information system visible. For this reason at this stage all the views are examined together.

In the second step a real concept (requirements definition) models the individual viewpoints of the applications system independent of implementation considerations. In the process, descriptive languages are chosen which are sufficiently formalized to provide a starting point for a consistent EDP-technical implementation.

In the third step, the creation of the EDP concept (design specification), the real models are adapted to the requirements of the user interfaces as regards implementation tools (e.g. database systems, network architectures or programming languages). However, at this point there is still no reference to specific products.

In the course of the fourth step, the technical implementation, the concrete translation of the requirements into physical data structures, hardware components and programming systems is undertaken (implementation description).

These four phases describe the creation of an information system and are therefore referred to as "build time". Thereafter, the completed system is delivered to the firm, so that the fifth operation and maintenance step can be added, which is referred to as "run time". This run time version of the information system and its support environment is not considered further below. This work thus restricts itself to the build time phases of information systems.

The real concept is very closely linked with the business economic application sphere, as is shown by the width of the arrow in figure 6. It should, however, be created largely independent of the implementation considerations, as is represented by the width of the arrow to the EDP concept. Both technical implementation and operation and maintenance are, in contrast, closely linked with the "device and product level" of information technology. Changes in information technology have an immediate impact on the kind of implementation and the operation of a system.

The phases cannot always be exactly separated from each other. As a result the assignment of methods, representations and results of the software design process is not always unambiguous. The phase concept should certainly not be interpreted as a strict sequencing of the development process according to the "waterfall" principle. Rather, a prototyping approach is also explicitly incorporated. But even in the case of evolutionary software development the descriptive levels are in principle given.

Using the phase concept the multifarious relationships between the resource view and the other components can be simplified. Initially, in the first two steps, each component is represented solely from the real viewpoint without implementation restrictions. Thereafter, the factual content is further specified in the framework of the EDP concept and in the implementation stage it is implemented using specific data processing techniques. Only in the third and fourth phases do resource considerations have an effect. The resources are therefore detailed in the course of these descriptions, insofar as is necessary.

153

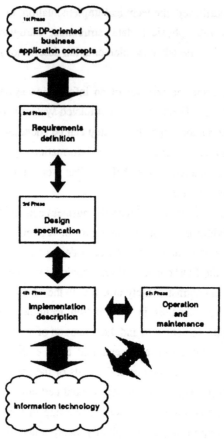

Fig. 6: Description phases dependent on the proximity to information technology

Since in the first step of process chain analysis and the formation of the business economics application concept the views are not yet separated, they are not actually part of the ARIS architecture of the information system. The components to be described therefore reduce to the model presented in figure 7 from the organization, process and data views each with three descriptive levels - the real concept, the EDP concept and implementation.

By subdividing the procedural model into views the relationships between these components are lost. However, since elementary relationships exist between data and functions and the organization these are reintroduced in their own components which intermediate between the elements. This is referred to as the control view.

Since the links between the elements create movements (data, in the form of events, initiate function, or functions alter data) the term control can serve to indicate this dynamic.

As a result, each component can in the first instance be described independently, the relationships to other components are then handled at the control level. Within control the three descriptive levels are also established with respect to their proximity to the resources. In this way the links to the other components can be created at every descriptive level.

Figure 7, therefore, represents the information system architecture. It consists of the following elements: functions, organization, data, and control. All the components are broken down in terms of their proximity to the information technology resources into the descriptive levels: real concept, EDP concept, and implementation.

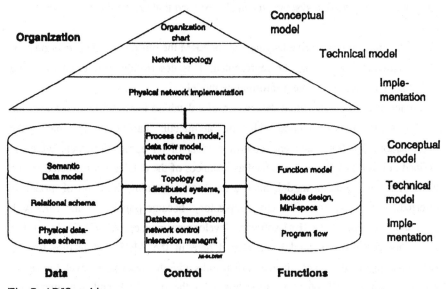

Fig. 7: ARIS architecture

3. Representation of the Information Model

Once the building blocks of the ARIS architecture for integrated information systems have been established, it is necessary to determine how their functionality can be described in greater detail.

In order to ensure that the interdependences between the individual blocks are also clearly established it is obvious that a uniform descriptive language should be chosen for all of the blocks. It is true that individual representational methods, such as data models, hierarchy diagrams, flow charts, or organigrams, have been developed to describe data, functions, and organizational aspects; however, they relate to the factual representation, that is, level 2 in figure 2. At the meta-level, that is, the description of the elements of the information system itself, a uniform language can be applied if it is capable of abstracting from the level-specific contents and reducing the methods to the objects to be represented and the relationships between them. Consequently, a descriptive language is chosen which merely establishes for each block the elements to be described and their relationships to each other.

Chen's entity-relationship model (ERM)[3] is generally suitable for representing objects and their relationships. Although it was developed for representing data structures for application systems, it can also be used to describe the meta-level.

Using the uniform descriptive language of the ERM the objects and their relationships of the individual views can be represented. This description is referred to as the information model, or the meta-information model.

Simultaneously, the conceptual description of a database is established, in which the specific applications developed within this architecture can be stored. That is, the organization, function, data and control models of an application area, which is defined at level 2 of figure 2, are held as instances of the database constructed on the basis of the information model. Such a database containing this kind of model, is referred to as a repository. The term "repository" became popular around 1989 with the announcement of the IBM software development concept AD/CYCLE.[26] The repository contains the models developed here in the ARIS architecture for the functions, organization, and data, and their links with the descriptive level 2 in figure 2 (that is the generalized application level) for the real, EDP and implementation concepts. The repository therefore constitutes the heart of an information system, and the information model of the repository is correspondingly significant, since it establishes the power of the descriptive elements.

The ERM consists of the elements entity or object types (represented by boxes) and relationships types (represented by rhombi). The relationship types are differentiated into the cardinalities 1:n, 1:1, n:m and m:1. Fig. 8 presents a rough information model of the ARIS architecture using these simple elements. The individual views are described by the object and relationship types representing them. The individual views are each presented within bold frames. As well as the function, data, organization and control views, the resource view is also explicitly represented. This implies that the gradual proximation to the resource level is not yet expressed in terms of a phase concept, but is generated by the relationship types "TRANSFORMATION, EXECUTION" between the entity type RESOURCES and the other views. This short-cut has the advantage that no terms need to be adopted from the EDP or implementation concepts. The information model of figure 8 gives a preliminary introduction into the means of representation and should be useful in making comparisons with other architectural concepts.

The starting point for the functional model of figure 8 are the enterprise goals which are to be pursued within the information system, or within the process chains and problem-solving approaches it represents. The enterprise goals are generally of hierarchical form. Global goals, such as "profit maximization", "winning a given share of the market" or "achieving a certain rate of growth" generate derived sub-goals such as "achieving a given turnover", "reducing costs by a certain amount" or "attaining a given product quality level".

The structure of the interdependent goals forms an n:m relationship within the entity type ENTERPRISE GOALS.

Certain functions must be carried out to achieve these goals. Examples of such functions are order processing, production or controlling. These can in turn be supported by derived sub-functions. The linking of functions with each other, and the supportive nature of functions with respect to goals, generates an n:m relationship within the entity type FUNCTION, as well as an n:m relationship between FUNCTION and ENTERPRISE GOALS.

On the left side the model of the data structures is presented. The entity type INFORMATION OBJECT refers to the object described by attributes within a database. It comprises events and conditions which can be represented by data. Relationships exist between information objects such as ORDERS, CUSTOMERS, etc. (e.g. which customer placed which order). These are expressed by an n:m relationship within the term INFORMATION OBJECT. Information objects which in terms of their contents belong to a self-contained area can be amalgamated into a data model. Since these may overlap an n:m relationship exists between data model and information object.

The central concept in the model of the organization view is the organizational unit. This can be defined as a department, position, or a larger unit such as an operational area on up to the entire enterprise. The structure of decision making powers or affiliation relationships between these areas gives rise to an n:m relationship within the entity type ORGANIZATIONAL UNIT. The n:m relationship thereby allows an area to be subordinate to several areas. This is the case, for example, if a factory is responsible for several higher level product areas.

The relationships between the three components are taken into account at the control level.

Functions can be interpreted as the transformation of input data into output data. Events initiate functions and are also the result of functions. These three interdependences are represented as relationships between INFORMATION OBJECT and FUNCTION.

The interdependence between ORGANIZATIONAL UNIT and FUNCTION is expressed by the PROCESSING ASSIGNMENT. Organizational units can be assigned to certain views of the INFORMATION OBJECTS, which is expressed by the relationship type DATA VIEW.

The information technology is represented by the entity type IT-RESOURCES. It is not broken down further, since the description of the relationships occupies the foreground. The relationship type TRANSFORMATION, EXECUTION is always assigned to each of the three models, so that their description within the views can be effected within the phase model in accordance with the architecture developed.

To represent these interdependences Chen's simple ERM model is extended, since relationships will be formed between the relationship types at the control level and the entity type RESOURCES. In this process the relationship types are first redefined as entity types and enclosed within boxes.

The meta-information model as ERM thus describes the objects of an information system (entity types) and the relationships existing between them. It describes all the views of the ARIS architecture developed here (functions, organization, data and their control) through the development levels (process chain analysis, real concept, EDP concept and implementation).

At the same time, it constitutes the conceptual schema of a database of the repository
for storing the relevant models at the application level (that is level 2 of figure 2).

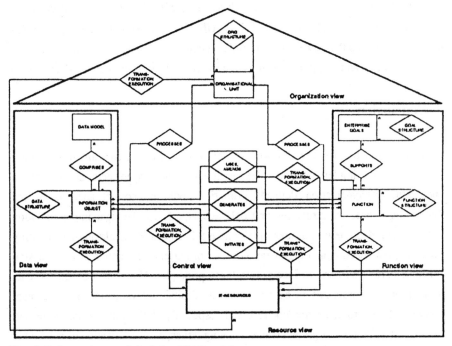

Fig. 8: Information model of the ARIS architecture

The four components of the meta-level
- general procedural model,
- ARIS architecture,
- descriptive language and ARIS information model,
- repository,

are thus developed and can be used as a basis for comparison with other architectural
concepts.

First of all the general procedural model, which contains the basic structure of the
process descriptions, establishes the levels to be described (ARIS architecture). For
each view the information model containing the objects to be described and their
relationships, is created with the help of the ERM descriptive language. Together
these generate the ARIS information model.

The repository is a database whose conceptual schema corresponds to the information model. The data stored contain the descriptions from level 2, that is the process and data models for specific applications such as PPC, sales, etc., but not their contents. Whereas the terms CUSTOMER, PART, EQUIPMENT are stored in the repository as entity types of a PPC model, for example, specific instances, that is the individual customers, parts and equipment entities, are stored in the PPC application databases.

4. Conclusion

Current approaches for the development of information systems are too strongly biased towards implementation. The architecture developed here shows that a successful implementation depends primarily upon the correct analysis of the underlying conceptual structures and only secondarily on the right implementation choices. The data view is an example, where this separation is already successfully practiced, but function and organization views of current information systems design methodologies also need to incorporate these principles. However, also on the data view, more emphasis has to be laid upon the design and validation of conceptual models. Many problems are not resolved, especially if the models are large and involve interdisciplinary project teams. Naming issues, the identification of synonyms and of type conflicts still lack an efficent and systematic approach. Reference models, which are generic for a particular type of industry, can be used to improve the quality and reduce the development effort for enterprise-specific data models.[6] Their utilization should be incorporated into ISDMs and the corresponding CASE-tools. Furthermore, the architecture shows a clear need for integrating data models with function and organization models. This shall be the final step to truly automating information systems design.

References

[1] Balzert, H.: Die Entwicklung von Software-Systemen. Mannheim 1982.
[2] Barker, R.: CASE* Method: tasks and deliverables. Wokingham, 1990.
[3] Chen, P.P.: The Entity-Relationship Model - Towards a Unified View of Data. In: ACM Transactions on Database Systems 1 (1976) 1, p. 9-36.
[4] Gutenberg, E.: Grundlagen der Betriebswirtschaftslehre, Band 1: Die Produktion. 24. ed., Berlin 1983.

[5] Halbert, J.: Data Integration in a Manufacturing Environment. In: Scheer, A.-W. (ed.) Proceedings of the Workshop Implementing CIM, Saarbrücken 1990, pp.227-235.

[6] Hars, A.; Heib, R.; Kruse, Chr.; Michely, J.; Scheer, A.-W.: Reference Models for Data Engineering in CIM. In: Computer Integrated Manufacturing - Proceedings of the 8th CIM-Europe Annual Conference, O'Neil, C.; MacConnail, P.; Van Puymbroeck, W. (eds.), Berlin 1992, p.249-260.

[7] Hars, A.; Klein, J.; Scheer, A.-W.: INMAS - A Uniform Approach to Data Exchange in Heterogeneous Environments. In Proth, J.-M. (ed.): Proceedings of the 8th International Conference on CAD/CAM, Robotics and Factories of the Future, Metz, France, August 17-19, 1992.

[8] Hildebrand, K.: Software Tools: Automatisierung im Software Engineering - Eine umfassende Darstellung der Einsatzmöglichkeiten von Software-Entwicklungswerkzeugen. Berlin 1990.

[9] Jorysz, H.R.; Vernadat, F.B.: CIM-OSA Part 2: Information View. In: International Journal of CIM, 3 (1990) 3/4, pp.157-167.

[10] Kremar, H.: Bedeutung und Ziele von Informationssytem-Architekturen. In: Wirtschaftsinformatik 32 (1990) 5, S.395-402.

[11] Lockemann P.C.; Dittrich, K.R.: Architektur von Datenbanksystemen, in: Lockemann, P.C.; Schmidt, J.W. (eds.): Datenbank-Handbuch. Berlin 1987, p. 87.

[12] Martin, J.: Information Engineering, Planning and Analysis. Englewood Cliffs, 1990.

[13] Olle, T.; Sol, H.; Tully, C.J. (eds.): Information Systems Design Methodologies: A Feature Analysis, Proceedings of the IFIP WG 8.1 Working conference on Feature Analysis of Information Systems Design Methodologies. Amsterdam 1983.

[14] Olle, T.W.; Hagenstein, J.; MacDonald, I.G.: Information Systems Methodologies: A Framework for Understanding. Wokingham 1988.

[15] Olle, T.W.; Verrijn-Stuart, A.A.; Bhabuta, L. (eds.): Computerized Assistance During The Information Systems Life Cycle. Proceedings of the IFIP WG 8.1 Working Conference on Computerized Assistance during the Information Systems Life Cycle, CRIS 88, Egham, England, 19-22 Sept. 1988, Amsterdam 1988.

[16] Preßmar, D.B.; Eggers, S.; Reinken, W.: Interaktive Entwurfsmethode zur computerunterstützten Herstellung betriebswirtschaftlicher Anwendungssoftware, in: Kurbel, K.; Mertens, P.; Scheer, A.-W. (eds.): Interaktive betriebswirtschaftliche Informations- und Kommunikationssysteme. Berlin 1989, p. 235-260.

[17] Rumbaugh, J. et al.: Object-Oriented Modeling and Design. Prentice Hall, Englewood Cliffs, 1991.

[18] Scheer, A.-W.: Architecture for Integrated Information Systems. Berlin, 1992.

[19] Scheer, A.-W.: Enterprise-Wide Data Modelling - Information Systems in Industry. Berlin 1989.

[20] Scheer, A.-W.: Principles of Efficient Information Management. 2nd ed., Berlin 1991, pp.35-43.

[21] Shlaer, F.; Mellor, F.: Object-Oriented Systems Analysis: Modeling the World in Data. Prentice Hall, Englewood Cliffs, 1988.

[22] Sol, H.: A Feature Analysis of Information Systems Desgin Methodologies. In Olle, T.; Sol, H.; Tully, C. (eds.): Information Systems Design Methodologies. Amsterdam 1983,

[23] Sommerville, I.: Software Engineering und Prototyping: Eine Konstruktionslehre für administrative Softwaresysteme. Berlin 1987.

[24] Strunz, H.: Zur Begründung einer Lehre von der Architektur informationsgestützter Informations- und Kommunikationssysteme. In: Wirtschaftsinformatik 32 (1990) 5, S.439-445.

[25] Tardieu, H.; Rochfeld, A.: La methode Merise. Vol.1, Paris 1983.

[26] Winter, F.; Maag, D.: AD/Cycle - Verstärkung für SAA? In: Information Management 5 (1990) 2, p.32-39.

The Use of a Lexicon to Interpret ER Diagrams: a LIKE project

Paul Buitelaar and Reind van de Riet

Free University
Department of Computer Science
de Boelelaan 1081
1081 HV Amsterdam

vdriet@cs.vu.nl

Abstract

In designing Information systems words are being used: words with a fixed meaning, such as keywords and words chosen by the designer denoting entities, relationships, attributes, values, actors, messages, etc. Usually these words have a certain meaning and usually their usage is according to that meaning. In this paper we will describe how a Lexicon, containing these words and their meaning, can be used fruitfully when combined with a CASE tool.

Keywords: CASE Tools; Conceptual Modelling; Lexicon; Object-Oriented Design

1 Introduction

The research reported in this paper has been carried out in the framework of the LIKE project. LIKE is a project in which researchers from Linguistics, Business Administration and Computer Science cooperate to investigate how Linguistic Instruments can be used in the area of Knowledge Engineering. One can think of Natural Language (NL) parsers, linguistic theories such as Functional Grammar (FG) and Lexicons. In this paper we will concentrate on the structure of a Lexicon which helps in the process of designing and building an Information and Communication System, ICS for short. As an example one can think of an office automation system where entities are represented as (active) objects, sending and receiving messages, inspecting and changing (object-oriented) databases.

In designing and building an ICS words are being used. In the requirements phase, words are used in NL sentences. These sentences express the specifications in a rough and (usually) ambiguous way. In the analysis phase more formal mechanisms are being used such as picture-based CASE tools (e.g. Software through Pictures -StP-

[Wasserman and Pirchner87]) and formal languages, with a precise (logical) semantics, to specify conceptual models, such as CPL (Conceptual Prototyping Language), which was developed within our group [Dignum and van de Riet91]. At this level words are being used to denote entities, relationships, agents, messages, etc. On the level of prototyping, where the design of the ICS can be tested by simulations with the MOKUM system [van de Riet89], again words are being used to name types, objects, collections, etc. Finally, at the implementation level, words are being used in data dictionaries and application programs.

Evidently, it would help the designers and programmers very much and the quality of the resulting software would be increased considerably, if all these words were used in a consistent way, corresponding to their meaning. For that purpose a Lexicon is needed containing these words with their meanings. This paper reports about an experiment in which the use of such a Lexicon has been studied.

The paper starts with a description of the experiment. It is shown how the CASE tool StP can be enhanced with a Lexicon to help the designer in specifying consistent diagrams. Then a short introduction is presented to CPL, the language we use for conceptual modelling. Further, some background knowledge on the history of a linguistic orientation in conceptual design and an overview of the structure and content of the Lexicon is given. Finally, a case study of the design of an Information System for a University Library is presented. The paper closes with our conclusions of the experiment.

In [Buitelaar and van de Riet92] we demonstrate also another use of the Lexicon. It is shown how the Lexicon can be used in generating CPL specifications from structured Natural Language sentences.

2 Short Description of the Experiment Reported in this Paper

In order to investigate whether the idea of using a Lexicon is a useful one, we performed the following experiment. First, we took a Universe of Discourse which is not too large, so that we could handle it, but large enough to be exposed to interesting problems. We chose a part of our University Library, described in a two-page document. Second, we decided to look at the picture-based CASE tool StP [Wasserman and Pirchner87] and whether this could be combined with the Lexicon into something useful.

This turned out to be fruitful. As a first approach we constructed a simple tool which used the Lexicon to check the diagrams produced by an information analyst. It checked the usage of words how they were attached to entities, relationships, active agents, attributes and data structures in ER Diagrams, Data Flow Diagrams and Data Structure Diagrams (ERD, DFD, DSD, respectively). However, the analyst had to indicate the different roles entities play in a relationship or as active agents in a communication.

Later we found out that the Lexicon could be used in a far more helpful way: not only could the usage of words be checked, the roles could be added. In fact it turned out that the combination of Diagrams and Lexicon provided enough information to generate CPL formulas more or less automatically from the (ER) Diagrams. It is about this experiment that we report in this paper (see figure below). In section 6 we will give details of this process.

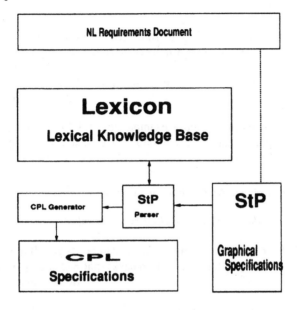

Fig. 1

3 An Introduction to CPL

The language CPL has been developed as a specification language as close as possible to natural language, but formal enough to specify the requirements of an ICS in a precise and unambiguous way. A formal semantics has been defined in [Dignum and van de Riet91]. Each CPL construct is translated into some form of (predicate, modal, deontic, temporal or dynamic) logic. A direct inspiration for CPL was Functional Grammar [Dik89], developed by Simon Dik, one of the participants in the LIKE project. The general form of a CPL specification is as follows:

```
Mode: Tense: Predication T1...Tn
            (id:....)
      (sit:....)
```

Mode =   **FACTUAL|MUST|NEC|PERMIT**
Tense =   **ACTION|DONE|PROSP|PERF|PRET**
Predication =   a relation between n terms T1...Tn, where a term denotes a
                (set of) object(s). Each object occurs in a specific role.

The 'id' part is for identification of the objects in the terms and the 'sit' part is to specify the situation in which this particular CPL sentence is supposed to hold. Mode and Tense say something about the modality and the time of the specification. For example, the following specification says, that the person with name 'John' is the parent of the person with name 'Mary'. PERF expresses that this fact (FACTUAL) is still valid.

FACTUAL: PERF: parent(**ref** = A in person)(**zero** = B in person)
        (**id:** has (**ref** = A in person) (**zero** = N in name)
                             (**id:** N = John))
        (**id:** has (**ref** = B in person) (**zero** = M in name)
                             (**id:** M = Mary))

Notice that the roles in the above example are: **ref** for referent, **zero** for 'not identified role' and **pat** for patient. In the following we shall also use: **ag** for agent and **go** for goal.

An example describing a precondition for an action:

A person can borrow three available books if he is a member.

PERMIT: ACTION: borrow(<1> **ag** = A in person) (<3> **go** = B in book)
        (**id:** has (**zero** = B in book) (**pat** = C in status)
                          (**id:** C = available))

        (**sit:** is_a (person) (member))

An example where an obligation for a person is specified. Note that the obligation may be violated by that person. However, it is not specified what should be done in such a case.

If a person borrows a book, he must return it within three weeks.

MUST: ACTION: return(**ag** = A in person) (**pat** = B in book) (**temp** = C in time)
            (**id:** C before T+3*week)

        (**sit: ACTION**: borrow(**ag** = A in person) (**pat** = B in book)
                (**temp** = T in time))

An example where an obligation for the (library) system is specified. This obligation is necessary (NEC):

If a user does not return a book then after one week the library sends him a reminder

NEC:ACTION: send(**ag** = A in library) (**pat** = B in reminder) (**rec** = C in user)
            (**temp** = T2 in time)
            (**id:** T2 = T1 + 1*week)

        (**sit:ACTION** ~return(**ag** = C in user) (**pat** = D in book)
            (**temp** = T1 in time))

4 A Linguistic Orientation in Conceptual Modelling

4.1 Some History

A linguistic orientation in conceptual design can be traced back to articles on the Entity Relationship approach [Chen76] and on early versions of the semantic datamodel [Smith and Smith77]. In the 80's we see the arrival of NIAM [Verheijen and Bekkum82], an information analysis method based on natural language analysis. NIAM is followed by other systems and methods, like DATAID [De Antonellis and Di Leva84], SAMPO [Auramäki et al88], TELL [Yonezaki90], GRAMMARS [Dijk et al89] and a system under developement at SISU [Dahlgren et al91].

In DATAID a linguistic filter to clean up the collected requirements has been specified. It includes the reduction of synonymical expressions to one expression and the resolution of homonyms by introducing suitable substitutes. It further makes implicit elements explicit and reduces repetitions and redundancies. Another system is SAMPO, of which an interesting feature is its use of 'speech act theory'. TELL is a natural language front end to software engineering, based on Montague grammar. GRAMMARS is a design method based on natural language analysis, much in the line of NIAM, but extended to incorporate also dynamic aspects of information systems.

4.2 The (Linguistic) Meaning of Diagrams and their Combinations

In order to make our position more clear let us describe the way we look at diagrams. An ER diagram represents relationships between some entities. Attributes can be attached to both entities and relationships. In the object-oriented paradigm we represent entities as (collections or classes of) objects and attributes as attributes of these objects. Linguistically speaking, entities correspond with nouns, attributes with adjectives / adverbs and relationships with verbs.

Diagrams which an information analyst can draw by means of a CASE tool are meant to define static structure and dynamic properties of the information system. Usually for the static structure one uses ER diagrams (ERD) and Data Structure Diagrams (DSD). For the dynamic aspects Data Flow Diagrams (DFD) are being used.

The situation is more complicated however. A DFD shows that there is some kind of communication between two processes by means of an arrow between two bubbles or boxes representing these processes. Furthermore there is a name and a DSD attached to this arrow so that the structure and name of the message which is sent can also be indicated. Evidently, when one wants to archive all messages in a database then the DFD together with the DSD's for the messages define the static structure of this database. So a DFD can be used to define static structure.

On the other hand one can attach to an ERD a dynamic aspect if it is combined with a Lexicon. The situation is that the Lexicon says what the roles are of the different entities connected to a relationship. When the relationship denotes an ACTION, and many do, one role is that of an AGENT. In fact it is exactly here that our experiment described in this paper focusses on: how to add these roles. So also the ERD may define dynamic properties.

The interesting observation is that the information in the Lexicon and the ERD in a sense makes the DFD more or less superfluous, because the Agent role (active object) in a relation, such as 'to borrow', is already specified in the Lexicon.

For instance considering *Students borrow books.*', we want the CPL formula belonging to this sentence to be:

ACTION: to_borrow_type (**ag** = student_type) (**pat** = book_type)

The tool we describe in section 6 uses the Lexicon to construct this formula from a simple ERD.

In the future we want to investigate how the Lexicon can be used in a combination of ERDs, DFDs, DSDs and ICDs (Information and Communication Diagram). The latter are a new type of diagram in which Communication and Information can be defined in a better way than with the current DFDs. In ICDs it should be possible to define cause-effect communication, as is done in a Petri net. Here we will base ourselves upon the work of Dietz, who is also a member of the LIKE project. Dietz uses linguistic notions in analyzing organizational problems concerning communication between 'subjects' (active objects) by means of so-called 'Communication Structure Diagrams' [Dietz92].

5 Content and Structure of the Lexicon

5.1 Introduction

The Lexicon consists of a syntactic and a semantic part. The latter we call Concept Lexicon [Nirenburg and Raskin87]. The Lexicon is indexed by words and phrases that are found in natural language. The Concept Lexicon is indexed by concepts, which are linked to words and phrases in the Lexicon. The syntactic part contains grammatical knowledge like part of speech (verb, noun, etc.).

The Lexicon is implemented in MOKUM, which is an object-oriented extension of Prolog [van de Riet89]. In MOKUM objects are defined by type definitions. The static part of the type definition comprises of the definition of (derived) attributes and constraints. In a derived attribute the value can be computed by means of Prolog rules. The dynamic part of a type definition consists of a script in which the behaviour of the objects of this type can be specified. The actual form is that of a finite state automaton: the object can (simultaneously) be in a (number of) state(s). The state transitions are governed by triggers. These triggers are usually messages sent by other objects or timers, set by the object itself.

For each linguistic construct (words, concepts, etc.) an objecttype is specified. These objecttypes are interrelated by a type hierarchy, which facilitates an efficient and conceptually clear way of describing linguistic generalizations. This approach is based on 'Typed Unification Grammar' [Uszkoreit88] and 'Inheritance Based Grammar' [Daelemans90].

5.2   The Concept Lexicon

The function of the Concept Lexicon is to supply the system with semantic knowledge on words, thus restricting the number of possible interpretations. For this purpose it has knowledge of the meanings of words from a domain specific sublanguage.

The structure of the Concept Lexicon is based on recent research in computational lexical semantics. Inspirations come from work on the Generative Lexicon [Pustejovsky89], Functional Grammar [Weigand89], Naive Semantics [Dahlgren88] and Subworld Concept Lexicons [Nirenburg and Raskin87]. Its main structure consists of three levels:

1. *Ontology*

   Primitive concepts, derived from CPL e.g. FACTUAL, PERMIT, SOA, etc.

2. *Common Sense*

   General concepts to be found in ordinary dictionaries, defined in terms of ontology primitives.

   In a later stage of the project we intend to use on this level the lexical database that was constructed on the basis of a machine readable dictionary by Willem Meijs and Piek Vossen, both members of the LIKE group [Dik, Meijs and Vossen91].

3. *Terminology*

   Domain specific concepts defined in terms of general concepts, augmented with knowledge that is specific for the domain.

   At this level the actual application of the Lexicon takes place. The higher levels (Ontology and Common Sense) are used only as a reference tool for generalizations to be made at the Terminology level.

The following figure shows a part of the Lexicon, which at the moment contains about 250 concepts and 200 words. The figure was generated by using the MOKUM animation facility that was implemented within our system to visualize the structure of the Lexicon [Croshere, Blom and van de Riet92]. The browser uses the graphical toolbox PCE [Anjewierden and Wielemaker89].

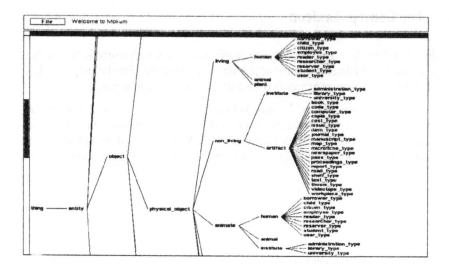

Fig. 2

5.3 Ontology

In the Ontology of the Concept Lexicon all basic notions of lexical semantic specification are introduced. Ontology concepts are the primitives of the specifications on the lower levels (Common Sense and Terminology). In this sense the Ontology constitutes the top of a lattice. The ordering of the lattice is based on the well-known is-a relationship. At the top of this lattice is the type ENTITY, which is differentiated into SOAs (State of Affairs), OBJECTs and ATTRIBUTEs.

SOAs are specified into ACTIONs, PROCESSes and STATEs:

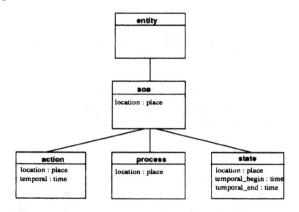

Fig. 3

OBJECTs are specified in a more-dimensional sublattice, of which we give the following example:

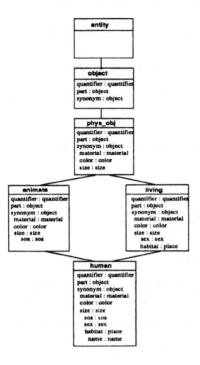

Fig. 4

ATTRIBUTEs are specified for instance as a QUANTIFIER or a STATUS:

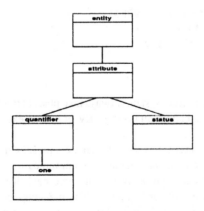

Fig. 5

5.4 Common Sense

Common Sense concepts are general concepts defined in terms of ontology primitives. Here (and on the Terminology level) the analysis is based mainly on [Pustejovsky89]. We distinguish the following substructures of lexical semantic structure.

Argument Structure   Arity and semantic types of the arguments of the function that is expressed by the concept. Argument Structure is reflected by the Argument Role attributes (AGENT, PATIENT, etc.) that are specified with predicative concepts in the Concept Lexicon.

Event Structure   Specification of the particular SOA type (ACTION, PROCESS, STATE) of the concept.

Example:

type to_receive_type **is_a** action
has_a agent:animate
has_a patient:object
has_a recipient:object.

Qualia Structure   Essential (but not necessary) attributes of the concept, according to Pustejovsky's distinction in Constitutive, Formal, Telic and Agentive roles.

Example: Constitutive (Prototypic features of a concept)

type car_type **is_a** physical_object
has_a manufacturer:company_type.

Example: Agentive (Prototypic SOA in which the concept acts)

type car_type **is_a** physical_object
has_a agentive:to_drive_type.

Example: Telic (Prototypic SOA in which the concept is used)

type book_type **is_a** physical_object
has_a telic:to_read_type
has_a agentive:to_write_type.

5.5 Terminology

Applications of the CL in actual systems always take place at the Terminology level. Restriction to a clearly distinct domain is necessary, or else an explosion of interpretations will occur.

Clarity in the definitions of the concepts that are represented in the Concept Lexicon is needed because vagueness, like in human communication, is not acceptable with computer systems. An information system at some bank has to know exactly what a customer means by 'deposit' or 'account'. The meanings of these words belong to the domain knowledge of 'banks'. So within domains some form of standardization is needed.

6   The University Library Case

6.1   Introduction

In this section we present a snapshot of a worked out example of linguistically motivated conceptual design, for further details see [Buitelaar and van de Riet92]. At the end of the paper an integrated ER diagram of the whole University Library case is to be found.

6.2   Example 1

As an example we take the following ER diagram:

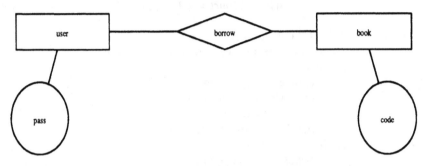

Fig. 6

The diagram is translated by a small C program into a set of Prolog facts:

    erd(borrow, [user, book]).

    has_a(user, [pass]).
    has_a(book, [code]).

The specifications are now available as input for our tool (StP-Parser / CPL-Generator), in order to check them and express their meaning in a formal way. The tool confronts the Prolog facts with the knowledge contained in the Lexicon, on the basis of which it makes the following inferences:

- USER is_a ANIMATE -> USER denotes an active object (= AGENT)

- BOOK is_a ARTEFACT -> BOOK has_a owner, size, color, use, etc.

- USER is_a HUMAN -> USER has_a sex, age, etc.

- BORROW -> RETURN

Finally, the tool generates the following CPL specification, considering the inferences just made. Note that '-' stands for NOT SPECIFIED by the information analyst. It is up to the analyst to add NOT SPECIFIED information to the specification, taking our tool as an advisory system for computer aided design.

FACTUAL: ACTION: to_return_type
    (location = -) (temporal = -)
    (agent = user_type)
     (whole =) (synonym =)
     (material = -) (color = -)
     (size = -) (sex = -)
     (habitat = -) (part = pass_type)
    (patient = book_type)
     (whole = -) (synonym = -)
     (material = -) (color = -)
     (size = -) (owner = -)
     (telic = -) (part = code_type)

(sit: **FACTUAL: ACTION:** to_borrow_type)
   (location = -) (temporal_begin = -) (temporal_end = -)
   (agent = user_type)
    (whole = -) (synonym = -)
    (material = -) (color = -)
    (size = -) (sex = -)
    (habitat = -) (part = pass_type)
   (patient = book_type)
    (whole = -) (synonym = -)
    (material = -) (color = -)
    (size = -) (owner = -)
    (telic = -) (part = code_type))

6.3 Example 2

Another example is the following ER diagram:

Fig. 7

Just one Prolog fact is generated from this diagram:

 erd(acquire, [library, book]).

The inferences that are made are:

- LIBRARY **is_a** INSTITUTE **is_a** ANIMATE -> LIBRARY denotes an active object (= AGENT)

- BOOK **is_a** ARTEFACT -> BOOK **has_a** owner, size, color, use, etc.

- LIBRARY is_a INSTITUTE is_a SOCIAL -> LIBRARY has_a function, processing, etc.

- ACQUIRE -> BENEFICIARY (for whom books are to be acquired)

The CPL specification then becomes:

FACTUAL: ACTION: to_acquire_type
                (location = -) (temporal = -)
                (agent = library_type)
                    (function =) (social =)
                (patient = book_type)
                    (whole = -) (synonym = -)
                    (material = -) (color = -)
                    (size = -) (owner = -)
                    (telic = -) (part = -)
                (beneficiary = -)

6.4 Some Problems

- Unfortunately not just one but many interpretations are generated by our tool. There are two reasons for this:

  - Many words have more than one meaning.

  - The semantic typing of roles is not sophisticated enough. Mostly more than one word can be a filler for more than one role.

- There is a danger of mapping each verb onto a relationship in ER diagrams.

  The verb 'to_reflect' for instance should of course not be treated in this way. No activity is expressed by this verb.

- In ER diagrams there is no possibility to express deontological operators like FACTUAL for factual, NEC for necessary, MUST for obligated and PERMIT for possible actions.

  In CPL however these distinctions are fundamental as a result of which the mapping from ER onto CPL becomes problematic. At the moment only a global solution is given for this problem in the sense that all actions are FACTUAL.

7 Conclusions

It is technically easy to combine StP and the Lexicon, because the Lexicon is structured as a Mokum object-oriented knowledge base which is based on Prolog. It was not necessary to change StP itself, a simple C program was made, which extracted the necessary information from StP's database (repository).

Neither was it a problem to interpret the (ER) diagrams by using the Lexicon in such a way that more information could be extracted from the diagrams than was put into them by the information analyst.

We have to admit, however, that the experiments reported in this paper are very limited. Actually, we did more experiments, with more ERDs and also with DFDs and DSDs. The main objection one could raise is that the Lexicon was very small with some 200 different words and some 250 different concepts. A Lexicon of practical use should be one hundred times as big. It does not need saying that to build such a Lexicon is quite an enterprise in itself. We are planning to do so within the LIKE context, using experiences of other LIKE partners [Dik, Meijs and Vossen91]. It is obvious that before doing so, extensive studies have to be made about such questions as how the Lexicon should be organized, what 'reasoning' capacities it should have (e.g. Inheritance) and whether it can be really used in building software. In other words there is still a long road to go. We have now explored only the beginning of this road.

We have demonstrated in this paper that the idea of using the meaning of words in tools for the design and construction of information systems is an interesting and viable one. Indeed it is in principle possible to enrich a CASE tool in such a way that diagrams get more meaning so that they can be used by information analysts and software designers in a more controlled manner, thereby enhancing the quality of the system designed.

8 Acknowledgements

We would like to thank Alco Blom for his support in programming matters, Hans Weigand for advice in linguistic and conceptual modelling problems, Robert Croshere for implementing the animation facility of MOKUM and Jan Wielemaker of the SWI institute in Amsterdam for giving us access to PCE.

9 Bibliography

[Anjewierden and Wielemaker89] PCE 3.6 User's Guide. Research report SWI, University of Amsterdam.

[Auramäki et al88] A speech-act based office modelling approach. ACM Transactions on Office Information Systems, Volume 6, Number 2, 126-152.

[Buitelaar and van de Riet92] A feasibility study in linguistically motivated object-oriented conceptual design. Research report Free University, forthcoming.

[Chen76] The Entity-Relationship Model: Toward a unified view of data. Transactions on Database Sytems, Volume 1, Number 1.

[Croshere, Blom and van de Riet92] An animation facility for MOKUM. Research report Free University, forthcoming.

[Daelemans90] Inheritance in Object-Oriented Natural Language Processing In: W. Daelemans and G. Gazdar (eds.) - Proceedings Workshop on Inheritance in Natural Language Processing, ITK Tilburg.

[Dahlgren88] Naive semantics for natural language understanding. Kluwer Academic

Publishers.

[Dahlgren et al91] Access to the Repository using Natural Language Knowledge. In: Proceedings Second Workshop Next Generation of Case Tools, Trondheim, May 1991.

[De Antonellis and Di Leva84] DATAID: A Database Design Methodology. IEEE Tutorial Notes 3.

[Dietz92] Modelling communication in organizations. In: R.P. van de Riet and R.A. Meersman (eds.) - Proceedings of the 1991 Workshop on Linguistic Instruments in Knowledge Engineering, Elsevier Science Publishers, 1992.

[Dignum and van de Riet91] How the modelling of knowledge bases can be based on linguistics and founded in logic. To appear in: Data and Knowledge Engineering.

[Dik89] A theory of Functional Grammar. Foris, Dordrecht.

[Dik, Meijs and Vossen91] LEXIGRAM: A lexico-grammatical tool for knowledge engineering. In: R.P. van de Riet and R.A. Meersman (eds.) - Proceedings of the 1991 Workshop on Linguistic Instruments in Knowledge Engineering, Elsevier Science Publishers, 1992.

[Dijk et al89] Taalkundige informatiesystemen ontwikkeld met GRAMMARS. Pandata Uitgeverij, Rijswijk.

[Nirenburg and Raskin87] The subworld concept Lexicon and the Lexicon Management System. In: Computational Linguistics, Volume 13, Numbers 3-4, 276-289.

[Pereira and Warren80] Definite Clause Grammars for language analysis - a survey of the formalism and comparison with augmented transition networks. Artificial Intelligence 13, p231-278.

[Pustejovsky89] The generative Lexicon. ms Brandeis University.

[van de Riet89] MOKUM: An object-oriented active knowledge base system. In: Data and Knowledge Engineering 4 (1989), p21-42.

[Smith and Smith77] Database abstractions: aggregation and generalization. Transactions on Database Systems, Volume 2, Number 2, 105-133.

[Uszkoreit88] From Feature Bundles to Abstract Data Types: New directions in the representation and processing of linguistic knowledge. In: A. Blaser (ed.) - Natural language on the computer, Proceedings scientific symposium on syntax and semantics for processing and man-machine communication, Heidelberg, FRG, February 1988. Lecture Notes in Computer Science 320.

[Verheijen and Bekkum82] NIAM: An Information Analysis Method. In: T.W. Olle et al (eds.) - Information Systems Design Methodologies: A feature analysis, North Holland.

[Wasserman and Pirchner87] A graphical, Extensible Integrated Environment for Software Developement. ACM SIGPLAN Notices, Vol. 22, No. 1, 1987, pp. 131-142.

[Weigand89] Linguistically motivated principles of knowledge base systems. Ph.D. Thesis, Department of Mathematics and Computer Science, Free University, Amsterdam.

[Yonezaki90] Natural language interface for requirements specification. In: Matsumoto and Ohno (eds.) - Japanese perspectives in software engineering. Addison-Wesley Publ., 41-76.

Appendix: ER Diagram of the University Library Case

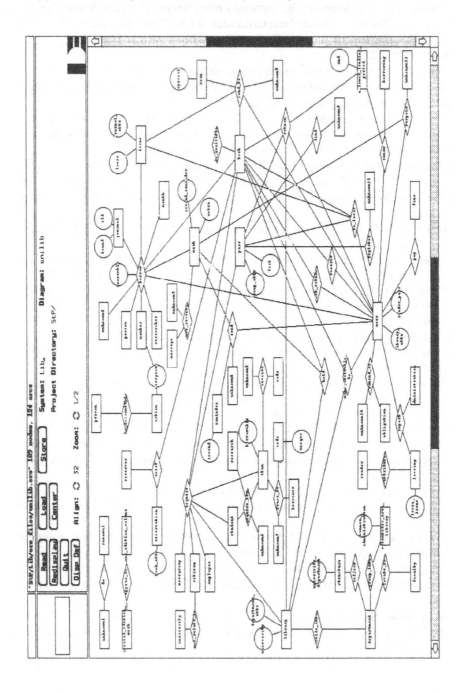

An Entity-Relationship-based Methodology for Distributed Database Design: An Integrated Approach Towards Combined Logical and Distribution Designs

Hong-Mei Chen Garcia[1] and Olivia Liu R. Sheng[2]

[1] Department of Decision Science, University of Hawaii, Honolulu, HI 96822 USA
[2] MIS Department, University of Arizona, Tucson, AZ 85721 USA

Abstract. This paper presents an integrated, general methodology (SEER-DTS Methodology) for relational homogeneous distributed database (DDB) design. The SEER-DTS methodology employs two ER-based data models: SEER (Synthesized Extended Entity-Relationship model) for static data modeling and DTS (Distributed Transaction Scheme) for dynamic data modeling. Rules are provided to transform the application semantics represented by SEER and DTS into "performance-oriented" logical and fragmentation design schemata. The formal treatment of distributed transaction information by DTS leads to an integrated requirement/distribution analysis and conceptual design as well as allows for a combined logical and fragmentation design. This simplifies the DDB designer's tasks and thus increases their effectiveness and productivity. The SEER-DTS methodology has been subjected to validation through a real-world case study and a laboratory experiment. Moreover, a computer-aided DDB design tool (Auto-DDB) which automates the SEER-DTS methodology has been prototyped.

1 Introduction

A homogeneous distributed database (DDB) is a collection of multiple databases logically integrated but physically distributed over a computer network [8,24]. DDB design is an alternative to centralized database design (CDB) for applications which have stringent performance/cost requirements. It is often claimed that a DDB design has potential advantages over a CDB design, including local autonomy, improved system performance, higher reliability and availability, and lower costs [8,17,20,24]. However, such advantages can only be achieved through proper DDB designs [17]. As distributed database (DDB) applications are increasing (driven by advances in networking and database technologies) [25], good DDB designs are difficult to achieve and expert designers are relatively few in number, an effective DDB design methodology is called for to help non-expert DDB designers manage design complexity and improve their productivity.

In the conventional DDB design methodological framework, the DDB design process is decomposed into several phases to handle design complexity (see Figure 1). DDB designers are assumed to perform the requirement analysis, conceptual design and logical design in the same manner as in a CDB design process. After generating a global logical design (a set of relations), the designers address distribution design problems (i.e., fragmentation design and fragment allocation design). Fragmentation design determines appropriate units for allocation or *fragments*, obtained by partitioning relations vertically or horizontally. Fragment allocation design determines the placement, replication and movement of fragments to different network sites.

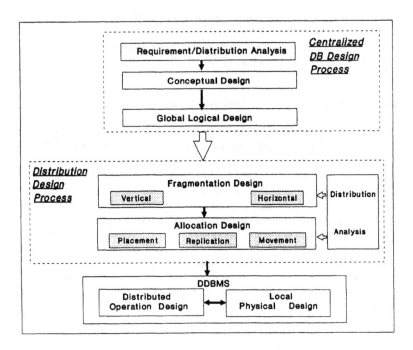

Fig. 1. Conventional DDB Design Process

Closer examination of the conventional methodology based on a real world DDB design case study [14,20] reveals that isolating of CDB design from distribution design appears to simplify the formulation of the problem but actually contributes to the complexity, inefficiency and ineffectiveness of DDB design. First, the separation ignores the impact of logical design on the distribution design. Relational logical design in a CDB design process primarily relies on normalization theory, which facilitates update processing but penalizes retrieval performance [12,29]. Taking a set of relations in higher normal forms (produced from a conventional CDB logical design process) as fragmentation design input may generate unnecessary fragments and thereby 1) exponentially increase the computational time/cost of fragment allocation design and 2) cause costly intra-site or inter-site joins of fragments during retrieval operations. Second, the separation prevents the easy transition of design inputs and design schema from CDB design to distribution design. Both"performance-oriented" logical design and distribution design require similar inputs which are acquired repeatedly. "Semantics-based" schema transformation (such as one in Logical Relational Design

Methodology (LRDM) [30] for CDB design) for distribution design was not offered to shield designers from dealing directly with complex DDB design theories/algorithms and decision models.

In view of these problems, a "good" general DDB design methodology must overcome the conventional separation of CDB and distribution design processes and resolve the DDB design problem in an integrated manner. Such a methodology is required 1) to acquire design inputs easily and effectively from the domain experts and to model the design inputs for use in all DDB design phases, 2) to provide seamless, structured transformation of design inputs and design schema from one design phase to the subsequent one, 3) to integrate database theories and algorithms that solve design subproblems into solving the DDB design as a whole, and 4) to be easily automated.

The SEER-DTS design methodology was developed to meet these requirements formulated through a case study of a real-world DDB design project [14,20]. In view of the end-user understandability and rich modeling capabilities of Entity-Relationship (ER) approach, the SEER-DTS methodology employs two ER-based data models: SEER (Synthesized Extended Entity-Relationship model) and DTS (Distributed Transaction Scheme) to facilitate DDB design from requirement analysis to distribution design. In the next section, we justify our ER-based approach for distributed data modeling and outline how the conventional separation of CDB and distribution designs could be bridged. In Section 3, the modeling constructs of SEER and DTS and their use for facilitating DDB design are presented. In Section 4, the SEER-DTS design process is described and design transformation rules are highlighted. Validation/automation of the SEER-DTS methodology and our conclusion are contained in Section 5.

2 The Methodology Development

This section presents our rationale for adopting ER-based models and a combined logical and fragmentation design process for our proposed DDB design methodology.

2.1 ER-based Approach to Distributed Data Modeling: SEER and DTS

Due to the need for acquiring DDB design inputs from domain experts and system users, we adopted the idea of semantic data modeling, a technique that has been effectively used in conceptual design to mediate between requirement analysis and logical design in CDB design [2,3,4,16,18,19,25,28,30]. Semantic data models provide logical data independence and serve as an effective communication/documentation means between users and designers. Techniques have been developed to transform conceptual schema in semantic data models into CDB logical schema in traditional data models (e.g., relational, hierarchical, network data models) for implementation [3,4,30].

The semantic data models and associated schema transformation techniques developed for CDB design are inadequate for DDB design, however. The inadequacy is twofold. First, data distribution design is concerned with dynamic information, e.g., transaction types, volume and frequencies of transactions at each site, number of access to objects by each transaction, and the original sites and result sites of the transactions [1,17,22,24,29]. Although the importance of dynamic modeling has been emphasized, most semantic data models developed for CDB design only model the static data structure of the database. TAXIS [5], ACM/PCM [6] and Event model [19] have included dynamic modeling, but these models are mainly concerned with procedural abstraction of transactions and have not modeled the distributed aspects of transactions. Nor have they discussed how to structure the transactions to facilitate DDB design. Second, DDB design relies on application knowledge to derive design heuristics. In particular, good selection predicates for horizontal fragmentation are often based on the subtyping of objects [17] and vertical fragmentation generally is based on decomposition of objects and "views" [9,17,22] (aggregation of attributes) of an object in different applications. Because most semantic data models have been developed for CDB design, subtyping (generalization) relationships have been used to derive designs that minimize storage redundancy. Different views of objects are derived only after a logical schema has been obtained. No effort has been made to address how the application semantics in a distributed environment can be represented and used for facilitating relational distribution design.

To overcome this inadequacy, we developed DTS to formalize the description of distributed transaction information and SEER, which has explicit constructs for facilitating relational distribution design. The guidelines for developing DTS and SEER include complete provisions for DDB design inputs, DDB design facilitation, end-user understandability, and easy automation. Separating SEER and DTS modeling results in the advantage of modularity, because the dynamic aspect will change more frequently than the static aspect. Furthermore, because users cannot be expected to have complete *a priori* application knowledge, the DTS modeling can deduce other possibly unanticipated static and dynamic information. DTS specifications can also serve as high-level application program specifications and can be used in DDB design simulation.

2.2 Bridging the Conventional Separation of CDB and Distribution Design

The conventional separation of CDB design and fragmentation design is ineffective and inefficient for both logical and fragmentation designs. Conventional logical design procedures primarily rely on normalization theory, which facilitates update processing and yet penalizes query retrieval performance. Researchers and practitioners investigating this problem have developed techniques that involve cost/benefit tradeoff analysis and "denormalization" heuristics to generate "performance-oriented" logical schema (see a survey in [14]). Denormalization principle states: *if two or more objects (relations) are very frequently retrieved together and are only very infrequently updated, and if full normalization would separate those objects, then the design should be denormalized to bring the objects together* [29]. This will avoid costly "join" operations in the DB implementation stage.

"Performance-oriented" logical design has to consider how the database is used, including transaction types, volume, frequencies, access type, etc. In the conventional DB design process where the two designs are separated, not only are design inputs to each repeatedly specified, but vertical fragmentation may further the degree of normalization or normalize already "denormalized" relations, because the conventional fragmentation design method takes a set of relations as design input without differentiating retrieval or update queries on these relations.

To remedy this problem, "performance-oriented" logical design and fragmentation design should be considered together, a natural association. From the viewpoint of physical design, relations and fragments essentially have one to one correspondence to physical files and subfiles. They both deal with the logical "clustering" of data items and determine the joins that a query might use and thus affect the query performance of the database. As a result, the logical and fragmentation designs should be combined, whereas schema design for objects in retrieval and update transactions should be separated due to performance consideration. "Denormalization" should only be applied where there is little penalty on update transactions and integrity control.

The SEER-DTS methodology therefore combines the logical and fragmentation design processes to generate a logical schema that preserves an accurate representation of real-world relationships while remaining oriented to efficient database performance. At the same time, a fragmentation schema which maximizes the performance of both DDB update and retrieval operations is generated. Static and Dynamic data modeling support (e.g. SEER and DTS) was developed to acquire the information needed for both designs in an integrated manner. In addition, design techniques were developed to advance the existing fragmentation methods by considering performance refinements of fragmentation design according to the transaction information modeled in DTS.

3 SEER and DTS for Distributed Database Modeling

In this section, the development and modeling constructs of SEER and DTS are detailed. The same modeling mechanisms are used for both.

3.1 Modeling the Static Structure - SEER

SEER is synthesized primarily from models [4,10,16,18,21,30] in the Entity and Relationship (ER) model family, which provides modeling expressiveness and ease of transformation from ER-based models to relational logical schema. The SEER constructs are graphically represented in Figure 2. As an extension of the ER model, SEER modeling is *object-based* (structurally object-oriented) and has three classes of objects: entities, attributes and relationships [4,10,15,18]. *Entities* are the principal data objects about which information is to be collected. For DDB design purposes, we model the size (cardinality) of the entities in SEER. Entities can be distinguished by the "strength" of their identifying attributes. Strong entities have internal identifiers that uniquely determine the existence of entity occurrences. Weak entities derive their existence from the identifying attributes of one or more "parent" entities. *Attributes* describes the properties of entities. There are two kinds of attributes, i.e., identifiers, which uniquely distinguish among the occurrences of an entity, and descriptors, which describe an entity occurrence.

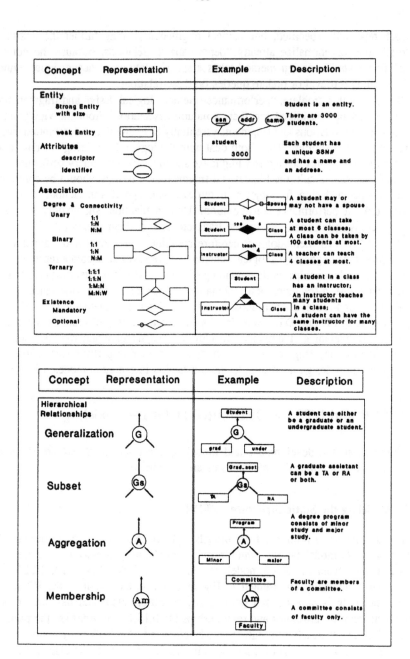

Fig. 2. SEER Constructs and Graphical Representations

Relationships relate one or more real-world entities. To support DDB design, the modeling of relationships in [10] is augmented. Relationships are nonhierarchical or hierarchical. A nonhierarchical relationship, called an **association**, relates one or more independent entities. (It corresponds to the relationships originally defined in the ER model.) Associations are described in terms of degree (number of entities participating in a relationship, e.g., unary, binary, ternary), connectivity (entity occurrence, 1 to 1, 1 to many, many to many), cardinality (the actual number associated with the "many" side), and existence (existence of an entity in an association is either optional or mandatory).

SEER models four types of hierarchical relationships, synthesized from abstraction mechanisms commonly used in database models, knowledge representation schemes and programming language constructs [5,6,18,23,27,30]. A **generalization** (*is-a*) relationship partitions an entity type (or class) into mutually exclusive subtypes (or subclasses). A **subset** relationship is also an *is-a* relationship except that every occurrence of the generic entity may also be an occurrence of other entities that are potentially overlapping subsets. An **aggregation** (*is-part-of*) relationship combines low-level objects into a composite object. A **membership** relationship is a special case of aggregation relationship. The component objects are of the same type. Generalization/subset relationships can naturally represent "subtyping" of objects to facilitate "performance-oriented" logical and horizontal fragmentation.

Existing data models implicitly specify an aggregation relationship by using attributes in an entity, a one-to-one or a one-to-many relationship. SEER explicitly models aggregation relationships so that the natural decomposition of an object is made obvious in order to facilitate vertical fragmentation design and so that the abstraction mechanism can be used to structure transactions. The distinctions between subset and aggregation relationships allow the integrity constraints among subtypes/components to be explicitly modeled.

3.2   Modeling the Dynamic Aspect - DTS

The development of DTS has employed such ideas from earlier transaction modeling research as the localization principle [6], procedural abstraction [5,6], exception handling, and using data abstraction mechanisms (e.g., generalization and aggregation) to organize transactions [5,6,19,23]. We further developed mechanisms (frame-based slots) for capturing properties/descriptions of transactions required by DDB design, according to several representative DDB design decision models [1,7,9,22]. The hierarchical structure permits easy automation for modular DB design.

A DTS models a *transaction* described by the following properties (slots).

Transaction-id. A transaction-id describes the *operation type* of a transaction (retrieve, insert, delete or update) and the *focal object*, which is the application "view" of real world objects such as forms or reports or queries in different applications [9,11]. Users can describe their transaction processing using a *transaction-id* without knowing pre-defined relations. *Operation types* of transactions are critical information for deciding what logical and fragmentation design rules (normalization or denormalization) should be applied. In Figure 3, the transaction-id Retrieve Transcript uniquely identifies a transaction of the type Retrieve that operates on a "form" Transcript. An DTS *focal object* corresponds to an entity in any hierarchical/nonhierarchical relationship or association, but not attributes in SEER (detailed transformation rules are in Section 4.1). The transaction-id also indicates if this transaction *is part of* (ispartof) or *is a* (isa) specialized type of a parent transaction. As shown in Example 2.1 and Example 2.2 (see Figure 4), the transaction Retrieve Student is *a part of* Retrieve Transcript and Retrieve Grad-Student *is a* specialized transaction of Retrieve Student.

Transaction Access. The access key and access method of a transaction are specified to indicate the volume as well as the searching pattern of a transaction in order to facilitate fragmentation design. For instance, in Example 1, **One**(SSN) means SSN is used to retrieve *one* student. Three types of accesses are defined in DTS. Random access (denoted as **One**) selects one instance of a given object. Sequential access (**All**) selects all or a large subset of instances of an object. Boolean query accesses (**Subset**) selects a group of instances based on simple or minterm predicates [24]. When Subset access is specified, the predicates should be specified for determining the candidate fragments. Given candidate fragments, the horizontal fragmentation is determined according transaction access types. Horizontal fragmentation benefits transactions that access one or a subset of objects (to be translated to relations) by leading to a smaller search space (i.e., searching for a graduate student vs. the whole student body.) Fragmentation is generally not appropriate for sequential search transactions because additional disk seek time is required to search for other fragments.

Statistics. The statistics of transactions are design parameters for logical, fragmentation and allocation designs. Statistics indicate the frequency and volume of each access of the transaction and model where data (transaction objects) are requested or sent. Here, we assume that the sites requesting the transactions are the same as the ones to which the results will be sent. If a transaction occurs at multiple sites, then total frequency as well as individual frequency at each site will be specified.

Related objects. *Related objects* are subordinate objects resulting from decomposition of the *focal object*. They allow users to think of the natural decomposition of a focal object and thereby facilitate conceptual design and fragmentation design. In Example 1 (Figure 3), Transcript is decomposed into related objects, Student, Class, and ~Grade. *Related objects* can also be attributes, in which case they are indicated by ~. In Example 1 (Figure 3), the related objects for Class are ~Course-No, ~Course-name, ~Section-No, and ~Instructor.

Procedures. A procedure states the integrity rules and provides control structures for dependent transactions which are identified by an *operation type* and a *related object*. Procedures are specified by the IF-THEN phrase. An *IF* clause specifies precondition for database operations (user-defined integrity constraints or business rules); a *THEN* clause defines dependent transactions (database operations). A dependent transaction can be an application transaction or an atomic transaction. An *application transaction* consists of one or more application or atomic transactions. An *atomic transaction* affects only an attribute or attributes of an object (an entity or a relationship in SEER). The DTS modeling will terminate at the atomic transaction level. The control structure (*And* and *Or*) in DTS corresponds to the hierarchical relationships in SEER and allows parent and dependent transactions to be related by aggregation/membership and generalization/subset, respectively, and processed by application

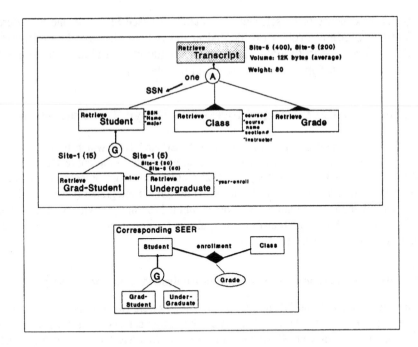

Fig. 3. DTS Graphical Representation and Corresponding SEER (Example 1)

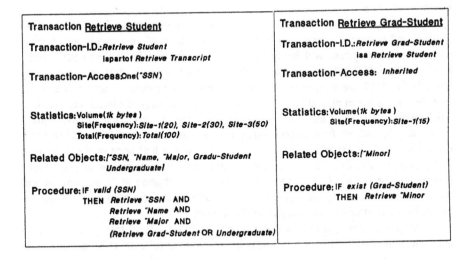

Fig. 4. DTS Textual Representation (Example 2.1 and Example 2.2)

programs in sequence or by selection. In example 2.1 (see Figure 4), the procedure of Retrieve Student involves two dependent transactions Retrieve Grad-Student "OR" Retrieve Undergraduate, meaning Grad-student and Undergraduate are two subtypes of Student and will be accessed by selection.

4 The SEER-DTS Design Process and Design Transformation

The SEER-DTS methodology 1) is based on SEER and DTS which have complete and consistent modeling mechanisms for providing inputs to the entire DDB design and facilitating DDB schema design, and 2) employs a design process in which requirement/distribution analysis and conceptual design are integrated (Design Activity I) and logical and fragmentation design are combined (Design Activity II). The design process is outlined here and transformation rules in the design process are highlighted. Please refer to [14] for detailed description.

4.1 Integrated Requirement/Distribution Analysis & Conceptual Design

As shown in Figure 5, the SEER-DTS methodology offers two-way design flexibility for the designers/users in Design Activity I: The design can start with DTS modeling (Entry from DTS) or with SEER modeling (Entry from SEER). Users can go back and forth between these two entry points but consistency control procedures should be followed to maintain consistency between SEER and DTS modeling.

Entry from DTS

DTS modeling is the mechanism that integrates requirement analysis, distribution analysis and conceptual design. In Step 1, the "global view" of transactions (S-level transaction) in a system will be captured in the Enterprise DTS hierarchical specification. The SEER-DTS methodology allows users to specify clusters (subsystems) through the DTS abstraction mechanism, aggregation or decomposition. The DTS modeling mechanism also allows flexible aggregation (reuse) of old transactions into new subsystems without affecting or duplicating existing transaction specifications.

In Step 2, analysis focuses on a subsystem or a subsubsystem (a logical or functional unit, such as Registration subsystem), which is a leaf node of the Enterprise DTS. Each **dominating** current and future transaction (routine and ad hoc) of a subsystem will be modeled using the DTS templates, anchoring at forms, reports and queries used in these systems (I-level DTS). DTS constructs help users to specify distribution information necessary for DDB design.

In Step 3, a corresponding SEER Diagram from an I-level transaction is generated. The main DTS-to-SEER transformation rules are as follows: 1) Model $i+1$-level objects which have an identifier (key) specified as an entity. Attach attributes. For instance, Student and Class in Example 1 (see Figure 3); 2) Model the $i+1$-level objects which have no identifiers of their own but have many related objects in the $i+2$-level transaction attached to it as a weak entity; 3) Set the $i+1$-level objects which have no identifiers of their own and do not have any related objects in $i+2$-level transaction as *candidate attributes for relationships* to be defined in the following

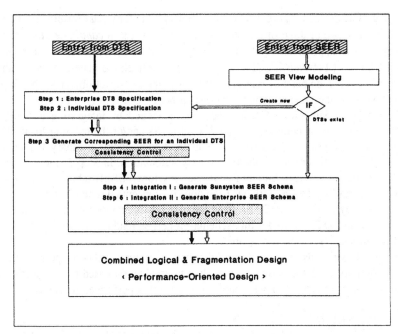

Fig. 5. SEER-DTS Design Process

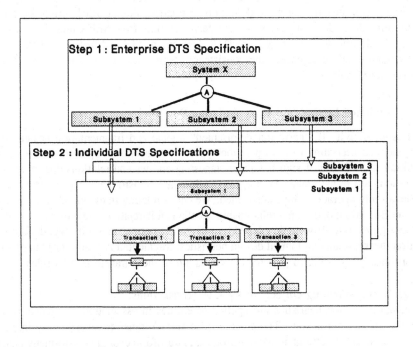

Fig. 6. System Level (*S*-Level) DTS Modeling

steps, e.g., Grade (see Figure 3); 4) Create binary or ternary relationships (use a role name) for any two or three of the entities involved; 5) Attach *candidate attributes for relationships* to appropriate relationships (i.e., Grade is the attribute of the relationship Enrollment between Student and Class); 6) Attach the generalization, subset, aggregation and membership relationships below the $i+1$-level object to the entities created, such as the generalization relationship below Student (see Figure 3).

In Step 4, a Subsystem SEER schema is generated by integrating corresponding SEER diagrams generated from an I-level DTSs and/or the existing local SEER schema in a subsystem. The SEER-DTS methodology adopts a binary ladder integration strategy [2] for its simplicity and easy automation. In Step 5, the Subsystem SEER schema is integrated into an Enterprise (or Global) SEER schema, which is not a trivial undertaking. Much work has been done on conceptual schema integration (see [2] for a survey). The SEER-DTS methodology extends previous work on conceptual design by using DTS to model interschema properties readily and help resolve type and key conflicts (see [14] for details).

Although we focus on requirement/distribution analysis and conceptual design in Design Activity I, identification of candidate fragmentation based on application semantics (e.g., data types, "views", subset predicates) is performed at the same time.

Entry from SEER

Many useful design guidelines for static data modeling [29] are integrated into the SEER-DTS methodology. Without DTS to anchor "focal" objects, the classification of entities and attributes and the definition of relationships in SEER might be relatively difficult. In addition, a new system design starting from SEER modeling has to repeat the design steps in Entry from DTS. Objects in DTS and SEER are compared and cross-referenced to ensure the consistency, correctness and completeness of the information acquired.

4.2 Combined Logical and Fragmentation Design

In Design Activity II, "performance-oriented" logical and fragmentation design will be generated according to the operation types of transactions: Update or Retrieve (include Insert). The design has three stages: 1) entities and relationships in update operations are transformed; 2) *marginal* entities are transformed; and 3) entities in retrieval-only operations are transformed. We call a relation transformed from an entity, an E-relation; one from a relationship is called an R-relation. Transformation rules for Design Activity II were developed by integrating normalization theory, denormalization theory, relational logical design heuristics, fragmentation design principles and algorithms. Please refer to [14] for the validation of these transformation rules.

Stage 1. Transforming Objects in Update Transactions.

First, normalization heuristics are applied to entities in association relationships involving update transactions. The general rules are: 1) transform every entity into an E-relation with the key and non-key attributes, 2) transform every many-to-many unary or binary relationship into a R-relation, and 3) transform each ternary relationship into an R-relation (see [14,29,30] for details). Second, transformation rules for hierachical relationships based on considerations for maximizing DDB design performance are applied. For example, the rules for transforming the generalization relationship are according to transaction access types:

- If a transaction is to exclusively process the supertype in the generalization relationship with access method "ALL", create a total of $3 + N$ E-relations for the supertype and $2 + N$ subtypes.
- If no transaction processes on the supertype (common attributes) exclusively with "All" access method, $2 + N$ E-relations should be created, Each consisting of common attributes and specialization attributes of a subtype. A vertical fragmentation (one fragment with specialization attributes and the other with common attributes) may be created for each of the $2 + N$ E-relations based on "views".

Vertical fragmentation is based on "views," e.g., subsets of attributes processed by different transactions (see Figure 7 for an example), and type disparity (image data type). Horizontal fragmentation is applied last according to the simple predicates associated with "Subset" transaction access type. If several transactions with different access types are operating on the same E-relation, the frequencies and volume of the conflicting transactions will be compared to determine the final horizontal fragmentation.

Stage 2: Handling "Marginal Entities."
Marginal entities are objects which have relationships with objects involving both retrieval and update operation types or opposite. An marginal object involving both types of operations should have already been transformed into an E-relation according to the rules for "Marginal entity" in Stage 1. The E-relation should include foreign keys from marginal entities in retrieval-only operations which it has 1-1 or M-1 relationships with. The M-M relationship between the marginal entities. should be transformed into an R-relation.

Stage 3: Transforming in Retrieval Only Transactions
The creation of relations for objects in retrieval-only transactions involves denormalization heuristics or materialization of "join" operations. The rules are restricted to materialize equi-join on the identifiers instead of non-key attributes to avoid a large volume of redundant storage space. Join on identifier domain is representative of the queries used in practice. The denormalization of entities in one-to-one and one-to-many relationships (creating multiple columns in an E-relation for the many-side entity) is straightforward. However, rules for the materialization of cross-product join for entities involved in many-to-many relationships are under very restrictive conditions. Often a "Half-Join" (a relation which materializes the join of an E-relation in M-M relationship with the R-relation transformed from the M-M relationship) is created to facilitate the the transaction with higher frequency and volume (see Figure 8 for an example). Horizontal fragmentation is created last according to the Subset access predicates, if any. Rules for derived fragmentation are also applied also.

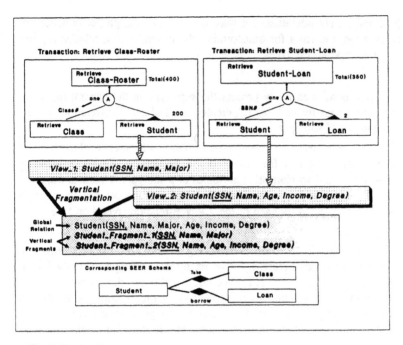

Fig. 7. Vertical Fragmentation based on "Views" (Example)

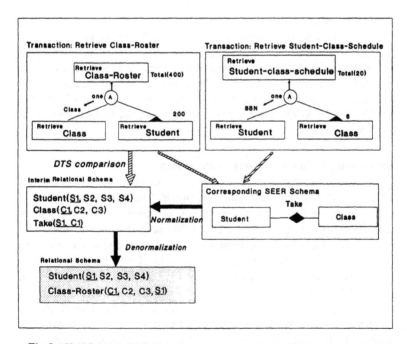

Fig. 8. "Half-Join" in CLD Stage 3: An Example of Transforming Entities in an Retrieval-Only Operations

5 Conclusion

As an initial effort, the SEER-DTS methodology aims at overcoming problems with the conventional separation of CDB and distribution design and resolving DDB design problems in an integrated manner. The applicability of the SEER-DTS methodology has been validated through a real world DDB design case study and a prototype of Auto-DDB. The research site for the case study was the Student Information Systems (SIS) at the University of Arizona . The unit of analysis was the application of the SEER-DTS methodology by novice DDB designers using a manual design mode. Novice DDB designers are defined as designers who lack DDB design experience and substantial DDB design knowledge.

The output of the SIS case study was used as a test case for the Auto-DDB prototype. Functionalities of the Auto-DDB prototype were incrementally developed according to the testing of the SIS case. (Please refer to [13,14] for the Auto-DDB architectural design and implementation.) The Auto-DDB prototype is an Microsoft Window Visual Basic application. So far, 25,000 lines of Visual Basic code have been implemented.

A laboratory experiment was conducted to compare the SEER-DTS methodology with a methodology (we call it the Conventional Best Methodology) which aggregates representative design techniques in a conventional DDB design methodology process (e.g., LRDM [30] for conceptual/logical design, Attribute Affinity Algorithm in [22] for vertical fragmentation design and horizontal fragmentation in [24] for horizontal fragmentation design). Used in the experiment were CASE tools which automated both methodologies with the same hardware/software platforms and the same window-based user interface. The results of the experiment showed that the SEER-DTS methodology in an automated design mode, performed by non-expert/novice DDB designers, produced better design outcomes in terms of design effectiveness (completeness and correctness) and efficiency (development time). However, there was no statistically significant difference between the two methodologies when compared for user-perceived ease of use. Further research is planned to continue developing and validating of the SEER-DTS methodology and associated CASE tools.

References

1. Apers, P.M.G., "Data Allocation in Distributed Database Systems." *ACM TODS*, Vol. 13, No. 3, Sep. 1988, pp. 263–304.
2. Batini, C., Lenzerini, M. and Navathe, S.B., "A Comparative Analysis of Methodologies for Database Schema Integration." *ACM Computer Surveys*, Vol. 18, No. 4, Dec. 1986, pp. 323–364.
3. Berman, Sonia. "A Semantic Data Model as the Basis for an Automated Database Design Tool." *Information Systems*. Vol. 11, No.2, pp. 149 -165, 1986.
4. Blaha, M.R., Premerlani, W.J. and Rumbaugh, J.E. "Relational Database Design Using an Object-Oriented Methodology," *Communications of ACM*, Vol. 31, No. 4, Apr. 1988, pp. 414–427.
5. Borgida, A., Mylopoulos, J. and Wong, H. K. T. "Generalization/Specialization As a Basis for Software Specification." in *On Conceptual Modeling: Perspectives from Artificial Intelligence, Databases, and Programming Language*. Edited by M. L. Brodie, J. Mylopoulos and J. W. Schmidt, 1984, pp. 88 - 117.
6. Brodie, Michael L. and Dzenan, Ridijanovic. "On the Design and Specification of Database Transactions." in *On Conceptual Modeling : Perspectives from Artificial Intelligence, Databases, and Programming Language*. Edited by M. L. Brodie, J. Mylopoulos and J. W. Schmidt, 1984, pp. 278 - 312.

7. Ceri, S., Navathe, S. and Wiederhold, G. "Distribution Design of Logical Database Schemas." *IEEE Transactions on Software Engineering*, Vol. SE-9, No. 4, July, 1983.

8. Ceri, S. and Pelagatti, G. *Distributed Databases : Principles and Systems*, McGraw-Hill, 1984.

9. Chang. S. K., and Cheng, W. H. "A Methodology for Structured Database Decomposition." *IEEE Transactions on Software Engineering*, Vol. SE-6, No. 2, pp. 205-218, March, 1980.

10. Chen, P. P. "The Entity-Relationship Model - Toward a Unified View of Data." *ACM Transaction on Database Systems, Vol. 1, No. 1*, March 1976, pp. 9 -36.

11. Choobineh, J., Mannino, M.V., Nunamaker, J. and Konsynski, B.R. "An Expert Database Design System Based on Analysis of Forms." *IEEE Trans. on Software Engineering*, Vol. 14, No. 2, Feb. 1988, pp. 242–253.

12. Dewan, R. M. and Gavish, B. "Models for the Combined Logical and Physical Design of Databases." *IEEE Transactions on Computers, Vol. 38, No. 7*, July 1989, pp. 955-967.

13. Garcia, Hong-Mei C. and Liu Sheng, Olivia R. "A semantics-Based Methodology for Integrated Computer-Aided Distributed Database Design." In the proceedings of *25th Hawaii International Conference on System Science*, January 1992.

14. Garcia, Hong-Mei C. " A Semantics-based Distributed Database Design Methodology: Towards Combined Logical and Fragmentation Designs and Design Automation." *Ph.D. Dissertation*, University of Arizona, 1992.

15. Gupta, Rajiv, ed. *Object-Oriented Database Systems with Applications to CASE, Networks and VLSI CAD*. Prentice-Hall, 1991.

16. Hammer, M., and Mcleod, D. "Database Description with SDM: A Semantic Data Model." *ACM Transactions on Database Systems, Vol. 6, No. 3*, Sept. 1981, pp. 351-386.

17. Hevner, L.R. and Rao, A. "Distributed Data Allocation Strategies." *Advances in Computers*, edited by M.C. Yovits, Academic Press, 1988, pp. 121–155.

18. Hull, R. and King, R. "Semantic Database Modeling: Survey, Applications, and Research Issues." *ACM Computing Surveys*, Vol. 19, No. 3, Sep. 1987, pp. 201–260.

19. King, Roger and McLeod, Dennis. "A Database Design Methodology and Tool for Information Systems." *ACM Transactions on Office Information Systems*, Vol. 3, No. 1, January 1985, pp. 2-21.

20. Liu Sheng, Olivia R. and Garcia, Hong-Mei C. "The Design of Medical Image Databases: A Distributed Approach." In *IEEE 1990 Conference Proceedings of IPCCC (Scottsdale, AZ, March 21-23, 1990)*, pp. 288-295.

21. Navathe, S. "Integrating User Views in Database Design." *Computer*, January, 1986, pp. 50 -61.

22. Navathe, S., Ceri, S., Wiederhold, S. and Dou, J. "Vertical Partitioning Algorithms for Database Design." *ACM Transactions on Database Systems*, Vol. 9, No. 4, Dec, 1984, pp. 680 - 710.

23. Ngu, H. H. "Conceptual Transaction Modeling." *IEEE Transactions on Knowledge and Data Engineering*, Vol. 1, No. 4, Dec. 1989.

24. Ozsu, M. T. and Valduriez, Patrick. *Principles of Distributed Database Systems*. New Jersey: Prentice Hall Inc., 1991.

25. Ozsu, Tamer M. and Valduriez, Patrick. "Distributed Database Systems: Where Are We Now?" *IEEE Computer*, August 1991, pp. 68-78.

26. Peckham, J. and Maryanski, F. "Semantic Data Models." *ACM Computing Surveys*, Vol. 20, No. 3, Sep. 1988, pp. 154–189.

27. Smith, J. M. and Smith, D. C. P. "Database Abstraction: Aggregation and Generalization." *ACM Transactions on Database System*, Vol. 20, No. 2. June 1977, 105 -133.

28. Storey, V.C. and Goldstein R.C. "A Methodology for Creating User Views in Database Design." *ACM TODS*, Vol. 13, No. 3, Sep. 1988, pp. 305–338.

29. Teorey, T. J. *Database Modeling and Design, the Entity-Relationship Approach*. San Mateo: Morgan Kaufmann Publishers, Inc., 1990

30. Teorey, T.J., Yang, D. and Fry, J.P. "A Logical Design Methodology for Relational Databases Using the Extended Entity-Relationship Model." *ACM Computing Surveys*, Vol. 18, No. 2, June 1986, pp. 197–222.

A Specification-based Data Model*

Munish Gandhi[†]

Edward L. Robertson[‡]

Computer Science Department, Indiana University, Bloomington, IN 47405-4101

Abstract

This paper presents a conceptual data model for engineered products ranging from software systems to physical objects. The presented model views the hierarchy of components that constitute a system as layers of alternating specification and implementation. If one considers the principles of abstraction and encapsulation, one can see that this viewpoint is quite natural. Abstraction implies that all implementations are implementations of *some* specification. Thus specifications may be regarded as directly "above" implementations. Encapsulation implies that implementations, at least conceptually, use specifications rather than other implementations to fulfill their goals. Thus, implementations may be regarded as directly "above" specifications.

This viewpoint has other advantages. It keeps specifications and implementations consistent with one another, models an evolving system nicely, and avoids version percolation problems naturally. It also suggests a way to separate local and global issues in system design.

1   Introduction

Engineered products, ranging from software systems to mechanical appliances, are built from components interacting in complex ways. While there are methods to model systems in each discipline we do not believe there is any model unifying the different approaches. Clearly there is a need for such an approach if only to handle products which use components from differing engineering technologies.

We present a minimal model that unifies mechanisms for system design, system configuration and system instantiation. We regard the model as an "engineering asset" which may be appropriately extended for purposes of a specific design environment. For example, the PMDB Project [12] has modeled the data relating to software development life cycle process used at TRW. Though the scope of the PMDB Project was much larger, it too attempted to develop a

---

*Partially supported by the Indiana Business Modernization and Technology Corporation.

[†]gandhim@cs.indiana.edu

[‡]edrbtsn@cs.indiana.edu

model that was not tied to specific methodologies and techniques. Rather, it produced a generic model which excluded implementation issues [13]. Another work which has objectives similar to ours is the data model (DODM) in the DAMOKLES project [5]. However, since DODM has been developed in context of the DAMOKLES system, the data model is closely tied to its implementation.

The presented model considers the specification for each component of a product as being closely linked to its implementation. The need for such an integration has been felt before. Swartout and Balzer [14] argue that even though software process models view specification and implementation as successive steps, in reality they influence one another. In other words, as software evolves both specifications and implementations undergo change. In fact, systems that integrate specifications in the design process are being developed currently. For example, the DEBYS (DEsign BY Specification) project intends to develop an integrated design and test environment for the design of electronic systems [11].

Our effort has been guided by a few general objectives. We explicate these as the following principles:

P1 The model should be general and flexible.

P2 Both the modeling notation and the model itself should be minimal.

P3 The model should represent designed objects.

P4 Specifications should be pre-eminent in the model.

Principles *P1* and *P2* are obviously intimately related. A minimal framework holds the fewest possible conflicts with a wide range of applications and offers the least resistance when adapted to a particular domain. Since familiarity and common acceptance complement minimality in facilitating adaptability, we use ER techniques as our notation. Likewise, *P3* and *P4* are related in their focus on design. Designed objects clearly arise because of an active process, but a data model should record the consequences of these activities rather than model the activities themselves. Hence the model captures only the structural relationships between the components of the product. Other interactions, especially those which are process oriented, are outside the core model. On the other hand, *P3* and *P4* sometimes require that certain aspects often considered incidental to the design process must be made explicit in capture and representation.

The development process is conceptually separated into design, configuration and manifestation stages. Each stage builds a distinct hierarchy. The components built during design constitute a design hierarchy, during configuration a definition hierarchy, and during manifestation an instance hierarchy.

- During design, development proceeds using alternate layers of specification and implementation. Further modifications are accommodated using the versioning mechanisms for both specifications and implementations.

- During configuration, a choice mechanism is provided to pick those versions of implementation which are most suited for assembling the system.

- During manifestation, the design for each component in the system assembly is materialised. This results in each materialised component getting an identity of its own.

In the next two sections we present the Specification-based Data Model (SBDM) using an E-R diagram. Section 2 reveals the entities and relationships needed to manage an evolving system design. Section 2.1 presents the specification entity, section 2.2 presents the implementation entity, and section 2.3 discusses how a system may be designed using the relationships between these entities. The configuration entity presented in section 2.4 is used to configure the system and the manifestation entity in section 2.5 allows configurations to be instantiated. Section 3 illustrates the above concepts by modeling a mechanical design, and an object-oriented software system. Finally, section 4 concludes the report by summarising some implications of the presented model.

A word on notations. Figure 1 is the only ER model in this paper using the traditional box and diamond notations and (min, max) pairs for cardinality/participation constraints. All other figures are instance diagrams using different shapes to distinguish various entity types and lines of various forms to distinguish relationships.

2 Design Components in SBDM

This section presents the Specification-based Data Model (SBDM) using the ER formalism [3] (Figure 1). The entities in the figure correspond to four important components in SBDM.

Specification Component encapsulates a formal statement of the objectives satisfied by its implementations and may be versioned to reflect an evolving design, or subtyped to represent a generalization hierarchy.

Implementation Component implements the objectives as specified by the specification component. This component may also be versioned.

Configuration Component selects implementations for a desired configuration. The containment of the configuration components specifies the relative placement of the implementations in a configuration.

Manifestation Component permits a distinction between those elements in final product which have the same definition, yet are distinctly instantiated. This is done by considering each element in the final product as a manifestation of the components in a configuration hierarchy.

2.1 Specification Component

A *Specification Component (SpecC)* is a precise statement of objectives expected to be satisfied by some objects. This statement has three parts – Interface Objectives, Behavioral Objectives and a Description (Figure 1). *Interface Objectives* define the protocol of the interaction between the objects and the external

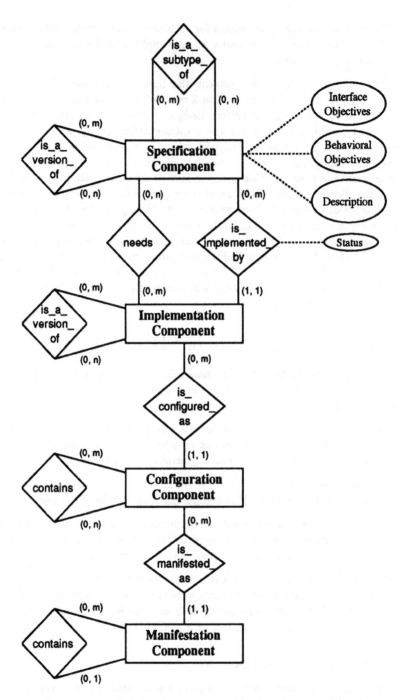

Figure 1: E-R Diagram for Specification-based Data Model

world. *Behavioral Objectives* define the functional characteristics expected of the object. The above two objectives should necessarily be syntactically or semantically verifiable. The *Description* section informally states non-verifiable and other miscellaneous objectives.

A specification may be versioned to reflect a maturing design. A SpecC *is_a_version_of* another if the former is directly derived from the latter. The graph formed by SpecCs and the *is_a_version_of* link between them is assumed to be a directed acyclic graph. The nodes of a connected component of this graph form a *specification set.*

SpecCs may also be arranged in a subtype hierarchy. A *is_a_subtype_of B* indicates that A is a specialization of B, or, alternatively, B generalizes A. The structure formed by considering SpecCs as nodes and *is_a_subtype_of* relationships as directed edges is again a directed acyclic graph.

2.2 Implementation Component

A Specification Component *is_implemented_by* an *Implementation Component (ImpC)* (Figure 1). This object necessarily satisfies the Interface Objectives of its specification. However, it only attempts to satisfy the Behavioral Objectives and the Description sections of its specification. The degree to which the ImpC satisfies the Behavioral Objectives is reflected in the *status* of the *is_implemented_by* link. As with specifications, the relationship *is_a_version_of* may be used to version implementations.

Implementations are not shared by specifications. If an ImpC A meets the functionality of two distinct SpecCs, then those SpecCs should be abstracted into a single SpecC which is implemented by A. This makes explicit the "union" of the two specifications. A specification set together with implementations for its elements constitute a structured group meeting similar objectives. Elements in this group of plans and implementations form a cohesive unit called a *functionality.*

2.3 Multi-level Design

A system is usually designed as a component hierarchy with "lower" levels refining or decomposing "higher" ones. In SBDM, SpecCs and ImpCs are fundamental to the design process and we refer to them collectively as *design components.* A single level design organises these design components to construct various functionalities. A multi-level design, in turn, organizes the functionalities heirarchically to form subsystems. This is done by linking an implementation of a higher functionality with specification of its constituent functionalities. Thus, an ImpC of the higher functionality *needs* SpecCs of the lower functionality (Figure 1).

The *needs* relationship between an implementation and a specification corresponds to those relationships among modules which define the software architecture. The semantic richness of such relationships necessitates at least two kinds of *needs.* The first, *uses,* indicates that an implementation uses the facilities

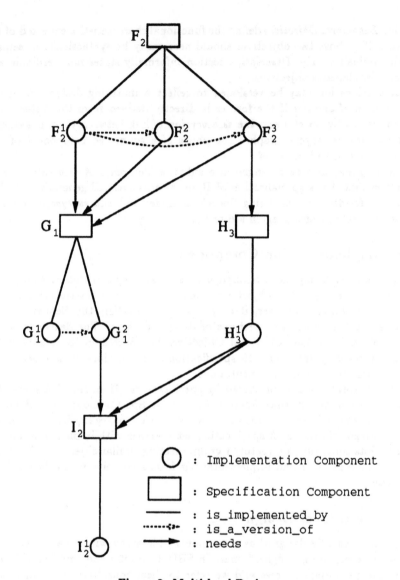

Figure 2: Multi-level Design

promised by the specification. A procedure call in a software system is a good example of this. The second, *is_composed_of*, indicates that a module is a part of another. This may occur, for example, in a mechanical assembly. An obvious difference between the two is that *uses* link between functionalities may form a cycle, the *is_composed_of* link may not.

Conceptually, the *needs* relationship could be considered as linking functionalities. However, linking functionalities rather than design components would result in a rigidly structured system. Designers must be free to allow different implementations within a functionality to decompose into different lower-level functionalities. A direct link like the *needs* relationship between ImpCs and SpecCs furnishes the model with such a flexibility. In Figure 2, for example, F_2^1 and F_2^2 need only G_1, F_2^3 needs both G_1 and H_3. We also allow multiple *needs* from an ImpC to a SpecC. These links indicate that several copies of the object specified by the SpecC are required. For example, H_3^1 requires two copies of I_2. The issue of copy identification is obviously relevant only for some technologies.

The structure of a multi-level design is similar to an AND-OR graph [1]. In Figure 2, the assembly of F_2^3 requires both G_1 and H_3. At G_1 and H_3 exactly one of the implementations is chosen, say, G_1^2 and H_3^1 respectively. Thus, SpecCs in multi-level design correspond to OR nodes and ImpCs correspond to AND nodes.

Systems which are built using alternating implementation and specification layers have significant advantages.

- A specification is part of the design and may be versioned with increasing knowledge about the system. This may be contrasted with the conventional viewpoint which essentially puts *all* specifications before implementations. Hence an evolving system is difficult to model, making the system difficult to manage. Furthermore, since a specification is in close proximity to its implementations it is easier to keep up with changes.

- Abstracting the requirements into the SpecC and having multiple implementations for the requirements allows one to concurrently experiment using different implementations.

- Version percolation is effectively controlled. A SpecC succinctly describes what is expected of its ImpCs. In Figure 2, the fact that there are two implementations of G_1 does not cause there to be two versions of F_2^3. Multiple versions of a specification are a different situation. Say G_1 has a version G_2. Since the contract between G_1 and F_2^i is still valid, there is no need for other versions F_2^*; but, by the same token, any attempt to use G_2 would require a new version. Even in this case, however, the versioning would (normally) stop at F_2.

On the process side, the designer of F_m^n may feel the need to be notified if G_2 is created. A design method using SBDM may easily incorporate

---

[1] The structure is not exactly an AND-OR graph because a subtype hierarchy may be present.

such a notification process. However, SBDM does not mandate it since it attempts to define only structural relationships among components.

- A decision as to whether a new object is just a version of a previous implementation or belongs to a new functionality is made rather trivially. If the new object satisfies the objectives stated in a SpecC then it should be in the implementation set of that specification. Otherwise, it constitutes a new functionality (and hence a new SpecC should be created to accommodate the new object).

- The design process becomes disciplined simply because new ImpCs are not allowed in the model before their specifications are defined.

2.4 Configuration Component

A configuration for a system may be defined as the relative functional arrangement of its subsystems. In other words, a configuration mechanism must not only identify the relevant subsystems but also specify their placement in the system structure. In SBDM, each functionality may have multiple implementations and each implementation may need yet other functionalities to fulfill its objectives. Thus, configuring a system would require a marking of an ImpC and, recursively, the ImpCs from each functionality it needs. This marking is done using the *Configuration Component (ConfC)*. The ConfCs themselves link to other ConfCs such that one *contains* another. This results in a structure which parallels that of the ImpCs in the system design.

We illustrate the mechanism by considering the scenario in Figure 3. To assemble a system with specification F_m, we mark an implementation F_m^n as being of interest by using a ConfC, say $C : F_m^n$ [2]. This is denoted by saying F_m^n *is_configured_as* $C : F_m^n$. For each specification G_x needed by F_m^n, a design version G_x^y is chosen and $C : F_m^n$ is linked to the ConfC for G_x^y, say $C : G_x^y$. Thus, $C : F_m^n$ *contains* $C : G_x^y$. If G_x^y *needs* other functionalities we repeat the above for specification G_x, where G_x^y is the ImpC of interest for G_x. Else, we are done.

Of course, it may not be necessary to explicitly create ConfCs and link them to get the desired configuration. A method of defaults may derive the configuration hierarchy automatically. The idea here subsumes that used in [4]. For each specification one may designate a distinguished object from its design set as *current*. To configure an object, we recursively construct it using the current versions of each functionality linked by the *needs* link. An atomic ImpC is configured using the ImpC itself. Obviously, configurations resulting from this method depend on the designations of current versions at configuration time [3].

---

[2] Note that there may be many ConfCs for an ImpC. Thus, $C : F_m^n$ does not represent a unique ConfC for the ImpC F_m^n. The same holds true for the ImpC G_x^y.

[3] To configure current versions for different platforms a constraint mechanism may be used. We do not elaborate of that mechanism here.

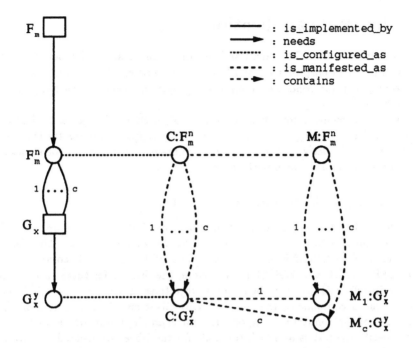

Figure 3: Configuring and Instantiating a system

2.5 Manifestation Component

[8] refers to the need for distinguishing an instance hierarchy and a definition hierarchy. The *Manifestation Component (ManC)* entity in SBDM together with the *contains* relationship enables us to explicitly create an instance hierarchy. Furthermore, the *is_manifested_as* relationship links the instance hierarchy with the definition hierarchy, which is built using the ConfC entity.

The instance for a ConfC, say $C : F_m^n$, is manifest as a manifestation component, say $M : F_m^n$. Because F_m^n (and hence $C : F_m^n$) is a composite, $M : F_m^n$ contains other manifestation components. These satisfy the following constraints:

- For each *contains* link from $C : F_m^n$ to $C : G_x^y$, $C : G_x^y$ *is_manifested_as* $M_1 : G_x^y$, ..., $M_c : G_x^y$, where c is the number of *contains* links. Each manifestation of $C : G_x^y$ is then related to $M : F_m^n$ by *contains*.

- Given a manifestation $M_a : G_x^y$, the ConfC from which the manifestation's parent in the instance hierarchy is manifest, is the same as, the parent of the ConfC in the definition hierarchy from which $M_a : G_x^y$ is manifest.

3   Example applications

SpecCs, ImpCs, ConfCs, ManCs and the structural relationships between them constitute an important part of SBDM. This section illustrates the wide applicability of these concepts by structuring systems from different engineering disciplines.

The first example considers the design of mechanical objects, and also illustrates the subtyping mechanism. The next example demonstrates the power of the model in designing products in a domain with a rich set of structural relationships, namely the object-oriented domain.

3.1   Design of Mechanical Objects

We apply SBDM to a mechanical design by modeling a (highly simplified!) decomposition of a car. Figure 4 displays a SBDM design of a car. The CAR is composed of an ENGINE and a BODY. The BODY in turn is composed of a CHASSIS, AXLE and WHEELs. As before, the SpecCs for these entities consist of Interface Objectives, Behavioral Objectives and a Description. In case of a physical component, the Interface Objectives specify the dimensions and positions of the connected components. For example, the interface for the axle may specify the radius at which the bolts for the wheel are located. Behavioral Objectives and Description sections may state those details of a part that will be used in the design of a product using this part as a subcomponent.

In our CAR design, each specification is implemented by at least one ImpC. The ENGINE specification has two implementations. The first is a Low Cost Engine and uses cheaper materials than the next which is a High Cost Engine. The ImpC for a product database will generally include a detailed design of the component. In addition, it may specify manufacturing details or vendor information if the part is supplied from outside.

When two constituent parts of a product interact with one another then the interaction should be specified in the implementation object that contains the interacting parts. For instance, even though the AXLE and the WHEEL are closely tied together, we do not link them with the *uses* relationship. The exact relationship between them is contained in the implementation of BODY. Thus, the *is_a_component_of* relationship between parts is the only *needs* relationship of relevance in a parts database.

A product database may also benefit from using a subtyping hierarchy. For example, consider the CHASSIS. We differentiate the 2 DOOR CHASSIS and the 4 DOOR CHASSIS at the specification level by creating SpecCs for them. These SpecCs may now be considered subtypes of CHASSIS. Note that in figure 4 we have an example of a design which is not exactly an AND-OR graph. Specifically, both CHASSIS and the nodes below it correspond to OR nodes.

To illustrate the configuration and manifestation mechanisms in SBDM, consider the right side of Figure 4. Here ConfCs are used to configure two types of cars. The 2-DOOR COUPE configuration uses the low cost engine and the 2-DOOR chassis. On the other hand, the 4-DOOR SEDAN uses the high cost

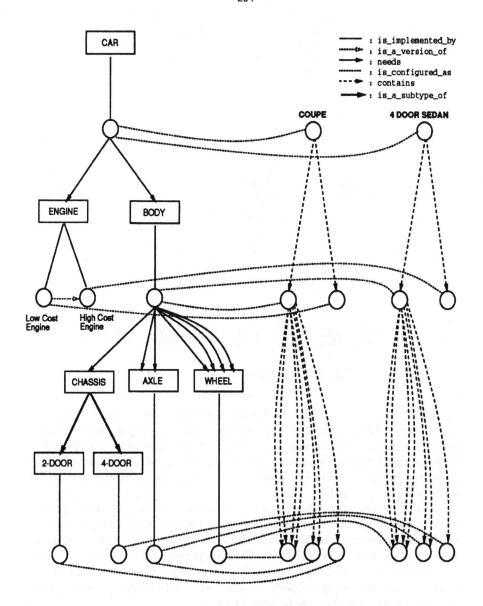

Figure 4: CAR: Design and Configurations

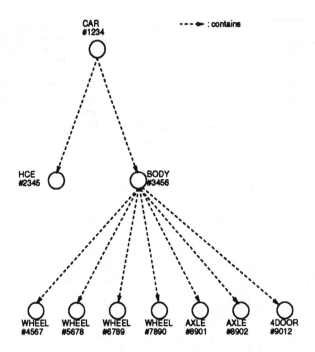

Figure 5: 4-Door Sedan: Manifestation

engine and the 4-DOOR chassis. Other subcomponents are the same for the two models. Note that we needed to link a version of an engine to a specific chassis. This is a constraint on the structure of the car and appears at a global level. Since the design stage handles essentially local concerns, we need a mechanism to handle the global constraints. The process of configuring a design using ConfCs provides such a mechanism.

After the local and the global concerns of the design have been handled in the previous stages, one may physically realize the product. Continuing our example (Figure 5), we manifest the ConfC for the 4-DOOR SEDAN. Manifestation provides an identity to each element. This is especially clear if we consider the wheels of the car. The design and configuration stages contained multiple references to the same design object. At the manifestation stage, however, each wheel is different and thus has its own identity.

3.2   Object Oriented Software Systems

We illustrate the applicability of SBDM to object oriented software systems in this subsection. Our examples use principles represented in the design approaches of Booch [2] and Meyer [10].

A specification for a family of objects in SBDM is very close to the notion of a class interface in object-oriented systems. It defines the communication

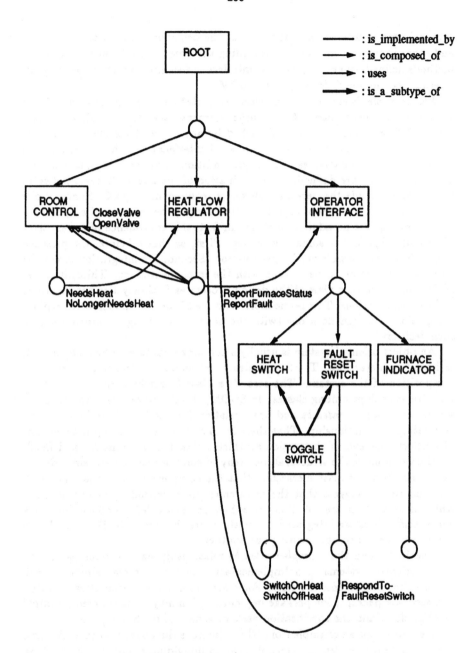

Figure 6: Home Heating System

protocol used to interact with the objects, the behavior expected of the objects, and other important information regarding the objects. And since most design methods define how exactly the class interface is specified, we can reuse the class interface as the SpecC for a class in SBDM.

For example, Booch defines a "class template" as a "means of documenting the meaning of each class". Among other elements, the class template contains fields and operations that can be reached by any client of the class (public interface) or a subclass of the class (protected interface). Furthermore, for each operation the parameters, result type, preconditions, postconditions, action, documentation, etc. are defined. An examination of the above elements indicates that it does include the necessary elements required in a SpecC. Hence, if one follows the Booch model of object oriented design, the creation of a SpecC for each class requires no additional effort. In fact, this equivalence of a class template and a SpecC has some advantages. First, as shown before, the presence of specifications controls version percolation. Second, the integration forces the class documentation to be in tune with the implementations. Third, it represents a more realistic view of the design process as it closely ties specifications and implementations. This is one more example of how our model forces explicit recognition of design decisions (with the hope of capturing documentation on such decisions).

An object oriented system is usually a complex structure embedding in itself at least two hierarchies. The first, a structural hierarchy, defines the structural composition of the system. The second, a class hierarchy, defines the inheritance relationships among classes. In SBDM, the structural hierarchy is represented by *is_implemented_by* and *needs* relationships and the class hierarchy by *is_a_subtype_of* relationship. That there is no subtype relationship between ImpCs reflects the level of abstraction at which a class hierarchy should be defined.

Conventionally, the structural hierarchy of components in a system is drawn separately from the class hierarchies that the components participate in. This may incorrectly suggest that the hierarchies are independent of one another, which of course they are not. Since class hierarchies are defined on specifications and specifications are integrated in the structural hierarchy, SBDM models the two hierarchies as complementing one another.

The ImpC and the *is_implemented_by* relationship have obvious parallel in object oriented systems. An Implementation Component may simply be the module that implements the class. For example, in ADA if each class is placed in a separate package, the package implementation may be considered an ImpC for that class (and the specification package a part of the SpecC).

We now adapt an example from [2] to illustrate the above concepts. A home heating system provides and controls heat to individual rooms in a home. The structure of one system is modeled in SBDM in Figure 6. The rooms have temperature sensors which allow the ROOM CONTROL to send messages to the HEAT FLOW REGULATOR whether it NeedsHeat or NoLongerNeedsHeat. The HEAT FLOW REGULATOR, which controls the furnace and the water valves in each room, responds by requesting the water valves to either OpenValve or CloseValve.

Thus the functionalities ROOM CONTROL and HEAT FLOW REGULATOR have a cyclical *uses* relationship between them. The HEAT FLOW REGULATOR also has to ReportFurnaceStatus regularly and ReportFault in case of some other failure.

The OPERATOR INTERFACE *is_composed_of* a FAULT RESET SWITCH, used to reset a fault, a HEAT SWITCH, to SwitchOn or SwitchOff the heating system, and a FURNACE INDICATOR, to indicate the status of the furnace. The FAULT RESET SWITCH and the HEAT SWITCH are both specialization of the class TOGGLE SWITCH. A root class is also used in the example to initialize and start up the system.

4 Summary

We have presented a model which uses a minimal set of concepts to unify mechanisms for system design, system configuration, and system instantiation. We also demonstrated the generality of the model using examples drawn from differing engineering domains.

A key concept in the paper is that a design hierarchy may be considered as a structure of alternating specifications and implementations. Either of these components may be versioned to realistically reflect an evolving system design and keep specifications and implementations consistent with one another.

The model records versions as independent objects related to each other by the *is_version_of* link. This may be contrasted with other approaches which use a specialized object to handle versions [1, 6, 5]. We believe our approach is more natural. It also makes the model independent of the underlying object management system which may or may not provide support for versioning. Similarly, we do not have specialized structures for composite objects. Instead, the composition relationship and the uses relationships are considered special cases of the *needs* relationship.

The presented versioning mechanism permits an intuitive configuration mechanism. A configuration simply selects desired implementations from the required functionalities. We do not make any real distinction between static and dynamic configurations [1, 7]. In fact, we consider the difference as being process oriented and hence not part of a data model.

Finally, manifestations are used to distinguish the instance hierarchy from the definition hierarchies [1, 9].

References

[1] D. Batory and W. Kim. Modeling concepts for VLSI CAD objects. *ACM Transactions on Database Systems*, 10(3):322–346, September 1985.

[2] G. Booch. *Object Oriented Design with Applications*. Benjamin/Cummings, Redwood City, California, 1991.

[3] P. P. Chen. The Entity-Relationship Model - Toward a unified view of data. *ACM Transactions in Database Systems*, 1(1):9–36, March 1976.

[4] H. T. Chou and W. Kim. A Unifying Framework for Version Control in a CAD Environment. In *Proceedings of the 12th VLDB conference, Kyoto, Japan*, pages 336–346, August 1986.

[5] K. R. Dittrich, W. Gotthard, and P. C. Lockemann. DAMOKLES - A Database Systems for Software Engineering Environments. In *Proceedings of an International Workshop on Advanced Programming Environments, Trondheim, Norway*, pages 353–371, June 1986.

[6] K. R. Dittrich and R. Lorie. Version support for engineering database systems. *IEEE Transactions on Software Engineering*, 14(4):429–437, April 1988.

[7] R. H. Katz. *Information Management for Engineering Design*. Springer-Verlag Computer Science Survey Series, Heidelberg, Germany, 1985.

[8] R. H. Katz. Toward a Unified Framework for Version Modeling in Engineering Databases. *ACM Computing Surveys*, 22(4):375–408, December 1990.

[9] D. McLeod, K. Narayanaswamy, and K. BapaRao. An approach to information management for CAD/VLST applications. In *Proceedings of the SIGMOD conference on Databases for Engineering Applications, San Jose, California*, pages 39–50, May 1983.

[10] B. Meyer. *Object-oriented Software Construction*. Prentice Hall International (UK) Ltd., Hertfordshire, HP2 4RG, 1988.

[11] K. D. Mueller-Glaser, J. Bortolazzi, and Y. Tanhuran. Towards a Requirements Definition, Specification, and System Design Environment. In *EURO-DAC Proceedings (to appear)*, 1992.

[12] M. H. Penedo and E. D. Stuckle. Integrated Project Master Database IR&D Final Report. Technical Report TRW-84-SS-22, TRW, December 1984.

[13] M. H. Penedo and E. D. Stuckle. TRW's SEE Saga. In *Software Engineering Environments - International Workshop on Environments, Chinon, France*, pages 25–56, September 1989.

[14] W. Swartout and R. Balzer. On the inevitable intertwining of specification and implementation. *Communications of the ACM*, 25(7):438–440, July 1982.

Data Dictionary Design : a Logic Programming Approach

Fiora Pirri

Dipartimento di Informatica e Sistemistica
Università di Roma "La Sapienza"
via Salaria 113, 00198 Roma, Italia
e-mail: pirri@vaxrma.infn.it

Clara Pizzuti*
CRAI
Località S.Stefano, 87036 Rende (CS), Italia
e-mail: clara@crai.it

Abstract

Some steps of the design of a data dictionary with the use of a particular methodology are represented by means of logic rules augumented with integrity constraints defining illegal data design. The presence of concepts incompatible among them is easily revealed by asking for satisfiability of integrity constraints. Furthermore, it is possible to obtain the hypotheses explaining the presence of illegality by exploiting *abductive reasoning*. To this end a new proposal for the computation of such hypotheses, based on an suitable manipulation of minimal three-valued models of the logic program, is presented.

Keywords: data dictionary design, entity-relationship model, logic programs, partial interpretations, abduction, explanations.

1   Introduction

The availability of an integrated description of all types of data, managed in a complex organization, together with their relations to other resources involved in an information system, is of great importance. In fact, such an availability of data description helps users to deeply understand their meaning. Creation of a

---

*This work has been partially supported by "Progetto Finalizzato Sistemi informatici e Calcolo Parallelo" of C.N.R..

data dictionary with a good methodology accomplishes this task, thus dictionary design constitutes an important step during the realization of an information system.

In this paper we propose to use *logic programming* to represent some steps of data dictionary design and *abductive reasoning* [10,6,8] to provide explanations for incompatibilities which can be generated during these steps. We assume as methodology for data dictionary design the one proposed by Batini et al. [2] which is based on the concept of local area schema, i.e. a data description realized with a given model, at different levels of abstraction. Data abstraction is realized through the introduction of *refinement*, which is a mechanism allowing for modeling the same portion of reality in terms of several schemata at different levels of abstraction. Refinements are formally defined through the introduction of *transformations* from a source schema to a target one. The methodology for data dictionary design performs a *multilevel integration* starting from the chain of refinements of local schemata and the sequence of transformations representing them, and generates an integrated schema. Unfortunately, integrating local chains may result in various kinds of incompatibilities due to a different user view of reality .

We propose to represent every local refinement chain with a particular set of rules, which can have also negative literals in their heads, augmented with integrity constraints defining illegal multilevel integrations, i.e. those allowing for incompatible concepts generation. The integration of a new local refinement chain thus just consists of adding to the logic program the rules representing it. If this new logic program admits at least a model then the knowledge on local refinement schemata contains incompatibilities. It is possible to provide the user with the possible causes which generate incompatibility by using *abductive reasoning*. We shall give a method to obtain the abductive explanations based on a suitable manipulation of the minimal partial models of the associated logic program.

The assistance given to the user during refinement chains integration, rebuilding the reasons of incompatibility, can be very useful both for the professional user, who can have at disposal an interactive tool of analysis, and the casual user, who can approach himself to this kind of problems with the help of a tool which guides him during this step of data dictionary design.

The paper is organized as follows: in Section 2 definitions of the structure and design of a data dictionary with the methodology of [2] are recalled, in Section 3 a logical framework for the structure and design of a Data Dictionary is described, in section 4 the computation the hypotheses explaining the source of incompatibility is addressed and, finally, in Section 5 some implementation issues are given.

2 The Data Dictionary

In this section we recall the structure and design of a data dictionary proposed in [2]. The data dictionary is the description of all types of data produced, managed, exchanged and maintained in an organization. The atomic objects stored in the data dictionary are schemata, i.e. data descriptions represented with a given model. The paper adopts the *Entity-Relationship model* as the data model of reference.

Definition 1 *A concept c is either an entity, denoted by a name, or a relationship among entities, denoted by $R(< name >, < list\_of\_names >)$ where $< name >$ is the name of the relationship and $< list\_of\_names >$ are names denoting entities, or a generalization hierarchy among entities, denoted by $H(< list\_of\_names >)$ where the first name of the list denotes the superset entity and the others the subset entities.*

With C we denote the set of all concepts defined, i.e. the language of the data dictionary.

Definition 2 *The structure of a data dictionary is a couple $\mathcal{D} = < \mathcal{F}, T >$, where $\mathcal{F} \subseteq 2^C$ and T is a set of bijective mappings (transformations) on $\mathcal{F}$.*

$\forall t, t' \in T$ and $A, B, C \in \mathcal{F}$ if $t : A \to B$ and $t' : B \to C$ then $t \circ t' \in T$ (for details see [11]).

We define on $\mathcal{D} = < \mathcal{F}, T >$ an indexation $f : C \to 2^{\mathcal{F}} \times I$, where I is a set of indexes, assigning to each concept $c \in C$ a subset of $\mathcal{F}$ as follows:

$$f(c) = \{S_i \in \mathcal{F} | c \in S_i, i \in I\}$$

The indexation f is injective, i.e. given two concepts $a, b \in C$ if $f(a) = \{S_0, \ldots, S_m\}$ and $f(b) = \{S_0, \ldots, S_m\}$, then $a = b$. Among the sets $\{S_0, \ldots, S_h\}$ associated with a given concept c, let S_0 denote the smallest set with respect to set inclusion.

Definition 3 *Let $S \in \mathcal{F}$. Let an indexation f, a set of transformations $\{t_0, \ldots, t_{n-1}, t\} \in T$, a concept c with smallest set S_0, be given. S is an ER-schema iff one of the following holds:*
1) $S = S_0$;
2) $\exists t_0 \ldots, t_i, t_j$ s.t. $S = t_i \circ \ldots \circ t_0(S_0)$ and $S' = t_j(S)$ (where S and S' do not necessarily belong to $f(c)$)
3) $S = S_n$ where $S_n = t_{n-1} \circ \ldots \circ t_0(S_0) = t(S_n)$

Note that the ER-schemata are either those elements of $\mathcal{F}$ obtained by a finite number of transformations applied to some smallest set S_0, associated with a concept c, or S_0 itself.

Given $\{t_0, \ldots, t_{n-1}, t\} \in T$ and a smallest set S_0, if $S_n = t_{n-1} \circ \ldots \circ t_1(S_0) = t(S_n)$, we call S_0 the source schema, S_n the target schema, i.e. the most refined schema since no further transformation will change it, $S_0, \ldots, S_n$ a sequence of schemata refinements and the composition $t_{n-1} \circ \ldots \circ t_0(S_0)$ the chain of refinement planes (or simply a chain of refinements) of S_n. The generation of the most refined schema S_n is thus described by means of a starting schema S_0

and a set of transformations $T' \subseteq T$ mapping S_0 in S_n. The schemata in the chain are chosen among the schemata in the sequence of refinements as the most representative for describing the process of generating a schema.

Example 1 *Let $\mathcal{F}$ contain the two following ER-schemata*
$S_0 = \{PUBLICATION\}$,
$S_1 = \{PUBLICATION, BOOK, PAPER,$
$\qquad H(PUBLICATION, BOOK, PAPER)\}$,
then $t : \mathcal{F} \rightarrow \mathcal{F}$ s.t. $t(S_0) = S_1$ maps the singleton PUBLICATION into the set containing the following concepts: PUBLICATION, BOOK, PAPER plus the generalization hierarchy H(PUBLICATION, BOOK, PAPER) where the superset entity is PUBLICATION and the subset entities are BOOK and PAPER.

Now, given $\mathcal{D} =< \mathcal{F}, T >$ we consider the following equivalence relations R_{New}, R_{Old} and $R_{Persistent}$, where each relation defines an equivalence class, as follows:
$\mathcal{D}/R_{New} = \{S \in \mathcal{F} | \forall < S_i, S_j > \in t, S = S_j - (S_i \cap S_j)\}$
$\mathcal{D}/R_{Old} = \{S \in \mathcal{F} | \forall < S_i, S_j > \in t, S = S_i - (S_i \cap S_j)\}$
$\mathcal{D}/R_{Persistent} = \{S \in \mathcal{F} | \forall < S_i, S_j > \in t, S = S_i \cap S_j\}$
For notational convenience we denote each equivalence class $\mathcal{D}/R_{New}$, $\mathcal{D}/R_{Old}$ and $\mathcal{D}/R_{Persistent}$ with, respectively, New_{S_i,S_j}, Old_{S_i,S_j} and $Persistent_{S_i,S_j}$, maintaining, in such a way, trace of the original couple $< S_i, S_j > \in t$ that has generated it.

Intuitively, Old_{S_i,S_j} is the set of concepts that are refined into new concepts, New_{S_i,S_j} represents the refined concepts and $Persistent_{S_i,S_j}$ those which do not need further refinement.

Example 2 *For the transformation t of the previous example :*
$New_{S_0,S_1} = \{BOOK, PAPER, H(PUBLICATION, BOOK, PAPER)\}$
$Old_{S_0,S_1} = \{\}$
$Persistent_{S_0,S_1} = \{PUBLICATION\}$

The methodology for building a data dictionary starts with the local chains of refinements, i.e. chains representing only a portion of reality of the overall information system, and generates a global schema by integrating the local ones performing a methodological step relatively new in the literature: the *multilevel integration*. This step presents some open problems which need to be investigated. Multilevel integration, in fact, may result in various kinds of incompatibilities. In order to discover and resolve them, the authors introduce the notion of *abstraction directed graph*, that is a synthetic description of the generative process underlying the sequence of refinements. We show the concept of abstraction graph by means of an example, see also Figure 1.

Example 3 *Let the following refinement chain be given:*
$t : \{RESIDENCE\}$
$\quad \rightarrow \{PERSON, TOWN, R(RESIDES, PERSON, TOWN)\}$
$t' : \{PERSON, TOWN, R(RESIDES, PERSON, TOWN)\}$

$\rightarrow \{PERSON, TOWN, MALE, FEMALE,$
$H(PERSON, MALE, FEMALE), R(RESIDES, PERSON, TOWN)\}$

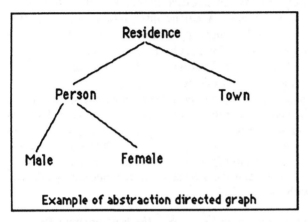

Fig. 1. The abstraction directed graph

The nodes of the graph are the entities appearing in the transformation, whereas there is an edge between two entities if one belongs to Old_{S_i,S_j} or, if this set is empty, to $Persistent_{S_i,S_j}$ and the other to New_{S_i,S_j}. Entities in the first two sets are chosen nondeterministically as representative entities of the transformation.

Local graphs are then integrated in a global graph. The presence of either a cycle or a semicycle in the global graph reveals an incompatibility in the generative process. Graphs having too many edges correspond to generative processes difficult to understand, thus some heuristics to reduce the graph complexity are considered.

In the following sections we shall propose a solution to this kind of problems based on logic programming.

3 The Logical Structure for the Data Dictionary

We assume a first order language $\mathcal{L}$, without function symbols. Constant and variables (terms), predicate symbols, connectives and quantifiers are defined as usual. An *atomic formula* or *atom* is either a propositional letter, $A, \ldots, P, Q$ or a predicate symbol applied to terms of $\mathcal{L}$. A *literal* is either an atomic formula (positive literal) or the negation of an atomic formula (negative literal).

If L is a literal, with $\overline{L}$ we denote its complement. A term, predicate or literal is *ground* if it is variable-free. A *clause* is a finite universally quantified disjunction $\forall y_1 \cdots \forall y_r (L_1 \vee \cdots \vee L_n)$ of literals with no free variables occurring in $L_1, \ldots, L_n$. A rule is a formula of the form $(\forall x)L \leftarrow L_1, \ldots, L_n$, where L is called the *head* of the rule and $L_1, \ldots, L_n$ the *body* of the rule. A negative logic program[1] is a set of rules. The declarative semantics for negative logic programs is given on the basis of partial Herbrand interpretations. A *partial Herbrand interpretation* is a set I_p of positive and negative literals s.t. if a literal does not belong to I_p then it is *undefined*. A partial interpretation of a negative program Π is a *partial model* $\mathcal{A}$ of Π if and only if $\mathcal{A}$ makes each rule of Π true on the basis of the Kleene truth-table. For details cfr. [11].

In the following we deal with a substructure of a Data Dictionary $\mathcal{D}' = < \mathcal{F}', T' >$, where only refinements are considered.

Let a chain of refinements $S_0, \ldots, S_n$ be given, for each couple $< S_i, S_{i+1} >$, a particular form of rule is defined. A rule $r : L \leftarrow L_1, \ldots, L_n$, is such that L is a literal of the form $new(c_k, a, l_h)$ with $c_k \in News_{S_i, S_j}$, a is the application area of interest[2], l_h is the abstraction level and $L_1, \ldots, L_n$ are literals either of the form $new(c_q, a, l_s)$ with $c_q \in Persistent_{S_i, S_j}$ and $l_s < l_h$, or $old(c_p, a, l_t)$ with $c_p \in Olds_{S_i, S_j}$ and $l_t < l_h$. For notational convenience, in the following we denote a sequence $S_{0_i}, \ldots, S_{n_i}$ with $S_0, \ldots, S_n$.

Definition 4 *Given a refinement chain $S_0, \ldots, S_n$, the logic program $P_{S_0, \ldots, S_n}$ associated with it is the set of rules of $\mathcal{L}_{\mathcal{F}}$ generated for each couple S_i, S_{i+1} for $0 \le i \le n - 1$.*

Example 4 *For the refinement chain constituted by the two schemata S_0, S_1 of Example 1, P_{S_0, S_1} is :*

1. $new(paper, purchase, 1) \leftarrow new(publication, purchase, 0)$

2. $new(book, purchase, 1) \leftarrow new(publication, purchase, 0)$

3. $new(H(publication, book, paper), purchase, 1)$
   $\leftarrow new(publication, purchase, 0)$

where *purchase* is the application area.

As we outlined in a previous section, one of the drawbacks during the *multilevel integration* is the possibility of having incompatibilities among the several local chains, due to a different user knowledge of the reality of interest. The most important incompatibilities happen when there is a circularity in the refinement of a concept, i.e. if a concept x is refined into a concept y, then y cannot be refined into x again. Furthermore, if a concept y is generated from a concept x in a local area, then its regeneration in another area is superfluous.

Remark. Given a negative logic program Π associated with a transformation, for any rule $new(x, a, l) \leftarrow new(y, a, l_1)$, if $l_1 < l$ then there is an incompatibility.

In order to avoid such problems, particular integrity constraints, defining the illegal multilevel integrations, are added to the logic program.

---

[1] this terminology is used in [7]

[2] by application area of interest we mean one of the possible subareas in which an information system can be organized on the basis of specific characteristics and properties.

Definition 5 *Given a refinement chain* $S_0, \ldots, S_n$ *and the associated logic program* $P_{S_0, \ldots, S_n}$, *the integrity constraints IC for it are closed formulae in* $\mathcal{L}_{\mathcal{F}}$ *of the form :*

$$\neg new(x, a, l) \leftarrow new(y, a, l_1), l_1 < l, new(y, a', l_2), new(x, a', l_3), l_3 < l_2$$
$$\neg new(x, a, l) \leftarrow new(x, a', l_1)$$

where variables are universally quantified.

The former integrity constraint says that a concept x of an application area a cannot be generated from a concept y of the same area if y was already generated from x in another area a'. The latter says that a concept x can not be generated in an area a if it was already generated into another area a'. Thus, if the logic program plus the integrity constraints admits at least a model, the knowledge on local refinement schemata contains incompatibilities. We have shown in [11] that there can be three possibilities: 1) IC are true in all the partial models of $P_{S_0, \ldots, S_n}$, 2) IC are true in some models, 3) IC are true in no model. In the former case we can conclude that, since incompatibilities are derived from the program, local refinement chains are badly defined. In the second case we can discard those models in which IC are true and, finally, in the latter case, there do not exist incompatible concepts.

At any time, the logic program represents the global schema obtained by integrating the local schemata provided by the several users until that moment, plus the integrity constraints necessary for performing a correct schemata integration. Suppose, now, a new user wants to add his piece of local knowledge to the global one. This just means to extend the logic program with the new set of rules. The problem that can now rise is if this program contains concepts incompatible among them. The presence of incompatibility is easily discovered asking for the satisfiability of the integrity constraint which can be expressed by means of the query :

$$\leftarrow \neg new(x, a, l)$$

meaning that for every new concept, if $\neg new(x, a, l)$ is true, then integrity constraints are satisfied and thus the logic program $P_{S_0, \ldots, S_n}$ contains incompatible concepts.

We now show the described process by means of an example based on the structure of a university. The university can be thought organized in two divisions, the *ADMINISTRATION* division and the *EDUCATION* division. The *EDUCATION* division is composed of three functional areas, an area concerns the schools (*SCHOOL AREA*), another the teachers (*PROFESSOR AREA*) and the other the courses (*COURSE AREA*). For simplicity we consider only refinement chains w.r.t. the entities, omitting the relationships and generalization hierarchy. The refinement chains for the three areas are:

SCHOOL AREA (abbreviated in *S_A*)
$t_1 : \{SCHOOL\} \rightarrow \{STUDENT, PROFESSOR\}$
$t_2 : \{STUDENT, PROFESSOR\} \rightarrow$
$\qquad \rightarrow \{STUDENT, PROFESSOR, EXAMINATION, COURSE\}$

PROFESSOR AREA (abbreviated in P_A)

$t_3 : \{PROFESSOR\} \rightarrow \{PROFESSOR, DEPARTMENT\}$

$t_4 : \{PROFESSOR, DEPARTMENT\} \rightarrow$
$\rightarrow \{PROFESSOR, DEPARTMENT, STUDENT\}$

COURSE AREA (abbreviated in C_A)

$t_5 : \{COURSE\} \rightarrow \{COURSE, PROFESSOR, EXAMINATION\}$

In Figure 2 the three local abstraction graphs are shown. In the SCHOOL AREA graph both STUDENT and PROFESSOR are chosen as representative entities of the second transformation, thus the former is connected to EXAMINATION and the latter to COURSE.

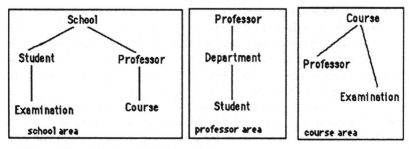

Fig. 2. Three local abstraction graphs

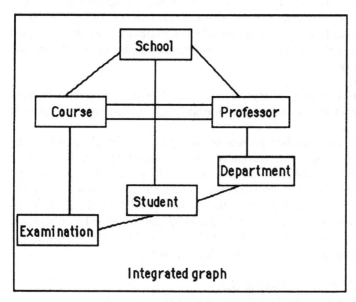

Fig. 3. The integrated graph

Note that there is a cycle between COURSE and PROFESSOR entities and both EXAMINATION and STUDENT are generated in two different areas.

The associated logic program P is :

1. $new(STUDENT, S\_A, 1) \leftarrow old(SCHOOL, S\_A, 0)$

2. $new(PROFESSOR, S\_A, 1) \leftarrow old(SCHOOL, S\_A, 0)$

3. $new(EXAMINATION, S\_A, 2) \leftarrow$
   $new(STUDENT, S\_A, 1), new(PROFESSOR, S\_A, 1)$

4. $new(COURSE, S\_A, 2) \leftarrow$
   $new(STUDENT, S\_A, 1), new(PROFESSOR, S\_A, 1)$

5. $new(DEPARTMENT, P\_A, 1) \leftarrow new(PROFESSOR, P\_A, 0)$

6. $new(STUDENT, P\_A, 2) \leftarrow$
   $new(PROFESSOR, P\_A, 0), new(DEPARTMENT, P\_A, 1)$

7. $new(PROFESSOR, C\_A, 1) \leftarrow new(COURSE, C\_A, 0)$

8. $new(EXAMINATION, C\_A, 1) \leftarrow new(COURSE, C\_A, 0)$

and the integrity constraints:

9. $\neg new(x, a, l) \leftarrow new(y, a, l_1), l_1 < l, new(y, a', l_2), new(x, a', l_3), l_3 < l_2$

10. $new(x, a, l) \leftarrow \neg new(x, a', l_1)$

Suppose, now, that the logic program contains only the rules regarding the SCHOOL and PROFESSOR AREAS and that the user wants to insert the program regarding the COURSE AREA (namely rules 7. and 8.). Thus he makes the query:

$Q: \leftarrow \neg new(x, C\_A, l)$

The three-valued semantics allows one to deduce $\neg new(PROFESSOR, C\_A, 1)$ and $\neg new(EXAMINATION, C\_A, 1)$. In fact, as already observed, there is a cycle between $COURSE$ and $PROFESSOR$ and the entity $EXAMINATION$ was defined in the $SCHOOL$ $AREA$.

Once discovered the presence of incompatibilities it should be very useful to have at disposal the causes explaining such incompatibilities. This can be obtained by exploiting *abductive reasoning*. In the next section, after a brief introduction to abduction, we shall show a method to find abducibles which will be applied to this example in order to obtain an explanation for $new(PROFESSOR, C\_A, 1)$.

4 Computing the Causes of Incompatibility

In this section a general specification for abduction is introduced, together with a new proposal for computing abductive explanations.

Definition 6 *An abductive framework F_A is a couple $F_A = <\Sigma, \Delta>$ where Σ is a set of sentences of $\mathcal{L}$ and Δ is a set of literals of $\mathcal{L}$ called abducibles.*

The above definition is mainly used in Logic Programming, where negation is not allowed in the head of a rule, in this paper Δ and Σ are equivalent.

Definition 7 *Given an abductive framework $F_A = <\Sigma, \Delta>$ and a sentence C (the observation), an explanation for C is a sentence ϕ, whose literals belong to Δ, if and only if*

1. $\Sigma \cup \{\phi\} \models C$;

2. ϕ *is minimal: for any sentence ϕ' s.t. $\phi' \supset \phi$, $\Sigma \cup \{\phi'\} \not\models C$*

Finally we should avoid the trivial condition of inconsistency, that is, if ϕ is inconsistent with Σ everything is derivable, i.e. both C and $\neg C$.

Definition 8 *A non trivial explanation for C is any ϕ s.t. $\Sigma \cup \{\phi\} \models C$ and $\Sigma \cup \{\phi\}$ is consistent.*

We say that an explanation is *obvious* when it is equivalent to the observation, i.e. when the observation is explained by itself.

Example 5 *Let Σ be :*

1. $father(X) \leftarrow married(X), has\_family(X)$

2. $head\_of\_family(X) \leftarrow father(X), has\_salary(X)$

The minimal explanations of $head\_of\_family(john)$ are :

a. $father(john) \wedge has\_salary(john)$

b. $has\_salary(john) \land married(john) \land has\_family(john)$

c. $head\_of\_family(john)$

where $head\_of\_family(john)$ is the obvious explanation.

The difficulty of generating abductive explanations is well known. The problem, in fact, has been shown to be *NP-hard* [4,15]. The approaches to compute abductive explanations can be divided into two main classes: *logic programming* based [14,6,8,9,5,13,3] and *clause* based [12]. In the former, explanations are computed using either *SLD-resolution* or stable model semantics whether in the latter by suitably manipulating the clauses.

A common drawback of all these approaches is that, assuming an abducible, because with present knowledge its negation cannot be proved, it does not prevent its later provability. Thus every time a new abducible is assumed, a consistency test is needed. Furthermore, abducibles are restricted to negative literals in the body of the rules.

We proposed [11] a new model-based method for abducibles computation which tries to overcome part of the outlined problems and which extends the previous approaches. In fact, we allow for negation in the heads of the rules and we effectively compute the hypotheses which explain a given observation.

Given a negative logic program Π and a query $\leftarrow C$, where C is any clause, an explanation for C can be obtained by suitably manipulating the minimal partial models of Π augmented with the query $\leftarrow C$ and then discarding those explanations inconsistent with Π.

Let us denote with $Th(M)$ the conjunction of all ground literals satisfied in a partial model M of the negative logic program Π.

Now, since we considered a finite language without function symbols, we have a finite Herbrand Base and the set of minimal partial models is in the set $2^{|\mathcal{L}|}$ where $|\mathcal{L}|$ is the cardinality of the language.

Theorem 1 *Let $M_1, \ldots, M_r$ be minimal partial models of $\Pi \cup \{\neg C\}$. Let S^* be*

$$S^* = CNF(Th(M_1) \lor \ldots \lor Th(M_r))$$

We call S^* a support set for explanations. Then the set S of explanations for C is

$$S = \{\neg\phi|\phi \text{ is a conjunct occurring in } S^* \text{ and } \neg\phi \text{ is consistent with } \Pi\}$$

Proof. [11].

Notice that a partial model is a set of both positive and negative ground literals, reflecting the fact that in a three-valued interpretation positive and negative information have the same importance.

In order to discard the set of inconsistent explanations, we devised a method based on the search of the irredundant sets of a bipartite graph over Π where the nodes are both the minimal partial models of Π and the literals occurring in Π. We have shown in [11] that this method is sound and complete, that is, it gives all and only the trivial explanations. We show this method by means of a simple example using a negative logic program.

Example 6 Let Π be:

$$a \leftarrow b$$
$$b \leftarrow \neg c, \neg a$$
$$d \leftarrow a, \neg b$$
$$c \leftarrow \neg b, e$$
$$\neg c \leftarrow \neg a$$

and we are looking for explanations for b which is not derivable from Π. Computing the minimal partial models of $\Pi \cup \{\neg b\}$ we obtain the following models: $M_1 = \{d, c, \neg b, a\}$ and $M_2 = \{d, \neg e, \neg b, a\}$. Computing the CNF of $Th(M_1) \vee Th(M_2)$ we obtain $(c \vee \neg e) \wedge d \wedge \neg b \wedge a$, that is, taking the negation, each of the propositions $(\neg c \wedge e)$, $\neg d$, b and $\neg a$ is a possible explanation (cfr. Theorem 1). Now, we have to take free from the trivial ones. From the method presented in [11] we take the minimal partial model of Π: $M_1^* = \{a, b\}$, $M_2^* = \{a, d, c\}$, $M_3^* = \{a, d, \neg t\}$; then we draw the bipartite graph associated to the models and the positive and negative literals occurring in it. Calculating the irredundant sets: $D_1 = \{a\}$, $D_2 = \{b, d\}$, $D_3 = \{b, c, \neg e\}$ we have that the negation of D_1 occurs in $\neg a$, and no other irredundant set occurs in the remaining explanations, therefore only $\neg a$ is the trivial explanation. In fact, it is easy to see that $\Pi \cup \{\neg a\}$ is inconsistent.

As we have observed in the previous section, from the given program P we had $\neg new(PROFESSOR, C\_A, 1)$ because of a cycle between the entities $PROFESSOR$ and $COURSE$. Suppose that the user is looking for an explanation.

We compute the minimal three valued models of the global logic program plus $new(PROFESSOR, C\_A, 1)$. Applying Theorem 1 we compute $CNF(Th(M_1) \vee \ldots \vee Th(M_5))$ obtaining the following explanations:

$E*_1 = new(COURSE, C\_A, 0) \wedge new(COURSE, S\_A, 2) \wedge$
$\qquad \wedge new(PROFESSOR, S\_A, 1)$
$E*_2 = new(COURSE, C\_A, 0) \wedge old(SCHOOL, S\_A, 0)$
$E*_3 = new(COURSE, C\_A, 0) \wedge new(STUDENT, S\_A, 1) \wedge$
$\qquad \wedge new(PROFESSOR, S\_A, 1)$
$E*_4 = \neg new(STUDENT, S\_A, 1) \wedge old(SCHOOL, S\_A, 0)$
$E*_5 = \neg new(PROFESSOR, S\_A, 1) \wedge old(SCHOOL, S\_A, 0)$
$E*_6 = \neg new(COURSE, S\_A, 2) \wedge old(SCHOOL, S\_A, 0)$
$E*_7 = \neg new(COURSE, S\_A, 2) \wedge new(STUDENT, S\_A, 1) \wedge$
$\qquad \wedge new(PROFESSOR, S\_A, 1)$

We now control which of the above is a consistent explanation. Consider the minimal partial models of the given logic program P without the query, where S denotes $STUDENT$, F denotes $SCHOOL$, P denotes $PROFESSOR$ and C denotes $COURSES$:

$$M_1 = \{new(S, S\_A, 1), new(P, S\_A, 1), new(C, S\_A, 2), \neg new(C, C\_A, 0)\}$$

$M_2 = \{\neg old(F, S\_A, 0),\ new(C, S\_A, 2),\ \neg new(C, C\_A, 0)\}$
$M_3 = \{\neg old(F, S\_A, 0),\ \neg new(S, S\_A, 1),$
$\qquad new(P, C\_A, 1),\ \neg new(C, S\_A, 2)\}$
$M_4 = \{\neg old(F, S\_A, 0),\ \neg new(S, S\_A, 1),\ \neg new(C, C\_A, 0)\}$
$M_5 = \{\neg old(F, S\_A, 0),\ \neg new(P, S\_A, 1),\ new(P, C\_A, 1)\}$
$M_6 = \{\neg old(F, S\_A, 0),\ \neg new(P, S\_A, 1),\ \neg new(C, C\_A, 0)\}$

Let us denote $M_1, \dots, M_6$ the above minimal partial models then we have the bipartite graph of Figure 4.

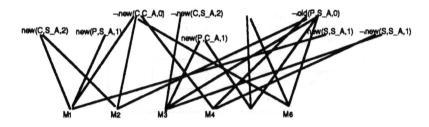

Fig 4. The bipartite Graph for detecting inconsistent explanations.

It is now easy to verify that, computing the irredundant sets of the bipartite graph, only the first three explanations are the consistent ones.

5 Discussion

As already observed, providing explanations for the incompatibilities generated during the step of multilevel integration because of the local, sometimes contradictory, knowledge owned by a user, is a very useful support tool to assist the user in this delicate phase of the design of a data dictionary. The logical framework devised in the paper could thus be thought as part of a *Knowledge Base Management System* which is able to elaborate the answers for the user in order to present them in a user-friendly way. In fact the interaction with the system should not be limited to just list a series of information perhaps incomprehensible for the user. For instance, as regard the application example, the answer explaining that adding the *professor* entity, which is defined as a refinement of the *course* entity, leads to an incompatibility, due to a circularity between these two entities in the refinement process, could be presented with entity-relationship diagrams as follows.

System: I already know that for the *school area* the refinement chain is :

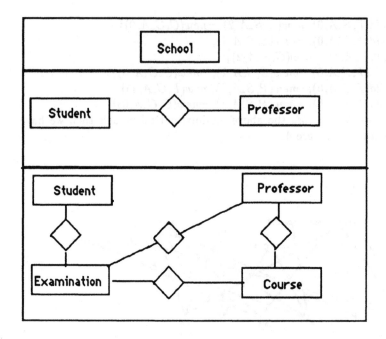

that is *course* is a refinement of *professor*.

You want, instead, assert the contrary, i.e. that *professor* is a refinement of *course* for the *course area*.

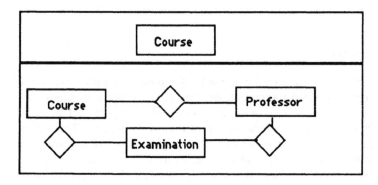

An interactive tool of this kind will help the user in improving his local knowledge of the world so that the final global schema represents the portion of reality of interest as closer as possible to the need of the end user.

6 Conclusions

Logic programming and abductive reasoning have been used during data dictionary design giving an insight of the power of both logic programming and abductive reasoning in representing and resolving some kinds of classical problems of the database world. The paper presented a logic approach to represent some steps of data dictionary design, with the methodology of Batini et al. [2] and the possibility to exploit *abductive reasoning* to provide explanations for the incompatibilities which can be generated during these steps. We are investigating in extending this kind of approach to all the phases of conceptual design to provide an helpful tool during this delicate phase of an information system realization.

7 Acknowledgements

We wish to thank Carlo Batini for many useful discussions and the anonimous referee for useful comments.

References

[1] K.R.Apt, H.A.Blair, A.Walker,"Towards a theory of declarative knowledge", in J.Minker ed. *Foundations of Deductive Database and Logic Programming*, pp.89-148, 1988, Morgan-Kaufmann.

[2] C. Batini, G. Di Battista, G. Santucci "Representation Structures for Data Dictionaries", *Technical Report*, 9, May, 1991, Università di Roma "'La Sapienza".

[3] F. Bry, "Intensional Updates: Abduction via Deduction" D. Warren and P.Szeredi, eds,*Logic Programming: Proc. 7th Intl. Conf. on Logic Programming*, pp.561-575, Cambridge, MA, 1990, MIT Press.

[4] T. Bylander, D. Allemang, M.C. Tanner and J.R. Josephson, "Some Results Concerning the Computational Complexity of Abduction", *Proc. First Int. Conf. on Principles of Knowledge Representation and Reasoning*, Toronto, pp.44-54,1989, Morgan-Kaufmann.

[5] P. M. Dung, "Negation as Hypotheses: an Abductive Foundation for Logic Programming", *Proc. 7th Intl. Conf. on Logic Programming*, pp. 3-17, 1991.

[6] K. Eshghi and R.A. Kowalski, "Abduction Compared with Negation by Failure", *Proc. 6th Intl. Conf. on Logic Programming*, pp. 234-254, 1989, MIT Press.

[7] D.Gabbay, E.Laenens, D.Vermair " Credoulous vs. skeptical semantics for ordered logic programs",*KR 91*, pp.208-217, Morgan Kaufman, 1991.

[8] A.C. Kakas and P. Mancarella, "Generalized Stable Models: a Semantics for Abduction", L.C.Aiello ed. *Proc. ECAI 90*, pp. 385-391, London, 1990, Pitman.

[9] A.C. Kakas and P. Mancarella, "On the Relation between Truth Maintenance and Abduction", *Proc. PRICAI 90*, pp. 438-443, Nagoya, Japan, 1990.

[10] H.J. Levesque, "A knowledge-level account of abduction" *Proc. IJCAI '89*, pp.1061-1067, Detroit, MI, 1989, Morgan-Kaufmann.

[11] F.Pirri and C.Pizzuti, '*Explaining Incompatibilities in Data Dictionary Design Through Abduction*, DIS, Technical Report, 1992, Università di Roma "'La Sapienza".

[12] R. Reiter and J. de Kleer, "Foundations of Assumption-Based Truth Maintenance Systems: Preliminary Report", *Proc. of the National Conference on Artificial Intelligence*, pp.183-188, 1987, Seattle, WA.

[13] K. Satoh and N. Iwayama, "Computing Abduction by Using the TMS", *Proc. 7th Intl. Conf. on Logic Programming*, pp. 3-17, 1991.

[14] M. Shanahan, "Prediction is Deduction but Explanation is Abduction", *Proc. of the 8th National Conference on Artificial Intelligence*, 1990, pp. 1055-1060, Boston, Ma.

[15] B. Selman and H.J. Levesque, "Abductive and Default Reasoning: A Computational Core", *Proc. of the 8th National Conference on Artificial Intelligence*, pp. 343-348, 1990, Boston, Ma.

Nesting Quantification
in A Visual Data Manipulation Language

Takao MIURA
SANNO College
Kamikasuya 1573 Isehara, Kanagawa, JAPAN
E-mail: miura@sanno.ac.jp

Abstract

In this paper we propose a new approach to provide us with (universal and existential) quantification in a visual data manipulation language called *PIM algebra*. Overall ideas are two basic constructs, one for universal ($\forall$) quantifier and another for existential ($\exists$) quantifier. Then a nesting feature is considered to obtain general expressive power. The major contribution of this paper is that, for every query specification with any depth of nesting of quantification, there is an equivalent *canonical* form which can be easily processed by database management systems.

Keywords – Databases, Visual Data Manipulation Languages, Quantifications, Expressive Power.

1 Introduction

1.1 Motivation

Recently new types of requirements in database processing capabilities have been increasing in several area of applications. Among them, a variety of sophisticated techniques for *end-user interface* are required although less progress has been made in this area. Many of traditional database query languages suffer from the fact that they are textually oriented and very formal. One of the solutions is certainly visual presentation of databases. It provides a high level of abstraction (modularity) to be understood easily, And the query formulation is possible by specifying parts of a diagram in any order while the operations could be validated interactively. All of building, browsing schemes and and constructing queries are accomplished using a same style of interface, that is, *point and click* interface.

One of the major deficiencies in visual approach is that there is no solid foundation nor theoretical basis. We have already proposed a visual data manipulation language *PIM*. We have shown that the language is *complete* in a sense that it has the equal expressive power of extended many sorted logic [16, 20]. Another defficiency is that it is hard to describe *scope* in a two dimensional syntax without loss of intuition, since we need two kinds of quantification, *universal* quantification and *existential* quantification.

Traditional investigations try to design the languages with a minimum number of constructs: *existential graph* contains only conjunction, negation and existential quantifier [6], *U-box* approach adds universal quantifier to SPJ queries [21]. Both follow a good principle but almost all investigations seem to suffer from complicated description; over-simplification produces inevitable complication. We propose *two kinds* of vehicles to describe quantification and scope. Then what kinds of new functionalities should be provided ?

In this paper, first we consider *E-pad* and *A-pad*. The former can be utilized for existential queries and the latter for universal queries. Then we describe how quantification are expressed in a nested way. The main result is that every query can be transformed into a canonical form which is suitable for processing.

1.2 Related Works

Let us briefly present related systems with an emphasis on quantification techniques that overlap those of PIM. The primary purpose of this survey is to see how well visual query languages have the capabilities of quantification.

SQL has a basic query construct SELECT .. FROM .. WHERE ... Although existential query is implicit in this construct, universal quantification can be made by ISNOTIN, NOT EXISTS and ALL. Query-By-Example is partially visual and has *SET* constructor which can serve as universal query, but scope capabilities are incomplete[24]. *Pasta-3* is a front-end system of a knowledge base and database system KB2 [13]. The basic construct is a table of QBE extended by boolean connectives and quantifiers. Scope is described by relative spatial position, left-to-right and top-to-bottom ordering just same as *textual* description. A form-based system has been proposed on nested relational model but the queries are textually described [1].

The several pioneer works have been done based on E–R model. GUIDE is the first graphics-based schema management system [22]. This system is visual but there is no query language nor no quantification. GQL is a much elegant visual language in a sense that the system always tries to find a *default path* between two nodes[23]. But it has no qunatification mechanism. The notable one is a system based on ECER (extended category E–R) model [5, 7]. The visual language is shown to be *complete* with respect to its algebraic language, which is again shown to be relationally complete. Unfortunately the scope cannot be specified in the quantified queries.

Visual languagaes based on *semantic data models* have been also proposed[14]. SKI is the first interactive schema manager, ISIS is the mouse based system [12]. Both systems require defining new *types* to specify queries by giving predicates textually. SNAP is a graphics-based language based on IFO [4] though the expressive power of the language remains unknown. Object oriented paradigm is yet another approach but these systems has no explicit quantification[9].

Several recent investigations propose *direct* quantification. A notable model ENIAM is another approach to describe conceptual schema and integrity constraints [6]. The visual description of constraints is based on *existential graph* including quantification and scope. Unfortunately it has no query capability. In E-R based approach, universal quantification is described with a *U-box*[21]. But it is assumed to interpret quantification in a resricted way and they miss generality. *DUO* is another approach based on a graph model to handle universal quantification that can be graphically represented[10]. But it seems to have the restricted interpretation.

PIM (Personal Information Management) algebra is defined as a visual language in a sense that it is a schema level *and* an instance level browser. Parts of PIM algebra seem similar to SNAP system since IFO is similar in spirit to AIS data model. Notable properties are : it can integrate complex objects with type concepts. It is *complete*, that is, we have a logic based language which has the equal power to this visual language. Here we extend PIM to have quantification capabilities.

1.3 Configuration

In section 2, we briefly describe a semantic data model *AIS* and algebraic capabilities of a visual data manipulation language. Section 3 focusses on quantification problem, nesting and views. In section 4 we give transformation rules to obtain standard forms which can be processed easily and efficiently. We conclude our discussion in section 5.

2 A Visual Data Manipulation Language

An interactive graphics-based system called *PIM* (Personal Information Management) is a general purpose schema management and query processing system for AIS. First of all, a brief overview of AIS model based on several examples is presented here. We peresent those features that are relevant for our discussion.

AIS (Associative Information Structure) data model consists of several primitive concepts that are well-known to semantic data models: entity types, complex-object types, inter-type relationship, ISA and general constraints. Similar to E-R model, *entities* (surrogates of objects in the real world) and *associations* (relationship among objects) are captured directly into modeling processes. An entity is said to have a *type* or an *entity type* if it shares certain common properties. We assume every type has non-empty, finite set of the entities, that is, there exist a finite number (and non-zero) of entities of the type. An association is assumed to have a *predicate* if it has certain common properties. A predicate has a set of distinct types, called *defined types*, that are enforced on related entities. An association must be identified by a predicate name p and the defined types with the entities. We assume every entity must have a type *Entity*. Also AIS provides a mechanism to describe *complex objects* by set and tuple constructors.

There is a natural correspondence between graph representation and AIS databases. Figure 1(a) contains a *data diagram* which shows 5 associations on two predicates *SELL* and *SUPPLY*. In this diagram of instance level, an entity is shown using a small circle (○), for example, m means an instance of type *SName*. A filled circle (●) is used to indicate an association. A set of entities are connected together by this notation. For example, s, $c1$ make one association. Figure 1(b) shows a *schema diagram* of this database. An entity type is indicated by set notation with a label and a predicate by a diamond (◇). A set symbol *SName* is contained in *Company*. This means a kind of generalization constraints, *SName ISA Company*. Therefore, for example, m must be a company. More detail discussion is in [2, 3, 18, 19].

Let us compare AIS with E-R model to understand our model easily. Roughly speaking there exist three points of clear distinction. First, no attribute concept is provided but is considered as relationship. Entities are not distingushed from attribute values. Secondly, in AIS one object has to be represented by one entity. That means one entity may have several entity types independent of type (class) hierarchy, or equivalently *mutiple inheritance* typing is allowed. The last point is that, to our knowledge, E-R model has no capability to describe *construction* of complex objects in a formal manner.

A visual data manipulation language, *PIM algebra*, has two dimensional syntax[15, 16, 20]. It displays parts of (or total) database schema, which are query *templates* described by graphical patterns such as sets and diamonds. Query specification can be made by several *E-pads* or just *pads*. Every pad corresponds to one of predicates in a database, it has selection-type conditions. Also it can have *overlap* conditions to equate two instances. When evaluating them, we can obtain a set of (parts of) associations that *match* the E-pads.

Example 2.1 (See figure 2)
Consider a query: 'Find departments who sell an item $c1$'.
As shown in figure 2(a), an E-pad consists of one diamond and several set symbols, indicating part of predicate definition. Figure 2(b) shows one of the answers. □

Generally an E-pad consists of three parts, *free variable* part X, *predicate* part P and *condition* part Θ. Free variables mean entity types to be asked, and they are underlined. Set symbols without underline are assumed to be existentially quantified. Conditions discussed in this paper are only boolean combination of equalities and inequalities for simplicity. Symbols in a set mean that an entity of the type are qualified. For instance, in figure 2(a), an underlined type *Dept* shows a free variable, a diamond *SELL* shows a predicate and a constant $c1$ means an equality condition. By this E-pad, a set of (part of) associations of $SELL$ are extracted from AIS databases if the item is $c1$.

Let us describe pads pads in a formal manner. Conceptually we can describe an E-pad as follows;

$$E(X \in A, P(XY), \Theta(XY)) = \{X \in A : (\exists Y \in B) P(XY) \wedge \Theta(XY)\}$$

where A, B means part of defined types of a predicate P, $X \in A$ means $(x_1 \in A_1) \cdots (x_n \in A_n), n \geq 0$ and $Y \in B$ means $(\exists y_1 \in B_1) \cdots (\exists y_m \in B_m), m \geq 0$. Quantified variables are bounded within a pad. We sometimes omit A, B if no confusion arises. Also we omit a condition part Θ if Θ is $TRUE$.

$$E(X, P) = \{X \in E_1 : (\exists Y \in E_2) P(XY)\}$$

A trivial query $\{X \in A : P(X)\}$ can be described by $E(X \in A, P(X))$. Every answer $< a_1 \cdots a_n >$ has the types $A = A_1 \cdots A_n$. An association of the predicate P is called to be *matched* if and only if it satisfies Θ. Then an answer is a part of this association (on A). Since every type has a finite and non-empty extension, the answers must be finite. The answer with no free variable is $TRUE$ if $P(Y)$ can be true. An E-pad seems just like SELECT X FROM P WHERE Θ in SQL [8].

An E-pad can be seen as a definition of a new predicate defined over $A \times < condition >$ where $< condition >$ represents a conceptual type not to be referred. This abstract predicate can be drawn again in a graphical manner. Figure 3 shows an abstract E-pad for figure 2(a).

An operation *structuring* is utilized for specifying disjunction. Also pads can be related each other by *overlapping*. It is utilized to equate two instances of underlined sets appeared in pads.

Example 2.2 Figure 4 shows fundamental queries.
(1) 'Find red items and the departments who sell them'.

$$E(v \in Item, SUPPLY(uvw), w =' red') \wedge E(x \in Dept, SELL(xy), v = y)$$

In figure 4(a), two E-pads (one is asking for $SELL$, another for $SUPPLY$) are *overlapped* over a set $Item$ indicating one fact that some items are shared.
(2) 'Find red items, blue items and the departments who sell both'.

$$E(v_1 \in Item, SUPPLY(uv_1w), w =' red')$$

$$\wedge E(v_2 \in Item, SUPPLY(uv_2w), w =' blue')$$

$$\wedge E(x \in Dept, SELL(xy), y = v_1)$$

$$\wedge E(x \in Dept, SELL(xy), y = v_2)$$

In figure 4(b), one department must sell red items *and* blue items at the same time.
(3) 'Find red or blue items and the suppliers who supply them'.

$$(E(v_1 \in Item, SUPPLY(uv_1w), w =' red') \wedge E(x \in Dept, SELL(xy), y = v_1))$$

$$\vee (E(v_2 \in Item, SUPPLY(uv_2w), w =' blue') \wedge E(x \in Dept, SELL(xy), y = v_2))$$

Figure 4(c) describes this query. $\square$

3 Quantification and Views

3.1 Quantification

In *E-pad* mechanism no quantification problem can arise since only free variables and existentially quantified variables are allowed. If we introduce universal quantification[1], we should consider *scope* for each variable.

Traditionally universal quantification has been considered a difficult concept for typical database users. For example there exist not a few people who feel hard to understand ALL or EXISTS in SQL syntax. It has not been fully integrated in many practical database languages. In fact, Query-By-Example[2] supports only part of the quantification. In this section, we introduce quantified queries. The basic idea is that we define another construct of universal quantification called an *A-pad*.

Example 3.1 Consider the following queries.
(1) 'Find departments such that all the items they sell are c1'.

$$(x \in Dept) : (\forall y \in Item)(SELL(xy) \rightarrow y =' c1')$$

(2) 'Find suppliers such that all the items they supply are *red*'.

$$(x \in SName) : (\forall y \in Item)(\forall z \in Color)(SUPPLY(xyz) \rightarrow z =' red')$$

(3) 'Find departments who don't sell c1'.

$$(x \in Dept) : \neg(\exists y \in Item)SELL(xy) \wedge y =' c1'$$

□

An A-pad consists of three parts just same as an E-pad; variables X and Y, a predicate $P(XY)$ and a condition Θ. We say a part of an association of P, $< a_1 \cdots a_n >$ *satisfies* this A-pad if all Y satisfying $P(< a_1 \cdots a_n > Y)$ satisfy $\Theta(< a_1 \cdots a_n > Y)$. The answers of an A-pad are defined as follows:

$$A(X; Y, P(XY), \Theta) = \{X \in E_1 : (\forall Y \in E_2)P(XY) \rightarrow \Theta(XY)\}$$

where $\forall Y \in E_2$ means $(\forall y_1 \in E_2^1) \cdots (\forall y_n \in E_2^n), n \geq 0$. A set of variables Y after the semicolon mean they are universally quantified. If there is no free variable, we may omit X. We omit a condition Θ if Θ is $FALSE$:

$$A(X; Y, P) = \{X \in E_1 : (\forall Y \in E_2)\neg P(XY)\}$$

A trivial query $\{X \in A : \neg P(X)\}$ can be described by $A(X, P(X))$.

Example 3.2 The queries in example 3.1 can be expressed in figure 5 as follows:
(1) $A(x; y, SELL(xy), y =' c1')$
(2) $A(x; yz, SUPPLY(xyz), z =' red')$
(3) $\neg E(x, SELL(xy), y =' c1')$
□

As in figure 5, an A-pad is similar to those of E-pads except it is surrounded by a bold box and Y are marked. If an A-pad has a constant c in a set symbol E_1, an answer $< a_1 \cdots a_n >$ satisfies this A-pad if all Y satisfying $P(< a_1 \cdots a_n > Y)$ satisfies the equality condition; the

---

[1] Or equivalently, negation causes scope problems.
[2] And so do the descendants like PARADOX

value on E_1 must be c. To separate E-pads from A-pads, E-pads are sometimes surrounded by solid box. Similarly negation of E-pads or A-pads can be described by dotted boxes (dotted solid boxes or dotted bold boxes). Note that every symbol outside a box has no scope restriction by a box though the opposite holds in [10, 21]. A-pads can be re-drawn in abstract form if any. That is, only entity types of free variables remain in the pad, other entity types disappear and an abstract type $< condition >$ contains a condition part.

There may exist variables Z that are not free nor universally quantified. In such case we assume Z are existentially quantifed before Y.

$$A(X; Y, P(XYZ), \Theta) = \{X \in E_1 : (\exists Z \in E_3)(\forall Y \in E_2)P(XYZ) \rightarrow \Theta(XYZ)\}$$

An A-pad is called *full* if there is no such Z.

Example 3.3 Consider the following two different queries.
(1) 'Find suppliers who supply all the items with some colors'.

$$\{x \in SName : (\forall y \in Item)(\exists z \in Color)SUPPLY(xyz)\}$$

(2) 'Find suppliers who supply all the items of only one color'.

$$\{x \in SName : (\exists z \in Color)(\forall y \in Item)SUPPLY(xyz)\}$$

□

According to our definition, the second query is described by a basic (but not full) A-pad[3] while the first cannot. By using view technique described later on, the reader can easily express general kinds of universal quantification.

We can discuss *overlaping* and *structuring* of A-pads just same as E-pads. Note overlapping can be applied only to set symbols that are underlined. It is perfectly OK to overlap E-pads and A-pads as well as A-pads and A-pads.

3.2   Nesting Pads

In SQL, one of the interesting features is the nesting query blocks to an arbitrary depth. Without this function, the expressive power is severely restricted[8, 11]. In PIM algebra, we introduce the nesting feature into a condition part of pads.

We say a pad Γ has *nested* conditions of a pad Δ if a condition part of Γ contains Δ. In PIM algebra, we can imagine that a box of a pad contains another box. Such nesting gives *scope* of variables.

Nested conditions discussed here are set-membership, set containment and set existence. First, let us consider the case that E-pads appear in set membership conditions. In PIM algebra, this condition is represented by an directed arrow from a set symbol to an *underlined* set symbol in the inner E-pad[4]. The inner E-pad may share the values of the outer pads. Non-membership can be described with a label **NOT** on arrows.

Example 3.4 Consider the following typical JOIN queries.
(1) 'Find departments who sell *red* items' (see figure 6(a)).

$$E(x \in Dept, SELL(xy), y \in E(v \in Item, SUPPLY(uvw), w =' red'))$$

This query shows set membership. The inner E-pad has its own *free* variables within the pad (*Item* in this case), i.e., bounded by a solid box.
(2) 'Find suppliers who supply *red* and *blue* items' (figure 6(b)).

$$E(x \in SName, SUPPLY(xyz),$$

---

[3]In fact, we have $A((x \in SName); (\forall y \in Item), \neg SUPPLY(xyz))$.
[4]Or we still plan to represent *pasting* pads; Pads are layered so that the inner E-pad is pasted to the outer pad.

$$z =' red' \wedge y \in E(v \in Item, SUPPLY(uvw), x = u \wedge w =' blue'))$$

This query shows that the inner pad may share *free* variables (x in this case) represented by overlapping underlined sets ($SName$ in this example).

(3) 'Find departments who do *not* sell *red* items'.

$$E(x \in Dept, SELL(xy), y \notin E(v \in Item, SUPPLY(uvw), w =' red'))$$

$$E(x \in Dept, SELL(xy), y \in A(v \in Item; uw, SUPPLY(uvw), w \neq' red'))$$

We have two styles of description(figure 6(c),(d)). □

We can discuss set existence condition by pads with no free variable of set-membership.

Nested conditions can be utilized for the description of set containment. We can determine truth value by comparing sets of answers of pads. In PIM algebra, these are given within a pad. In most cases, the inner pads may take over the values of the outer pad so that the truth value can be determined depending on these values. Graphically a directed arrow with a label SUBSET represents containments instead of set-membership.

Example 3.5 (See figure 7(a), (b))

(1) 'Find suppliers such that, for every item they supply, they supply the *red* item'.

$$A((x \in SName); (y \in Item), SUPPLY(xyz),$$

$$E(, SUPPLY(uvw), u = x \wedge v = y \wedge w =' red'))$$

In the query, the inner E-pad has no free variable[5]. An association of $SUPPLY$ becomes an answer if $SName$ value satisfies $SUPPY(xy'red')$ for every $Item$ y that x supplies.

(2) 'Find suppliers that supply same *red* items if they supply *blue* items.

$$E(x \in SName, SUPPLY(xyz),$$

$$E(v, SUPPLY(xvw_1), w_1 =' blue') \subseteq E(v, SUPPLY(xvw_2), w_2 =' red'))$$

□

3.3 Nesting Predicates

We can extend a pad in such a way that a predicate part P may be predicates, E-pads, A-pads or their boolean combination. In other words, we can define *nested predicates*. If a predicate part consists of only one E-pad (one A-pad), the predicate part is called an *E-view* (*A-view* respectively). The mechanism has more expressive power than basic constructs. For example, we can give an example that cannot be described only by basic pads.

Example 3.6 Consider the query that is impossible to describe in example 3.3 (see figure 8): 'Find suppliers who supply all the items with some colors'. Using nesting feature, this can be expressed by an A-pad :

$$A((x \in SName); y, E(xy, SUPPLY(xyz)))$$

□

Nested predicate expression can be described in two ways. If a predicate part consists of only predicate symbols, the syntax can be seen as a view name. If there exist duplicate names among defined types, they are appropriately qualified or renamed. If a predicate part is nested, then there exits a directed arrow from an inner pad to an outer predicate with an appropriate name.

---

[5] In SQL, it corresponds to a keyword EXISTS.

Example 3.7 Consider the following queries.
(1) 'Find departments and suppliers such that the department sells the items sold by the suppliers.' (see figure 9(a)).

$$E((x \in Dept)(y \in SName), SELL(xz) \wedge SUPPLY(yuv), u = z)$$

(2) 'Find suppliers such that, for every item they supply, they also supply the $r'd$ items' (figure 9(b)).

$$A(x \in SName; y, E(xy, SUPPLY(xyz)),$$

$$x \in E(u \in SName, SUPPLY(uvw), v = y \wedge w =' red'))$$

(3) 'Find suppliers such that, for every item, if there exists all the colors of the items supplied by the supplier, then the item must be p' (figure 9(c)).

$$A(x \in SName; y, A(xy; z, SUPPLY(xyz)), y =' p'))$$

□

4 Simplification

4.1 Canonical Pads

Canonical pads are E-pads or A-pads are suitable for efficient processing. Formally we say an E-pad $E(X, \beta(XY), \Theta)$ is *canonical* if

(1) β consists of boolean combination of predicates and simple conditions.
(2) And, Θ consists of boolean combination of predicates and simple conditions.

Similarly we say an A-pad $A(X; Y, \beta(XYZ), \Theta)$ is *canonical* if

(1) Θ consists of boolean combination of predicates and simple conditions. And,
(2-1) β consists of a succesive canonical A-pad (called an A^n pad[6]).
(2-2) Or β consists of boolean combination of predicates and simple conditions.

In short, canonical pads are one of the following forms:

(1) $E(X, \beta(XY), \Theta)$
(2) $A(X; Y, A^n(XYZ, \beta(XYZ)), \Theta)$

where β and Θ mean boolean combination of predicates and simple conditions. For example, unnested E-pads are canonical; the first and the last queries in example 3.7 are canonical but the second is not.

Given nested pads, we have to evaluate the inner pads for each value in predicate parts of the outer pad but we can examine canonical E-pads by conventional database techniques. Possibly this observation allows us to improve the efficiency dramatically.

From now on we show that every pad can be transformed into a canonical pad. That is, we will transform nested conditions and nested predicates into unnested ones. The basic idea is similar to the optimization technique of SQL queries [11]. Because of the space limitation, we skip all the proofs.

---

[6]That is, a canonical A-pad whose predicate part consists of a canonical A-pad whose predicate part ····

4.2 Decomposing Pads

First of all, let us discuss decomposition rules of condition parts. The condition parts are assumed to be in disjunctive normal form and all $p(X), \neg p(X)$ in condition parts are described by trivial pads $E(X, p(X)), A(X, p(X))$ respectively where p means predicate symbols. Then there remain only simple conditions ; $x =' c', x \neq' c', x = y, x \neq y$.

The following lemma makes evaluation easier.

Lemma 1 Assume a condition Θ has boolean connectives $\vee, \wedge$. Then pads with the conditions can be simplified as follows:

(1) $E(X, P(XY), \Theta_1 \wedge \Theta_2) = E(X, P(XY) \wedge \Theta_1, \Theta_2)$

Especially we can *remove* condition part if no Θ_2 appears.

(2) $A(X; Y, P(XYZ), \Theta_1 \wedge \Theta_2) = E(X, A(XZ; Y, P(XYZ), \Theta_1) \wedge A(XZ; Y, P(XYZ), \Theta_2))$

(3) $E(X, P(XY), \Theta_1 \vee \Theta_2) = E(X, P(XY), \Theta_1) \vee E(X, P(XY), \Theta_2)$

(4) $A(X; Y, P(XYZ), \Theta_1 \vee \Theta_2) = A(X; Y, P(XYZ) \wedge \neg \Theta_1, \Theta_2)$

Especially we can *remove* condition part if no Θ_2 appears.

□

All E-pads (A-pads) become free of disjunctive connectives (conjunctive connectives respectively) by decomposing them. On the other hand, conjunction of E-pads (disjunction of A-pads) can be *moved* to predicate parts.

The second kind of decomposition concerns simplification of nested conditions. The next two lemmas say that nested conditions can be transformed into unnested ones.

Lemma 2 (Membership) Let $\beta(Y)$ be a pad that has Y as free variables and γ be a pad with no free variable.

(1) $E(X, P(XY), \Theta \wedge (Y \in \beta(U))) = E(X, P(XY) \wedge \beta(Y), \Theta)$

where $\beta(Y)$ is obtained by replacing all U by Y.

(2) $A(X, P(XY), \Theta \vee (Y \in \beta(U))) = A(X, P(XY) \wedge \neg \beta(Y), \Theta)$.

(3) $E(X, P(XY), \Theta \wedge \gamma) = E(X, P(XY) \wedge \gamma, \Theta)$.

(4) $A(X, P(XY), \Theta \vee \gamma) = A(X, P(XY) \wedge \neg \gamma, \Theta)$.

□

Lemma 3 (Containment) Assume there are two E-pads $E_i(X) = E(X, \beta_i(XY_i), \Theta_i(XY_i))$ and two A-pads $A_i(X) = A(X; U_i, \beta_i(XU_iV_i), \Theta_i(XU_iV_i))$ where $i = 1, 2$.

(1) $(\forall X)E_1(X) \subseteq E_2(X)$ can be described by

$$A(; X, A(X; Y_2, A(XY_2; Y_1, \beta_1(XY_1) \wedge \neg \beta_2(XY_2), \neg \Theta_1) \wedge$$
$$A(XY_2; Y_1, \beta_1(XY_1), \neg \Theta_1 \vee \Theta_2)))$$

(2) $(\forall X)E_1(X) \subseteq A_2(X)$ can be described by

$$A(; X, A(X; Z_2, A(XZ_2; Y_2Y_1, \beta_1(XY_1) \wedge \beta_2(XY_2Z_2), \neg \Theta_1 \vee \Theta_2)))$$

(3) $(\forall X)A_1(X) \subseteq E_2(X)$ can be described by

$$A(; X, A(X; Y_2, A(XY_2; Z_1, A(XY_2Z_1; Y_1, \beta_1(XY_1Z_1) \wedge \neg \beta_2(XY_2), \Theta_1)) \wedge$$
$$A(XY_2Z_1; Y_1, \beta_1(XY_1Z_1), \Theta_1 \vee \Theta_2))))$$

(4) $(\forall X)A_1(X) \subseteq A_2(X)$ can be described by

$$A(; X, A(X; Z_2, A(XZ_2; Y_2Z_1, A(XY_2Z_1Z_2; Y_1, \beta_1(XY_1Z_1) \wedge \beta_2(XY_2Z_2), \Theta_1 \vee \Theta_2))))$$

□

By lemma 1 and lemma 3, all the nested conditions can be represented as pads in predicate parts. So we can assume that every pad has no disjunction, no conjunction and no pad in its condition part.

Next let us consider how to decompose predicate expressions. We assume a predicate expression is in disjunctive normal forms.

Lemma 4 Let $\beta_i(X)$ be a predicate expression or a pad expression with free variables X.
(1) An E-pad over disjunction can be decomposed into two E-pads.

$$E(X, \beta_1(XY) \vee \beta_2(XY), \Theta) = E(X, \beta_1(XY), \Theta) \vee E(X, \beta_2(XY), \Theta)$$

(2) An A-pad over disjunction can be transformed into an E-pad that has two A-pads in the predicate part.

$$A(X; Y, \beta_1(XYZ) \vee \beta_2(XYZ), \Theta) = E(X, A(XZ; Y, \beta_1(XYZ), \Theta) \wedge A(XZ; Y, \beta_2(XYZ), \Theta))$$

(3) An E-pad with negated predicate part can be described by an E-pad over A-view.

$$E(X, \neg\beta_1(XY), \Theta) = E(X, A(XY, \beta_1(XY)), \Theta)$$

(4) An A-pad with negated predicate part can be described by an A-pad over A-view.

$$A(X; Y, \neg\beta_1(XYZ), \Theta) = A(X; Y, A(XYZ, \beta_1(XYZ)), \Theta)$$

□

By this lemma, we can decompose pads into ones that have no disjunction nor negation in predicate parts. As a result we can assume every pad or every pad within a pad is of the form $E(X, \beta(XY), \Theta)$ or $A(X; Y, \beta(XYZ), \Theta)$ where β is in conjunctive form $\alpha_1 \wedge \cdots \wedge \alpha_n$, α_i is a predicate, a pad or a simple condition. As fo rconjunction, there exists no clear characterization and we cannot decompose the structure any more.

4.3 Synthesizing Conjunction

By the decomposition rules, we can assume predicate parts are in conjunctiove forms. In this subsection we show these can be synthesized into one pad. First of all, we discuss *negation* problem.

Lemma 5 (Negation) We have the following relationship between E-pads and A-pads.
(1) $\neg E(X, \beta(XY), \Theta) = A(X, \beta(XY), \neg\Theta)$
(2) $\neg A(X; Y, \beta(XYZ), \Theta) = A(X; Z, A(XZ; Y, \beta(XYZ), \Theta))$

□

For instance, two pads of an example 3.4 (3) are equivalent. Now we prove that conjunctive combination of pads can be synthesized into one. Remember we can generate boolean combination of pads; conjunction of pads, disjunction of pads and difference of pads. The techniques show all the results also can be described by single pads.

Lemma 6 (Conjunction) Let $E_i(X_i) = E(X_i, \beta_i(X_iY_i), \Theta_i)$ be E-pads and $A_i(X_i) = A(X_i; Y_i, \gamma_i(X_iY_iZ_i), \Gamma_i)$ be A-pads. Moreover assume no common variable exists among X_i, Y_j, Z_k except X_i and X_j. The followings hold without increasing nesting depth.
(1) Conjunction of two E-pads can be expressed by one E-pad. That is,

$$E_1(X_1) \wedge E_2(X_1) = E(X_1X_2, \beta_1(X_1Y_1) \wedge \beta_2(X_2Y_2), \Theta_1 \wedge \Theta_2)$$

(2) Conjunction of two A-pads can be expressed by one A-pad. That is,

$$A_1(X_1) \wedge A_2(X_2) = A(X_1X_2; Y_1Y_2, \gamma_1 \vee \gamma_2, (\Gamma_1 \wedge \Gamma_2) \vee (\Gamma_1 \wedge \neg\gamma_2) \vee (\neg\gamma_1 \wedge \Gamma_2))$$

(3) Conjunction of an A-pad and E-pad can be expressed by an A-pad.

$$A_1(X_1) \wedge E_2(X_2) = A(X_1X_2; Y_1, \gamma_1(X_1Y_1Z_1) \vee \neg\beta_2(X_2Y_2) \vee \neg\Theta_2, \Gamma_1 \wedge \beta_2 \wedge \Theta_2)$$

□

Lemma 7 (Conditions) Let β predicate expression or a pad expression, and $\Theta(X), \Gamma(Z)$ be conditions. The followings hold without increasing nesting depth.

(1) $E(X, \beta, \Theta) \wedge \Gamma(Z) = E(XZ, \beta, \Theta \wedge \Gamma)$

(2) $E(X, \beta, \Theta) \vee \Gamma(Z) = E(XZ, \beta \vee \Gamma, \Theta \vee \Gamma)$

(3) $A(X; Y, \beta, \Theta) \wedge \Gamma(Z) = A(XZ; Y, \beta \vee \neg\Gamma, \Theta \wedge \Gamma)$

(4) $A(X; Y, \beta, \Theta) \vee \Gamma(Z) = A(XZ, \beta, \Theta \vee \Gamma)$

□

By these above synthesizing rules, we can assume that predicate parts of pad consist of just one pad or boolean combination of predicates (or negation) and simple conditions.

4.4 Synthesizing Nested Predicates

In this subsection let us discuss nested predicates.

Lemma 8 (NestedPredicates) Let $\beta(W)$ be a predicate expression or a pad expression with free variables W. Nested predicate can be simplified into unnested ones as follows:

(1) An E-pad of E-view can be unnested to an E-pad.

$$E(X, E(XY, \beta(XYZ), \Theta_1), \Theta_2) = E(X, \beta(XYZ), \Theta_1 \wedge \Theta_2)$$

(2) An E-pad of A-view can be unnested to an A-pad.

$$E(X, A(XY; Z, \beta(XYZW), \Theta_1), \Theta_2) = A(X; Z, \beta(XYZW) \vee \neg\Theta_2, \Theta_1 \wedge \Theta_2)$$

(3) An A-pad of E-view can be unnested to an A-pad.

$$A(X; Y, E(XYZ, \beta(XYZW), \Theta_1), \Theta_2) = A(X; YW, \beta(XYZW), \neg\Theta_1 \vee \Theta_2)$$

□

Lemma 8 says that successive nested predicates can be simplified into one level nest if it is not a successive A-view (i.e., A-view over A-view over $\cdots$). In the case of successive A-views, we have the following results.

Lemma 9 (NestedPredicates) Assume we have an A-pad over A-view.

$$A(X; Y, A(XYZ; W, \beta(XYZWU), \Theta_1), \Theta_2))$$

(1) If no W part appears, this can be described by an unnested A-pad.

$$A(X; YU, \neg\beta \vee \Theta_1, \Theta_2)$$

(2) If no Y, U part appears, this can be described by an unnested E-pad.

$$E(X, \beta \vee \Theta_2, \neg\Theta_1 \vee \Theta_2)$$

(Proof) □

No general simplification can be made to successive A-views. This is the case that we have to implement by means of sophisticated techniques like physically organized structures.

By applying synthesizing rules, every decomposed pad can be synthesized equivalently into an E-pad or an A-pad over succesive A-views where the innermost pad consists of boolean ($\vee, \wedge$) combination of predicates, simple conditions and their negation. In our words, we can get to *canonical* pads.

4.5   Synthesizing Canonical Pads

By the above discussion, we can say that every pad is decomposed into boolean combination of canonical pads. In this subsection we show the transformation rules to synthesize canonical pads and conditions into one canonical pad.

We have already discussed negation of pads, conjunction of pads and pads with conditions. Here we show disjunctive case.

Lemma 10 (Disjunction) Let $E_i(X_i) = E(X_i, \beta_i(X_iY_i), \Theta_i)$ be E-pads and $A_i(X_i) = A(X_i; Y_i, \gamma_i(X_iY_iZ_i), \Gamma_i)$ be A-pads. Moreover assume no common variable exists among variables except X_i and X_j. The followings hold without generating any new nested conditions.

(1) Disjunction of two E-pads can be expressed by an E-pad.

$$E_1(X_1) \vee E_2(X_2) = E(X_1X_2, \beta_1 \vee \beta_2, (\beta_1 \vee \Theta_2) \wedge (\beta_2 \vee \Theta_1) \wedge (\Theta_1 \vee \Theta_2))$$

(2) Disjunction of two A-pads can be expressed by an A-pad.

$$A_1(X_1) \vee A_2(X_2) = A(X_1X_2; Y_1Y_2, \beta_1(X_1Y_1Z_1) \wedge \beta_2(X_2Y_2Z_2), \Gamma_1 \vee \Gamma_2)$$

(3) Disjunction of an E-pad and an A-pad can be expressed by an A-pad.

$$A_1(X_1) \vee E_2(X_2) =$$

$$A(X_1X_2; W_1W_2, ((\gamma_1(X_1W_1Z_1) \wedge \neg\beta_2(X_1Y_2)) \vee \gamma_1(X_1W_2Z_1)) \wedge$$

$$\neg(\Gamma_1(X_1W_1Z_1) \wedge \neg\gamma_1(X_1W_2Z_1)) \wedge$$

$$\neg(\neg\gamma_1(X_1W_1Z_1) \vee \beta_2(X_1Y_2)) \wedge (\Gamma_1(X_1W_2Z_1) \vee \Theta_2(X_2Y_2)),$$

$$\Gamma_1(X_1W_1Z_1) \wedge (\Gamma_1(X_1W_2Z_1) \vee \Theta_2(X_2Y_2)))$$

Lemma 11 (Composition) Conjunction of canonical pads is equivalent to a canonical pad, and so is true for disjunction of canonical pads. Similarly conjunction (disjunction) of canonical pads and simple conditions is equivalent to a canonical pad.

□

To summarize above lemmas, we have our main result.

Theorem 1 Every pad can be transformed equivalently into a canonical pad.

Example 4.1 Let us apply our methods to other previous examples (see figure 10(a),(b)).
(1) An example 3.4 (1) contains set membership. We can simplify the pad into a canonical E-pad:

$$E(x \in Dept, SELL(xy) \wedge SUPPLY(uyw), w =' red')$$

(2) An A-pad over E-view with membership in an example 3.7 (2) can be transformed into a canonical A-pad:

$$A(x; y, E(xy, SUPPLY(xyz)), x \in E(u, SUPPLY(uvw), v = y \wedge w =' red'))$$
$$= A(x; y, E(xy, SUPPLY(xyz)) \wedge E(x, SUPPLY(xyw), w =' red'))$$
$$= A(x; y, E(xy, SUPPLY(xyz) \wedge SUPPLY(xyw), w =' red'))$$
$$= A(x; yzw, SUPPLY(xyz) \wedge SUPPLY(xyw), w =' red')$$

□

4.6   Processing Canonical Pads

A canonical E-pad $E(X, \beta(XY), \Theta)$ can be processed by the following strategy.

(1) Evaluate $\beta(XY)$ part. This can be processed by using conventional techniques since there exists no recursive nested predicate.

(2) For each $a_1 a_2$ in the result of (1), examine whether Θ is satisfied or not. If it is, put a_1 into answers.

This strategy acts like SPJ queries. And it is possible to process (1) and (2) in a pipeline fashion. A canonical A-pad $A(X; Y, A^{*}(XYZ, \beta(XYZ)), \Theta)$ can be processed by the following strategy.

(1) Obtain $A^{*}(XYZ)$ view. Then make groups by each XZ value.

(2) For each xz value in each group of (1)

(2-1) For each y value in the group

(2-1-1) examine whether Θ is satisfied or not.

(2-1-2) If not, quit testing of xz and skip to the next value.

(2-1-3) If all the y values satisfy Θ, put x into answers.

This strategy acts like division. And it is possible to process each group of (2) in parallel.

Let us comment on our result in terms of PIM algebra. Generally E-pads are pasted at circles and diamonds in AIS diagrams. On the other hand, the main theorem assures that canonical pads allow us to paste pads only at diamonds since pads can appear only in predicate parts. Although there exist some cases that further simplification cannot be applied, we can optimize them after obtaining intermediate results. That corresponds to abstraction by which we can consider predicate definition as a unit in a two dimensional syntax of PIM queries.

5   Conclusion

In this paper we have proposed how quantification be expressed and evaluated in a visual data manipulation language. basic ideave introduced two kinds of pads, E-pads and A-pads which represent existential queries and universal queries respectively. Pads carry own scope so that they can be constructed and processed in a nested way. Canonical pads represent alternative basic constructs that are suitable for processing queries. We have shown transformation algorithms by which we can obtain canonical pads from general pads.

In a companion paper[17], we consider how complex objects can be processed in a visual data manipulation language. Also we discuss aggregate operators in the context of complex objects.

Acknowledgement

The author thank Prof.I.Kobayashi (SANNO College) and Prof.H.Arisawa (Yokohama National University) for the encouragement of this research.

References

[1] Adiba, M. and Collet, C.: Management of Complex Objects as Dynamic Forms, VLDB (1988), 134-147

[2] Arisawa,H. and Miura,T.: Formal Approach to Database Description, IEEE *COMPCON* (1984), 463-470

[3] Arisawa,H. and Miura,T.: On the Properties of Extended Inclusion Dependencies, VLDB (1986), 449-456

[4] Bryce,D. and Hull,R.: SNAP, A Graphics based Schema Manager, *Data Engineering* (1986), 151-164

[5] Campbell, D.M., Embley, D.W. et al : Graphical Query Formulation for an Entity-Relationship Model, IEEE *Trans. On Data and Knowledge Eng.* 2-2 (1987), 89-121

[6] Creasy, P.: ENIAM - A More Complete Conceptual Schema Language, VLDB (1989), 107-114

239

[7] Czejdo,B., Elmasri, R. et al.: A Graphical Data Manipulation Language for an Extended Entity Relationship Model, IEEE *Computer* (1990) March, 26-36

[8] Date, C.J.: A Guide to The SQL Standard (1990), Addison-Wesley

[9] Gyssens, M., Paredaens, J. and Van Gucht, D.: A Graph Oriented Object Model for Database End User Interface, SIGMOD (1990), 24-33

[10] Houchin, T.: DUO:Graph-based database Graphical Query Expression, to appear in *Future Database Systems* (1992)

[11] Kim, W.:On Optimizing an SQL-like nested Query, ACM TODS 7-3 (1982), 443-469

[12] King, R. and Melville, S.: The Semantic Knowledge Interface, VLDB (1984), 30-37

[13] Kuntz, M. and Melchert, R.: Pasta-3's Graphical Query Language, VLDB (1989), 26-29

[14] Larson,J.A.: A Visual Approach to Browsing in a Database Environment,IEEE *Computer* (1986) June, 62-71

[15] Miura,T.: Desktop Schema Evolution, *Database Symposium For Advanced Applications* (1991), 67-75

[16] Miura,T.: A Visual Data Manipulation Language for a Semantic Data Model, IEEE *COMPSAC* (1991), 212-218

[17] Miura,T.: On Optimizing Complex Objects Queries in A Visual Data Manipulation Language, in preparation

[18] Miura,T. and Arisawa,H.: Logic Approach of Data Models - Data Logic, *Future Database Systems* (1990), 143-151

[19] Miura,T., Moriya, K. et al.: On the Irreducible Non First Normal Form Relations, *Info.Syst.* 12-3 (1987), 229-238

[20] Miura, T. and Moriya,K: On the Completeness of Visual Operations for a Semantic Data Model, to appear in IEEE *Trans.On Data and Knowledge Eng.* (1992)

[21] Whang, K.Y., Malhotra, A. et al.: Supporting Universal Quantification in a Two Dimentional Database Query Language, *Data Engineering* (1990), 68-75

[22] Wong,H.K.T. and Kuo, I.: GUIDE, a graphical user interface for database exploration, VLDB (1982), 22-32

[23] Zhang, Z.Q. and Mendelzon, A.: A Graphical Query Language for Entity Relationship Databases, *E-R Conf.*(1983), 441-448

[24] Zloof, M.: Query By Example, IBM System Journal 16 (1977), 324-343

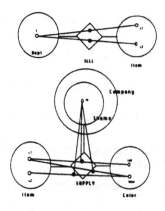

Figure 1(a): Data Diagram

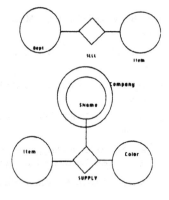

Figure 1(b): Schema Diagram

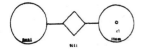

2(a): An E-pad over SELL

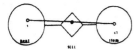

2(b): Example Answers

Figure 2: An E-pad Query

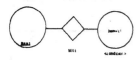

Figure 3: An Abstract E-pad Query

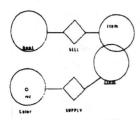

Figure 4(a): Overlapped Query

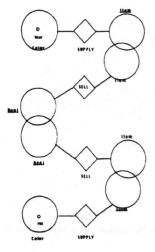

Figure 4(b): Overlapped Query

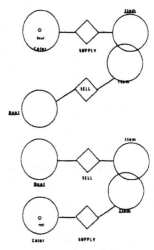

Figure 4(c): Disjunctive Query

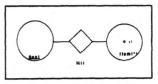

5(a): A(x;y,SELL(xy),y='c1')

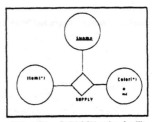

5(b): A(X;yz,SUPPLY(xyz),z='red')

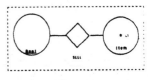

(c) ˉ E(x,SELL(xy),y='c1')

Figure 5: A-pads Queries

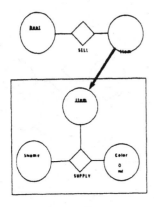

Figure 6(a): E-pad Nested by E-pad

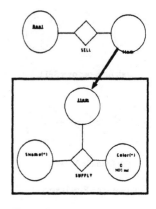

Figure 6(d): E-pad Nested by A-pad

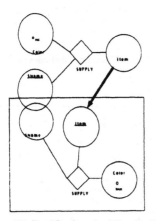

Figure 6(b): E-pad Overlapped and Nested by E-pad

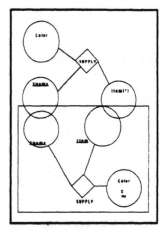

Figure 7(a): Nested E-pad as Existence Condition

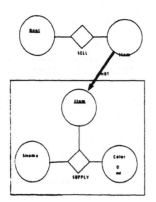

Figure 6(c): E-pad Negated and Nested by E-pad

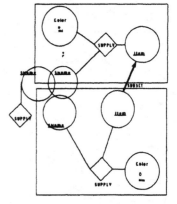

Figure 7(b): Nested E-pad as Subset Condition

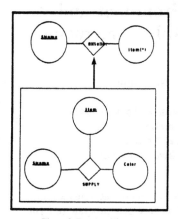

Figure 8: E-pad as View

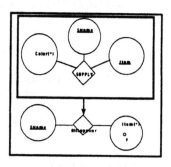

Figure 9(c): A-pad over A-view

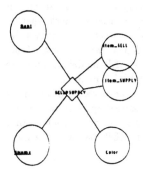

Figure 9(a): View Pad

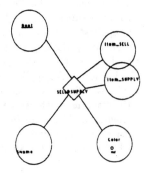

Figure 10(a): Simplification

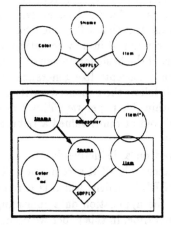

Figure 9(b): A-pad over E-view

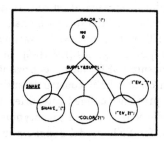

Figure 10(b): Simplification

An EER Prototyping Environment and its Implementation in a Datalog Language

Norbert Kehrer and Gustaf Neumann

Vienna University of Economics and Business Administration
Department of Management Information Systems
Augasse 2–6, A–1090 Vienna, Austria
kehrer@wu-wien.ac.at, neumann@wu-wien.ac.at

Abstract. In this paper we present an approach to represent schema information, application data and integrity constraints as a logic program in form of Datalog. The schema information is supplied as an enhanced entity relationship (EER) model which is transformed by a one-to-one mapping into a set of ground facts. The application data corresponding to the schema is also represented by ground facts in a single table. In order to check whether the application data conforms to the given schema, a set of integrity rules is defined by Datalog rules which expresses the dependencies (mostly functional and inclusion dependencies) implied by the EER model. In order to check whether the application EER model is a valid EER model a meta EER model is defined. Any application EER diagram is an instance of the meta EER diagram which can be specified using the proposed application data representation. The same integrity rules can be used to check the conformance between the application data and the application EER diagram, the meta EER diagram and the application EER diagram.

1 Introduction

The entity relationship (ER) approach is undoubtably a very popular tool for the communication between a database designer and a user of a database system. In our opinion the reason for the popularity is due to the fact that ER models have a graphical representation and that ER models can be mapped in a systematic way to a relational database schema [TYF86]. Extensions of the basic formalism of Chen [Che76] were proposed by various authors to capture concepts like generalization [SS77] or categories [EWH85]. In this paper we will follow the enhanced entity relationship (EER) flavor as presented in [EN89]. Within this paper we will not deal with certain EER constructs such as composite, derived or multi-valued attributes and predicate defined categories or sub-/superclasses.

We will present a prototyping environment based on a deductive database system for EER model designers in the form of an executable EER specification. To accomplish this goal we develop a representation of EER models, which is derived from a meta EER model, and a representation of the application data consisting only of a single table, which can be provided at design time. In this paper we do not focus on the generation of efficient information systems for production use, rather we provide a tool for a database designer to model EER applications together with its data, to experiment with various design approaches and to refine the EER model if necessary. The provided integrity constraints may be used to check the consistency of both, the application EER model (by checking it against the meta EER model) and the application data. In order to obtain an efficient information system using a relational database system the standard mapping techniques can be applied. This paper does not, however, address application issues like transactions, locking, user interfaces, output, etc.

2 Using a Deductive Database System for EER Modelling

Relational databases represent extensional knowledge (facts) in the form of tables. Deductive databases enhance relational databases by deduction rules, which are used to derive new facts from given facts. As a uniform representation of facts and rules Datalog clauses are used. A pure Datalog clause is a logical implication of the form "$A \leftarrow B_1 \wedge \ldots \wedge B_n$", where A and the B_i are positive (non-negated) literals without any function symbols. If the premise of the Datalog clause is empty ($n = 0$) it is referred to as a fact otherwise it is called a rule.

In this paper we use the deductive database system SYLLOG [WMSW90], which provides a near-English representation of facts and rules and a comfortable user interface. It extends pure Datalog by the possibility to have negated literals in the premise of a rule as long as the database remains stratified [ABW87]. SYLLOG is implemented using a backchain iteration procedure which gives clear semantics to stratified logic knowledge bases. The syntax of SYLLOG facts and rules will be described when needed.

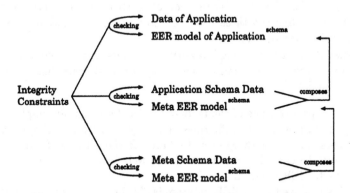

Fig. 1. Using general EER constraints to check application and schema integrity

In our approach a given application EER diagram is mapped one-to-one to a set of facts. The application data will be given as facts as well. By applying general consistency rules we are able to check the conformance of data and schema (see Figure 1). These consistency rules are implemented in SYLLOG, where one can easily generate explanations for inconsistent data. In general, our approach does not rely on the SYLLOG system. The same logic formulation can be used in a different syntactic form in a Prolog based environment [KN92], or could be implemented in systems capable of dealing with negations in stratified Datalog programs such as LDL [NT89] or RDL [KMS90]. Since in our representation schema and data are kept in the same database, we can use a meta EER diagram to reason about the well-formedness of application EER diagrams by applying the general integrity constraints. The application schemas are formulated as instances of the meta EER diagram. Similarly the well-formedness of the meta EER diagram is checked. The resulting checked data-base has the form of a Datalog program which can be extended with deduction rules or additional constraints (which exceed the expressiveness of the EER methodology) as needed by the application. Such constraints will be discussed in the section about the meta EER model.

Our work was influenced by [DZ88], who developed a first order specification of inference rules together with a set of integrity constraints for a graphical information systems specification language. In contrast to our work, a new formalism called LOCS is proposed. We based our work on the well established and well known EER approach. The paper of [DZ88] does not mention any attempt to check the well-formedness of the application schema using the same integrity constraints.

3   Representing EER-Diagrams and its Data in Datalog

The information contained in EER diagrams can be separated into two components:

1. An extensional part containing the names of the concepts used in the EER mo-del, a certain classification of these concepts (attribute, entity type, relationship type), the links between these basic concepts and the definition of certain pro-perties of the concepts, and
2. an intensional part containing integrity constraints and deduction rules. In this paper we are concerned primarily with integrity constraints that are induced by the EER model.

The extensional part consists of the facts of the EER schema plus application data, the intensional part of EER specific rules and optionally additional application spe-cific constraints. The integrity rules will be used to check the conformance between the schema and the data. In order to check the well-formedness of a schema we will introduce a meta EER diagram.

The extensional part of an EER diagram is obtained by performing a one-to-one mapping from the diagram to a set of facts. We represent EER diagrams in terms of the links between basic EER concepts. These links are either roles, attributes, generalizations, or categories. For denoting weak entity types an additional fact type is needed.

The schema representation consists of the following SYLLOG sentences (words starting with a prefix like *some-*, *the-* and *a-* are logical variables in SYLLOG. Words differing only in their prefix denote the same variable):

1. One-to-one mapping of roles:
   Role a-role-name a-rel-name an-ent-name the-cardinality the-participation

where *the-cardinality* is either *One* or *Many* and *the-participation* is either *Partial* or *Total*. In EER diagrams roles are arcs connecting entity types and relationship types. All roles are labelled with their names and their cardinalities (1 for *One*, n or m for *Many*). Thick role arcs denote total participations, thin lines denote partial participations.

2. One-to-one mapping of attributes:

   Attribute an-att-name a-mt-name of-type

   where *of-type* is either *Simple* or *Identifying*. *a-mt-name* is the name of a modelled type, i.e. an entity type or a relationship type. Graphically attributes are drawn as ellipses, identifying attributes are underlined.

3. One-to-one mapping of generalizations:

   Generalization a-gen-name the-supertype the-disjointness the-completeness
   G-sub a-gen-name an-ent-name

   where *the-disjointness* is either *Overlapping* or *Disjoint* and *the-completeness* is either *Partial* or *Total*. Generalizations are denoted in the diagrams as undirected arcs leading from a supertype to a small circle containing either a *d* (for disjoint subclasses) or an *o* (overlapping subclasses) which is connected with arrows pointing to the entity types of the subclasses. A thick line between the supertype and the small circle indicates a total generalization. In cases where a supertype has a single subtype a partial overlapping generalization is assumed. In our representation a unique generalization name (*a-gen-name*) is used to represent the circle symbol. The supertype of a generalization is included in the predicate *Generalization*. Subtypes are specified in a separate table *G-sub*.

4. One-to-one mapping of categories:

   Category a-cat-name an-ent-name the-completeness C-super a-cat-name an-ent-name

   where *the-completeness* is either *Partial* or *Total*. Categories are drawn in diagrams like generalizations except that the character *u* is used in the circle and there is only one arrow from the circle to the category entity type.

5. Identification of weak entity types:

   Identifies a-rel-name a-weak-ent-name

   Weak entity types and identifying relationship types are drawn in a gray box using a thicker line style.

3.1 A simple Application Schema and its Extensional Representation

The schema representation introduced above will now be used to represent a sample application EER diagram (Figure 2). It should be noted that this mapping is easy enough to be done by a fairly simple transformation program. We have developed such a program that transforms EER diagrams drawn with the graphical editor TGIF [Che91] into a relational schema conforming to the schema representation. Since the EER diagram of Figure 2 contains only entity types, relationship types and attributes it suffices to use *Role* and *Attribute* sentences.

In SYLLOG a table is written as a SYLLOG sentence followed by two lines line followed by the values. All facts are ground (i.e. variable free).

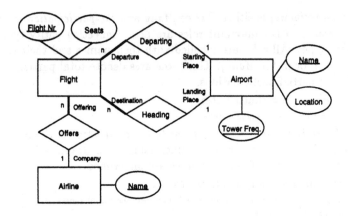

Fig. 2. An EER Diagram Specifying a Simple Airline Information System

Role the-name	the-relationship-type	the-entity-type	the-cardinality	the-participation
Starting-Place	Departing	Airport	One	Partial
Departure	Departing	Flight	Many	Total
Landing-Place	Heading	Airport	One	Partial
Destination	Heading	Flight	Many	Total
Company	Offers	Flight	Many	Total
Offering	Offers	Flight	One	Partial

Attribute the-attribute	the-entity-type	the-type-of-attribute
Name	Airport	Identifying
Location	Airport	Simple
Tower-Freq	Airport	Identifying
Flight-Nr	Flight	Identifying
Seats	Flight	Simple
Name	Airline	Identifying

3.2 A Set of Instances for the Airline Schema

In order to make the EER diagram executable it is necessary to store the data for
the diagram in the same SYLLOG knowledge base. To achieve maximal flexibility we
decided to use a fairly atomistic representation schema based on so called *Observations*. An observation is a fact determining that some attribute (or role) belonging
to a certain entity type (or relationship type) has for a given object a certain value.
Thus all instances of the EER schema are defined by a single predicate *Observation*
with four arguments. The following patterns are possible:

Observation some-attribute some-entity-type some-tuple-identifier some-value or
Observation some-attribute some-relationship-type some-tuple-identifier some-value or
Observation some-role some-relationship-type some-tuple-identifier some-value

The first two arguments refer to the schema information, the third argument *tuple-
identifier* is used to group the various *Observations* to a certain tuple (aggregation).
The *tuple-identifier* uniquely determines the object in the database. The tuple identifier is a concept comparable to the surrogate in [Cod79].

Note that a representation based on *Observations* allows us to cope with null values (no observation available) or with multi-valued attributes (several observations with identical first three arguments and different fourth arguments) in a simple way.

Observation the-attribute	the-modelled-type	the-tuple-id	the-value
Name	Airline	Airline1	Aua
Name	Airline	Airline2	Malev
Name	Airport	Airport1	Wien-Schwechat
Location	Airport	Airport1	Schwechat
Tower-Freq	Airport	Airport1	123
Name	Airport	Airport2	Jfk
Location	Airport	Airport2	New-York-City
Tower-Freq	Airport	Airport2	222
Flight-Nr	Flight	Flight1	123
Seats	Flight	Flight1	130
Flight-Nr	Flight	Flight2	234
Seats	Flight	Flight2	170
Starting-Place	Departing	Departing1	Airport2
Departure	Departing	Departing1	Flight1
Landing-Place	Heading	Heading1	Airport1
Destination	Heading	Heading1	Flight1

One might argue that this representation is very atomistic and hard to use. Nevertheless the representation allows us to reference EER concepts from integrity rules in a very general way and simplifies schema modifications significantly (e.g. introducing a new attribute).

In order to provide a more traditional view of the data specified in the *Observation* facts one might provide rules. A SYLLOG rule consists of one or several SYLLOG sentences (premises) followed by a single line and one or several SYLLOG sentences (conclusions). The following two SYLLOG rules show how to make the data more accessible and how to specify additional rules which are not expressible in the EER model (recursively defined transitive closure).

Observation Flight-Nr	Flight	some-tuple-flight	some-flight
Observation Seats	Flight	some-tuple-flight	some-seats
Observation Offering	Offers	some-tuple-offers	some-tuple-flight
Observation Company	Offers	some-tuple-offers	some-tuple-airline
Observation Name	Airline	some-tuple-airline	some-airline
Observation Departure	Departing	a-tuple-departing	some-tuple-flight
Observation Starting-Place	Departing	a-tuple-departing	some-airport-a
Observation Destination	Heading	a-tuple-heading	some-tuple-flight
Observation Landing-Place	Heading	a-tuple-heading	some-airport-b
Observation Name	Airport	some-airport-b	the-place-b
Observation Name	Airport	some-airport-a	the-place-a

some-flight is a flight of some-airline from the-place-a to the-place-b with some-seats seats
one can fly from some-place-a to some-place-b

one can fly from some-place-a to some-place-b
one can fly from some-place-b to some-place-c
one can fly from some-place-a to some-place-c

Rules like the first one can be found by applying a procedure as suggested in [TYF86], [Teo90], or [EN89] to transform an EER model into a relational schema. These procedures are oriented towards generating a small number of relations together with their attributes. Those relations are used as conclusions of SYLLOG rules where the attributes are stated as variables. The premises of the rules are formed by grouping together the *Observations* that are needed to specify the variables in the conclusion. Both the generation of a relational schema and the grouping of the *Observations* can be done automatically, so the advantages of the representation of the data as *Observations* and of the possibility to easily access the data can be utilized without additional effort.

The transformation into relations with a high number of attributes can entail some disadvantages: If a particular *Observation* is missing to form such a many-attribute relation, either the whole relation tuple will be omitted or a special representation for null values is needed. This null value problem occurs if an attribute is missing or when a partial n-to-1 relationship type is represented as additional attributes of the table corresponding to an entity type. An simple solution for missing attributes would be to use another integrity constraint that forbids missing values. This constraint would be very similar to the constraint that each role in a relation must be specified, which is discussed in the next section. A solution for the partial relation problem would be to map such relationship types to separate tables.

4   General Integrity Constraints of the EER Model

In this section we will present a set of general integrity constraints which can be used to check whether the instances of an EER diagram conform to the restrictions entailed by this EER diagram. We describe the different types of integrity constraints and show how integrity checking can be implemented using stratified Datalog knowledge bases in SYLLOG. It is assumed that the EER diagram is represented as a set of facts for the predicates resulting from the one-to-one mapping of the meta EER diagram (*Attribute, Role*, etc.) and that the instances of the EER diagram are given as ground facts using the predicate *Observation*.

As both are available – namely, the information about the EER model and the instances of the model – we are able to check the integrity of a database with one general set of integrity constraints. Unlike other approaches [TYF86, MS89, EN89] which generate their own set of integrity constraints for each EER model, we only have one set of integrity constraints which can be used for any EER model.

An integrity constraint is formulated in SYLLOG as a deduction rule with the conclusion stating that the constraint is violated. The premise of the rule states the conditions for the violation and combines predicates referring to EER schema information and the *Observation* predicate containing the instances. To make the rules shorter and more readable we have introduced auxiliary predicates.

4.1   Functional Dependencies

Marking attributes as identifying and the specification of cardinalities of 1 in relationship types in an EER model are ways to express functional dependencies on the modelled data.

A functional dependency (FD) is a constraint on a relation R which states that the values of a tuple on one set of attributes X uniquely determine the values on another set Y of attributes. FDs are specified in the form $X \Rightarrow Y$ and are formally defined by the following implication [Mai83, GV89]:

$$t_1(X) = t_2(X) \rightarrow t_1(Y) = t_2(Y)$$

t_1 and t_2 are two different tuples of R. If the values on the set of attributes X are the same in t_1 and t_2 then the values on the attribute set Y have to be the same. A FD is violated if there exist two tuples which have the same values in X and different values in Y. We will use the following informal representation for describing functional dependencies:

$$value(some\text{-}fieldX, some\text{-}typeX) \Rightarrow \text{value(some-fieldY,some-typeY)}$$

where $value(some\text{-}fieldX, some\text{-}typeX)$ is seen as a function returning a set of corresponding attributes of the underlying universal relation. The notation $tupid(some\text{-}type)$ is a shorthand for $value(tupid, some\text{-}type)$. $tupid$ stands for the tuple identifier (see Section 3.2) which can be seen as a pseudo attribute in the underlying relation.

The arguments of $value$ refer to concepts of the EER model. The first argument typically contains *field*, *role* or *attribute*, where *field* is a generalization of *role* and *attribute*. The second argument of $value$ denotes the modelled type mt to which the first argument belongs. It might contain *entity-type* or *relationship-type*, or their generalization mt. *weak-entity-type* is a subset of *entity-type*, *non-weak–type* stands for mt excluding *weak-entity-type*. A FD with an atomic left hand side can be expressed in SYLLOG by the following rule:

two observations with different values in [the-att-RHS the-mt-RHS] are the-t1 the-t2
not: two observations with different values in [the-att-LHS the-mt-LHS] are the-t1 the-t2
_____
ATOMIC [the-att-LHS the-mt-LHS] does not determine value of [the-att-RHS the-mt-RHS]

This rule defines the violation of a functional dependency of the type $value(field\text{-}LHS, mt\text{-}LHS) \Rightarrow value(field\text{-}RHS, mt\text{-}RHS)$ (where *field* denotes an atomic attribute). Since in our representation both the values and the tuple identifiers are accessible in the same way, we could express dependencies of the form $value(field\text{-}LHS, mt\text{-}LHS) \Rightarrow tupid(mt\text{-}RHS)$ or $tupid(mt\text{-}LHS) \Rightarrow value(field\text{-}RHS, mt\text{-}RHS)$ or $tupid(mt\text{-}LHS) \Rightarrow tupid(mt\text{-}RHS)$ with the same ease.

In cases where the left hand side of a functional dependency is not atomic (like: $AB \rightarrow C$), the representation in a Datalog language is more complicated since since the arguments have to be function symbol free and no list of attributes can be specified. It is necessary to reformulate sentences of the form *"the dependency is violated if for any different RHS all LHS are equal"* into *"...no elements of the LHS are allowed to be different"*. Now we can use a syllogism to generate the left hand side attributes and proceed as follows:

two observations with different values in [the-attR the-mtR] are the-t1 the-t2
not: different observations on LHS for *some-dependency* exist in the-t1 the-t2, context [the-attR the-mtR]
_____
value of [the-attL the-mtL] does not determine value of [the-attR the-mtR] for *some-dependency*

Some syllogism that concludes [the-attL the-mtL] *in context* [the-attR the-mtR]
two observations with different value in [the-attL the-mtL] are the-t1 the-t2
_____
different observations on LHS for *dependency* exist in the-t1 the-t2, context [the-attR the-mtR]

The test whether two tuples of the modelled type of the left hand side are different is done by a special syllogism which determines the items of the left hand side of the FD. For each type of non-atomic left hand side one wants to use a specialized syllogism (like the second rule) has to be given, which is referenced by an integrity rule using the variable *dependency*. Examples for non-atomic LHS are given later.

Identifying attribute determines tuple identifier: For each identifying attribute *att* of a modelled type of the EER schema there exists a functional dependency between *att* and the tuple identifier of the form:

$$value(identifying\text{-}att, non\text{-}weak\text{-}type) \Rightarrow tupid(non\text{-}weak\text{-}type)$$

This corresponds to the definition of an identifying attribute as an attribute whose values can be used to identify an entity uniquely [EN89], because in our approach an entity is represented by its tuple identifier.

In SYLLOG this is formulated by a rule which contains the conditions for the violation of the functional dependency as its premises and states the attribute and modelled type which violates the FD as conclusion.

Attribute the-att the-mt identifying
the-mt is a non-weak modelled type
ATOMIC [the-att the-mt] does not determine value of [tupid the-mt]

---

fd of the-att -> tuple identifier in the-mt is violated

It has to be noted that the identifying attribute of weak entity types does not determine the weak entity [Che76], but together with the owner entities it does. Therefore we need a separate rule to check this functional dependency violation for weak entity types. It states that the identifying attribute together with the tuple identifier(s) of the owner(s) determine the tuple identifier of the weak entity type:

$$value(identifying\text{-}att, weak\text{-}ent) \cup tupid\text{-}owner(weak\text{-}ent) \Rightarrow tupid(weak\text{-}ent)$$

Tuple identifier determines single-valued attributes: Chen defined an attribute as a function which maps an entity set or a relationship set into a value set [Che76]. For our representation this means that the value of each single-valued attribute of the modelled type *mt* is determined by the tuple identifier of *mt*:

$$tupid(modelled\text{-}type) \Rightarrow value(any\text{-}field, modelled\text{-}type)$$

We need not check the constraint that the identifying attribute determines the values of the other attributes of non-weak entity types, because it follows from the two previous constraints:

$$value(identifying\text{-}att, non\text{-}weak\text{-}type) \Rightarrow tupid(non\text{-}weak\text{-}type) \wedge$$
$$tupid(non\text{-}weak\text{-}type) \Rightarrow value(any\text{-}attribute, non\text{-}weak\text{-}type) \rightarrow$$
$$value(identifying\text{-}att, non\text{-}weak\text{-}type) \Rightarrow value(any\text{-}attribute, non\text{-}weak\text{-}type)$$

All fields determine tuple identifier: Since entity types and relationship types refer to sets of values [Che76] all fields together (attribute fields or role fields) must be unique.

$$value(all\text{-}fields, non\text{-}weak\text{-}type) \Rightarrow tupid(non\text{-}weak\text{-}type)$$

This rule is expressed in SYLLOG as:

```
a-mt is a non-weak modelled type
value of [all-fields a-mt] does not determine value of [tupid a-mt] for ALL-FIELDS
```
```
fd of all-fields -> tuple identifier in a-mt is violated
```
```
Field some-field the-mt
two observations with different value in [some-field the-mt] are a-t1 a-t2
```
```
different observations on LHS for ALL-FIELDS exist in a-t1 a-t2, context: [all-fields the-mt]
```

This is an example of a FD where the left hand side is not atomic, but consists of all fields of a modelled type. Therefore we define a syllogism to determine two tuples of a modelled type *the-mt* where at least one observation of a field of *the-mt* differs in these tuples. The FD violation is checked using the rule for a non-atomic left hand side which is described at the beginning of this section.

The constraint for weak entity types can be formulated as

$$value(all\text{-}fields, weak\text{-}type) \cup tupid\text{-}owner(weak\text{-}type) \Rightarrow tupid(weak\text{-}type)$$

Entities participating in a relationship type with cardinality *One*: Each role *r* of a relationship type *rel* in which an entity type participates with cardinality *One* is determined by all other roles of *rel* together [TYF86]:

$$value(other\text{-}roles, rel\text{-}type) \Rightarrow value(one\text{-}role, rel\text{-}type)$$

This constraint is independent of the degree of the relationship type.

4.2 Inclusion Dependencies

The use of relationship types, generalizations, and specializations in EER models indicates that entity or relationship sets are subsets of some other entity or relationship set. The property of being a subset of another set is covered by inclusion dependencies. An inclusion dependency(ID) of the form $A \subseteq B$ is violated iff there exists a value of field A which is not a value of field B. In SYLLOG this is expressed by the following rule:

```
one observation of [some-field1 some-mt1] is the-value
not: one observation of [some-field2 some-mt2] is the-value
```
```
value of [some-field1 some-mt1] is not a value of [some-field2 some-mt2]
```

Like the rule for FD violations this rule may be used to check inclusion dependencies between field values in any combination.

Participating entities included in entity type: The values of a role of a relationship type must be tuple identifiers of the participating entity type:

$$value(role, rel\text{-}type) \subseteq tupid(participating\text{-}entity\text{-}type)$$

In SYLLOG the ID is checked by the integrity rule:

Role the-role the-rel the-ent the-card the-part
value of [the-role the-rel] is not a value of [tupid the-ent]

---

role the-role of the-rel is not included in entity type the-ent

Note that in our representation we use the artificial tuple identifiers as contents of role fields. These tuple identifiers should be replaced by the corresponding contents of an identifying attribute in the final application. By using the tuple identifiers in roles we can postpone the design decision concerning which identifying attribute should be used to a later step.

Totally participating entity types: For entity types which participate totally in a relationship type the previous ID has to hold in the other direction, too. Each tuple identifier of an entity type e must be a value of a role in which e participates totally:

$$tupid(totally\text{-}participating\text{-}entity\text{-}type) \subseteq value(role, rel\text{-}type)$$

Generalizations: A generalization may be total or partial. A total generalization specifies the constraint that every entity in the superclass must be a member of some subclass in the specialization [EN89]. For our representation this means that in a total generalization with supertype *super* there must be at least one subclass *sub* for each tuple identifier T of *super*, where T is included in *sub*:

$$tupid(supertype) \subseteq tupid(at\text{-}least\text{-}one\text{-}subtype)$$

There is also an inclusion dependency $tupid(subtype) \subseteq tupid(supertype)$ for both partial and total generalizations. In our representation we guarantee through the use of deduction rules that the tuple identifiers of supertypes are also tuple identifiers of the subtypes. Therefore this ID needs not to be checked.

Categories: As for generalizations there are deduction rules to assure that tuple identifiers of the superclasses are also tuple identifiers of the subclass in a category and that the attributes are inherited. This mechanism may not be applied to partial categories, because not every entity of a supertype has to be a member of the subclass. Instead the members of the subclass in partial categories have to be stated explicitly. Therefore we will have to check if the tuple identifiers and attribute values of a subclass in partial category occur in one of the superclasses specified for the category, which is expressed by the inclusion dependencies:

$$tupid(subclass) \subseteq tupid(some\text{-}superclass)$$
$$value(att, subclass) \subseteq value(att, some\text{-}superclass)$$

The mechanism of attribute inheritance will be described in a later section.

All roles in a relationship must be specified: In each relationship instance the associated entities have to be specified. This constraint is violated if there are two different roles *role1* and *role2* in a relationship type *rel* and the set of tuple identifiers of *rel* which have a value for *role1* is a proper subset of the tuple identifiers of *rel* having a value for *role2*. This can be expressed as: for every tuple identifier that has a value for *role1* there must be a value for *role2* also.

$$tupid(role1, rel\text{-}type) \subseteq tupid(role2, rel\text{-}type)$$

which is expressed in SYLLOG as:

```
Role the-role1 the-rel the-ent1 the-card1 the-part1
Role the-role2 the-rel the-ent2 the-card2 the-part2
tupid of [the-role1 the-rel] is not a tupid of [the-role2 the-rel]
```
---
not all roles specified in relationship type the-rel

4.3 Naming Constraints in Observations

The following naming constraints restrict the names of modelled types and tuple identifieres in observations.

Naming of modelled types and fields: Whether the fields and modelled types appearing in *Observation* facts are specified in the schema cannot be checked by one of the above dependencies, because the rules only refer to data integrity whereas these naming conventions are like inclusion dependencies between data and schema representation. Therefore we use separate consistency rules.

An observation containing a *field* of a modelled type *mt* does not conform to the schema if *field* or *mt* have not been specified in the corresponding schema.

```
Observation a-field a-mt a-tuple-id a-value
not: Field the-field the-mt
```
---
schema conformity violated by tuple the-tuple-id of [the-field the-mt]

Unique Tuple Identifiers: Modelled types not occuring in any hierarchy (generalization or category) must have unique tuple identifiers. This can be expressed as a FD stating that the tuple identifier of a modelled type determines the name of the modelled type:

$$tupid(non\text{-}hier\text{-}mt) \Rightarrow name(non\text{-}hier\text{-}mt)$$

For entity types that occur in a hierarchy the case is more complicated. First we define the concept of a root entity type as

$$root\text{-}ent = top\text{-}gen\text{-}ent \cup level1\text{-}disj\text{-}ent$$

where *top-gen-ent* refers to the top entity type of a generalization hierarchy and *level1-disj-ent* refers to a direct subtype of a disjoint generalization. The constraint

$$tupid(root\text{-}ent) \Rightarrow name\text{-}supertype(root\text{-}ent)$$

states that a tuple identifier of a root entity type determines the name of its super-type. For disjoint generalizations this means that the name of any direct subtype is determined by its tuple identifier. Additionally, the name of the top entity type of a generalization is determined by its tuple identifiers, i.e. tuple identifiers in a generalization hierarchy do not appear in other generalization hierarchies.

We do not allow entities to appear in different (non-connected) categories. This is expressible by the FD that the tuple identifier of a superclass in a category determines the name of the category:

$$tupid(ent\text{-}in\text{-}cat) \Rightarrow name(cat)$$

This constraint prevents also nested categories.

4.4 Type Hierarchies

The concepts of the generalization and category allow the construction of a hierarchy of entity types. In our representation we use a mechanism for the inheritance of attributes in that hierarchy and for the inclusion of tuple identifiers of one entity type in other entity types. It is built upon the following rules:

- In a generalization the tuple identifiers and attributes which were stated in an *Observation* for a subtype become tuple identifiers and attributes of the super-type. The entity – represented by the tuple identifier – belongs to both types. The name of the supertype is an alias for the name of the subtype. Therefore we call this process "aliasing".
- In a total category the attributes specified for a superclass are inherited to the subclass, and the tuple identifiers of the superclass become tuple identifiers of the subclass (aliasing).

Nonetheless, additional *Observations* may be specified for the superclass in a gene-ralization and for a subclass of a category. Therefore the corresponding inclusion dependencies, which we described earlier, have to be checked.

The inheritance of attributes and the aliasing of tuple identifiers is performed by SYLLOG deduction rules for a predicate called *Observation-In-Hierarchy*. This pre-dicate has the same arguments as *Observation* and covers all *Observations* plus the ones that result from the inheritance mechanism. Actually the integrity constraint definitions are based upon this predicate except in the cases where *Observation* is used explicitly.

4.5 Integrity Checking in Syllog

The checking of the integrity constraints is performed by querying the constraint violations which were defined above. If there is a positive answer the database is inconsistent.

The integrity rules can be extended to include the tuple identifiers of the vio-lated *Observations*. In such cases the answers to queries contain the observations which violate the constraint, and a set of observations which represents a consistent database can be generated. Such a consistent subset is comprised of the answers to the predicate *Consistent observation* which may be defined as follows:

fd of the-id-att -> tuple identifier in the-mt is violated for tuple the-ti

---

inconsistent observation the-id-att the-mt the-ti

role [the-r the-rel] not included in entity type the-ent for tuple the-ti

---

inconsistent observation the-r the-rel the-ti

Observation the-field the-mt the-ti the-value
not: inconsistent observation the-field the-mt the-ti

Consistent observation the-att the-mt the-ti the-value

The integrity of an inconsistent database can be recovered by deducing the consistent observations and replacing the set of *Observation* facts by the set of consistent observations. This new set of observations is not necessarily a consistent database, because due to the deletion of the inconsistent observations other integrity constraints (e.g. inclusion dependencies) might now be violated. So the process of integrity checking and generation of consistent observations has to be repeated until no more inconsistent observations can be detected (fixed point).

This iterative process of recovering the integrity of a database is necessary, because the integrity constraints are based upon the predicate *Observation* and therefore use the stored facts regardless of the recognition of some of these facts as inconsistent observations by other integrity constraints. One possible solution would be to use the predicate *Consistent observation* instead of the basic *Observation* predicate in the integrity constraints, but here the problem arises that the knowledge base becomes unstratified and cannot be used with traditional inference mechanisms.

4.6   Generating Meaningful Explanations

If the database is inconsistent, it is important to know the reasons for the integrity violations in order to update the database appropriately. SYLLOG offers the facility to generate explanations of the answers it gives. This facility can be used to detect the reasons for integrity constraints violations. A rule to check the consistency of the whole database can be defined as:

not: some FD is violated
not: some ID is violated
not: the schema conformity is violated
...

---

general integrity constraints hold

fd of the-identifying-att -> tuple identifier in the-mt is violated

---

some FD is violated

fd of all-fields -> tuple identifier in a-mt is violated

---

some FD is violated
...

The integrity of a database may be checked by submitting the query **"general integrity constraints hold"** to SYLLOG. If the answer is *"No"* the database is violated and an explanation like the following may be generated.

general integrity constraints hold
=================================

  Sorry, no

  Because....

not : some FD is violated
not : some ID is violated
not : the schema conformity is violated
...

---

general integrity constraints hold

schema conformity violated by tuple t123 of [country airline]

---

not : the schema conformity is violated

Observation country airline t123 Austria
not: Field country airline

---

schema conformity violated by tuple t123 of [country airline]
...

The items in italics could not be proved by SYLLOG. This explanation shows that in tuple *t123* there is a value for an undefined attribute *country* of the entity type *airport*. By using different groupings of the premises of the rule that checks the integrity of the database different aspects of integrity violations may be covered and different explanations are generated. E.g., if we use the following rules to check the integrity, we obtain for each violating modelled type an explanation of the inconsistency.

not: fd of the-id-att -> tuple identifier in the-mt is violated
not: role the-role of the-mt is not included in entity type the-ent
not: schema conformity violated by tuple the-tuple-id of [the-field the-mt]
...

---

general integrity constraints hold for modelled type the-mt

the-mt is a modelled type
not: general integrity constraints hold for modelled type the-mt

---

general integrity constraints violated

5 Using a Meta EER Diagram to Reason about the Well-formedness of EER Models

So far, we are only able to check whether some given data conforms to the integrity constraints of a given EER diagram. In a next step it will be checked whether the EER diagram is a valid EER diagram. This task is performed by using the meta

EER diagram of Figure 3 and by a few further integrity constraints which are not expressible in the meta EER diagram.

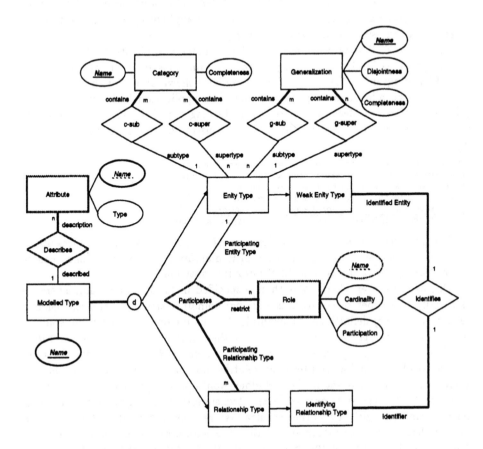

Fig. 3. A Meta EER Diagram

The meta EER diagram in Figure 3 can be read as follows: The central EER concepts are *entity type* and *relationship type*. Both of these concepts are generalized to *modelled types*. Since a modelled type is either an entity type or a relationship type the generalization is disjoint. A modelled type might be described by *attributes*, which is identified by a name and characterized by its *type* (simple or identifying). Since the names of attributes are only unique per modelled type, *attribute* is a weak entity type with *modelled type* as owner.

Entity types and relationship types can be connected via roles. Roles are identified using a name and have a cardinality and a participation value. The role names are unique per relationship type, each occurrence of a relationship type participates in the *participates* relation (total participation). Each *weak entity type* (a subtype of entity type) is identified by an *identifying relationship type* (subtype of relationship type) and vice versa. The enhanced ER constructs of the *category* and the *generalization* are used to define hierarchies of entity types. A generalization (identified by name, characterized by the attributes *disjointness* and *completeness*) has one entity type a supertype and might have several (one or many) entity types as subtypes. A *category* has one subtype and several supertypes.

The meta EER diagram may be used to represent application EER diagrams which appear as its data. We can perform the same one-to-one mapping from the meta EER diagram to the schema facts as we have shown above for the airline EER diagram. In an additional step, the schema of an application EER diagram can be specified in form of observations for the meta diagram. The mapping back to the schema representation used by the integrity constraints above can be achieved by deduction rules like:

```
Observation Name        Attribute   some-att some-attribute-name
Observation Type         Attribute   some-att the-type-of-attribute
Observation Description Describes    some-rel some-att
Observation Described    Describes   some-rel some-mt
Observation Name         an-et-or-rt some-mt  some-mt-name
```
Attribute some-attribute-name some-mt-name the-type-of-attribute

Using the schema information of the meta EER diagram and the instances above, the well-formedness of the application EER diagram (the airline schema) can be checked by applying the general EER integrity constraints.

One can, however, check more than is specified in the EER diagram. There are essentially two types of constraints missing: domain restrictions and exclusion of certain (recursive) definitions. An example of a missing domain restriction would be to specify that the *participation* of a *role* is either *total* or *partial* (or that the *role* in which a weak entity type participates in an *identifying Relationship* must be *total*, the names of roles and attributes of an relation must be disjoint). An example of an EER construction that should be forbidden would be if an entity-type is *owner* of itself (or if a *subtype* is its own *supertype*, two supertypes in a generalization do not have a common root). Two other constraints are that each relationship type must have at least two roles attached and that the names of attributes and roles perl relationship type are disjoint. Such constraints (we call them application specific constraints as opposed to the general constraints) can easily be added.

```
not: a relationship has at least two roles
...
```
application specific constraints hold for METAEER

```
Role some-role-name1 the-rel some-entity1 some-c1 some-p1
Role some-role-name2 the-rel some-entity2 some-c2 some-p2
not: some-role-name-1 equals some-role-name2
```
a relationship has at least two roles

general integrity constraints hold
application specific constraints hold for some-application

database for some-application consistent

As demonstrated above one can easily derive the schema information of the application EER diagram from observations of the meta EER diagram. Since the meta EER diagram itself is an EER diagram it can be represented and checked in the same way.

In order to check the consistency between the application schema and its data it is only necessary to store the observation information and to use deduction rules like above. Thus, none of the instances of the one-to-one mapping introduced in an earlier section must be available in form of facts, since these sentences might be formulated as deduction rules based on observations. One could even rewrite the integrity constraints to access the observation information of the schema directly which would make the deduction rules for *Attribute* and the like unnecessary.

If the meta EER diagram is specified in terms of instances of itself (using *Observation*), the same general and application specific integrity rules (as introduced the previous section) can be applied to check the well=formedness of the meta EER model as well.

6 Conclusion and Future Work

In this paper we have presented a set of general integrity constraints for EER models which we have implemented using a stratified Datalog program. In our prototyping environment checking all constraints of the meta and application EER model with sample data takes about ten seconds elapsed time on a medium sized IBM mainframe. We concentrated our efforts on a clear representation of the rules and did not consider runtime aspects in the formulation.

Integrity checking is however the most naive approach to exploit the integrity information, since it might be too costly for reasonably sized databases. A large improvement in performance could be achieved, when only relevant rules are tested on each update.

As pointed out in an earlier section it would be desirable not only to check the whole database, but rather to compute the set of consistent tuples or observations, ignoring the invalid (or incomplete) information during the computations of an application. As a consequence either a layering of the integrity constraints must be introduced (e.g. first compute the set of consistent observations using only integrity-constraint-1, apply integrity-constraint-2 on its results, and so on), or to specify the integrity constraints recursively, which leads to nonstratified knowledge bases. The disadvantage of the first approach is that the layering of the integrity constraints might be very hard (for n integrity rules exist $n!$ different layerings), the disadvantage of the second approach is that most implemented deduction methods rely on stratified programs.

A problem of a different nature is the missing modularity of our approach. When several EER models are kept in a single knowledge base (e.g. a meta EER model and several application EER models), the user has to take care that the names of the modelled types do not interfere. Our integrity checking rules can detect many clashes, but a better approach is to introduce an EER diagram name, which can be specified as an additional argument in the *Observation* facts.

Although our approach has several shortcomings, we think it might lead to better understanding of EER modeling and of integrity checking in general, and that our system is a very powerful prototyping system and case designer, in which traditional relational databases could be easily integrated.

References

[ABW87]   C. Apt, H. Blair, A. Walker: *"Towards a Theory of Declarative Knowledge"*, in: Minker (ed.): *"Foundations of Deductive Databases and Logic Programming"*, Morgan Kaufmann, Los Altos 1987.

[Che76]   P.P. Chen: *"The Entity-Relationship Model – Toward a Unified View of Data"*, ACM Transactions on Database Systems, 1:1, March 1976.

[Che91]   W.C. Cheng: *"Tgif 2.6 - A Xlib based drawing facility under X11"*, available via anonymous ftp from export.lcs.mit.edu, May 1991.

[Cod79]   E. Codd: *"Extending the Database Relational Model to Capture More Meaning"*, Transactions on Database Systems, 4:4, December 1979.

[DZ88]   P.W. Dart, J. Zobel: *"Conceptual Schemas Applied to Deductive Database Systems"*, Information Systems, Vol. 13, 1988.

[EN89]   R. Elmasri, S.B. Navathe: *"Fundamentals of Database Systems"*, Benjamin/Cummings, Redwood City 1989.

[EWH85]   R. Elmasri, J. Weeldreyer, A. Hevner: *"The Category Concept: An Extension to the Entity-Relationship Model"*, International Journal on Data and Knowledge Engineering, 1:1, May 1985.

[GMN84]   H. Gallaire, J. Minker, J. Nicolas: *"Logic and Databases: A Deductive Approach"*, ACM Computing Surveys 16, 2, June 1984.

[GV89]   G. Gardarin, P. Valduriez: *"Relational Databases and Knowledge Bases"*, Addison-Wesley, Reading 1989.

[KMS90]   G. Kiernan, C. de Maindreville, E. Simon: *"Making Deductive Databases a Practical Technology: A Step Forward"*, in: Proceedings of the ACM SIGMOD, Atlantic City, USA, May 1990.

[KN92]   N. Kehrer, G. Neumann: *"Treating Enhanced Entity Relationship Models in a Declarative Style"*, in: A. Voronkov (ed.), *"Logic Programming – First Russian Conference on Logic Programming, Irkutsk, Russia, September 1990 – Second Russian Conference on Logic Programming, St. Petersburg, Russia, September 1991 – Proceedings"*, Lecture Notes in Artificial Intelligence, Springer-Verlag: Berlin 1992, pp. 263–270.

[Mai83]   D. Maier: *"The Theory of Relational Databases"*, Computer Science Press, Rockville 1983.

[MS89]   V. M. Markowitz, A. Shoshani: *"On the Correctness of Representing Extended Entity-Relationship Structures in the Relational Model"*, in: J. Clifford, B. Lindsay, D. Maier (eds.): *"Proceedings of the 1989 ACM SIGMOD International Conference on the Management of Data"*, ACM, New York 1989.

[NT89]   S. Naqvi, S. Tsur: *"A Logic Language for Data and Knowledge Bases"*, Computer Science Press, New York 1989.

[SS77]   J. Smith, D. Smith: *"Database Abstractions: Aggregation and Generalization"*, ACM Transactions on Database Systems, 2:2, June 1977.

[Teo90]   T.J. Teorey: *"Database Modeling and Design: The Entity-Relationship Approach"*, Morgan Kaufmann, San Mateo 1990.

[TYF86]   T.J. Teorey, D. Yang, J.P. Fry: *"A logical Design Methodology for Relational Databases Using the Extended Entity-Relationship Model"*, ACM Computing Surveys 18, 2, June 1986.

[WMSW90] A. Walker (ed.), M. McCord, J.F. Sowa, W.G. Wilson: *"Knowledge Systems and Prolog"*, 2nd Edition, Addison-Wesley, Reading 1990.

A Theory for Entity-Relationship View Updates

Tok-Wang Ling   Mong-Li Lee

Department of Information Systems & Computer Science
National University of Singapore
10 Kent Ridge Crescent
Singapore 0511

Abstract. The traditional problem of updating relational databases through views is an important practical problem that has attracted much interest. In this paper, we examine the problem of view update in Entity-Relationship based database management systems [17] where the conceptual schema is represented by a normal form ER diagram [16] and views may be modelled by ER diagrams. We develop a theory within the framework of the ER approach that characterizes the conditions under which there exist mappings from view updates into conceptual schema updates. Concepts such as virtual updates and three types of insertability are introduced.

1. Introduction

Views are external schemas. They increase the flexibility of a database by allowing multiple users to see the data in different ways. They offer a measure of protection by letting users have access to only part of the data and preventing the users from accessing data outside their view. They provide logical independence by allowing some changes to be made to the conceptual schema without affecting the application programs.

For a view to be useful, users must be able to apply retrieval and update operations to it. These operations on the view must be translated into the corresponding operations on the conceptual schema instances. [19] describes how we can automatically generate the external-to-conceptual mapping and the conceptual-to-internal mapping of an ER based DBMS. Using this mapping, retrievals from a view can always be mapped into equivalent retrievals from the conceptual schema.

A mapping is also required to translate view updates into the corresponding updates on the conceptual schema. However, such a mapping does not always exist, and even when it does exist, it may not be unique [6]. The problem of updating relational databases through views is an important practical problem that has attracted much interest [1, 2, 3, 7, 8, 10, 11, 12, 13, 15, 23]. The user specifies queries to be executed against the database view; these queries are translated to queries against the underlying database through query modification [24]. One of the problems in updating through views lies in determining whether a given view modification can be correctly translated by the system. To define an updatable view, a view designer must be aware of how an update request in the view will be mapped into updates of the underlying relations. In current practice, updates must be specified against the underlying database rather than against the view. This is because the problem of updating relational databases through views is inherently ambiguous [11]. How this ambiguity is handled is an important characteristic that differentiates various approaches to supporting view updates. Yet, none has been able to handle the view update problem satisfactorily.

There are two approaches to the problem of mapping view updates. One approach is to regard the conceptual schema and view as abstract data types [10]; the view definition not only describes how view data are derived from the conceptual schema instances, but also how operations on the view are mapped into (that is, implemented using) operations on the conceptual schema [22, 23]. This approach is dependent on the database designer to design views and their operational mappings and to verify that the design is correct; that is, that the conceptual schema operations indeed perform the desired view operations "correctly".

The second approach is to define general translation procedures [2, 4, 7, 11, 13, 15]. These procedures input a view definition, a view update, and the current schema instances. They produce, if possible, a translation of the view update into conceptual schema updates satisfying some desired properties. [7] develops a theory within the framework of the relational model that characterizes precisely the conditions under which there exist mappings from view updates into conceptual schema updates satisfying various properties. He formalize the notion of update translation and derive conditions under which translation procedures will produce correct translations of view updates. However, the problem of choosing among several alternative updates sequences that might be available for performing a desired relational view update still exists. Our approach to view update in the ER approach eliminates this problem.

[11] analyses the possible translations of particular classes of update operations for relational views and obtains the semantics of the application to choose among the alternative translations from a dialog with the database administrator at view-object definition time. However, Keller's update policy of translating deletion or insertion against a selection view into a modification of the operand view or base relation has some problems. For example, consider the relation EMP which contains each employee's number, name, location, and whether the employee is a member of the company baseball team. Given the following view definition,

    Select *
    From EMP
    Where Baseball = 'Yes'

[12] proposes that the request to delete an employee from the view should be translated into a modification of the Baseball attribute value to 'No'. However, complication arises when the domain of the selection attribute has more than two values or the selection condition is a conjunction of terms.

On the other hand, there has been a lack of literature in the area of view update for the ER approach. The problem of view update in the ER approach is quite different from that in relational databases as views in ER approach are not necessarily flat relations. Furthermore, the ER approach uses the concepts of entity types and relationship sets and incorporates some of the important semantics about the real world which helps us in resolving ambiguity when translating view updates. For instance, the special relationship sets such as ISA, UNION etc in the ER approach reflects inheritance in the real world. In this paper, we examine the problem of view update in Entity-Relationship based database management systems [17] (which is quite different from relational databases) where views may be modelled by ER diagrams. Section 2 gives the terminologies used in this paper. Section 3 explains what is meant by view updatability in ER approach. We develop a theory within the framework of the ER approach that characterizes the conditions under which there exist mappings from view updates into conceptual schema updates in section 4.

2. Terminologies

[5] proposes the ER approach for database schema design. It uses the concepts of *entity type* and *relationship set*. An entity type or relationship set has *attributes* which represent its structural properties. An attribute can be *single-valued, multivalued or composite*. A minimal set of attributes of an entity type E which uniquely identifies E is called a *key* of E. An entity type may have more than one key and we designate one of them as the *identifier* of the entity type. A minimal set of identifiers of some entity types participating in a relationship set R which uniquely identifies R is called a key of R. A relationship set may have more than one key and we designate one of them as the identifier of the relationship set. Note that there are entity types in which entities cannot be identified by the values of its own attributes, but has to be identified by its relationship with other entities. Such an entity type is called a *weak entity type* and the relationship set which is used to identify the entity is said to be an *identifier dependent relationship set*. If the existence of an entity in one entity type depends upon the existence of a specific entity in another entity type, such a relationship set and entity type are called *existence dependent relationship set* and weak entity type. An entity type which is not a weak entity type is called a *regular entity type*. A relationship set which involves weak entity type(s) is called a *weak relationship set*. A relationship set which does not involve weak entity types is called a *regular relationship set*. In the ER approach, *recursive* relationship sets and *weak* relationship sets such as *existence dependent* (EX) and *identifier dependent* (ID) relationship sets are allowed. We can also have special relationship sets such as *ISA, UNION, INTERSECT* etc. For more details, see [16].

Using the ER approach in a systematic way, we can construct ER based external views. An entity type in an ER external view is called an *external or view entity type*. There is a one-to-one correspondence between the entities of a view entity type and the entities of some entity type which is called the *base entity type* of the view entity type, in the conceptual schema. A relationship set in an ER external view is called an *external or view relationship set*. Unlike the view entity type, the relationships of a view relationship set may not have a one-to-one correspondence with the relationships of any relationship set in its corresponding conceptual schema. A view relationship set can be derived by applying some join, project, and/or selection operations on one or more relationship sets and special relationships such as ISA, UNION, INTERSECT, etc [17].

An attribute in a view is called an *external or view attribute*. A view entity type may include some or all the attributes of its base entity type. A view entity type may also include attributes from an entity type which is connected to its base entity type by one or more relationship sets in the conceptual schema. We define a *derivation* as a list of conceptual schema relationship sets which are involved in natural joins to obtain a view attribute. If a view attribute A has a *derivation* $<R_1, R_2, ..., R_n>$, where R_i is a relationship set in the conceptual schema, $1 <= i <= n$, then we call A a *derived attribute*. The base attribute of A can be in R_n or in some participating entity type of R_n. We can obtain a *derived relationship set* from by joining all the relationship sets in the attribute derivation. A derivation also specifies how a view relationship set is obtained from the relationship sets in the conceptual schema. A special case of derived attributes occurs if the derivation of a view attribute A contains only special relationship sets. We call such attributes *inherited attributes*. *Multi-level attribute inheritance* is allowed. If a view attribute A has associated with it some functions or arithmetic expressions, then we call A a *computed attribute*. A view attribute can also be obtained from a combination of computation and derivation, or computation and inheritance. We consider such an attribute as computed. For more details, see [14].

[14] proposes an ER schema and view data definition language. Figure 2 shows an ER external view which is based on the example medical database in Figure 1. We illustrate the view definition obtained during the construction of this external view in an ER based DBMS Workbench [18]. This is a user-friendly graphical tool which allows the design of database conceptual schema, definition of user views based on a schema, and formulation of queries and updates against a view. The view definition for Figure 2 is as follows. The keywords are in italics.

```
VIEW DOCTPAT OF MEDICALDB
    VIEW ENTITY TYPE EMPLOYEE  /*By default, base and view entity types have same name*/
        ( ATTRIBUTES ( EMPNO,   /*Base attribute is in base entity type of EMPLOYEE*/
                        HNAME DERIVED ( <EMPLOYS> ) OWNER ( HOSPITAL ) )
        IDENTIFIER ( EMPNO ) )
    VIEW ENTITY TYPE DOCTOR
        ( ATTRIBUTES ( EMPNO, QUAL,
                        NAME INHERITED ( <UNION> ) OWNER ( EMPLOYEE ),
                        AGE INHERITED ( <UNION> ) OWNER ( EMPLOYEE ),
                        DNAME DERIVED (<ATTACHTO>) OWNER (DEPARTMENT))
        IDENTIFIER ( EMPNO ) )
    VIEW ENTITY TYPE PATIENT
        ( ATTRIBUTES ( REGNO, PNAME, AGE, SEX,
                        BEDNO DERIVED ( <OCCUPY> ) OWNER ( OCCUPY ) )
        IDENTIFIER ( REGNO ) )
    VIEW ENTITY TYPE NURSE
        ( ATTRIBUTES ( EMPNO, RANK )
        IDENTIFIER ( EMPNO ) )
    VIEW RELATIONSHIP SET ATTD-DOCTOR
        ( PART-VIEW-ENTITIES ( DOCTOR, PATIENT )
                /*PART-VIEW-ENTITIES indicates participating view entity types*/
        IDENTIFIER ( DOCTOR, PATIENT )
        DERIVATION ( <WORKSWITH> ) )
    VIEW RELATIONSHIP SET ATTD-NURSE
        ( PART-VIEW-ENTITIES ( NURSE, PATIENT )
        IDENTIFIER ( NURSE, PATIENT )
        DERIVATION ( <INCHARGE, OCCUPY> ) )
    ISA ( PART-VIEW-ENTITIES ( DOCTOR, EMPLOYEE )
        DERIVATION ( <UNION> ) )
    ISA ( PART-VIEW-ENTITIES ( NURSE, EMPLOYEE )
        DERIVATION ( <UNION> ) )
```

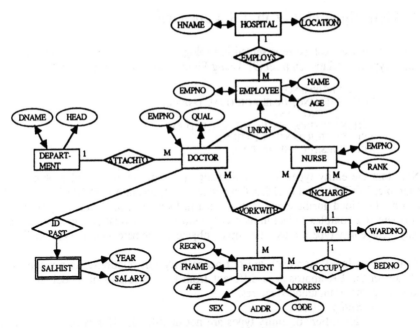

Figure 1: An Example ER Medical Database

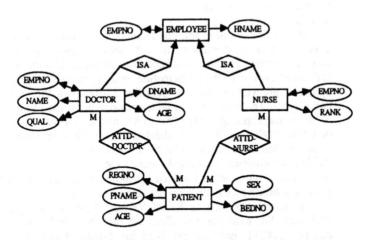

Figure 2: An Example ER External View of Conceptual Schema in Figure 1.

3. View Updatability in ER approach

An ER user view can be represented in Prolog by using a predicate symbol for each entity type and relationship set [9]. Using Figure 2 as an example, we have

> EMPLOYEE (EMPNO, HNAME).
> DOCTOR (EMPNO, NAME, AGE, QUAL, DNAME).
> NURSE (EMPNO, RANK).
> PATIENT (REGNO, PNAME, AGE, SEX, BEDNO).
> ATTD-DOCTOR (DOCTOR, PATIENT).
> ATTD-NURSE (NURSE, PATIENT).

Note that the entity types in a relationship set predicate are complex objects. For example, DOCTOR and PATIENT are complex objects in ATTD-DOCTOR. QUAL is a multi-valued attribute and is thus a list in DOCTOR predicate. Any composite attribute is a complex object in its owner (entity type or relationship set) predicate. Any weak entity type is a list of complex objects in the parent entity type predicate.

Thus, views in ER approach are not necessarily flat relations. As a result, view update in the ER approach is different from that in relational model. It has the following important unique features.

1. *Entity Types*

   Identifiers of entity types are not modifiable. This is because they are used as object identifiers in the relationship sets in which the entity types participate in. Modification of entity type identifiers will cause undesirable updating anomalies. The insertion of an entity requires the identifer value to be defined.

2. *Relationship Sets*

   Identifiers of relationship sets can be modified without causing any side effects or updating anomalies. This is because a relationship specifies the way participating entities are related. The attributes of a relationship set and the identifiers of the participating entity types can be modified. No update is allowed on the non-identifier attributes of the participating entity types. The insertion of a relationship requires the identifer values of all the participating entity types to be defined. It violates the meaning of a relationship set in an ER database if we allow insertion to occur when only the identifier of a relationship defined.

3. *Multivalued Attributes and Weak Entity Types*

   Weak entity types are set-valued attributes in the parent entity type predicate. Multivalued attributes are also sets in the owner predicate. We use set operations such as REMOVE and APPEND to update such attributes. For example, to reflect the fact that Dr Chew, employee number 114211, has just received his MFRC degree and will be transfered to the pediatrics department, we can have the following Prolog goal to update the view entity type DOCTOR in Figure 2.

   > ?- retrieve (doctor (114220, Name, Age, Qual, Dname)),
   >   append (Qual, ['MFRC'], NewQual),
   >   modify (doctor (114220, Name, Age, Qual, Dname),
   >   doctor (114220, Name, Age, NewQual, pediatrics)).

4. *Special Relationship Sets*

Special relationship sets such as ISA, UNION, INTERSECT etc are actually constraints and hence cannot be updated. However, inherited attributes can be modified using the identifiers of the participating entity types in these special relationship sets.

We have the following principles that guide us in updating ER views.

1. There must be a clear one-to-one correspondence between the objects (attributes, entity types and/or relationship sets) in the view and the underlying database schema. That is, there must *no ambiguity of origin* in the view objects.

2. The result of a view update must not violate the definition of the view. This is because a user will not be able to retrieve the new updated data through the view since they do not meet the conditions specified by the view. We can enforce such an update rule by including the selection criteria of views in the mapping rules.

3. Side effects that are results of the system's actions to ensure that changes in a view requested are consistent with the rest of the database are permitted. The following definition introduce the concept of *virtual update* to refer to such side effects.

Definition 1 : Let A be a subset of the attributes of an entity type or a relationship set in a view. Let B be an attribute in the entity type or relationship set such that B $\notin$ A. If the value of the base attribute of B is a function of the values of the base attributes of A, then the modification of any of the attributes in A will cause the system to retrieve or re-compute the corresponding value of B whenever the value of B is required. We call such an action *virtual update*.

Note that virtual updates are automatically carried out by the system and not the user to maintain database consistency after a view update. Virtual updates are important in the following cases.

1. Computed attributes in a view are not directly modifiable by the user. But their values can be implicitly updated by the system.

2. Let E be the base entity type of a view entity type E'. Suppose E' contains attributes A_1, A_2, ...A_k whose base attributes are not in E but in another entity type F connected to E by relationship sets R_1, R_2, ..., R_n. If the base attribute of A_1 is the identifier of the entity type F, and A_1 has been determined to be modifiable in the view entity type E', then the modification of A_1 will cause the system to retrieve the corresponding values of the attributes A_2, ...A_k whenever these values are required.

3. Let $<R_1, R_2, ..., R_n>$ be the derivation of a view relationship set R'. Suppose R' contains attributes A_1, A_2, ...A_k whose base attributes are in an entity type E, where E is a participating entity type in some relationship set in the derivation, say R_i, for some i where $1 <= i <= n$. If the base attributes of A_1 is the identifier of E, and A_1 has been determined to be modifiable in the view relationship set R', then the modification of A_1 will cause the system to retrieve the values of the attributes A_2, ...A_k whenever these values are required.

4. A Theory for ER View Update

Next, we give a theory within the framework of the ER approach that characterizes the conditions under which there exist mappings from view updates into conceptual schema updates. Note that an entity type or relationship set is updatable if and only if the entity type or relationship set is deletable, modifiable or insertable. We first examine the conditions under which a view entity type or relationship set is deletable or modifiable. A view entity type or relationship set is deletable (or modifiable) if we are able to delete (or modify) some corresponding entities or relationships in the database without violating any of the three view update principles stated in section 3.

Definition 2 : A *key-preserving projection* is a projection of an entity type or relationship set which includes a key of the entity type or relationship set.

Theorem 1 : Any view entity type is deletable. Let E be the base entity type of a view entity type E'. Any view attribute of E' whose base attribute is in E and is not part of the identifier of E is modifiable.
Proof : Trivial. ∎

Two sets of attributes X and Y in the relational model are said to be *functionally equivalent* if and only if $X \rightarrow Y$ and $Y \rightarrow X$. We can determine the functional equivalence of these two sets of attributes using Armstrong's axioms [21].

Definition 3 : Two sets of entity types E_i and E_j are *functionally equivalent* w.r.t. a derivation $<R_1, R_2, ..., R_n>$, denoted $E_i \leftrightarrow E_j$, if and only if we can establish that the set of identifiers of the entity types in E_i is functionally equivalent to the set of identifiers of the entity types in E_j from the functional dependencies in the relationship sets $R_1, R_2, ..., R_n$.

Figure 3 shows an ER diagram in which A is functionally equivalent to B w.r.t. $<R_1>$, but $A \rightarrow B$, $B \nrightarrow A$ w.r.t. $<R_2>$. Since $B \leftrightarrow C$ in R_3, we can conclude that $A \leftrightarrow C$ from the functional dependencies in $<R_1, R_3>$ (or we can say that $A \leftrightarrow C$ w.r.t. $<R_1, R_3>$) by transitivity.

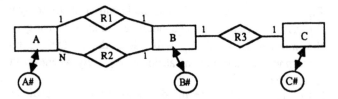

Figure 3: An ER diagram to illustrate the functional equivalance of entity types.

Definition 4 : Let E_i be the set of participating entity types of a relationship set R_i whose identifiers form a key of R_i. Similarly, let E_j be the set of participating entity types of another relationship set R_j whose identifiers form a key of R_j. We say that

R_i and R_j are *functionally equivalent*, denoted $R_i \leftrightarrow R_j$, w.r.t. a derivation $<R_1, R_2, ..., R_n>$ if and only if E_i and E_j are functionally equivalent w.r.t. $<R_1, R_2, ..., R_n>$.

Theorem 2 : Let R be a view relationship set with the relationship derivation $<R_1, R_2, ..., R_n>$. R has the following updatability if and only if R is functionally equivalent to some relationship set R_i w.r.t. $<R_1, R_2, ..., R_n>$ where $i \in \{1, 2, ..., n\}$:

      1. R is deletable and
      2. R is modifiable for those attributes which are also attributes of R_i.

Proof : If the view relationship set R is functionally equivalent to some conceptual schema relationship set R_i w.r.t. $<R_1, R_2, ..., R_n>$, where $i \in \{1, 2, ..., n\}$, then we have a one-to-one correspondence between the relationships of R and the relationships of R_i. Thus when we delete a relationship of R, we delete the corresponding relationship of R_i which is retrieved using the key value of R. Moreover, when we modify the values of the attributes of a relationship of R, the corresponding attributes' values of the corresponding relationship in R_i retrieved using the key value of R are modified. Otherwise, if R is not functionally equivalent to any of the relationship set R_j w.r.t. $<R_1, R_2, ..., R_n>$, where $j \in \{1, 2, ..., n\}$, then there will not be a one-to-one correspondence between the relationships of R and the relationships of R_j. R_j is not the base relationship set of R and the system will not be able to determine uniquely the relationship to be deleted or modified. ∎

Corollary 1 : A view relationship set obtained from a *key-preserving* projection of a base relationship set is modifiable and deletable. ∎

Theorem 1 restricts the modifiable attributes of a view entity type to those view attributes whose base attributes are in the base entity type of the view entity type. However, we can apply the argument used in proving theorem 2 to extend the modifiable attributes of a view entity type to include derived attributes.

For example, the single-valued derived attribute DNAME in the view entity type DOCTOR in Figure 2 can be modified as follows. We observe that the base attribute of the key of the view entity type DOCTOR and the key of the conceptual schema relationship set ATTACHTO are functionally equivalent w.r.t. <ATTACHTO>, thus resulting in a one-to-one correspondence between the view entities in DOCTOR and the relationships in ATTACHTO. Hence, when we modify the value of the derived attribute DNAME of a view entity in DOCTOR, the value of the base attribute of DNAME in the corresponding relationship in ATTACHTO retrieved using the key value of DOCTOR is modified.

We generalize this concept of modifying single-valued derived attributes of a view entity type when certain conditions are satisfied in the following theorem.

Theorem 3 : Let E be the base entity type of a view entity type E'. Let A be a single-valued attribute of E' with the attribute derivation $<R_1, R_2, ..., R_n>$. If the base attribute of A is the identifier of some entity type F, a participating entity type in

R_n, then A is modifiable if and only if the derived relationship set of A is functionally equivalent to R_n w.r.t. $<R_1, R_2, ..., R_n>$.

Proof : The derived relationship set R of the view attribute A is constructed by joining all the relationship sets in the attribute derivation of A and projecting out all the participating entity types of $R_1, R_2, ..., R_n$ except E and F. Note that the construction of the derived relationship set is similar to the construction of view relationship sets. There is a one-to-one correspondence between the relationships of R and the relationships of R_n if and only if R is functionally equivalent to R_n w.r.t. $<R_1, R_2, ..., R_n>$. If the base attribute of A is an identifier of F, then it is part of the relationship set R_n. If A is a single-valued attribute in E', then there is a one-to-one correspondence between the entities in E' and the relationships in R. Hence A is modifiable if and only if R is functionally equivalent to R_n w.r.t. $<R_1, R_2, ..., R_n>$. ■

Note that we do not allow the modification of any multivalued derived view attribute A as it will be ambiguous. Each value of A, which is a set, will correspond to a set of relationships in the conceptual schema and there is no unique translation of the modification request.

Corollary 2 : Let E be the base entity type of a view entity type E'. If E' contains a single-valued attribute A whose base attribute is not in E, but is the identifier of another entity type F which is connected to E by some regular binary relationship set R, then A is modifiable. ■

Corollary 3 : Let E be the base entity type of a view entity type E'. Let A be a single-valued attribute of E' with the attribute derivation $<R_1, R_2, ..., R_n>$. If the base attribute of A is an attribute of R_n, then A is modifiable if and only if the derived relationship set of A is functionally equivalent to R_n w.r.t. $<R_1, R_2, ..., R_n>$. ■

We next consider insertion in the ER approach. A view entity type or view relationship set is insertable if we are able to insert some corresponding entities or relationships into the database without violating any of our three view update principles stated in section 3. Moreover, the entities or relationships inserted into the ER database are subjected to meet the domain constraints, the key constraints, as well as the referential constraints in the case of a relationship insertion.

Theorem 4 : A view entity type is insertable if and only if the identifier of its base entity type is included in the view.
Proof : Trivial. ■

Corollary 4 : A view entity type obtained from the selection of a base entity type is always updatable. ■

Theorem 5 : Let R be a view relationship set with relationship derivation $<R_1, R_2, ..., R_n>$. R is insertable for those attributes which are also the attributes of some relationship set R_i where $i \in \{1, 2, ..., n\}$ if R is functionally equivalent to R_i w.r.t.

$<R_1, R_2, ..., R_n>$ and all the participating entity types of R_i are also the base entity types of the participating view entity types of R.

Proof : If R is functionally equivalent to some relationship set R_i w.r.t. $<R_1, R_2, ..., R_n>$, then we have a one-to-one correspondence between the relationships of R and the relationships of R_i. R_i is a base relationship set of R. Thus, the insertion of a new relationship into R will be translated into an insertion of a corresponding relationship into R_i. Now, to insert a relationship into the database, we require the identifier values of its participating entities to be given. Thus, we can only insert a new relationship into R if all the participating entity types of R_i are also the base entity types of the participating view entity types of the view relationship set. ■

Corollary 5 : A view relationship set obtained from the selection of a base relationship set is always updatable. ■

We refer to the class of view relationship sets that are determined to be insertable by theorem 5 as *Type 1 insertable*. We can always find the mapping to translate any insertion requests on these Type 1 insertable relationship sets. For example, Figure 4 shows a view relationship set R_v obtained from a join of two conceptual schema relationship sets R_1 and R_2, that is, derivation is $<R_1, R_2>$. A', B' and C' are the view participating entity types of R_v whose base entity types are A, B and C respectively. R_v is functionally equivalent to both R_1 and R_2. Hence, R_v is Type 1 insertable with respect to both R_1 and R_2. To insert a relationship (a, b, c) into R_v, we insert the relationships (a, b) and (b, c) into R_1 and R_2 respectively if they do not already exist in database. Otherwise, if both the relationships exist in the database, we reject the insertion.

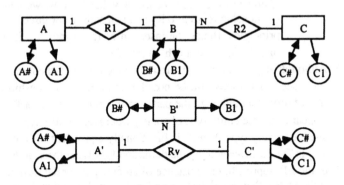

Figure 4: A view relationship set Rv obtained from a join of the conceptual schema relationship sets R1 and R2.

However, the class of view relationship sets which are Type 1 insertable is very restrictive. For example, Figure 5 shows a view relationship set R_w obtained from a join of the two conceptual schema relationship sets R_1 and R_2 in Figure 4, that is, derivation is $<R_1, R_2>$. Here, the common entity type B has been projected out from the view. Although R_w is not Type 1 insertable, but it is possible to insert a relationship (a, c) into R_w without violating any of our view update principles. We first check if a is participated in some relationship in R_1, that is, if there exists an entity b of B such that the relationship (a, b) is in R_1. If the relationship (a, b) exists in R_1 and the relationship (b, c) does not exist in R_2, then we can insert (b, c) into R_2. Otherwise, we reject the insertion.

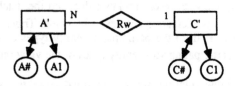

Figure 5: A view relationship set Rw obtained from a join of the conceptual schema relationship sets R1 and R2 with the common entity type B projected out.

We have a few observations from the second example.
1. Two possible situations can occur when we insert a relationship (a, c) into R_w. We try to retrieve the identifier value of B from R_1 using the key value of A'.
   Case 1: The relationship (a, b) does not exist in R_1.
   > That is, a is not participated in any of the relationships in R_1. For this case, there is no way we can insert the relationship (a, c) into R_w. Hence we reject the insertion.
   Case 2: The relationship (a, b) exists in R_1.
   > Using the retrieved identifier value b of B, we can insert a relationship (b, c) into R_2 and still satisfy our three view update principles. Hence the insertion of (a, c) into R_w is translated into the insertion of (b, c) into R_2.
2. Although R_w is not Type 1 insertable according to theorem 5, but we have seen that it may still be possible to insert a relationship into R_w. We observe that although the participating entity type B of R_2 does not appear as a base entity type of some participating entity type of R_w, but the base entity type A of A' is functionally equivalent to B w.r.t. $<R_1>$. R_w is *Type 3 insertable* by the definition following theorem 6.
3. In the ER approach, the existence of an entity in a relationship could be defined as either *mandatory or optional*. If we know that the existence of the entity type A in the relationship set R_1 is mandatory, then we can always retrieve the identifier value of B in R_1 given a key value of A. Thus, we can always find the mapping to translate any insertion requests on R_w. R_w is *Type 2 insertable* by the definition following theorem 6.

Definition 5 : Suppose an entity type E_{i_0} is involved in a relationship set R_{i_0} with another entity type E_{i_1}, and E_{i_1} is involved in a relationship set R_{i_1} with an entity type E_{i_2}, and so on, and eventually we have an entity type $E_{i_{j-1}}$ involved in a relationship set $R_{i_{j-1}}$ with an entity type E_{i_j}. If the existence of E_{i_k} is mandatory in R_{i_k} (which may be n-ary) for all k, $0 <= k < j$, then we say that the existence of E_{i_0} is *transitively mandatory* in the relationship R which is obtained from a natural join of all the relationship sets R_{i_k}.

We will now define the concepts of Type 2 insertable and Type 3 insertable formally.

Theorem 6 : Let R be a view relationship set with the relationship derivation $<R_1$, R_2, ..., $R_n>$. R is insertable for those attributes which are also the attributes of some relationship set R_i where $i \in \{1, 2, ...,n\}$, if R is functionally equivalent to R_i w.r.t. $<R_1, R_2, ..., R_n>$, and for each participating entity type E of R_i
either   1. E is a base entity type of some participating view entity types of R,
or   2. E is functionally equivalent to some entity type F w.r.t. a derivation T such that F is a base entity type of some participating view entity type of R and T is either $<R_1, R_2, ..., R_{i-1}>$ or $<R_{i+1}, R_{i+2}, ..., R_n>$. ∎

We call the class of view relationship sets that are determined to be insertable by the above theorem as *Type 3 insertable*. Moreover, if the existence of the entity type F in the above theorem is transitively mandatory in the relationship set which is obtained from a join of a set of relationship sets in the derivation T, then we call this class of view relationship sets as *Type 2 insertable*. For example, the view relationship set R_w in Figure 4 has a relationship derivation $<R_1, R_2>$ and the entity type A is functionally equivalent to B w.r.t. $<R_1>$. R_w is Type 2 insertable if A is mandatory in R_1. Otherwise, R_w is Type 3 insertable. In both cases, R_2 is the base relationship set of R_w, that is, R_w is insertable w.r.t. R_2. Note that if a view relationship set is Type 2 insertable, then any relationship insertion request is subjected only to domain and key constraint checks. On the other hand, if a view relationship set is Type 3 insertable, then any relationship insertion request is not only subjected to domain and key constraint checks, but is also dependent on the contents of the database.

Corollary 6: If a view relationship set is Type 1 insertable, then it is also Type 2 insertable. If a view relationship set is Type 2 insertable, then it is also Type 3 insertable. ∎

We conclude in the following theorem that if a view relationship set is not Type 3 insertable, then it is not insertable.

Theorem 7 : If a view relationship set is not Type 3 insertable, then it is *not* insertable.
Proof : We will give an outline of the proof here.
Let R be a view relationship set with the relationship derivation $<R_1, R_2, ..., R_n>$. If R is not Type 3 insertable, then by theorem 6, for each of the relationship sets R_i, $1 <= i <= n$, either R is not functionally equivalent to R_i w.r.t. $<R_1, R_2, ..., R_n>$, or there exists some participating entity type E of R_i such that E is not the base

entity type of any participating view entity type of R, and E is not functionally equivalent to any entity type F w.r.t. derivation T such that F is the base entity type of some participating view entity type of R and T is either $<R_1, R_2, ..., R_{i-1}>$ or $<R_{i+1}, R_{i+2}, ..., R_n>$.

Now if R is not functionally equivalent to R_i w.r.t. $<R_1, R_2, ..., R_n>$, then we do not have a one-to-one correspondence between the relationships of R and the relationships of R_i. The insertion of any new relationship into R cannot be translated into an insertion of some relationship into R_i. Therefore, R_i is not the base relationship set of R.

If there exists some participating entity type E of R_i such that E is not the base entity type of any participating view entity types of R, and E is not functionally equivalent to any entity type F w.r.t. a derivation T such that F is the base entity type of some participating view entity type of R and T is either $<R_1, R_2, ..., R_{i-1}>$ or $<R_{i+1}, R_{i+2}, ..., R_n>$, then there is no way we can obtain the identifier value of E during an insertion of R. Therefore, R_i is not the base relationship set of R.

Hence, if R is not Type 3 insertable, then for each of the relationship sets R_i, $1 <= i <= n$, R_i is not the base relationship set of R. Therefore, R is not insertable. ∎

Theorem 4 restricts the attributes of a view entity type which can be given values in an insertion of a view entity to those view attributes whose base attributes are in the base entity type of the view entity type. However, we can allow values to be given to derived attributes of a view entity type in an insertion of a new entity without violating any of our view update principles.

For example, we may want to insert a new doctor into the view entity type DOCTOR in Figure 2, and at the same time give the name of the department the doctor is attached to. This insertion request can be translated into an insertion of a corresponding entity into the base entity type of DOCTOR and an insertion of a relationship into the conceptual schema relationship set ATTACHTO. The new relationship which is inserted into ATTACHTO is created using the identifier values of its two participating entity types, DOCTOR and DEPARTMENT, that is, the user-given values for the attributes EMPNO and DNAME which are both in the view entity type DOCTOR. We have a one-to-one correspondence between the relationships in ATTACHTO and the entities in the view entity type DOCTOR since the identifier of ATTACHTO is functionally equivalent to the key of the view entity type DOCTOR. Hence, when we give a value to the derived attribute DNAME in an insertion of a new view entity into the view entity type DOCTOR, a new relationship is inserted into the relationship set ATTACHTO in the database in addition to the insertion of a corresponding entity into the base entity type of DOCTOR.

We say that a view attribute of a view entity type or view relationship set is *insertable* if values can be given to it in an insertion of a new view entity or view relationship into the view entity type or view relationship set respectively. We generalize the concept of *insertable derived attributes* in the following theorem.

Theorem 8 : Let E be the base entity type of a view entity type E' and let A be a *derived* attribute of E' with the attribute derivation $<R_1, R_2, ..., R_n>$ such that R_n is a binary relationship set. Suppose E_n is a common entity type of R_{n-1} and R_n, and F is the other participating entity type of R_n such that the base attribute of A is the identifier of F. A is insertable if

1. the derived relationship set R of A is functionally equivalent to R_n w.r.t $<R_1, R_2, ..., R_n>$, and

2. E is functionally equivalent to E_n w.r.t. $<R_1, R_2, ..., R_{n-1}>$, and

3. E is transitively mandatory in the relationship set which is obtained from a join of the relationship sets $R_1, R_2, ..., R_{n-1}$.

Proof : Recall that the derived relationship set R is obtained by joining all the relationship sets in the attribute derivation of A and projecting out all the participating entity types of $R_1, R_2, ..., R_n$ except E and F. There is a one-to-one correspondence between the relationships of R and the relationships of R_n if and only if R is functionally equivalent to R_n w.r.t. $<R_1, R_2, ..., R_n>$. If E is functionally equivalent to E_n w.r.t. $<R_1, R_2, ..., R_{n-1}>$, and E is transitively mandatory in the relationship set obtained from a join of the relationship sets $R_1, R_2, ..., R_{n-1}$, then R is Type 2 insertable with respect to R_n. If the base attribute of A is the identifier of F, then it is part of the relationship set R_n. Therefore, if A is a single-valued attribute in E', then when A is given a value during an insertion of a view entity into E', we can insert a new relationship into the binary relationship set R_n using the retrieved identifier value of E_n and the given value of A. If A is a multivalued attribute in E', then a set of values S will be given to A during an insertion of a view entity into E'. In this case, we will insert |S| new relationships into R_n. Each of these new relationships is created using the retrieved identifier value of E_n and a value in S. These insertions will not cause any violation of our view update principles. Hence, A is insertable. ■

Corollary 7: Let E be the base entity type of a view entity type E'. If E' contains an attribute A whose base attribute is not in E, but is the identifier of another entity type F which is connected to E by some regular binary relationship set R, then A is insertable. ■

Corollary 8: An inherited attribute is insertable. ■

Based on the above theory developed, we have an algorithm to systematically determine the updatability of view entity types and view relationship sets in a view. In addition, this algorithm also determines the different types of insertability for view relationship sets. Interested readers can refer to [20] for details of this View Updatability Algorithm. We also have a View Update Translation Algorithm [20] to translate a view update request into the corresponding database update based on the results obtained from the View Updatability Algorithm. Information regarding the updatability of a view generated from the View Updatability Algorithm is stored in the data dictionary. The View Update Translation Algorithm will use these information during any view update request translation.

We have seen that it is trivial to delete an entity from a deletable view entity type. However, to insert a new entity into an insertable view entity type, we may need to take into consideration the presence of inherited and/or derived attributes. If we have derived attributes in the view entity type, then in addition to the insertion of a corresponding entity into the base entity type of the view entity type, we will need to insert a corresponding relationship into some relationship set. For example, to insert a new doctor into the view in Figure 2, we have the Prolog goal

?- insert (doctor (116790, 'H. Goh', 35, ['MBBS', 'MMed'], surgery)).

The View Update Translation Algorithm will translate this view insertion request into the following three facts to be inserted into the database.

doctor (116790, ['MBBS', 'MMed']).
       /* Base attributes of EMPNO and QUAL are in base entity type */
employee (116790, 'H. Goh', 35).
       /* NAME & AGE are inherited attributes with derivation <UNION>*/
attachto (116790, surgery).
       /* DNAME is a derived attribute with derivation <ATTACHTO> */

To modify a particular doctor in the view entity type DOCTOR in Figure 2, we use the given key value of the doctor to retrieve and modify the corresponding doctor entity in the database if the attribute QUAL is given a new value. If either one or both the attributes NAME and AGE are given new values, we modify the corresponding employee entity. If the attribute DNAME is given a new value, we modify the corresponding attachto relationship. Similar forms of translations can be carried out for view update requests on relationship sets. View relationship sets deletions and modifications are trivial. For view relationship set insertions, we need to consider the three types of insertability.

5. Conclusions

We have proposed a theory within the framework of ER approach which characterizes the conditions under which there exist mappings from view updates into conceptual schema updates. We allowed the concept of virtual updates which are carried out by the system to ensure that changes in a view requested are consistent with the rest of the database. This is important in cases where the value of a view attribute cannot be changed by the user but whose value is a function of the values of other modifiable view attributes. With the concept of derivations, we are able to handle view updates involving derived attributes, relationship set joins and multilevel inheritances through the special relationship sets ISA, UNION etc. We have also defined three types of insertability for view relationship sets. We can always find the mapping to translate any insertion requests on Type 1 insertable view relationship sets. If a view relationship set is Type 2 insertable, then any view relationship insertion request is subjected to domain and key constraint checks. On the other hand, if a view relationship set is Type 3 insertable, then any view relationship insertion request is not only subjected to domain and key constraint checks, but is also dependent on the contents of the database. We have also seen that if a view relationship set is Type 1 insertable, then it is also Type 2 insertable. If a view relationship set is Type 2 insertable, then it is also Type 3 insertable. Moreover, we proved that if a view relationship set is not Type 3 insertable, then it is not insertable.

Based on the theory, we have developed the View Updatability Algorithm and the View Update Translation Algorithm. These algorithms also take into consideration the three types of insertability for view relationship sets. [16] has an algorithm which gives a unique translation of a normal form ER diagram to a set of relations. Hence, any update in the ER approach can be translated uniquely to an equivalent update in the relational database. Note that our approach to view update is intended to fit into the framework of a general and systematic approach to the whole question of view updating.

References

1. F. Bancilhon and N. Spyratos: Update semantics and relational views, ACM Trans. Database Systems 6 (4), 1981.
2. T. Barsalou, et. al: Updating Relational Databases through Object-Based Views, Proc. of the 1991 ACM SIGMOD Int. Conf. on Management of Data, May 1991.
3. C.R. Carlson and A.K. Arora: The updatability of relational views based on functional dependencies, Third International Conputer Software and Applications Conference, IEEE Computer Society, 1979.
4. M.C. Chan: Translation templates for updates issued on relation views, Tech. Report 35, Dept. of Comp. Science, Monash University, Melbourne, Australia, April 1983.
5. P.P. Chen: The Entity-Relationship Model: Toward a Unified View of Data, ACM Transactions on Database Systems vol 1, no 1, 1976, pp 166-192.
6. E.F. Codd: Recent Investigations in a Relational Database System, Information Processing 74, North Holland, Amsterdam, 1974, pp 1017-1021.
7. U. Dayal and P.A. Bernstein: On the correct translation of update operations on relational views, ACM Trans. Database Systems 7 (3), 1982.
8. A.L. Furtado, C.K. Sevcik and C.S. Santos: Permittting updates through views of databases, Information Systems 4 (4), Pergamon Press, Great Britain, 1979.
9. J. Grant and T.W. Ling: Database Representation and Manipulation Using Entity-Relationship Database Logic, Proc. of Methodologies for Intelligient Ststem IV, Elsevier Science Pub. Co., 1989, pp 102-109.
10. J. Guttag: Abstract data types and the development of data structures, Communications of ACM 20 (6), 1977, pp 396-404.
11. A.M. Keller: Algorithms for translating view updates to database updates for views involving selections, projections and joins, 4th PODS, ACM, March 1985.
12. A.M. Keller: Choosing a view update translator by Dialog at view definition time, Proc. of the 12th International Conference on Very Large Databases, 1986.
13. R. Langerak: View Updates in Relational Databases with an Independent Scheme, ACM Transactions on Database Systems, Vol 15, No 1, March 1990, pp 40-66.
14. M.L. Lee: An Entity-Relationship Based Database Management System, a thesis submitted for the degree of Master of Science, National University of Singapore, 1992.
15. S.B. Legg and K.J. McDonell: Translating update requests on user views, technical report 77, Department of Computer Science, Monash University, Melbourne, Australia, Nov 1986.
16. T.W. Ling: A Normal Form for Entity-Relationship Diagrams, Proc. 4th International Conference on Entity-Relationship Approach, 1985.

17. T.W. Ling: A Three Level Schema Architecture ER based Database Management Systems, in: March, S.T. (ed), Entity-Relationship Approach, North Holland, Amsterdam, 1987, pp 205-220.

18. T.W. Ling and M.L. Lee: A Graphical Entity-Relationship Based Database Management System Workbench, Proc. 4th International Workshop on Computer-Aided Software Engineering, 1990, pp 480-495.

19. T.W. Ling. and M.L. Lee: A Prolog Implementation of an ER based DBMS, Proc. 10th Int. Conf. on ER Approach, 1991, pp 587-605.

20. T.W. Ling and M.L. Lee: View Update in Entity-Relationship Approach, to be submitted for publication, 1992.

21. D. Maier: Theory of Relational Databases, Computer Science Press, 1983.

22. L. Rowe and K.A. Schoens: Data abstractions, views and updates in RIGEL, in Proc. ACM-SIGMOD International Conf. on Management of Data, 1979, pp 71-81.

23. K.C. Sevcik and A.L. Furtado: Complete and compatible sets of update operations, in International Conf. on Management of Data (ICMOD), 1978.

24. M. Stonebraker: Implementation of integrity constraints and views by query modification, Proc. ACM SIGMOD Int. Conf. on Management of Data, San Jose, 1975, pp 65-78.

Transforming Conceptual Data Models into an Object Model

Rudolf Herzig* and Martin Gogolla

Technische Universität Braunschweig, Informatik, Abt. Datenbanken
Postfach 3329, W–3300 Braunschweig, Fed. Rep. Germany
e–mail: {herzig|gogolla}@idb.cs.tu-bs.de

Abstract. In this paper a conceptually simple structural object model focusing on object types, attributes and ISA relationships is introduced. The model is derived mainly from an extended Entity-Relationship approach, but concepts from other semantic and object-oriented models have influenced its features. It is shown how high-level conceptual data models can be mapped to this model, and to what extent the object model subsumes classical modeling paradigms.

1 Introduction

In recent years numerous data models for the conceptual modeling of information systems have been proposed. Among them there are semantic data models like SDM [13], IFO [3] and (extended) ER models [8, 9, 24, 31, 34, 10], complex object models like [1, 18, 26], purely object-based models like FDM [28] as well as object-based models with complex values such as [22]. All the approaches have different motivation, terminology, and aims. Here we aim to show you how some of these models can be translated into a conceptually simple object model (OBM), which can serve as a common basis for the constructs employed in those approaches.

Our object model is mathematically precisely defined, i.e., it is given an abstract syntax and formal semantics, and it is complete, since we gave semantics to the query and integrity specification component in [12], and to the data manipulation component in [14], by using a well-defined calculus.

As should become clear, the object model is not intended to be a tool for conceptual modeling. For this task one of the well-known semantic data models offering high-level modeling primitives should be used. The purpose of the object model is to provide a kind of target model for the logical design, i.e., the chosen design should be translated into it. In this respect the role of the object model should be seen analogously to the role played by the relational model to the logical design. However, although the object model is conceptually simpler than high-level semantic models, it is clearly much richer than the relational model. More importantly, it is still rich enough to apply results obtained in its simple context to more complex ones. For instance, the calculus defined for the object model may be applied to IFO in a straightforward manner.

The paper is organized as follows. In Sect. 2 a fictitious conceptual data model summarizing concepts of a number of semantic data models is introduced, and in Sect. 3 it is shown how this model can be mapped into our object model which is conceptually much

---

* This work was funded by the German Ministry for Research and Technology (BMFT) under Grant No. 01 IS 203 D.

simpler because it deals with atomic object types only. While Sect. 2 adopts a rather informal view, the object model is subject to rigorous mathematical semantics in Sect. 3. The object model is related to other modeling paradigms like complex object models and purely object-based models in Sect. 4. Finally, our observations and conclusions are given in the last section.

2 A fictitious conceptual data model

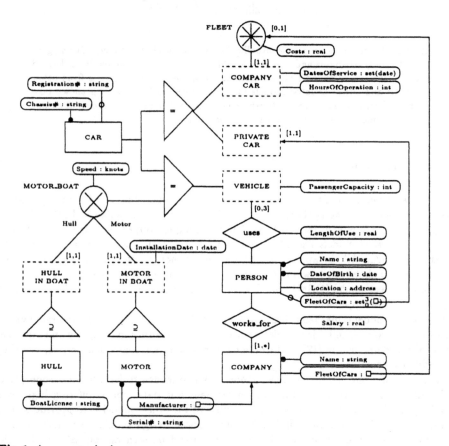

Fig. 1. A conceptual schema

Let us look at the conceptual schema in Fig. 1. The schema combines modeling primitives of IFO [3], the ER model [8], and an extended ER approach [10], covering the following fundamental data abstractions of the semantic data models (cf. [27, 17, 25]):

Object types are used to collect physical objects (entities) in the world such as PERSONs, MOTOR_BOATs, or conceptual objects such as COMPANYs. This abstraction is called *classification* in the literature. Typically, a semantic data model provides means to specify *atomic types* and type constructors for building *complex types*.

- Atomic object types are usually distinguished either as being *printable* (literal or lexical object types, LOTs), e.g. string, or *abstract* (non-lexical object types, NOLOTs [33]), e.g. PERSON. In the following, printable object types are called "data types", whereas the notion "object type" is used for abstract object types only. In Fig. 1 object types (entity types) are depicted by rectangles.

- The symbols ⊛, ⊗ and ◇ denote complex object types. To be more specific, we have a *set object type* (association [5], collection [18], grouping [13]) FLEET, a *tuple object type* (aggregation [29], composition [18]) MOTOR_BOAT, and the *relationship types* uses and works_for. Members of set object types are sets over an underlying type, whereas members of both tuple object types and relationship types are ordered n-tuples. Of course, relationships can be seen as (tuple) objects, and it would be possible to combine tuple object types and relationship types under one single heading, but this addresses an advanced level of abstraction[2].

Attributes given by ovals are used to model properties of objects. Several kinds of attributes can be identified.

- First we have *data-valued* attributes, such as Name : PERSON → string.
- In contrast, attributes ranging over abstract object types, such as Manufacturer : MOTOR → COMPANY, are called *object-valued*.
- Both data- and object-valued attributes are allowed to be *multi-valued*, e.g., FleetOfCars : PERSON → set(PRIVATE_CAR).

ISA relationships form the third fundamental component of semantic data models. In Fig. 1 ISA relationships are represented by triangles which we call **distributors**. Object types on the base line of a distributor are called input types, and object types on the pointed side are called output types. Distributors take objects of the input types and associate them with output types. The distribution is "lax" in the sense that there may be objects in the input types, which are not associated with any output type.

If an input object is associated with an output type, this brings about a role object or *aspect* of this object to be created. All objects in the output types originate from this mechanism. Therefore, the output types of distributors are also called **ISA-dependent types**. In contrast, object types which do not appear on the output side of any distributor are called **base types**. We assume that there are no cyclic ISA relationships. Consequently, we have for every ISA-dependent object an underlying base object. In Fig. 1 ISA-dependent object types are represented as base object types except for a dashed line as boundary of the rectangle.

Depending on the number of the input types and the output types of a distributor, two special kinds of ISA relationships can be ascertained, namely *specialization* and *categorization*:

- If there is only input type, then specializations, such as the specialization of a MOTOR to a MOTOR_IN_BOAT, are modeled. If there are several output types at the same time, we have *disjoint specializations*, such as CAR to COMPANY_CAR and PRIVATE_CAR.
- If there is only output type, then categorizations [9] are modeled. For example, both STUDENTs and TEACHERs may act as BORROWERs in a lending library. By an additional constraint (see below), categorizations can be extended to generalizations by demanding that each input object of a distributor must be assigned to the output type, as in the case of generalizing CARs and MOTOR_BOATs to VEHICLEs.

---

[2] A similar distinction was made in [34] by the notion of *abstract* and *associative* relationships.

The concepts specialization and categorization overlap if there is only one object type on each side of a distributor.

To summarize the basic modeling primitives we maintain that object types are the fundamental building blocks of a semantic data model schema, and that there are three ways to express relationships between the different object types: to relate objects we can build complex object types, or make use of attributes modeling functional relationships, or distribute objects to ISA-dependent types.

Up to now we have described the basic modeling primitives. The schema in Fig. 1 includes some further features which can be characterized as *structural restrictions*.

Object participation constraints: The participation of objects in complex objects can be limited by lower and upper bounds, e.g., every MOTOR_IN_BOAT must be installed in exactly one MOTOR_BOAT, every COMPANY_CAR must appear in exactly one FLEET, for every COMPANY there must be at least one PERSON working for it, and each VEHICLE must not be used by more than three PERSONs. Object participation constraints are used in many semantic data models, e.g. IRIS [11], in particular they cover cardinality constraints and existence dependencies in ER models [9].

Cardinalities wrt. multi-valued attributes: The cardinality of a set appearing as a value of a multi-valued attribute can be restricted by lower and upper bounds, too, e.g., every PERSON must not own more than three PRIVATE_CARs given the attribute FleetOfCars (or more precisely PERSON.FleetOfCars).

Cardinalities wrt. ranges of attributes: In some cases we need cardinalities even for the ranges of attributes. In our example it is not permitted for a FLEET to belong to more than one COMPANY via the attribute FleetOfCars, and a PRIVATE_CAR must belong to exactly one PERSON. Hence COMPANY.FleetOfCars can be characterized as a *non-overlapping* attribute, and PERSON.FleetOfCars is non-overlapping and moreover *exhaustive*. Both attribute restrictions are known from SDM [13], for example.

Mandatory attributes: We assume that the interpretations of all object types include a special element ⊥ representing the *undefined* or *null value*. Consequently, all attributes are *optional* by default. The optionality can be excluded by a constraint. In the example schema optional attributes are distinguished from mandatory attributes by a circle (○), i.e., Registration# and PERSON.FleetOfCars are optional attributes, whereas all other attributes are mandatory.

Bi-directional ISA relationships: In general, triangles represent ISA relationships directed from the output side to the input side (every MOTOR_IN_BOAT is a MOTOR, but a MOTOR is not necessarily a MOTOR_IN_BOAT). To express that an ISA relationship also holds for the other direction, as it is in case of *generalizations* (every CAR and every MOTOR_BOAT is a VEHICLE) and *partitions* (i.e. covering disjoint specializations) (every CAR is either a COMPANY_CAR or a PRIVATE_CAR), the corresponding triangle can be marked by '='.

Key concept: The identity of abstract objects is not visible to the user. But especially with respect to updates it is necessary that the user is able to refer to a distinct object. Therefore, we have for each base object type at least one key attribute denoted by a thick dot (●). The key integrity assures that each base object can be identified uniquely by the values of its key attributes. For complex object types and ISA-dependent types we do not need a key concept, because the identity of each complex object is already given by the construction of the object, and an ISA-dependent object inherits its identity from the underlying base object.

In the next section the conceptual schema of Fig. 1 is mapped into a simple formal data model. Provided that this model finds an implementation, this might be considered as a logical design step within database design process [30, 7].

3 Formal Definition of an Object Schema

In this section we present the basic terms relevant to our notion of an object schema. We distinguish between a data level given by a *data signature* DS and an object level given by an *object schema* over DS. The data signature contains a finite set of *data types* (or printable object types) together with a set of operations and predicates defined upon them. In contrast to (abstract) object types the semantics of data types is fixed. From a semantic point of view, the data level is the kernel of the object level because abstract objects can be observed only by means of data types used as attribute domains.

For all terms discussed in this section we give precise mathematical definitions employing mainly the notions set and function.

Axiomatic conventions. Let $|\mathbf{SET}|$ denote the class of sets, $|\mathbf{FISET}|$ the class of finite sets, $|\mathbf{FUN}|$ the class of total functions and $|\mathbf{REL}|$ the class of relations. There are the obvious inclusions $|\mathbf{FISET}| \subseteq |\mathbf{SET}|$ and $|\mathbf{FUN}| \subseteq |\mathbf{REL}| \subseteq |\mathbf{SET}|$. Assume sets $S, S_1, \ldots, S_n \in |\mathbf{SET}|$ are given. Then $F(S)$ denotes the restriction of the powerset $P(S)$ of S to finite sets, S^* the set of finite lists over S, S^+ the set of finite non-empty lists over S, and $S_1 \times \ldots \times S_n$ the Cartesian product of the sets $S_1, \ldots S_n$. Finite sets are written as $\{c_1, \ldots, c_n\}$, lists as $\langle c_1, \ldots, c_n \rangle$, and elements of the Cartesian product as $(c_1, \ldots, c_n)$.

3.1 Data Level

The syntax of a data signature gives the names of the data sorts and the operations and predicates upon them. We assume certain sorts (e.g., int, real, string) and standard operations (e.g., $+_{\mathbf{int}}$: int $\times$ int $\rightarrow$ int) and predicates (e.g., $\leq_{\mathbf{int}}$: int $\times$ int) to be predefined. The semantics of a data signature associates a (possibly infinite) set with every sort name, and functions and relations with the operation and predicate names. This interpretation will be fixed once and for all and will not change. In the following formal definition we shall only consider names of data types, i.e., data sorts. A complete definition of a data signature, including data operations and predicates, can be found in [12].

Definition 1 (data sorts). The syntax of data sorts is given by a finite set DATA-SORT. The **semantics of data sorts** is given by the total function $\mu[\text{DATASORT}]$: DATASORT $\rightarrow |\mathbf{SET}|$ such that $d \in$ DATASORT implies $\perp \in \mu[\text{DATASORT}](d)$. □

Predefined sorts like int, real, string these sorts have the 'usual' semantics, e.g., $\mu[\text{DATASORT}](\mathbf{int}) = \mathbb{Z} \cup \{\perp\}$. The element $\perp$ denotes the 'undefined' value. We require every data sort d (and later every object type o) to contain $\perp$, because it is necessary to have such a value as result of incorrect applications of operations, e.g., the division by zero always results in $\perp$. We assume the interpretations of all data sorts (and later object types) to be disjoint, which is partially achieved by including the name or token of a type into the structure of values.

Besides the standard applications, the data signature may contain user-defined sorts, operations and predicates. With respect to user-defined sorts, atomic data types (e.g. enumeration types such as color = {green, yellow, red}) are possible as well as arbitrary complex data types definable by *sort expressions*.

Definition 2 (sort expressions). Let a set S ∈ |SET| together with a (semantic) function $\mu[S] : S \rightarrow |SET|$ (such that $\perp \in \mu[S](s)$ for every $s \in S$) and a set A of (attribute) names be given. The **syntax of sort expressions over S** is given by the set EXPR(S) determined by the following rules.

(i) If $s \in S$, then $s \in$ EXPR(S).
(ii) If $s \in$ EXPR(S), then **set(s)** ∈ EXPR(S).
(iii) If $s_1, \ldots, s_n \in$ EXPR(S) and $a_1, \ldots, a_n \in$ A with $a_i \neq a_j$ for $i \neq j$, then
tuple($a_1:s_1, \ldots, a_n:s_n$) ∈ EXPR(S).
(iv) If $s_1, \ldots, s_n \in$ EXPR(S) and $a_1, \ldots, a_n \in$ A with $a_i \neq a_j$ for $i \neq j$, then
union($a_1:s_1, \ldots, a_n:s_n$) ∈ EXPR(S).

The **semantics of sort expressions over S** is a total function
$\mu[\text{EXPR}(S)] : \text{EXPR}(S) \rightarrow |SET|$ determined by the following rules.

(i) $\mu[\text{EXPR}(S)](s) := \mu[S](s)$.
(ii) $\mu[\text{EXPR}(S)](\text{set}(s)) := F(\mu[\text{EXPR}(S)](s)) \cup \{\perp\}$.
(iii) $\mu[\text{EXPR}(S)](\text{tuple}(a_1:s_1, \ldots, a_n:s_n)) :=$
$(\{a_1:\underline{s}_1 \mid \underline{s}_1 \in \mu[\text{EXPR}(S)](s_1)\} \times \ldots \times \{a_n:\underline{s}_n \mid \underline{s}_n \in \mu[\text{EXPR}(S)](s_n)\}) \cup \{\perp\}$.
(iv) $\mu[\text{EXPR}(S)](\text{union}(a_1:s_1, \ldots, a_n:s_n)) :=$
$\{a_1:\underline{s}_1 \mid \underline{s}_1 \in \mu[\text{EXPR}(S)](s_1)\} \cup \ldots \cup \{a_n:\underline{s}_n \mid \underline{s}_n \in \mu[\text{EXPR}(S)](s_n)\} \cup \{\perp\}$. ☐

A complex data type **graph** is constructed by **tuple(N:nodes, E:edges)** in which nodes is given by **set(node)**, edges by **set(tuple(Start:node, End:node))**, and node is an enumeration type. For instance, (N:{ 1,2 }, E:{ (Start:1, End:2), (Start:1, End:1) }) is a proper value of type **graph**. The constructor **union** allows the modeling of alternatives. For example, a data type **amount** could be given by **union(Dollar:int, Sterling:int)**, and **Dollar:10** or **Sterling:5** are possible values of type **amount**. Besides the proposed further type constructors like **list** or **bag** (multiset) are possible.

Sort expressions induce a number of **aggregate functions** like **CNT** counting the elements in a set, **IN** representing the element-of relation, operations selecting components of a tuple or alternatives of a union. and many other operations and predicates. For details we refer to [12].

3.2 Object Level

The object schema is the central notion of this section. The syntax of such a schema introduces names for object types, for distributors which make some object types to ISA-dependent types, and for attributes of objects. The semantics of an object schema associates sets and functions with these items. For instance, for every object type there is a (finite) set of current objects, and for every attribute name there is a function giving the current value of the attribute for every object. These sets and functions constitute a (database) state, which can be altered in the course of time (in contrast to the interpretation of the data types, which is fixed). The connection to the data signature is established via data-valued attributes.

Definition 3 (object schema). Let a data signature DS be given. The **syntax of an object schema OBM(DS) over DS** is given by

- the finite sets BASE_OBJTYPE, ISA_OBJTYPE, ATTR, DISTR,
- and the total functions

source :	ATTR	$\to$ OBJTYPE,
destination :	ATTR	$\to$ EXPR(SORT),
parent_distr :	ISA_OBJTYPE	$\to$ DISTR,
input :	DISTR	$\to F(\text{OBJTYPE}) - \{\emptyset\}$,
key :	BASE_OBJTYPE	$\to \text{ATTR}^+$.

OBJTYPE = BASE_OBJTYPE $\cup$ ISA_OBJTYPE refers to the set of all object types and SORT = DATASORT $\cup$ OBJTYPE to the set of all basic sorts. The function *output* : DISTR $\to F(\text{ISA\_OBJTYPE})$ is defined by $output(d) := \{ o \mid parent\_distr(o) = d \}$. If $a \in$ ATTR with $source(a) = o$ and $destination(a) = s$, this is denoted as $a : o \to s$. If $d \in$ DISTR with $input(d) = \{i_1, \ldots, i_m\}$ and $output(d) = \{o_1, \ldots, o_n\}$, this is denoted as $d(i_1, \ldots, i_m \supseteq o_1, \ldots, o_n)$.

There are some syntactical restrictions:

- For $key(o) = \langle a_1, \ldots, a_n \rangle$ there is $a_i \neq a_j$ for $i \neq j$, and $a \in key(o)$ implies $source(a) = o$.
- The function *parent_distr* has to be surjective.
- (*) It is not permitted for $obj\_dep^+(o, o)$ to hold for some $o \in$ OBJTYPE, where obj_dep^+ is the transitive closure of the relation obj_dep defined by: if $o_1 \in$ ISA_OBJTYPE and $o_2 \in input(parent\_distr(o_1))$ or $o_1 \in$ BASE_OBJTYPE and there is a key attribute $a \in key(o_1)$ with $a : o_1 \to s$ and o_2 appears in the construction of the sort expression s, then $obj\_dep(o_1, o_2)$ holds.

The semantics of an object schema OBM(DS) over DS is given by the total functions

- $\mu[\text{BASE\_OBJTYPE}]$: BASE_OBJTYPE $\to |\text{FISET}|$ such that $o \in$ BASE_OBJTYPE implies $\bot \in \mu[\text{BASE\_OBJTYPE}](o)$,
- $\mu[\text{DISTR}]$: DISTR $\to |\text{FUN}|$ such that $d(i_1, \ldots, i_m \supseteq o_1, \ldots, o_n)$ implies $\mu[\text{DISTR}](d) : \bigcup_{k=1}^{m} \mu[\text{OBJTYPE}](i_k) \to \{o_1, \ldots, o_n\} \cup \{\bot\}$,
- $\mu[\text{ISA\_OBJTYPE}]$: ISA_OBJTYPE $\to |\text{FISET}|$ such that $o \in$ ISA_OBJTYPE implies $\mu[\text{ISA\_OBJTYPE}](o) :=$

  $\{ o{:}\underline{b} \mid b \in$ BASE_OBJTYPE and $\underline{b} \in \mu[\text{BASE\_OBJTYPE}](b)$ and
        there are $o_1, \ldots, o_n \in$ ISA_OBJTYPE with $o_n = o$ such that
          $\mu[\text{DISTR}](parent\_distr(o_1))(\underline{b} \quad) = o_1$ and
          $\mu[\text{DISTR}](parent\_distr(o_2))(o_1{:}\underline{b} \quad) = o_2$ and

                      $\vdots$

          $\mu[\text{DISTR}](parent\_distr(o_n))(o_{n-1}{:}\underline{b} \,) = o_n \, \} \cup \{\bot\}$,

- $\mu[\text{ATTR}]$: ATTR $\to |\text{FUN}|$ such that $a : o \to s$ implies
  $\mu[\text{ATTR}](a) : \mu[\text{OBJTYPE}](o) \to \mu[\text{EXPR(SORT)}](s)$, and
  - if $o \in$ BASE_OBJTYPE and $a \in key(o)$, then $\mu[\text{ATTR}](a)(\underline{o}) = \bot$ implies $\underline{o} = \bot$.

For $o \in$ BASE_OBJTYPE, $key(o) = \langle a_1, \ldots, a_n \rangle$, $a_i : o \rightarrow s_i$ $(i = 1, \ldots, n)$ the function $id_o : \mu[\text{BASE\_OBJTYPE}](o) \rightarrow \mu[\text{EXPR(SORT)}](\text{tuple}(a_1{:}s_1, \ldots, a_n{:}s_n))$ is defined by $id_o(\underline{o}) := (a_1{:}\mu[\text{ATTR}](a_1)(\underline{o}), \ldots, a_n{:}\mu[\text{ATTR}](a_n)(\underline{o}))$ iff $\underline{o} \neq \bot$, and $id_o(\bot) = \bot$. **Key integrity:** $\underline{o}_1, \underline{o}_2 \in \mu[\text{BASE\_OBJTYPE}](o)$ with $id_o(\underline{o}_1) = id_o(\underline{o}_2)$ implies $\underline{o}_1 = \underline{o}_2$.

$\mu[\text{OBJTYPE}]$ and $\mu[\text{SORT}]$ are determined by the corresponding μ's on the right-hand side of the equations above. For all $s_1, s_2 \in$ SORT there is $\mu[\text{SORT}](s_1) \cap \mu[\text{SORT}](s_2) = \{\bot\}$. Every function $\mu[\text{ATTR}](a)$ and $\mu[\text{DISTR}](d)$ has to preserve the undefined value, e.g., $\mu[\text{ATTR}](a)(\bot) = \bot$, and so on. $\qquad\qquad\qquad\qquad\qquad\square$

Let us now consider the textual object schema in Fig. 2 belonging to the conceptual schema in Fig. 1. The schema is denoted in a linear way. Specifications enclosed in < > contain information about the logical object identity, i.e., the key group for base object types and the parent distributor for ISA-dependent object types. Please note that specifications starting with '/' are to be ignored at this stage. The syntax of the object schema is given by the sets:

```
BASE_OBJTYPE  = { CAR, HULL, ..., FLEET, uses, works_for }
DISTR         = { specialization_HULL, ..., generalization_VEHICLE }
ISA_OBJTYPE   = { HULL_IN_BOAT, MOTOR_IN_BOAT, ..., VEHICLE }
ATTR          = { Chassis#, Registration#, ..., PassengerCapacity }
```

We assume that attributes of the same name defined on different object types remain distinguishable by using the object type as a prefix, e.g., PERSON.Name and COMPANY.Name.

The elements of BASE_OBJTYPE are called **base object types.** With respect to the example of Fig. 1 the notion "base object type" includes (base) entity types $\square$, set object types $\circledast$, tuple object types $\otimes$, and relationship types $\diamond$. The set of actual objects belonging to an object type o is given by $\mu[\text{BASE\_OBJTYPE}](o)$.

$$\mu[\text{BASE\_OBJTYPE}](\text{CAR}) = \{\underline{c}_1, \ldots, \underline{c}_m\} \cup \{\bot\}$$
$$\mu[\text{BASE\_OBJTYPE}](\text{MOTOR\_BOAT}) = \{\underline{mb}_1, \ldots, \underline{mb}_n\} \cup \{\bot\}$$

Throughout the paper the underbar notation will always indicate a value of semantic domain. For base object types, the values $\underline{c}_i$, $\underline{mb}_j$, etc. represent *abstract object identifiers* (OIDs, surrogate keys), which belong to real world entities. We are not going into the subject of the structure of object identifiers, because we assume that object identifiers are internal values not visible to the user.

The elements of DISTR are called **distributors;** they are represented by triangles in Fig. 1. A distributor d may be regarded as a rearrangement of object types associating with every object in the input types an output type. The distribution is "lax" in the sense that there might be objects in the input types appearing in none of the output types if they are mapped to the 'undefined type'.

$$\mu[\text{DISTR}](\text{partition\_CAR}) : \{\underline{c}_1, \ldots, \underline{c}_m\} \cup \{\bot\} \rightarrow \{\text{COMPANY\_CAR}, \text{PRIVATE\_CAR}\} \cup \{\bot\}$$
$$\mu[\text{DISTR}](\text{generalization\_VEHICLE}) : \{\underline{c}_1, \ldots, \underline{c}_m\} \cup \{\underline{mb}_1, \ldots, \underline{mb}_n\} \cup \{\bot\}$$
$$\rightarrow \{\text{VEHICLE}\} \cup \{\bot\}$$

In contrast to base object types, the semantics of object types on the output side of distributors are fixed by the semantics of the "parent" distributor. Therefore, the output types given by the set ISA_OBJTYPE are called **ISA-dependent object types.** In Fig. 1 ISA-dependent object types are represented by a dashed box $\vdots\vdots$.

```
schema example
  base_objtypes
    CAR           < Chassis# : string >
                  Registration# : string /optional;
    HULL          < BoatLicense : string >;
    MOTOR         < Manufacturer : COMPANY, Serial# : string >;
    PERSON        < Name : string, DateOfBirth : date >
                  Location : address,
                  FleetOfCars : set(PRIVATE_CAR)
                                    /optional /multi[0,3] /inv[1,1];
    COMPANY       < Name : string >
                  FleetOfCars : FLEET /inv[0,1];
    MOTOR_BOAT    < Hull  : HULL_IN_BOAT /inv[1,1],
                    Motor : MOTOR_IN_BOAT /inv[1,1] >
                  Speed : knots;
    FLEET         < Members : set(COMPANY_CAR) /inv[1,1] >
                  Costs : real;
    uses          < P : PERSON, V : VEHICLE /inv[0,3] >
                  LengthOfUse : real;
    works_for     < P : PERSON, C : COMPANY /inv[1,*] >
                  Salary : real;

  isa_objtypes
    HULL_IN_BOAT  < specialization_HULL >;
    MOTOR_IN_BOAT < specialization_MOTOR >
                  InstallationDate : date;
    COMPANY_CAR   < partition_CAR >
                  DatesOfService  : set(date),
                  HoursOfOperation : int;
    PRIVATE_CAR   < partition_CAR >;
    VEHICLE       < generalization_VEHICLE >
                  PassengerCapacity : int;

  distributors
    specialization_HULL      HULL;
    specialization_MOTOR     MOTOR;
    partition_CAR            CAR /strict;
    generalization_VEHICLE   CAR, MOTOR_BOAT /strict;
```

Fig. 2. Object schema

$$\mu[\text{ISA\_OBJTYPE}](\text{COMPANY\_CAR}) = \{ \text{COMPANY\_CAR}:\underline{c} \mid \underline{c} \in \{\underline{c_1}, \ldots, \underline{c_m}\} \text{ and }$$
$$\mu[\text{DISTR}](\text{partition\_CAR})(\underline{c}) = \text{COMPANY\_CAR} \}$$
$$\mu[\text{ISA\_OBJTYPE}](\text{VEHICLE}) = \{ \text{VEHICLE}:\underline{o} \mid \underline{o} \in \{\underline{c_1}, \ldots, \underline{c_m}\} \cup \{\underline{mb_1}, \ldots, \underline{mb_n}\}$$
$$\text{and } \mu[\text{DISTR}](\text{generalization\_VEHICLE})(\underline{o}) = \text{VEHICLE} \}$$

We did not formulate the semantics of ISA-dependent object types in such a way that $\mu[\text{ISA\_OBJTYPE}](o) := \{\underline{i} \mid \mu[\text{DISTR}](d)(\underline{i}) = o \}$, because we want the interpretations of all object types to be disjoint (with the exception of $\bot$). The acyclity of the object type dependency graph discussed below guarantees that there are no cycles in ISA relationships. In consequence, for every ISA-dependent object $\underline{o}$ (of type o) there will always be a base object $\underline{b}$ and n ISA-dependent object types o_i with $parent\_distr(o_i) = d_i$ $(i = 1, \ldots, n)$ so that

$$\underline{b} \xrightarrow{\mu(d_1)} o_1; \quad (o_1{:}\underline{b}) \xrightarrow{\mu(d_2)} o_2; \quad \cdots; \quad (o_{n-1}{:}\underline{b}) \xrightarrow{\mu(d_n)} o_n; \quad (o_n{:}\underline{b}) = (o{:}\underline{b}) = \underline{o} \quad (n \geq 1) .$$

The object $\underline{b}$ is called the underlying base object or *ISA root* of $\underline{o}$. $o{:}\underline{b}$ could be read as "base object $\underline{b}$ playing role o". Formally, $o{:}\underline{b}$ establishes a new object distinguishable from $\underline{b}$, but in the data manipulation component of the object model inheritance can be supported in both directions (!) by implicit type conversions (see [12]). In an ISA hierarchy it is possible for there to be several derivation paths for a single ISA-dependent object:

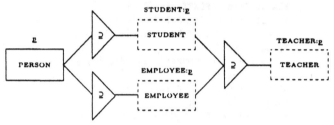

For example, the ISA-dependent object TEACHER:$\underline{p}$ comes already into being if one of the objects STUDENT:$\underline{p}$ or EMPLOYEE:$\underline{p}$ is distributed to TEACHER.

Remark. The semantics chosen for ISA-dependent types is non-standard. To preserve disjointness of types, we particularly refrained from employing subtypes to describe ISA relationships. In our opinion a role object or *aspect* should be strictly disassociated from its origin, because a role object can show its own observation and its own behavior. Nevertheless, the dependency of an aspect on its parent object remains still reflected within the concepts of our approach. IFO, for example, takes the other view. In an IFO schema, ISA-dependent types are represented as *free nodes*. The *derived type* of a free node is determined by specialization and generalization edges. Applied to our example schema of Fig. 1, the derived type of HULL_IN_BOAT is HULL, and the derived type of VEHICLE is $\oplus(\mathrm{CAR}, \otimes(\mathrm{HULL}, \mathrm{MOTOR}))$, i.e., instances of VEHICLE would be either instances of CAR, or composite objects built from instances of HULL and MOTOR.

The elements of ATTR are the **attribute names**. In Fig. 1 attributes are depicted by ovals. $\mu[\mathrm{ATTR}](a)$ gives the attribute values of objects.

$$\mu[\mathrm{ATTR}](\mathbf{Chassis\#}) : \{\underline{c_1}, \ldots, \underline{c_m}\} \cup \{\bot\} \to A^* \cup \{\bot\} \ (= \mu[\mathrm{DATASORT}](\mathbf{string}))$$

The ranges of attributes can be given by arbitrary complex sort expressions. Attributes can relate to data or object sorts (single-valued attributes), and second tuple-, set- or union-valued attributes are possible. Deeper nesting allows the representation of *context-dependent* information [16]. Please note that components of tuple expressions are accessible by (attribute) names. Hence, attributes mapping to complex sort expressions relate to *complex attributes* as proposed in [24], for example.

We mentioned that the identity of base objects is invisible to the user. Hence, we can speak of an *abstract identity* of objects. It is difficult to obtain a specific base object, especially with respect to updates on objects. When such an update is to be carried out, the target object has to be described associatively through some related objects or values. However, there might be situations in which an update can only be performed as an update on sets, because there is no way to reference a distinct object. In order to facilitate object access, we offer a **key concept** providing base objects with an additional *logical identity*. One or more attributes of a base object type can be put together to form a *key group* of the object type, e.g., *key*(MOTOR) = ⟨ Manufacturer, Serial# ⟩. Every key group creates an object generating function (or fetch operation) for the associated base object type, being MOTOR^{GEN} : COMPANY × string → MOTOR in our example. The key integrity ensures that this object generating operation is well-defined. The function returns ⊥ if there is no abstract object with the given key values. In principle, we could assign more than one key group to a base object type achieving several logical access paths for abstract objects, as it has been proposed in SDM [13], but for simplicity we are not considering this aspect in this paper.

The key concept plays a crucial role in case of complex object types which are to be mapped into an object schema, because it allows the **simulation of complex object types** by atomic ones without losing the natural identity of composed objects. In more precise terms we are replacing *internal structure* by *attribute structure* [16], but we are retaining the means to express internal structure by keys. So, the aggregation type MOTOR_BOAT is modeled by turning the roles Hull and Motor to single-valued key attributes, and the association type FLEET is mapped to an atomic type with a multi-valued key attribute **members** denoting the members of a fleet. From a logical (user) point of view, nothing changes. In fact, the natural identity of constructed objects is split up to an *abstract identity* given by an object identifier (e.g., $\underline{mb}$ for a MOTOR_BOAT), and a *logical identity* given by the key attributes (e.g., $id_{\text{MOTOR\_BOAT}}(\underline{mb})$ = (Hull : $\underline{h}$, Motor : $\underline{m}$), in which $\underline{h}$ represents a HULL and $\underline{m}$ a MOTOR).

ISA relationships and object-valued key attributes lead to certain *object dependencies* in an object schema (see Fig. 3). The global structure of an object schema is restricted by condition (∗) in the definition of an object schema demanding that there are no cycles in the object type dependency graph.

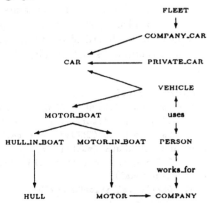

Fig. 3. Object type dependency graph

In summary we have SCHEMA=(BASE_OBJTYPE, ISA_OBJTYPE, ATTR, DISTR), and μ[SCHEMA] = (μ[BASE_OBJTYPE], μ[ISA_OBJTYPE], μ[ATTR], μ[DISTR]). The semantics of an object schema μ[SCHEMA] is also called a **state** σ belonging to the schema. We define π[SCHEMA] as the set of all **possible states** Σ. State transitions between possible states are described by *elementary update operations*.

Apart from the fact that the object model includes the key concept as a base modeling primitive, the object model can be seen as a submodel of an **Extended Entity-Relationship** approach [10]. For this model a well-defined **EER calculus**, taking into account data operations on arbitrary user-defined data sorts and aggregate functions, was described in [15, 12]. By including object generating operations this calculus can be applied to the object model. Hence, the query component of the object model is well-understood. In addition, the calculus can be adopted to specify constraints on database states.

3.3 Constraints on Database States

The formal object schema only includes the basic modeling primitives as there are object types, attributes and ISA relationships represented by distributors. The one and only structural restriction which is covered by a formal object schema is the key concept. This is necessary, because we want all abstract objects to be accessible by printable data in every possible database state. However, there are further structural restrictions specified in Fig. 2 by expressions beginning with '/' which are yet not covered by the object schema. These structural restrictions can be regarded as *embedded constraints* (cf. [34]), because they could be included in the formal definition in a straightforward manner. We did not do so, because in the first place we wanted to keep the formal definition simple. Secondly, when structural restrictions are integrated in the formal definition, we also have to ask if these restrictions are consistent, i.e., if possible schema instances exist which satisfy all constraints. Last but not least, structural restrictions directly complicate the definition of elementary update operations to database states, i.e., even elementary updates will sometimes escalate into transactions. For example, the insertion of a MOTOR_BOAT requires the specialization of a HULL to a HULL_IN_BOAT, the specialization of a MOTOR to a MOTOR_IN_BOAT, the insertion of a MOTOR_BOAT, and the generalization of the MOTOR_BOAT to a VEHICLE, together with the specification of the attributes InstallationDate, Speed, and PassengerCapacity, to satisfy all embedded constraints.

In our approach we view embedded constraints as a simple form of general **explicit integrity constraints**, which can be described by using formulas from the above mentioned calculus. For example, structural restrictions given in Fig. 2 can also be expressed by the following formulas.

- Object participation constraints /inv[min, max]:
  - $\forall$(mib:MOTOR_IN_BOAT) CNT-{ mb | (mb:MOTOR_BOAT) $\wedge$ Motor(mb)=mib } = 1
  - $\forall$(cp:COMPANY)   CNT-{ wf | (wf:works_for) $\wedge$ C(wf)=cp } $\geq$ 1
  - $\forall$(f:FLEET)   CNT-{ cp | (cp:COMPANY) $\wedge$ FleetOfCars(cp)=f } $\leq$ 1
- Cardinalities wrt. multi-valued attributes /multi[min, max]:
  - $\forall$(p:PERSON)   DEF(FleetOfCars(p)) $\Rightarrow$ CNT(FleetOfCars(p)) $\leq$ 3
- Mandatory attributes (not /optional):
  - $\forall$(mib:MOTOR_IN_BOAT) DEF(InstallationDate(mib))
- Bi-directional ISA relationships /strict:
  - $\forall$(c:CAR)   DEF(COMPANY_CAR(c)) $\vee$ DEF(PRIVATE_CAR(c))
  - $\forall$(c:CAR)   DEF(VEHICLE(c))

Similar formulas may be used to describe more complex constraints, for example, covering constraints for ISA-dependent types, disjoint/covering/partition constraints across the object participation in multiple relationship types (see [34]), object participation constraints addressing more than one coordinate at a time [23], or general computable constraints [17]. By means of (static) explicit integrity constraints the set of all possible states

Σ is reduced to a set of **consistent states** Σ_C. Transitions between consistent database states are described by *complex update operations* (transactions) being generally sequences of elementary update operations.

At the end of this section, in Table 1 various semantic data models are described according to some of their structural aspects. Most of those aspects have been mentioned above. For details on comparison criteria for semantic data models consult [27, 32, 17, 25, 16], for example. We are now leaving semantic data models and turning to data models which are simpler, by concentrating on only a few modeling constructs. For most of these models there are actual implementations. Hence they can be considered as models for logical design.

Table 1. Comparison of semantic data models

| | ER [8] | FDM [28] | SDM [13] | IFO [3] | extended ER models | | | | OBM |
					ECR [9]	ERC [24]	ORAC [34]	EER [10]	
Objects:									
- key concept	emb		✓		emb	emb		emb	✓
- set object types			✓	✓					
- tuple object types				✓			✓		
- relationship types	✓				✓	✓	✓	✓	
Attributes:									
- single-valued	✓	✓	✓	✓	emb	emb	emb	✓	✓
- multi-valued		✓	✓	✓	✓	✓	✓	✓	✓
- object-valued		✓	✓	✓				✓	✓
- complex				✓		✓	✓	✓²⁾	✓
- context-dependent				✓¹⁾					
- n-argument		✓							
ISA relationships:									
- specialization		✓	✓	✓	✓		✓	✓	✓
- disjoint specialization			ext		ext		ext	✓	✓
- partition			ext		ext		ext	emb	emb
- categorization					✓		✓	✓	✓
- generalization				✓	ext		✓	emb	emb

√: explicit support   emb: embedded constraint   ext: external constraint
¹⁾ fragment concept   ²⁾ value-based domains only

4 Relating the Object Model to Various Modeling Paradigms

In this section we relate our object model to two classical database modeling paradigms, formed by purely value-based and purely object-based data models. With the well-known supplier example we shall try to show that both classical directions can be faithfully simulated by the object model. In consequence, the object model also bears comparison with recent data models which take advantage of both directions by combining their capabilities.

4.1 Complex Object Models including Nested Relations

A relational database schema DB consists of a set of database relation names $R_1, \ldots, R_n$, in which each relation R_i is associated with a tuple expression T_i having only atomic data sorts as components. Complex object models [1, 18, 26] extend the relational model by allowing the components of a relation to be arbitrary complex type expressions. Hence, a complex object schema can be seen as a single type DB:tuple(R_1:set(T_1),...,R_n:set(T_n)), and a database instance is a rather complex value of type DB (see Fig. 4). The focus of complex object models is in objects with *internal structure*, i.e., complex objects are directly represented by (printable) complex values. For example, (SNo:2324, Name:(Last:"Miller", First:"Tom"), Cities:{"Berlin", "New York"}) is a possible object of type SUPPLIER. Indeed, the term "complex object models" should be replaced by the term "complex value models" to avoid confusion of concepts. It should be clear that we do not need the object level of our object model to simulate complex object models, because values can be already described by the data level.

```
DB:tuple( SUPPLIER:set(tuple(SNo:int, Name:tuple(Last:string, First:string),
                        Cities:set(string))),
        PART    :set(tuple(PNo:int, Name:string, Price:int)),
        SUPPLY  :set(tuple(SNo:int, PNo:int, Quantity:int)) )
```

Fig. 4. Complex object model schema

Complex object models are of captivating simplicity but they have known drawbacks in respect of the representation of object identity. Since real world entities are modeled by tuple values or possibly key values in those tuples, those values are to be repeated whenever a reference to an entity is needed within another object. This leads to superfluous data in both instances and schema. The redundancy at the schema level adds unnecessary complexity to the types, and creates the potential for error when creating or modifying the database types. The redundancy at the data level complicates the algorithms for update propagation [16]. A solution to this problem is given by the introduction of a further level of indirection, called *object identity* [20], which is the fundamental principle of object-based data models. In our object model object identity is supported by abstract object identifiers.

```
schema DB
  base_objtypes
    SUPPLIER < SNo:int, Name:tuple(Last:string, First:string),
               Cities:set(string) >;
    PART     < PNo:int, Name:string, Price:int >;
    SUPPLY   < SNo:int, PNo:int, Quantity:int >;
```

Fig. 5. Object schema simulating complex objects

In Fig. 5 it is shown how complex object types might be simulated within an object schema. Such a simulation means adding abstract object identity but making no use of it. In the case of complex objects it is not possible for there to be *shallow-equal* objects [6], e.g., two different SUPPLIERs with the same values in all components. In principle, this is possible in the object model, because in an object schema instance SUPPLIERs are primarily represented by abstract object identifiers, and not by (tuple) values. However, by specifying all attributes as keys, it is possible to obtain the tuple values as an isomorphic copy of abstract object identifiers. Please note that in Fig. 5 only the naive translation is considered. Relational constraints like *key dependencies* (e.g., SNo is a key for SUPPLIER, PNo a key for PART, and (SNo,PNo) a key for SUPPLY), or *inclusion dependencies* (foreign keys, referential integrity) (e.g., SUPPLY.SNo → SUPPLIER and SUPPLY.PNo → PART), can serve as the basis for further improvement.

4.2 Pure Object-Based Models

Pure object-based models form the counterpart to the value-based complex object models. In pure object-based models every single data item is considered as an object with identity, and complex objects are modeled by *attribute structure*. FDM [28] is a notable example of this class of models.

```
SNo:    SUPPLIER → SNO              PNo:   PART → PNO
Name:   SUPPLIER → COMPOSED_NAME    Name:  PART → PNAME
Cities: SUPPLIER → set(CITY)        Price: PART → PRICE

First:  COMPOSED_NAME → FIRSTNAME   Quantity: SUPPLIER × PART → QUANTITY
Last:   COMPOSED_NAME → LASTNAME    ...
```

Fig. 6. Attribute structure of FDM

An FDM schema (see Fig. 6) is given by a set of object types (upper case items in Fig. 6). Relationships between object types are established via a set of single or multi-valued attributes. As shown by the attribute Quantity, the domain of an attribute can be given by the Cartesian product of object types (n-argument attribute). In an FDM schema instance a set of actual objects is associated with every object type o, called the *active domain* of o, and a function f is assigned to every attribute a, so that the domain of f is the active domain of the source of a (the Cartesian product of the active domains if a is an n-argument attribute), and the range of f is contained in the active domain of the target of a (or the finite powerset of the target of a if a is multi-valued). Actual objects may be distinguished either as *printable* such as objects of the types SNO, CITY, FIRSTNAME, etc., or as *abstract* such as objects of the types PART, SUPPLIER and COMPOSED_NAME. For example, the above supplier could be represented by an abstract object $\underline{s}$ of type SUPPLIER with SNo($\underline{s}$) = 2324, Name($\underline{s}$) = $\underline{cn}$, and Cities($\underline{s}$) = {"Berlin","NewYork"} where $\underline{cn}$ denotes an abstract object of type COMPOSED_NAME.

Simulating an FDM schema by an object model schema (see Fig. 7) means modeling all object types in FDM as base object types in the object model, because only those types have a time-varying interpretation[3]. Since the object model does not directly support n-argument attributes, tuple domains have to be modeled by explicit object types, e.g., the object type SUPPLY has been added. Significantly, in FDM a printable object like 5 or "abc" enjoys the same rights as an abstract object such as $\underline{s}$ representing a SUPPLIER. For example, it is possible to have an object type NAME with printable names in isolation,

---

[3] Please note that in Fig. 7 we have used a variant of the object model in which a base object type is allowed to have an empty key group. This is because FDM does not take care of object access.

```
schema DB
  base_objtypes
    SUPPLIER      SNo:SNO, Name:COMPOSED_NAME, Cities:set(CITY);
    PART          PNo:PNO, Name:PARTNAME, Price:PRICE;
    SUPPLY        < S:SUPPLIER, P:PART > Quantity:QUANTITY;

    SNO           < Sno:int >;
    COMPOSED_NAME Last:LASTNAME, First:FIRSTNAME;
    CITY          < Name:string >; ...
```

Fig. 7. Object schema variant simulating FDM

i.e., the existence of printable objects does not depend on associated abstract objects. Printable object types in simulation are associated with a single key attribute ranging over a data type, thus having printable values as isomorphic copies of abstract identifiers.

Remark. There have been also approaches to object identity without leaving the framework of complex object models by the use of *printable object identifiers*, thus making the vehicle of object identity visible to the user. The resulting models can be considered to be hybrids of value-based and object-based data models (see [16] on this topic). A model which gives a good example for this is LDM [21].

Besides simplifying object reference, the concept of object identity allows *object sharing*, which avoids redundancy in data and schema, *cyclic object modeling*, which breaks with the strict hierarchical structure of complex object models, *encapsulation of object structure* as in object-oriented programming, and *updates on objects* which also makes the definition of update propagation easier. But as pointed out in [22] or [16], and as it becomes clear in Fig. 7, pure object-based models have severe drawbacks, since they force the user to define a new object type every time a complex value is needed. For example, the object types COMPOSED_NAME, SNO and CITIES are dispensable, as there are no other object types sharing objects with these types. In particular, objects of these types do not belong to entities "in the world". Next we turn to models which take advantage of both complex object models and pure object-based models by combining their modeling capabilities.

4.3 Object-Based Models with Complex Values

A model generalizing complex object and object-based models was presented in [22]. In the model of [22] *classes* and *types*, and *objects* and *values* are differentiated. Objects are members of classes and have an identity, while *values* as members of types are items without identity. The type system induced by the model is actually being used in the database programming language O_2. We draw some parallels to our object model in Table 2.

In [22] a schema is defined as a function σ which associates a type with every class (see Fig. 8). Let $o \in$ OBJTYPE be given in our object model, and let $a_1, \ldots a_n \in$ ATTR be all attributes defined on o with $a_i : o \rightarrow s_i$. Then we could view o as a class with $\sigma(o) = \text{tuple}(a_1{:}s_1, \ldots, a_n{:}s_n)$. A domain is defined as a function δ which associates a value with every object identifier determining the state of an object base. Let $\underline{o}$ be an object of type o. Then we have $\delta(\underline{o}) = (a_1{:}\mu[\text{ATTR}](a_1)(\underline{o}), \ldots, a_n{:}\mu[\text{ATTR}](a_n)(\underline{o}))$. However, there is a difference between [22] and our object model with respect to the interpretation of types. In [22] subtype rules make it possible that the value (a:5,b:7) is associated with the type

Table 2. The model of [22] compared with the object model

notions in [22]	counterpart in object model
class (name) $c \in \mathcal{I}_C$	object type $o \in$ OBJTYPE
object (identifier) $\varrho \in \mathcal{I}_O$	$\varrho \in \dot{\mu}[\text{OBJTYPE}]$
type $t \in S$	sort expression $s \in$ EXPR(SORT)
value $v \in \mathcal{V}$	$\underline{s} \in \dot{\mu}[\text{EXPR(SORT)}]$
schema $\sigma : \mathcal{I}_C \rightarrow S$	object types and attributes
domain $\delta : \mathcal{I}_O \rightarrow \mathcal{V}$	given by $\mu[\text{ATTR}]$
interpretation	
of types: compatible values	fixed by $\mu[\text{EXPR(SORT)}](s)$
of classes: compatible objects	given by $\mu[\text{OBJTYPE}](o)$

```
σ(SUPPLIER)= tuple(SNo:int, Name:tuple(Last:string, First:string),
                   Cities:set(string))
σ(PART)    = tuple(PNo:int, Name:string, Price:int)
σ(SUPPLY)  = tuple(s:SUPPLIER, p:PART, Quantity:int)
```

Fig. 8. Schema according to [22]

`tuple(a:int,b:int)`, but also with the types `tuple(b:int,a:int)` and `tuple(b:int)`. Clearly, in the object model the given value can only be of the first type.

```
schema DB
  base_objtypes
    SUPPLIER < SNo:int >
             Name:tuple(Last:string, First:string), Cities:set(string);
    PART     < PNo:int > Name:string, Price:int;
    SUPPLY   < S:SUPPLIER, P:PART > Quantity:int;
```

Fig. 9. Final object schema

In Fig. 9 the final object schema is stated. It is equivalent to the schema of Fig. 8 with the exception that in an object schema we have additional means for logical object identity by the presence of keys. We should note that the final schema is obtained also from the schema of Fig. 5 regarding further relational key dependencies and referential integrity. But clearly, the easiest way to obtain an adequate object schema is to use a high-level semantic data model for conceptual design (see Sect. 2), and then map it to an object schema as a matter of logical design (see Sect. 3).

5 Conclusion

After having translated the various data models into our object model we feel that these data models and the relationships among them can be much better understood. We have considered quite different models from several areas and we have tried to point out the distinctions and the common elements in the different approaches. Perhaps our attempts are a first step towards unifying the concepts and terminology of different approaches. At least it is an attempt to provide a common basis for understanding the various data models.

The main idea of the object model was the simulation of complex object types like tuple, set or relationship types by atomic object types with keys, or in other words, the replacement of internal structure by attribute structure, which unifies data-manipulation. With respect to ER models we emphasize that recent ER extensions in the field of aggregation object types [34] or relationships over relationships [31] are also captured by the object model. Secondly we stress the fact that, in spite of dropping subtypes, our object model still provides a simple framework for modeling different kinds of ISA relationships.

By mapping Entity-Relationship and object-oriented data models to the same approach we feel that we are bridging the gap between Entity-Relationship and object-oriented approaches [4] and pointing out the similarities between both worlds. However, future work must also address the integration of object behavior into the object model, for example by using *events* as shown in [19].

References

1. S. Abiteboul, C. Beeri, M. Gyssens, and D. Van Gucht. An introduction to the completeness of languages for complex objects and nested relations. In Abiteboul et al. [2], pages 117–138.

2. S. Abiteboul, P.C. Fischer, and H.J. Schek, editors. *Nested Relations and Complex Objects in Databases*, Springer LNCS series, Vol. 361, 1989.

3. S. Abiteboul and R. Hull. IFO – A formal semantic database model. *ACM Trans. on Database Systems.*, 12(4):525–565, 1987.

4. C. Beeri. A formal approach to object oriented databases. *Data & Knowledge Engineering*, 5(4):353–382, 1990.

5. M.L. Brodie and D. Ridjanovic. On the design and specification of database transactions. In M.L. Brodie, J. Mylopoulos, and J.W. Schmidt, editors, *On Conceptual Modelling - Perspectives from Artificial Intelligence, Databases, and Programming Languages*, pages 277–306, Springer (New York), 1984.

6. J. Van den Bussche and J. Paredaens. The expressive power of structured values in pure OODB's. In *Proc. 10th ACM Symp. Principles of Database Syst.*, pages 291–299, 1991.

7. S. Ceri, editor. *Methodology and Tools for Database Design.* North-Holland, Amsterdam, 1983.

8. P.P. Chen. The Entity-Relationship model – Towards a unified view of data. *ACM Trans. on Database Systems.*, 1(1):9–36, 1976.

9. R. Elmasri, J. Weeldreyer, and A. Hevner. The category concept: An extension to the entity-relationship model. *Data & Knowledge Engineering*, 1:75–116, 1985.

10. G. Engels, M. Gogolla, U. Hohenstein, K. Hülsmann, P. Löhr-Richter, G. Saake, and H.-D. Ehrich. Conceptual modelling of database applications using an extended ER model. To appear in *Data & Knowledge Engineering*, 1992. Preliminary version: Informatik-Bericht Nr. 90-05, Technische Universität Braunschweig (Germany), 1990.

11. D.H. Fishman et al. IRIS: An object-oriented database management system. *ACM Trans. on Office Information Systems*, 5(1):46–69, 1987.

12. M. Gogolla and U. Hohenstein. Towards a semantic view of an extended entity-relationship model. *ACM Trans. on Database Systems.*, 16(3):369–416, 1991.

13. M. Hammer and D. McLeod. Database description with SDM: A semantic database model. *ACM Trans. on Database Systems.*, 6(3):351–386, 1981.

14. R. Herzig and M. Gogolla. On data manipulation in an object model. Internal report, Technische Universität Braunschweig (Germany), February 1992.

15. U. Hohenstein and M. Gogolla. A calculus for an extended entity-relationship model incorporating arbitrary data operations and aggregate functions. In C. Battini, editor, *Proc. 7th Intl. Conf. on Entity-Relationship Approach*, Rome (Italy), pages 129–148. North-Holland, Amsterdam, 1988.

16. R. Hull. Four views of complex objects: A sophisticates's introduction. In Abiteboul et al. [2], pages 87–116.

17. R. Hull and R. King. Semantic database modelling: Survey, applications, and research issues. *ACM Computing Surveys*, 19(3):201–260, 1987.

18. R. Hull and C.K. Yap. The Format model: A theory of database organization. *J. ACM*, 31(3):518–537, 1984.

19. R. Jungclaus, G. Saake, and T. Hartmann. Language features for object-oriented conceptual modeling. In T.J. Teorey, editor, *Proc. 10th Intl. Conf. on Entity-Relationship Approach*, San Mateo (California), pages 309–324, 1991.

20. S.N. Koshafian and G.P. Copeland. Object identity. In *Proc. ACM Intl. Conf. on Object Oriented Programming Systems, Languages and Applications*, Portland (Oregon), pages 406–416. ACM, New York, 1986. (Special Issue of SIGPLAN Notices, Vol. 21, No. 11, 1986).

21. G.M. Kuper and M.Y. Vardi. A new approach to database logic. In *Proc. 3rd ACM Symp. Principles of Database Syst.*, pages 86–96, 1984.

22. C. Lécluse and P. Richard. Modeling complex structures in object-oriented databases. In *Proc. 8th ACM Symp. Principles of Database Syst.*, Philadelphia (Pennsylvania), pages 360–368, 1989.

23. P. Lyngbaek and V. Vianu. Mapping a semantic database model to the relational model. In *Proc. ACM SIGMOD Symp. on Management of Data*, San Francisco (California), pages 132–142. ACM, New York, 1987.

24. C. Parent and S. Spaccapietra. Complex objects modeling: An entity-relationship approach. In Abiteboul et al. [2], pages 272–296.

25. J. Peckham and F. Maryanski. Semantic data models. *ACM Computing Surveys*, 20(3):153–189, 1988.

26. H.J. Schek and M. Scholl. An algebra for the relational model with relation-valued attributes. *Inf. Syst.*, 11(2):137–147, 1986.

27. M. Schrefl, A M. Tjoa, and R.R. Wagner. Comparison criteria for semantic data models. In *Proc. Intl. Conf. on Data Engineering*, Los Angeles (California), pages 120–125. ACM, New York, 1984.

28. D. Shipman. The functional data model and the data language DAPLEX. *ACM Trans. on Database Systems.*, 6(1):140–173, 1981.

29. J.M. Smith and D.C.P Smith. Database abstractions: Aggregation and generalization. *ACM Trans. on Database Systems.*, 2(2):105–133, 1977.

30. F.J. Teorey and J.P. Fry. *Design of Database Structures.* Prentice-Hall, Englewood Cliffs, N.J., 1982.

31. B. Thalheim. Extending the entity-relationship model for a high-level, theory-based database design. In J.W. Schmidt and A.A. Stagny, editors, *"Next Generation Information System Technology"*, *Proc. 1st Int. East/West Database Workshop*, Kiev (USSR), 1990, Springer LNCS series, Vol. 504, pages 161–184, 1990.

32. S.D. Urban and L. Delcambre. An analysis of the structural, dynamic, and temporal aspects of semantic data models. In *Proc. Intl. Conf. on Data Engineering*, Los Angeles (California), pages 382–387. ACM, New York, 1986.

33. G.M.A Verheijen and J. Van Bekkum. NIAM: An information analysis method. In T.W. Olle, H.G. Sol, and A.A. Verrijn-Stuart, editors, *Proc. "Information Systems Design Methodologies: A Comparative Review"*, pages 537–590, North-Holland 99, 1982.

34. G. Wei and T.J. Teorey. The ORAC model: A unified view of data abstractions. In T.J. Teorey, editor, *Proc. 10th Intl. Conf. on Entity-Relationship Approach*, San Mateo (California), pages 31–58, 1991.

Meta Object Management
and its Application to Database Evolution[*]

Markus Tresch   and   Marc H. Scholl

Department of Computer Science, Databases and Information Systems
University of Ulm, D-W 7900 Ulm, Germany
<tresch,scholl>@informatik.uni-ulm.de

Abstract. In this paper, we address the problem of supporting more flexibility on the schema of object-oriented databases. We describe a general framework based on an object-oriented data model, where three levels of objects are distinguished: *data objects, schema objects*, and *meta-schema objects*. We discuss the prerequisites for applying the query and update operations of an object algebra uniformly on all three levels. As a sample application of the framework, we focus on database evolution, that is, realizing incremental changes to the database schema and their propagation to data instances. We show, how each schema update of a given taxonomy is realized by direct updating of schema objects, and how this approach can be used to build a complete tool for database evolution.

1   Introduction

There is an increasing need for *database evolution facilities*, offering more flexibility on the logical structure of object-oriented databases (OODBs). On the one hand, schema evolution is the basic prerequisite for better support of database *extensibility* and *reusability*, which is a big promise of object-oriented systems; and on the other hand, database integration has a renaissance, since the integration of *federated databases* and *interoperability of multidatabase systems* has become urgent. In addition, new aspects arise from the fact that not only the logical schemas of the databases can evolve, but also existing data must be migrated and integrated. Either of these demand more dynamics of database schemas.

Evolution in databases addresses the problem that the logical structure of a database is likely to undergo changes during lifetime, even if a database is already populated with objects. There are many reasons for that [6]: *schema design* can be a stepwise development of a schema from scratch; *schema tailoring* consists in slight adaptations of existing schemas (e.g. extension with new components); *schema restructuring/reorganization* is used after significant, non-trivial changes; and *schema versioning* allows to record and manage a history of schemas.

Most current OODBS products and prototypes do not allow free and dynamic changes of the schema. Some of them provide a limited set of special purpose

---

[*] Work done while at Department of Computer Science, ETH Zürich, Switzerland

schema update methods, and restrict their application to unpopulated (empty) databases. If modifications of populated databases are allowed, the problem is how to propagate the changes to the instances. One either includes a data migration utility to adapt existing data objects to the changed schema, or an other mechanism (screening, versioning) has to ensure consistency between data and structure.

An early investigation of type changes in populated databases exists for EN-CORE [26]. This work addresses the effects of type changes to objects and to programs that use objects of the type. The impact of type polymorphism on schema evolution is investigated in [18]. The first systematic analysis of desirable schema evolution possibilities was done for the ORION data model [2, 3], where a set of necessary schema updates was listed and organized in a taxonomy. Similar enumeration can also be found for the O_2 [31] and the GemStone DBMSs [21]. The schema update primitives of these taxonomies are realized as special purpose methods for schema management. Another approach is to provide a complete end-user tool to assist in transforming database schemas [15].

Schema evolution is in fact an important issue for ER databases, because even relational, hierarchical, network, or object-oriented databases use an ER-approach for conceptual DB design [12], or for representation of external schemas [16].

Our approach was to built a *uniform model* and *general framework* for investigation of the above mentioned database evolution and integration issues. In the following, we introduce the main components of the framework, which in turn reflects the structure of this paper:

Object model and algebra: As the basis of the framework, the object-oriented data model COCOON with its algebraic query and update language is used (Section 2). However, notice that the basic ideas of the framework are not strongly bound to this specific object model; it can be replaced by any object-oriented data model, especially an object-oriented entity-relationship approach [17, 20] with an algebra or a calculus [19].

Three object levels: In this model, a separation of database objects into three disjoint subsets is introduced: data objects, schema objects, and meta-schema objects (Section 3). Hence, also (meta-)schema objects are modeled as objects like others, we allow that the generic query and update operators can be applied on objects of each of these three sorts and there is no difference in the syntax and semantics of the algebraic operators, whether they query or update data, schema, or meta-schema objects. Even though representation of the meta-schema within the same model is not a new idea, such meta-data usually serve only for documentation purposes. That is, only *retrieval* is allowed. In contrast, here we investigate also the feasibility of *updates* to meta-objects.

Elementary Operations: Based on this separation, we focus into special applications, implementing elementary operations for database evolution or database integration (Section 5.1). We thereby concentrate in this paper on the application of the framework to schema evolution, and show how to realize schema update operations by applying the algebraic query and update algebra to meta-objects. Consequently, the use of generic update operators as "schema evolution and integration language", instead of special purpose schema evolution methods, has the advantage that: (i) the functionality of these operators is formally defined with a clear semantics [14] and has no unpredictable side-effects; (ii) they handle integrity constraints, that is, no update leaves the database in an inconsistent state w.r.t. these constraints. The remaining problem is to propagate the modifications from the schema level down to the data object level. We will show that this can be achieved straight-forward due to the clear semantics of schema updates.

Advanced Operations: Next, the elementary operations are encapsulated into advanced, user-oriented tools for database evolution. The purpose of this is to capture more semantics and insure higher level integrity constraints (Section 5.2). Database integration using the framework, as an other sample application of the framework is presented in [25].

2 An Object Model and Algebra

The framework we present throughout this paper is based on the COCOON object model. We very briefly review the key concepts of the object model and the algebra, referring to the literature for more details [24, 23].

2.1 Basic Concepts

The COCOON object model is an object-function model in the sense of [4, 5]. Its basic constituents are objects, functions, types, and classes:

Besides **data**, which can be atomic (numbers, strings) or constructed (tuples, sets), there are **objects** that are instances of abstract object types (AOTs). Objects can be manipulated by a set of applicable operations.

Functions are the generalized abstraction of attributes (stored or computed), relationships between objects, and update methods (with side-effects). They can be single- or set-valued. Functions are described by their name and signature. The implementation is given separately, in the object implementation language (OIL), which is not described here any further.

Types describe the common interface to all of its instances. So, a type is defined by a name and a set of applicable functions. This set is the union of the functions explicitly defined to belong to the type and those inherited from the types of the acyclic isa relationship. The subtype relationship that is used for type-checking corresponds to the subset relationship of the function sets. Thus, instances of one type are also instances of its supertypes (multiple instantiation). The root of this lattice is the predefined type **object**.

Classes are strictly distinguished from types [4]. Classes are typed collections of objects. So every class c has an associated member type $mtype(c)$ and an actual extension $extent(c)$, the set of objects in the class. We define the extent of a class to include the members of all its subclasses. Thus, objects can be member of multiple classes at the same time (multiple class membership). Besides the subset property the subclass relationship states that the member type of a subclass must be the same type or a subtype of its superclasses' member types. The top class of the subclass hierarchy is the class **Objects**.

COCOON features that are usually not found in other object-oriented models are the possibilities to define class predicates and views. Class predicates are either necessary or necessary and sufficient conditions that have to be fulfilled by the class members. **Views** can be defined by queries of arbitrary complexity and can be regarded as a special kind of classes, because their extent and their member type is sufficiently defined by the query. Thus, classes with necessary and sufficient predicates are regarded as a special kind of views, since also their extent is populated automatically.[1]

EXAMPLE 1: As a running example, we use the following database *Business*, defined by COOL type and class declaration statements.[2]

> **define database** *Business* ;
>> **define type** *person* **isa object** = *name:* **unique** *string* **not null** ,
>>> *age: integer* ;
>> **define type** *employee* **isa** *person* = *salary: integer* ,
>>> *empl: company* **inverse staff** ;
>> **define type** *company* **isa object** = *ident:* **unique** *string, city: string* ,
>>> *staff:* **setof** *employee* **inverse** *empl* ,
>>> *bran:* **setof** *company* **not cyclic** ;
>> **define class** *Persons : person* **some Objects** ;
>> **define class** *Youngs : person* **all** *Persons* **where** *age<30* ;
>> **define class** *Employees : employee* **some** *Persons* ;
>> **define class** *Companies : company* **some Objects** ;
>> **define view** *PublEmpls* **as project** [*name,empl*] (*Employees*) ;
> **enddb** .

The two classes *Persons* and *Youngs* have both the same type, *person*. Moreover, the class *Youngs* is defined as a subclass of *Persons*, holding exactly those persons that satisfy the class predicate *age* < 30. The selector **all** in the **where** clause (in contrast to **some**) indicates that the class predicate is necessary and sufficient, such that the member objects of class *Youngs* are automatically computed from those of *Persons*. The projection view *PublEmpls* hides the *age* and *salary* properties, such that users of this view only see *name* and *empl* functions.

In addition to class predicates, there is a possibility to define constraints for functions: (i) **not null** functions are not allowed to have undefined values, (ii) **unique** functions must have distinct values, (iii) **not cyclic** functions ensure that no object has itself as result of that function (even if applied repeatedly), and (iv) **inverse** means that two functions are inverse to each other.   ◇

---

[1] Updating views is discussed in [23].

[2] We use the convention that type names are in lower-case letters and in singular, whereas class or view names are in plural and start with an upper-case letter.

2.2 Generic Query and Update Operations

The query and object manipulation language COOL was designed as an extension of (nested) relational algebra. It provides a collection of generic query operators with object-preserving semantics. That is, they return (some of) the already existing input objects, instead of generating new (copies of) objects.

As query operations we provide selection of objects (**select** $[P](C)$), projection (**project** $[f_1, \ldots, f_n](C)$), extension (**extend** $[f_i :=< expr_i >, \ldots](C)$), and the set operations (**union, intersection, difference**). Variables can be used as temporary names ("handles") for objects, since objects are typically unnamed, due to the set-oriented style of the language. So this is the way how to refer to objects and results of previous algebra expressions.

Besides query operators, COOL also provides a collection of generic update operators (cf. [14] for a formal definition). The main advantage of general purpose update operations is that their semantics is known by the system. That is, they maintain model-inherent integrity constraints like uniqueness or acyclicity of functions, and class predicates. We will see later how we exploit by this property, when schema updates are defined by such generic update operations. In the remainder of this paper we will make use of the following operations:

Insert takes as argument a class C and a list of assignments of values to functions. If the function assignments in the assignment list do not conflict with the respective constraints of all functions, a new object as instance of C's member type is created, and initialized with the function values given in the assignment list. In case the new object satisfies C's class predicate, it is also added to the extent of class C. As a result, a reference to the newly created object is returned, and can therefore be assigned to a variable, e.g.:

$john :=$ **insert** $[name:='John\ Smith',\ age:=31]\ (Persons)$;

Delete destroys objects consistently. It takes an object as its only argument. This object is removed from all classes, sets, and variables, in case that no function constraint is violated. For example:

delete $(paul)$;

Add and **remove** have a "weaker" effect: they have no impact on the existence of objects. Rather, an existing object can be added to or removed from classes or sets. They take an object and a set of objects as parameter:

add $[john]\ (staff(ibm))$;
remove $[dec]\ (Companies)$;

Both operators may change the type of objects dynamically. Consider $john$, which is an instance of type $person$. Adding it to the class of $Employees$, makes $john$ an instance of type $employee$, in addition to including him in IBM's staff.

Set assigns new function values for given arguments. It takes two arguments: a list of assignments and an object. As in the case of the **insert** operation, the newly assigned function values must respect the function constraints.

set [*salary:= 1.1*salary*] (john);

It is essential to notice that generic update operations are refused and therefore not processed, if they would conflict with any function constraints (unique, not null, not cyclic). Consider for example the **insert** -statement above, where a new person object with name "John Smith" is created. Since the *name* function is defined to be unique, the update would be rejected, if there already were a person with this name.

Violation of class predicates is handled different [23]. The class predicate is checked after execution of the update operation, and if necessary, the changed objects are reclassified. Note that changing values of objects, for example with the set-operator, may need such a reclassification of objects. Consider for example the object *john*. Changing its age from 31 to 29 would immediately classify it down in the hierarchy, by adding it to the class *Youngs*. The treatment of inverse functions is similar to reclassification: If a function value is changed, this update is propagated automatically to the inverse function, such that the constraint is maintained.

3   Three Levels of Objects

For every COCOON database, the set of actually stored persistent objects is denoted by $\mathcal{O} = \{\ldots, o, \ldots\}$. Each of these objects has a specific state σ, such that $v_{ij} := \sigma(f_i)(o_j)$ is the actual value returned by applying function f_i on object $o_j \in \mathcal{O}$.[3] The states of all objects in $\mathcal{O}$ together form the actual state of the database.

Definition 3.1 (Database) A database is a tuple $DB = <\mathcal{O}, \sigma>$, where

1. $\mathcal{O}$ is the finite set of persistent objects in the database, and
2. σ is the state of the database. □

Consider for example the variable *john* of type *person* and the function *name* that is applicable on instances of that type (*name: person → string*). The actual value of function *name* might be the set: $\{\langle john, \text{'John Smith'}\rangle, \langle mary, \text{'Mary Hughs'}\rangle\}$, such that for instance, $\sigma(name)(john) = \text{'John Smith'}$.

3.1   Meta-Schema, Schema, and Data Objects

A closer look at the set of objects $\mathcal{O}$ reveals, that they are build up of three pairwise disjoint sorts, each of which is placed on a different level: the meta-schema level, the schema level, and the data level:

---

[3] In our model, all functions are partial, such that when applied on an object, their values can be undefined. For this case, the state $\sigma(f_i)(o_j)$ is defined to be the null value $\perp$. Later, we will see, that this lazy evaluation strategy is very useful for schema update propagation.

- *meta-schema level objects:* the objects describing the meta-schema of the database. There is a predefined fixed set of meta-objects, building the database kernel, being always part of a database. Meta level objects are the meta-types $\mathcal{T}_M$, the meta-functions $\mathcal{F}_M$, and the meta-classes $\mathcal{C}_M$.

$$\mathcal{O}_{meta} = \{ \ \underbrace{type,\ set\text{-}type,\ fcn\text{-}type,\ object\text{-}type,}_{} $$
$$\underbrace{function,\ class,\ class\text{-}def,\ view\text{-}def,}_{\mathcal{T}_M} $$
$$\underbrace{Types,\ Set\text{-}Types,\ Fcn\text{-}Types,\ Object\text{-}Types,}_{} $$
$$\underbrace{Functions,\ Classes,\ Class\text{-}Defs,\ View\text{-}Defs,}_{\mathcal{C}_M} $$
$$\underbrace{tname, functs, localf, supert, etype, dom, ran,}_{} $$
$$fname, sign, unique, notnull, notcyclic, inverse, $$
$$\underbrace{cname, extent, auto, mtype, pred, superc, query}_{\mathcal{F}_M} \ \} $$

- *schema level objects:* the objects describing the schema of the application database. They are application dependent and are created as instances of meta-types. Schema objects are distinguished in application types $\mathcal{T}_A$, application functions $\mathcal{F}_A$, and application classes $\mathcal{C}_A$.

$$\mathcal{O}_{schema} = \{ \underbrace{t_1, \ldots, t_k,}_{\mathcal{T}_A} \underbrace{f_1, \ldots, f_m,}_{\mathcal{F}_A} \underbrace{c_1, \ldots, c_l}_{\mathcal{C}_A} \} $$

- *data level objects:* the primary level objects, representing the user data stored in the database. They are created as instances of application-schema types.

$$\mathcal{O}_{data} = \{ o_1, \ldots, o_n \} $$

Objects are created top-down: Whereas an "empty" database holds only meta-level objects, later, the schema level objects are created during the database design phase. Finally, the use of the database generates data level objects. Figure 1 illustrates instance-of relationship between objects and types of the three different levels.

3.2 Database Schemas

A database schema is a representation of the structure (syntax), semantics, and constraints on the use of a database in the data model. In our model, this is given by classes, types, and functions.

Thus, the schema of a COCOON database $DB = \langle \mathcal{O}, \sigma \rangle$ is represented as a triple $< T, F, C >$, with T a set of objects representing types, F a set of objects representing functions, and C a set of objects representing classes. The set of all types, functions, and classes in the database is denoted as $\mathcal{T}, \mathcal{F}, \mathcal{C}$. These sets are identical with the active domain of the meta-types (*type, function, class*) and the extent of the meta-classes (*Types, Functions, Classes*).

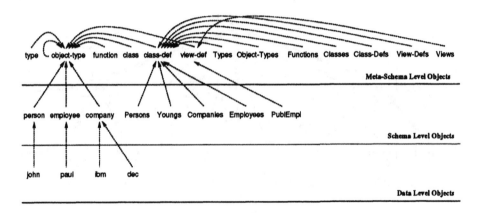

Fig. 1. *Instance-of relationship (drawn as dashed arrows) between meta-schema, schema, and data level objects. Data level objects are instances of schema level types. Schema level types are themselves represented by type objects, that are instances of meta-level types. The meta-level types are represented by meta-level objects. Notice, that the object object-type is instance of the type that it represents (which does not mean that it is "instance of itself").*

The meta-schema is a special schema, the schema of the meta-database. It is represented by the meta-level objects of Section 3.1 and defines the data model itself. Figure 2 gives a graphical overview of the meta-schema, and a definition in COOL notation can be found in Appendix A.

Definition 3.2 (Meta Database Schema) The meta-schema of a database $DB = < \mathcal{O}, \sigma >$ is given as the triple $\mathcal{S}_{Meta} = < \mathcal{T}_M, \mathcal{F}_M, \mathcal{C}_M >$. □

The application-schema holds application level objects. It defines the conceptual schema of the database application.

Definition 3.3 (Application Database Schema) The application schema of a database $DB = < \mathcal{O}, \sigma >$ is given as the triple $\mathcal{S}_{Appl} = < \mathcal{T}_A, \mathcal{F}_A, \mathcal{C}_A >$. □

3.3 Queries and Updates to Objects of Different Levels

So far, we introduced a distinction of objects into three sorts, according to the role they play within a database application. Nevertheless, all of them are ordinary objects, such that queries and updates of the COOL language apply. Of course, the effect of an operation depends on the level of its input objects.

Data Level Operations retrieve or change data level objects. These are the ordinary operations as we know them from Section 2.2.

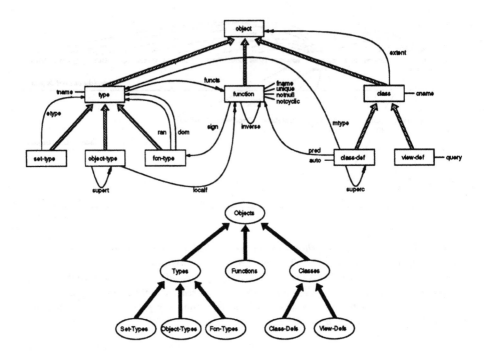

Fig. 2. *The meta-database schema is a hierarchy of meta-types $\mathcal{T}_M$ (rectangles) with their meta-functions $\mathcal{F}_M$ (lines with one arrowhead mean single-valued functions, with two arrowheads set-valued functions), and a hierarchy of meta-classes $\mathcal{C}_M$ (ellipses). Subtype relationship is shown with gray arrows, whereas subclass hierarchy is indicated using black arrows.*

$Q_1 : name(john)$ $U_1 : \mathbf{set}\ [name:='hans\,'](john)$
$Q_2 : \mathbf{select}\ [name='john\,'](Persons)$ $U_2 : \mathbf{delete}\ (john)$

For example, getting the name of object *john* (Q_1), selecting all persons with name *'john'* (Q_2), changing John's name to *'hans'* (U_1), or deleting the object *john* (U_2) .

Schema Level Operations operate on objects representing the schema. Retrievals work straightforward without additional effort. As an example, query Q_3 gets the name of the application type *person*, and Q_4 returns all objects representing types with name *'person'*.

$Q_3 : tname(person)$ $U_3 : \mathbf{set}\ [tname:='people\,'](person)$
$Q_4 : \mathbf{select}\ [tname='person\,'](Types)$ $U_4 : \mathbf{delete}\ (person)$

In contrast to query operators, direct manipulation of schema objects (U_3, U_4) needs further consideration, since these updates finally realize **schema evolu-**

tion. The usual way to make basic updates to the schema objects is by using a data definition language (DDL), as it was introduced in Section 2.1 (e.g., **define type** *employee* **isa** ...). Advanced changes to schema objects, like e.g. modifying types, are normally implemented in a schema manipulation language (SML).

Such a special language is used, because these operations can yield "side-effects", that must be regarded carefully. Consider for example update U_3, changing the name of type *person* to *'people'*, or U_4 even deleting the type *person*. We will cover the following questions: There are some functions applicable to instances of type *person* (*name, age, ...*), should they be deleted together with the type? When the type *person* is removed, what will be the member type of the classes *Persons* and *Youngs*? What will be the new supertype of *employee*? What about propagation of schema changes to existing data objects like *john*. What happens with the instances of a deleted type?

Meta-Schema Level Operations operate on objects representing the meta-schema. Again, queries can be used quite straightforward. So, Q_5 returns the name of the meta-type *type*, and Q_6 selects a set of all types with name *'type'*.

Q_5 : *tname(type)* U_5 : **set** [*tname:='interface'*](*type*)
Q_6 : **select** [*tname='type'*](*Types*) U_6 : **delete** (*type*)

Updates U_5, U_6 are changes to the meta-schema. As an example, U_5 renames the type *type* to *'interface'*, and U_6 even destroys the type *type*. These updates are generally not allowed, since they change the basic ingredients of the data model. Anyway, some elementary modification to the meta-schema could be very useful, i.e. for **model tailoring** by adding specialized types and classes, derived functions, or meta-views [13], and for preparing for the coupling of multiple DBMS [25].

Mixed Level Operations involve different levels within one operation. To do this, we need an additional operator, that provides the possibility to change the level: **apply** [*f*] (<*set-expr*>). It applies a function *f* to a set of objects in <*set-expr*>. E.g. query Q_7 first finds all classes *c* from the meta-class *Class-Defs*, where the function *name* can be applied; then the expression **select** [*name = 'john'*](*d*) is run for each of these classes, now called *d*.

Q_7 : **apply** [**select** [*name = 'john'*](*d*)]
         (*d* : **select** [*name* ∈ *functs(mtype(c))*] (*c: Class-Defs*));

Notice, that the selection on *Class-Defs* returns a set of schema level objects, whereas the later selection gives data level objects. Such mixed level facilities give additional expressive power to the language, but static type checking becomes impossible in some cases [10].

4 Prerequisites for Updating Schema Objects

Direct changes to schema objects (cf. U_3, U_4, U_5, U_6 in Section 3.3) have additional "side-effects". Thus, before we show how the schema updates are implemented, we investigate the feasibility of these operations, namely completeness and correctness, as well as the propagation of meta-schema and schema level updates to other levels.

4.1 A Taxonomy of Schema Updates (Completeness)

Some schema changes are quite simple, whereas others need complete reorganization of the database. The latter can often be decomposed in a sequence of more elementary changes.

Below, a taxonomy of primitive schema updates is presented, which is minimal and complete in the sense that all possible schema transformations can be built up by (a combination of) these updates. Since a schema is a triple $< T, F, C >$, we categorize schema changes into updates to type, function, and class objects respectively:

(1)   *UPDATING TYPES*
(1.1)   create/delete a type object
(1.1.1) create a new type object
(1.1.2) delete an existing type object
(1.2)   changes a type object
(1.2.1) change the name
(1.2.2) change the supertypes
(1.2.3) change the local functions

(2)   *UPDATING FUNCTIONS*
(2.1)   create/delete a function object
(2.1.1) create a new function object
(2.1.2) delete an existing function object
(2.2)   change a function object
(2.2.1) change the name
(2.2.2) change the function signature
(2.2.3) change the function constraints

(3)   *UPDATING CLASSES*
(3.1)   create/delete a class object
(3.1.1) create a new class object
(3.1.2) delete an existing class object
(3.2)   change a class object
(3.2.1) change the name
(3.2.2) change the auto tag
(3.2.3) change the member type
(3.2.4) change the class predicate
(3.2.5) change the superclasses
(3.2.6) change the query expression

A similar taxonomy was first introduced for the ORION data model [3], where all supported schema changes are classified into changes to an edge, changes to a node, and changes to the contents of a node.

4.2 Insuring Schema Correctness

Since not every arbitrary triple $< T, F, C >$ of types, functions, and classes is a correct schema, we must make sure that schema updates transform a database structure into another correct state. Thus, the ORION, O_2, and GemStone data models provide a set of *schema invariants*. These are conditions that have to be satisfied by any valid schema. Similar, in our model the schema constraints R1, ..., R14 below determine the basic characteristics of a COCOON schema, such that a schema is correct, if it satisfies these conditions.

To ensure that these conditions are respected at any time, they are translated into integrity constraints of the meta-schema (unique, not null, not cyclic). In the sequel, we explain the constraints in the COCOON meta-schema: [4]

Unique Naming Constraints (R1, R2, R3) guarantee, that there are no two types, functions, or classes with the same name. Notice that these are the internal names, after solving any naming conflicts from multiple inheritance, or overloading respectively.

(R1) for all types $t, t' \in T, t \neq t'$: $tname(t) \neq tname(t')$
(R2) for all functions $f, f' \in F, f \neq f'$: $fname(f) \neq fname(f')$
(R3) for all classes $c, c' \in C, c \neq c'$: $cname(c) \neq cname(c')$

The unique naming constraints are expressed by declaring the meta-functions *tname, fname, cname* to be **unique** in the meta-type definition.

Closure Constraints (R4, ..., R12) ensure schema closure in the sense that the following objects must be part of the schema:

(R4)   for all object-types $t \in T$: $localf(t) \subseteq F, \; supert(t) \subseteq T$
(R5)   for all set-types $t \in T$: $etype(t) \subseteq T$
(R6)   for all function-types $t \in T$: $dom(t) \subseteq T, \; ran(t) \subseteq T$
(R7)   for all functions $f \in F$: $sign(f) \in T$
(R8) $inverse(f) \in F \; \lor \; inverse(f) = \bot$
(R9) $inverse(f) = f' \iff inverse(f') = f$
(R10) for all class-defs $c \in C$: $mtype(c) \in T, \; superc(c) \subseteq C$
(R11) $pred(c) \in F$
(R12) for all view-defs $v \in C$: $query(v) \in expression$

To implement closure constraints, the meta-schema must follow two restrictions. First, in the meta-schema, all functions, that are not allowed to be undefined, have a **not null** constraint. Second, the active domain of the meta-types are by definition identical to the extent of the corresponding meta-class (cf. Section 3.2).

Acyclicity Constraints (R13, R14) ensure that supertype and superclass relationship do not end up in a cycle. Thus, no type can be supertype of itself, and no class superclass of itself.

(R13) for all object-types $t \in T : t \notin supert^*(t)$
(R14) for all class-defs $c \in C$: $c \notin superc^*(c)$

The acyclicity of the supertype/superclass relationship is implemented by adding a **not cyclic** constraint to the meta-function *supert/superc*, and is therefore checked automatically.

---

[4] The semantics of the meta-functions *tname, localf, supert, ...* is explained in the meta-schema in Appendix A. In addition, $supert^*$, $superc^*$ are defined as the transitive closure of *supert*, and *superc* respectively.

Implementing schema invariants for unique naming, closure, and acyclicity as constraints in the meta-schema is a very natural approach: since the application schema includes constraints for data level objects, constraints for schema level objects must be defined in the meta-schema. We use the generic update operations of COOL to change the schema level. Since they are defined to respect constraints, schema invariants are maintained automatically.

Thus, whenever a COOL update is performed to a schema level object in order to implement schema modifications, which would result in an incorrect database schema, this update will be rejected by the system.

4.3 Propagation to Data Level Objects (Type-Validness)

Figure 1 showed the *instance_of* relationship between types and objects. We mentioned that types define the interface (a set of functions) to their instances. The following definition gives the notion of *type-valid databases* [27], which means that every instance must match the definition of its type at any time:

Definition 4.1 (Type-Valid) A database $DB = <\mathcal{O}, \sigma>$ is type-valid, iff $\forall$ types $t \in \mathcal{T} : o \ instance\_of \ t \ \Rightarrow \ \exists! \ \sigma(f)(o) \in range(f), \ \forall f \in functs(t)$. $\Box$

In other words, a database must fulfill two requirements to be type-valid: (i) whenever the type-checker allows a function f to be applied on an object o (that is, iff f is in the interface of a type t and o is an instance of t), then the state $\sigma(f)(o)$ must be well defined; and (ii) the value of the state must match the range type of f.

Since types are represented by schema objects, we have therefore strong consistency requirements between objects of the schema level and of the data level, such that updates to objects representing types must propagate to updates on objects of the data level below.[5] However, we allow direct updating of schema level objects, but want to avoid that afterwards a migration utility must be called to adapt data level objects.

4.4 Implementation Considerations

A type evolution strategy, where all objects are kept type-valid on the physical level at any time, is usually called propagation by *immediate (eager) conversion* (e.g., realized in the GemStone system [21]). In the context of schema evolution, this is a very costly strategy: after any type change all instances may have to be converted. Therefore, two main alternatives to eager instance conversion have been proposed: (i) *delayed (lazy) conversion* is a strategy, where instances are only converted on demand, i.e., at the moment when they are touched the first time after the type change by a read or write operation. In combination with *screening*, one can even avoid to convert instances after a read, because screening is a kind of "logical" instance conversion, where objects are interpreted in the

---

[5] Notice, that the same situation shows between the meta-schema level and the schema level as well.

new definition (e.g., ORION [3]); and (ii) *type versioning* is a strategy where a new version of a type is created whenever a type is modified. Instances created after the change, belong to the new version [26, 1], and the same object may be viewed through different versions of the schema.[6]

Our approach was to realize a more "sophisticated" state function $\overline{\sigma}$, based on a combination of the above strategies, that keeps databases type-valid without any instance conversion. For this purpose, the database state of Section 3 was enhanced, such that each value of a function is carrying in addition information about its type $(type(f)(o))$. Whenever, the type checker allows the application of function f to object o, $\overline{\sigma}$ looks up in the database for the state $\sigma(f)(o)$.

$$
\overline{\sigma}(f)(o) := \begin{cases}
\sigma(f)(o) & \text{, if } type(f)(o) \preceq range(f), \\
cast(\sigma(f)(o)) & \text{, if } type(f)(o) \preceq object \text{ and } range(f) \preceq object, \\
transf(\sigma(f)(o)) & \text{, if } type(f)(o) \not\preceq object \text{ or } range(f) \not\preceq object, \\
\bot & \text{, otherwise.}
\end{cases}
$$

If there is no actually defined value for $f(o)$ in the database – for example, because f was added by a schema update after o has been created – $\overline{\sigma}$ returns a null value ($\bot$). If there is a value and it matches the range type of f, which is the ordinary case, $\sigma(f)(o)$ is retrieved.

Moreover, $\overline{\sigma}$ transforms values that do not match the range type of f – for example, because the signature of f was modified by a schema update in between –, using the *cast* or *transf* operator. The *cast* operator maps objects from one object type into an other object type, as it is known from other strictly typed languages [14]. The *transf* operator does a similar transformation for value types. It is mainly a table of mapping rules between integers, strings, booleans, etc.

With this definition of $\overline{\sigma}$, we can show:

Theorem All schema changes of the taxonomy, performed on a COCOON database $< \mathcal{O}, \overline{\sigma} >$ using COOL algebra operators, leave the database type-valid, w.r.t. to the modified state function $\overline{\sigma}$.

Implementing the database state like this, direct updates to schema objects can be performed, and the database is kept type-valid without explicit propagation to instances. The proof is just a case analysis following the explanations in Section 5.1.

5 Database Evolution as a Sample Application

So far, the framework is built such that we can allow a user to make direct schema object updates. We make now use of the above prerequisites and turn to a specific purpose of the framework: database evolution.

---

[6] It is finally a matter of performance trade-offs, which of these alternatives is chosen ([11] gives a performance comparison of immediate vs. delayed conversion).

5.1 The Taxonomy with Direct Updates to Schema Objects

The first step towards realizing schema evolution operations is to find a corresponding COOL algebra expression on schema objects for each of the update primitives in the presented taxonomy. We do that in the following and mention the constraints that are checked to satisfy schema correctness as well as how propagation to existing instances (data level objects) is resolved.

Creating new Schema Objects. Schema objects are created with the generic **insert** statement, by inserting a new object into one of the meta-classes *Object-Types, Functions, Class-Defs* or *View-Defs*. Thereby, the initial values of the new objects are to be specified. All given parameters must satisfy unique naming, not null, and not cyclic constraints.

$$(1.1.1) \; t := \textbf{insert} \; [tname := n_t, \; localf := \{ \; f_1, \ldots, f_n \; \}, \; supert := \{ \; t_1, \ldots, t_l \; \}]$$
$$(\textit{Object-Types});$$

Since the set of functions *localf(t)* that is associated with the newly created type is already existing, this schema update is simply the assignment of a type name the a set of functions, and does not propagate to data level objects.

$$(2.1.1) \; f := \textbf{insert} \; [fname := n_f, \; sign := dom\_ran, \; unique := uq,$$
$$notnull := nn, \; notcyclic := nc, \; inverse := f_i] \; (\textit{Functions});$$

After creation, the new function is not in a type interface, no object has a value for the new function, and therefore no explicit propagation is needed.

$$(3.1.1) \; c := \textbf{insert} \; [cname := n_c, \; auto := as, \; mtype := t_m,$$
$$pred := p_c, \; superc := \{ \; c_1, \ldots, c_n \; \} \;] \; (\textit{Class-Defs});$$
$$v := \textbf{insert} \; [cname := n_c, \; query := qr] \; (\textit{View-Defs});$$

Classes can be created either by a class definition (insertion into the meta-class *Class-Defs*) or as a view (insertion into the meta-class *View-Defs*). Since the extents of views and *all*-classes are defined by necessary and sufficient conditions, they are populated automatically if necessary.

Deleting schema objects. Applying the **delete** operator to a type, function, or class object removes it from the database schema. Deletion of schema objects may be refused, if it violates the closure constraint.

$$(1.1.2) \quad \textbf{delete} \; (t);$$

Deletion of a type does not propagate to the instance level. This operation simply removes the assignment of a named type object to a set of applicable functions (cf. generating a type). The instances of that type remain in the database, and all functions of the type interface are still applicable.

$$(2.1.2) \quad \textbf{delete} \; (f);$$

After deletion of a function object, that state of this function becomes useless. Nevertheless, there is no need for immediate removal of the values of f for data objects, because the type checker would no longer permit the application of f to an object.[7]

In case that the function f is part of a class predicate or query defining a view, deleting f could result in a run-time error. We discuss this problem below.

(3.1.2) **delete** (c);

Deletion of a class has no influence on the class members.

Changing the name of schema objects. Names of types, functions, or classes can be changed, using the generic **set** operator to assign a new name string.

(1.2.1) **set** $[tname:= n_t]$ (t); (3.2.1) **set** $[cname:= n_c]$ (c);
(2.2.1) **set** $[fname:= n_f]$ (f);

These changes must follow the unique naming constraint. Changing object names does not need to be propagated any further.

Changing the type interface. Using the generic **add** and **remove** operators, a type object t_i can be added or removed to/from the type interface in order to change the set of supertypes. Similarly, a new function object f_i can be added or removed to/from the set of locally defined functions.

(1.2.2) **add** $[t_i]$ $(supert(t))$; (1.2.3) **add** $[f_i]$ $(localf(t))$;
          remove $[t_i]$ $(supert(t))$;   **remove** $[f_i]$ $(localf(t))$;

In case of adding supertypes or local functions, new functions become applicable to all instances of t: e.g., if o is an existing instance of t, then $\sigma(f_i)(o)$ becomes type-valid. But, following our lazy propagation strategy (cf. Section 4.3), the state of the data objects can remain unchanged, because σ returned a null value anyway.

After removing the function f_i from the type interface, the application of f_i to an object o in context of this type would not pass the type checker. Thus, it does not matter whether the actual value is kept in the database state.

Changing the function signature. The signature of a function object can be changed directly, by assigning a new object ft (of type fcn-$type$), using the generic **set** operator.[8]

(2.2.2) **set** $[sign:= ft]$ (f);

---

[7] Deleting the values of f from the database is an implementation issue. It could be done later, e.g. in a clean-up phase, cf. Section 4.3.

[8] For the considerations here, we assume, that for each desired combination of domain and range, there already exists a function type object that represents it. For example, *obj_set_employee* for signature with domain *object* and range *set of employee*.

Altering the range of a function may cause that existing instance values must be transformed to other types. This is done by the cast-option in the state function. If the domain is restricted, the type-checker avoids the use of these function for an object that is not instance of the new domain; if the range gets more general, substitutability guarantees that function values are still valid. Anyhow, all changes of the signature are handled by the σ-function according to Section 4.3.

Changing the function constraints. For changing the function constraints, one must distinguish between two cases: those making the constraint more restrictive (setting unique, not null, not cyclic to true) and those making it less restrictive (setting constraints to false). Only the former ones give problems, because there could be data objects already in the database that do not follow the new more restrictive constraints.

(2.2.3) **set** $[unique:= uq]$ (f);   **set** $[notnull:= nn]$ (f);
         set $[notcyclic:= nc]$ (f);   **set** $[inverse:= f_i]$ (f);

Changing class properties. Properties of classes can be changed by assigning new selector as, membertype t_m, or class predicate p_c.

(3.2.2) **set** $[auto:= as]$ (c);   (3.2.5) **add** $[c_i]$ $(superc(c))$;
(3.2.3) **set** $[mtype:= t_m]$ (c);   **remove** $[c_i]$ $(superc(c))$;
(3.2.4) **set** $[pred:= p_c]$ (c);   (3.2.6) **set** $[query:= qr]$ (c);

Since the extent of a class is not stored but computed (no matter whether defined as a class or as a view), changing these class properties has no effect on instances, but simply needs recomputation of the extent. Assigning a new query or an new predicate needs of type-checking (see below).

5.2 Embedding Schema Updates into Methods

Although all schema update primitives have been mapped into an algebra expression, isolated use of these updates may not be adequate or desirable for many reasons:

- Since a small update on a schema object may have serious effects on databases, it may be useful to ensure additional pre and post conditions for such an update.
- If a direct update violates model inherent integrity constraints (uniqueness, not null, or not cyclic), the operation is just rejected. It may be more adequate, if meaningful error messages were returned.
- The user's authorization to make the schema update must be checked. In general, this is done using a normal authorization model for objects [22], and applying it to the schema objects. Anyway, some special restrictions to schema updates may be checked globally, e.g. forbidding that meta-types are deleted.

- The meta-schema does not contain any information about physical design issues. Physical descriptors for the classes and functions may be given explicitly together with a schema update. As an example, consider that some views or derived (computed) functions may be materialized, indexes should be created, objects may be clustered, or statistics on the transaction load should be kept.
- Run-time information for dynamic type-checking or function bindings is not part of the meta-schema as well. If for example the predicate of a class is changed, it must be type-checked for that no run-time error can occur; and since functions (e.g., queries of a view definition) can be derived from others, we have to represent dependencies between functions. This problem is known as "behavioral consistency" [30].
- Finally, user defined semantics may be added. For example, one may want to enforce, that deleting a class includes deletion of all instances.

EXAMPLE 2: Consider deletion of type objects $(U_{1.1.2})$. The following method requires that before type t is deleted, t is not a meta-type and that t is not used somewhere else.

> **procedure** *delete_type (t : object-type)* **is**
>   *— delete an existing type object (update 1.1.2 of the taxonomy)*
> **require**
> $t \notin MetaTypes$ **and**
>   **select** *[t ∈ supert] (Object-Types)* = ∅ **and**
>   **select** *[t = etype] (Set-Types)* = ∅ **and**
>   **select** *[t = dom* **or** *t = ran] (Fcn-Types)* = ∅ **and**
>   **select** *[t = mtype] (Class-Defs)* = ∅
> **begin**
>   **delete** *(t);*
> **end** *— delete_type*   ◇

We therefore propose that updates to schema objects should only happen encapsulated into save schema update methods. In an object-oriented system, these methods can be implemented as overriding of the standard methods of the meta-types.

6   Conclusion and Future Work

We presented a general framework for investigation of database evolution based on an object-oriented data model and an object algebra for queries and updates.

The contribution of this framework is threefold. First, we introduced a system where schema and meta-schema objects are treated as ordinary objects, and the meta-schema is fully available to the user. Beyond, we defined the semantics of the generic update operators such that they can be applied on any object, independent of whether it belongs to a schema or the data level. Finally, we showed that this approach is powerful enough to realize schema evolution, such that a taxonomy of desirable schema change primitives can be implemented as direct updates to schema objects. They will respect integrity constraints on the schema and they will also leave the database in a type-valid state.

The object model COCOON and its algebra COOL are currently being implemented as a prototype system, respecting the separation of database object into the three different levels [29]. We have defined all primitives for schema updates, and have been setting up a collection of higher level evolution operations, based on these primitives. They will facilitate complete schema design, tailoring, and restructuring. Finally, as a long time goal, we are working towards a tool that supports users in extending and reusing databases. The framework is open in the sense that schema evolution is only one sample application. As a second one, we started to study the feasibility of database integration [25]. We showed, how the distinction of the three object levels can be used for making multidatabases interoperable.

Furthermore, we are extending our meta-schema for physical database design and "behavioral consistency". Information must be included about the implementation (computed/stored) of functions, materialization of class/view extents, and clustering of objects. To detect run-time type errors, function bindings and dependencies between function and query expressions are to be stored.

Acknowledgments. The authors are indebted to Hans-Jörg Schek, Christian Laasch, and Klaus Gaßner for their helpful discussion on the paper. A preliminary version of the framework was presented in [28].

References

1. J. Andany, M. Leonard, and C. Palisser. Management of schema evolution in databases. In *Proc. 17th Int'l Conf. on Very Large Data Bases (VLDB)*, Barcelona, Spain, September 1991.
2. J. Banerjee, H. Chou, J.F. Garza, W. Kim, D. Woelk, and N. Ballou. Data model issues for object-oriented applications. *ACM Trans. on Office Information Systems*, 5(1), January 1987.
3. J. Banerjee, W. Kim, H.J. Kim, and H.F. Korth. Semantics and implementation of schema evolution in object-oriented databases. In *ACM SIGMOD Record 1987*, San Francisco, February 1987.
4. C. Beeri. Formal models for object-oriented databases. In DOOD89 [7].
5. C. Beeri. New data models and languages – the challenge. In *Proc. ACM Symp. on Principles of Database Systems*, San Diego, California, June 1992.
6. E. Casais. *Managing Evolution in Object-Oriented Environments: An Algorithmic Approach*. Phd thesis, Centre univ. d'informatique, Université Genève, 1991.
7. *Proc. 1st Int'l Conf. on Deductive and Object-Oriented Databases (DOOD)*, Kyoto, Japan, December 1989.
8. *Proc. 2nd Int'l Conf. on Deductive and Object-Oriented Databases (DOOD)*, Munich, Germany, December 1991.
9. *Proc. 7th Int'l Conf. Entity-Relationship Approach*, Rome, Italy, November 1988.
10. J. Göers and A. Heuer. Definition and application of metaclasses in an object-oriented database model. Inst. für Informatik, TU Clausthal, Germany, June 1991.

11. G. Harrus, F. Velez, and R. Zicari. Implementing schema updates in an object-oriented database system: A cost analysis. Technical report, GIP Altair, Le Chesnay Cedex, France, 1990.

12. G. Kappel and M. Schrefl. A behavior integrated entity-relationship appraoch for the design of object-oriented databases. In ER88 [9].

13. W. Klas. *A Metaclass System for Open Object-Oriented Data Models*. PhD thesis, Technische Universität Wien, January 1990.

14. C. Laasch and M. H. Scholl. Generic update operations keeping object-oriented databases consistent. In *Proc. 2nd GI-Workshop on Information Systems and Artificial Intelligence (IS/KI)*, FAW Ulm, Germany, February 1992.

15. B.S. Lerner and A.N. Habermann. Beyond schema evolution to database reorganization. In *Proc. Int'l Conf. OOPSLA/ECOOP*, Ottawa, Canada, October 1990.

16. T.W. Ling. External schemas of entity-relationship based data base management systems. In ER88 [9].

17. S.B. Navathe and M.K. Pillalamarri. OOER: toward making the E-R appraoch object-oriented. In ER88 [9].

18. S.L. Osborn. The role of polymorphism in schema evolution in an object-oriented database. *IEEE Trans. on Know. and Data Engineering*, 1(3), September 1989.

19. C. Parent, H. Rolin, K. Yétongnon, and S. Spaccapietra. An ER calculus for the entity-relationship complex model. In *Proc. 8th Int'l Conf. Entity-Relationship Approach*, Toronto, Canada, October 1989.

20. C. Parent and S. Spaccapietra. About entities, complex objects and object-oriented data models. In *Information System Concepts - An In-depth Analysis*, *Proc. of IFIP WG 8.1 Working Conference*, Namur, October 1989.

21. D.J. Penney and J. Stein. Class modification in the GemStone object-oriented DBMS. In *Proc. Int'l Conf. on Object-Oriented Programming Systems and Languages (OOPSLA)*, October 1987.

22. F. Rabitti, E. Bertino, W. Kim, and D. Woelk. A model for authorization for next-generation database systems. *ACM TODS*, 16(1), March 1991.

23. M.H. Scholl, C. Laasch, and M. Tresch. Updatable views in object-oriented databases. In DOOD91 [8].

24. M.H. Scholl and H.-J. Schek. A relational object model. In *Proc. 3rd Int'l Conf. on Database Theory (ICDT'90)*, Paris, 1990.

25. M.H. Scholl, H.-J. Schek, and M. Tresch. Object algebra and views for multi-objectbases. In *Proc. Int'l Workshop on Distributed Object Management*, Edmonton, Canada, August 1992.

26. A.H. Skarra and S.B. Zdonik. Type evolution in an object-oriented database. In *Research Directions in Object-Oriented Programming*, 1987.

27. L. Tan and T. Katayame. Meta operations for type management in object-oriented databases. In DOOD89 [7].

28. M. Tresch. A framework for schema evolution by meta object manipulation. In *Workshop on Foundations of Models and Languages for Data and Objects*, Aigen, Austria, September 1991.

29. M. Tresch and M.H. Scholl. Implementing an object model on top of commercial database systems. In *Workshop on Foundations of Database Systems*, Volkse, Germany, May 1991.

30. E. Waller. Schema updates and consistency. In DOOD91 [8].

31. R. Zicari. A framework for schema updates in an object-oriented database system. In *Proc. 7th Int'l Conf. on Data Engineering (ICDE)*, Kobe, Japan, April 1991.

A The Meta Schema

In the sequel, we define the COCOON meta-schema. Usually the purpose of a meta-schema is twofold: (i) to describe the object model using its own notation, and (ii) to represent data dictionary information. Nevertheless, since the scope of this paper is schema evolution, our meta-schema is only given and explained as far as it is necessary to define the semantics of schema updates.

As proposed in Definition 3.2, the meta-schema is composed of meta-types and meta-classes. The first meta-type represents data and object types. That is, each COCOON type is represented by an object, being instance of the following meta-type:

> **type** *type* **isa** *object* =
> > *tname* : **unique** *string* , // type name
> > *functs* : **set of** *function* ; // functions, applicable to
> > > the type's instances

Most types are defined by users in order to specify the interface of an abstract object type (i.e. to define the signatures of the applicable functions). As usual in object-oriented systems, such types can be ordered in type-hierarchies. The meta-type *object-type* is a specialized subtype:

> **type** *object-type* **isa** *type* =
> > *localf* : **set of** *function* **not null** , // local functions, inde-
> > > pendent of inheritance
> > *supert* : **set of** *object-type*   // explicitly defined
> > > **not null not cyclic** ,   supertypes of the type

Whereas *localf(t)* are the functions defined to be applicable to *t*'s instances independent of inheritance, for an abstract object type, the set of all applicable functions *functs(t)* is derived by the union of the local functions *localf(t)* and the functions inherited from the supertypes:

$$funcs(t) := localf(t) \bigcup_{t_i \in supert(t)} funcs(t_i)$$

Notice, that type checking is based on all functions *functs(t)*, not only on the local ones. We distinguish for each type t between explicit and implicit supertypes. The former ones are those explicitly assigned with the meta-function *supert(t)*, whereas the implicit ones are derived from the set of applicable functions as follows:

$$t \preceq t' \iff funcs(t) \supseteq funcs(t')$$

That is, a type t' is supertype of t, if the applicable functions of t are a superset the functions of t'.

In addition to abstract object types, two more subtypes represent constructed data types: the set and function types. Since these types are normally created and managed internally by the system, most of them are unnamed.

type *set-type* **isa** *type* =
>   *etype* : *type* **not null** ; // the type of the elements in the set

type *fcn-type* **isa** *type* =
>   *dom* : *type* **not null** , // the domain type of the function
>   *ran* : *type* **not null** ; // the range type of the function

The second meta-type represents COCOON functions. They are named, have a signature, and their values can be restricted by a set of constraints.

type *function* **isa** *object* =
> | *fname* : | **unique** *string* **not null** , | // function name |
> | *sign* : | *fcn-type* **not null** , | // function signature |
> | *unique* : | *boolean* **not null** , | // uniqueness constrain |
> | *notnull* : | *boolean* **not null** , | // not undef constraint |
> | *notcyclic* : | *boolean* **not null** , | // cycle free constraint |
> | *inverse* : | *function* **inverse** *inverse* ; | // inverse function |

Information about the implementation of the function (e.g. whether the function result is stored or computed), is intentionally excluded from the meta-schema, since this is irrelevant for schema evolution.

The third meta-type represents COCOON classes.

type *class* **isa** *object* =
>   *cname* : **unique** *string* **not null** , // class name
>   *extent* : **set of** *object* ;   // actual class members

Since we treat views as classes with implicitly defined type and extension, two subtypes of meta-type *class* are distinguished: those defined as a class, and those defined as a view.

type *class-def* **isa** *class* =
> | *auto* : | *boolean* **not null** , | // (see below) |
> | *mtype* : | *type* , | // explicit member type |
> | *pred* : | *function* , | // the class predicate |
> | *superc* : | **set of** *class* | // explicit super classes |
> | | **not null not cyclic** , | |
> | *pmemb* : | **set of** *object* ; | // potential class members |

type *view-def* **isa** *class* =
>   *query* **not null** : *expression* , // query defining the view

The value of *auto(c)* is true, iff the class *c* is defined with the selector **all**. In these cases the system can decide whether an object belongs to the extent of a class. If classes are defined by the selector **some** there are just necessary conditions defined. The information about class membership is specified by the user in terms of adding and removing objects to/from a class explicitly. This information is stored by the set *pmemb* that represents the potential members of a class. These are objects that are added to a class, but need not to fulfill the class predicate (for more detail see [14]). *extent(c)* derives the actual set of member objects (extent) of a class, i.e. a subset of *pmemb* which elements fulfill the class predicate. The actual derived member type of the class objects is either equal to *mtype(c)*, if a member type is explicitly defined, or otherwise, it must be derived from the member type of *c*'s superclasses and class predicate.

Together with each meta-type, there is a meta-class holding the actual instances of the meta-type.

> **class** *Types* : *type* **some** *Objects* ;
> **class** *Set-Types* : *set-type* **some** *Types* ;
> **class** *Fcn-Types* : *fcn-type* **some** *Types* ;
> **class** *Object-Types* : *object-type* **some** *Types* ;
>
> **class** *Functions* : *function* **some** *Objects* ;
>
> **class** *Classes* : *class* **some** *Objects* ;
> **class** *Class-Defs* : *class-def* **some** *Classes* ;
> **class** *View-Defs* : *view-def* **some** *Classes* ;

In addition, the following view collects all classes with implicitly defined extent. That is, the view-defined classes and the class-defined ones with an **all** - selector:

> **view** *Views* **as** *View-Defs* **union select** [*auto(c)*] (*c: Class-Defs*);

Modelling of Audio/Video Data

Christian Breiteneder
Simon Gibbs
Dennis Tsichritzis

Centre Universitaire d'Informatique, Uni Dufour,
24 rue du Général-Dufour, CH-1211 Geneva 4, Switzerland.
{chris, simon, dt}@cui.unige.ch.

Abstract. Advances in data compression are creating new possibilities for applications combining digital audio and digital video. These applications, such as desktop authoring environments and educational or training programs, often require access to collections of audio/video material. This paper introduces audio/video, or "AV", databases and discusses the key problem of data modelling in the context of time-based media. Extensions needed for modelling basic audio/video structures and relationships are described. These extensions, which include temporal sequences, quality factors, derivation relationships and temporal composition, are applied to an existing audio/video data representation.

1 Introduction

A number of key technologies are being developed that are likely to result in much greater use of digital audio and digital video data. These developments include advances in high-bandwidth networks, improvements in storage media, faster graphics hardware, and greater availability of special-purpose audio and video processors. Perhaps the most significant event is the development of real-time compression and decompression hardware for digital video. The compressed video has data rates comparable to bus and disk bandwidths and so opens the possibility of video recording and playback from conventional secondary storage devices.

The presence of digital audio and video, or what we call AV data, poses a challenge to the database community. Databases for managing AV are needed for a number of reasons. First, AV data places enormous demands on storage. For instance a single *second* of high-quality digital video may consume tens of Mbytes. Very large capacity "tertiary" storage systems are appropriate. These AV storage systems will benefit from database functionality allowing shared use and efficient access. Second, AV data often goes through an editing or "post-production" process during which particular segments are selected and combined. Rather than copying immense amounts of data, the edited segments consist of links to the original data. Hypermedia applications also create interlinked AV data. The result is that a single AV segment may be referenced in many places. Such dependencies should be managed by a database system so that referenced data is not accidentally deleted or unnecessarily duplicated. Third, many AV design and production tools rely on "clip media" – audio and video snippets, graphics and raster images, animation sequences, and pieces of music – intended to be combined and reused.

Large collections of clip media are now being introduced, primarily on CD-ROM. As designers acquire and augment these collections, they are encountering basic problems in data management. Databases that organize and query clip media are needed. Current multimedia database systems are not suitable, primarily because they lack support for AV data.

In the following section we provide background information on AV database systems and summarize a number of emerging AV data representations. Section 3 identifies issues related to modelling AV data in general. These issues are then illustrated and further refined in section 4 by developing a data model for an existing AV representation.

2 AV Database Systems

What are AV database systems and how do they differ from database systems in general? It appears that support for AV data will require major changes to system architecture and the nature of the application interface. To better see these changes, we now give a short description of AV database systems and describe several existing AV data formats.

Informally, an *AV value* is a sequence of digital audio or digital video data elements. Each AV value has a *data rate*. This quantity is critical in determining the storage and processing requirements of AV data, its existence is the primary difference between AV and other forms of data. Examples of AV values include CD encoded audio, MIDI[1] sequences, CCIR 601[2] digital video, and various compressed digital video formats. An *AV database system* is a software / hardware entity capable of storing a large number of AV values, controlling their concurrent access, *and* providing their real-time transfer to applications.

In a companion paper [3] we expand the above definitions and explore their implications on the nature of AV database systems. Here we summarize some of the characteristics distinguishing AV database systems from other systems:

specialized hardware The production, consumption and processing of AV values (examples of processing include format conversion, filtering, compression and rendering) often requires special hardware such as analog-to-digital and digital-to-analog converters, digital signal processors, and graphics pipelines. It should be possible to place some of these hardware elements under control of the database system.

applications may specify scheduling With AV databases, certain forms of scheduling should be under application control. Since system resources (buffers, processor cycles, bus bandwidth, network bandwidth) are limited it is possible for application requests to tie up resources, or the database itself, for significant periods of time. Consequently, concurrent access to AV data may require explicit scheduling (in particular, resource pre-allocation) by applications.

---

1. MIDI, or *Musical Instrument Digital Interface*, is a standard for communicating with musical devices.
2. A digital video standard developed by an international association of broadcasters.

asynchronous, stream-based interface to applications   With conventional database systems, interaction between the application and the system resembles a call-by-value procedure: the application assembles a request, issues it to the database system, and then waits to receive a reply. With AV data this form of interaction is not suitable. Interfaces based on multiple tasks, stream redirection, and asynchronous notification are more appropriate than a simple issue-request / receive-reply protocol.

applications may specify data placement   Assuring physical data independence can severely diminish the usability of an AV database system since certain operations may require exclusive access to storage resources. The alternative is to make visible to the application some aspect of the physical storage structure so that AV data can be assured to be available when needed.

data representation based on "quality factors"   There are many alternatives for encoding and compressing digital video and digital audio. Application programs need not be aware of representations used by the database system. Instead applications should specify data representation indirectly, in terms of AV "quality factors." These factors include, for example, video resolution and audio fidelity.

There are a number of emerging data formats allowing the combination of digital audio and digital video. Since many of these may not be familiar to the database community we will give a short summary of several formats:

DVI – The David Sarnoff Research Center has developed a digital video technology known as *Digital Video Interactive* or *DVI* [4][6][10]. Intel acquired the rights to DVI technology and, through its *ActionMedia* boards, supports DVI on PCs. DVI is based on two digital video formats: *Production-Level Video* (PLV) and *Real-Time Video* (RTV). PLV uses a proprietary compression algorithm which allows VHS quality video to be produced from a data rate of about 1 Mbit/sec. The algorithm performs *interframe* compression which exploits similarities between successive frames. This requires considerable computation, and even with costly hardware is difficult to achieve in real-time (3 seconds per frame have been reported [6]). Application developers obtain PLV compression via service facilities established by Intel. PLV decompression, on the other hand, can be performed in real-time by the ActionMedia boards. Thus, while applications cannot record PLV, they can play it back. Applications that need to record digital video, use the second DVI format. The RTV format results in data rates similar to those of PLV, however the video quality will be poorer and the frame rate may be reduced. DVI software makes use of a multimedia format, called the *AVSS file format*, where multiple tracks of PLV, RTV, digital audio, and other temporal data, can be interleaved into a single linear data structure. The DVI software and hardware then perform the real-time composition and synchronization needed to playback AVSS files.

MPEG – The *Moving Pictures Expert Group* (MPEG), an ISO working group, has proposed a video compression standard based on interframe coding and Discrete Cosine Transform (DCT) techniques [5]. The initial MPEG proposal for video, known as "phase I", leads to data rates of, like DVI, about 1 Mbit/sec for VHS quality video. A further "phase II" proposal is envisaged where data rates of up to 10 Mbit/sec will be used for near-broadcast quality video. MPEG is also working on standards for digital audio and combined (audio-video) data streams. MPEG has broad industrial participation and products based on MPEG have already been announced.

JPEG – The *Joint Photographic Experts Group* (JPEG), another ISO working group, has developed an image compression standard intended for continuous-tone colour and grayscale images [11]. JPEG can also be used with digital video by treating each frame as an image to be compressed independently. Hardware implementations of JPEG are capable of compressing and decompressing medium resolution images (640 x 480 pixels) at video frame rates and are the basis of several computer-based digital video editing systems. For a given frame rate and resolution, JPEG-compressed video will have a higher data rate than interframe compression techniques such as MPEG and DVI's PLV, but since frames are compressed independently, it is an easier matter to rearrange the order of the frames and to playback in reverse or at variable rates.

CD-I – *Compact-Disc Interactive* (CD-I) is a self-contained multimedia system developed by Philips and Sony [9]. CD-I specifies a data format allowing digital audio of various qualities, digital images of various resolutions, and arbitrary application data, to be stored on a CD. Support for MPEG video has now also been announced. CD-I players provide audio/video output by attachment to normal television receivers, they can support several interface devices including infrared keypads and joysticks. The player contains a powerful processor running a real-time operating system. This processor is responsible for de-interleaving the CD data stream and transferring separated audio and video data to particular decoders and output processors. The processor is typically under control of an application program loaded from the disc. It is this program which provides interactivity; it determines how to respond to input events, which portions of the disc should be played, and how the various data streams are to be composed and synchronized.

QuickTime – *QuickTime* [1] is an addition to System 7 (the Macintosh operating system) allowing real-time synchronized playback of digital audio and digital video. QuickTime is extensible; "components" can be added for decoding and encoding new data representations. The initial release includes several decoders intended for synthetic (computer-generated) images and natural (continuous tone) images. Multiple tracks of digital audio and video data are combined in a *movie* file, which can then be played by QuickTime on the various Macintosh platforms. Section 4 will discuss the movie format in more detail.

Director – MacroMind *Director* is a popular multimedia authoring application for the Macintosh [7]. Director is based on a multi-track data structure (also called a movie) where individual tracks may contain graphic objects, audio and MIDI events, timing information, and interactive scripts. The main tool provided by Director is the "score editor," used to specify track contents, how multiple graphics tracks are to be combined and overlaid, and the timing constraints between tracks. A second tool is used to playback and interact with a Director movie. In addition to the Macintosh, Microsoft's multimedia extension to Windows [8] supports playing of Director movies.

3 AV Data Modelling

Existing representations for combining audio and video data often involve similar structuring mechanisms. For instance, among the representations described in the previous section, aggregates of "tracks" are common, as are structures based on time series. An AV data model must provide abstractions that correspond to these structures and which can be used to specify a database schema. We now describe the basic concepts needed by AV data models.

3.1 AV Primitives

We will follow a bottom-up approach and first introduce terms for the basic building blocks of AV data:

Data Types and *Data Elements*   A *data type* governs the encoding and interpretation of *data elements*. Examples of data types include the familiar IntegerType and FloatType. Each data element has a *size*, which can be thought of as its length in bytes. If all elements of a data type, T, are of the same size we say T has fixed-size elements.

AV Types and *AV Elements*   Certain data types are used to encode digital audio or digital video data. Examples of these *AV types* include CDaudioType and JPEGvideo-Type. An *AV element* is an element of an AV type. For the types just mentioned, elements would be a single sample of CD audio or a single frame of JPEG video.

3.2 AV and Time

AV is time-based. This has two important implications: first the handling (retrieval, storage, and processing) of AV data is subject to real-time constraints, and, second, temporal correlations may occur in AV data. Satisfaction of real-time constraints (as opposed to their specification) is a performance and implementation issue rather than a data modelling issue. What is important to AV data modelling is the ability to specify temporal correlations. In other words, an AV data model must address the *timing* of AV data.

Continuous Time Value   A continuous time value is simply a measurement of time using some agreed upon units.

Discrete Time Coordinate System   A discrete time coordinate system, D, is a mapping from discrete time values to continuous time (a discrete time value is an integer). The mapping is of the form D: $i = (1/f)i$, where f is called the *frequency* of the coordinate system. We will indicate specific discrete time systems by D_f. Some examples are D_{30}, for North American video, D_{25} for European video, D_{24} for film, and D_{44100} for CD audio.

Temporal Value   A temporal value is a finite sequence of tuples of the form: $<e_i, s_i, d_i>$, $i=1, \ldots n$. Each temporal value is based on a data type T and a discrete time coordinate system D. In particular, the e_i are data elements of type T, and the s_i and d_i are values referring to the system D. The value s_i is called the start time of e_i and d_i is its duration. Start times and durations must satisfy: $s_{i+1} \geq s_i + d_i$, $s_{i+1} > s_i$ and $d_i \geq 0$. Various special forms of temporal values can be identified:

- *AV value*: T is an AV type,
- *fully covered value*: $s_{i+1} - s_i = d_i$ for $i = 1, \ldots n-1$,

- *uniform value*: the value is fully covered and $d_i = 1$ for $i = 1, ... n-1$,
- *constant rate value*: the value is uniform and elements have the same size.

For example a CD audio sequence is a constant rate value, elements have the same size and occur uniformly. A JPEG encoding of NTSC video frames would be uniform (since frames occur every 1/30th of a second) but not constant rate since the encoded frames vary in size. Video representations that avoid repeating identical frames are fully covered, but non-uniform. Finally, MIDI sequences, where data elements correspond to musical events, are not fully covered.

3.3 AV Abstractions

We now define several abstractions that provide higher-level descriptions of AV values.

Quality Factors Video compression algorithms such as JPEG, MPEG and those used in DVI and QuickTime are *lossy*, encoding followed by decoding is not an identity transformation. Loss of information can be thought of as a reduction in image quality. The amount of information lost can be controlled by selection of parameters used during encoding. However, these parameters should not be visible at the data modelling level, instead video quality should be specified via descriptive *quality factors*. A video quality factor could be an expression of the form:

$$w \times h \times d$$

indicating a video resolution of width w and height h pixels, and a depth of d bits per pixel. Other alternatives could be descriptions such as "VHS quality" or "broadcast quality."

Temporal Entity Type A temporal entity type is specified by an expression of the form $N[T, \{Q\}, \{D\}]$, where N is the name of the entity type, T is its underlying data type, Q an optional quality factor, and D its discrete time coordinate system. D need not be specified if: 1) temporal values based on T always use the same time system, (e.g., CDaudioType values always use D_{44100}) or, 2) different instances of N are allowed to refer to different time systems. An instance of a temporal entity type, specified as above, is a temporal value based on the data type T and referring to the discrete time coordinate system D if present. Finally, if T is an AV type then N is an *AV entity type*, examples are:

    VideoEntity[JPEGvideoType, 480x640x8, D_{30}]
    VoiceEntity[PCMaudioType, D_{16000}]
    MusicEntity[CDaudioType]
    MIDI-Entity[MIDI-Type]
    AudioEnvelopeEntity[IntegerType, D_{2205}]

For example, instances of VideoEntity, would be sequences of JPEG encoded video frames, of good quality, and occurring at a rate of 30 frames per second.

Derivation Relationships A number of relationships occur between temporal entities. Of particular interest are relationships that indicate how one entity is *derived* from another. As with other relationships, derivation relationships can be represented as instances of relationship types, attributes of the type are parameters that govern the derivation. Useful derivation relationship types include Translation (the start times of a value are uniformly displaced), Concatenation (a value is added to the end of another value), Selection (a sub-value is extracted), and Conversion (a value is "resampled", the simplest case would be changing a value based on D_{2n} to one based on D_n by dropping every second element). Generally there are constraints on the types of entities related by derivation relationships. For example, a VoiceEntity could not be concatenated to a VideoEntity or obtained from a VideoEntity by conversion.

Derivation relationships are essential to AV databases for a number of reasons. First, they reduce storage costs by allowing alternative views to be constructed without the need for replication. Second, modification operations can be performed more efficiently. For example, to delete a video sub-sequence one could copy and reassemble the frame data, but it would be much more efficient to simply alter a derivation relationship. Finally, derivation relationships provide physical data independence by separating derived values from the underlying stored data. It should also be noted that derived values can be converted to non-derived values if need be. For instance, a CD authoring application would perform such a conversion in order to obtain the actual data to be laid out on the disc.

Temporal Composition　A special relationship, known as *temporal composition*, is used to represent groups of temporally correlated entities. Such groups require synchronized presentation and are the basis of multimedia, for instance both television and film consist of temporally correlated audible and visual values. A *simple entity* is a temporal entity (either derived or non-derived). A *composite entity* is a group of entities related by temporal composition. The group may contain both simple entities and other composite entities.

AV Data Diagram　An AV data diagram is a directed graph where nodes correspond to temporal entities (either simple or composite) and arcs correspond to derivation relationships and temporal composition relationships. For example, consider a composite

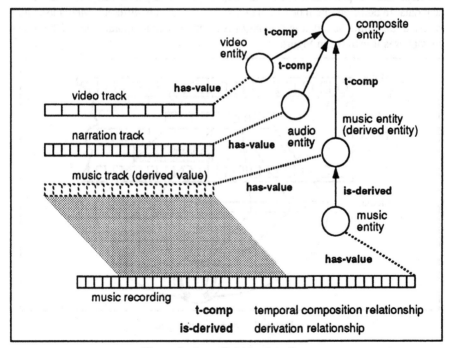

Figure 1　An audio/video data diagram.

entity consisting of two audio tracks (one for music, the other for narration) and a single video track. The narration has been specially recorded while the music track is derived from an existing recording. The AV data diagram for this example is shown in Figure 1, here we also indicate entity values by rectangular nodes (attached to their corresponding entity by a dashed line).

4 A Data Model for Audio/Video Data

In this section, a data model for AV data is presented which is based upon the general concepts of the previous section and the QuickTime movie format. We will not discuss this format in detail but rather focus on the principal issues which have to be expressed in a general model for AV data. The section consists of three parts. In the first part, we define the various audio/video types of the AV data model in a specialization hierarchy. The second subsection focuses on temporal composition and time attributes and introduces the top layer of a nested ER diagram [2] that we see as a general model for temporally composite AV data. This diagram is refined in the third subsection by the introduction of additional entities which describe various derivation relationships more precisely.

In general, we will follow the terminology suggested for QuickTime which uses a so-called "movie" metaphor. Movies represent digital videos combined with sound. Movies are temporally composed of tracks. Tracks are derived from media that refer to the actual temporal values. There exist several reasons for tracks not directly referring to the temporal values stored on an external device. All of them can be subsumed under the term data independence. The media roughly gives a logical description of the physical data. In addition, the index of media and stored data is different. Media uses *time information* while the index is *data address* for the stored temporal values. The movie metaphor is illustrated in Figure 2.

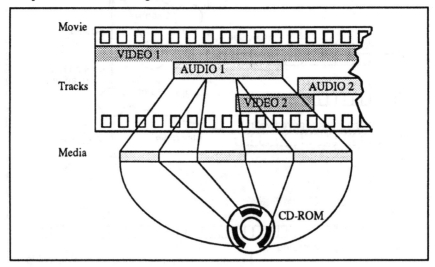

Figure 2 The movie metaphor.

4.1 AV Types

Media and tracks in a movie are of a specific AV type. The various types of audio/video data we consider to be relevant include images, graphics, video and audio. Generally, AV types can be separated into audio and visual types. The latter can be further separated into still types such as images, video stills, graphics, and moving video types. The reason for the differentiation of visual and audio types is that these two media have different requirements with respect to internal storage (e.g., compression) and final presentation. For the presentation of visual types, more information (spatial information) is needed to define how and where a certain image or video is presented (e.g., the placement and size of the window, etc.). A possible specialization hierarchy of AV types is shown in Figure 3, we now look at some of these specializations in more detail.

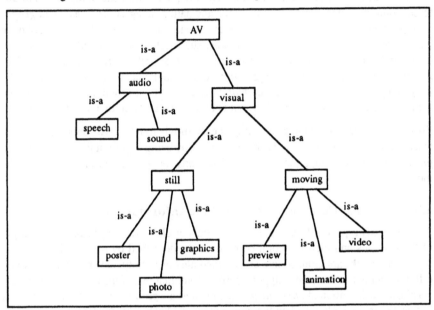

Figure 3 Specialization hierarchy of audio/video types.

Audio Types. Audio types usually do not involve a complex specification for the purpose of presentation to the user. However, there are certain attributes that deal with presentation – volume and balance are examples. In QuickTime, every movie owns these two attributes as well as every track entity. The volume attribute of a track has a slightly different meaning than that of a movie as this attribute is relative to other tracks. The volume attribute of a track is scaled to the setting of the corresponding movie volume. For example, a setting less than 1.0 for a specific track results in a proportionally quieter playback of that track relative to the loudness of the other tracks in that particular movie. In addition, each track has its own balance setting. Subtypes of audio are speech and sound, where sound is defined as everything that is not speech. As with the audio/video distinction, it is the use of different compression techniques for these two types that requires their differentiation.

Visual Data Types. Generally, visual types require the specification of a presentation area. In QuickTime, this spatial information includes such things as a presentation region, clipping region, matte, bounds region, and transformation matrix. The presentation region describes the window needed to display the visual data. The clipping region and bounds region identify the portion of visual data that will appear. Mattes, which allow graduations of transparency, are used to accomplish mask operations. A transformation matrix is used for translation, rotation, and scaling. The various regions, mattes, and transformation matrices refer either to a movie in its entirety or to a track. The spatial information of a track is composed with that of the movie during playback.

Still and Moving Visual Types. Visual types can be further differentiated into *still* and *moving*. This distinction is a matter of different requirements concerning time and different compression techniques for synthetic and natural imagery. The *photo* and *graphics* types both refer to still images. Photos are images that vary smoothly or do not have large areas devoted to edges, borders, or other sharp details. Photos will generally refer to "natural" images with continuous tone in contrast to synthetically generated *graphics* images where sharp edges and large regions of constant colour are possible. Similarly, the difference between *video* and *animation* is again one of origin, the *animation* type is best for synthetic imagery while *video* is best for natural continuous tone material.

Posters and Previews. QuickTime allows each movie to have two "abbreviated" representations: A *poster* is a single frame selected as being representative of a movie, a *preview* is a short video, typically of 1 to 3 seconds, again serving as a summary of the movie.

4.2 Temporal Composition and Time Information

A *movie* entity type may be composed of several correlated temporal values. The length of these values and their temporal correlation are described by *track* entity types. In some cases tracks are grouped into an intermediate *layer* entity. Layers are used for two different purposes: first, they support reuse of combinations of tracks, and second, layers allow the definition of *alternate groups*. In alternate groups, one, and only one, track is selected from the layer when the movie is played back. This is often used for audio information supplied in several languages within a movie. Another use of alternate groups occurs when a track is suitable for playback only in a certain environment.

To insure data independence of the various movie entities from the actual stored data, an entity type called *media* is introduced. The media entity type is responsible for the logical description of the physical data representation of a given temporal value. Since a specific media entity can be referenced in many different tracks, changes in, for example, the actual storage of data, need only be reflected in the media entity and not in all the tracks where it is used. Each track entity is derived from one media entity, so the connectivity of the relationship type is 1:n. Only track and media entity types refer to AV types and relationships between track and media entities can only be defined if the entities involved are of compatible AV types. The ER diagram describing the structural layout of these entity types is shown in Figure 4. In this figure, two special types of relationship are used: *t-comp* (temporal composition) and *is-derived* (entity derivation).

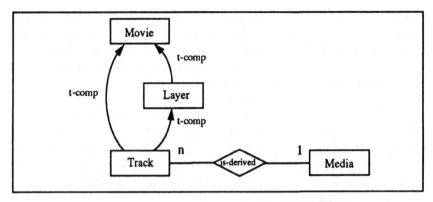

Figure 4 ER diagram for the Movie, Track and Media entity types.

Naturally, time has a major significance for time-based data, so we start with a description of how time is represented. Time-based data in general, refer to a time scale and a context in which it is evaluated (called a time coordinate system). The time scale defines the number of time units that pass per second in a given time coordinate system. For example, a time coordinate system with time scale 1 (D_1) measures time in seconds, while a time coordinate system having time scale 30 (D_{30}) would measure thirtieths of a second. A particular point in time in a time coordinate system is represented using a time value which is expressed in terms of the time scale of the underlying time coordinate system. Time coordinate systems (for movies and media) in this context are always considered to be finite and having a maximum value.

The movie, track and media entity types own attributes describing time information. However, only movie and media entities have their own time coordinate system (specified by a *Time Scale* attribute), whereas track entities depend upon the time system of the movie entity they take part in. Time values relating to a movie entity or a media entity refer to the entity's time scale and have to be between 0 and the duration of the movie or media entity. The origin of a movie entity is determined by the *Start Point* attribute, this refers to the time value at which playback commences. Table 1 compares the various time information attributes owned by these three entity types.

In addition, all three entity types own time attributes for keeping the information about *creation time* and *modification time* (these do not refer to movie or media time scales and therefore are not included in the table).

Movie	Track	Media
Duration	Duration	Duration
Time Scale		Time Scale
Start Point	Start Point	

Table 1 Summary of time information.

Example. To clarify the various dependencies between the movie, track and media entity types, entities of a specific example are presented. Consider a movie entity containing information about the city of Geneva and its sights. Information included is either still or moving video, or sound information. The movie is offered in three different languages: German, English, and French (see Figure 5). To keep movie productions flexible, each video scene is included in its own track, allowing for the rearrangement and insertion of new material since complete tracks can be re-grouped rather easily.

The entities comprising the Geneva movie are depicted in Figure 5. Attributes of the entities are used as headings. Only a small number of the attributes necessary to describe the various entities are shown in the example. In the tables that appear, rows refer to a single entity. The movie contains an alternate group out of which a specific language for playback can be selected.

4.3 Derivation Relationships

One of the main goals of a data model for audio/video data is to allow sharing of data among movies. To this end, a mechanism must be provided that supports modifications of the media values without influencing the use of the same data by others. Modifications of audio/video data in this context are limited to the change of sequence or the removal of unwanted subsequences. The mechanism for this purpose, called derivation, requires the definition of relationships between the various parts of a movie entity. In the discussion we will follow a bottom-up approach and start with the derivation of media samples from data samples.

4.3.1 Data-to-Media Derivation Relationships.

Generally, a temporal value is a sequence of elements. In QuickTime, these elements are called *media samples,* and each media entity defines a sequence of media samples. Media samples, the elements of the lowest level of temporal composition, are derived from data samples which may be video frames, images, or audio samples. The relationship between a media entity and actual data is not trivial. The ER diagram in Figure 4 shows the temporal composition of a movie. We use this diagram as the top level of a nested diagram and extend it by entity types and relationships for the definition of this derivation (Figure 6).

Within the media entity type a number of dependent entity types appear. These entity types are necessary for the specification of the derivation of a particular media entity and therefore depend upon its existence. The derivation has two purposes. It converts the physical location of a data sample into the media time coordinate system, and it allows selection and rearrangement of data samples in a sequence of media samples. The data-to-media relationship can be seen as a mapping from the media abstraction to physical storage, and so may be thought of as beyond the concern of logical data modelling. However, we believe it to be an important aspect of AV data modelling. In one sense, an AV value is simply a (very likely) large "blob" of data. It is not until a data-to-media mapping has been provided that it is possible to interpret this data as a sequence of audio or video samples (or perhaps a sequence in which these are interleaved). Thus it is the data-to-media mapping that provides the *semantics* of AV data – it identifies samples and specifies their ordering.

334

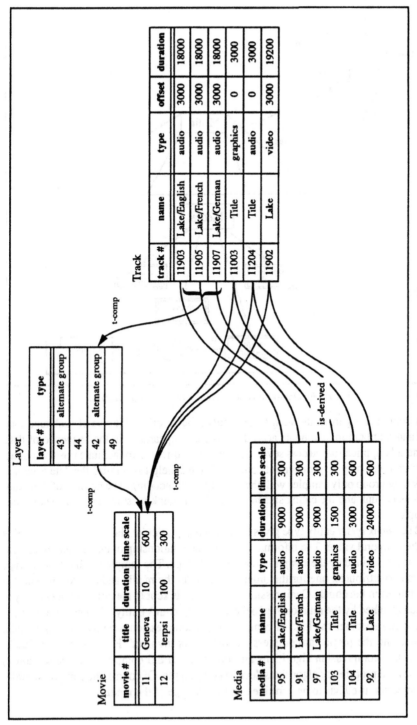

Figure 5 Instance diagram for temporal composition and derivation.

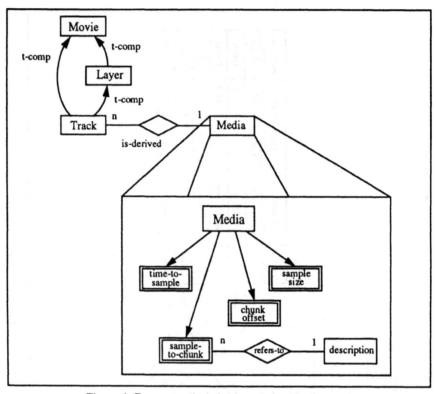

Figure 6 Data-to-media derivation relationship diagram.

Looking at Figure 6, the *sample size* entity type describes the size of each data sample and numbers the elements according to their appearance in the sequence of data. Generally applications access several samples in sequence. To facilitate this form of access, samples may be grouped into *chunks*. Chunks help to optimize the data access as they may group only samples with the same type of encoding. The number of data samples in a chunk and the chunk size may vary, but a chunk must include at least one data sample.

The *chunk offset* entity type gives the offset of a particular chunk from the beginning of the temporal value. The information about the relationship of chunks and data samples is maintained by the *sample-to-chunk* entity type. The sample-to-chunk entity type owns two attributes, one for the order of chunks in the media and one for the number of samples in the chunk. Compression information is kept in the *description* entity type which is linked by the relationship to the sample-to-chunk entity. The description entity essentially specifies the kind of compression/decompression used by a specific media sample and the particular compression parameters involved. For example, in Quick-Time, five compression algorithms are provided – JPEG compression (see section 2) and several proprietary algorithms developed by Apple. Of course, the compression/decompression used has to be permitted on the AV type of the media.

As the various samples in the media are referenced by media time only, a reference is necessary that allows the mapping of media time into sample location. This information is kept in the *time-to-sample* entity type. Entities of this type have two attributes, one giving the sample duration in media time and the other a sample span. As all entries in the table are ordered, an entry can describe several subsequent samples of the same duration. If all samples in the media have the same duration (which is the case for audio samples) the table would have one single entry, i.e. the number of samples and their duration in media time.

Information about chunks and samples is split over several entity types because sample size and chunk offset have entries for every instance of samples and chunks, respectively. Time-to-sample and sample-to-chunk entity types, however, do not require entries for each entity. Information in these tables can be aggregated according to the variation of sample duration or the number of samples belonging to a chunk.

Example. An example will explain the description of a media value by these entity types and the transformation of media time to data sample location in more detail. We refer to the example depicted in Figure 5 and consider the media *Lake*. The AV type of this media entity is video and video samples, in general, have varying durations due to the way they are compressed. A media entity specifies an ordering of the samples. Samples are grouped into chunks which are ordered as well. A media entity is illustrated in Figure 7, the entity contains eight samples distributed into five chunks. At the bottom of the figure the actual data value and the chunks chosen to derive the media sequence are illustrated. It can be seen that the order of the chunks in the stored data is not necessarily the same as the order of chunks in the media. This may be the result of a reordering, or it may be a natural consequence of the fact that certain compression schemes lead to intermixed samples (as in interframe encoding schemes where certain frames are interpolated from earlier and later "keyframes"). It should also be noticed that the "index" in both sequences is different. The index is a *data address* for the data samples and *time* for the media samples.

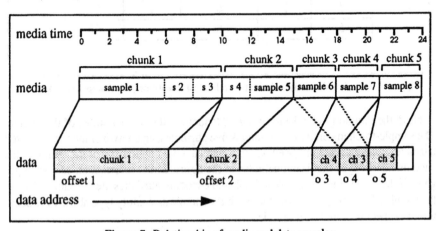

Figure 7 Relationship of media and data samples.

To specify this derivation, a number of entity types are relevant. Since samples in the media are referenced by time the sample number, first, has to be identified by accessing the time-to-sample entity. The entity has four attributes in this example: sample number, sample span, sample start time, and sample duration. Actually, not all of these attributes are necessary – the basic two attributes (see above) have been augmented by two derived attributes to increase understandability. As depicted in Figure 8, an entry for every media sample is not required. Samples with the same duration can be aggregated to one entry. Only the data of the first sample of this subsequence is kept in the table. The sample span indicates the number of samples with the same duration. This kind of aggregation requires only one entry, if the sample size is fixed.

Time-to-sample

sample number	sample span	sample start time	sample duration
1	1	0	6
2	3	6	2
5	4	12	3

Sample-to-chunk

chunk number	chunk span	start sample in chunk	samples/ chunk	encoding
1	1	1	3	E1
2	1	4	2	E1
3	2	6	1	E1
5	1	8	1	E2

Figure 8 Data / media sample derivation relationship entities (time/sample/chunk tables).

Next, the sample-to-chunk entity is used to identify the chunk number of the sample. The sample-to-chunk entity type contains five attributes, again, two of them are derived attributes. One attribute has been added to indicate the relationship of the chunk to the encoding entity type that is not depicted in the figure. Entity information can be aggregated if the values for the samples/chunk and encoding attributes are the same. Finally, the chunk offset entity type, together with the sample size entity type allow the allocation of a specific stored data sample.

4.3.2 Media-to-Track Derivation Relationships

As mentioned earlier, every track refers to exactly one media. In the media the references to data samples are defined. Out of these references a track may select only portions of data which are defined as instances of the *edit-list* entity type (Figure 9).

The edit-list entity stores information about the track time to media time mapping. Each list entry specifies a single "edit" and contains a track duration attribute, a media time attribute, a media rate field, and an identifier. The track duration field specifies the playing time for the edit. The media time field identifies where the edit occurs in the underlying media sequence. The rate attribute describes the rate at which the particular media is to be played. Tracks are independent of each other in the sense that they can be individually added, deleted or shifted within a movie. However, tracks within the same movie are temporally correlated, since they refer to the same time coordinate system (that of the movie) and playback must honour this correlation by maintaining synchronization.

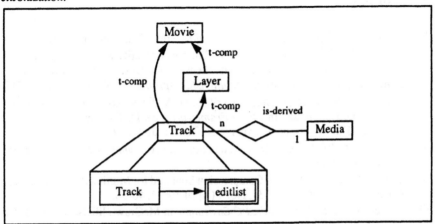

Figure 9   Media-to-track derivation relationship diagram.

4.3.3 Track-to-Movie Derivation Relationships

The derivation relationships between tracks and a movie are straightforward. There are only two issues which have to be taken into consideration: the computation of time and the identification of grouping. One essential issue for the derivation is the specification of active tracks. Only active tracks can take part in the playback of a movie. Out of an alternate group only one track can be active. For each track, a temporal offset specifies at which time after the movie has been started playback of the track is to begin.

5   Conclusion

This paper addresses general concepts for the modelling of audio/video data. Temporal sequences, quality factors, and two important abstractions, called temporal composition and entity derivation, are introduced to support the modelling task in this domain. Temporal composition denotes a special kind of aggregation based upon time. Derivation provides flexibility in editing and viewing AV data. Modelling concepts are applied to an AV format that is used by an existing software product for the definition, manipulation, and presentation of digital audio and video.

The advent of digital audio and video signifies a new challenge for the database community. The huge amount of storage required by the new data types, the control of shared data, and the retrieval of stored images, graphics, audio and video sequences require the employment of database management systems. The characteristics of time-based data, however, have not yet received sufficient consideration by this community. Audio/video data require the solution of several issues in database research, the extension of existing multimedia database features and the investigation of data modelling abstractions and data models.

References

[1]   Apple Corp., *QuickTime Developer's Guide*. Preliminary version, 1991.

[2]   Carlson, C. R., Ji W., and Arora, A. K. The Nested Entity-Relationship Model – A Pragmatic Approach to E-R Comprehension and Design Layout. *8th International Conference on the Entity-Relationship Approach*, Chicago 1989, 203-217.

[3]   Gibbs, S., Breiteneder, C., and Tsichritzis, D. Audio/Video Databases: An Object-Oriented Approach. In *Object Frameworks*, ed. D. Tsichritzis, Centre Universitaire d'Informatique, Université de Genève, July 1992.

[4]   Green, J. The Evolution of DVI System Software. *Commun. of the ACM*, Vol. 35, No. 1 (Jan. 1992), 53-67.

[5]   Le Gall, D. MPEG: A Video Compression Standard for Multimedia Applications. *Commun. of the ACM*, Vol. 34, No. 4 (April 1991), 46-58.

[6]   Luther, A. *Digital Video in the PC Environment*. McGraw-Hill, New York, 1991.

[7]   MacroMind Inc. *Director Studio Manual*, Version 3.0, 1991.

[8]   Microsoft Corp. *Microsoft Windows Multimedia Programmer's Workbook*, 1991.

[9]   Preston, J.M. (ed.) *Compact-Disc Interactive: A Designer's Overview*, Kluwer, Deventer NL, 1987.

[10]   Ripley, G.D. DVI – A Digital Multimedia Technology. *Commun. of the ACM*, Vol. 32, No. 7 (July 1989), 811-822.

[11]   Wallace, G.K. The JPEG Still Picture Compression Standard. *Commun. of the ACM*, Vol. 34, No. 4 (April 1991), 30-44.

SUPER - Visual Interaction with an Object-based ER Model

Annamaria Auddino, Yves Dennebouy, Yann Dupont, Edi Fontana,
Stefano Spaccapietra and Zahir Tari

Ecole Polytechnique Fédérale - DI - Laboratoire Bases de Données
IN - Ecublens   1015 Lausanne   Switzerland
auddino@elma.epfl.ch

Abstract

SUPER is a project aiming at the specification and development of a consistent set of visual user interfaces covering all phases of the database lifecycle.

In this paper we discuss the basic principles which, in our opinion, should underline a global approach to visual interaction with advanced data models. Visual interaction in SUPER environment is based on direct manipulation of objects and functions, providing users with maximum flexibility during schema definition as well as query formulation. Graphical interactions are easy to manage, and take advantage of the support of a simple but powerful modelling paradigm. Visual data manipulation is assertional and object-based. The environment offers multiple interaction styles, well-suited for various categories of users. Interaction styles are consistent over the various functions and editors.

To support the discussion, SUPER schema and query editors are analyzed, focusing on functionalities, and the underlying design choices, rather than precisely describing how they operate. An example of query formulation shows the rules used to govern interactions with users.

1 Introduction

Visual interaction had a drastical evolution during the eighties. WYSIWYG techniques (What You See Is What You Get) are nowadays standard for personal computing, while the WIMP metaphor (Windows, Icons, Menus, Pointing devices) governs user interaction with larger systems on workstations (and is moving into personal computing as well). Consequently, researchers try to master the many existing possibilities for human computer interaction. User Interface Management Systems (UIMS) are becoming popular as an answer to this question.

Despite this evolution, users of database management systems are still bound to classical textual languages, namely SQL. Although proposals for visual languages have been well known at least since 1975, thanks to QBE [37], research on visual interfaces still has to produce a global, recognized framework, consistent with the actual state of the art in data modelling techniques.

Indeed, graphical data definition techniques is the only area where a large consensus has been achieved on the marketplace. A number of tools exist, which offer graphical facilities for the definition of a database schema, according to concepts of the entity-relationship (ER) approach. They are eventually complemented with an automatic translation into a relational schema. Some tools also provide functionalities for describing application processes (usually through dataflow diagrams, sometimes with

Petri nets) and consistency checks. As far as we know, no commercial tool proposes a graphical manipulation language.

Several prototypes providing graphical DBMS interfaces have also been developed. Some of them only support graphical data definition: [8], [2]. DDEW [26] extends the definition process to all phases of database design, providing an integrated environment from user requirements to physical design. Some other tools provide both schema definition and visual querying facilities: ISIS [13], SNAP [6], [28], Pasta-3 [18, 19].

A few prototypes support visual data browsing, rather than query formulation: [21], ZOO [27], OdeView [1]. Finally, some prototypes only provide an aid for query formulation, to relieve users from constraints of textual syntax: [20], for instance, uses syntax graphs to guide users through the formulation of a relational query. Outside the scope of this presentation are toolkits for the design of graphical DBMS interfaces, like FaceKit [17], which belong to research in UIMS.

Existing prototypes can be classified according to the underlying data model (the following list of prototypes is not meant to be exhaustive):

- Entity-Relationship model: [8], [35], [36], [10], [21], [28], [26], [7], [14],[18], [9], [19];
- Object-Oriented model: [11], [27], [24], [17], [1];
- Semantic Data model: [16], [13], [6], [2];
- Relational model: [37], [15], [20], [23], [29].

The SUPER project is based on ERC+, an object-based extension of the entity-relationship model designed to support complex objects and object identity [33]. The goal of this project is to produce an integrated CASE tool (whose underlying model is ERC+) supporting interactions during all the life cycle of a database. To that extent, we first built a graphical definition and manipulation interface, providing users with a consistent approach to both functionalities. A data manipulation and a data browsing tool will deal with updates and navigation at the occurrences level.

Moreover, a view definition tool will allow users to build views over an existing schema. Conversely, a view integration tool will allow to build an integrated schema from a set of user views. This last tool will be the kernel of a future database design tool, covering, as in DDEW, the various phases in this activity. At this purpose, some others tools are planned for schema normalization, restructuring and evolution.

This global approach will provide the user with the same interaction paradigms all along his/her dialogs with the different components of the DBMS, during both design and operation on the database. Moreover, ERC+ modelling provides the user of a database with the same objects as the real world of interest to him/her.

It should be clear that the main concern of SUPER is to design clear, clean, easy, precise and uniform user interaction methods. SUPER may be used as a front-end to a relational or an object-oriented DBMS. It is not our aim to develop it as a self-contained complete DBMS.

The next section discusses the basic principles governing the design of DBMS user interfaces, and shows which choices have been made in SUPER. Section 3 briefly recalls the characteristics of the ERC+ approach, which will be used in the sequel to illustrate the functionalities of the graphical interface. Section 4 presents the main characteristics of the data definition interface (the schema editor), while section 5 gives an overview of how users can define queries on the database. Finally, the conclusion summarizes the main features of the project and presents future and ongoing extensions.

2 Guidelines for SUPER Interfaces

In the last decade, the need for user-friendly interfaces to large systems (including DBMSs), has generated numerous contributions to the topic. The field has grown mature enough to stress the importance of sound principles for the design of good interfaces (see [31], for instance). This section discusses some aspects we felt are of major concern for visual DBMS interfaces.

2.1 Direct Manipulation

The first goal in visual interfaces is to avoid the use of complex command languages. Some graphical conventions should be adopted, to make visible on the screen both the objects being manipulated and the functions used to manipulate them. Users may interact with the system through direct click and point specifications. This paradigm is known as *direct manipulation* [30] and it is a de facto standard for graphical, bit-mapped workstations provided with a multiwindowing system and a mouse.

The advantages of this approach are: first, users may permanently see the information they work on (for instance, the schema diagram). Secondly, users immediately see the impact of their actions through the visual representation. Finally, users can perform physical actions (like selecting and dragging an object) to modify the graphical representation, or activate dedicated functions (through menus, labelled buttons, dialog boxes and so on) to manipulate available application objects. A direct manipulation interface is easy to learn for novice users, easy to remember for occasional users (with knowledge of the domain of use) and rapid enough for expert users.

2.2 Unconstrained User Behavior

A second important goal is to provide users with freedom from having to follow a predefined pattern in their interaction with the system. Whenever actions are not atomic, the users should be allowed to start some action and move to another one without having completed the first one. Moreover, they should not be compelled to perform a set of actions in a predefined sequence.

Some of the existing prototypes do not adhere to this principle. For instance, the schema editor described in [8] forces users to complete a consistent specification of objects at creation time (e.g. entities with at least one attribute). Many graphical query languages (as the one described in [10] and QBD [7]) impose some fixed sequencing of steps, at least for building the query subschema and for its restructuring. Other interfaces do not explicitly state what are the built-in constraints. Only some less demanding interfaces allow users to leave definition of objects incomplete, as in Schemadesign [28] or in SNAP [6]. Pasta-3 supports a high degree of flexibility in user interactions.

SUPER fully supports unconstrained user behavior, both for schema editing and for query formulation. Each tool is responsible for checking user actions, ensuring the desired level of consistency among the actions.

2.3 Well-Suited Graphical Representations

There is no general agreement about what should be a good graphical representation for displaying schema diagrams, queries or data resulting from query evaluation.

Icons seem to be one of the most appealing visual representations. IBS [12] uses icons for representing object types. In SDMS [15] and SICON [14] icons are appropriately placed in a spatial framework, to browse data in an easy way.

Databases with a large number of object types require the users to memorize a large number of iconsand their manipulation can confuse users [31]. Moreover, when coping with many icons, their design is not an easy task. The result may be that an icon is meaningful for its designer, but not for users. Consequently, iconic languages may require as much, or even more, learning time than a textual representation.

Most of the existing prototypes based on semantic models (ER, SDM or IFO) use graphs to represent the conceptual schema of a database. However, they use different formalisms for schema diagrams. For instance, Pasta-3 [19] characterizes the type of nodes by a different character style (plain for entities, bold for relationships), instead of using different graphic symbols. Schemadesign uses the same graphical notation for multivalued attributes as for relationships, which can be rather misleading for users. In ZOO [27] knowledge is represented by a graph of icons, where edges are associated to either classes or objects and arcs represent the relationships between items. Again, users are confronted with the problem of distinguishing items through a large number of different icons.

Some prototypes use colors or patterns to display objects. For instance, GUIDE [35] represents with different colors partial queries embedded in a complex query. DDEW [26] uses different colors and patterns to express links cardinality. ISIS [13] associates to each class an unique fill pattern; this pattern can be used in an attribute definition to express its value class (i.e. a reference), with eventually a white border if the attribute is multivalued. However, the use of patterns is a little clumsy and not immediate for the user. As for icons, the automatic generation of patterns may cause problems when the number of classes becomes too large.

We took simplicity and minimality as guidelines. SUPER keeps the basic ER symbols: rectangles for entity types, diamond boxes for relationship types. Attributes are simply displayed as names attached to the parent object by a line (different line drawings are used according to cardinalities). Generalizations are shown with usual arrows. These symbols are well understood by users.

2.4 Multiple User Profiles

Human-computer interfaces should take into account the existence of several categories of users [31]. Novice or occasional users need basic functionalities accessible through easy to understand graphical displays. For data definition, for instance, these users will build small schemas, picking graphical symbols and putting them together as in a drawing tool. Expert users might favour the definition of a schema via menus and dialog boxes. Moreover, it should be possible to create a schema definition from a textual file imported from some other tool: in this case, the graphical approach is of no use.

To support diverse interaction styles, SUPER provides two modes of operation for schema definition, each mode having its associated window. The graphical mode is based on direct manipulation, while in the alphanumeric mode schema objects are defined through dialog boxes. There is no notion of "mode switch", as both modes are active in parallel: users may freely go from one to the other, any time during the interaction. When the graphical window is used, dialog boxes are prompted with default information, which users may change, if needed. If objects are defined in the alphanumeric mode, a corresponding diagram is automatically generated. Therefore, the two modes are equivalent, the schema editor keeping them synchronized: all visible representations of the same object are automatically updated when users modify its definition. These two representations are different ways to show the overall schema (i.e. they can both be used to display all available information). They are not complementary representations of different aspects of the schema.

Some of the existing DBMS interfaces do have a notion of mode switch and do not allow for a global view of the schema. For instance, in [2] users have to enter a textual environment to specify properties of classes, whereas classes and their relationships can be specified only in a graphical environment: the two representations are neither simultaneously displayed nor equivalent. In Schemadesign there are different modes for the definition of entities and relationships on the one side, and their properties on the other side. The ER graph and the inheritance lattice used by Pasta-3 are an example of complementary, but not equivalent representations of a diagram. ISIS provides several different views of a schema, as the so-called "inheritance forest view", in which all class definitions are displayed; users may expand an object into the associated semantic network by clicking on it. Again, the main shortcoming is the impossibility of having a simultaneous display of the two representations and even of the semantic networks associated to two different classes.

2.5 Consistent Paradigms

User interfaces should avoid different modes of operation, or different dialog styles, when switching from one function to the other. For instance, it is usual to base data manipulation on the same schema representation as the one used at schema definition time [35] [36] [10] [13] [6] [7] [9].

However, this kind of consistency is not always achieved. For instance, several interfaces use the ER paradigm for data modelling, while offering manipulation facilities which are close to those defined for relational databases, or presenting the resulting data as relational tuples rather than ER objects [10] [21] [7] [9]. Pasta-3 supports query formulation directly on the schema diagram, but also uses QUEL-like displays for predicates [18]. A consistency example may be found in SNAP, where the same formalism ("comparitor arcs") is used both for the conceptual schema and for predicate specification: however, only very simple predicates can be specified.

2.6 Assertional Data Manipulation

The experience from textual interfaces shows that assertional languages are to be preferred, w.r.t. procedural ones, especially for non expert users. Visual DBMS interfaces should therefore depart from requiring queries to be formulated as a strict sequence of operations (programming steps), to be executed in the order they are specified. In [9] queries are specified as a sequence of operators (graphical counterpart of an underlying algebraic language), which transform at each step the subschema into a new one. On the contrary, users should be allowed to independently specify the different components of their query. This not only alleviates the user's task, but also leaves the editor with the possibility of optimizing query processing. Moreover, users should be able any time to modify any stated part of the query, either to correct errors or to refine some incomplete specification. This seems to us the only way to put into practice, for data manipulation, the unconstrained user behavior principle.

2.7 Object Management

The evolution of modelling requirements has highlighted the need of keeping application objects when implemented onto a DBMS. According to the principle of consistent paradigms, data manipulation interactions should support objects, without making them vanish into a set of relations.

While in relational interfaces a query defines a single resulting relation, in object-based interfaces the resulting object type is an attribute tree showing only value attributes. As reference attributes bear object identities, they have to be replaced in the resulting structure by either an object identifier or the whole value of the referenced object (referenced object are embedded into the referencing one).

In visual database interfaces, the structure of the result is defined by building the so-called *query subschema*, i.e. the desired restriction of the underlying database schema. This subschema can be unambiguously interpreted if it has a hierarchical structure, with no cycles in it. If a cycle is kept, to express recursion, query formulation must explicitly state the path to follow to explore the cycle (linearization of the cycle).

Relational-like visual interfaces can support graphs as final query subschemas, as they produce the result by generating a flat join among all relations in the final graph [9]. Object-based interfaces transform the subschema into a hierarchy by identifying one of the object types in the subschema as the "root" of the query [10]. All other object types in the subschema are accordingly turned into attributes of the root object type. SUPER follows this strategy (with appropriate refinements, as discussed in § 5.2).

3. The ERC+ Model

ERC+ is an object-based extension of the entity-relationship model, specifically designed to support complex objects and object identity. Object types may bear any number of attributes, which may in turn, iteratively, be composed of other attributes. The structure of an object type may thus be regarded as an multiple attribute tree. Attribute complexity and multivaluation express the usual product and set constructs of the object-oriented approach, with the advantage that they may simultaneously apply at the same node. Attributes, entities and relationships may be valued in a multiset (i.e. not excluding duplicates). An object identity is associated to entities and relationships, i.e. different instances may have exactly the same values for their attributes. Two generalization relationships are supported on entities: the classical "is-a" and an additional "may-be-a" relationships [32]. The former corresponds to the well-known generalization concept; the latter has the same semantics, but does not require an inclusion dependency between the subtype and the type. A complete discussion of the features of the model may be found elsewhere [33] [32].

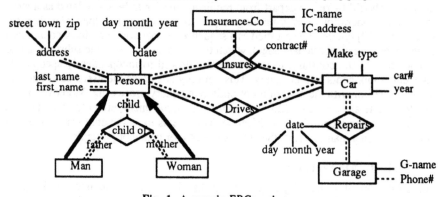

Fig. 1. A sample ERC+ schema

Figure 1 shows a sample ERC+ diagram; a single continuous line is used to represent a 1:1 link, a single dotted line represents a 0:1 link, a double dotted line represents a

0:n link, a double line (once dotted, once continuous) represents a 1:n link. Arrows represent generalizations.

Formal manipulation languages (an algebra and an equivalent calculus [25]) have been defined. The functionalities provided by the algebraic operators include the classical operations of *projection* and *selection* on one entity type and *union* of two entity types.Specific to ERC+ is the *reduction* operator, which allows the elimination of the values of an attribute not satisfying a given predicate. Most important is the relationship-join (*r-join*, in short) operator. If E1, E2, ..., En is the set of entity types linked by a relationship type R, the r-join of E1 with E2, ..., En via R builds a new entity type (and the corresponding population) with the same attributes as E1 plus an additional attribute, named R, whose components are the attributes of R, E2, ..., En. A *spe-join* operator allows the joining of entity types participating into a given generalization.

Every operation results in the creation of a new entity type, with its attributes, relationships and population derived from the operands through specific rules. Operations may thus be combined into expressions of arbitrary complexity.

4 Schema Editor

The schema editor is a visual data definition interface, providing two modes for schema definition. Each mode has a separate display window, identified by the name of the schema being edited and labelled by the corresponding operation mode. Users may work simultaneously on several schemas with different modes. In the *graphical* mode, the designer builds an ERC+ diagram by direct manipulation. The user picks the graphical symbols from a palette and positions them into the workspace provided in the associated window. The symbols in the palette correspond to ERC+ constructs (entity, relationship, link, attribute, generalization). In the *alphanumeric* mode, forms-like representations of ERC+ constructs (called *object boxes*) are provided by the editor for entering data definitions. Different object boxes are shown in figure 2.

Standard editing operations are available through pull-down menus. "Schema", "Edit" and "Dictionaries" menus are available in both windows, and provide the same functionalities. The "Schema" menu contains the usual operations for opening, saving, creating a schema. The "Edit" menu offers cut, copy and paste facilities, as well as undo and redo. The "Dictionaries" menu gives access to a global dictionary or any of the specialized dictionaries (entities, relationships, attributes). The "Options" menu in the graphical window contains purely graphical manipulations (changing the layout, rearrange object disposal, etc.) and is therefore specific to this window. Conversely, functionalities for creating a new schema (or modifying an existing one) are provided in the "Creation" menu when in the alphanumeric mode. They are equivalent to the definition of schema elements through the graphical palette.

4.1 Information Display

Figure 2 shows the schema diagram for a hypothetical application for an Insurance company. Each object in the diagram has been created by first selecting the corresponding graphical symbol in the palette and then clicking in the workspace to position the object. Creating an object displays the corresponding object box (alternatively, it may be displayed using the alphanumeric Creation menu). Newly created objects receive a standard name, which can be changed in the corresponding alphanumeric object box. An object box contains text entry areas (e.g. object's name and comment), radio buttons for predefined choices (cardinality specification, for instance) and list-bars referring to objects directly attached to the current object. The entity box (Person) in figure 2 shows list-bars for attributes, links and generalizations defined on an entity type. A list-bar for components of a complex attribute is included in the attribute box (address). List-bars have been chosen as a standard technique to link objects. Clicking on a list-bar displays the corresponding scrollable list of attached objects. Two such lists are shown in figure 2, one for links on the Person entity type, one for components of the address attribute.

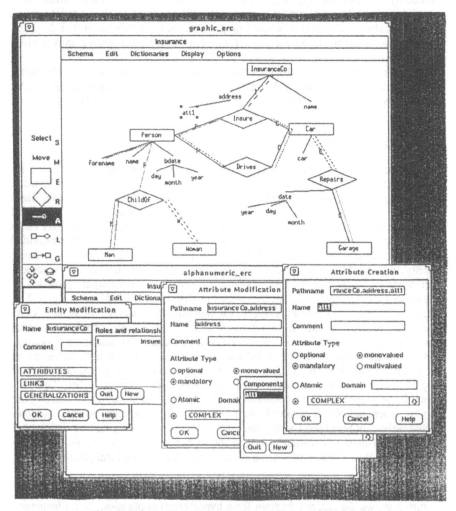

Fig. 2. Screen display showing schema editor windows
(after creation of a new attribute, whose default name is att1)

Lists have a standard behavior. They group objects of the same type, attached to the same parent element (the latter is the schema for dictionary lists). Clicking on an object in a list displays its object box. Clicking on the New button in the list box displays an empty object box for adding a new object to the list. Using object boxes, list-bars and the attached lists, users may navigate through the schema and add or modify objects as needed. Top-down definition strategies are very easily performed.

ERC+ diagrams are stored with spatial information, so that the diagram may be later displayed as it was at creation time. For schemas defined in the alphanumeric mode, SUPER automatically builds and displays the corresponding diagram. As governing this process is a complex task, our implementation leaves it up to the users to adjust the diagram if they dislike it. For readability, the user may hide attributes.

Flexibility in the schema design process is enhanced by the possibility to leave object definitions incomplete. Users may, for instance, define entity types, and come back later to these objects to attach attributes or add generalizations. Incomplete schema definitions may be saved and reused in another session. At any time, a validation function may be activated to check whether the actual schema definition is consistent with model rules. If inconsistencies or incompleteness are detected, they are reported to the user. However, some model rules have to be permanently enforced (uniqueness of entity names, for instance) in order to avoid ambiguities.

Finally, users may quit the editor any time. When they continue schema editing, their work on the schema is reactivated in exactly the same state as it was at the time of interruption.

4.2 Flexibility, Reusability and Backtracking

Besides the above usual editing functions, SUPER includes the additional facilities of redundancy, reusability and backtracking to make users' task as easy as possible.

Redundancy is intended to provide flexibility. It allows the users to view their schema through two equivalent representations. Accordingly, some functionalities have been implemented redundantly, so that users may access them directly through the representation they are using. For instance, an object may be created graphically, or in several alternative ways in the alphanumeric mode. A new attribute, for instance, can be created either by activating the Creation menu, or clicking on the New button in the attribute list attached to its parent object. Whichever way is used, it will result in displaying an attribute creation box, where users will enter the attribute definition.

This kind of flexibility is sometimes criticized as being confusing for users. We believe it might indeed be confusing if the alternatives appear within a single context, with users not having a criteria to choose from. On the contrary, if the alternatives are provided along different paths, it avoids the burden of explicitly moving from the context they are in to the context which provides the desired function.

Reusability allows the users to reuse definitions of objects in the current schema or in another schema. *Cut, copy* and *paste* operations may be used to move an object, delete it, or create a similar object elsewhere. The object here may be a single object (an entity type, ...), or a collection of objects (a set of attributes may be copied from various existing objects and in one shot attached to an entity type), or a subschema (a set of interrelated objects obeying some given model constraints: for instance, no isolated attributes, links and generalizations must be with their source and target objects). A *duplicate* operation is provided. It creates an object identical to the original one and bearing the same connections.

Finally, backtracking is supported through *undo* and *redo* operations. This allows the users to recover from erroneous actions and restore the previous state. Typically, if a user clicks on a Cancel button instead of the nearby OK button, all actions performed on the object would be lost. By undoing the erroneous click, he/she will get a second chance.

4.3 Browsing

The current version of SUPER supports schema browsing. Users may scroll the schema diagram to display the desired part of it. The alphanumeric mode allows schema browsing by navigation from one object to another through existing connections in between. This navigation may use object boxes (as shown in figure 2) to allow user to see all informations about the objects on the path. A similar navigation may also be performed using a simultaneous display of the various dictionary lists. For instance, the selection of an entity type in the entity types list will automatically display its attributes, relationships and generalizations or specializations, if any, in the corresponding list. However, the only information users get in such a navigation are the names of the objects. To know more about a specific object, users have to click on its entry in the appropriate list, to activate its object box (the information contained in the object box is then only available for inspection, to prevent conflict between different actions on the same object).

5 Query Editor

This section discusses the features concerning query formulation in the SUPER environment. For more details about the query editor, see [4]. The steps which compose this process are the following:
- *Selecting the query subschema*: the portion relevant to the query is extracted from the database schema.
- *Creating the query structure*: the subschema is transformed into a hierarchical structure (as discussed in § 2.7).
- *Specifying predicates*: predicates are stated on database occurrences, so that only relevant data is selected.
- *Formatting the output*: the editor is provided with data items to be included into the structure of the result;
- *Displaying resulting data*.

The whole process may be rather complex, and therefore difficult to master for novice users. As these users are the main target of visual interfaces, we believe that visual query languages should take advantage of the above multistep structure. Indeed, clear separation between the steps alleviates users' mental load and improves the chances of correct formulation. The sequence of steps is logically meaningful: for instance, predicates cannot be defined before the query subschema is determined. Users can any time modify any stated part of the query to correct or refine the current formulation.
SUPER implements step separation, by using the following specific windows for the different steps:
- the *database schema* (DBS) window is a read-only window used to display the diagram corresponding to a schema (figure 3);
- the *working schema* (WS) window displays the subschema, extracted by the user, relevant for a query (figure 5);
- the *selection window* (SW) displays the structure of the resulting entity type, and it is used for expressing predicates and the attributes to be kept in the result (figure 6);
- the *result window* (RW) displays the set of resulting occurrences (figure 8).

5.1 Selecting the Query Subschema

This step configures the schema to contain only those objects which are involved in the query (equivalent to an "open subschema ..." command in textual languages). The DBS window is used to extract the query subschema through a sequence of "point and click" specifications. To speed up this process, the semantics of the clicks can be tailored either as "keep" or as "delete" the designated object. Implicit designation is sometimes used: gql/ER [36], for instance, automatically adds to the query subschema the path in between two selected objects (in case of multiple paths, the "most likely" one is chosen). QBD [7] uses a similar technique, which can be refined with additional constraints (on the length of the path, for instance). It also allows predicates on attribute names to select all entity types with such attributes.

In SUPER, the "point and click" specifications copy objects in the WS window. The user can choose between a traditional *Copy-Paste* mode (objects are copied without relating them to objects already in the WS) and an *Expand* mode, where objects are copied and connected to a start entity type previously selected in the WS window.

Some automatic selection is embedded in SUPER. If the user clicks on a role, the complete relationship type is transferred in the WS. If the relationship is binary, the start entity type changes to the new one. Clicking on a distant object is possible if there is a smallest path to the object. For instance, the user cannot click on a relationship which has two roles leading to the start entity type.

5.2 Restructuring the Query Subschema

Once a query subschema is defined, proper query formulation may start. However, some interfaces introduce an additional step, to transform the subschema into a specific pattern. In [10] the query subschema is transformed into a hierarchical structure. The root of the hierarchy is selected by user. [21] follows the same approach, but the transformation is complemented with a generation of nested forms, visualizing the hierarchical structure. QBD provides a query-like transformation language for schema modification.

In SUPER, graphical data manipulations are based on the underlying ERC+ algebra. The result of a query is a syntactical tree whose root is an entity with constraints expressed as predicates. In [4] we discuss the use of tree representation of queries.

In our editor, the user identifies the root of a query hierarchy. A graph in a tree is transformed by first removing cycles. The removal of cycles could not be an automatic process as there are many interpretations of the cycle itself.

In the SUPER query editor, the user can break cycles by removing some vertices or some nodes of the graph or by disconnecting some links. *Disconnection* means that the designated link is detached from the linked entity type and attached to a (newly automatically created) copy of that entity type.

Another facility, *pruning*, is used to remove objects (attributes, entity types, ...) which are not used in the query, i.e.appearing neither in the format of the result nor in a predicate. There are some additional facilities like the product to create an artificial link between two entities.

5.3 Specifying the Predicates

Once the user has created a correct query structure, the corresponding hierarchy is displayed in the SW as a single entity type with all other informations as attributes. Appropriate modifications, if needed, can be made in the SW; otherwise, the user will proceed with the specification of predicates.

Predicates against complex objects may be rather clumsy. For the simplest ones (comparison of a monovalued attribute with a constant) a graphical counterpart may easily be defined. A simple specification technique is to click on the attribute, select a comparison operator from a menu, and finally type the value or choose one from a list. For complex predicates (involving several quantifiers, for instance), there might be no simple way to express it graphically. Menus are sometimes used for syntactic editing of predicates ([10] or ISIS [13]). In gql/ER, QBE-like forms are used to specify conditions on the selected nodes. Only a few interfaces use a graphical formalism for expressing predicates (see, for instance, Pasta-3 [18] or SNAP [6]).

In this paper we focus on functionalities, instead of discussing the best graphical solution for predicate specification. A predicate is any logical expression involving attributes of the entity type resulting from the previous step. The predicate implements the selection operator if it is attached to the root or the reduction operator if it is attached to an attribute. The domain of a predicate is the set of quantified variables.

Predicates are expressed by using a *predicate box* associated to the root of the hierarchy. Subpredicates are automatically generated when the user designates the attributes involved in the predicate. By default (as in Pasta-3), the equality operator is used for clauses and the existential quantifier is assumed for multivalued attributes. Every attribute which appears several times in one or several predicates is duplicated as many times in the SW. This is the graphical counterpart of the use of variables in textual languages.

Evaluation of the predicates can be done in any order. Each intermediate step usually builds a potential query that can be interpreted (a syntactic validation) and executed (a semantic validation on an existing database) in the fourth window.

5.4 Formatting the Output

By default, the SW defines the structure of the resulting entity type. However, the users may wish to discard some of the attributes, kept up to now only because of some predicate to be defined on them. The SW has to provide for a "hide" (or, conversely, "show") operation, to define which attributes are to be discarded (or kept in). The hiding (or the showing) of a complex attribute also hides (or shows) all its component attributes.

5.5 Displaying Resulting Data

The last phase is the display of instances representing the result of the query. SUPER displays resulting entities according to their hierarchical structure, into a nested tabular form (NT mode) or into an entities browser form (EB mode). Users can choose between the two kinds of presentation through a switch mode radio button.

Relational interfaces display occurrences in a tabular form. SNAP provides the user with the choice between the tabular format and a NF^2 format, where occurrences are arranged into "buckets". [21] uses the nested forms representation to display the results of data browsing. GUIDE [35] and VGQF [23] allow the user to choose among different formats. In OdeView [1] complex objects can be displayed through a text or picture representation; the user can click on buttons to display all related objects.

5.7 Additional Facilities

Additional functionalities supported by SUPER allow to store queries for later reuse or modification, as well as evaluation of partial queries. The latter is useful for query debugging. Suppose the user is confronted with a result different from what was expected, without recognizing what is the problem within the formulation. The query can be broken into two or more separate queries by disconnecting some links. Independent evaluation of the subqueries can be performed to identify what changes have to be made. After this refinement, the original, corrected query can easily be rebuilt by unification of the duplicated entity types created by the previous disconnection.

5.8   A Sample Query

This section illustrates the process of query formulation in SUPER. Let us assume the user wants to formulate the following query:

Select name and address of people who insure a 1984 Ford

on the schema of figure 1. The corresponding diagram will be displayed in the DBS window. The corresponding diagram will be displayed in the database window. The user begins by picking the relationship type Insures, that will be copied into the WS window, together with the linked entity types (Person, Insurance-Co and Car) and all their attributes (figure 3).

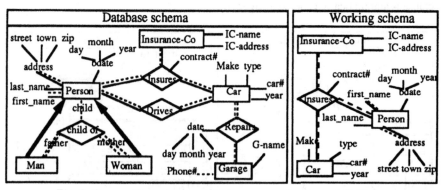

Fig. 3. Query editor windows showing query subschema definition

Next, assume the user designates Person as the root of the hierarchy. Figure 4 shows the contents of the selection window.

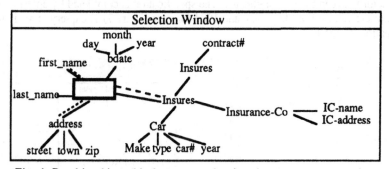

Fig. 4. Resulting hierarchical structure, showing the root as an empty box

The resulting structure contains many attributes the user is not interested in. Consequently, he/she will return to the WS window and prune unnecessary objects.

The attributes name and address of Person are needed for result display, while **Make** and year of entity Car will be used for predicate specification. Pruning will change the contents of windows, as shown in figure 5.

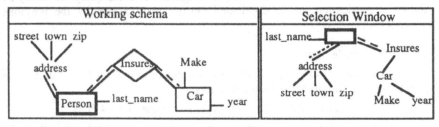

Fig. 5. The updated query subschema and corresponding hierarchical structure

The definition of a predicate is made through a predicate box, displayed in the SW. The user designates the attributes (Make and year) involved in the predicate. As the Insures attribute (to which Make belongs) is multivalued, a modifiable "exist Insures" clause is automatically generated (figure 6).

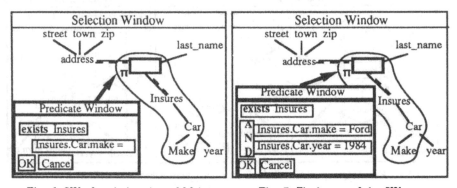

Fig. 6. SW after designation of Make   **Fig. 7.** Final state of the SW

While designating the second attribute (year) the user also has to specify the logical connector between the two predicates. The specification is completed by entering the appropriate values: Ford for Make and 1984 for year (figure 7).The query is ready for evaluation (figure 8).

	address			
last_name	street	town	zip	
Deneuve	Regent St	London	GB-1001	
	Taft Ave.	Loveland	CO-80535	
Hey	74 Burnet Rd	Austin	TX 78750	
	Taylor Hall	Austin	TX 78712	
Yamayoto	6 Kagusha	Fukuoka	JP-816	

Fig. 8. Result of the evaluated query in the entities browser and the nested tabular form

6 Conclusion

Development of good and powerful visual interfaces is a major current challenge for database system designers. Despite an important investment of research efforts in the general domain of user interfaces, database users are still confronted with textual languages for their interaction with a DBMS. Most of the tools available on the marketplace are limited to data definition facilities. For graphical data manipulation, a few prototypes have been developed to support modern, object-based modelling approaches. However, they do not seem to consistently support all of the desired functionalities. For these reasons we believe more research and experiments are needed to fulfill the goals attached to visual interfaces.

The development of the SUPER environment is intended as a contribution in this direction. Our aim is to use well specified paradigms, consistently over all the phases related to database operation. This includes, of course, data definition and data manipulation, but also considers database design activities, with a particular emphasis on view definition and view integration.

Visual interaction in SUPER environment is based on direct manipulation of objects and functions, providing users with maximum flexibility during schema definition as well as query formulation. Graphical interactions are easy to manage, and take advantage of the support of a simple but powerful modelling paradigm. Visual data manipulation is assertional and object-based. The environment offers multiple interaction styles, well-suited for various categories of users.

The schema editor has been implemented in C++, in a UNIX environment (Sun workstations), complemented with the user interface InterViews [22]. The SUPER environment implementation is based on a toolbox approach. This approach is discussed in [3]. The query editor is currently being implemented. For more details about the architecture of the SUPER environment, see [5].

The next step concerns the specification of a view definition graphical facility. Its first goal will be to allow users to define views over an existing schema. Secondly, we intend to develop a similar tool for definition of views in the initial phase of database design, as a formal way to express user requirements. These views will be used as input to an integration tool, which will automatically perform their integration according to explicitly defined interview correspondences [34]. Finally, more tools will be specified to cover the other phases of the database design process.

Acknowledgments

The authors are indebted to Prof. Bharat Bhargava and Prof. Kokou Yétongnon for many useful suggestions to previous versions of this paper. They also want to express their gratitude to Claude Vanneste and Bull France for their cooperation in the ergonomics of SUPER editors.

References

[1]   R. Agrawal, N. H. Gehani, J. Srinivasan: "OdeView: The Graphical Interface to Ode", in *Proc. of ACM SIGMOD '90, Int'l Conf. on Management of Data*, pp. 34-43, Atlantic City, 1990

[2]   A. Albano, L. Alfò, S. Coluccini, R. Orsini: "An Overview of Sidereus, a Graphical Database Schema Editor for Galileo", in *Advances in Database*

Technology - EDBT '88, J. W. Schmidt, S. Ceri, M. Missikof eds., Springer-Verlag, pp. 567-571, 1988

[3]   A. Auddino, E. Amiel, B. Bhargava: "Experiences with SUPER, a Database Visual Environment", in *Proc. of the 2nd Int'l Conf. on Database and Expert Systems Applications - DEXA '91*, pp. 172-178, Berlin, 1991

[4]   A. Auddino, Y. Dennebouy, Y. Dupont, E. Fontana, S. Spaccapietra, Z. Tari: "SUPER: A Comprehensive Approach to Database Visual Interfaces", in *Proc. of IFIP WG 2.6 2nd Working Conf. on Visual Database Interfaces*, pp. 359-374, Budapest, 1991

[5]   A. Auddino, E. Amiel, Y. Dennebouy, Y. Dupont, E. Fontana, S. Spaccapietra, Z. Tari: "Database Visual Environments based on Advanced Data Models", in *Proc. of the Int'l Workshop on Visual Interfaces - AVI '92*, pp.., Rome, 1992

[6]   D. Bryce, R. Hull: "SNAP, a Graphics-Based Schema Manager", in *Proc. of the 2nd IEEE Int'l Conf. on Data Engineering*, pp. 151-164, Los Angeles, 1986

[7]   T. Catarci, G. Santucci: "Query by Diagram: A Graphic Query System", in *Proceedings of the 7th Int'l Conf. on Entity-Relationship Approach*, pp. 157-174, Rome, 1988

[8]   E. Chan, F. Lochovsky: "A Graphical Database Design Aid Using the Entity-Relationship Model", in *Entity-Relationship Approach to Systems Analysis and Design*, North-Holland, pp. 259-310, 1980

[9]   B. Czejdo, R. Elmasri, D. W. Embley, M. Rusinkiewicz: "A Graphical Data Manipulation Language for an Extended Entity-Relationship Model", *IEEE Computer*, Vol. 23, No. 3, pp. 26-36, March 1990

[10] R. A. Elmasri, J. A. Larson: "A Graphical Query Facility for ER Databases", in *Entity-Relationship Approach - The Use of ER Concept in Knowledge Representation*, P. P. Chen ed., North-Holland, 1985, pp. 236-245

[11] D. H. Fishman et al.: "Iris: An Object-Oriented Database System", *ACM Transactions on Office Information Systems*, Vol. 5, No. 1, pp. 48-69, January 1987

[12] C. Frasson, M. Er-radi: "Principles of an Icons-Based Command Language", in *Proc. of ACM SIGMOD '86, Int'l Conf. on Management of Data*, pp. 147-151, Washington, 1986

[13] K. J. Goldman, S. A. Goldman, P. C. Kanellakis, S. B. Zdonik: "ISIS, Interface for a Semantic Information System", in *Proc. of ACM SIGMOD '85, Int'l Conf. on Management of Data*, pp. 328-342, Austin, 1985

[14] I. P. Groette, E. G. Nilsson: "SICON, an Iconic Presentation Module for an E-R Database", in *Proc. of the 7th Int'l Conf. on Entity-Relationship Approach*, pp. 137-155, Rome, 1988

[15] C. F. Herot: "Spatial Management of Data", *ACM Transactions on Database Systems*, Vol. 5, No. 4, pp. 493-514, December 1980

[16] R. King, S. Melville: "SKI: A Semantics-Knowledgeable Interface", in *Proc. of the 10th Int'l Conf. on Very Large Databases*, pp. 30-33, Singapore, 1984

[17] R. King, M. Novak: "FaceKit: A Database Interface Design Toolkit", in *Proc. of the 15th Int'l Conf. on Very Large Data Bases*, pp. 115-123, Amsterdam, 1989

[18] M. Kuntz, R. Melchert: "Pasta-3's Graphical Query Language: Direct Manipulation, Cooperative Queries, Full Expressive Power", in *Proc. of the 15th Int'l Conf. on Very Large Data Bases*, pp. 97-105, Amsterdam, 1989

[19] M. Kuntz, R. Melchert: "Ergonomic Schema Design and Browsing with More Semantics in the Pasta-3 Interface for E-R DBMSs", in *Entity-Relationship*

Approach to Database Design and Querying, F. Lochovsky ed., North-Holland, 1990

[20] J. Larson, J. B. Wallick: "An Interface for Novice and Infrequent Database Management System Users", in *AFIPS Conference Proceedings, National Computer Conference*, vol. 53, pp. 523-529, 1984

[21] J. Larson: "A Visual Approach to Browsing in a Database Environment", *IEEE Computer*, vol. 19, no. 6, pp. 62-71, June 1986

[22] M. A. Linton, J. M. Vlissides, P. R. Calder: "Composing User Interfaces with InterViews", *IEEE Computer*, vol. 22, no. 2, pp. 8-22, February 1989

[23] N. H. McDonald: "A MultiMedia Approach to the User Interface", in *Human Factors and Interactive Computer Systems*, Y. Vissiliou ed., Ablex Publishing Corp., 1984, pp. 105-116

[24] A. Motro, A. D'Atri, L. Tarantino: "The Design of KIVIEW: An Object-Oriented Browser", in *Proc. of the 2nd Int'l Conf. on Expert Database Systems*, pp. 17-31, Tysons Corner, 1988

[25] C. Parent, H. Rolin, K. Yétongnon, S. Spaccapietra: "An ER Calculus for the Entity-Relationship Complex Model", in *Entity-Relationship Approach to Database Design and Querying*, F. Lochovsky ed., North-Holland, 1990

[26] D. Reiner et al.: "A Database Designer's Workbench", in *Entity-Relationship Approach*, S. Spaccapietra ed., North-Holland, 1987, pp. 347-360

[27] W.-F. Riekert: "The ZOO Metasystem: A Direct Manipulation Interface to Object-Oriented Knowledge Bases", in *Proc. of European Conf. on Object-Oriented Programming - ECOOP '87*, pp. 145-153, Paris, 1987

[28] T. R. Rogers, R. G. G. Cattell: "Entity-Relationship Database User Interfaces", in *Proc. of the 6th Int'l Conf. on Entity-Relationship Approach*, pp. 323-335, New York, 1987

[29] L. A. Rowe, P. Danzig, W. Choi: "A Visual Shell Interface to a Database", *Software - Practice and Experience*, vol. 19, no. 6, pp. 515-528, June 1989

[30] B. Shneiderman: "Direct Manipulation: A Step Beyond Programming Languages", *IEEE Computer*, vol. 16, no. 8, pp. 57-69, August 1983

[31] B. Shneiderman, *Designing the User Interface - Strategies for Effective Human-Computer Interaction*, Addison-Wesley, 1987

[32] S. Spaccapietra, C. Parent, K. Yétongnon, M. S. Abaidi: "Generalizations: A Formal and Flexible Approach", in *Management of Data*, N. Prakash ed., Tata McGraw-Hill, 1989, pp. 100-117

[33] S. Spaccapietra, C. Parent: "ERC+: an Object-based Entity-relationship Approach", in *Conceptual Modelling, Databases and CASE: an Integrated View of Information Systems Development*, P. Loucopoulos, R. Zicari eds., John Wiley, 1992

[34] S. Spaccapietra, C. Parent: "View Integration: A Step Forward in Solving Structural Conflicts", *IEEE Transactions on Data and Knowledge Engineering*, 1992

[35] H. K. T. Wong, I. Kuo: "GUIDE: Graphic User Interface for Database Exploration", in *Proc. of the 8th Int'l Conf. on Very Large Databases*, pp. 22-32, Mexico City, 1982

[36] Z. Q. Zhang, A. O. Mendelzon: "A Graphical Query Language fort Entity-Relationship Databases", in *Entity-Relationship Approach to Software Engineering*, Davis et al. eds., North-Holland, 1983, pp. 441-448

[37] M. M. Zloof: "Query By Example", in *AFIPS Conference Proceedings, National Computer Conference*, vol. 44, pp. 431-438, 1975

Natural Language Restatement of Queries Expressed in a Graphical Language

Gabriella Bono and Paolo Ficorilli

Dipartimento di Informatica e Sistemistica
Università degli Studi di Roma "La Sapienza"
Via Salaria 113, 00198 Roma, Italy

Abstract. Various works have been proposed to simplify the interaction between casual users and databases. Too powerful tools, however, can cause the user to lose control of the many operations performed. A natural language restatement of the query has seemed the best way to assure the user about the accuracy of the formulation of his/her intents. The result of this work has been the individuation of general criteria to obtain natural languages restatements from a single query expressed in a graphical language on Entity-Relationship schemas.

1 Introduction

During the last decade several institutes have worked at the realization of user-friendly interfaces in order to endow general users with easy instruments to investigate a database, such as hierarchical view [1], value of the data [2], extended Entity-Relationship Model [3] or network of entity and relationship kinds [4].

Starting from this, the research has been continued in the field of natural language. For example, ERROL [5] is a query language within the Entity Relationship Model (ERM) [6] that takes advantage of the possibilities posed by the linguistic analogies of the ERM by using constructs similar to the natural language sentence combination. The role that an entity set plays in a relationship set is labeled with a verb. These verbs are then used for unambiguous queries. DESPATH [7] is a data manipulation language for another variation of the ERM in which relationships are given meaning via a pair of predicates. These predicates are invariably labeled using verb phrases.

As far as it regards Italian, such prototypes seem to be absent, although studies have been done in semantic interpretation of natural language [8, 9] and in malformation of sentences [10].

To obviate those deficiencies, a system has been built to guide the user through a natural language restatement of queries expressed in a graphical language. This system has characteristics that can be explained via the following several steps to rendezvous with the casual user [11]:

1. A simple data model, the ERM, has been selected.
2. A high level logic as internal target, which always produces well-formed, complete, unambiguous and meaningful queries, QBD*, has been used.
3. A way to assure the user that the system has interpreted the user's intent correctly and that the user has well-expressed his/her own intent has been studied. The chosen check is that of synthesizing, from the formal query, a

precise restatement of the user's query in a natural language system. It should be noted that the system does not build long sentences in order to obtain natural language restatements as legible as possible. The study of previous similar works [12] has proved that this is the way to obtain a good compromise between natural language and readability.

4. Query formulation has been separated from database search. The actual search for the desired data is commenced only after the user and the system are in complete agreement on the user's intent. For this reason the user can always see the natural language restatement of the query in order to have both a complete knowledge of what he is handling and the possibility for correcting possible mistakes before saving and executing the query. Some diagnostic messages have been introduced for this purpose, for example to inform the user that his query will not visualize any attribute in the final result. An other aim of the restatement is that of helping the user to understand the meaning of the database when he sees it for the first time and to guide him during the formulation of complex intertwined queries that involve the same concepts more than once.

This paper is organized as follows: section 2 presents QBD* architecture. Section 3 shows the structure of a sentence. Section 4 presents some short cuts, which are important to reduce the number of words that are in a sentence, with obvious attention to not lose important information. In Section 5 some aspects of the prototype are discussed and finally, in Section 6, the conclusions and some future developments are presented.

2 The Graphical Language QBD*

This section presents a general overview of the system [13]. We assume that the DBMS is based on the relational model, although this is not a strict requirement.
The general architecture of the system is based on three main modules:

1. The Graphical Interface enables the user to query the database. The query is expressed on an E-R schema and is built using the graphical commands available in the interface.
2. The Translator analyzes the queries and, using the target (relational) schema, translates the non-recursive queries into relational algebra expressions, and the recursive ones into programs in a host language.
3. The DBMS Interface translates the algebraic expression into a query formulated in terms of the target DBMS.

During the query formulation activity, the user is provided with a large set of facilities. In fact, the user may first interact with the conceptual schema to understand its information content by means of a *top-down browsing* mechanism; then, using the location primitives, she/he may extract the subschema containing the concepts involved in the query (schema of interest). During this phase, the user may perform transformations on the schema of interest, by means of replacing primitives, bringing it "close to the query"; in this way, a (temporary or permanent) user view, which may be helpful in the subsequent activities of query formulation, is built. Finally, the user may resort to the navigational primitives in order to complete the specification of the query, defining all its procedural characteristics. A complex query may be expressed through a sequence of elementary operations, each one represented by a navigation or a selection on the conceptual schema; even typical textual operations (e.g., conditions on attributes) are reduced to easy graphical interactions. It is worth noting that the above interactions should be seen as a kit of tools that will be chosen by the user according to his needs.

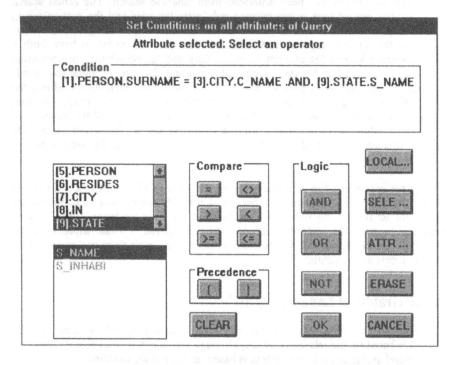

Fig. 1. The Graphical Interface

Fig. 1 shows how the user interacts with the graphical interface to establish conditions and attributes to see in the final result.

3. The Structure of a Sentence

This work has been thought as a tool integrated in QBD*. Starting from a query that is a path of concepts from an ER schema, it proposes several principles, as language independent as possible, for a natural language restatement of queries. The translating techniques are based on the observation that entities and relationships are well-connected respectively with nouns and verbs. Therefore, adding prepositions and articles, the system is able to build simple sentences.

At the beginning [14] it was thought of just for a particular syntax of the query (that characteristic of QBD*) and for a particular language (the Italian). During the drafting of the work, however, we noticed that the same could have been easily fitted to an other syntax or to an other language, as it will be shown in this paper.

The following step has been to carry out a comparative study of Italian and English grammars [15, 16, 17, 18, 19, 20], focusing our attentions on nouns, gender and number of nouns; definite and indefinite articles and their use; verbs; syntax of clauses and sentences. The result of the study is that many grammatical structures are common to the two languages: the kinds of clause (main, depend and co-ordinate), the members of a clause (subject, predicate and object), the declension of nouns (gender and number), the use of the definite and indefinite article and the indirect objects. Yet the two languages show differences in: the position of the subject of a clause (in English subject always proceeds the verb) the use of relative pronouns (distinguishing person from thing and animal) and the exceptions in use of articles (countable or uncountable nouns and geographic names).

Starting from the previous observations, every effort has been made to obtain restatement structures as general as possible in order to avoid an excessive increase of the execution time of the algorithm that should be linear in the number of selected concepts and attributes.

The translator of a query is built by a set of sentences. All the sentences are characterized by subject, verbal predicate, direct or indirect object and possible indirect complements due to local conditions established on concept attributes. Therefore each sentence will be built by two entities: one relative to the subject and one to the object. The selected path is split in several subpaths, each one composed by two entities opportunally linked. From now on we will refer to the first and to the second entity of a generic subpath.

Italian preserves the order of the selected concepts during the translation, English does not. In fact in English when the entity which has the role of subject in the sentence follows the relationship, it will be always placed before the verb and the system will split[1] the restatement after translating the subpath.

When the readability rules concur, the sentences that translate each subpath are merged. In fact each subpath has the last entity equal to the first entity of the following subpath. Therefore such an entity, with the possible local conditions established on its attributes, will be translated only once. In order to estimate the

---

[1] To split a repropositions means to begin a new sentence

readability of the sentences translated by the system, a score is used. Such a score derives from studies by R. Flesh [21] about readability rules focused on the average number of words and syllables for each sentence. Such studies has been fitted to the Italian language by R. Vacca and V. Franchina [22].

An example[2] is shown in Fig. 2 when the system reproposes the second subpath CITY-BORN-PERSON. The restatement does not keep the order: *a person named Paolo* (PERSON) *was born* (BORN) *in the city* (CITY).

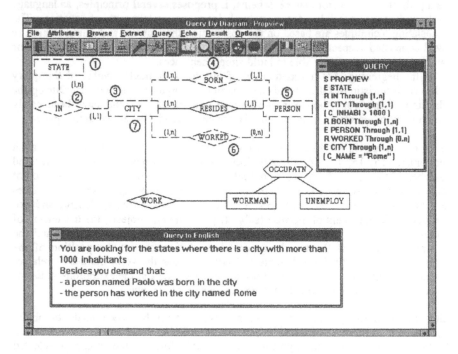

Fig. 2. A general example

3.1 Entities

To translate an entity the system has to define:

1. The gender and the number of the noun of the entity.
2. The kind of article of the noun, definite or indefinite.
3. The position of the noun in the sentence.

When a path is composed by more than one subpath, the first entity of a subpath (except the first subpath) is always the second entity of the previous subpath. The noun of the first entity of a generic subpath is expressed only when the clause which it belongs to is the first of a sentence, otherwise a pronoun or an adverb replaces the noun. Each time the restatement is split, the first entity of the next subpath will be

---

[2] In the figures the number near each concept represents the selecting order of the concepts in the query path. The conceptual query is that produced by QBD* and analysed by our system

translated, whereas the possible local conditions established on its attributes will not because they will already have been translated in the previous sentence.

A set of examples is now reported to show how the system handles the gender and the number of a noun and its article. When translating a noun of the first entity, the system will consider:

1. The conditions that could be established on a primary key of the second entity and the cardinalities of the second entity in the eventual relationship that could link it with the first. Fig. 2 shows that since the second entity (CITY) from the first subpath (STATE-IN-CITY) has no condition of equality on a primary key, the noun of the first entity (STATE) will be declined plural (*states*). Since the maximal cardinality of the second entity (CITY) is 1, if there had been a condition of equality on a primary key of the second entity, the noun of the first entity (STATE) would have been declined singular and its article would have been definite (e.g., You are looking for *the state* where there is the city named Rome).

2. If the clause which the sentence belongs to is the opening one or not. Fig. 2 shows that the number of the noun of the first entity (CITY from the subpath CITY-BORN-PERSON and PERSON from the subpath PERSON-WORKED-CITY) is that of the previous sentence and that its article is always definite (*the city; the person*).

3. The conditions established on a primary key of the first entity. If there is a condition of equality on a primary key of the first entity, its noun will be declined singular and its article will be always definite (e.g., You are looking for *the state named Italy*).

4. Whether the definite article is used before the noun or not and whether both the singular and the plural of the noun exist or not. In fact the system can manage the nouns which have no singular (e.g., *scissors*), those which have no plural (e.g., *milk*) and those with the same form for both the singular and the plural (e.g., *means*). It is worth remembering that there are nouns before which no definite article can be used (e.g., You are looking for *breakfast* made of milk). Moreover, the system handles collective nouns which require the singular form of the verb (e.g., You are looking for *the news* which is announced by John Landis).

The declension of the plural of a noun is easier in English than in Italian because the former has fewer rules and exceptions than the latter. The same holds for the use of the definite article: English has only one article (*the*), Italian has six.

When translating a noun of the second entity, the system will consider:

1. The conditions established on a primary key of the second entity. Fig. 2 shows that since there is a condition of equality on a primary key (name = Rome) of the second entity (CITY) from the third subpath (PERSON-WORKED-CITY), its noun will be declined singular (*city*) and its article will be definite (*the*). But if there had been no condition of equality on a primary key of the second entity (CITY from the subpath STATE-IN-CITY and PERSON from CITY-BORN-PERSON), the noun would have been declined singular (*city; person*) and its article would have been indefinite (*a*).

2. If the singular of the noun does not exist. When the noun is definite plural and there is no condition of equality on a primary key, the article will be obviously omitted (e.g., You are looking for people who wear *glasses*).

3. Whether the indefinite article is used before the noun or not (e.g., You are looking for the passengers who travel with *luggage*). It is worth noting that while in English there are some nouns for which it is impossible to use the indefinite article, in Italian the use of the indefinite article before some nouns is a pure aesthetic question.

The English use of the indefinite article (*a, an*) is easier than the Italian because, unlike the latter, the former has no elision of vocals and its article has no gender, that is it does not vary according to the male or female gender of the noun.

3.2 Local conditions

Establishing conditions on the attributes of a concept specifies important information about the concept itself. Thus, it is necessary to translate such information near what it refers to.

The system is able to join each local condition composed by the tern[3] attribute-condition-second term of the comparison to an appropriate indirect object. The presence of more local conditions will be translated by a sequence of indirect objects.

Since there are different kinds of attributes (numbers, dates and strings) the system will translate them in different ways, according to the different conditions and to the second term of the comparison: in fact the system can compare an attribute to a constant or to an attribute of the same concept (e.g., You are looking for the teachers whose name is not *Paul* or is the same as *their surname*). It is worth noting that the words expressing the attribute can be singular or plural and can follow or precede the condition. The conditions are then expressed according to the kinds of attributes the system can handle.

An attribute can belong to an entity or to a relationship. Since we translate each local condition with an indirect object, it is often better to refer it to a noun and not to a verb. For this reason, we have decided to translate the local conditions about the attributes of a relationship as local conditions of one of the two entities linked by the relationship. Only particular local conditions will be translated after the restatement of the relationship, as it will be shown in the following paragraphs.

Numerical Attributes. The system can repropose a tern including a numerical attribute in different order, according to:

1. The second term of the comparison: constant or attribute; two terns which differ only for the second term of the comparison may be translated in different order (e.g., *with less than 2 sons*; *with less sons than brothers*).
2. The kind of the condition; two terns which differ only for the kind of the condition may be translated in different order (e.g., *whose number of sons is not 2*; *with more than 2 sons*).
3. The number (1 or more than 1) of the terns with the same numerical attribute as first term of the comparison which are translated in the same way; in this case the information about the attribute is translated only when it is necessary (that

---

[3] In this section we will refer *tern* to each local condition

is the first time) and it is not repeated for each term (e.g., *with more than 2 sons, but less than 6*).

4. The number of the natural language expressions of the attribute. In fact there are:

A a kind of numerical attribute which, merely for stylistic reasons, can be translated in two ways according to the kind of the condition and to the second term of the comparison;

B another kind of numerical attribute which is always translated with the same expression, independently of the condition and of the second term of the comparison.

The attributes belonging to *A* have two possible expressions for their natural language restatement: one composed by a group of indeclinable words and another composed by a group of declinable words, possibly completed by a group of indeclinable words which can precede or follow it. The attributes belonging to *B* have only one expression composed by a group of indeclinable words. For example, the numerical attribute showing the number of sons of age of a person belongs to *A*: in some cases it will be translated by a group of indeclinable words (e.g., You are looking for the people *whose number of sons of age is different from 3*), other times it will be translated by declinable words followed by a group of indeclinable words (e.g., You are looking for the people *with more than 3 sons of age* or You are looking for the people *with more than 1 son of age*). In this example the group of English indeclinable words that complete the expression follows the declinable word, but there are attributes where the order of the groups of words is reversed (e.g., You are looking for the people *who own 1 big house*). Obviously the declension of the declinable words depends on the value of the constant: 1 or more than 1. It is worth noting that there is no correspondence between the two languages about declinable and indeclinable words which compose the expression of an attribute belonging to *A*.

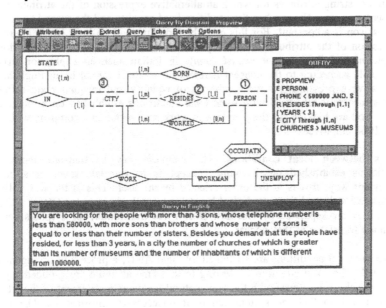

Fig. 3. Numerical attributes restatement

Fig. 3 shows the different structures used to translate the terns. A difference between the two languages is that, in some cases, English needs the possessive adjective (*his, her, its, their,* according to the concept the attribute refers to) before the expression of the second term of the comparison. Another difference is that Italian has a more complicated use of the article (as shown in section 3.1) and often links the preposition with the definite article that follows it.

Date Attributes. The system distinguishes between a date attribute refered to an entity (e.g., *whose date of starting activity precedes 01/01/78*) and one refered to a relationship with the second term of the comparison constant. In the last case the restatement omits the translation of the attribute and the natural language expressions of the different kinds of condition depend on the meaning of the relationship. For instance, the condition $> =$ can be translated in different ways: You are looking for the people born *after or on 01/01/78* in the city named Rome or You are looking for the people who have worked *since 01/01/78* in a company with more than 1000 employees.

String Attributes. The system can handle string attributes, giving the conditions appropriate expressions. There are different structures to translate a tern including this kind of attribute. In all these structures the natural language expression of the attribute is composed by a group of indeclinable words. When there are more terns with the same string attribute translated in the same way, the standard expression is omitted, but the first time it is necessary (e.g., You are looking for the people *whose name precedes Smith in alphabetic order, but follows their surname*; You are looking for the cities *the name of which is different from London, follows Cardiff in alphabetic order but precedes Oxford*).

There are string attributes for which an alternative expression of the attribute makes the sentence more fluent when the condition is of equality and the second term of the comparison is a constant. For this case the structure will be built by an alternative expression of the attribute followed by the constant (e.g., You are looking for the people *named Paul or not named John*). In Italian such an expression may be declinable according to the concept it refers to, while it cannot be in English. The alternative expressions for the conditions of equality and inequality are different. This structure is also used with some local conditions established on a relationship (e.g., You are looking for the people who work *as director* in a company with more than 1000 employees).

Links between local conditions. The simplest way to translate more local conditions established on the same concept is to translate them in a context dependent way, that is in the order selected by the user. This is the way followed when the local conditions are linked by at least one logic operator OR or NOT, or when they are separated by brackets. During the translation, the symbols between them are translated as they appear.

When the local conditions are all linked by logic AND, a process of arrangement is executed. The local conditions referring to the same attribute are grouped together and, in each group, those with the same natural language restatement of the attribute are grouped so that the system can omit unnecessary information. The groups composed by only one local condition are established first and, in each new subgroup, those with a condition of equality are established first. The groups of local conditions that contain at least one local condition with a condition of equality are translated first. Before translating the logic ANDs, the system will count the number of the local conditions. In fact usually a logic AND will be translated by the comma. If it separates the last local condition of a group from the last but one of the same group, the local condition will be introduced by the conjunction *but*. If there are at least 2 groups, the logic AND before the last group will be translated by *and* (e.g., You are looking for the cities near Rome, with less than 3 stadiums *and* with more than 1000000 inhabitants, *but* less than 2000000).

3.3 Attributes the user wants to know

The attributes the user wants to know are translated at the end of the natural language restatement of the query. For all the attributes, except those about the first selected entity, which are distinguished in English by the possessive adjective, the name of the concept they refer to will be added to the natural language expression of the attribute. If the same concept is selected more than once and if the user wants to see some attributes in the final result, each time the concept is selected, the system will distinguish them according to the following rules:

1. If an entity is selected more than once and if, each time the user asks to see its attributes in the final result, the couple of concepts (one relationship and one entity) that precedes the entity is different, such a couple will be translated in order to distinguish the entities having the same name.

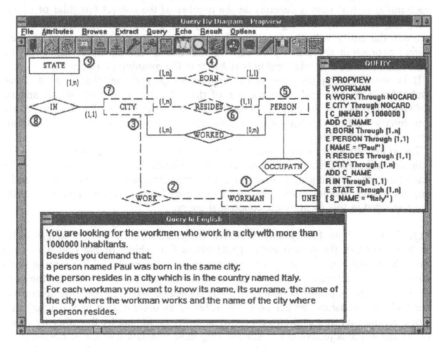

Fig. 4. Restatement of attributes the user wants to know

Fig. 4 shows a query in the final result of which are present the attributes showing the name of the city each time the entity CITY is selected. Since the couples that precede the entity CITY in the path (WORK-WORKMAN and RESIDES-PERSON) are different, they are translated after the entity CITY in the final result. It is worth noting that the system notes if an entity belonging to a couple is the first selected entity or it is not, using opportunely the definite or indefinite article (... *city where the workman works ... city where a person resides*).

2. If the couple of concepts that precedes the entity is the same, the system will analyse the quadruplet, the sextuplet, and so on until it will be different.

If the user asks to see only the attributes of the main entity, such attributes will be translated at the beginning of the restatement. For example, if in Fig. 4 the user had asked to see only the name and surname of the workmen, the restatement would have been *You are looking for the name and surname of the workmen who work in a city ...*

3.4 Relationships

A verbal expression can include prepositions, adverbs, articles, nouns and pronouns. Thus its structure will be:

[introducing part] verb [completing part] [preposition]

where the introducing part is usually an adverb or a pronoun; the verb depends on the mood, the tense, the form (positive or negative) and the number of the subject. The completing part is a group of words, completing the verb, which may be declinable; in that case it depends on the number of the subject (singular or plural) and, only in Italian, on the gender of the subject (male or female). Prepositions can precede the entity with the function of indirect complement. The reason to use a verbal expression and not a pure verb to translate a relationship is that often the semantic meaning of a relationship is richer than the meaning of a pure verb.

It is worth noting that the verbal expression depends on the kind of clause (subordinate or principal), the number of the subject (singular or plural) and the different direction of the path (each elementary path is composed by two entities and one binary relationship between them; the relationship has two different meanings according to the entity that precedes it in the selected path).

The system handles cyclic relationships and roles of relationships too.

Since until now QBD* allowed to use n-ary relationships via a path composed by one entity, the relationships, a second entity, the relationship, a third entity, and so on, our system handles n-ary relationships as many binary relationships because they are presented in this form by the conceptual query.

Fig. 5 shows how the system translates the relationships. In the subpath CITY WORKED PERSON the second entity (PERSON) is the subject of the sentence, so in English the order of the concepts is reversed (a *person* named Paul has *worked* in the *city*) and the restatement is split. In the subpath PERSON - FATHER - PERSON the order of the concepts is preserved and the role is translated with the verbal expression of the cyclic relationship (the person *is the father of an other* person named John). It is worth noting that in a cyclic relationship an entity is distinct by the other by means of the indefinite adjective *other*. Considering their translation of the attributes in the final result, we see that the relationships belonging to the couples preceding the entity PERSON (WORKED-CITY and FATHER-PERSON) are translated in a different way compared to the translation in the path (the person *who is the son of an other person* Vs the person *is the father of an other person*; the person *who has worked in a city* Vs a person *has worked in the city*).

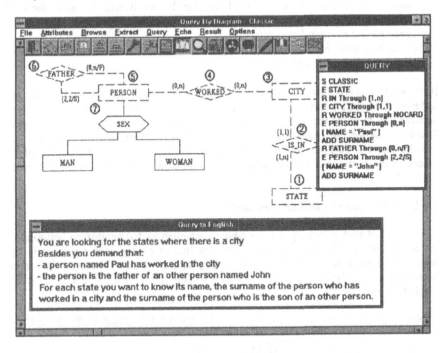

Fig. 5. Relationships restatement

3.5 Links between entities not directly linked

During the formulation of a query it is possible to connect two entities which are not directly linked by a relationship, comparing their attributes with the same domain. This operation is called bridge. The terms attribute_of_an_entity - condition - attribute_of_an_other_entity are translated as indirect objects of the noun relative to the entity which has the role of first term of the comparison and they are placed after its possible local conditions.

There are four kinds of structures to translate the term $attribute_1$ - condition - $attribute_2$, with $attribute_1$ belonging to $entity_1$ and $attribute_2$ belonging to $entity_2$, as shown in Fig. 6:

1. A structure only used for the numerical attributes which can be translated in two ways, when the condition is not that of equality or inequality (*with more sons than the unemployed's brothers*).
2. A structure only used when $attribute_1$ is equal to $attribute_2$, the condition is of equality and they are both string attributes (*named as an unemployed*). If there are terms translated by this structure, they will be placed before the others.

3. A structure used for all kinds of attributes, provided that attribute$_1$ is the same as attribute$_2$. If entity$_1$ is animal or thing, the English pronoun *of which* will follow attribute$_1$, which will be preceded by the definite article *the*; otherwise *whose* will precede attribute$_1$. The demonstrative pronoun will be declined according to the number of attribute$_1$ (in Italian it will be also declined according to the gender of attribute$_1$) (*whose surname precedes that of an unemployed in alphabetic order*).

4. A structure used for all the other kinds of terns (e.g., *whose birthdate precedes the deathdate of an unemployed*).

It is worth noting that the natural language expressions of the conditions are different according to the kind of attributes (numerical, date or string). The links between the terns of the bridge are the same of that shown in the part about Local Condition. After the translation of a bridge, the restatement will be split and the possible local conditions of the second entity which composes the bridge will be placed in the next sentence (the unemployed, *whose surname is Brown*, was born in the city).

3.6 Global conditions and set operations

At the end of each subquery it is possible to establish global conditions between all the attributes with the same domain. The structure of each global condition is the same for all the kinds of attribute (numerical, date or string). The only difference between the two languages is the use of the possessive case, which is typically English.

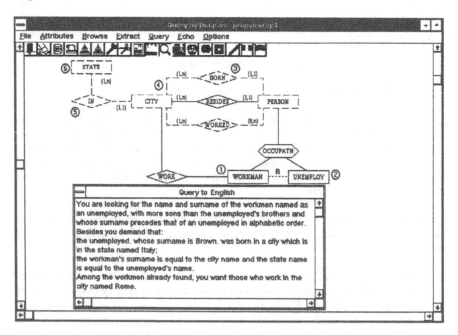

Fig. 6. Restatement of links between entities not directly linked, global conditions and set operations

It is worth noting that the natural language expressions of the global conditions are different according to the kinds of attribute and that the links between them are the same of that shown in the Local Condition section. An example is shown in Fig. 6 (e.g., *the workman's surname is equal to the city name and the state name is equal to the unemployed's name*). About the distinction between the selections of the same concepts more than once holds what said in 3.3.

The system can also reformulate the set union, intersection and difference operations which can connect more subqueries. The system has a standard restatement for each set operation. An example is shown in Fig. 6 for the set intersection operation (e.g., *Among the workmen already found, you want those ...*).

4 Short Cuts

Several short cuts have been used to simplify the restatement. There are entities for which a condition of equality, followed by a constant established on some particular attributes which are primary key for the entity, can allow the omission of the natural language restatement of the entity the attribute refers to (first kind of short cut). For instance, *You are looking for the cities where John Brown has worked* is better than *You are looking for the cities where the person first named John and surnamed Brown has worked* or *You are looking for the people who work in IBM* is better than *You are looking for the people who work in a company the name of which is IBM*.

Sometimes several concepts are used only to connect two entities (that we call first and last entity), in fact there are neither conditions established on their attributes nor attributes that must be showed in the final result.
There are examples where such a rule cannot be applied. For instance, in a schema with the path TEACHER - NOT LIKE LIVING - CITY - IN - STATE, the relationship NOT LIKE LIVING is strongly connected with the entity CITY, because a teacher may not like living in a city that is in Italy, but he may like living in Italy. Thus the query will be restated as: You are looking for the *teachers who do not like living in a city which is in Italy*.

To apply this short cut it is necessary to check if there are others paths between the first and the last entity. If such paths exist, the system will translate the sentence belonging to the first two entities and will check again the remaining untranslated path. Thus, if only one path remains and the short cut can be applied, the system will apply it.

Fig. 7 shows that a short cut can not be applied to the whole path of concept because there is an other path between the entity TEACHER and the entity STATE (TEACHER - STUDIED - PRIVATE SCHOOL - OF - STATE). Therefore, the system will translate the first subpath (TEACHER-STUDIED-PUBLIC SCHOOL) and it will apply the short cut to the remaining subpaths (PUBLIC SCHOOL - IN - CITY - IS IN - STATE). It is worth noting that the replacement of the entity CITY with the entity STATE is possible only because the relationship IS IN relative STATE keeps unchanged its semantics.

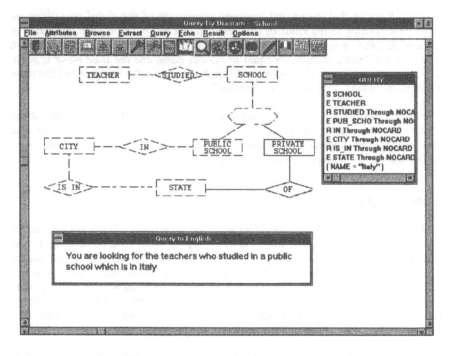

Fig. 7. A complete example of short cut use

5 Implementation Issues

A prototype of a tool for supporting the natural language restatement of a query has been implemented using the C-Windows language on a personal computer.

This tool works with Italian and is the result of a collaboration with the Language Science Department of the University of Rome "La Sapienza" and with the Computer & MicroImage S.p.A.. The program, executed on a i486 machine, has showed a good response time (less than 1 second) with middle dimensional schemas (about a hundred attributes and fifty concepts).

Presently we are working at the realization of a prototype for the English natural language restatement dealt with in this paper. A single and effective structure for both the textual data has been built in order to translate the query in English and Italian at the same time, according to the user's demand. The general architecture of the system, as showed in Fig. 8, is based on four main modules:

1. The *Filter* points out the concepts where the first kind of short cut can be applied and finds the chains of concepts used only to connect couples of entities. If the second kind of short cut can be applied, the system will replace each chain with the relationship expressing the short cut. *Entity Textual Information* and *Relationship Textual Information* are the set of the natural language information of the entities and of the relationships.

2. The *Condition Organizer* orders the (local or global) condition in order to avoid the repetition of unnecessary information. *Attribute Textual Information* is the set of the natural language information of the attributes.
3. The *Final Result Analyzer* establishes where the attributes to see in the final result have to be placed: at the beginning or at the ending of the restatement.
4. The *Translator*, finally, translates the conceptual query in a natural language query. *Rules* are the set of gender, number and conjugation rules. *Standard Words* are the set of standard expressions used in the restatement. They are distinguished in *conditions* (which point out that there are additional information according to the different kinds of attribute which the condition refers to) and *introducing expressions* (which are the set of expressions used to introduce each kind of sentence)

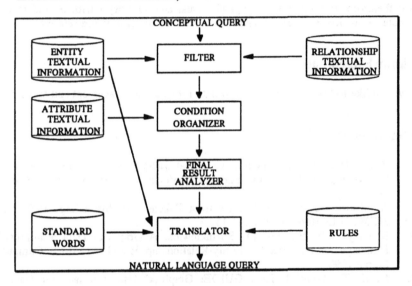

Fig. 8. The Architecture

6 Conclusions and Future Developments

The Computer and Microimage S.p.A. is working at the realization of a tool supporting QBD* and integrating a natural language module (the figures of this paper refer to the prototype). This tool has made possible the checking of the result of this research with potential clients, who have proved very interested in the natural language restatement of the query.

To meet the clients' requirements for a restatement of the query in a fluent language, one of the main obstacles faced has been that of limiting the amount of textual information handled by the system.

There are many subjects that could be still investigated. It could be useful to work out a way to check the accuracy of the query. For example, looking for the teacher John Brown born in a city, without asking to see any information about the entity CITY or the entity TEACHER in the final result, is a logic sentence. In fact the query would be that aimed to find out whether the city where John Brown was born is in the database or not. On the contrary, looking for the teacher John Brown born in a city, asking to see only the name of the city in the final result, is not a well formulated query. A well formulated query would be that aimed to find out the name of the city where John Brown was born.

It could be interesting to investigate about the use of different language styles according to different users (formal, informal, technical, schematic, ...), the customization of the dictionary, the possibility to create the query directly in natural language and the study of a version that produces logic sentence too.

Given the general tendency to use multimedial databases, we are thinking of a way to repropose the new kinds of attribute in natural language. The restatement will have, therefore, to include time, logical, visual and auditory attributes and textual attributes on which the user will establish conditions of information retrieval.

Acknowledgements

We would like to thank Professor Carlo Batini for his encouragement and support.

References

1. R. A. Elmasri, J. A. Larson: A Graphical Query Facility for ER Database. In: Proceedings of the 4th International Conference on ER Approach, Chicago 1985
2. A. Motro: Constructing Queries from Tokens. In: Proceedings 1986 ACM SIGMOD Conference, pp. 144-152
3. B. Czejdo, R. Elmasri, M. Rusinkiewicz: A Graphical Data Manipulation Language for an Extended Entity-Relationship Model. In: IEEE Computer, March 1990
4. H. K. T. Wong, I. Kuo: GUIDE: Graphical User Interface for Database Exploration. In: Proceedings of the 8th International Conference on Very Large Data Base, Mexico City September 1982, pp. 22-32
5. V. M. Markovitz, Y. Raz: Errol: an Entity-Relationship, Role Oriented, Query Language. In: ER Approach to Software Engineering, Davis Jajodia & Yeh, North-Holland, 1983, pp. 329-346
6. P. P. Chen: The Entity-Relationship Model: Toward a Unified View of Data. In: ACM Transactions on Database Systems, Vol. 1, No. 1, March 1976, pp. 9-36
7. W. Roesner: Despath: An ER Manipulation Language. In: Proceedings of the 4th International Conference on ER Approach, Chicago 1985, pp. 72-81
8. G. Toffoli, A. Giannetti: Un Sistema realistico per la Comprensione di Sequenze di Frasi. In: Primo Congresso della Associazione Italiana per l'Intelligenza Artificiale, Novembre 1989, pp. 50-58
9. P. Terenziani, L. Lesmo: Un Sistema a Regole per l'Interpretazione Semantica del Linguaggio Naturale. In: Primo Congresso della Associazione Italiana per l'Intelligenza Artificiale, Novembre 1989, pp. 40-49

10. A. Lavelli, O. Stock: Quando l'Input non è una Frase: una Soluzione basata su Chart per alcuni Fenomeni di Malformatezza. In: Primo Congresso dell'Associazione Italiana per l'Intelligenza Artificiale, Novembre 1989, pp. 59-67

11. E. F. Codd: Seven Steps Rendezvous with the Casual User. In: Data Base Management, Klimbie & Koffeman, North- Holland, 1974, pp. 179-200

12. J. A. Wald, P. G. Sorenson: Explaining Ambiguity in a Formal Query Language. In: ACM Transactions on Database Systems, Vol. 15, No. 2, June 1990, pp. 125-161

13. M. Angelaccio, T. Catarci, G. Santucci: QBD*: A Graphical Query Language with Recursion. In: IEEE Transactions on Software Engineering, 16, 10, pp. 1150-1163

14. P. Ficorilli: Riproposizione in linguaggio naturale di un'interrogazione espressa in un linguaggio grafico. Tesi di laurea in Ingegneria Elettronica. Universita' degli Studi di Roma "La Sapienza", Febbraio 1991

15. Dizionario Enciclopedico Italiano. Istituto della ENCICLOPEDIA ITALIANA fondato da Giovanni Treccani, 1974

16. T. De Mauro: Guida all'Uso delle Parole. Editori Riuniti, Libri di base, 1980

17. M. Dardano, P. Trifone: Grammatica Italiana. Zanichelli

18. A. V. Martinet, A. J. Thomson: A Practical English Grammar. Oxford University Press, 1985

19. Otto-Jespersen: Essential of English Grammar. George Allan and Unwin, 1976

20. M. Swam: Basic English Usage. Oxford University Press, 1986

21. R. Flesh: The Art of Readable Writing. Collier_Macmillan, 1949

22. V. Franchina, R. Vacca: Taratura dell'indice di Flesch su testo bilingue italiano-inglese di un unico autore. In: Atti dell'incontro di studio, Istituto di Filosofia dell'Università degli studi di Roma "La Sapienza", pp. 26-27 Giugno 1986

A Temporal Query Language
Based on Conceptual Entities and Roles

Ramez Elmasri   Vram Kouramajian

Computer Science Engineering Department

The University of Texas at Arlington

Arlington, Texas 76019–0015

Fax: (817) 273-2548   Telephone: (817) 273-3785

{elmasri, kouramaj}@cse.uta.edu

Abstract

In our previous work [ElEK90], we introduced a Semantic Temporal model based on the Extended Entity-Relationship model (STEER), where we proposed new classification concepts for temporal/conceptual objects and relationships. We defined temporal constraints and outlined rules for preserving temporal integrity constraints.

In this paper, we propose a temporal query language based on the STEER data model. The query language is a temporal extension of GORDAS [ElWi81, ElWu90], which is a formal, high-level, user-friendly query language for the Extended Entity-Relationship model. The temporal query language derives its power and flexibility from the distinction between temporal and conceptual objects, and from temporal and conceptual relationships. It provides natural and high level temporal element constructor operators that simplify temporal query expressions.

1 Introduction

There are several issues to be considered when adding the temporal dimension into database systems and data models; these include temporal query languages [Snod87, ElWu90, WuDa92], efficient physical storage of temporal data [AhSn88, ElWK90, ElJK92], and temporal semantic constraints [ElEK90]. Recently, research in temporal databases has increased rapidly; and has been applied primarily in the context of the relational model of data [Snod87, GaYe88, NaAh89, Jens90], and to a lesser extent, in conceptual data models [SeSh87, ElWu90, WuDa92]. However, these approaches have a fundamental pitfall, in that they fail to consider the semantics associated with time. In a previous paper [ElEK90], we proposed a Semantic Temporal model based on the Extended Entity-Relationship model (*STEER*). We introduced new classification concepts that distinguish between conceptual and temporal objects. A conceptual object, once it is created, can always be referenced at any future time, whereas a temporal object, which we call an entity role, has a specific existence lifespan. For example, information concerning a *STUDENT* conceptual object can be referenced even after the student has completed his studies. However, the role of that entity as an *ENROLLED-STUDENT* has specific start and end times that define its lifespan. In [ElEK90], we characterized the properties of entities (conceptual objects), entity roles (temporal objects) and (temporal and non-temporal) attributes, defined temporal constraints among entity roles, differentiated between temporal and conceptual relationships, and outlined rules for preserving temporal integrity constraints.

Our work here complements our previous research [ElEK90] by proposing temporal query language constructs based on the *STEER* data model. The query language is a temporal extension of *GORDAS* [ElWi81, ElWH85, ElWu90], which is a formal, high-level, user-friendly query language for the Extended Entity-Relationship model. The temporal query language derives its power from the distinction between temporal/conceptual objects and relationships. It provides natural and high level temporal element constructor operators that simplify temporal query expressions. It takes advantage of the fact that attributes and relationships of a role type and its owner entity type are public to each other and can be inherited; and hence it gives queries the flexibility to specify selection conditions and to retrieve information involving attributes of a role or an entity type by referring to each other's attributes. It allows temporal element constructor operators to be defined over entities, entity roles and temporal attributes. It supports temporal version restriction operators and allows multiple temporal scopes in a temporal projection.

The remainder of this paper is organized as follows. In section 2, we review the *STEER* data model. In section 3, we present constructs for temporal boolean expressions, temporal selection and temporal projection. Section 4 describes the temporal query language constructs. Finally, section 5 contains a conclusion and planned future work.

2 Review of the STEER Model

The *STEER* data model [ElEK90] maps the real world into basic concepts closer to the human perception of the real world. Critical to the model is the semantic role that time plays in classification of objects. In section 2.1, we describe the representation of time we use. Section 2.2 reviews our model.

2.1 Representing Time

Let T be a countably infinite set of totally ordered discrete time points, where T is denoted as $T = \{t_0, t_1, \ldots, t_{now}, t_{now+1}, \ldots\}$, and t_{now} represents the current time point which is continuously increasing. We define a *time interval*, denoted by $[t_l, t_u]$, to be a set of consecutive equidistant time instances, that is the totally ordered set $\{t_l, t_{l+1}, \ldots, t_u\} \subset T$. Interval representation has an important shortcoming. Since the set of all intervals in T is not closed under set operations, [GaYe88] suggested the concept of temporal elements. A *temporal element* is a finite union of time intervals, denoted by $\{I_1, I_2, \ldots, I_n\}$ where I_i is an interval in T. The intervals have to be disjoint in the canonical temporal element representation [NaAh89].

In temporal databases, it is customary to include a number of different time dimensions. Two of the most common ones are *valid time* and *transaction time* [Snod87]. Additional time dimensions are also possible and sometimes necessary [JeSn91]. Because of space limitations, we will consider only the valid time in this paper.

2.2 The Temporal Data Model

The *STEER* model [ElEK90] distinguishes between conceptual objects and temporal objects and between conceptual relationships and temporal relationships. Below, we present only those features that are relevant for the discussion in this paper.

2.2.1 Conceptual Objects: Entities

Our goals are to define guidelines for determining the basic aspects of an object's life time. The conceptual existence of an object does not directly correspond to the birth, death, and change of the object. Objects need to be modeled in a mini-world when they become of interest. For example, employees exist in the real world as persons. However, they become objects of interest to a company only when the company wants to hire them. At this point, the company may still want to record previous information about these persons. If an employee leaves the company, the employee remains an object of interest as long as the company still wishes.

Each conceptual entity e has an *existence time*, denoted by ET, which is unrelated to the concept of lifespan. The *start time point ST* of the existence time refers to the time the concept of the entity is materialized. There is no *end time point* of an existence time. The end time can be considered to be infinity in our model, because a concept (an entity) once realized never ceases to exist. The only time that characterizes an entity is the start time of its existence. Hence, $ET = [ST, \infty)$. We also use the notation $T(e)$ to refer to the existence time of an entity e.

There are two important ramifications in associating existence time with entities:

1. We can define and treat future planning concepts using similar mechanisms to those used for historical concepts

2. We can enhance the power of query languages and simplify their constructs while dealing with conceptual objects, by using start time point of existence time as the earliest possible time the entity can be referenced.

An *entity type* is a set of entities of the same type; that is, entities that share the same properties. An entity type is diagrammatically represented by a rectangular box (see Figure 1).

2.2.2 Temporal Objects: Roles

Entities describe one aspect of the real world, the conceptual one. The other aspect is captured by temporal objects. The classification of objects as temporal and conceptual gives our model the capability to faithfully represent the way people perceive the real world. Temporal objects materialize the active role that conceptual objects play in the temporal dimension.

We call a temporal object an *entity role*, since it represents the time that the entity is participating in that role. A *role type* is a set of entity roles of the same type; that is, roles that share the same properties. Each role type is associated with a single entity type called its *owner entity*. Hence, $owner(entity\ role) = entity \Leftrightarrow role(entity) = entity\ role$. A role type is diagrammatically represented by a dotted rectangular box, and connected to an owner entity as shown in Figure 1. Each entity role ro of a role type RO is associated with a temporal element $T(ro) \subset [t_0, \infty)$ which gives the lifespan LS of the role.

The following general set of rules must hold on roles:

1. Start time of the lifespan of an entity role must be greater or equal to the start time of the existence time of the (conceptual) owner entity. This implies a top-down approach in creation of role types; that is, before a role is created its corresponding (owner) entity must exist.

2. A role type is restricted exactly to one owner entity type.

3. A role type can have only temporal attributes.

4. (Temporal) attributes of a role type are *public* to the owner entity type; that is, an owner entity refers to these attributes as though they are attributes of the owner entity.

5. Similarly, (temporal and non-temporal) attributes of an entity type are public to all associated role types.

6. A role can access all relationship instances for relationship types in which the owner entity participates.

7. Similarly, an entity can access all relationship instances for relationship types in which the associated role participates.

2.2.3 Conceptual Relationships

A *conceptual relationship type* R of degree n has n participating entity types $E_1, \ldots, E_n$. Each *relationship instance* r in R is an n-tuple $r = < e_1, e_2, \ldots, e_n >$ where each $e_i \in E_i$. Each relationship instance r in R has an existence time ET. The start time of the existence time of a relationship instance must be greater or equal to the start time of the existence time of each of the participating entities; that is, $ST(r) \geq ST(e_i)$ for each $e_i \in E_i$ $(i = 1, 2, \ldots, n)$.

2.2.4 Temporal Relationships

Our model supports temporal relationships. A *temporal relationship type* TR of degree n has n participating entity types (role types) $O_1, O_2, \ldots, O_n$ where all O_is are either entity types $(O_i \equiv E_i)$ or role types $(O_i \equiv RO_i)$. Each *temporal relationship instance* tr in TR is an n-tuple $tr = < o_1, o_2, \ldots, o_n >$ where all o_is are either entities $(o_i \equiv e_i, e_i \in E_i)$ or entity roles $(o_i \equiv ro_i, ro_i \in RO_i)$.

Each temporal relationship instance tr in TR is associated with a temporal element $T(tr)$ which gives the lifespan of the temporal relationship instance. If the participating objects are entity roles, then the lifespan of the temporal relationship instance must be a subset of the intersection of the lifespans of the roles; and if the participating objects are entities, then the start time of the lifespan of the temporal relationship instance must be greater or equal to the start times of all existence times of the entities.

2.2.5 An Example

Consider the example database schema in Figure 1, which describes a simplified organization for part of a *UNIVERSITY* database. The database includes the (conceptual) entity types *PERSON*, *STUDENT*, *FACULTY*, *COURSE*, and *SECTION*. Any entity instance that is a member of any of these entity types is associated with an existence time. The entity types *STUDENT* and *FACULTY* are subtypes of the entity type *PERSON*. The role types are diagrammatically represented by a dotted rectangular box, and connected to their owner entity types. The role types and their owner entities are:

owner(LIVING–PERSON) = PERSON
owner(ENROLLED–STUDENT) = STUDENT
owner(CURRENT–FACULTY) = FACULTY
owner(VALID–COURSE) = COURSE
owner(ACTIVE–SECTION) = SECTION

The conceptual relationship types are:

CS between *COURSE* and *SECTION*
TAUGHT between *FACULTY* and *SECTION*
TRANSCRIPT between *STUDENT* and *SECTION*

The temporal relationship types are:

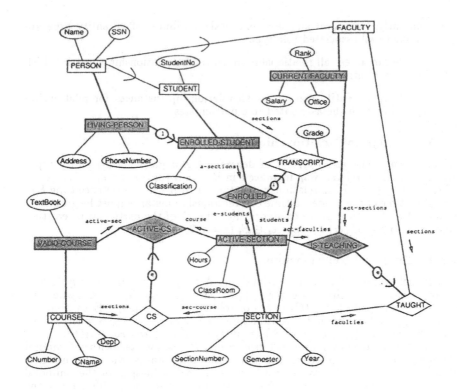

Figure 1: A Temporal EER Schema for Part of a UNIVERSITY Database

ACTIVE-CS between *VALID-COURSE* and *ACTIVE-SECTION*
IS-TEACHING between *CURRENT-FACULTY* and *ACTIVE-SECTION*
ENROLLED between *ENROLLED-STUDENT* and *ACTIVE-SECTION*

Figure 1 also depicts temporal constraints among roles and among relationships. (For a complete description of temporal constraints, see [ElEK90].)

3   Temporal Query Language Constructs

In *non-temporal* databases, a typical query will select certain entities based on boolean predicates that involve attribute values of an entity (and of related entities). Following that, certain attributes or relationships of each of the selected entities are displayed. Other queries involve aggregate functions on groups of entities or their attributes. In a *temporal database*, selection criteria may be based not only on attribute values but also on temporal conditions. In addition, once an entity is selected, the user may be interested in displaying the complete history of some of its attributes or relationships, or to limit the displayed values to a certain time interval. To allow for temporal constructs in queries, we will use the concepts of temporal boolean expressions, temporal selection conditions (or temporal predicates), and temporal projection [ElWu90].

A *(temporal) boolean expression* is a conditional expression on the attributes and relationships of an entity (or an entity role). For example, a boolean expression can be *Classification = 'Senior'*. The boolean condition when applied to one entity e (or one entity role ro), evaluates to a function from $T(e)$ (or $T(ro)$) to { *TRUE, FALSE, UNKNOWN* }. We call this function a temporal assignment.

The *true_time* of a boolean expression, c, denoted by $[\![c]\!]$, evaluates to a temporal element for each entity e (or each entity role ro). The temporal element is the time for which the condition is *TRUE* for e (or ro). As an example, the boolean condition *Classification = 'Senior'*, when applied to an *ENROLLED-STUDENT* ro (Figure 1), returns a function from $T(ro)$ to { *TRUE, FALSE, UNKNOWN* }. If $T(ro)$ is equal to [9/1/83, 8/31/87], and the student classification was senior during [9/1/86, 8/31/87], the temporal assignment result would be: { [9/1/83, 8/31/86] → *FALSE*, [9/1/86, 8/31/87] → *TRUE* }. The value for the true_time $[\![$ *Classification = 'Senior'* $]\!]$ would be [9/1/86, 8/31/87].

Next we define a *(temporal) selection condition*, which compares two temporal elements using the set comparison operators $=$, $\neq$, $\supseteq$, and $\subseteq$. When applied to an entity type (or class), it evaluates to those entities that satisfy the temporal selection condition. For example, consider the following temporal selection condition applied to the *ENROLLED-STUDENT* entity role type of Figure 1:

$$[\![\text{Classification} = \text{'Senior'}]\!] \supseteq [9/1/86, 5/31/87]$$

This selects all *ENROLLED-STUDENT* entity roles whose classification was *'Senior'* during the period [9/1/86, 5/31/87]. The condition is evaluated for each *ENROLLED-STUDENT* entity role individually, and returns either a *YES* or *NO* answer. All entity roles for which the answer is *YES* are selected.

We also define *temporal projection*. This is applied to a temporal entity and restricts all temporal assignments (attributes and relationships) for that entity to a specific time period specified by a temporal element T.

Temporal selection conditions are used to select particular entities based on temporal conditions, whereas temporal projections are used to limit the data displayed for the selected entities to specific time periods. Temporal boolean conditions may be used as components in the expressions for both temporal selections and temporal projections.

4   The Temporal Query Language

Much of the flexibility and power provided by a query language is dependent on the data model. Our temporal query language derives its simplicity and
expressiveness from the *STEER* data model; in particular from the distinction
between temporal and conceptual objects, and temporal and conceptual relationships. The query language used is a temporal extension of *GORDAS* [ElWi81,
ElWH85, ElWu90]. We briefly recall that *GORDAS* is a functional query language with two clauses: *GET* and *WHERE*. The *WHERE*–clause specifies conditions for the selection of entities from a *root entity type*, while the *GET*–clause
specifies the information to be retrieved for each selected entity. For example,
consider the following (non-temporal) *GORDAS* query specified on the database
of Figure 1:

Q1: **GET** < Name, SSN, < CName **of** sec-course, Semester, Year >
     of sections > **of** STUDENT
     WHERE Address of STUDENT = 'Arlington'

Here, the root entity type, specified at the end of the *GET*–clause, is *STU-
DENT*. The *WHERE*–clause is evaluated individually for each entity in the root
entity type, and selects each entity that satisfies the *WHERE*–clause. In this
query, each *STUDENT* entity who lives in *'Arlington'* is selected. (Note that
the *Address* attribute is visible to *STUDENT* by being inherited from *LIVING-
PERSON* via *PERSON* as we will describe in section 4.1.) The *of STUDENT* in
the *WHERE*–clause is optional, and can be left out. For each selected entity, the
GET–clause retrieves the student *Name*, *SSN* (both inherited from *PERSON*)
and *sections*, and for each of the student's sections the *CName*, *Semester* and
Year are retrieved. The connection names such as *sec-course* and *sections* are
used to specify related entities of the root entity type in a functional way as
though they were attributes of root entities. Hence, the path *sections of STU-
DENT* specifies the *SECTION* entities related to each *STUDENT* entity via
the *TRANSCRIPT* relationship. A full discussion of non-temporal *GORDAS* is
outside the scope of this work, and is given in [ElWi81, ElWH85].

In temporal *GORDAS*, we will adopt the philosophy that a non-temporal
GORDAS query is also valid, and will default to the current database state.
Hence, if a temporal *GORDAS* query is specified with no temporal selections
or projections, we will assume that a snapshot of the database is taken at the
time instant t_{now} when the query is evaluated, and the query is processed using
this database state. This will make it possible to specify both temporal and
non-temporal queries on the database within the same framework.

In section 4.1 we discuss temporal projection and introduce additional temporal element constructor operators. Section 4.2 presents temporal selection.
Section 4.3 describes temporal version restriction operators. Finally, section 4.4
introduces operators that allow multiple temporal scopes in a temporal projection.

4.1   Temporal Projection

A temporal query may involve a temporal selection condition or a temporal
projection condition or both. The general philosophy of *GORDAS* is to maintain
a clean separation between the specification of conditions for selection of entities
(in the *WHERE*–clause) and the specification of information to be displayed
(in the *GET*–clause). To maintain this philosophy, we will specify a temporal
projection on the data to be displayed at the end of the *GET*–clause, as in
[ElWu90]. For example, consider the query to retrieve the history of the *Address*
and *PhoneNumber* of *'John Smith'* during the period 1985 to 1990:

Q2: **GET** < Address, PhoneNumber > **of** PERSON : [1/1/1985, 12/31/1990]
     WHERE Name = 'John Smith'

The term *PERSON* : [1/1/1985, 12/31/1990] at the end of the *GET*–clause specifies that the temporal assignment for *'John Smith'* is to be retrieved during the period [1/1/1985, 12/31/1990]. On the other hand, the next query is non-temporal, and displays the current (at time instant t_{now}) *Address* and *PhoneNumber* of *'John Smith'*:

Q3: **GET** < Address, PhoneNumber > **of** PERSON
    WHERE Name = 'John Smith'

As seen from query *Q2*, the temporal projection of selected entities is specified by a temporal element at the end of the *GET*–clause. The temporal element may be a time period (as in *Q2*) or may itself be derived from the database for each entity (as in *Q4* below). For example, suppose we want the full history of the *Address* and *PhoneNumber* of *'John Smith'*:

Q4: **GET** < Address, PhoneNumber > **of** PERSON : ET
    WHERE Name = 'John Smith'

This retrieves the values of address and phone number over the whole existence time (*ET*) of the entity. If *:ET* is left out, only the current *Address* and *PhoneNumber* (at time instant t_{now}) are retrieved.

Temporal attributes of a role type are *public* to the owner entity type; that is, an owner entity can refer to these attributes (through inheritance) as though they are attributes of the owner entity. Similarly, (temporal and non-temporal) attributes of an entity type are *public* to all associated role types. The definition of attributes and relationships of a role type and its owner entity type as public to each other gives queries the flexibility to specify selection conditions and to retrieve information involving attributes of a role or an entity type by referring to each other's attributes. For example, in queries *Q2*, *Q3* and *Q4*, the entity *PERSON* is able to refer to the attributes *Address* and *PhoneNumber* of the entity role *LIVING–PERSON* since the owner of *LIVING–PERSON* is the entity *PERSON*. Notice that we can specify similar queries to the queries *Q2*, *Q3* and *Q4* by referring to *LIVING–PERSON* explicitly, as in *Q5*, *Q6* and *Q7*, since they only display temporal attributes:

Q5: **GET** < Address, PhoneNumber > **of** LIVING-PERSON
      : [1/1/1985, 12/31/1990]
    WHERE Name = 'John Smith'

Q6: **GET** < Address, PhoneNumber > **of** LIVING-PERSON
    WHERE Name = 'John Smith'

Q7: **GET** < Address, PhoneNumber > **of** LIVING-PERSON : LS
    WHERE Name = 'John Smith'

However, *Q6* and *Q7* will only retrieve entities that are *LIVING–PERSON*s at time t_{now}, whereas *Q3* and *Q4* may retrieve deceased persons (since conceptual entities have no end time) but then find that their attributes may be *NULL* at time t_{now}.

The projection of (temporal) attributes over a lifespan displays information about a conceptual entity during the time period it participates as a particular entity role. For example, in the next query, the history of the *Address* and *PhoneNumber* of *'John Smith'* is retrieved, during the time he was an enrolled student:

Q8: **GET** < Address, PhoneNumber > **of** ENROLLED-STUDENT : LS
    WHERE Name = 'John Smith'

Here, the *Address* and *PhoneNumber* history are retrieved only during the lifespan (*LS*) that 'John Smith' exists in the *ENROLLED-STUDENT* entity role. If *:LS* is left out, the current *Address* and *PhoneNumber* are retrieved if end time $ET(LS) \geq t_{now}$; if $ET(LS) < t_{now}$, the entity will not be selected since it is not valid as an *ENROLLED-STUDENT* any more.

The next query retrieves all sections that 'John Smith' has completed:

Q9: **GET** < CName of sec–course, Semester, Year > of SECTION
   WHERE Name of students of SECTION $\supseteq$ {'John Smith'}

In this query, there is no need to project the query result over a time period since the attributes *Semester* and *Year*, and the relationship *CS* (specified by *sec-course*) are non-temporal attributes and relationship of *SECTION*, and hence always exist. It is this type of query that becomes cumbersome to specify when no distinction is made between temporal and conceptual objects, as in [ElWu90]. For instance, if the root entity *SECTION* of query *Q9* is replaced by *ACTIVE-SECTION*, we get all sections that 'John Smith' is currently enrolled in:

Q10: **GET** < CName of sec–course, Semester, Year > of ACTIVE-SECTION
   WHERE Name of e–students of ACTIVE-SECTION $\supseteq$ {'John Smith'}

This query is implicitly temporal since it refers to the temporal entity role *ACTIVE-SECTION*. The query displays the current (at time instant t_{now}) sections that 'John Smith' is enrolled in. The capability to express such temporal queries by referring to an entity role without explicit reference to time is one of the advantages of this model.

A temporal query may explicitly specify a temporal projection that is derived from a temporal boolean expression. For example, suppose we want the history of *Name*, *Office* and *Salary* of each *CURRENT-FACULTY* entity role only when the value of its attribute *Rank* was either 'Assistant Prof' or 'Associate Prof':

Q11: **GET** < Name, Office, Salary > of CURRENT-FACULTY
   : ⟦ (Rank = 'Assistant Prof') **OR** (Rank = 'Associate Prof') ⟧

In this case, a different time projection is applied to each selected entity role based upon the time that entity was an assistant or associate professor; that is, the time restriction is correlated to each individual entity role.

When we deal with temporal intervals and elements in *STEER*, we need additional functionalities that are not needed in other temporal query languages [ElWu90]. For instance, ⟦*entity* : *ET*⟧ − ⟦*role* : *LS*⟧ returns the time period (temporal element) when an entity does not participate in a specific role. Hence, to retrieve the *Name*, *SSN*, and *Salary* of each faculty during the time period she/he is not *CURRENT-FACULTY* (e.g. on sabbatical or working for industry), we write:

Q12: **GET** < Name, SSN, Salary > of FACULTY
   : ⟦ FACULTY : ET ⟧ − ⟦ CURRENT-FACULTY : LS ⟧

Here, the *Name*, *SSN*, and *Salary* of a faculty are retrieved only during the period ⟦ *FACULTY* : *ET* ⟧ − ⟦ *CURRENT-FACULTY* : *LS* ⟧, which is different for each selected entity. Note the difference between the temporal expression in queries *Q11* and *Q12*. In both queries *Q11* and *Q12*, temporal element constructor operators are used to define temporal elements at the end of the *GET*–clause. However, in query *Q11*, the boolean condition $c = (\,(\,Rank = 'Assistant\ Prof'\,)$ **OR** $(\,Rank = 'Associate\ Prof'\,)\,)$ is based on a boolean predicate that involves attribute values of an entity role, whereas in query *Q12*, the boolean condition refers only to the existence time of *FACULTY* and the lifespan of *CURRENT-FACULTY*. In query *Q11*, the temporal element at the end of the *GET*–clause is the true_time of a boolean condition, whereas in query *Q12*, the temporal element is the difference between two true_times, namely the existence time of a *FACULTY* entity and its lifespan as a *CURRENT-FACULTY* entity role.

The next query retrieves the history of the *Name*, *Address* and *PhoneNumber* of living persons during the period they were not enrolled students:

Q13: **GET** < Name, Address, PhoneNumber > of PERSON
    : [LIVING-PERSON : LS] − [ENROLLED-STUDENT : LS]

The usual set theoretic operations of *UNION*, *INTERSECTION*, *DIFFERENCE* and *COMPLEMENT* can be combined with temporal element constructor operators. Both previous queries *Q12* and *Q13* use the *DIFFERENCE* operator. The next query uses the *COMPLEMENT* operator to retrieve the history of the *Name*, *Address* and *PhoneNumber* of persons before they become faculty members:

Q14: **GET** < Name, Address, PhoneNumber > **of** PERSON
    : **COMPLEMENT** [FACULTY : ET]

The idea of applying a temporal boolean condition to entity roles and entities can be extended to temporal attributes. The true_time of a boolean condition reduced to a temporal attribute name is represented as [*temporal_attribute* : *time_period*]. This corresponds to the true_time of the *temporal_attribute* during *time_period*. For example, the next query retrieves the history of the *Name*, *StudentNo*, *CName*, *Semester* and *Year* of enrolled students during the period they had a valid *Classification* (that is, a *Classification* value that is not *NULL*):

Q15: **GET** < Name, StudentNo, < CName **of** sec-course, Semester, Year >
    of sections > **of** ENROLLED-STUDENT : [Classification : LS]

4.2 Temporal Selection

Next, consider the specification of temporal conditions to select entities. These will usually involve the specification of temporal selection predicates in the *WHERE*–clause. For example, consider the query to retrieve the *Name* and *PhoneNumber* of all persons who lived in *'Arlington'* on 3/30/1992:

Q16: **GET** < Name, PhoneNumber > of LIVING-PERSON : [3/30/1992]
    WHERE [Address = 'Arlington'] ⊇ [3/30/1992]

In query *Q16*, the *WHERE*–clause is a temporal selection condition. For each *LIVING-PERSON* entity role, it first calculates the temporal boolean expression $c = ($ *Address* = *'Arlington'* $)$; if the true_time [c] ⊇ [3/30/1992], the temporal selection condition evaluates to *YES* and the *LIVING-PERSON* entity role is selected by the *WHERE*–clause. Note that it is still necessary to specify the temporal projection [3/30/1992] again in the *GET*–clause since leaving it out would retrieve the current *Name* and *PhoneNumber* of each selected entity rather than those on 3/30/1992.

The next query retrieves the *SectionNumber* and *ClassRoom* of all active sections that were held in room *'EB119'* during the period 1990–1991:

Q17: **GET** < SectionNumber, ClassRoom > of ACTIVE-SECTION
    WHERE ([ClassRoom = 'EB119'] ∩ [1/1/1990, 1/12/1991]) ≠ ∅

When we deal with time periods, we sometimes need to access the first and last time points of temporal elements. For example, to retrieve the *Name*, *SSN* and *Address* of all current students who lived in *'Arlington'* when they first enrolled as a student, we write:

Q18: **GET** < Name, SSN, Address > **of** ENROLLED–STUDENT
     WHERE [Address = 'Arlington'] $\supseteq$ ST(LS)

Here, the temporal selection condition evaluates to *TRUE* if $[c] \supseteq ST(LS)$, where $c = ($ *Address = 'Arlington'* $)$. The term $ST(LS)$ means the start time point of a lifespan. Note that $ST(LS)$ is implicitly applied to *ENROLLED–STUDENT* since it is the root entity role. This can also be written as $ST($[*ENROLLED–STUDENT : LS*]).

The lifespan of an entity role can be a continuous time period. This may happen if either an entity role has come into existence in the mini-world and never ceased to exist, or an entity role has come into existence for a while then has ceased to exist and has never reexisted in the mini-world. In order to support the concept of continuous and discontinued lifespans in our query language, we introduce the keywords *CONTINUOUS* and *DISCONTINUED*. For example, suppose we want to display the courses that have been continuously taught every semester:

Q19: **GET** < Cname, CNumber, Dept > **of** VALID–COURSE
     WHERE CONTINUOUS LS

This is similar to the temporal *ALWAYS SINCE* operator in temporal logic [Srip88].

As a final example, note that a name related with any lifespan besides the root entity must be explicitly specified in a temporal query. For instance, the next query explicitly specifies the lifespan of attribute *Address* in the *WHERE–*clause , and retrieves the *Name*, *SSN* and *Address* of all current students whose initial *Address* value was *'Arlington'*:

Q20: **GET** < Name, SSN, Address > **of** ENROLLED–STUDENT
     WHERE [Address = 'Arlington'] $\supseteq$ ST([Address : LS])

4.3   Temporal Version Restriction Operators

In the *STEER* data model, the complete history of an entity (or an entity role) is kept. The temporal versions of an entity (or an entity role) are ordered and queries may be restricted to specific versions of an entity (or an entity role). A temporal version restriction operator may be specified in the *GET* or *WHERE* clause of temporal *GORDAS* queries. The syntax of our version restriction operator is:

$$: ([NAME] \ : \ INTERVAL \ < INDEX >)$$

where the term [*NAME*]: is optional and the term *INTERVAL* < *INDEX* > is required. The term [*NAME*] is a true_time, where *NAME* may be either a boolean condition, or may be reduced to an entity name, an entity role name, or a temporal attribute. The term *INTERVAL* < *INDEX* > indicates a projection either over a single interval if < *INDEX* > is an integer or over a range of intervals if < *INDEX* > is an integer range. (Note that we assume that the intervals of a temporal element are disjoint and in the canonical temporal element representation.) As an example, the version restriction operator :(*INTERVAL 1*), when applied to a *CURRENT-FACULTY* entity role *ro*

(Figure 1) restricts the temporal element to the first interval of its lifespan. In this case, the term ⟦ *NAME* ⟧: is not used in the version restriction operator :(*INTERVAL 1*). However, if the term ⟦ *NAME* ⟧: is used in the version restriction operator such as :(⟦ *Address* ⟧ : *INTERVAL 1*), then when it is applied to a *CURRENT-FACULTY* entity role *ro* (Figure 1) it restricts the temporal element to the first interval of the lifespan of attribute *Address*.

The next query retrieves the *Name* and the first three *Salary* values for each faculty:

Q21: **GET** < Name, Salary : (**INTERVAL** 1 to 3) > of FACULTY

The term :(*INTERVAL 1 to 3*) in the *GET*-clause specifies that the projection displays the first three *Salary* values for each *FACULTY*. Notice that once a temporal version restriction operator appears in either the *GET* or *WHERE* clause of a query, we immediately deal with the full temporal entity in that clause, rather than the current entity version only.

Temporal operators may be nested and are evaluated from *left to right*. For example, suppose we want to display the *Name, SSN* and the current *Address* for each person whose first *Address* was 'Houston' and third *Address* was 'Arlington':

Q22: **GET** < Name, SSN, Address > of PERSON
    WHERE (Address : (**INTERVAL** 1) = 'Houston') **AND**
             (Address : (**INTERVAL** 3) = 'Arlington')

The term *Address : (INTERVAL 1) = 'Houston'* in the *WHERE*-clause means that we first apply the temporal ordering restriction operator :(*INTERVAL 1*) and then compare it with = 'Houston'. Similarly, the term *Address : (INTERVAL 3) = 'Arlington'* in the *WHERE*-clause means that we first apply the temporal ordering restriction operator :(*INTERVAL 3*) and then compare it with = 'Arlington'.

As seen from queries *Q21* and *Q22*, if the term ⟦ *NAME* ⟧: is omitted from the version restriction operators, then the term *INTERVAL < INDEX >* is applied to the specific attribute. However, if we would like to display the *Name* and *PhoneNumber* of a person during the time period she/he first lived in 'Arlington', we could write:

Q23: **GET** < Name, PhoneNumber : (⟦ Address = 'Arlington' ⟧
    : **INTERVAL** 1) > of PERSON

In this case, the true_time of the boolean expression *c = (Address = 'Arlington')* is evaluated for each entity and then the temporal element is assigned to the first interval of each true_time. Note that the projection over *PhoneNumber* may result with multiple values. However, we could even further restrict the previous query, *Q23*, by displaying only the first value of the *PhoneNumber*:

Q24: **GET** < Name, PhoneNumber : (⟦ Address = 'Arlington' ⟧
    : **INTERVAL** 1) : (**INTERVAL** 1) > of PERSON

Temporal version restriction operators are not limited to attributes; they may be applied to entities and therefore restrict queries to a specific range of lifespans. For example, the next query displays the *Name, SSN, Address, PhoneNumber, CName, Semester, Year* during the second interval of the lifespan of each *ENROLLED-STUDENT* who currently lives in 'Arlington':

Q25: **GET** < Name, SSN, Address, PhoneNumber, < CName **of** course,
Semester, Year > **of** a–sections > **of** ENROLLED-STUDENT
: (**INTERVAL** 2)
WHERE Address = 'Arlington'

As a final example, note that any restriction condition specified on an entity is
applied before any other restriction operator is applied to its attributes. Hence,
if we would like to display for current full professors, their *Name*, and the initial
Salary as associate professors, we could write:

Q26: **GET** < Name, Salary : (INTERVAL 1) > **of** CURRENT-FACULTY
: 〚 Rank = 'Associate Prof' 〛
WHERE Rank = 'Full Prof'

4.4 Temporal Scope Operators

In the *GORDAS* language, one can reference the attributes of an entity related
to the root entity by using a connection name. In the temporal *GORDAS*, related
entities must be projected over the temporal elements of connection names. To
generalize our temporal projection capabilities, we introduce the scope operator,
denoted by *SCOPE*, which overwrites the temporal projection of a root entity
(or related entities). For example, if we would like to retrieve the *Name* and
Rank attribute values of each current faculty during their $LAST - 1$ interval but
we would like to retrieve their initial *Salary*, we could write:

Q27: **GET** < Name, Rank, Salary : **SCOPE(INTERVAL** 1) >
of CURRENT-FACULTY : (**INTERVAL** LAST - 1)

In this case, the *SCOPE* operator at the end of *Salary* attribute overwrites
the temporal projection at the end of the *GET*–clause.

5 Conclusions

In this paper, we proposed temporal query language constructs based on the
STEER data model [ElEK90]. The query language is a temporal extension of
GORDAS [ElWi81, ElWH85, ElWu90]. The temporal query language derives its
power from the distinction between temporal/conceptual objects and relationships. It provides natural and high level temporal element constructor operators
that simplify temporal query expressions. These operators utilize the entity existence times and the role lifespans in query formulations, without having to
refer explicitly to time values. They also use the concepts of boolean conditions,
true_times, and temporal projections [ElWu90].

Our query language allows temporal element constructor operators to be defined over entities, entity roles and temporal attributes. It supports temporal
version restriction operators and allows multiple temporal scopes in a temporal projection. In addition, the concept of *CONTINUOUS* and *DISCONTIN-
UED* temporal elements can be used to specify conditions such as *ALWAYS* and
SOMETIME from temporal logic.

We are currently working on query optimization techniques for processing
complex temporal queries by utilizing temporal indexing techniques such as the
time index [ElWK90] and the monotonic B^+-tree [ElJK92].

References

[AhSn88] Ahn, I., and Snodgrass, R. Partitioned storage for temporal
databases. In *Information Systems*, 13(4), (1988).

[ElEK90] Elmasri, R., El-Assal, I., and Kouramajian, V. Semantics of temporal data in an extended ER model. In *9th Entity-Relationship
Conference* (October 1990).

[ElJK92]   Elmasri, R., Jaseemuddin, M., and Kouramajian, V. Partitioning of time index for optical disks. In *IEEE Data Engineering Conference*, (February 1992).

[ElWK90]   Elmasri, R., Wuu, G., and Kim, Y. The time index: An access structure for temporal data. In *VLDB Conference*, (August 1990).

[ElWH85]   Elmasri, R., Weeldreyer, J., and Hevner, A. The category concept: An extension to the ER model. In *Data and Knowledge Engineering* (June 1985).

[ElWi81]   Elmasri, R., and Wiederhold, J. GORDAS: A formal high-level query language for the ER model. In *2nd Entity-Relationship Conference* (October 1981).

[ElWu90]   Elmasri, R., and Wuu, G. A temporal model and query language for ER databases. In *IEEE Data Engineering Conference*, (February 1990).

[GaYe88]   Gadia, S., and Yeung, C. A generalized model for a temporal relational database. In *ACM SIGMOD Conference* (June 1988).

[Jens90]   Jensen, C. Towards the realization of transaction time database systems. *Ph.D. Dissertation, University of Maryland*, (December 1990).

[JeSn91]   Jensen, C., and Snodgrass, R. Temporal specialization and generalization. *Technical Report, University of Arizona*, (November 1991).

[NaAh89]   Navathe, S., and Ahmed, R. A temporal data model and query language. In *Information Sciences* (1989).

[SeSh87]   Segev, A., and Shoshani, A. Logical modeling of temporal data. In *ACM SIGMOD Conference* (June 1987).

[Snod87]   Snodgrass, R. The temporal query language *TQUEL*. In *ACM TODS 12 (2)*, (June 1987).

[Srip88]   Sripada, S. A logical framework for temporal deductive databases. In *VLDB Conference*, (August 1988).

[WuDa92]   Wuu, G., and Dayal U. A uniform model for temporal object-oriented databases. In *IEEE Data Engineering Conference* (February 1992).

On the Design of Object-Oriented Databases

Zahir TARI

Ecole Polytechnique Fédérale , Laboratoire de Bases de Données
IN - Ecublens, 1015 Lausanne, Switzerland
zahir@lbdsun.epfl.ch

Abstract. This paper proposes a practical approach for designing object-oriented databases. Users start by describing their database applications with a semantic data model combined with a rule model. The semantic data model allows for the representation of the structural aspect of database applications. The rule based model uses first order logic formula to define general constraints and behaviour. We propose a conceptual language, called Conceptual Definition Language, which allows for simultaneous design of structural and behavioural aspects of database applications. The produced conceptual schema is mapped into an object-oriented database by preserving all access paths associated to the conceptual schema, and by decomposing formula into atomic formula which can be directly implemented into methods of the target object-oriented database.

1. Introduction

Database applications become more and more complex. Consequently, many database researchers have tried to define richer data models to deal with advanced applications (CAM, CAD, etc.). Object-oriented data models are an example: they allow complex objects, shareability of objects, abstraction hierarchies, object identity and encapsulation [2]. Several object-oriented database systems are now available on the market (e.g., ORION [16], GEMSTONE [5], ONTOS [20], and O_2 [7], and other).

The use of object-oriented data models for conceptual modelling pose some problems [1, 12, 15]. Generally speaking, object-oriented data models are weak in their capabilities in modelling structure and behaviour aspects of database applications. Among their limitations, we find:
- an inadequacy in representing and manipulating various complex relationships of database applications. Object-oriented data models do not provide a formal syntax and semantics to express relationships as abstract notions. The information about relationships may be stored redundantly and distributed to many participating objects rather than gathered into a single object. Additionally, all relationships are represented as references between two objects. Some relationships, such as n-ary relationships, cannot be properly represented.
- a lack of explicit representation and management of the constraints as an element of a database system. Thus, the constraints are only partly expressed and their

semantics is buried into a method of a class, even though they are related to many different classes.

Semantic data models represent structural aspects of database applications in a way more appropriate than object-oriented data models. Various relationships and integrity constraints can be easily specified. But the semantic data models lack to express the behaviour of databases. Many models (e.g., Taxis [18], SHM+ [4] and INSYDE [13], and other) were proposed to integrate behaviour modelling. Some researchers focus on providing formalisms for the specification of behaviour in terms of logic programs (e.g., Caddy [10] and T_{ROLL} [14], and other). They use a logic-oriented way of modelling to specify behaviour of objects.

We follow the same orientation as Caddy and T_{ROLL}, and add new mechanisms to semantic data models to take into account the behaviour of database applications. We propose an extension of the entity-relationship data definition language, called *Conceptual Definition Language* (CDL), to model behaviour using extended first order logic. As shown in figure 1, users may describe their applications with separate models. They may also use the CDL to model both the structural and the behavioural information within the classes. The produced conceptual schema is mapped into the target object-oriented database system by preserving all its access paths which represent paths used by user queries. Formula of classes are implemented as methods by decomposition into atomic formula which represent an elementary operation within an object. Atomic formula are easily mapped into a method.

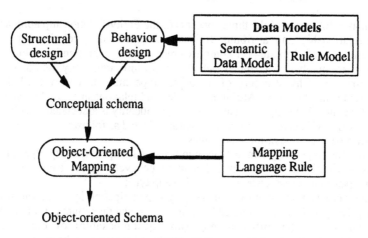

Fig. 1. Different steps of the design methodology.

The methodology is illustrated using the extended entity-relationship model ERC+ [23] and the O_2 object-oriented database system [17].

This paper is organized as follows. In the next section we describe the models used at the conceptual level. Section 3 gives a short presentation of the O_2 system. Section 4 describes the methodological framework of the transformation of a conceptual schema into O_2 system. Section 5 concludes on the contribution of our approach and introduces future works.

2 Conceptual Modelling

This section gives an overview of the different models used at the conceptual level. First we describe the semantic data model ERC+ for structural modelling. Secondly, we propose and extend first order logic language for modelling constraints and behaviour of database applications. We present an overview of a unified model which integrates all information related to a database.

2.1 Structural Modelling

Semantic data models are powerful tools for modelling structural aspects of database applications (see [11] for a survey). These models were developed to provide a higher level of abstraction for modelling data, allowing database designers to think of data in ways that correlate more directly to the real world. The semantic data models are based on well-known concepts such as classification, aggregation and generalization.

Many semantic data models are now available (Chen's data model [6], Taxis [18], SDM [9], ERC+ [23], and other) and they are used within database design tools. Among these existing semantic data models, we have chosen to use the ERC+ data model as starting point for object-oriented modelling. The main reason is that the ERC+ data model is "closer" to object-oriented data models in structural modelling. We here describe some of the basic concepts of the ERC+ data model. For more detail, we refer to [23].

ERC+ makes full usage of the three concepts of the Entity-Relationship approach [6]: entity, relationship and attribute. It is an extended entity-relationship model, specifically designed to support complex objects and object identity. Object types may bear any number of attributes, which may in turn, iteratively, be composed of other attributes. The structure of an object type may thus be regarded as an unconstrained attribute tree. Attributes, entities and relationships may be valued in a multiset (i.e. not excluding duplicates). An object identity is associated to entities and relationships. ERC+ characteristics may be summarized as follows:

- entity types bear one or more attributes;
- relationship types may connect any number of participating entity types and may have attributes as well; they are said to be cyclic if the same entity type participates more than once in the relationship type;
- a role name is associated to each entity type participation in a relationship type. The participation is characterized by its minimum and maximum cardinalities;
- attributes may be either atomic (non decomposable) or complex, i.e. decomposable into a set of component attributes, which may be either atomic or complex; an attribute is also characterized by its minimum and maximum cardinalities (mandatory/optional, monovalued/ multivalued);
- the generalization relationship is supported through the well-known is-a relationship.

Figure 2 shows a sample ERC+ diagram. The square boxes represent entities and the diamond boxes represent relationships. A single continuous line represents a 1:1 link (mandatory monovalued), a single dotted line represents a 0:1 link (optional monovalued), a double dotted line represents a 0:n link (optional multivalued), a double line (once dotted, once continuous) represents a 1:n link (mandatory multivalued). Arrows represent generalizations.

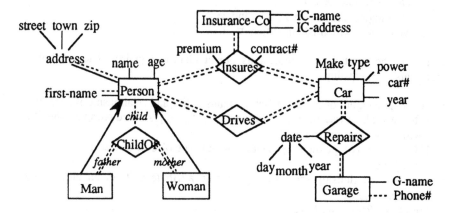

Fig. 2. An example of ERC+ schema

2.2 Behavioural Modelling

The behaviour refers to behaviour properties (i.e. operations and their relationships). Until recently, most of the semantic modelling research concentrated on specifying the structural aspects of constructed types and relationships between them, rather than on the behaviour components. SHM+ [4], INSYDE [13] and Taxis [18] are the most known systems which integrate behaviour modelling. SHM+ and INSYDE develop control mechanisms that closely follow the structure of semantic schemas. Taxis provides tools for modularizing the specification of database transactions and can support a wide class of interactive data management applications.

Logic is a powerful language for specifying constraints and behaviour of databases [8, 22]. The integration of rules in a conceptual data model is not a new topic. Several semantic data models allow dynamic modelling with logic (e.g., Caddy [10], TROLL [14] and Morse [5]). Various formalisms have been proposed for the specification of behaviour in terms of logical programs. We follow the same direction as Caddy and TROLL, and propose a logic language to model behaviour.

In the following, we present an extended first order logic for specifying the behaviour of an ERC+ schema. Behaviour of an object is represented as a closed formula associated to entity and relationship types. Formula are restricted to at most one implication symbol. Three basic domains are used in the data model: the string domain, the real domain, and the integer domain. A complex domain is defined by using the tuple and the set constructors on the basic domains. The alphabet in which formula are defined is defined by the following sets:
- A set of constants: composed of (i) the union of basic domains (integer, real, string), (ii) complex domains derived by using recursively the set and the tuple constructors on the basic domains, (iii) object identifiers, (iv) union of entity, relationship and attribute names.
- A set of variables taking their values on the previous set of constants.

- The symbols $\in$ and : .
- A set of comparison operators which contains ==, >, $\geq$, <, $\leq$, ...
- A cardinality function *card*.
- A set of logical connectors $\wedge$, v, $\neg$ and $\Rightarrow$.
- Universal and existential quantifiers $\forall$, $\exists$.

Note that the symbol "==" represents object identity equality. The symbol "=" represents value equality.

Let C be an element of the set which contains entity and relationship names of the alphabet, and t be a variable on C. Variable $t.A_1.A_2...A_n$ is called *path variable* if the following conditions are satisfied:
- If C is an entity type then A_1 is either an attribute of C or a relationship in which C participates.
- If C is a relationship then A_1 is either an attribute of C or an entity which participates to C.
- For each j, $2 \leq j \leq n$, we have:
  - If A_j is an attribute then A_k is an attribute of A_{k-1}, $j+1 \leq k \leq n$.
  - If A_j is an entity type then A_{j+1} is either an attribute of A_j or a relationship in which A_j participates.
  - If A_j is a relationship type then A_{j+1} is either an attribute of A_j or an entity type which participates to the relationship A_j.

Let t be a variable on the entity type Person (figure 1). The variables t.address.town, t.Drives and t.Insures.Car.type are path variables.

A *term* is either a variable, a path variable, or a cardinality function.

Atomic formula are obtained by using terms as follows:
- A term is an atomic formula.
- If x is a variable and E is an entity type, then x *isa* E is an atomic formula.
- If Φ_1 and Φ_2 are atomic formula, then $\Phi_1 \varphi \Phi_2$ is an atomic formula, where $\varphi \in \{=,==,\geq,\leq\}$ or φ is either the symbol ":" or $\in$.
- If Φ is an atomic formula, then $\neg\Phi$ is an atomic formula.

Examples:
- w: Car is an atomic formula.
- w: Car, w.Car.power $\geq$ 500 is an atomic formula.
- w_1: Car, w_2: Car, w_1.power $\geq$ w_2.power is an atomic formula.
- p: Person, (p isa Man) is an atomic formula.
- p: Person, (p isa Woman) is an atomic formula.

With the concept of atomic formula, one can construct a set of syntactically *well formed formula* (in short, formula) as follows.
- An atomic formula is a formula.
- If Φ, Φ_1 and Φ_2 are formula, then $\Phi_1 v \Phi_2$, $\Phi_1 \wedge \Phi_2$ and $\Phi_1 \Rightarrow \Phi_2$ are formula.
- If Y is a variable and Φ is a formula, then $\exists Y \Phi_Y$, and $\forall Y \Phi_Y$ are formula.

Examples:
- $\forall$ p, p: Person, p.age $\leq$ 200 is a formula.
- $\forall$ p, p: Person, (p.age $\geq$ 18) $\Rightarrow$ card(p.address.town) $\geq$ 2 is a formula.
- $\forall$ p: Person, (p isa Man) $\vee$ (p isa Woman) is a formula.

The last constraint defined as ($\forall$ p: Person, p: person, (p isa Man) $\vee$ (p isa Woman)) means that a given person must be either a man or a woman. It models the well-known exclusive constraint.

A formula is defined by a name and a logic description, called the body of the formula. Two different formula may have the same name and different bodies. This is generally done when a constraint of a given class is refined in one of its sub-classes. In this case, the local formula of the class is firstly considered (checked) before using the inherited formula.

Formula are associated to entity and relationship types. Generally speaking, formula which are associated to entity types refer to a local object and those associated to relationship types refer to many objects. Variables can be quantified existentially or universally.

The presented extended first order logic allow users to model behaviour aspects of an ERC+ schema. Here, we illustrate the use of the proposed logic language to model the constraints of the schema in figure 1.

- Constraint C1: *The age of a person must be less or equal to 150*
  $\forall$ x, x: Person, x.age $\leq$ 150.

- Constraint C2: *All addresses of one person should be in the same town*
  $\forall$ x, $\forall$ y_1, $\forall$ y_2, x: Person, y_1: Person.address.town, y_2: Person.address.town, ($y_1 \in$ x.address.town) $\wedge$ ($y_2 \in$ x.address.town) $\Rightarrow$ ($y_1 = y_2$).

  Note that this constraint may be also represented as the following:
  $\forall$ x, $\forall$ y, $\forall$ z_1, $\forall$ z_2, x: Person, y: Person.address, z_1: Person.address.town, z_2: Person.address.town, ($y_1 \in$ x.address)$\wedge$($z_1 \in$ y.town)$\wedge$($z_2 \in$ y.town) $\Rightarrow$ ($z_1 = z_2$).

- Constraint C3: *If the age of a person is less than 20 and he/she drives a car with power greater than 10, then the insurance premium is at least equal to 5000 [3]*
  $\forall$ y, $\forall$ w, y: Insures, w: Drives, (w.Person.age $\leq$ 20) $\wedge$ (w.Car.power $\geq$ 10) $\wedge$ (y.Person == w.Person) $\wedge$ (y.Car == w.Car) $\Rightarrow$ (y.premium $\geq$ 5000).

2.3 Conceptual Definition Language

Here we describe an extension of a data definition language to integrate formula into entity and relationship types. This language is called *Conceptual Definition Language (CDL)*. Classes defined with CDL allow users to describe their applications by integrating both the static and behaviour of objects within a single class. Some predefined classes are available for describing all information of database applications. These classes are EntityClass and RelationshipClass which correspond to entities and relationships of applications. A generic class factorizes all information associated to all classes, called *CDLClass*. This partial hierarchy of predefined classes is illustrated in figure 3.

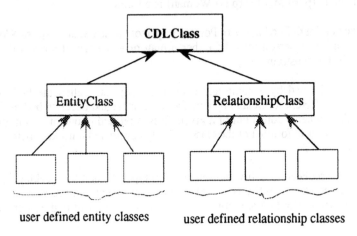

Fig. 3. The partial hierarchy of classes

Classes are build up of two parts: the type part and the rule part. The type is defined by using tuple and set constructors on predefined types such as integer, real and string types. The rule part contains a set of formula. The general definition of a class is the triple <N,T,C> where N is the name, T the type and C is the set of rules. Relationship classes, i.e. subclasses of the RelationshipClass, in addition to properties of CDLClass have a set of associated participant entities called the role parts. The following example shows some entity and relationship classes of the schema illustrated in figure 2:

/* *Entity Class Person* */
Person **SubClass** EntityClass with
    Type [(1:1) name: String; (1:n) first-name: String; (1:1) age: Real;
          (1:n) address: [(1:1) street: Integer; (1:1) town: String; (1:1) zip:Integer]
    Rules
        (C0) Self.age $\leq$ 150;
        (C1) $\forall y_1, \forall y_2, y_1$: Person.address, y_2: Person.address.town,
            y_2: Person.address.town, $(y_1 \in$ Self.address.town) $\wedge$
            $(y_2 \in$ Self.address.town) $\Rightarrow (y_1 = y_2)$;
end.

/* *Subclasses of Person* */
Woman is Person.
Man is Person .

/* *Relationship class Drives* */
Insures **SubClass** RelationshipClass with
    Roles (0:n) Person
          (0:n) Car

(1:n) Insurance-Co

Type [(1:1) contract# : String; (1:1) premium: Real]

Rules

(C3) $\forall$ y, y: Drives, (y.Person.age $\leq$ 20)$\wedge$(y.Car.power $\geq$ 10) $\wedge$
(Self.Person == y.Person) $\wedge$ (Self.Car == y.Car)
$\Rightarrow$ (Self.premium $\geq$ 5000);

end.

Note that in the type part of classes, a user specifies explicitly the cardinalities of attributes and roles. All information of user applications are expressed explicitly within the type, rule and role parts of classes.

A conceptual schema is a set of classes defined with the conceptual definition language and related by inheritance links. The inheritance mechanism is based on sub-typing, which is defined by set inclusion. The mechanism is extended to take into account inheritance of formula associated to a class. A class inherits not only the type of its super-class but also its rules. The inheritance property can be modelled as follows. We assume the existence of two functions *type* and *rule* applied to a class returning respectively the type and the rules of that class. If C_1 is a subclass of C_2 then $type(C_1) \geq type(C_2)$ and $rule(C_1) \subseteq rule(C_2)$. We allow re-definition of rules in subclasses. This allows refinement of constraints.

There is no inheritance of the role part of relationship classes, as this is not allowed in the ERC+ data model.

3. Object-Oriented Data Models

An object-oriented database system is a database system which supports an object-oriented data model. These models support basic concepts like complex objects, shareability of objects, abstraction hierarchy, object identity and encapsulation [2].

In this paper, we have chosen to give a short presentation of the O_2 data model. The interested reader will find a detailed description in [17].

The O_2 data model supports two kind of concepts: *objects* and *values*. Objects are instances of classes, and values are instances of types. Objects are encapsulated (i.e., their value is only accessible through methods), whereas values are not- their structure are known to the user, and they are manipulated by primitive operators. Manipulation of objects is done through *methods*, which are procedures attached to the objects. Object sharing structure (*type*) and behaviour (*methods*) are grouped into classes.

Types are constructed recursively using the O_2 atomic types (e.g., integer or bitmap), classes from schema and the *set*, *list* and *tuple* constructors. An O_2 schema is a set of classes related by inheritance links and/or composition links, as well as the attached methods.

Though O_2 is a multi-language, the methods are coded in the O_2C language. O_2C is a C-like programming language which allows (i) class declaration, (ii) object instanciation (i.e., message passing) and (iii) value manipulation by means of primitive operators.

4. Conceptual Schema Mapping

The purpose of this section is to present the methodological framework of the transformation of a conceptual schema produced by CDL into the O_2 object-oriented data model.

Several proposals for mapping a conceptual model into an object-oriented database have been given [3, 19, 21]. These approaches propose a set of mapping rules which are specific to the used data models. Furthermore, they are restricted to the mapping of the structural aspect of a conceptual schema.

Our approach is quite different from existing ones. We propose a general framework of the transformation of a conceptual schema into an object-oriented database system. We introduce the concept of access path preserving to map the structural aspects of a conceptual schema, and we propose a way to implement formula by its decomposition into basic formula, called atomic formula. Each atomic formula relates to a single class and is directly mapped into a method.

4.1 Structural Mapping

There is a close correspondence between the concepts of ERC+ and those of O_2. This correspondence is shown in table 1. Both models allow structured types and object identity. The structural part of classes are ERC+ concepts.

ERC+ concept	$\Leftrightarrow$	O_2 concept
entity class		class
relationship class		class
type of a class		type of a class
object identifier		object identifier
object		object
simple attribute		atomic type
complex attribute		structured type
generalization		inheritance

Table 1. Correspondence between ERC+ and O_2 concepts

The mapping strategy for the transformation of the structural part of a conceptual schema into an O_2 schema is based on the principle of *access path preserving*. An access path is a path that allows the navigation from a class to other classes and attributes of a schema. The navigation is done either vertically, in which case attributes of the original class are selected in the access path, or horizontally, in which case referenced classes of the original class are selected.

Using the schema of figure 2, Person—Drives—Car and Person—address—street are access paths but address-street is not. In other words, the access to the attribute address can be done from accessing to the class Person.

The main advantage of access paths is that they can be a basis for a query language. For example, the following queries
- What are the names of the persons living in Lausanne ?
- What are the names of the persons who drive BMW cars ?

use the access paths Person—name, Person—address—town, Person—Drives, Drives—Car, Car—make. These access paths of the conceptual schema represent the possibility for the user to navigate through information of a database for manipulation. Obviously, the mapping should preserve the contents of a database. In other words, every query q, on the conceptual schema S, which uses a set of access paths $\omega(q)$ must have a corresponding query q', on the object-oriented schema S', which produces the same result, as shown in figure 4. Consequently, $\omega(q)$ should be equivalent to $\omega(q')$. This can be done by mapping each access path of S into exactly one access path of S'.

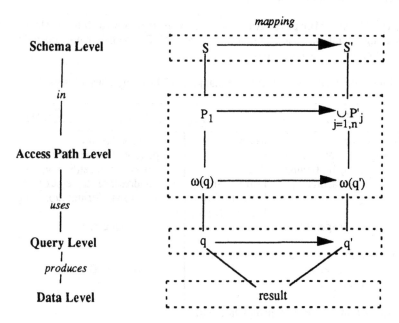

Fig. 4. Structural mapping principle

The path P_1, as shown in figure 4, may be mapped into a set of access paths P'_j if the corresponding class of P_1 is mapped into a set of classes which contain P'_j. As said above, we have chosen to map each path of a conceptual schema into a single path of the target schema.

Using the principle of access path mapping and the correspondence between the concepts of ERC+ and O_2 data models, a general mapping can be achieved by mapping each access path C_{ERC+}—A_1—A_2—...—A_n of an ERC+ schema into an access path C_{O2}—A_1—A_2—...—A_n of the corresponding O_2 schema, where C_{ERC+} is the name of a class and C_{O2} is its image class in the O_2 database. For example, Person—address—street is an access path of the entity class Person. The mapping of the latter into an O_2 class $Person_{O2}$ should preserve that access path. Thus, $Person_{O2}$—address—street is an access path of $Person_{O2}$.

Vertical navigation is done by using *internal access paths* i.e., access paths which are embedded in an entity or a relationship class. Horizontal navigation is done by using *external access paths* i.e., access paths which use entity and relationship classes. For example, Person—name and Person—address—street are internal access paths, and Person—Drives is an external access path. Given a class E, we note by $\psi(E)$ the set of all external access paths of E, and by $\lambda(E)$ the internal access paths. Obviously the constraint $\omega(E) = \psi(E) \cup \lambda(E)$ is satisfied.

The mapping of static information into an object-oriented model is done by mapping both the external and the internal paths into a single class. In the following, we propose some mapping rules.

Entity Class Mapping. An entity class E is mapped into a class E' by preserving the internal and external access paths of E. The following constraint must be satisfied $\lambda(E') = \psi(E) \cup \lambda(E)$.

The following example illustrates the mapping of the entity class Person:

Class	$\Rightarrow$	O_2 class

Person SubClass EntityClass with
Type [(1:1) name: String;
     (1:n) first-name: String;
     (1:n) address: [(1:1)street: String;
                 (1:1) town: String;
                 (1:1) zip: Integer]
     (1:1) age: Integer
		add class **Person**
		type tuple (name: String;
		   first-name: set(String);
		   address: set(tuple(street: String;
		      town: String; zip: Integer)
		
		age: Integer;

Drives SubClass RelationshipClass with Roles (0:n) Person (0:n) Car		drives: set(Drives);

Insures Subclass RelationshipClass with
Roles   (0:n) Person
        (0,n) Car
        (1,n) Insurance-Co
		insures: set(Insures);

ChildOf Subclass RelationshipClass with
Roles   (0:1)Person
        (0,n) Woman
        (0,n) Man
		childof: ChildOf)

Note that not all access paths of the classes Drives, Insures and ChildOf are considered in the mapping of the class Person, since they do not contain the class Person. For example, the access path Drives–Car does not concern the class Person.

Relationship Class Mapping. The mapping of a relationship class is quite similar to the one we proposed for entity classes. The following example illustrates the mapping of the class Insures:

Class	$\Rightarrow$	O_2 class

Insures SubClass RelationshipClass with
Role   (0:n) Person
         (0,n) Car
         (1,n) Insurance-Co
 	
Type [(1:1) contact#: String;
        (1:1) premium: Real]
end.
		add class **Insures** with
		type tuple (person: Person;
		car: Car;
		insurance-co: Insurance-Co;
		
		contract#: String;
		premium: Real)

Cardinality Constraints Mapping. Cardinality constraints are a special case of integrity constraints. They are explicitly specified in ERC+ schemas. We study the methods which will implement these constraints.

Attribute cardinality. A cardinality constraint is a couple of values (m,n) which respectively specify the minimum and the maximum number of attribute values. The test is performed on the maximal and minimal cardinality of the value of the attribute. The following example shows how to map such constraints:

/* Description of class E */
E SubClass E1 with
Type   [(a_1,b_1) A_1: [(a_{12},b_{12}) A_{12}: [... , (a_{1j},b_{1j}) A_{1j} : *type of* A_{1j}] ...]
       •••
       (a_n,b_n) A_n : *type of* A_n]

The cardinality constraint (a_{1j},b_{1j}) of A_{1j} is implemented as follows:

method *CheckCardinalityOfA$_{1j}$*: boolean in class E
body *CheckCardinalityOfA$_{1j}$*: boolean in E
    O_2C { if((count(Self$\rightarrow$A$_{11}\rightarrow$A$_{12}\rightarrow$ ...$\rightarrow$A$_{1j}$)$\geq$ m &&
        count(self$\rightarrow$A$_{1j}\rightarrow$A$_{12}\rightarrow$...$\rightarrow$A$_{1j}$) $\leq$ n)
        then {return (true);} else return (false);}

Link Cardinality. Methods implementing cardinality constraints of a link are similar to those of an attribute. The cardinality constraints of a link between relationship R and entity E could be transformed into a method *"CheckRoleCardinalityRE"* of a class E which checks both maximum and minimum cardinalities of the attribute r in class E.

4.2 Behavioural Mapping

The correspondence between the concepts of the logic language we use and O_2C concepts is given in table 2. The variables of a formula are path variables defined on a conceptual schema; atomic formula can be directly mapped into O_2C methods.

Logic Language $\Leftrightarrow$	O_2C concept
constant	constant
path variable	variable
function card	count function
atomic formula	method
formula	method

Table 2. Correspondence between the logic language and O_2 concepts

We assume that for each attribute X_j of a class X, the method *GetValueX$_j$* which returns the value of that attribute, is automatically generated during the mapping of the class X. If we assume that $X—X_1—...—X_j$ is an access path, then the method GetValueX$_j$ is defined as Self$\to X_1 \to X_2 \to ... \to X_{j-1} \to X_j$. The latter is an instance of the path $X—X_1—...—X_j$, where Self is an instance of X, and Self$\to X_1 \to X_2 \to ... \to X_r$ is an instance of $X—X_1—X_2—...—X_r$ for $1 \leq r \leq j$.

We use the table of correspondences and the generated methods for attributes to implement formula in a O_2C procedural language. The principle of mapping formula to methods is based on the concept of symmetry between the structure of a conceptual schema and the associated formula [4]. Consequently, each formula Φ of a class is decomposed into a set of atomic formula ∇_j, which in their turn relate to a single class. Formally, $\Phi = \nabla_1 \theta_1 \nabla_2 ... \nabla_{n-1} \theta_{n-1} \nabla_n$ where $\nabla_j = (Y_j \varphi_j \zeta_j)$ and $\theta_j \in \{\wedge, \vee\}$ for each j in $\{1,...,n\}$. φ_j is either a comparison-, or the set membership operator, and Y_j and ζ_j are either access path variables of X, or constants. The proof of formula decomposition is as follows: assume that $\nabla_j = (Y_{C1} \varphi_j Y_{C2})$ where Y_{C1} and Y_{C2} are variables of classes C_1 respectively C_2. ∇_j is decomposed into two atomic formula by introducing a new constant ξ as follows: $\exists \xi, (Y_{C1} = \xi) \wedge (\xi \varphi_j Y_{C2}) = \nabla_{C1} \wedge \nabla_{C2}$. The atomic formula ∇_{C1} and ∇_{C2} relate to the classes C_1 and C_2.

Given a given formula Φ of a class X, there exist a set of atomic formula $\nabla_1,..., \nabla_n$ such that $\Phi = \nabla_1 \theta_1 \nabla_2 ... \nabla_{n-1} \theta_{n-1} \nabla_n$. Each atomic formula $\nabla_j = (Y_j \varphi_j \zeta_j)$ is easily implemented in a procedural language, since it corresponds to a primitive behaviour of on an object. The different steps of the implementation of the formula Φ are the following:

- Step 1: *Variable mapping*
  Each variable of the formula Φ is mapped into a variable. Depending on the variable quantifier, a specific language keyword is used.
- Step 2: *Atomic formula mapping*
  The formula Φ is implemented by mapping each atomic formula $\nabla_j = (Y_j \varphi_j \zeta_j)$ into the procedural language as (GetY$_i$ φ_i ζ_j). The corresponding method of Φ is the following:

$(GetY_1 \ \varphi_1 \ \zeta_1) \ \theta_1 \ (GetY_1 \ \varphi_1 \ \zeta_1) \ ... \ (GetY_{n-1} \ \varphi_{n-1} \ \zeta_{n-1}) \ \theta_{n-1} \ (GetY_n \ \varphi_n \ \zeta_n)$
where θ_j are logical connectors.

Consider the formula C3 of the class Insures which has the following body:

$\forall$ s, s: Drives, y: Insures, (s.Person.age $\leq$ 20) $\wedge$ (s.Car.power $\geq$ 10) $\wedge$
(s.Person == y.Person) $\wedge$ (s.Car == y.Car) $\Rightarrow$ (y.premium $\geq$ 5000))

The variable which relates to class Insures, i.e. the variable y, is generally called *global variable* and the other variables, i.e. the variable s, are called *local variables*. Some transformations of the formula C3 may be done. For example, C3 is equivalent to

$\forall$ s, s: Drives, y: Insures, $\neg$ ((s.Person.age $\leq$ 20) $\wedge$ (s.Car.power $\geq$ 10) $\wedge$
(s.Person == y.Person) $\wedge$ (s.Car == y.Car)) $\vee$ (y.premium $\geq$ 5000)

However, the latter version of the formula is more expensive to evaluate than the following form

$\neg$ ($\exists$ y, y: Insures, (s.Person.age $\leq$ 20) $\wedge$ (s.Car.power $\geq$ 10) $\wedge$
(s.Person == y.Person) $\wedge$ (s.Car == y.Car) $\wedge$ (y.premium $\geq$ 5000))

The different steps of the mapping of the constraint are the following:
- Step 1: *Mapping of variables*

  y $\qquad\qquad\qquad\Rightarrow\qquad$ self
  $\forall$ s, s: Drives $\qquad\Rightarrow\qquad$ O_2 Drives χ
  $\qquad\qquad\qquad\qquad\qquad$ for (χ in Drives$_s$ ...)
  Where Drives$_s$ represents the set object of the class Drives.

- Step 2: *Mapping of atomic formula*

s.Person.age$\leq$20	$\Rightarrow$	($\chi\rightarrow$GetPerson)$\rightarrow$GetAge $\leq$20
s.Car.power$\geq$10	$\Rightarrow$	($\chi\rightarrow$GetCar)$\rightarrow$GetPower$\geq$ 10)
s.Person == y.Person	$\Rightarrow$	($\chi\rightarrow$GetPerson == Self$\rightarrow$GetPerson)
s.Person == y.Car	$\Rightarrow$	($\chi\rightarrow$GetCar == Self$\rightarrow$GetCar)
y.premium $\geq$ 5000	$\Rightarrow$	(Self $\rightarrow$GetPremium) $\geq$ 5000

Finally, we obtain the following code of the method which implements C3:
add class **Insures**
type tuple (car: Car; person: Person; insurance-co: Insurance-Co;
            Premium: real; Contract#: String)
method *CheckRule1*: boolean

body *CheckRule1*: boolean in class Insures
O_2C { O_2 Drives χ, res: boolean; res = true;
        for (χ in Drives$_s$ when
        ($\chi\rightarrow$GetPerson)$\rightarrow$GetAge$\leq$ 20) && ($\chi\rightarrow$GetCar)$\rightarrow$GetPower $\geq$ 10) &&
        (Self$\rightarrow$GetPerson == $\chi\rightarrow$GetPerson) && (Self$\rightarrow$GetCar == $\chi\rightarrow$GetCar) &&
        ! (if (Self $\rightarrow$ GetPremium $\geq$ 5000) then {res = false});
        if(res == false {return(false);} else return(true);}

The constraint methods should be activated during an insertion or update of an object. Functional dependencies, represented as formula, can be easily implemented according to the previous mapping rule. Given a class X, a functional dependency is expressed as $X_1 X_2 ... X_n \rightarrow Y$, and corresponds to the following constraint formula:

DF1: $\forall i_1, \forall i_2, i_1: X, i_2:X, (i_1.X_1 = i_2.X_1) \wedge (i_1.X_2 = i_2.X_2) \wedge ... \wedge (i_1.X_n = i_2.X_n)$
$\Rightarrow (i_1.Y = i_2.Y)$

If we assume that i_1 is a global variable, then the code of the method which implements DF1 is the following:

```
/* Description of class X */
Add class X
method DF1: boolean
```

```
/* The code of DF1*/
body DF1: boolean in class X
    O2C { O2 X χ; res: boolean; res = true;
            for ( χ in Xs when (Self→GetValueX1 = χ→GetValueX1) &&
            ....
                (Self→GetValueXn = χ →GetValueXn) &&
                ! (Self→GetValueY = χ → GetValueY))
            then { res = false});
            if (res == false { return (false);} else return (true); }
```

The integrity constraint (name, first-name) → age of the schema of figure 2 is implemented as follows:

```
method CheckConstraint: boolean
body CheckConstraint: boolean in class Person
    O2C {O2 Person v; res: boolean; res = true;
            for ( v in Persons when (Self→name == v → name) &&
            (Self → first-name == v → first-name) &&! (Self → age == v → age))
            {res = false}); if (res == false {return(false);} else return(true);}
```

Dynamic constraints are predicates specified over a sequence of states. A considerable amount of dynamic constraints can be expressed in terms of the initial state and the final states. Such constraints are extended formula with temporal predicates such as *always* and *sometimes*. These extended formula are implemented in the same way as proposed above.

5. Conclusion

In this paper, we proposed a practical approach for designing object-oriented databases. First, we extended the semantic data model ERC+ with an extended logic language to be able to model behaviour of objects. The logic language expresses concepts of ERC+ in appropriate way. The proposed conceptual definition language extends entity and relationship types to integrate formula as a part of their descriptions. The obtained conceptual schema (structural and behaviour) is mapped into the O_2 object-oriented data model by preserving all its access paths. The formula of an ERC+ schema are decomposed into atomic formula, and implemented into a procedural language.

Current work concerns semantic normalization [24] in semantic data models which take into account user point of views (conceptual aspects). The normalization process will be integrated in the step of conceptual modelling.

Future works concern the implementation of a CASE tool based on the proposed methodology. This tool will be based on an expert system. A formal definition of the conceptual modelling language will be the subject of a forthcoming publication.

References

1. A. Albano, G. Ghelli, R. Orsini: A relationship mechanism for a strongly typed object-oriented database programming language. In Proc. of the 17th Int. Conf. on Very Large Data Bases, Sept. 1991, pp. 565-575.
2. M. Atkinson, F. Bancilhon, D. DeWitt, K. Dittrich, D. Maier, S. Zdonik: The Object-Oriented Database System Manifesto. In. Proc. of Int. Conf. on Deductive and Object-Oriented Database Systems, Dec. 1989, pp. 40-57.
3. M. Bouzeghoub, E. Metais: Semantic modelling of object oriented databases. Proc. of the 17th Int. Conf. on Very Large Data Bases, Sept. 1991, pp. 3-14.
4. M. L. Brodie, D. Ridjanovic: On the development of data models. In: M. L. Brodie, J. Mylopoulos, Y. Schmidt (eds.): On Conceptual Modelling. Springer-Verlag 1984, pp. 19-48.
5. R. Bretl et al.: The Gemstone Data Management System. In: W. Kim, F. H. Lochovsky (eds): Object-Oriented Concepts, Databases and Applications. Addison Wesley Publishing Company, 1989.
6. P. Chen: The Entity-Relationship Model-Toward a Unified View of Data. ACM TODS, 1(1), 1976.
7. O. Deux and al.: The story of O_2. Special Issue of IEEE transactions on Knowledge and Data Engineering, 2(1), March 1990.
8. H. Gallaire, J. Minker, J. M. Nicolas: Logic and databases: a deductive approach. ACM Computing Surveys, 16(2), 1984.
9. M. Hammer, D. McLeod: Database Description with SDM: A Semantic Database Model. ACM TODS, 6(3), 1981.
10. U. Hohenstein, K. Hülsmann: A Language for specifying static and dynamic integrity constraints. In Proc. of the 10th Int. Conf. on the Entity-Relationship Approach, Oct. 1991, pp.389-416.
11. R. Hull, R. King: Semantic database modelling: Survey, Applications, and Research Issues. ACM Computing Surveys, 19 (3), 1987.
12. S. Hwang, S. Lee: The Object-Oriented Relationship System for Managing Complex Relationships. In Proc. of Int. Symp. on Database Systems for Advanced Applications, April 1991, pp. 391-400.
13. R. King, D. McLeod: A database design methodology and tool for information systems. ACM Trans. Off. Inf. Syst., 3(1) , 1985, pp. 2-21.
14. R. Jungclaus, G. Saake: Language features for Object-Oriented Conceptual Modelling. In Proc. of the 10th Int. Conf. on the Entity-Relationship Approach, Oct. 1991, pp. 309-324.

15. M. F. Kilian: Bridging the gap between O-O and E-R. In Proc. of the 10th Int. Conf. on the Entity-relationship Approach, Oct. 1991, pp. 445-458.
16. W. Kim, J. F. Garza, N. Ballou , D. Woelk: Architecture of the ORION Next-Generation Database System. IEEE Transactions on Knowledge and Data Base Engineering, 2(1), 1990.
17. C. Lécluse, P. Richard: The O_2 programming language. In Proc. of the 15th Int. Conf. on Very Large Data Bases, Aug. 1989, pp. 411-422.
18. J. Mylopoulos, H. K. T. Wong: Some features of the TAXIS data model. In Proc. of the 6th Int. Conf. on Very Large Databases, 1980.
19. J. Nachouci, M. P. Chastang, H. Briand: From entity-relationship diagram to an object-oriented database. In Proc. of the 10th Int. Conf. on the Entity-Relationship Approach, Oct. 1991, pp. 459-481.
20. Ontologic Inc.: ONTOS Object Database Documentation. Version 1.5, 1990.
21. D. Ravalet, H. Briand: Transformation d'un schema entité-association en base de données orientées objets. In Proc. of the 3rd Int. Workshop on Software Engineering and its applications, Dec. 1990, pp. 289-303.
22. R. Reiter: Towards a logical reconstruction of relational database theory. In On Conceptual Modelling, Book, Springer-Verlag eds., 1984, pp. 191-223.
23. S. Spaccapietra, C. Parent: ERC+: an object based entity-relationship approach. In: P. Loucopoulos, R. Zicari (eds.): Conceptual Modelling, Databases and CASE: An Integrated View of Information Systems Development. John Wiley, 1992.
24. Z. Tari, S. Spaccapietra: Semantic Normalization in Object-Based Models. Technical Report, EPFL/DI/LBD.

"Part" Relations for Object-Oriented Databases

Michael Halper, James Geller, and Yehoshua Perl

Institute for Integrated Systems, CIS Department
and
Center for Manufacturing Systems
New Jersey Institute of Technology
Newark, NJ 07102 USA

Abstract. It has long been recognized that the "part" relation is an extremely useful modeling tool. This is especially true in areas such as manufacturing, design, graphics, and document processing. In this paper, we present a comprehensive conceptual model for parts in the context of object-oriented database (OODB) systems. Our model captures the semantics and functionality of a variety of part relations with characteristics such as exclusiveness/sharing, multi-valuedness, cardinality restriction, ordering, essentiality, dependency, and value propagation. Our notion of exclusiveness extends previous work by refinement into two kinds, inter-class and intra-class exclusiveness. Dependency in our model is permitted from both the part to the whole object, and vice versa. We also present a general mechanism for upward and downward value propagation along the part relation. Of note is the fact that we realize the part model without having to introduce any extraordinary new constructs into the underlying OODB data model. The part relation itself is represented as an object class whose instances represent the actual part connections between instances of the participating classes. By elevating the part relation to the status of a "first-class citizen," we are following in the tradition of the ER and other semantic data models.

1 Introduction

The specialization (*is-a*) relation has long been the cornerstone of semantic [26] and object-oriented data models [2, 5, 10]. Another relation which has begun to receive considerable attention is the "part" relation. The need for part decomposition can be found in many advanced modeling domains, many of which have been targeted as testing grounds for object-oriented database (OODB) systems. In fact, a number of such systems have included intrinsic support for the part relation (e.g., [21, 23, 25, 29]). An example application is a database used in a manufacturing enterprise, where, after all, the main activity is the assembly of collections of parts into whole products. The part relation is also used extensively in CAD systems [22] and computer graphics [11].

Part decomposition has generated interest in Artificial Intelligence and related fields, where much attention has been paid to the part relation as it occurs in the context of logical syllogisms [31]. In particular, the question of the part relation's transitivity has been investigated [7]. The part relation has also been investigated in the context of connectionist networks (e.g., [18]).

In previous work [12, 16], we have investigated different kinds of part relations for graphical deep knowledge [13]. In this paper, we present a conceptual model for "parts" in the context of an OODB. This conceptual model (henceforth referred to as the *part model*) comprises a variety of part relations and their realization above an existing OODB data model. Characteristics of the different part relations include exclusiveness/sharing, multiplicity, cardinality restriction, ordering, essentiality, dependency, and upward/downward value propagation.

The ORION part model [21] distinguishes between four types of part relations, derived by imposing two types of constraints, exclusiveness and dependency, on *weak* references (what we call relationships). The *exclusiveness* constraint permits a "whole" object to put an exclusive hold on a part. In this paper, we further refine the exclusiveness property into two kinds, intra-class and inter-class exclusiveness. *Dependency* gives the schema designer the ability to make a part dependent on the existence of the whole: If the whole is deleted, the part is deleted automatically. Our model extends this idea and permits the specification of dependency in both directions, from the whole to the part, and vice versa. ORION allows a part relation to be set-valued. Our model includes the ability to impose cardinality constraints on the part relation. For example, we can say that a car has exactly four tires or a truck has between four and eighteen.

The part model of SNOOD [25] addresses the problem of value propagation (or selective inheritance) where values of certain attributes are made available at different levels of the part hierarchy. In our representation, we introduce a general mechanism for performing both upward and downward value propagation along the part relation.

An important aspect of our part model is the fact that we have avoided introducing any extraordinary new constructs into the underlying OODB model. We exploit features of OODBs which have been widely investigated and studied. Our model elevates part relations to the level of classes and objects: The part relation between two classes is represented as an object class in its own right, with its instances representing the actual part connections between pairs of objects from the participating classes [1, 8, 23, 28]. In this sense, our model is close to the ER [6] and other semantic models [26], where both entities and relationships are viewed as "first-class citizens."

The rest of the paper is organized as follows. In the next section, we discuss the underlying OODB model. In Section 3, we define the different part relations included in our model. Section 4 contains the details of incorporating these relations into the OODB. Conclusions and a discussion of future work are found in Section 5.

2 Preliminaries

In this section, we present features whose presence we assume in the underlying OODB model. While these features are common to existing OODBs, we closely follow the terminology of the Vodak Modeling Language [9] and the Dual Model [14, 15, 24]. An OODB relationship is a (named) property of an object which references another object. (At the schema level, we say that the relationship is a property of one class referring to another.) A relationship which does not refer to some object is said to be nil-valued.

A multi-valued relationship references a set of objects. Explicit upper and lower bounds can be placed on this set's cardinality [3], yielding a *range-restricted* relationship. We assume that our underlying OODB supports two other types of such constraining relationships, *essential* and *dependent*. An *essential relationship* is one which must always refer to an existent object (i.e., which may not be nil). It is equivalent to a range-restricted relationship whose upper and lower bounds are both equal to one. A *dependent relationship* from a class **A** to a class **B** exists if the existence of an instance of **A** depends on the existence of an instance of **B**. The deletion semantics for such a relationship is as follows: If an instance a of **A** references an instance b of **B**, and b is deleted, then a is also deleted.

A *path method* [14] is one which traverses a path through an object's composition hierarchy [20] to retrieve some data value. In other words, it is a sequence of messages passed along such a path. The concept is similar to the notion of *path expression* introduced in [5].

In [17], we introduced a graphical notation for the specification of OODB schemata, which will be employed throughout the paper. The conventions are: A class is represented as a box enclosing the name of the class (Fig. 5). An attribute is an ellipse which circumscribes a name. A single-valued relationship is denoted by a labeled, single-lined arrow pointing from the source class to the target class. A multi-valued relationship is similar, but the arrow is dual-lined (Fig. 11). A relationship is designated dependent (essential) with the addition of an extra arrow head (a circle). A path method is represented as a labeled, broken-lined arrow directed from the class of definition to the data item it accesses.

3 Definitions of the Part Relations

Our part model comprises a number of different part relations, defined with the following characteristics: exclusiveness/sharing, single-valuedness/multi-valuedness, cardinality range-restriction, ordering, and essentiality. There are also two part relations which express dependency semantics, and two others which permit value propagation along the part relation link.

Before getting to the specific definitions, let us define the terminology we will be using when discussing the part relations. Following Winston *et al.* [31], we will occasionally refer to the "part" relation as the *meronymic* relation. A part will be called a *meronym*, while the whole will be called the integral object or *holonym*. We will sometimes refer to the class of a part as the meronymic class; likewise, the class of the integral object will be referred to as the holonymic class. For example, an instance e of class **engine** would be a meronym and an instance c of class **car** would be a holonym. The classes, **engine** and **car**, would be the meronymic and holonymic classes, respectively.

Part relations in general can be divided along the lines of *exclusive* and *shared* [21, 25]. Designating a part relation exclusive means that the integral object is the sole owner of the part object. The need for exclusiveness arises when modeling *physical* (or *extensive*) objects [31] such as cars or buildings. In order to capture the semantics of such applications, the part relation must permit the explicit statement and enforcement of the fact, e.g., that cars do not share engines.

Part relations which are not exclusive are called *shared*. A shared part relation puts no restrictions on the way other objects can reference an object which is already part of some integral object. A part can be freely shared among several holonyms. For example, many memoranda may share the same textual body, or two books (compilations) may share the same chapter.

The exclusive/shared dichotomy is supported in a number of existing OODB part models (e.g., [21, 25]). In our model, we further refine the notion of exclusiveness by defining two kinds, *inter-class* and *intra-class* exclusiveness.

While it is the case that no two cars can share an engine, it is also the case that a car and an airplane cannot share one either. Therefore, the exclusive part relation between the classes **car** and **engine** has ramifications for the entire database topology, restricting not only "part" references from cars but from objects belonging to other classes as well. We call such a part relation *inter-class exclusive* because the reference restriction applies across all classes. There are times, however, when we would like to enforce the exclusive reference restriction only within a single class, and relax it otherwise. In other words, we want to be able to enforce the following: The fact that an object a of class **A** has a part reference to an object b of class **B** disallows any other instance of **A** from claiming b as its part, but does not disallow an instance of a class other than **A** from doing so. Let's look at an example where this restriction is relevant.

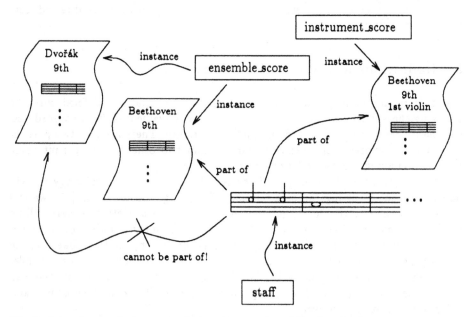

Fig. 1. Intra-class exclusive part relations in a music publication database

Consider a music publication system. The score for an orchestral composition is typically available in two formats, the full (or ensemble) score and individual instrument scores. The "staff object" representing the music to be played, e.g., by the first

violin section in Beethoven's Ninth Symphony can be modeled as part of both an
ensemble score object and an instrument score object. However, it cannot be part of
more than one ensemble score because different musical compositions do not have
identical music played by the same instrument. For example, the music for the first violin section is not the same for Dvořák's Ninth as it is for Beethoven's Ninth (Fig. 1).
Thus, the part relation between the classes **ensemble_score** and **staff** is intra-class
exclusive. The same is true of the part relation between **instrument_score** and
staff. See Fig. 1 for an illustration of this scenario.

Another example of the intra-class exclusive link is found between
ensemble_score and **score_expression_sequence**. A score expression sequence is
the line above the staff of a musical score containing annotations such as "Allegro"
(Fig. 2). As tempo markings and other such performance notation vary from score
to score, an expression sequence object will always be part of only a single ensemble
score. In contrast, the same score expression sequence will constitute a part of all instrument scores associated with a particular ensemble score. Thus, the part relation
between **ensemble_score** and **score_expression_sequence** is intra-class exclusive,
while that between **instrument_score** and **score_expression_sequence** is shared.

Fig. 2. An ensemble score and its score expression sequence

Single-valued part relations are those where the holonym can have only one
meronym of the given type. For example, a car has only one engine. When holonyms
can have many components of the same type, the relation is *multi-valued*, as with a
car and its doors. To enhance expressiveness, our part model includes a number of
variations of the multi-valued part relation.

The *range-restricted* part relation puts constraints on the number of meronyms
that an integral object can have, allowing explicit upper and lower bounds to be
placed on the relation's cardinality. For example, an engine can be required to have
between four and twelve cylinders. The upper or lower bound may be omitted,
indicating an "n or greater" or "0 to n" semantics.

The *fixed-cardinality* part relation is a special case of the range-restricted relation
with upper and lower bounds of equal value. If only engines with six cylinders are

being modeled in the database, then a fixed-cardinality relation of degree six would be used.

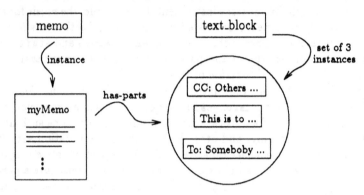

Fig. 3. Inadequate representation of memo

Another special type of multi-valued relation, the *ordered part relation*, accommodates an ordering among parts. For example, a memo can be modeled as the composition of a header, body, and carbon copy (CC) section. These latter objects can be modeled as "text block" objects. Hence, it might seem possible to represent **memo** with a fixed-cardinality part relation of degree three to **text_block** (Fig. 3). But throwing components together in a set with cardinality three does not preserve the ordering among them. In fact, there is no way to tell the header from the body, etc. Our ordered part relation resolves this problem by allowing an ordering to be specified among the parts.

An *essential* part relation requires the holonym to have exactly one part of the given type. It is therefore equivalent to the fixed-cardinality relation of degree one. An example is the relation between a car and its frame.

Dependency semantics are often desired when modeling with parts. If a large integral object, such as a CAD drawing, is deleted, then we may want to have all its parts deleted, so that these need not be searched out and deleted separately. Our model provides a *"part-to-whole" dependent* part relation for this purpose.

There are also times when a *"whole-to-part" dependency* is desired. Referring back to our music publication system, consider what happens when a particular instrument is removed from the orchestration of a score, meaning that the staff containing the instrument's music is removed from the ensemble score. In such a case, the staff object is deleted from the database. Since an instrument score consists of only a single staff, and since the staff contains the music, the deletion of its staff leaves an instrument score with no music at all. Therefore, the instrument score should be deleted as well. So it is sensible to make **instrument_score** dependent on **staff**. Our model provides this complementary "whole-to-part" dependent part relation.

In our part model, we define a general mechanism for value propagation [25] from both the meronym to the holonym, and vice versa. Value propagation refers to the flow of a data value across the part connection. As a modeling tool, it is useful for expressing certain functional dependencies between integral objects and their parts. As an example, the attribute *age* of a car can be taken to be identically equal to the age of its frame. Hence, the value of *age* should be propagated upward through the part link from the **frame** to **car**. Such an arrangement not only alleviates the need to explicitly store *age* with **car**, it also eliminates the burden of having to maintain the functional dependency. By propagating the attribute's value, we insure that it is the same at both **car** and **frame**.

The direction of flow may also be from the whole to the part. Such a scheme captures the case where a data value of the whole determines something about its parts. For example, if a filing cabinet is composed of steel, then its drawers are probably composed of steel, too. In general, we could opt to model drawers such that they are always composed of the same material as their filing cabinets. We stress that within our part model, such an arrangement would not represent a default (see, e.g., [27]) and would not be defeasible, but would represent a definitive modeling decision. All drawers would be required to obtain their material make-up from their filing cabinets.

4 Realization of the Part Relations

In this section, we discuss our realization of the above mentioned part relations. Before getting to the specifics, we introduce our basic approach which is to represent the part relation as a type of object class—objects, in this case, representing relationships between other objects [1, 8, 23, 28].

4.1 Generic Part Relation

Assume that we have two classes, **A** and **B**, and we wish to define a part relation between them such that **B** is the meronymic class and **A** is the holonymic class. The syntax for skeletal definitions of the two classes can be seen in Fig. 4, where the line in the definition of **A** containing the keyword **has-part** indicates the part relation to **B**. Included in the **has-part** specification is an optional selector "myB" which can used by an instance of **A** to reference its part. The selector may be omitted, in which case the name of the meronymic class is used by default. To improve readability, an optional corresponding **is-part-of** can be placed in the meronymic class, as we have done for **B**. Normally, this is not needed and just introduces unnecessary coupling between the definitions. However, there are two types of part relations (discussed below) which do require this explicit reference to the holonymic class.

To realize the part relation between the two classes, our system expands the **has-part** construct into a subschema of its own. The system automatically defines an object class **B-PART-A** and connects it via the relationships *holonym* and *meronym* to **A** and **B**, respectively. The system also adds relationships *p1* to **A** and *w1* to **B**. The names *p1* and *w1* ("p" for part, and "w" for whole) are chosen arbitrarily by the system so as not to conflict with the names of any other properties of the class. As mentioned above, a selector (e.g., "myB" of **A** in Fig. 4) is used to retrieve the part from within the integral object. This "selector" is actually the name of a path method [14] defined by the system as the final step in the subschema expansion and

```
class A
    has-part(myB:B)

class B
    is-part-of(A)
```

Fig. 4. Incomplete definitions of A and B

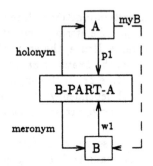

Fig. 5. Schema expansion for Fig. 4

added to the definition of the holonymic class. The method is defined such that it traverses *p1* to the relation object (i.e., an instance of B-PART-A) and returns the part object's OID which it obtains as the value of *meronym*. The entire subschema expansion for the part relation between A and B is shown pictorially in Fig. 5.

This realization was chosen for a number of reasons. First, the arrangement does not require the introduction of any extraordinary new OODB modeling constructs. In fact, all the different part relations can be obtained by making straightforward modifications to the basic configuration. The arrangement also permits traversal from the whole to the part, and vice versa. Furthermore, the mechanism offers a convenient way of performing value propagation along the part hierarchy. Finally, as an object in its own right, the relation can be endowed with attributes in a similar fashion to relationships in the ER and other semantic models.

4.2 Exclusive and Shared Part Relations

The part relation between **instrument_score** and **staff**, introduced above, will be used to demonstrate the realization of the *intra-class exclusive* link between an integral object and its part. The (partial) definitions of two classes, **instrument_score** and **score**, from the music publication database are shown in Fig. 6. Note that the **has-part** specification in **instrument_score** has been changed to **has-intra-excl-part**.

The subschema expansion for this part relation (Fig. 7) is actually the same as the one presented above for the generic example. The key point here is that the relationship *w1* is defined by the system to be single-valued. Because of this, an instance of **staff** may only be related to a single instance of **staff-PART-instrument_score**. This, in turn, means that it can be part of only one **instrument_score**. Hence, the particular instrument score has an exclusive hold on the staff with respect to other instrument scores. However, the configuration in no way precludes an instance of another class (e.g., an ensemble score), with its own part connection to **staff**, from making such a reference. Thus, the configuration indeed captures the desired intra-class exclusive part semantics.

Before introducing the *inter-class exclusive part relation*, we need to discuss the generic system operation **make-part-of** which is used to establish a part connection between a pair of objects. The operation takes two arguments, the OIDs of the inte-

```
class score                    class instrument_score
   attributes:                    subclass-of(score)
     title: titleType             has-intra-excl-part(stf:staff)
     dedication: string           has-part(score_expression_sequence)
     year: yearType             attributes:
     opus_number: integer         instrument: instrumentType
     pages: integer
   relationships:
     composed_by: composer
```

Fig. 6. Some class definitions from music publication OODB

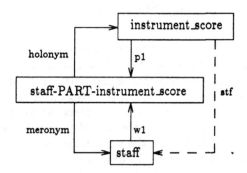

Fig. 7. The part relation between instrument_score and staff

gral object and the part. For instance, assume that we have an instrument score SC and a staff ST. Invoking make-part-of(SC, ST) causes the following actions to take place. First, an instance of the class staff-PART-instrument_score is created, and its relationships *holonym* and *meronym* are assigned values of SC and ST, respectively. After that, the relationships *p1* of object SC and *w1* of object ST are given the value of the OID of the new part relation object.

Because one inter-class exclusive part relation affects all the part relations of a meronymic class, it is not possible for the system to properly enforce the semantics of the restriction just by relying on the structure of the subschema expansion between the pair of classes. An operational approach is required. Our approach is to augment the writer methods [19] for the wi's, the relationships automatically installed in the meronymic class by the system. The augmentation is such that the methods enforce the "make-component" rule defined in [21], as explained in the following.

Assume that we have a class B which is the meronymic class in n different part relations. The holonymic classes are A1, A2, ..., An. The system-defined relationships emanating from B to the part relation classes B-PART-A1, B-PART-A2, ..., B-PART-An are $w1$, $w2$, ..., wn, respectively (Fig. 8). The part relation between A1 and B is taken to be inter-class exclusive.

Let z be the OID of the instance of B-PART-A1 created when make-part-of is invoked with a pair of OIDs, a and b, representing instances of A1 and B, respectively. Instead of just assigning $w1$ the value z when it is invoked by make-part-of, the

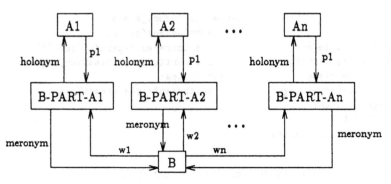

Fig. 8. A meronymic class with multiple part relations

writer method does the following. It scans the relationships $w2$ through wn of the instance b searching for values other than nil. If it finds such a value, it knows that b is already part of an object other than a and thus cannot be grabbed exclusively by a. The writer then refuses to perform the assignment of z to $w1$. This failure implies the failure of **make-part-of** and guarantees the maintenance of the inter-class exclusive reference constraint. In the case of an intra-class exclusive or shared part relation, the writer method for the concomitant wj need only check the wi's of inter-class exclusive relations for nil values; a meronym can participate freely in other intra-class exclusive or shared relations so long as it is not in any inter-class exclusive relation.

Syntactically, we represent the inter-class exclusive relation by replacing **has-part** with **has-inter-excl-part**. In Fig. 9, we see an inter-class exclusive part relation between the classes **car** and **engine**.

```
class car
    subclass-of(vehicle)
    has-inter-excl-part(engine)
    attributes:
    model: modelType

class engine
    attributes:
    model: engineModelType
    fuel: gasOrDiesel
```

Fig. 9. Classes car and engine

```
class instrument_score
    subclass-of(score)
    has-intra-excl-part(staff)
    has-shared-part
         (score_expression_sequence)
    attributes:
    instrument: instrumentType
```

Fig. 10. Instrument_score with shared part

A *shared part relation* is obtained in our model when the system-defined relationship $w1$ is made multi-valued. By doing this, meronyms can be associated with many part relation objects, and thus with many integral objects. In Fig. 10, we show a revised version of the class **instrument_score** which indicates that many such objects can share the same score expression sequence. Note that **has-part** is replaced by **has-shared-part**. The schema expansion for this part relation is shown pictorially in Fig. 11, where *w1* appears as a dual-lined arrow to indicate its multiplicity.

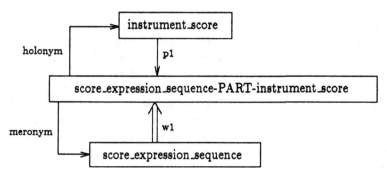

Fig. 11. Shared part relation of **instrument_score** and **score_expression_sequence**

4.3 Single- and Multi-valued Part Relations

Instrument scores, because they contain music for a single instrument, require only one staff. Hence the part relation between the classes **instrument_score** and **staff** is *single-valued*. In our realization, a single-valued part relation is obtained when the relationship *p1* of the meronymic class is defined to be single-valued (Fig. 7). This implies that an instance of **instrument_score** can be related to at most one instance of **staff-PART-instrument_score**, and consequently to only one staff.

On the other hand, ensemble scores are defined to have many staves, and so the part relation between the two respective classes is *multi-valued* (Fig. 12). The **has-part** construct, in this case, is modified with a pair of curly brackets surrounding its argument, conveying the fact that there are a set of parts from the given class. The schema expansion for the multi-valued part relation is obtained by defining *p1* to be multi-valued, as in Fig. 13. In this way, instances of the holonymic class can be related to any number of instances of the part relation class, and therefore any number of instances of the meronymic class.

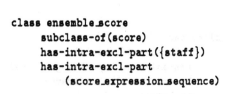

```
class ensemble_score
    subclass-of(score)
    has-intra-excl-part({staff})
    has-intra-excl-part
        (score_expression_sequence)
```

Fig. 12. Multi-valued part relation

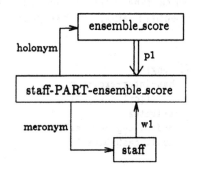

Fig. 13. Realization of Fig. 12

4.4 Range-restricted, Fixed-Cardinality, and Essential Part Relations

Above, we used the example of the engine with between four and twelve cylinders to define the *range-restricted part relation*. Here, we use the same example to discuss the realization. Syntactically, the range-restriction is expressed by adding a numerical range extension to the set notation as in Fig. 14. (The syntax used here is similar to Sowa's pluralization notation [30]). In terms of the subschema expansion, the range-restriction is obtained by placing upper and lower bounds on the cardinality of the relationship *p1* of the holonymic class [3, 4]. The subschema expansion for the part relation between the classes is shown graphically in Fig. 15. The numerical range 4–12 in parentheses following *p1* is our notation for the range constraint on this multi-valued relationship.

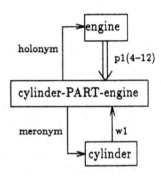

```
class engine
    has-inter-excl-part
        ({cylinder}:4-12)
    attributes:
    model: engineModelType
    fuel: gasOrDiesel
```

Fig. 14. Engines with 4 to 12 cylinders

Fig. 15. Realization of Fig. 14

As the *fixed cardinality* and *essential* part relations are special cases of the range-restricted relation, their realizations are readily derived from the one just presented. Syntactically, however, we employ a different notation for each of these. For the fixed-cardinality relation, a single number is shown after the colon, instead of the numerical range (Fig. 16). The numerical range and curly brackets are omitted for an essential relation, and **has-part** is replaced by **has-essential-part** (Fig. 17).

```
class engine
    has-inter-excl-part
        ({cylinder}:6)
    attributes:
    model: engineModelType
    fuel: gasOrDiesel
```

```
class car
    subclass-of(vehicle)
    has-inter-excl-part(eng:engine)
    has-essential-part(frame)
    attributes:
    model: modelType
```

Fig. 16. Engines with exactly 6 cylinders

Fig. 17. Car with essential part frame

4.5 Ordered Part Relation

The class memo, discussed above, will be used to introduce the realization of the *ordered part relation*. The **has-part** specification for this relation includes a list of selectors in square brackets before the meronymic class's name (Fig. 18). Each element of the list is a selector for a single part object. (Cf. the generic part relation with the optional selector above.) To realize this part relation, the system places three relationships in memo, rather than one as with the other part relations discussed so far. It also creates three path methods to function as the selectors for the parts from within the holonyms. In general, the integral class must be equipped with n new relationships and methods. The schema expansion for the part relation between memo and **text_block** can be seen in Fig. 19.

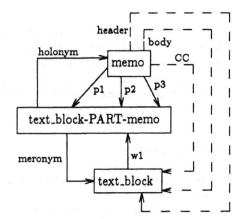

```
class memo
  has-intra-excl-part
    ([header, body, CC]:text_block)
```

Fig. 18. Definition of class memo

Fig. 19. Realization of Fig. 18

4.6 Dependent Part Relations

The realizations of the two kinds of *dependent part relations* can be derived by further refining the relationships *p1* and *w1* of the generic subschema expansion with dependency. As an example of the *"part-to-whole" dependent part relation*, assume that block is dependent on engine: If an engine is deleted from the database, its block is deleted, too. The definitions of these classes in Fig. 20 show that here, for the first time, an explicit reference (is-dependent-part-of) to the holonymic class is needed in the meronymic class. In the schema expansion in Fig. 21, we see that both *w1* and *holonym* are dependent (with dependency indicated by a double-headed arrow). Thus, if an instance of engine is deleted, the related instance of block-PART-engine is deleted, which in turn causes the deletion of the related block.

Referring back to our music publication system, we will use the part relation between the classes instrument_score and staff to demonstrate the realization of *whole-to-part* dependency. Remember that an instrument score contains a single

```
class engine
    has-inter-excl-part(block)
  attributes:
    model: engineModelType
    fuel: gasOrDiesel

class block
    is-dependent-part-of(engine)
```

Fig. 20. Engine and dependent part block

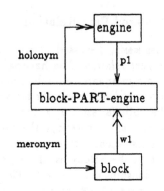

Fig. 21. Realization of Fig. 20

staff, and this staff contains all the music for the score. Without its staff, an instrument score contains no music at all. Thus, it is reasonable to make **instrument_score** dependent on its part **staff** (Fig. 22). To realize the dependency, the system designates *p1* and *meronym* dependent (Fig. 23), which causes deletions to be propagated from **staff** to **instrument_score** through **staff-PART-instrument_score**.

```
class instrument_score
  subclass-of(score)
  has-intra-excl-part-depends-on(staff)
  has-shared-part
      (score_expression_sequence)
  attributes:
    instrument: instrumentType
```

Fig. 22. Instrument_score with dependency

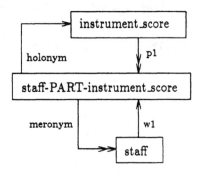

Fig. 23. Realization of Fig. 22

4.7 Part Relations with Value Propagation

The realization of upward value propagation is illustrated with the example of the propagation of *age* from **frame** to **car**. In Fig. 24, we show the textual definitions of these two classes, where the argument **frame** to the **has-part** statement is further qualified by the name of the attribute (*age*) whose value is to be propagated. In general, this secondary argument can be any method which is part of the meronymic class's public interface and which returns a data value.

To realize the propagation, the system installs, in the receiving class, a method which performs a traversal to the sending class and retrieves the value of interest (Fig. 25). In the figure, we see that the class **car** is augmented with the path method "age." The method operates as follows. It first crosses *p1* and arrives at the class

```
class car
    subclass-of(vehicle)
    has-inter-excl-part(eng:engine)
    has-essential-part(frame(age))
    attributes:
    model: modelType

class frame
    attributes:
    age: ageType
```

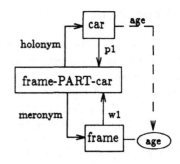

Fig. 25. Realization of Fig. 24

Fig. 24. Car with propagation of *age*

frame-PART-car. From there, it follows *meronym* to the class **frame** and accesses its namesake, the attribute *age* (through the selector method).

A similar scheme allows a value to be propagated down the part relation. Let's look at the example of the filing cabinet and its drawers (Fig. 26). Here, as in the case of part-to-whole dependency, an **is-part-of** statement is placed in the meronymic class. And as with **has-part** above, the argument to **is-part-of** is given an argument of its own (*material*), which is the property whose value is to be propagated. We once again emphasize that this value propagation is not a default: the value of a drawer's material is defined to be that of its filing cabinet.

```
class filing_cabinet
    has-inter-excl-part({drawer})
  attributes:
  material:
     one-of {steel, aluminum,...}

class drawer
    is-part-of
     (filing_cabinet(material))
```

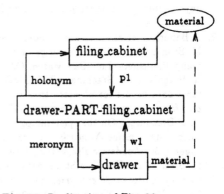

Fig. 26. Filing_cabinet with propagation of *material*

Fig. 27. Realization of Fig. 26

The realization of the downward propagation is analogous to that of upward propagation. Whereas for upward propagation, a method is installed by the system in the holonymic class, for downward propagation, a method is added to the meronymic class. In the example, a method "material" is installed in **drawer** to retrieve the value of the attribute *material* defined for **filing_cabinet** (Fig. 27).

5 Conclusion

In this paper, we have presented a comprehensive part model for OODB systems. Our model comprises a number of different part relations with characteristics such as exclusiveness/sharing, multi-valuedness, cardinality range-restriction, ordering, essentiality, dependency, and value propagation. All the relations were realized without modifying the underlying OODB data model. As a refinement of previous work, we have distinguished between two kinds of exclusiveness, intra-class and inter-class exclusiveness. The concept of dependency was refined to allow it in two directions, both from the part to the whole, and vice versa. We have also presented a general mechanism for upward and downward value propagation along the part relation.

In the tradition of the ER and other semantic data models, we have realized the part relation as a class whose instances represent the actual part connections between objects of the participating classes. Because of this, there is the possibility of defining attributes and even methods on the relation. In future work, we will consider how to exploit such capabilities. For example, the position of an integrated circuit on a circuit board might very well be stored as an attribute of the part relation between the respective classes.

An important issue is that of the transitivity of the part relation, which impacts on value propagation and "parts-explosion" retrieval. Ordinarily, transitivity is tacitly assumed. However, work in AI and related fields [7, 31] has shown that such an assumption is ill-founded. This issue is currently under investigation.

References

1. A. Albano, G. Ghelli, and R. Orsini. A relationship mechanism for a strongly typed object-oriented database programming language. In *Proc. VLDB '91*, pages 565–575, 1991.
2. J. Banerjee et al. Data model issues for object-oriented applications. In M. Stonebraker, editor, *Readings in Database Systems*, pages 445–456. Morgan Kaufmann Publishers, Inc., San Mateo, CA, 1988.
3. A. Borgida, R. J. Brachman, D. L. McGuinness, and L. A. Resnick. CLASSIC: A structural data model for objects. In *Proceedings of the 1989 ACM SIGMOD Conference on Management of Data*, Portland, OR, May 1989.
4. R. J. Brachman. On the epistemological status of semantic networks. In N. V. Findler, editor, *Associative Networks: Representation and Use of Knowledge by Computers*, pages 3–50. Academic Press, Inc., New York, NY, 1979.
5. R. Bretl et al. The GemStone data management system. In W. Kim and F. H. Lochovsky, editors, *Object-Oriented Concepts, Databases, and Applications*, pages 283–308. ACM Press, New York, NY, 1989.
6. P. P.-S. Chen. The Entity-Relationship Model: Toward a unified view of data. *ACM Transactions on Database Systems*, 1(1):9–36, 1976.
7. D. A. Cruse. On the transitivity of the part-whole relation. *Journal of Linguistics*, 15(1):29–38, 1979.
8. O. Diaz and P. M. Gray. Semantic-rich user-defined relationships as a main constructor in object-oriented databases. In *Proc. IFIP TC2 Conf. on Database Semantics.* North Holland, 1990.
9. D. Fischer et al. VML - The Vodak Data Modeling Language. Technical report, GMD-IPSI, Dec. 1989.

10. D. H. Fishman et al. Overview of the Iris DBMS. In W. Kim and F. H. Lochovsky, editors, *Object-Oriented Concepts, Databases, and Applications*, pages 219–250. ACM Press, New York, NY, 1989.

11. J. Geller. *A Knowledge Representation Theory for Natural Language Graphics*. PhD thesis, SUNY Buffalo CS Department, 1988. Tech. Report 88-15.

12. J. Geller. A graphics-based analysis of part-whole relations. Research Report CIS-91-27, NJIT, 1991.

13. J. Geller. Propositional representation for graphical knowledge. *Int. J. Man-Machine Studies*, 34:97–131, 1991.

14. J. Geller, E. Neuhold, Y. Perl, and V. Turau. A theoretical underlying Dual Model for knowledge-based systems. In *Proc. of the First Int'l Conference on Systems Integration*, pages 96–103, Morristown, NJ, 1990.

15. J. Geller, Y. Perl, and E. Neuhold. Structure and semantics in OODB class specifications. *SIGMOD Record*, 20(4):40–43, Dec. 1991.

16. J. Geller and S. Shapiro. Graphical deep knowledge for intelligent machine drafting. In *Tenth Int'l Joint Conference on Artificial Intelligence*, San Mateo, CA, 1987. Morgan Kaufmann Publishers, Inc.

17. M. Halper, J. Geller, Y. Perl, and E. J. Neuhold. A graphical schema representation for object-oriented databases. In *IDS92, Int'l Workshop on Interfaces to Database Systems*, July 1992.

18. G. E. Hinton. Representing part-whole hierarchies in connectionist networks. In *Proceedings of the 10th Cog. Sci. Soc. Conference*, pages 48–54, 1988.

19. S. E. Keene. *Object-Oriented Programming in Common Lisp*. Addison-Wesley Publishing Co., Inc., Reading, MA, 1989.

20. W. Kim. A model of queries for object-oriented databases. In *Proceedings of the 15th Int'l Conference on Very Large Databases*, pages 423–432, 1989.

21. W. Kim, E. Bertino, and J. F. Garza. Composite objects revisited. In *Proceedings of the 1989 ACM SIGMOD Int'l Conference on the Management of Data*, pages 337–347, Portland, OR, June 1989.

22. B. MacKellar and F. Ozel. ArchObjects: Design codes as constraints in an object-oriented KBMS. In J. Gero, editor, *AI in Design '91*. Butterworth-Heinemann Ltd., 1991.

23. B. MacKellar and J. Peckham. Representing design objects in SORAC. To appear in *AI in Design '92*, 1992.

24. E. Neuhold, Y. Perl, J. Geller, and V. Turau. Separating structural and semantic elements in object-oriented knowledge bases. In *Proc. of the Advanced Database System Symposium*, pages 67–74, Kyoto, Japan, 1989.

25. G. T. Nguyen and D. Rieu. Representing design objects. In J. Gero, editor, *AI in Design '91*. Butterworth-Heinemann Ltd., 1991.

26. J. Peckham and F. Maryanski. Semantic data models. *ACM Comp. Surveys*, 20(3):153–189, Sept. 1988.

27. E. Rich and K. Knight. *Artificial Intelligence*. McGraw-Hill, Inc., New York, NY, second edition, 1991.

28. J. Rumbaugh. Relations as semantic constructs in an object-oriented language. In *Proc. OOPSLA '87*, pages 466–481, Oct. 1987.

29. J. Rumbaugh, M. Blaha, W. Premerlani, F. Eddy, and W. Lorensen. *Object-Oriented Modeling and Design*. Prentice Hall, Englewood Cliffs, NJ, 1991.

30. J. F. Sowa. *Conceptual Structures, Information Processing in Mind and Machine*. Addison-Wesley Publishing Co., Inc., Reading, MA, 1984.

31. M. E. Winston, R. Chaffin, and D. Herrmann. A taxonomy of part-whole relations. *Cognitive Science*, 11(4):417–444, 1987.

Unified Class Evolution by Object-Oriented Views

Svein Erik Bratsberg

Div. of Computer Systems and Telematics
The Norwegian Institute of Technology
N-7034 Trondheim, Norway. E-mail: sebra@idt.unit.no

Abstract

Object-oriented databases are said to support evolution and incremental development. On the schema level, a firm restriction in this evolution is that it can only be done by evolving class hierarchies downwards by subclassing. We show a unified approach to class evolution in object-oriented databases, where class hierarchies are allowed to grow in all directions, covering for evolution situations like generalisation, specialisation, and class versioning. We show how to make the evolution transparent, allowing existing and new clients to coexist and be clients of the same (existing and new) objects. A design of this approach based on object-oriented database views is shown.

1   Introduction

In most database applications there is a need for letting the schema evolve. There are several reasons for this. There may be design flaws that are not discovered before (some of the) applications are implemented and the database is populated. The domain being modelled is evolving, new applications having new requirements are incorporated into the database, and schemas and databases developed independently may have to be integrated.

Object-oriented databases may be viewed as extending structural databases by making parts of what previously were in the applications shared in the database. This means that the schema designer has to consider both structural and behavioural aspects of the domains to be modelled. We think this means that there is a larger potential for having to evolve the schema. One of the reasons for this is that *encapsulation* reduces the possibilities of letting each application give their own interpretation to the data. This is a result of that it is hard to factor out what really is shared semantics (implemented by behaviour) and what is application-specific interpretations.

This paper has three main parts. The first part (Section 3) presents our object model, including the organisation of classes into hierarchies and how they evolve. Object-oriented databases are said to support evolution and incremental development. On the schema level this is mainly done through the subclassing and dynamic binding mechanisms, by allowing the class hierarchy to evolve downwards (creating subclasses). By separating the organisation of the intensional and extensional dimensions of classes, we show another approach where the class hierarchy may evolve in all directions. This covers for the typical evolution situations of subclassing, and generalisation, which allows for creating superclasses from existing classes, see [SN88] and [Ped89]. In addition it covers what is known as type versioning [Zdo90].

The second part of the paper (Section 4) treats two problems introduced by evolving the schema: there are existing objects and clients to take care of. *Type change transparency* [ABB+83] allows for existing clients and objects to exist by creating new versions of the types and converting the objects back and forth between the versions. We generalise this into *class evolution transparency* by introducing a general method for describing and maintaining consistency of objects being member of several classes.

The third part of the paper (Section 5) shows that our classes are very similar to database views, and shows how they may be realised by object-oriented views.

2 Related Work

Various kinds of class evolution problems have been studied in object-oriented databases. We will classify these according to if they update existing classes (*destructive*) or not (*additive*).

Specialisation is a simple, additive evolution technique that adds new classes to a class hierarchy, usually by *subclassing*. Subclasses inherit properties from their ancestors, possibly rejecting, redefining and adding properties. In databases, the extent of the subclass is automatically a subextent of the extent of the superclass.

Several authors [SN88, Ped89] recognise that the opposite to specialisation, namely *generalisation* is needed. This is caused by initially designed classes which were not abstract or general enough, or that an integration of the set of objects in different classes is wanted. Generalisations may be destructive or additive. [SN88] is an additive approach, which solves *name* and *scale differences* in generalisations by the use of *context colouring* and *message forwarding*.

Class surgery is a destructive approach which lets updates be done to class hierarchies. Traditional approaches [BKKK87, DZ91] define invariants of the class hierarchy, categorise atomic changes to the class hierarchy, and give actions to what should be done to ensure that the class hierarchy and the objects are consistent upon each category of change. Class surgery lets the class hierarchy be kept in a single, "correct" form, but disallows users to disagree about a class design, and may result in loss of information (destructive surgery).

Class versioning is an additive evolution providing for class (type) change transparency. This means that the old version of the class is retained, and that the two class versions will have the same extent. The rational is that old clients of the class should be allowed to coexist with the new clients and to share the extent. This avoids conversion of the clients to conform to new class versions. Conversion might be an error-prone and costly process. Class versioning also prevents information to be lost. [ABB+83] supports class versioning by *substitute read* and *write functions*, [SZ87] by *error handlers*, [Zdo90, Cla92] by *multiple views* to objects.

Database views [GPZ88, KDN90, Ber92] is a general technique for having derived information, and it may successfully be used for class evolution. However, often it is not possible to create objects of views and it is not possible to add representation in views with respect to the *base classes*, which is necessary in the general class evolution situation.

As we have seen, there are diverse work being done on class evolution, but none really covers the spectrum of evolution situations. We will now show an approach which covers for several of the evolution techniques that are mentioned.

3 Class Evolution

3.1 Object Model

An *object* possesses an *object identifier* (OID) and a set of properties described by the intent. All objects have distinct object identifiers, thus an object identifier is unique. An *intent* is a named set of properties. It is used to create and interpret objects. An object created from one intent "is of that intent". The intent is used to describe the common "form" and "behaviour" shared by the objects created from that intent. An *extent* is a special set of objects. To every intent we will connect an extent with the same name as the intent and being the set of objects created from the intent. An object created from the intent will be a *member* of the extent. We will assume a one-to-one and onto mapping from extents to intents. We name an intent–extent pair a *class*.

As will be further treated in Section 3.2, an object is created in one class, but may be *added* to other classes. *Adding* an object to a class is similar to creating an object in that class, but adding does not result in creating new object identifiers.

A *property* is either an attribute or an operation. An *attribute* is a named description of state of an object. The state of an attribute is a *value* of a specific *attribute domain*. All attributes are "typed", in the sense that they can only hold values of the associated attribute domain. An attribute may have a *default value*, i.e. a value it will automatically achieve if no other value is specified upon creation and adding the object to a class. We divide attribute domains into *basic*, predefined like int, float, link (references) and user-defined enumerations, and *composite* which are constructed by the use of e.g. array and set.

An intent may have *operations*, which are shared by all objects of that intent. An operation is a description of behaviour. An operation is *requested* as a property of an object (of the class it is defined within), and it is executed in the context of that object. The binding between an operation request and an operation is static. An operation may be a *mutator* which is an operation changing the state of an object. An operation may also be an *observer*, which is an operation which only reports on the state of an object.

Every property of an intent will either be public or private. A *public* property is accessible for all objects, while a *private* property is only accessible for the object itself.

3.2 Intent Hierarchies and Extent Graphs

The main reason for us to separate the intent and extent dimensions of classes is that we want to have separate organisation of hierarchies of intents and extents.

Intents may be organised in inheritance hierarchies, named *intent hierarchies*. An intent C_2 may inherit a set of properties P from an intent C_1. Then there is an *inheritance link* from C_2 to C_1. The semantics of the inheritance link is *copying*, i.e. intent C_2 behaves equally if P is defined locally or inherited from C_1. An *intent hierarchy* is a directed acyclic graph (DAG), where the vertices correspond to intents and the edges correspond to inheritance links.

Until now, we have said that an object will be a member of the class that it is created in, and that it may be added to other classes. We will now introduce a mechanism to let an object *automatically* be added to classes. An *extent propagation link* is a directed edge from extent C_2 to extent C_1. This will be written as $C_2 \Rightarrow C_1$. The semantics of the extent propagation link is that an object being a member C_2, will also be a member of C_1. Related to the terminology introduced in Section 3.1, this means that *creating* an object o in C_2 implies *adding* o to C_1. The notation $C_2 \Leftrightarrow C_1$ is a shorthand notation for $C_2 \Rightarrow C_1$ and $C_2 \Leftarrow C_1$.

An *extent graph* is a directed graph $D = (V, E)$ such that

1. V is a set of extents.

2. E is a set of extent propagation links.

In Figure 1 we see an example of an extent graph with its corresponding intent hierarchy. There are four classes Person (P), Student1 (S1), Student2 (S2), and Teacher (T). An object that is created in S1 will be propagated to S2 and P, and an object created in T will be propagated to P. As we see in the figure, we have made use of cycles in the extent graph.

An object may exist in all classes of a connected subgraph of an extent graph. We will not allow for adding an object to a class that is not in the connected subgraph that the object was created in. The rational for this is that all classes that an object *can* be a member of, are connected by extent propagation links either directly or transitively. Note that given two classes connected by an extent propagation link, $C_2 \Rightarrow C_1$, and an object o being a member of C_1, it is allowed to add this object to C_2. But this have to be done manually in contrast to the automatic propagation done by extent propagation links.

We may view extent propagation links as flow of copies of object identifiers between extents. But in addition to this, with each propagation link, there

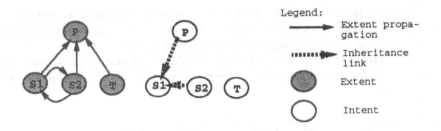

Figure 1: Extent graph and intent hierarchy.

are some property consistency relations (treated in Section 4) that describe the relationships between the properties of the classes being connected.

In Figure 1 it may look like there are some superfluous extent propagations. Objects in S1 and S2 are propagated both directly and through each other to P. With respect to object identifiers these multiple propagation paths are superfluous. But it may happen that the property consistency relations are different between those two paths, such that an object in P is a "join" of identical objects (objects having the same object identifier) in S1 and S2. An object in S1 may be identical to an object from S2, but may have different properties and values. The "join criterion" is object identity, but in case of integration of independently developed classes, the "join criterion" may be user-defined (treated in [Bra92]).

3.3 Class Evolution Definition

An *extent evolution* is an addition of extents and extent propagations to an extent graph D_1, creating a new extent graph D_2, such that D_1 is a directed subgraph of D_2. An *intent evolution* is an addition of intents and inheritance links to an intent hierarchy I_1, creating a new intent hierarchy I_2, such that I_1 is a directed subgraph of I_2. A *class evolution* is an extent evolution and an intent evolution, such that there is a one-to-one and onto mapping from the new extents to the new intents.

There is a one-to-one and onto mapping from the extents to the intents, but an extent graph and its corresponding intent graph do not have to be isomorphic. If it is introduced cycles in the extent graph, they cannot be isomorphic. In Figure 1, the extent graph and intent hierarchy are not isomorphic, e.g. the inheritance link between P and S1 is in the opposite direction to the extent propagation. The intent hierarchy indicates the partial order of creation of classes (e.g. the intent P is created based on the intent S1), while the extent graph does not.

Class evolution is related to the evolution of object-oriented design. Literature [SN88, Ped89] indicates that class hierarchies are likely to be discovered and developed in all directions, and especially in the opposite direction of the subclass direction. To cater for this, we have factorised out the intent and extent dimensions from the traditional class hierarchy. These two dimensions of classes have different characteristics w.r.t. evolution. Intent inheritance is a construct for reuse and organisation of intensional descriptions, and is inherently evolved downwards. Extent hierarchies may evolve in all directions, and are not sensitive to when abstractions are discovered. We will use the extent graph as the main conceptual organisation vehicle for objects. For conceptual class browsing, the extent graph will be used, but for developers, browsing the intent hierarchy may also be useful.

We will now give some typical examples of evolution (illustrated in Figure 2):

1. *Generalisation*: Adding a new class (C_g) with one or several extent propagations going into it from a set of classes (C_1 through C_n).

2. *Specialisation*: Adding a new class (C_s) with one or several extent propagations going out from it and into a set of classes (C_1 through C_n).

3. *Class versioning*: Adding a new class (C_v) with one extent propagation going from and one into the same (existing) class (C_1).

4. *Class connection*: Two *existing* classes (C_1 and C_2) will be connected by adding suitable extent propagations between them ($C_1 \Rightarrow C_2$, $C_1 \Leftarrow C_2$, or $C_1 \Leftrightarrow C_2$).

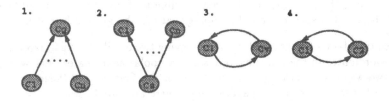

Figure 2: Typical class evolution situations.

4 Object Consistency

Extent propagation ensures that an object is a member of several classes. The properties associated with an object in two classes that are connected by an extent propagation link, are often partly overlapping. *Object consistency* means that for one object, the classes agree upon the overlapping properties. With respect to maintenance, "agreeing upon" means that if an object is mutated in one class, the other class will have to do a similar mutation to the overlapping properties.

4.1   Attribute Consistency Relations (ACR)

When we have two classes, C_1 and C_2, that are connected by an extent propagation link, there may be some attributes of C_1 and C_2 that are dependent on each other. C_1 and C_2 must agree upon the values of the dependent attributes of all objects that are member of both classes.

Consider class C_1 having attributes a_1 through a_n, and class C_2 having attributes b_1 through b_m. Class C_1 and class C_2 are connected by an extent propagation link (the direction of the link is not of importance in this discussion). An attribute, a_i of C_1 may either be *independent* or *dependent* of the attributes b_1 through b_m. Connected to the extent propagation link, we will describe all attributes that are dependent on attributes of the other class. The dependencies will be described by *attribute consistency relations (ACRs)*. These relations exist in two categories:

- **Derivable relation:**

$$(x_1, ..., x_k) = \mu(y_1, ..., y_p)$$

   Attributes x_1 through $x_k \in \{a_1, ..., a_n\}$ are derivable from attributes y_1 through $y_p \in \{b_1, ..., b_m\}$ using the attribute mapping μ.

- **Non-derivable relation:**

$$(x_1, ..., x_k) = \phi(y_1, ..., y_p)$$

   Attributes x_1 through $x_k \in \{a_1, ..., a_n\}$ are dependent on all attributes y_1 to $y_p \in \{b_1, ..., b_m\}$, but it is not possible to derive them. As will be seen below, ϕ is special kind of mapping that may be given different meanings.

Given two classes CartLoc and PolarLoc, having two attributes each, representing the coordinates in the plane by cartesian and polar coordinates. Below, we see the two-way extent propagation link between the CartLoc and PolarLoc classes. Connected to the extent propagation link, there are two ACRs.

CartLoc	$\Leftrightarrow$	PolarLoc
(x, y)	$=$	$\mu_1(rho, theta)$
$\mu_2(x, y)$	$=$	$(rho, theta)$

The pair (x, y) is derivable from $(rho, theta)$ using the attribute mapping μ_1, and $(rho, theta)$ is derivable from (x, y) using the attribute mapping μ_2.

Given a non-derivable ACR, $(x_1, ..., x_k) = \phi(y_1, ..., y_p)$, where a client attempts to mutate one of the attributes y_1 through y_p. The following different policies are possible:

1. Insert *null values* in the non-derivable attributes x_1 through x_k, meaning that the values of the xs are not known. The correct values for the xs will be inserted manually when they are known.

2. Deny mutator requests (updates) to y_1 through y_p, because we do not have an "updatable dependency", similar to the policy of the weak attribute equivalences of [LNE89].

We may also allow inconsistencies to appear by omitting to specify dependencies, which gives the responsibility for maintaining the dependencies to the clients. Which policy to choose may be dependent on the profile of the requests.

We will study ACRs that appear in special groups, named attribute consistency groups. Given two classes, C_1 with attributes a_1 to a_n and C_2 with attributes b_1 to b_m, an extent propagation link $C_1 \Leftarrow C_2$, a non-null subset A of the attributes a_1 to a_n, and a non-null subset B of the attributes b_1 to b_m. Let D be the largest non-null subset of $dom(A)^1$, R the largest non-null subset of $dom(B)$, such that there exist a mapping $\mu : D \rightarrow R$ and an inverse mapping $\mu^{-1} : R \rightarrow D$. Then the quadruple (A, B, μ, μ^{-1}) is an *attribute consistency group (ACG)*.

If D is a proper subset of $dom(A)$, μ is said to be a *partial mapping*, and we introduce an *extended mapping*, μ',

$$\mu' : dom(A) \rightarrow R$$

defined as

$$\mu' = \begin{cases} \mu & \text{if } (x_1, \dots, x_k) \in D \\ null & \text{else} \end{cases}$$

If D is equal to $dom(A)$, μ is a *complete mapping*.

For non-derivable relations, we will define ϕ to be a mapping that is *null* for all elements in the domain. This means that all ACRs involve mappings that never are *null* (complete), sometimes are *null* (extended), or always are *null* (non-derivable). ACGs consist of two ACRs. We will allow for ACGs (A, B, μ_1, μ_2) where μ_1 is complete or extended, and μ_2 is complete, extended, or partial. This means that an ACG consists of either two derivable relations, or one derivable relation and one non-derivable relation.

4.2 Shared Representation for Attributes

Now, we will explore the possibility of using shared representation for attributes from the different classes. By analysing the ACRs connected to an extent propagation link, we can tell if the attributes may be shared. Shared representation provides for "automatic consistency maintenance" since there is no way of representing any disagreement. When using separate representation, object consistency defined by ACRs will be implemented using operation consistency relations, as will be explained in Section 4.3.

Given an ACG (A, B, μ, μ^{-1}), where μ is complete and μ^{-1} is complete (i.e. R is equal to $dom(B)$). The basic representation scheme is that the two sets of attributes are represented separate. The other approach is to represent these

---

[1]Let A be the set of attributes x_1 to x_k ($x_i \in a_1..a_n$). $dom(A)$ is then a shorthand for $dom(x_1) \times \dots \times dom(x_k)$.

attributes shared, that is, we may let one of the attribute sets (e.g. A) be represented, and use the mappings to observe and mutate the other attributes (B). As the mapping is complete and has an inverse, this is always possible.

The example from Section 4.1 has the ACG $(\{x, y\}, \{rho, theta\}, \mu_1, \mu_2)$, where both mappings μ_1 and μ_2 are complete. This means that we may choose to represent these either separately or shared. For shared representation we may choose to represent either $\{x, y\}$ or $\{rho, theta\}$. If we choose to represent $\{x, y\}$, for all requests (both observer and mutator) to the attributes rho and $theta$, we must map to the attributes x and y.

Shared representation is also possible for ACGs where μ or μ^{-1} are not complete, but the choice of which attribute set to represent may be bounded by the mappings and the choice of policy for managing non-derivability.

4.3 Operation Consistency Relations (OCR)

Operation consistency relations may be seen as a special case of database triggers, which are used for realising ACRs where separate storage is chosen. It may also be seen as an alternative to ACRs.

An *operation consistency relation* (OCR) is an "operation" that is automatically requested when a given operation is requested. An OCR cannot be requested explicitly, only implicitly upon a normal operation request. Like an ACR, an OCR is specified in connection with an extent propagation link between two classes $C_2 \Rightarrow C_1$. An OCR consists of a *timing mode*, an operation signature, and a body. The timing mode is either *before* or *after* (explained below). The operation signature, $op(i_1, ..., i_k)$, corresponds to a signature of an operation op' from one of the classes C_2 or C_1. When op' is requested, the OCR will get a copy of the actual parameters, and the body of the OCR will be executed either before or after the execution of op' (depending on the timing mode).

There are two *timing models* for how the consistency is maintained.

1. *Eager consistency maintenance* means that the consistency is maintained busily upon mutation of objects. This will be accomplished using *after* timing.

2. *Lazy consistency maintenance* means that the consistency is maintained upon the time of observing a property that is "inconsistent". This is accomplished by *before* timing.

After timing for an OCR, is such that when op' is requested in C_1 for an object o, the body of the OCR is executed *after* op' has executed. The utilisation of this construct is when op' is a mutator. The body of the OCR will then ensure that the o in C_2 is consistent with respect to o in C_1.

Before timing for an OCR means that when op' is requested in C_1 for an object o, the body of the OCR will be executed *before* the operation op' is executed for o in C_1. With this timing mode, the body of the OCR will ensure that o in C_1 is made consistent before it is accessed. The utilisation of this construct is when op' is an observer operation which has related mutator operations for the same object in other classes.

OCRs are specified in connection with an extent propagation link $(C_2 \Rightarrow C_1)$. Similar to the ACRs, all operation signatures specified to the left of an OCR $(op(i_1, ..., i_k) \rightarrow ...)$, has a corresponding operation in C_2, while all operation signatures specified to the right of an OCR $(... \leftarrow op(i_1, ..., i_k))$ correspond to operations of C_1.

Taken the coordinate example from Section 4.1, we specify two ACRs for each variable, such that we get four ACRs. Eager consistency maintenance means that upon every mutator request, the respective mapping (μ_3 through μ_6) is applied to mutate the dependent attribute. This example is partly illustrated below[2]:

$$
\begin{array}{lcl}
\text{rho } (\mu_3 \text{ (x (),y ()))}; & \leftarrow & \textbf{After x (new\_x)} \\
\text{theta } (\mu_4 \text{ (x (),y ()))} & & \\
\textbf{After rho (new\_rho)} & \rightarrow & \text{x } (\mu_5 \text{ (rho (), theta ()))}; \\
& & \text{y } (\mu_6 \text{ (rho (), theta ()))}
\end{array}
$$

Lazy consistency maintenance means that when observing an attribute, it is checked whether it is consistent w.r.t. its dependent attributes. If it is not, a mapping is applied to make it consistent. A realisation of this approach requires to register if an attribute holds the "correct" (i.e. the most recent) value. This will be done using "dirty flags", where the meaning of "x being dirty" is that an attribute that x is dependent on (rho or $theta$), has been mutated since the last time x was mutated. We assume the cost of setting and checking flags to be lower than the cost of mutating the attribute. The following set of OCRs outlines parts of a realisation of this approach:

$$
\begin{array}{lcl}
\text{if x is "dirty" then} & \leftarrow & \textbf{Before x ()} \\
\text{x}(\mu_7(\text{rho(),theta()})) & & \\
\text{unset "dirty flag" of x} & & \\
\text{set "dirty flag" of rho and theta} & \leftarrow & \textbf{After x (new\_x)} \\
\textbf{Before rho ()} & \rightarrow & \text{if rho is "dirty" then} \\
& & \text{rho}(\mu_3(\text{x(),y()})) \\
& & \text{unset "dirty flag" of rho} \\
\textbf{After rho (new\_rho)} & \rightarrow & \text{set "dirty flag" of x and y}
\end{array}
$$

It is also possible to use OCRs directly for maintaining object consistency, without describing the dependencies between attributes. This is a reasonable approach where it is a large discrepancy between the representations, but the operations are quite similar. The advantages of this are that encapsulation does not have to be broken if it is only operations that are public, and that the representation does not have to be understood if the operations are understood. The use of OCRs directly has some disadvantages: it does not allow for reasoning about representation, and it has the timing mode and error-handling policy hard-coded.

---

[2]For every attribute a, we assume an observer operation a(), and a mutator operation a(new_a).

4.4 Consistency Maintenance and Encapsulation

The extent and intent dimensions of our approach may be seen as mechanism to loosen the rather strict mechanism of subclassing, and to unify this with similar mechanism like generalisation and class versioning. We think that subclasses (or generally classes connected by extent propagation links) are special clients of each other, and not ordinary clients. In some sense they are different "views" to the same objects. In this setting, if one should retain to strong integrity (by forbidding encapsulation to broken by subclasses), the superclass "view" would be in some sense superior to the subclass "view". We would like our system to treat generalisation equally well as subclassing. With respect to this, treating classes and subclasses equal with respect to encapsulation is important. If we disallowed encapsulation to be broken, the advantages of ACRs would only be available for attributes being public.

The main disadvantage of breaking encapsulation is that the integrity of an object may be broken. A class may be viewed as having certain *invariants*, which are satisfied whenever no operations of the class is executing. When granting other classes rights to break the encapsulation, this integrity may be lost.

5 Object-Oriented Views

5.1 View Design

Our concept of classes and objects is very similar to database views. A view in [HZ90] consists of a type and a query, which correspond to the intent and extent of our classes. Objects exist in many classes which may have overlapping properties. Maintaining object consistency is essentially the same problem as maintaining consistent views. [GPZ88] defines a static view as a triple (A, B, f) where A is a base data abstraction, B is the view data abstraction, and f is a mapping between the states of A and B. Updatability and consistency of views are dependent on if there exist complete mappings and inverses between the base and the view. This corresponds in our case to two classes C_1 and C_2 connected by an extent propagation link, and having the attribute consistency group (A, B, f, f^{-1}).

We will now show a design of the concepts introduced in Section 3 and 4 based on object-oriented views. A class consists of an intent and a query to represent the extent. In addition, we need operation consistency relations to maintain object consistency when shared representation is not used.

As we saw in Section 4.2, there are two ways we may represent attribute consistency groups: either shared or separate. When using shared representation, the choice where to represent the attributes is dependent on the extent propagation link between the corresponding extents. Given the two classes C_1 and C_2 having the attribute consistency group (A, B, μ, μ^{-1}), the following situations of shared representation are possible.

$$C_1 \Leftrightarrow C_2: \quad \text{Shared in either } A \ (C_1) \text{ or } B \ (C_2)$$
$$C_1 \Leftarrow C_2: \quad \text{Shared in } A \ (C_1)$$

The choice of where to have the shared representation is dependent on the profile of the requests. Upon evolution, it may be wise to let the existing objects retain their representation. This means that in the $C_1 \Leftrightarrow C_2$ case, the choice may often be given by the class that was created first.

Having shared representation corresponds to the normal view situation, where the view is represented as a query that is evaluated upon request. Separate representation corresponds to materialisation of views [CW91]. In this case, our OCRs play the same role as the production rules of [CW91].

We will use shared representation as long as possible. Each class will have a *local extent*, which is used to represent objects temporarily or permanently, depending on if it is a choice of shared representation. In addition it may represent the objects created in this class, and the properties that cannot be represented shared elsewhere. The extent will then be defined as a query to the local extent, and depending on the representation, to other extents which should propagate objects to this extent. For clients, it should not be possible to tell if the object is represented locally or if it is queried from other classes.

A query is issued towards an extent requesting properties. The properties requested in the query may be evaluated in one of two ways:

1. The properties are represented and evaluated locally in this extent.

2. Query objects from other extents into the local extent (creating a temporary object) and request the properties of the local intent to work on the temporary representation.

In case 1, mutation of objects will be handled directly. In case 2, it will be handled by creating a temporary representation of the object in the local extent, and use OCRs to maintain the object consistency. Creation of objects will be handled similarly: the created object may have to represented locally, or mapped to other classes.

We will use an "objectified" version of the relational query algebra as an example query language. The query algebra is set-oriented: the input to and the output from queries are sets of objects. All operators are object-preserving, meaning that the indentity of the input objects are retained in the output.

- *Identity-preserving selection*:

$$\sigma_P(S)$$

  This operator selects all objects, which satisfies the predicate P, from the set of objects S. The result set will be a subset of the input set. The original set of objects S will very often be an extent (which is named). The name of an extent may be used in formulas as an abbreviation for unconditional selection.

- *Identity-preserving projection*:

$$\pi_{p_1,p_2,\ldots,p_N}(S)$$

This operator projects the properties p_1 through p_N from the set of objects S. The result objects are the same objects as the input objects, but only the projected properties will be available for further processing of the result. A property p_i may be renamed in the projection, giving it a different name in the result than in the input.

- *Object join*: An object may be vertically fragmented (having representation in several classes), which requires the capability of joining it from different classes.

$$S_1 \bowtie S_2$$

The set of objects in S_1 (having a specific intent) is joined with the objects in S_2 (having another intent). This operator corresponds to the *outer join* in relational algebra. The result set of objects is the union of the sets of objects S_1 and S_2 (joined on OID), and the resultant objects will have the union of the properties of the properties of the objects in S_1 and S_2. If an object is not represented in one of the classes being joined, *null values* will be inserted for these properties of this object in the result.

- *Set operators*: The query algebra has the set operators *union* ($\cup$), *intersection* ($\cap$), and *difference* ($-$).

With this view design of classes, class evolution means that we may have to evolve the extent definition of classes and to add operation consistency relations. Existing queries which represent extents, may have to be extended upon evolution. The existing intents and objects are retained, such that existing clients will continue to work. As pointed out in Section 4.1, the clients may have to treat *null* values that did not appear prior to the evolution.

5.2 Examples of Class Evolution

We will give some examples of class evolution. The syntax of intent definitions is similar to the syntax of class definitions in C++.

The first example is a class versioning example based on one from [Cla92]. The intent of Student1 is defined below.

```
intent Student1 {
public:
  string              name;
  string              addr;
  degree_program      pgm;
  class_domain        cl;
  set-of(link(Course)) course;
};
```

Below, the initial definition of the extent of Student1 is given. The L-subscript on a class name designate the local extent.

$$extent\,(\text{Student1}) = \text{Student1}_L$$

Student2 is a new version of the Student1 class, i.e. Student1 $\Leftrightarrow$ Student2. The intent of Student2 inherits one property from the intent of Student1.

```
intent Student2 inherits Student1
    excluding addr, pgm, cl, course {
  public:
    string          phone;
    int             id_numb;
    link(Teacher)   advisor;
    int             cl_year
};
```

The attributes of these two class versions are related in the following ways:

Student1	$\Leftrightarrow$	Student2
name	=	name
pgm	=	$\phi_1(\text{advisor})$
$\phi_2(\text{pgm})$	=	advisor
cl	=	$\mu_1(\text{cl\_year})$
$\mu_2(\text{cl})$	=	cl_year

The name attribute is the same in both classes – thus they constitute an ACG. addr and id_numb are independent. cl and cl_year are derivable from each other, and constitute an ACG. pgm and advisor are non-derivable from each other. We let name and cl_year of Student2 be represented shared with name and cl in Student1. phone, id_numb, and advisor must be represented separate in Student2 since they cannot be derived from Student1. The non-derivable relations between pgm and advisor will be handled by OCRs (not shown here).

The extent definition of Student1 is unchanged, while the extent of Student2 is defined below:

$$extent\,(\text{Student2}) =$$

$$\pi_{\text{name,cl\_year}=\mu_2(\text{cl})}(\text{Student1}) \bowtie \pi_{\text{phone,id\_numb,advisor}}(\text{Student2})$$

The next example shows a generalisation of the Student1, Student2 and Teacher classes into the Person class. The Teacher class has encapsulated the name and address representation by two observer operations get_name and get_addr. The private properties are not shown.

```
intent Teacher {
  public:
    string                  get_name ();
    string                  get_addr ();
    set-of(link(Course))    course;
};
```

The intent of Person is defined by inheriting from the intent of Student1.

```
intent Person inherits Student1
   excluding pgm, cl, course {
 public:
   string  phone;
   int     year_of_birth;
};
```

The Person class adds the year_of_birth property with respect to the classes that it generalises. The name, address, and phone attributes are in ACGs with the corresponding attributes in Student1 and Student2. In this example, we must represent objects created from the Person class in the local extent because they should not be propagated to any of the other classes. The objects existing in the Student classes will partly be represented as they are, and partly be extended in the Person class (the year_of_birth attribute). Since the Teacher class has the name and address encapsulated, we must use separate representation, and use OCRs to maintain the consistency (not shown). The extent of Person is defined below:

$$extent\,(\text{Person}) =$$
$$\text{Person}_L \cup$$
$$\pi_{\text{name,addr}}(\text{Student1}) \bowtie \pi_{\text{phone}}(\text{Student2}) \bowtie \pi_{\text{year\_of\_birth}}(\text{Person}_L)$$

Figure 1 shows the resulting extent graph and intent hierarchy of the examples. The labels are abbreviations of the class names, e.g. T corresponds to Teacher. The correspondence between extent and intent is by equal names.

6 Conclusions and Further Work

Our approach to class evolution may be seen as a unified method covering several existing evolution techniques. We separated the intensional and extensional dimension of classes to allow them to exist in separate hierarchies, and introduced property consistency relations to describe and maintain the consistency of objects being member of several classes. The main contribution of the paper is to show that by loosing up the rather strict concept of subclassing, we allow for evolving class hierarchies in all directions. The object consistency problem created by this semantics is essentially the same as the consistency problem known from database views [GPZ88]. A design of our classes using object-oriented views was shown.

We are working on extending the work further into integration of classes that are developed independently (an initial approach may be found in [Bra92]). This introduces several new problems. First, different existing objects may represent the same conceptual object, such that integration of objects and object identifiers must be done as well. Second, modelling discrepancies may make the recovering of similarities of different classes harder.

Acknowledgements

Discussions with Stewart M. Clamen improved the section on object consistency substantially. Reidar Conradi and Arne-Jørgen Berre made comments to the paper.

References

[ABB+83] M. Ahlsén, A. Björnerstedt, S. Britts, C. Hultén, and L. Söderlund. Making Type Changes Transparent. In *Proceedings of IEEE Workshop on Languages for Automation, Chicago*, pages 110–117. IEEE Computer Society Press, Nov. 1983.

[Ber92] E. Bertino. A view mechanism for object-oriented databases. In *A. Pirotte, C. Delobel, and G. Gottlob, editors. Advances in database technology - EDBT '92: International Conference on Extending Database Technology, Vienna, Austria, March 23-27, 1992* pages 136–151, Springer-Verlag LNCS, Mar. 1992.

[BKKK87] J. Banerjee, W. Kim, H.-J. Kim, and H. F. Korth. Semantics and Implementation of Schema Evolution in Object-Oriented Databases. In *Proceedings of ACM/SIGMOD (Management of Data)*, pages 311–322, May 1987.

[Bra92] S. E. Bratsberg. Integrating independently developed classes. In *M. T. Özsu, U. Dayal, and P. Valduriez, editors. Distributed Object Management, Proceedings from International Workshop, August 19-21, 1992, Edmonton, Canada.* Morgan Kaufmann Publishers, 1992.

[Cla92] S. M. Clamen. Type Evolution and Instance Adaptation. Technical Report CMU-CS-92-133, School of Computer Science, Carnegie Mellon University, Pittsburgh, PA 15213-3890, USA, 1992.

[CW91] S. Ceri and J. Widom. Deriving production rules for incremental view maintenance. In *Proceedings of the Sixteenth International Conference on Very Large Databases, Barcelona, Spain (VLDB '91)*, pages 577–589, Sep. 1991.

[DZ91] C. Delcourt and R. Zicari. The Design of an Integrity Consistency Checker (ICC) for an Object Oriented Database System. In *P. America, editor. European Conference on Object-Oriented Programming, Geneva, Switzerland, July 1991*, pages 97–117. Springer-Verlag LNCS 512, 1991.

[GPZ88] G. Gottlob, P. Paolini, and R. Zicari. Properties and update semantics of consistent views. *ACM Transactions on Database Systems*, 13(4):486–524, Dec. 1988.

[HZ90]   S. Heiler and S. Zdonik. Object Views: Extending the Vision. In *Sixth International Conference on Data Engineering*, pages 86–93. IEEE Computer Society Press, Feb. 1990.

[KDN90] M. Kaul, K. Drosten, and E. J. Neuhold. ViewSystem: Integrating Heterogeneous Information Bases by Object-Oriented Views. In *Sixth International Conference on Data Engineering*, pages 2–10. IEEE Computer Society Press, Feb. 1990.

[LNE89] J. A. Larson, S. B. Navathe, and R. Elmasri. A Theory of Attribute Equivalence in Databases with Applications to Schema Integration. *IEEE Transactions on Software Engineering*, 15(4):449–463, Apr. 1989.

[Ped89] C. H. Pedersen. Extending ordinary inheritance schemes to include generalization. In *Proceedings of the ACM Conference on Object-Oriented Systems, Languages and Applications (OOPSLA), New Orleans, 1989*, pages 407–417, Oct. 1989.

[SN88]   M. Schrefl and E. J. Neuhold. Object class definition by generalization using upward inheritance. In *Fourth International Conference on Data Engineering*, pages 4–13. IEEE Computer Society Press, Feb. 1988.

[SZ87]   A. H. Skarra and S. B. Zdonik. Type Evolution in an Object-Oriented Database. In *B. Shriever and P. Wegner, editors. Research Directions in Object-Oriented Programming*, pages 393–415. MIT Press, 1987.

[Zdo90] S. B. Zdonik. Object-Oriented Type Evolution. In *F. Bancilhon and P. Buneman, editors. Advances in Database Programming Languages*, pages 277–293. Addison-Wesley Publishing Company, 1990.

Lecture Notes in Computer Science

Springer-Verlag Berlin Heidelberg New York London Paris Tokyo Hong Kong Barcelona Budapest

Lecture Notes in Computer Science

For information about Vols. 1–559
please contact your bookseller or Springer-Verlag